THE TIMELY AND THE TIMELESS

THE TIMELY
AND THE
TIMELESS

Jews, Judaism and Society
in a Storm-tossed Decade

Dr. Immanuel Jakobovits

Chief Rabbi of the United Hebrew Congregations
of the British Commonwealth of Nations

VALLENTINE, MITCHELL—LONDON

Published in Great Britain in 1977 by
VALLENTINE, MITCHELL & CO. LTD.
Gainsborough House,
11 Gainsborough Road, London, E11 1RS, England

© 1977 Dr. Immanuel Jakobovits

ISBN 0 85303 189 4

Printed in Great Britain by
Billing & Sons Ltd
Guildford, London and Worcester

CONTENTS

A Personal Prologue   ix

Chapter One: Israel—Sanctuary or Asylum?
"Shall your brothers go to war . . . ?"   3
The Infamy of Munich   7
From Tears to Joy   11
The Jewish Destiny—The Spiritual Challenge of the Yom Kippur War   17
Zion—Sanctuary or Asylum?   34
Zionism Today: Vision, Illusion and Reality   43

Chapter Two: Anglo-Jewry—Tradition in Transition
Spiritual Leadership—The Heritage of Priest, Prophet and King   53
Milestones and Millstones   61
The Provincial Contribution to Anglo-Jewry   69
Anglo-Jewish Melting-Pot: The Fusion of Natives and Immigrants   78

Chapter Three: World Jewry—The Quest for Survival
The Reunification of Jerusalem and the Reunification of the
    Jewish People   83
Our People's Challenge to Rabbis   87
Orthodoxy's Strengths and Weaknesses   96
The Enlarged European Community—Its Jewish Significance   99
The Crisis of Survival   103
Visiting the Soviet Union: Two Articles   109

Chapter Four: Religion and Society—Beyond our Confines
Inter-Faith Relations—Advances and Limits   119
An Instrument of Amity   122
Human Rights and Human Duties   125
Moral Challenges before the Mass Media   130
Religion in Public Life   135
Letter to the Queen   142

Chapter Five: Passover and New Year Broadcasts
Acting Today, Asking Tomorrow (Passover 1967)   147

Promise and Fulfilment (Passover 1968) 151
Creation and Judgement (New Year 1968) 155
Reaching the Moon: Two Perspectives (New Year 1969) 159
Racial Equality—What Can Jews Contribute? (Passover 1970) 163
The Relevance of Religion (Passover 1971) 167
The Meaning of Prayer and Confession (New Year 1971) 171
Science—Master or Servant? (Passover 1972) 175
Constant Exodus (Passover 1974) 179
From the Four Corners (Passover 1976) 183

**Chapter Six: Jewish Education and Jewish Identity:
What Makes and What is a Jew?**
A Phoenix from the Ashes 189
Jewish Education—Is the Alarm Justified? 192
Life-Line to Survival 197
Jewish Identity: Three Essays 199
    (1) Who is a Jew? 199
    (2) Stemming Intermarriage—Why and How? 205
    (3) To Convert or Not to Convert? 210
The 'Who is a Jew' Crisis 215

Chapter Seven: Studies in Jewish Law, Thought and History
Marriage and Divorce in the Sources of Jewish Law 221
The Ashkenazi and Sephardi Pronunciation in Prayer 236
The Religious Significance of Israel Independence Day 249
Samson Raphael Hirsch—A Reappraisal of his Teachings and
    Influence in the Light of our Times 251
Conformity and Diversity in the Jewish Historical Tradition 259
The Evolution of the British Rabbinate since 1845—
    Its Past Impact and Future Challenges 268

**Chapter Eight: Halachah in Modern Times—Applying Timeless
Principles to Timely Conditions**
Halachah in Modern Jewish Life 281
Halachic Abstracts 288
    The Six-Day War 288
    The Jewish Holy Places 289
    The Occupied Territories 297
    Mitzvah Observance for Space Travellers 299
    Letterheads 302
    Mourning Laws for Babies 303
    Strikes 303
    Car Fuel Payment 305
    Children's Services 306
    Changing Prayer Rites 306
    Israeli Cantors 307
    The Agunah Problem 308
    Reform Marriages 311

Reform Mixed Marriages   312
Medical Halachah   314
Artificial Insemination   317
The Blind in Jewish Law   319
Rabbis and Deans   320

Chapter Nine: Medical Ethics

The Jewish Contribution to Medical Ethics   331
Population Explosion—The Jewish Attitude to Birth-Control   338
Jewish Views on Abortion   348
Medical Experimentation on Humans   362
The Medical Treatment of Animals in Jewish Law   368
Tay-Sachs Disease and the Jewish Community   379
Euthanasia   384

Chapter Ten: Homiletical Memories of America   384

Exploring America—and Judaism   387
Farewell to America   408
Index   429

A PERSONAL PROLOGUE

Few decades, if any, have seen more dramatic convulsions in human and Jewish affairs than the past ten years. Telescoped into this fleeting era has been an extraordinary succession of momentous changes and upheavals. What was once one world, largely dominated by the Judaeo-Christian civilisation, has been fragmented into three rival blocks, with the newly emerging "Third World" seeking to impose a novel political and economic colonialism on the rest. Terrestrial beings have landed on the lunar surface, whilst lunatics rule over rich chunks of the terrestrial surface. The decade has witnessed the rise of the permissive society; the fall of superpower dominance; and the decline of the affluent age. In Jewish life, we have seen the failure of secular nationalism as the answer to anti-Semitism and Jewish insecurity; the ecstasy and the agony of the Six-Day and Yom Kippur Wars; the wondrous awakening of Soviet Jewry; the remarkable shift in communal emphasis on Jewish education; and an entirely new awareness of our responsibilities to Jewish students. Altogether there has been a terrifying acceleration in the pace of history, leaving those harried pace-setters in positions of leadership ever less time to deliberate on ever more fateful decisions.

This book, in great part, is a search for Jewish responses to these cataclysmic developments.

Its selection of writings and addresses, composed (with a few exceptions) within the past ten years, was originally intended as a sequel to my *Journal of a Rabbi*, first published in 1966, which covered the preceding twenty-five years. But, though similar in scope and presentation, indeed often in the opinions expressed, the present work naturally reflects the rather different character and experience of the position I have occupied since I assumed my present office early in 1967. The vistas and responsibilities in the exercise of religious jurisdiction over several hundred congregations and other institutions in Britain and the Commonwealth hardly bear comparison with my previous rabbinical experiences in London, Ireland and New York, varied as these were.

The ensuing chapters also lay bare more personal aspects which I want to spell out in all frankness.

Elevation to an exalted and time-hallowed public position bestows not only high honours—it also exacts its penalties. Two of them I find especially irksome. One is the all too common expectation, particularly among communal office-holders, to be conventional: to "do things as they have always been done", and conversely not to do or say things that have never been done or said; in my case, to represent and incarnate the Establishment with a capital "E". The other is the severe curtailment of opportunities for literary and scholarly work, imposed by the ceaseless procession of public commitments which, however necessary, and expected of leadership, distract the mind and divert one from academic pursuits.

This volume, in a sense, records efforts to overcome both disabilities. It neither shuns the uninhibited expression of many controversial opinions nor hides the evidence of occasional retreats into the sheltered world of thought, history and literature. It is not, of course, meant as an autobiography, except in several rather indirect ways, although to an extent, every book of this nature reveals something of its author. In some respects, the reasons for this incidental self-portrayal are due to quite objective factors; others are highly subjective. If I here dwell in some detail on the relationship between book and author, it is in order to explain its contents, the choice of subjects, and the mental, ideological and practical attitudes, no less than the external promptings, responsible for their presentation.

To begin with, the book is autobiographical in so far as it chronicles many of the principal events in which I was involved during the past decade, and my reactions to them. While my office imposes many burdens, there are also ample compensations. Not least among these is the chance to observe the making of history at close quarters, to meet and befriend many leading actors in the drama of contemporary life, and occasionally to play some small role in historic events.

It is by virtue of the public office entrusted to me that I had the opportunity to experience such momentous events as addressing some 10,000 fellow-Jews at the Royal Albert Hall on the outbreak of the Six-Day War in one of the most emotionally-charged experiences one is likely to encounter in one's life-time, conscious that the feelings that day scarcely had a parallel in 2,000 years of history; the exhilaration to be, a week later, among the very first Jews at the Western Wall and at the tombs of Rachel and our Patriarchs just restored to Jewish sovereignty after 1,900 years of alien rule, followed by some thirty visits to Israel since then for numerous conferences and consultations; articulating the extreme joys of an entire community at unique occasions like the centenary of the United Synagogue and Israel's Silver Jubilee, and our extreme sorrows in the wake of the Munich Olympic massacre and of the Yom Kippur War; being the first Chief Rabbi from the West officially to visit the Soviet Union; presenting Jewish social teachings before 5,000 of Britain's most distinguished industrialists as guest-speaker of the Institute of Directors; planning and launching major communal enterprises like the Torah Corps, the Jewish Universities Chaplaincy Board and the Jewish Educational Development Trust, which have helped significantly to reverse the trends of religious and educational decline by providing the human and financial resources for important new projects; being the first Chief Rabbi to be honoured, together with his wife, with an invitation to be the Queen's personal guests at Windsor Castle—these are precious privileges the excitement of which I feel moved to share with the wider public.

Such experiences have combined with the benefits of frequent travel in this country and abroad—on pastoral or speaking tours which have taken me since 1967 to virtually all major Jewish communities, from Scandinavia to South Africa, and from both American continents to the Antipodes down under as well as to the principal Jewish communities in Russia beyond the Free World's frontiers. These global peregrinations have helped me to evaluate current events in a manner enjoyed by few others in comparable positions of community service, whether lay or rabbinical. My views cannot but be affected by the impact of my continual encounter with Yeshivah heads and university dons, with government leaders and schoolchildren, with church dignitaries and newspaper editors, with hospital patients and despaired drop-outs of society, with the faithful in synagogues and the faithless in marriages, with zealots and rebels, with implacable critics and loyal supporters. My professional horizons inevitably encompass the entire panorama of the social landscape—its high peaks of nobility and visionary leadership, its deep valleys of depravity and deprivation, its wide rivers of contention dividing communities and opinions, and its vast plains of mediocrity, indifference and inconsequential existence.

In terms of personal moods and views, these chapters unavoidably reveal a mosaic, perhaps a jumble, of contrasts and contradictions: hopes and disappointments, elation and depression, unanswered questions and questionable answers, doubts and certainties, a hankering after authority as well as after non-conformity. Maybe these complexities and perplexities mirror the confusion of our turbulent age in which inconsistency and instability seem to be the only consistent and stable features.

Less accidental in submitting my thinking to public scrutiny is the exposure of my special interests and preferences. I do not hesitate to admit that I know of, and seek, more rewarding activities than interminable meetings and ceremonial functions, interspersed by a constant stream of appointments and a voluminous correspondence. Exciting and essential as many of these occupational hazards often are, they cannot compare to the thrills of speaking to a group of students, or simply teaching a sixth-form class, or preparing and delivering a paper for some professional seminar or communal conference —pursuits which usually also yield more enduring results, as this volume testifies.

More specifically, this book highlights my specialised concern with Jewish medical ethics, and the application of Jewish teachings to modern thinking and living generally. To these fields I continue to devote as much spare time as I can find and to contribute whatever expert knowledge I may have gained through study and practical experience.

Obviously most indicative of my personal commitments and attitudes, perhaps even my obsessions and certainly my limitations, are the items dealing with topical issues. Having an innate aversion to platitudes, or to voicing views which are widely accepted and which therefore do not require my endorsement, I may well have a tendency to lean in the opposite direction —a disposition to swim against, rather than with the stream; emphasising challenge more than attainment, dissent more than consent, innovation more than preservation, and seeking stimulation rather than acclaim. I commonly divide speakers into two categories: those who say what people want to hear, and those who say what (they believe) people ought to hear. I try to have myself counted among the latter. Hence, I have never allowed the generally assumed proprieties of my office, including an aloofness from controversy, to override the dictates of my conscience and convictions. Religious influence, to my mind, can never be exerted by applause-catching campaigns or be imposed by votes. The price of inheriting the mantle of Israel's traditional seers and mentors, however inadequately it fits, is a constant readiness to face the risks of loneliness, unpopularity and even defamation.

My readers, therefore, will find no lack of unconventional opinions, sometimes to the point of near-heresy in the eyes of the religious, communal and national establishments. I decried the futility of the secularist dream "to solve the Jewish problem" by "normalising" the Jewish condition through Statehood long before the Yom Kippur War finally shattered this illusion, just as I persistently proclaimed my conviction that the abandonment of our national assignment as "a light unto the nations" and a holy people would be liable to render Jewish survival both questionable and meaningless. I did not wait for spectacular hijacks and murderous outrages to be reminded, and to remind others, of the wretched plight of Arab refugees and the sensitivities of the Jewish conscience to this human tragedy. My strictures of rabbinic shortcomings were no less sparing than my criticisms of diehard lay policies in the conduct of communal affairs, and no more discreet than my impatience with minds closed to new ideas and enterprises. I denounced wanton terrorism directed against innocent lives with the same conviction as I attacked the cheapening of human life by the devotees of euthanasia and abortion on demand, or the immorality of inflicting indiscriminate suffering on innocent third-parties through nationally crippling strikes. Nor, when addressing myself to particular groups, have I shrunk from condemning the unethical abuses of freedom in journalism or medicine, or the insufficient concern with the spiritual reclamation of the Jewish masses among leading Torah sages, or the over-centralisation of religious authority in my own office.

I claim no monopoly of truth for my views. I simply assert the right to express them, and I willingly submit them to public criticism and discussion. For, concomitant to my frequent advocacy of persuasion rather than compulsion in the effective exercise of spiritual leadership nowadays, is my affirmation that only through the tensions of argument, controversy ("for the sake of Heaven") and even provocation can the dynamics of progress be generated.

In making my selections from a rather bulky accumulation of material, I have used among the major criteria for what to include, apart from intrinsic interest, the diversity of the items discussed and the significance of the occasions prompting them. Excluded are most of my sermons, all letters to the press, forewords to books, contributions to encyclopedias, annual New Year reviews, obituaries and memorial addresses, messages to organizations, and many other literary exercises. Nevertheless, in a collection of utterances and writings drawn from such a far-flung variety of platforms and forums, I found it difficult to avoid some repetitiveness of ideas and expressions.

In some cases I deleted more or less identical passages already used elsewhere. But occasionally I found that such omissions would have broken up the continuity of thought or removed a major argument from a particular presentation. Hence, I crave the reader's forbearance if here and there he discovers phrases, perhaps occasionally whole paragraphs, already familiar from previous pages. Such repetitions, too, faithfully reflect traits from which I—presumably among some other writers and public speakers—am not free.

*　　*　　*　　*　　*

In offering this harvest of my more recent writings to the public, I am all too keenly aware of the debt I owe to many for their indispensable help in producing these fruits. In a unique category is my wife who has provided me with a cheerful home and constant inspiration, tempered by the priceless benefit of healthy criticism. Sheltering the saplings of my toil in the sunny climate of her companionship, she has helped to ensure that the plants will be well rooted in the soil and yet, with affectionate tending, reach upwards towards heaven, protected against the buffetings of the elements. I seek the understanding of those others whom I cannot mention individually, but I must acknowledge the painstaking help of Mr. Moshe Davis who freely applied his skills and experience to supply seminal ideas, to prune overgrown branches and to enhance the market prospects of the finished products. Indeed, there is hardly an item produced in the past five years which did not pass his careful scrutiny in the course of production.*

Scarcely less important to this produce has been the irrigation of challenge and opportunity provided by the people and the community it is my privilege to serve. Their invitations to speak or lecture generated the demand which created the supply; the stimulation of their questions and problems fertilised my thinking, and the distinguished platforms they made available to me served as the rich soil without which no seeds would have brought forth any fruit. To all of them, I dedicate this thanksgiving offering as a token of my affection and in humble prayer that it, in turn, will produce seeds which will yield fresh fruits in the fields of Jewish endeavour and human understanding.

* I also acknowledge with much gratitude the kind permission for the reprint of articles and other contributions published in *The Times*, *The Times Educational Supplement*, *The Observer*, *The Journal of Jewish Studies*, *Tradition*, *L'Eylah*, *The Proceedings of the Association of Orthodox Jewish Scientists*, as well as in publications issued by *The Case Western Reserve University Press* and the *Soncino Press*.

First Jew wins Templeton Prize for Progress in Religion

NEW YORK (AP) — Britain's Chief Rabbi Immanuel Jakobovits this week became the first Jew to win the $800,000 Templeton Prize for Progress in Religion, the world's richest award.

Jakobovits, 70, was cited for his "moderation and compassion on Arab-Israeli issues," his "enlightened approach to interfaith relations, and his originality in interpreting traditional values of Judaism."

The Templeton was founded by American investment manager John M. Templeton and was first given in 1973. It is kept larger than the Nobel Prizes in science, literature and other fields to show that religion is more important.

Past winners include Mother Teresa, writer Alexander Solzhenitsyn and evangelist Billy Graham. The Templeton has gone to Protestants, Roman Catholics, Hindus, an Eastern Orthodox, a Buddhist and a Muslim.

Jakobovits, born in Konigsberg, Germany, fled the Nazi terror as a teen-ager. He was chief rabbi of Ireland from 1949 to 1958.

He was appointed chief rabbi of Great Britain and the Commonwealth in 1967. He was knighted by Queen Elizabeth in 1981 and made a titled member of the House of Lords in 1988, the first rabbi to hold a seat there.

While rabbi of New York's Fifth Avenue Synagogue from 1958 to 1967, he broke ranks with fellow Jews in condemning the 1962 U.S. Supreme Court decision banning Bible readings and prayers in public schools.

Virtually every other Jewish leader backed the court, saying such practices violated church-state separation. But Jakobovits argued that Jews should not seek to reduce religious influence in society.

Also differing with other Jews, he advocated federal aid or tax relief for parochial schools.

Jakobovits called the award "the supreme moment of my life." 1991

Chapter One

ISRAEL

Sanctuary or Asylum?

"SHALL YOUR BROTHERS GO TO WAR...?"

Nearly thirty years ago my illustrious predecessor, Chief Rabbi Dr. Hertz, addressed a massed assembly in this very hall to arouse the conscience of the world on the catastrophe that lay ahead for European Jewry. Alas, the cry was too weak and too late to avert disaster.

Today we have reached another turning-point in Jewish history, perhaps more fateful than any in our long and chequered past. From the land of our first oppression in biblical days a new oppressor has arisen—a tyrant so cruel that he does not flinch from using poison gas on his own Arab brothers— with the avowed and often-proclaimed aim to destroy Israel and to drive its population into the sea.

We are here this evening to make quite sure that we will not be too weak and not be too late this time. We are not going to have another holocaust in the martyred history of our people. The hope of two millennia, and the toil and sacrifice of two decades, is not now going to wiped out in two weeks or two months.

Israel, as we were foretold in the Bible, *hen am levadad yishkon*, "a people that will dwell in loneliness" (Nu. 23:9), is the only nation on earth without alliances—except for the Jewish communities. We are Israel's only allies. We are assembled here this evening to make it clear that an attack on Israel is an attack on every Jewish community throughout the world, and that we are at least as united in the defence of the land that is dear and cherished by us as our adversaries are in their resolve to destroy us.

I make no apology for having called last week, before the Board of Deputies of British Jews, upon the Anglo-Jewish community to mobilise all its resources in the defence of Israel. Nor will I ever be deterred from doing my religious and my moral duty in this moment of our people's anguish by anyone coming forth with the dangerous nonsense of dual loyalties.[1]

Let me try, as plainly as I can, to clear up this diabolical confusion. As a British citizen, England is my country. As a Jew, Israel is my people. When my father and my mother, my brothers and sisters, are in danger of being murdered, I will defend them whatever their nationality, and if I were not to do so, then my fellow-citizens would have nothing but contempt for me. I am, therefore, overcome with grief, I am sickened to the depths of my

---

Address delivered on the outbreak of the Six-day War at the Royal Albert Hall, London, on 5 June 1967.

heart, by the spectacle of some Jews who, having previously betrayed their God and betrayed their religion, are now publicly calling upon their fellow-Jews to betray their people.

But, together with you, I am proud and elated by the magnificent response of the overwhelming majority of our community in rising to this historic occasion. We have been flooded with volunteers who wish to offer their lives and their service to our people, and with those who are coming forward to give of their means towards the consolidation of Israel in this hour of trial.

This grave emergency calls first upon the Jewish people. We hear tonight an anguished cry, a cry that Moses once uttered when two of our tribes of Israel wanted to remain on the other side of the Jordan without participating in the battle that lay ahead for the rest of them, and he said to them: *Ha'achechem yavou' lamilchamah ve'atem teshvu po*; "Shall your brothers go to war and you will remain and sit idly by here?" We are not asked, thank God, to go to war or surrender lives. But we are asked to identify ourselves and make common cause with those who do, so that not merely they will live, but that we will live as a self-respecting community.

You may ask, "What can I do in this emergency?" The industrialist who gives a million or the little Jewish child who pours out his heart in prayer to God to have mercy over our people, the volunteer who gives his service in order to prop up Israel's economy, or our communal leaders who now fight for Jewish survival against the scourge of assimilation with redoubled vigour —they all stand in the front-line of the battle against Jewish extinction. They all help to make sure that together we prevail.

Specifically, my office in trying to co-ordinate, and to assist in, the gigantic efforts that will be demanded of us, has taken a number of steps, together with the Haham. First, I have convened a Conference of Rabbis and Ministers from all over the country for tomorrow to consult together on the help we can render in directing and co-ordinating efforts to mobilise our community, and indeed to mobilise public opinion on a local as well as a national level. Second, we have opened an office, an Israel Emergency Office, to receive enquires and direct offers of help. Third, we are asking all synagogues during the present emergency to remain open all day for those who wish, in a moment of anxiety or inspiration, to commune with their Creator and seek the strength and comfort of which we stand in need in this awesome moment of test and trial. Two-and-a-half million Jews cannot, by the ordinary laws of nature, win out against fifty million adversaries without the help of God, and side by side with our material mobilisation we are going to mobilise our spiritual resources to storm the gates of Heaven and plead to God to be at our side in this moment of destiny and danger. Fourth, we are appealing to all members of our community, during this crisis, to curtail personal parties and functions and to use the resources that had been set aside for these purposes as contributions to Israel that it may prevail. Fifth, we are asking Jewish communal organisations throughout the country during this emergency to suspend all campaigns for communal projects, with the sole exception of any venture connected with the intensification of the Jewish education of our own children. For, let us make no mistake—the battle of Jewish survival is being fought in our own midst just as grimly as in Israel. How can we survive, and what kind of a people are we going to be, if our children will be aliens to our heritage; and if we are going to suffer more casualties than our troubled and martyred people has already sustained through massacre, through repression and through assimilation in the past thirty years?

There also goes out from us here a call to the British nation. An Israeli friend of mine, a member of the Knesset, told me a few years ago of an interview he had had at the White House with the then President Truman. He asked the President what made him decide on the day of the establishment of Israel to give his historic recognition to the newly born State. Mr. Truman answered that he felt "Providence had summoned me to complete the Balfour Declaration". Tonight, in this fiftieth year of the Balfour Declaration, Britain is being summoned by Providence and destiny to complete the Balfour Declaration. I plead with the leaders of Parliament with us here and, through them, the leaders of this great and gallant nation, which also was once in the depths of danger and appealed to the world to come to its rescue. I plead with them as a Bible-loving people: You can help to make not just Jewish history but British history.

And we call upon the nations of the world. Israel is the only nation that has been created by the United Nations. We are surely, as anyone with the scantiest knowledge of Jewish history knows, a peace-loving people. Never in our history have we embarked on building empires by aggression. Never in our history have we gone out on crusades in order to convert others to Judaism by force. Throughout our history we have been at the receiving end of persecution. We have never meted out persecution to others. Tonight, on this evening of Jewish solidarity, how we think of our three million brethren in the Soviet land who, if they only could, would join with us and whose spokesmen we are, and who are a living witness that we are victims of persecution and will never impose persecution, let alone extermination, on others. Let the world take up our cause. We have four thousand years of history behind us to prove our case. We will get along in peace and construc- tive endeavour with our Arab cousins and neighbours.

Let me conclude on a note of confidence. We are told in the Book of Books: "And it shall be, when you draw nigh to war, that the priest, the spiritual leader, shall approach and speak to the people, and shall say to them: *Shema Yisrael*, Hear, O Israel, you draw near this day to war against your enemies; let not your heart be faint, fear not, nor be alarmed, neither be affrightened at them, for the Lord your God will go with you, to fight for you against your enemies to save you" (Deut. 20:2–4).

May I mention to you, as a token of the spirit of the land which today has been plunged into war, that I was advised through the Israel Embassy that, on this first day of war, the children of Israel went to school and took examinations at school. Likewise, the Ambassador has told me that since the delivery of the mail in Israel has been taken over by the youngsters, it has become more efficient and more expeditious that ever before. That is the spirit of the newly born Israel, and that is going to be our spirit.

We cry out on this evening of decision to God, the guarantor of Israel's survival. In the words that we recite every time we open the Holy Ark, "*Vayehi Binso'a Ha'Aron Vayomer Mosheh Kumah Hashem Veyafutsu*

Oyevechah Veyanusu Mesan'echah Mipanechah". And as the Holy Ark of Jewish history is once again on the march, we call out "O Lord, arise and scatter Your enemies and let those that hate You flee from before You!" We also call out to our brothers and sisters assembled here this evening. We hear a distant cry from our brothers in Israel, and I am here to convey it to you. That cry is identical with the words which the British nation, through its greatest son, once used when it was in danger and addressed itself to others. Our Israeli brethren call to us tonight: "Give us the tools, and we will finish the job."

May we so acquit ourselves of one of the greatest challenges of Jewish history that we may, with God's help, on next Iyar 5 celebrate the 20th Anniversary of Israel with greater joy, with greater comfort, and indeed with a greater assurance of permanent peace than ever before.

NOTE

1. The Chief Rabbi's call had aroused the spectre of "dual loyalties" in a bitter and widely publicised attack by a well-known Jewish columnist in *The Daily Mail* a week earlier.

THE INFAMY OF MUNICH

Over a hundred years ago the German-Jewish scholar, Leopold Zunz, founder of the modern "Science of Judaism", wrote in an immortal passage quoted by George Eliot in *Daniel Deronda*:

"If there are ranks in suffering, Israel takes precedence of all nations;

if the duration of sorrows and the patience with which they are borne ennoble, the Jews can challenge the aristocracy of every land;

if a literature is called rich in the possession of a few classic tragedies—what shall we say of a national tragedy lasting many centuries, in which the poets and the actors are also the heroes?"

Suffering and martyrdom, death and grief through terror and assassination are not new in the Jewish experience.

What can better remind us of this than the coincidence of this Day of Mourning and this Memorial Service for the latest victims to the horrors of hate and violence with today's Fast of Gedaliah, a fast we have observed for 2,500 years to remember with timeless sorrow the assassination of Gedaliah, the Governor of Judah appointed by the Babylonians after their capture of Jerusalem in 586 BCE? Our remembrance has not faded over the millennia, and to this day we commemorate his death with which the first Jewish Commonwealth finally came to an end. If the tribulations of our people are extraordinary in their duration and intensity, our memories of them are no less enduring and acute.

Yet, last week's tragic events at Munich have a poignancy and a significance which, even in our martyred history, are without precedent.

There is the ultimate depravity in the sordid story of man's inhumanity to man when young, sprightly sportsmen leave their young country to join the world's greatest spectacle of human harmony and international friendship, and then return in coffins, slain in cold blood after 20 hours of horror, manacled and blindfolded.

There is the ultimate heart-break, personal and national, when little babies, too small to mourn, are turned into orphans, young wives condemned to widowhood and aged parents forced to bury their children, in some cases their only child, and when an entire people is bereaved of gallant sons,

Address delivered at the Memorial Service for the Israel Olympic victims of the terrorist outrage in Munich, held at the Hendon Synagogue, London, on 11 September 1972.

some of them survivors of the Nazi Holocaust and others only recently restored to the Land of their Fathers after heroically prevailing over the agony of their cruel repression and the long wait for their liberation behind the Iron Curtain.

And there is the ultimate pain caused by tearing open old wounds and rubbing salt into them when such a crime is perpetrated in the very cradle of the movement which became the Jewish people's most diabolical oppressor, a site only a few miles away from the notorious concentration camp which not so long ago was soaked with Jewish blood, and a city which has given its name to one of history's most infamous betrayals by the disastrous appeasement of murderers.

But we have gathered in this house of worship as well as in synagogues throughout our community not merely to join in the world-wide expression of shock and grief, of outrage and condemnation. Still under the spell of the religious inspiration we have drawn from our New Year services yesterday and the day before, we have come here today to seek the solace and moral instruction of our faith at this time of grief and bewilderment.

In the past few days we have heard and read countless statements by the world's leading statesmen and church dignitaries, by journalists and numerous other personalities in public life. But here we want to be comforted and guided by the voice of our own hard-tried and long-tested heritage.

How would our Hebrew Prophets—the most perceptive and far-sighted commentators of all times on contemporary events, on the fortunes and misfortunes of our people—how would they have reacted to a calamity of such national poignancy and such universal ramifications? They would surely have turned, in their inspired vision and fiery eloquence, both to the nations of the world and to their own people.

To the nations, I believe, their words would ring out clear with a double message: First, an expression of gratification that at last the peoples of the world have not left Israel to endure its tribulations alone, on its own.

In the past, we have all too often borne our ordeals in utter loneliness. When six million Jews were brutally done to death in a bloodbath unmatched in the annals of man, we had to weep by ourselves. The nations did not lower their flags to half-mast, there was no memorial meeting for the victims attended by leading representatives of the world's nations, great and small; the conscience of mankind was hardly stirred by that monstrous tragedy inflicted on our people.

How different this time, when the world has shared the trauma of our anguish, when we have received the most touching messages of sympathy from thousands of human brothers in positions high and low, from leaders of nations, and races, and creeds in all parts of the globe, and when at last we hear a universal outcry for concerted action to liberate the human race from the intolerable stain of wanton terror against the innocent.

In acknowledging this momentous advance towards the ideals of human brotherhood our Prophets were the first to preach, they might also have added a warning: The values of human life and dignity, no less than peace, are indivisible.

The twentieth century has shown abundantly that when the Jew is a victim of injustice and persecution, he is but the first and others follow. Hitler began by unleashing his terror against the Jews; he finished by plunging the world into the most costly and calamitous war in all history, with consequences from which we still suffer in our restless world.

Significantly, an evil dictator in Uganda began by expelling Israelis whose purpose was to upbuild his country; next he expelled British subjects who had contributed so much to his people; and finally he turned against thousands of his own former nationals.

Let the world know that if terror is tolerated when endured by any minority, and when those who protect terrorists and give succour to them remain unconstrained and beyond the reach of international law and justice, then eventually the forces of terror and lawlessness erode the entire fabric of human society. The present mood of mankind encourages us in our hope that this warning is now widely understood.

To our own people, stricken with grief, our Prophets would speak in more intimate and familiar terms. They surely would first of all have seen the reality of Israel's colossal achievement in the wider perspective of the place of the Jew in the contemporary world and in history. Gone are the days when Jews suffered pogroms, persecution and repression, and no one heard their cry or pleaded their cause before the family of nations. It is only through the existence of the Jewish State and its defence of Jewish interests that the conscience of the world has been aroused and involved on a global scale. Without Israel's corporate expression of the Jewish voice, the three million Jews of Soviet Russia might still languish in utter silence; neither we nor the world would be alert to their suffering and respond to the challenge of their ordeal. Were it not for Israel, groups of Jews might be butchered anywhere in the world, and few voices would be raised in sympathy and still fewer in meaningful protest. How immense therefore, must be our thanksgiving in this 25th year of Israel's rebirth, a rebirth foretold and promised by our Prophets.

But our Prophets would also not have allowed a moment of Jewish national grief such as this to pass without searching and probing the Jewish conscience, asking how far we have fulfilled our national purpose and implemented our part of the Covenant with God from whom we now seek consolation and reassurance,

Whenever we fast and mourn, we recite *Selichot*, prayers for forgiveness, as we did this morning. In the Jewish view there is no national suffering without national failings. Apart from summoning us to far greater religious and spiritual exertions in general, our Prophets would have emphasised particularly the moral call to share in the ordeals of others, as we want others to share in ours.

It has always been the Jewish characteristic that our compassion extends to all who suffer, even our enemies. Our Sages tell us that the 100 notes of the *Shofar* which we sound on the New Year are meant to echo the 100 sighs that rose from the bereaved mother in Sisera, when he was slain in his battle against the Jewish people in biblical times.

We are to feel the anguish of all mothers who lose their children, and our Prophets would surely expect us to sense even the grief of the mothers of the evil assassins. They would also expect us not to be insensitive to the enormous human tragedy of hundreds of thousands who still suffer the indignity and deprivation of refugeedom, a fate with which we ourselves are all too familiar.

But above all, they would issue a stirring call to our people to labour ceaselessly for the fulfilment of our historic assignment. They might even question some aspects of the Olympic ideal as quite alien to Judaism, much as we applaud the invaluable contribution of these competitions to the promotion of human fellowship and international goodwill. But whilst we participate in these Games under a torch lit on Mt. Olympus idealising the holiness of beauty and physical perfection, let us recall that this was a creed against which our Maccabean forebears once fought bitterly. Without their victory over these very ideals embraced by Hellenism there would have been no survival of Judaism, nor 160 years later the emergence of Christianity and eventually of our entire Western civilisation.

Our ultimate purpose is to light a new torch—*"or chadash al Ziyon ta'ir"*—not on Mt. Olympus, but on Mt. Zion, a torch which will be a light unto the nations, through which we will illumine the inner splendour of man and bring the illumination of our prophetic ideals of social justice and human brotherhood to the ends of the earth.

How wonderful it would be if one day we could initiate international competitions around a flame lit in Jerusalem which would exalt spiritual striving, and which would bring together all moral pioneers who compete for the alleviation of suffering, the eradication of poverty, the elimination of vice and crime, the conquest of disease, and the banishment of selfishness and materialism—a spectacle which would focus the eyes of the world on an arena dedicated to the beauty of holiness and the soul of man.

We have entered a New Year. May we be blessed with a beneficient response to our fervent prayers at this penitential season: "Our Father our King, annul the designs of those who hate us!" "Our Father our King, do it for the sake of those who were slain for Your holy Name," that their sacrifice be not in vain.

Speed the day when "the just shall see and be glad, as iniquity shall close her mouth, and all wickedness shall be altogether consumed like smoke, when You cause the rule of violence to pass away from the earth."

May we and all our fellow-humans, having sown in tears reap in joy, as we see fulfilled the beautiful words in Hannah's song which we read in the portion from the Prophets at our New Year Service: "He will preserve the feet of His faithful ones, while the wicked will be put to silence in darkness; for no man shall prevail by force. The Lord shall judge the ends of the earth, and He shall give strength unto His ruler, and exalt the horn of His annointed."

May the New Year bring the blessings of peace and fellowship to Israel and to all our human family, as we witness the realisation of the promise: "Zion will be redeemed through justice, and those who return to her through righteousness."

FROM TEARS TO JOY

We are assembled at this solemn service, united with the entire House of Israel the world over in festivity and thanksgiving, to mark an occasion unique in the perspective of history and without parallel among the convulsive happenings of our exciting times. Never before in the annals of man has any nation or group of people celebrated an event which is only a quarter-of-a-century old and which yet took millennia to evolve, plan and eventually turn from dream to reality. In expressing our infinite pride and joy at this epoch-making event, and in reflecting on its significance, it is right that we should first of all pay homage to the visionaries and dreamers, to the inspired leaders and pioneers, and to the builders and fighters who have co-operated with Providence to the fulfilment of Its age-old design.

The Psalmist speaks of Jerusalem as עיר שחוברה לה יחדו —"a city which is joined altogether". The Talmud interprets this as עיר שהיא עושה כל ישראל חברים —"the city which turns all Jews into partners", referring to Zion's capacity to unite the Jewish people in a unique togetherness. The establishment of Israel in 1948 was the culmination of an effort which indeed drew its inspiration and national energy from every epoch of Jewish history, from every stratum of Jewish literature, and from every section of the Jewish people.

ROOTS IN HISTORY

The reborn Jewish State is like a tree, deriving its nourishment from a mighty network of roots embedded in every layer of past Jewish experience. These roots stretch back to the Torah, which provided the original Divine mandate for the Jewish title to the Land and its sanctification, and which records the summons of Aliyah to the Land as the first commandment given to the first Jew. These roots extend to the Hebrew Prophets, who constantly affirmed the Divine promise of the Jewish people's eventual return to Zion following their dispersion among the nations. They spring from the Talmudic era which, having guided the transformation of our people from a life of national independence to exilic existence, instilled the faith in our return to Zion and the rebuilding of Jerusalem in every daily prayer; in every Grace-after-meals;

Address delivered at the 25th Israel Independence Day Service at St. John's Wood Synagogue, London, on 6 May 1973.

in every greeting, whether of joy when founding a Jewish home or of sorrow when comforting mourners. These roots reach out to the Golden Age of the Spanish period, which sublimated the love of Zion in the passionate poetry of Yehuda Halevi and the arduous Aliyah to the Holy Land of Nachmanides and others; and to the mystic school of Luria and Karo, which flourished in Safed in the sixteenth century as a direct forerunner of the modern Yishuv.

The more immediate antecedents of the Zionist movement and its evolution to the present day have likewise drawn their inspiration from the interplay and partnership of virtually every strand in the fabric of Jewish thought and ideology within the past century and a half. In the ever-growing momentum of the Zionist idea there were fused together the religious fervour of spiritual pioneers like Rabbis Zvi Hirsch Kalischer and Judah Alkalai, in the second quarter of the nineteenth century, with the secular nationalism of social revolutionaries and humanists like Moses Hess and Leon Pinsker, in the second half of that century. Among the vital forces that have produced the Jewish State are blended the rudimentary Zionism of Nathan Birnbaum, who coined the world Zionism in 1890; the political Zionism of Theodor Herzl, who created the Zionist Organisation in 1897; the cultural Zionism of Achad Ha'am, who fixed his gaze upon Zion as our spiritual centre; and the fusion of these trends called "synthetic Zionism" by Chaim Weizmann, whose sagacious leadership traversed the forty-year wilderness from the post-Herzl period to the Presidency of the newly born State of Israel.

Towards the triumphant consummation of the Zionist ideal laboured militants like Nordau and Jabotinsky, as well as pacifists like Magnes and Buber; aristocrats like Brandeis and Herbert Samuel, as well as socialists like Ben Gurion and Golda Meir; Orthodox rabbinical sages like Rabbis Kook and Maimon as well as Reform leaders like Stephen Wise and Abba Hillel Silver. Zion truly proved "a city joining us altogether", the cause through which Jews of every generation, of every persuasion and of every motivation, were drawn together in a common hope and a common triumph.

Of course, this young plant of the new State, with its powerful roots struck deep and broad in Jewish history, could not have sprouted forth to produce its first-fruits in our generation without the fertilisation and irrigation of much blood, sweat and tears. The Psalmist, too, uses an agricultural metaphor when, referring the Restoration of our people to Zion "the Lord will return the captivity of Zion," he asserts "those who sow in tears will reap in joy".

OUT OF THE DEPTHS . . .

Just as the creation of all life is accompanied by the pangs of labour and the loss of blood, so did every major thrust leading to the rebirth and consolidation of our national independence result from the agony of suffering, persecution and slaughter. In 1840 it was the Ritual Murder charge against the Jewish community of Damascus that sparked Alkalai's conversion to Zionism. Forty years later the Chovevei Zion movement led by Lilienblum and Pinsker was galvanised by the pogroms in Rumania and Russia, especially after the assassination of Czar Alexander II in 1881. Some 15 years later the endemic scourge of western anti-semitism manifested in the Dreyfus Affair precipitated Herzl's metamorphosis from his assimilationist beliefs into his Zionist zeal. In the growing turmoil of the past six decades it was left to the cataclysmic events of the First World War to produce the Balfour Declaration and the ultimate disaster of the Second World War and the Nazi Holocaust to generate the superhuman energies for the final push towards the birth of the new State, a state itself born and defended in the martyrdom of three wars, at the cost of much precious blood.

FIRST FRUITS

Now, 25 years after the momentous event, we begin to reap in joy the first-fruits of the countless seeds sown in tears over the centuries. What luscious outsize fruits this young sturdy plant has already produced! In but one generation, Israel has already become the world's leading centre of Torah learning and intensely religious living; proportionately it has given a haven to more refugees than any other country in history; it has achieved greater ethnic integration and equality for the most diverse tribes in two and a half decades than the advanced civilisation of America did in 100 years; it has a higher rate of literacy, scientific progress and economic growth than any other developing country; it has more academic institutions, greater democratic freedom, more stable government, than any other state in the region. Its leaders and diplomats are men and women of outstanding ability and dedication; its army has earned the respect of friends and foes alike, and its contributions to the development of other emergent nations have set a rare example of a struggling nation stretching out a helping hand to sustain the struggles of others who seek national independence and economic self-sufficiency.

Equally significant are the fruits of Israel now exported in an increasing measure to the Jewish communities of the Diaspora. By now we may truly say that more than we contribute to Israel through financial, moral and political support, does Israel contribute to the enrichment of our lives. Israel has intensified our Jewish pride and self-respect. Where the synagogue and the Jewish school no longer proved effective in retaining the Jewish loyalties of some, Israel has restored to countless Jews their Jewish identity and harnessed some of their finest talents, otherwise lost to the community, in the cause of the Jewish people. Moreover, the wondrous rebirth of Israel has spawned the miraculous reawakening of Soviet Jewry, has helped to stimulate the phenomenal growth of Jewish day schools throughout the world, has revived interest in Hebrew and Jewish studies, and has given new meaning and purpose to the struggle for Jewish survival.

Altogether, Israel—partly through the continuing urgency of its needs and partly through its centrality in contemporary Jewish affairs and thought—has become the principal dynamic of Jewish communal activity the world over. With Israel supplying many of our Jewish teachers and helping to train others, sustaining most of our fund-raising work and much of our cultural life, providing a magnet for students, communal leaders, pilgrims and tourists to recharge their spiritual batteries by visiting the Land, and not least arousing our Jewish conscience and involvement through the almost daily reports on and challenges to Israel in our newspapers and other mass media, it is clear that without Israel much of the vitality of Jewish life and the vibrancy of Jewish spirit in the Diaspora communities would be blighted.

FESTIVALS OF SALVATION

On this anniversary, then, we have more reason to rejoice and to render thanks to the Almighty than we have had for the past twenty centuries. Where all our other festivals celebrate events which occurred thousands of years ago, this newest festival in the Jewish calendar marks an event for which we have waited thousands of years and which many of us witnessed with our own eyes. Significantly, *Yom Ha'atzmaut* combines features of the other three festivals of national salvation in our calendar: the Passover deliverance from bondage to freedom, the Purim victory over anti-semitic persecution and aggression, and the surrender of the "many into the hands of the few" of Chanukah. In the rise of Israel our generation has seen the combination of all three triumphs brought about by Divine help and human valour: millions of Jews have been liberated from oppression and humiliation, the counsel of those who hate us has been confounded, and vast armies bent on our destruction have been put to flight by but a fraction of their number.

Yet, in one important respect our latest festival seems to differ fundamentally from its most notable predecessor, Passover, the original festival of our freedom. Pesach celebrated the beginning of our Exodus, not its conclusion; its records our departure from Egypt, not our entry into the Holy Land. In fact, neither Divine legislation nor Jewish tradition have ever fixed a date to commemorate Joshua's conquest of the land, or any other conquest, as a day worthy of special celebration. Passover feasts the start of the journey, not its end. The Jewish calendar immortalises the opportunity for gaining and utilising national independence rather than its fulfilment; for in the Jewish scale of values we hail effort rather than success.

Against the backdrop of our millennial history and our destiny as *Am Hanetzach*, the people of eternity, a period of 25 years, however eventful, is but a tiny and insignificant slice of time. *Yom Ha'atzmaut* will rank as a permanent and distinguished marker in our calendar, alongside our other traditional festivals, only if we regard it as opening rather than closing one of the great epochs of the Jewish experience; if we look upon the 5th of Iyyar 1948 as the beginning and not the end in our hard and long struggle for the realisation of our ultimate Jewish destiny. The real challenges of Jewish independence are yet to be met.

All the colossal achievements behind us provide but the springboard for a mighty national effort to reach the goals of our historic assignment. Passover was but the forerunner of Shavuot, our people's encounter with God at Sinai; it was the condition for our sanctification of the Land under Joshua forty years later; it was the curtain-raiser for the drama which led to the achievement of our spiritual glory with the building of the Temple under King Solomon 480 years later. So does the deliverance of *Yom Ha'atzmaut* in our time summon us to set our national sights on the essential ideals still unfulfilled: the striving for peace, the continued ingathering of our exiles, the promotion of righteousness in human and international relations, the search for Jewish identity and unity of purpose consonant with our historic traditions, and the resumption of our role as the People of the Book that, living "not by might nor by power but by My spirit", will advance the moral order and spiritual commitment of mankind at large.

CONFRONTATION WITH THREE FAITHS

The tasks besetting Israel and the Jewish people are formidable indeed. Quite apart from the pressing problems of national security, economic stability and social and religious harmony, the restoration of independence, by a strange twist of fate, has in different ways precipitated a direct confrontation with all the three monotheistic faiths generated out of Israel's spiritual energies. There is the confrontation with Islam, now the world's principal breeding-ground for hostility against our people; the confrontation with Christianity, which has yet not come fully to terms with the Jewish return to Zion and its theological implications; and even the confrontation with Judaism itself which must still evolve a dynamic response to the modern experience of Jewish statehood, just as the Jewish people must yet rediscover the timeless values of its religious faith, to provide a national purpose transcending the quest for physical survival and material prosperity. This applies with special urgency in an age when the gulf between Jews and Judaism is constantly widening. There can be no survival of Jews without Judaism, as our history has amply proved, any more than there can be Judaism without Jews. The State of Israel can clearly prosper on the strength of its age-old roots and vindicate the millennial tribulations of its nurture only if it is dedicated to both propositions.

At this festive milestone to mark Israel's semi-jubilee, then, we have reached the end of a new beginning in Jewish history. The founding generation in the upbuilding of the State is being succeeded by its sons. The challenges we have met and those which still confront us recall another unique epoch in Jewish history, the establishment of the first Jewish Commonwealth, when the first incumbent of the Davidic dynasty was to be succeeded by his heir.

King David had united the tribes of Israel, consolidated their sovereignty in the Promised Land, and secured Jerusalem as Israel's eternal capital. Undaunted by overwhelming odds, he had slain Goliath, and waged many wars in the defence of Israel. But as a bloodstained warrior he was denied his dearest wish, to build the Temple in Jerusalem, symbolising Israel's spiritual splendour. This had to await the accession of his son, Solomon—מלך שהשלום שלו—"the King of Peace", as his very name implies. Untarnished by the agonies of battle, the scars of war, the heroics of conquest and the self-righteousness bred by conflict, only he could succeed in directing his and the nations's energies to Israel's ultimate purpose: the revelation of God and the elevation of man.

DAVIDS AND SOLOMONS

The first 25 years of Israel's reborn statehood represent the generation of

Davids, a generation of pioneers cast in an heroic mould, bravely battling against and prevailing over many a Goliath, a generation bent single-mindedly on hoisting the Star of David to flutter proudly and invincibly over the ramparts of Zion and Jerusalem,

We pray that the next 25 years may witness the rise of the new generation, a generation of Solomons, blessed in peace to concentrate with equal determination on rebuilding the sanctuaries of our people, uniting the ingathered tribes of Israel in the pursuit of spiritual excellence and our national vocation as a beacon of social justice, ethical rectitude, moral discipline and religious fervour.

On this most auspicious occasion, and for the first time collectively, we send forth our heart-felt greetings to, and invoke Divine blessings upon, Israel's new first citizen, President Katzir. We pray that he may usher in a new Solomonic age of wise leadership, enduring tranquillity and lasting spiritual grandeur. If Israel's first President, bearing the name Weizmann, literally "the man of wheat", personified the struggle, hardship and sacrifice of sowing the seeds of Jewish independence in tears, may President Katzir, as his Hebrew name denotes, symbolise the rich harvest of peace and immortal achievement reaped in joy to fulfil the beautiful promise of yesterday's Haftorah from the Prophet Amos:

"Behold, the days come, says the Lord, that the ploughman shall overtake the reaper, and the treader of grapes him that sows seed; and the mountains shall drop sweet wine and all the hills shall melt. And I will turn the captivity of My people Israel, and they shall build the waste cities and inhabit them; and they shall plant vineyards and drink the wine thereof; they shall also make gardens, and eat the fruit of them. And I will plant them upon their land, and they shall no more be plucked up out of their land which I have given them, says the Lord your God."

THE JEWISH DESTINY—THE SPIRITUAL CHALLENGE OF THE YOM KIPPUR WAR

Our meeting happens to coincide with one of the most infamous anniversaries of all times. On 30 January, forty-one years ago, the Nazi gangsters came to power in Germany, leading within ten years to the most catastrophic blood-bath in our history, but leading indirectly also within fifteen years to our finest hour, the rise of Israel, born out of the resolve and idealism generated by the travail of the preceding years.

The Yom Kippur War has certainly likewise been a major turning-point in Jewish history. Its immediate consequences have caused great heartbreak, but its more long-term effects, if we will only learn the right lessons, may well turn its curse into a blessing, by not only bringing us closer to the prospect of peace, but by bringing the Jewish State closer to the ideals which stirred the vision of our Prophets and our thinkers and martyrs through the ages. The War, then, opened up for all Jews an entirely new era, calling for a long hard new look at the revolutionary course of Jewish history and the progressive realisation of the Zionist dream.

SPIRITUAL CRISIS

I am, therefore, grateful to the Honorary Officers of the United Synagogue and its Israel Committee for their willing response to my suggestion to convene this special meeting of leaders, both spiritual and lay, of our synagogue community and some of Anglo-Jewry's principal organisations. Convinced, as I am, that the convulsive changes in Jewish fortunes and prospects precipitated by the Yom Kippur War, represent, above all else, a profound spiritual crisis of momentous proportions, I have for some time felt the urge to share with you, and through you with my fellow-Jews, especially the religious element, some reflections on the deeper significance of these epoch-making events in the perspective of our historical and religious experience. After all, we are not novices in battling against the most fearful odds and we have prevailed over all our tribulations because we were a people steeled by history and sustained by religious faith.

Some of my assessments and conclusions I have previously, in part, presented to public audiences in Israel—once in Tel Aviv two months ago

Lecture delivered before the Ministers and Councils of the United Synagogue and communal leaders at the Hendon Synagogue, London, on 30 January 1974.

and again in Jerusalem ten days ago. The reception accorded to them, including the strictures they contained, encouraged me to set them forth for delivery to you, duly revised in the light of numerous discussions with religious and national leaders, as well as with many ordinary Israeli citizens.

My remarks, let me add, are intended to deal with the Jewish condition as a whole; they are not meant to relate to the impact of the present crisis specifically on Anglo-Jewry. Nevertheless, I hope that my message may stimulate some collective response by this great community which has played such a notable role in the rise and consummation of Zionism and which could now, once again, make some original contributions in charting a fresh and safe course for the storm-tossed ship of the Jewish destiny.

SALUTARY EFFECTS

Out of the agony of this War, which followed so unexpectedly the ecstasy of the Six-day War, have flowed much blood and tears, many anxieties and fears. But from it have also already emerged some altogether salutary effects.

The War has united the Jewish people more firmly than ever before, even than in 1967, drawing Israel and the Diaspora intimately together by both a sense of common loneliness and a growing feeling of mutual dependence. Moreover, out of the disillusionment with the past and concern for the future has sprung up an unprecedented search for deeper spiritual values, especially among Israel's youth, now largely at the fronts. And, not least in importance, our past inclination to self-righteousness has given way to intense soul-searching, to frank self-criticism, where previously any unconventional opinions were often rejected as unnecessary or even unpatriotic.

These welcome developments make it less hazardous than before to undertake an agonising reappraisal, a stocktaking to which Jews everywhere, sharing a common destiny, must contribute whatever they can. In our situation, questions are as vital as answers, for without questioning the past, we shall not avoid its pitfalls and failures in the future. And the proper cure for an affliction can only come after its correct diagnosis which is itself revealed by asking the right questions.

GUILT OF OURSELVES AND OTHERS

Now, my remarks are addressed to Jews, and especially religious Jews. They are founded on the firm belief, constantly upheld in Jewish teachings, that we ourselves are solely responsible for our national fate, certainly in the Land of Israel, to which the doctrine of collective reward and punishment is invariably limited in the Bible. In the final analysis, we suffer or prosper as a nation, not through the capricious conduct of others but only through our own failure or merit. Of course, this does not in any way gloss over the guilt of our enemies and their friends. For instance, the specious claim, repreated *ad nauseam*, that territory acquired by war may not be retained even for self-defence and security, reeks of particularly odious hypocrisy when it comes from the lips of Arabs whose vast empires across Asia and Africa were all conquered by the sword, or from Russia which still subjugates half of Eastern Europe by annexation and military occupation as a strategic security-belt, or even from France and Britain whose territorial acquisitions by force, some retained to this day, dwarf all conquest made by Jews in 4,000 years of history.

But whatever blame attaches to them or to others for our tribulations cannot invalidate the authentic teaching of Judaism on the philosophy of Jewish history as proclaimed throughout our sacred literature, and as enshrined in the Psalmist's words: "If only My people would hearken unto Me, and Israel walk in My ways, I would subdue their enemies and turn My hand against their adversaries."

PROVIDENCE AND MIRACLES

The mere fact that a tiny people restored to a little land, with few natural resources, continues to be at or near the very heart of the major political, economic and strategic upheavals besetting the entire world, affecting the fortunes of super-powers and small nations alike, is itself the surest indication that the millennial drama of God's special relationship with Israel is far from played out. A numerically insignificant nation cannot bestride the front-pages of the world's newspapers for twenty-five years without serving a special purpose in the evolution of man's history.

But let me caution against an overemphasis of miracles, as is so common today in the quest for religious authenticity. Maimonides already warned against interpreting even biblical miracles as serving to prove God or to legitimise His messengers (*Hil. Yesodei Ha-Torah 8:1*).

The quite extraordinary events of Israel's first twenty-five years have induced perhaps an undue tendency to look for a constant succession of miracles. There is something less than genuine faith and more than a trace of over-bearing presumption in the widely current assertion: "In Israel, he who does not believe in miracles is not a realist."

True enough, if miracles are events which confound human calculations, wrought by a Higher Intelligence, some no doubt did occur in the latest War, too. With only six hundred troops and under a hundred tanks defending the fortifications in the South against overwhelmingly superior forces, and Israel having thrown back the Syrian invaders against similar odds after they had rolled across and down the Golan Heights to threaten Northern Israel with a deluge of blood and destruction, the outcome was nothing short of one of Jewish history's greatest wonders. Thanks to Divine help and the superhuman heroism of Israel's valiant youth, there was averted a catastrophe of near-holocaust proportions, with potentially devastating effects on Jewish existence everywhere. Yet even these colossal military feats—which, in themselves, may well eclipse the achievements of the Six-day War—are now almost irrelevant to Israel's predicament.

For alas, not all miracles were in Israel's favour. Equally against all rational anticipation were Israel's astounding unpreparedness, the unexpected strength and unity of the Arabs, and the stunning capitulation overnight, under oil-blackmail, of virtually all of Israel's friends, with but a few exceptions, notably the United States and Holland. There are circumstances, it seems, when we are not the sole beneficiaries of miracles. We may do well to analyse

these circumstances if, as in the past, we are once again to merit the special
solicitude of Israel's Guardian.

"ECHA?"—"HOW? WHY?"

In the war's grim aftermath many questions remain as yet unanswered. They
can all be summed up in the single Hebrew word expressing the classic Jewish
reaction to adversity and bewilderment: "*Echa?*"—"How? Why?"How could
it all happen? Why did a proud self-assured people, enjoying relative prosperity
and security behind the trusted shield of the proven strength and superb skill
of its defence forces, so suddenly find the props of its faith challenged, the
land plunged into grief and gloom, the Jewish nation faced again with fear
for its safety and survival, and the world brought to the brink of nuclear
confrontation and economic chaos?

The Commission of Enquiry set up by the Israel Government will no
doubt report in due course on the military, political and intelligence miscalculations responsible for the reverses, probably only to confirm and embellish facts
already known or suspected. But nothing could compound these errors more
than to believe that the factors leading to the war and its consequences were
limited, or even mainly attributable, to these miscalculations. The war
revealed a spiritual crisis at least as alarming and critical as lapses in the
sphere of logistics. It marked the collapse of an attitude of mind, of a whole
philosophy of life, no less than the collapse of a military strategy and of a
foreign policy. It slaughtered some very sacred cows and exploded quite a few
hallowed myths just as ruthlessly as it brought to an untimely end thousands
of precious lives and dashed many cherished hopes and assumptions.

Let it be stated at once and emphatically: We are all responsible for our
predicament and we can exonerate from blame neither secular Zionism nor
the religious parties, neither our national leadership nor our rabbinical
establishment, neither non-observant nor observant Jews, neither in Israel
nor in the Diaspora. We are united in guilt as we must be united in repentance
and a common endeavour to overcome our difficulties. None of us can undo
the past; but we all can and must learn our lessons to secure the future.

THE FALLACY OF SECULAR ZIONISM

The spiritual crisis may well trace its origin to the fallacious premises on
which the earliest secular Jewish nationalists based their dreams, plans and
policies. They, and their successors to the present day, believed that the
restoration of Jewish national independence in Zion would solve "the Jewish
problem". Ignoring the perennial lessons of our history and faith, they sought
to turn their backs on our past traditions and the spiritual ingredients in the
mystique of Jewish survival, convinced that, if only we had a state like all
other nations, we would "normalise" the Jewish condition and lose the
"peculiarity" responsible for our sufferings and persecution. The boon of
sovereignty—with a government, an army, a diplomatic corps, universities
and all the trappings of statehood—would make us accepted as an equal

among the nations and, by removing the "abnormalcy" of our homelessness, eliminate anti-Semitism.

What an idle dream this was! The Yom Kippur War has shattered this illusion. Jews today are as different, as "peculiar", and as lonely as they ever were. Far from having solved "the Jewish problem", the Jewish State has highlighted it. The "abnormalcy" of the Jewish condition—with all its attendant prejudices and dangers—has now been extended from individual Jews and scattered Jewish communities to the Jewish people as a whole. Despite the enormous spiritual, cultural, scientific, technological and material resources Israel, both in ancient and modern times, has invested into building up the civilisation of the Western World and helping the newly emergent nations, we are now the loneliest people on earth. In a world in which the moral order has broken down, we have been shamelessly forsaken by former friends and subjected to the very "double standards" of treatment and judgement by the international community it was the dream of the secularist Zionists to eliminate in the process of making us "equals"—like the rest of the world.

Of course, Israel's achievements are immeasurable—its restoration of Jewish pride and self-respect; its ingathering of the exiles and provision of a haven for millions of hunted Jews; its immense contributions to Jewish learning and culture; its social and scientific pioneering; its intense enrichment of Jewish life everywhere; its revitalisation of Jewish education and communal activity, stimulating the re-identification of countless Jews who would otherwise have been lost to our people—to mention just some of the priceless benefits which far outweigh, and amply compensate for, whatever costs Jewish statehood has imposed on us. But the one thing the Jewish State could not, must not, and never will achieve is to turn us into a nation like all other nations, losing our historic identity as a unique people.

THE FUTILE QUEST FOR EQUALITY

Did we really have to wait for the Yom Kippur War to expose the futility of the attempt to "normalise" the Jewish experience by wresting it from its spiritual moorings? Where was our sense of logic, where were our historical and religious traditions? These should have forewarned us against such an enterprise. Without our national distinctiveness as religious pioneers and moral path-finders, committed to the destiny assigned to us at Sinai and by our Prophets, if we succumb to be being like all other peoples, what purpose is to be served by Jewish survival altogether? Surely our forebears did not endure so much cruel martyrdom "for the sanctification of the Divine Name", nor offer thanks to God daily that "He has not made us like the nations of other lands, and not placed us like other families of the earth and our lot like all their multitude", in order that in the end we should glory in being a people just like all others, or even boast the finest army in the world! Would it make sense to establish a Jewish State as a bulwark against individual assimilation only to find it turning into an instrument of national assimilation?

After all, many larger and more powerful nations have been consigned to the dusty pages of history; who mourns them, who misses them? Even without a Jewish people, the progress and development of industry and agriculture, science and general culture would still continue apace. So, by what justification do we claim the right of survival after four thousand years of existence, already far beyond the life-span of other nations—and at a time when millions of human beings die from the onslaughts of poverty, starvation and violence in different parts of the globe?

What entitles us to demand the sympathy and support of the international community for our survival, even at the risk of world peace and economic stability—other than our special role to be "a light unto the nations", striving as a model society to enrich mankind with incomparable spiritual and moral contributions as we did in the past? This alone was and remains our national *raison d'être*.

SPIRITUAL EXPORTS AND IMPORTS

In pursuing the phantom of equality and mirage of normality rather than the unique goals of our Prophetic destiny, we reversed the flow of national features, of virtues and vices, in our trade of ideas with the nations. Instead of exporting the ideals and values peculiar to the Jewish spirit—the whole range, from humility, moral excellence and profound faith to the discipline of life trained by the regimen of religious observances—we all too often imported from our exile the base materialism, the social and moral depravities to which we had been exposed. The whole ethos of our national existence became widely contaminated by these alien imports. In the end, the benefits of equality escaped us, as the nations still do not treat us as equals, whilst the liabilities of equality afflict us, as we now sadly experience, like all other peoples, rising rates of delinquency, divorce, illegitimacy, social inequality, if not downright discrimination, and many other evils which erode society at large.

I would go further. In our obsession with "normality" our national independence itself was frequently expressed in forms utterly alien to Jewish thought. Was it really necessary, or consistent with the Jewishness of the Jewish State, to idolise power and organise military parades in the Holy City to celebrate Israel Independence Day, or to ape non-Jews by participating in ephemeral events which glorify the pagan cult of the human body, its strength or its beauty—an affront to the Jewish moral conscience which once sparked the Maccabean revolt against Hellenism?

Instead of the torch lit on Mt. Olympus, should we not rather have remembered our role as "a light unto the nations", and carried to the world the illumination of Mt. Sinai and the enlightenment of Mt. Zion, encouraging a competitiveness of the spirit, with the award of accolades for the best formulae to secure understanding among nations and races, honesty in society, pride in work, integrity in business, fidelity in marriage and nobility in human conduct generally?

Hard as we may have tried, Jonah-like, to escape from our Divine mission, by becoming a people like all others through the secularisation of the Jewish national purpose, our recent traumatic experience has shown that if we do not freely accept the uniqueness of Israel, it is providentially imposed on us against our will. "Behold, a people that dwells alone" is as true of us today as it was when first spoken by Balaam, when we first emerged as a nation to defy the rest of the world and eventually to inspire it with our teachings. Individually, many Jews may opt out. Nationally, we cannot run away from our destiny.

"MY POWER AND THE MIGHT OF MY HAND . . ."

Another myth shattered by the war was the exaggerated belief, uncritically accepted among many secularist and religious Jews alike, in the invincibility and infallibility of the military establishment as the sole guarantor of Israel's security and Jewish survival. Also, the much hailed statement "What matters is what Jews do, not what non-Jews think", to the extent that it is applied to our relations with the international community, now has a rather hollow ring, as we decry the hostility of world opinion. In the past, we cared very much about the good name of Jews and Judaism among non-Jews. The whole concept of *Kiddush Ha-Shem* is based on this concern, and we abandon it only at our extreme peril.

This unconcern with the views of others has, alas, exacted a terrible price. So has this over-confidence in our own strength. A personal experience brought this home to me when, visiting a church dignitary of international standing to seek his intervention for our prisoners, I took the opportunity to ask him why the Church had not protested against the brutal aggression on Yom Kippur, and he answered me: "We were so confident that Israel would defeat her enemies in a few days that it simply did not occur to us to raise our voice in defence of Israel." Inadequate as this answer was to me, I then understood how far we had become the victims of our over-confidence.

". . . BUT BY MY SPIRIT"

No one questions the obvious fact that a powerful army was, and remains, an indispensable condition for Israel's security. Yet, even the most gallant, the best trained and equipped army of a small people like Israel cannot always expect to prevail over vastly more numerous forces, with well-nigh limitless hardware, and with scarce concern for their casualties, unless it is sustained by a faith and a Power transcending all physical strength. Otherwise, how could Israel, like "a sheep among seventy wolves" in the imagery of the Talmud, have outlived all its past oppressors? In the Jewish experience, there is realism as well as idealism in Zechariah's ringing words "Not by might nor by strength, but by My spirit", recited annually in our synagogues at the very time when we celebrate the Maccabean victory of the "few over the many".

That victory has a special relevance today, quite apart from the inequality of the contestants then and now. The battle against the Hellenists twenty-one centuries ago was not merely a military conflict, heroic as the Maccabees were. Nor were their war aims in liberating their country limited to securing the survival of their people. They were but the means to the higher end of preserving the integrity of Judaism, of restoring the sanctity of the Temple and cleansing it from its pagan defilement. As a result, the battle was not only won; it changed the entire course of human history. Thanks to it, Judaism survived against the rising tide of Hellenism, making possible the emergence of Christianity 160 years later and of Islam 600 years after that.

SURVIVAL OF JEWS AND JUDAISM

Herein lies the third factor which requires a fundamental transformation of attitudes. For the first time in our history, which was always precarious, our dominant concern has become "Jewish survival". In God's original covenant with our people, He made Himself responsible for our survival, so long as we undertook to be responsible for the survival of His Torah. The agreement worked until our generation. Now we have reversed the roles: We worry about the survival of Jews, and we leave it to Him to care about the survival of His faith. This cannot work.

The struggle for Jewish survival must be elevated to the fight for Judaism's future. There can be no Jews without Judaism any more than Judaism without Jews. The Jewish people can exist, and serve a purpose, only as an indispensable instrument to uphold and exemplify the teachings of Judaism. Otherwise Jewish survival becomes meaningless and even questionable, because the Jewish people would be redundant.

In this supreme battle for Judaism, Jews inside and outside Israel can and must engage equally, thus serving as a further vital bond to unite them. In the final analysis Israel is bereaved both when Jews are lost by war and by assimilation and indifference. Grievous as have been our casualties in Israel's wars, it would be idle to pretend that the massive, self-inflicted losses by defection, intermarriage and apathy have not caused an even greater numerical drain on our human resources. These crippling losses now probably run at the rate of tens of thousands annually; to reduce them will require the same concern and determination as a military operation to prevent war casualties.

JEWS BY PROXY

In the double crisis, eroding both the quantity and quality of Jews in addition to threatening their security, Israel and the Diaspora will increasingly now have to merge their respective roles in a common drive to consolidate the Jewish spiritual commitment. Paradoxically, while the establishment of the Jewish State has greatly intensified Jewish consciousness and identification in communities everywhere, it has also weakened the main common demoninator between them. In the Diaspora, many Jews have found vicarious refuge for the expression of their Jewish identity in the existence and support of Israel. For them, living as Jews by proxy has conveniently replaced the personal discipline of Jewish living. In Israel, again, large numbers of Jews have found in their national allegiance a substitute for traditional Jewish loyalties. For these Jews, the Diaspora became the vicarious haven of their residual Jewishness, as poignantly attested by the many Israelis who discover their Jewish feeling and identity only when they visit the Diaspora and find communication with their faith and with fellow-Jews in the synagogue. Thus Jewish statehood helped to accelerate the secularisation, or de-spiritualisation, of Jewish life both at home and abroad, leading to an ever widening gap between Jews and Judaism.

The Yom Kippur War will force us to recognise that a secularist Jewish State, itself a contradiction in terms, cannot be viable in the long run, as we will find the ultimate answer to many of our most pressing problems in a growing emphasis on our spiritual assets.

"THE RIGHTEOUS SHALL LIVE BY HIS FAITH"

Reference has already been made to the indispensability of staunch religious faith as an essential corrective to the gross imbalance between Israel's very limited resources and the vast hostile forces engulfing it. We have now seen how insignificant are the combined wealth and influence of all the Jews in the world as compared with the financial and political power wielded by the Arabs through their oil weapon alone.

Faith of a similar calibre will also be required to bring to our people the healing gifts of solace, comfort, encouragement and inspiration at a time of acute distress, when the morale of some may flag and cause widespread panic and despondency. After all, even an individual who, whilst enjoying good health, disregards religious practice, turns to his religion for strength when stricken with illness. How much more does this now apply to the Jewish people as a whole if we are to brace ourselves with fortitude and confidence to endure our ordeals and to face the tribulations ahead. Many accounts from Israel's battlefields confirm the tremendous inspiration and uplift the religious soldiers gave to their spiritually impoverished brothers-in-arms, and few will doubt that the only element which can never be completely broken and demoralised by adversity is the religious community, for whom Jewish life has meaning even in suffering, and dignity even in desolation, and purpose even when ultimate fulfilment tarries.

EDUCATIONAL STARVATION

Today, any Jewish child denied the opportunity to cultivate this faith for lack of an intensive religious education and environment is deprived not only of his birthright but of his capacity to weather the storms which may threaten his life as a Jew. It is an invitation to national despair, if not suicide, to allow the continuation of a state of affairs in which the majority of children in Israel receive no religious instruction whatever in their schools and never even see Jews at prayer, and in which most Jewish children elsewhere at best obtain a totally inadequate Jewish education, usually stopping well before it can even begin to exercise its influence on a mature mind. After Yom Kippur, who would dare to stand idly by whilst our youth grow up as spiritual cripples in this way? This would be tantamount to criminal negligence on our part.

The strengthening of our spiritual commitment will also help to bring about an urgently needed change in our sense of values. A society in which the pursuit of wealth and pleasure is the *summum bonum*, the car a status symbol, and the concern with rights rather than duties the driving force of the social ethic, such a society is decadent, as so painfully borne out by the bankruptcy of our affluent civilisation. Jewish society has prevailed over the decline and fall of others because it made the pursuit of righteousness the ultimate goal, learning the status symbol, and the submission to the Law the dynamic of the national ethic.

SPIRITUALITY IN JEWISH LIFE

To ensure greater spirituality and improve the quality of Jewish life, there must be a shift in our national (and communal) scale of priorities and public recognition. For instance, financial resources are certainly vital to sustain the fabric of our corporate existence. But if wealth alone becomes the main qualification for communal honour and respect, it is bound to devalue the coinage of the spirit and inflate the currency of material success. In a truly Jewish society, the teacher, the scholar, the thinker, the man of piety and moral nobility generally, must command at least the same power and respect. In the hierarchy of leadership, too, men of vision, competence and culture, rather than mere party-faithfuls, will have to reach the top if we are to harness our finest brains in the tough struggles ahead. Such a return to Jewish traditional values would also, incidentally, help to regain the involvement in Jewish affairs of numerous gifted talents, especially of the younger generation, whose disenchantment with the bureaucratic and materialistic value system of our age has alienated them.

Of course, neither the Hebrew language nor what is commonly understood by Israeli culture, including a knowledge of the Bible, can be a substitute for spirituality. The truly Jewish character cannot be determined merely by the tongue in which one speaks, or the books one reads, or the music one sings. Judaism is historically a sham and morally a futile absurdity if it is wrenched from its halachic bearings. Nationally, such a disembodied form of Judaism is self-destructive. In our contemporary dilemma, the relevance of religious observance is not far to seek. A few illustrations will suffice.

THE ALTERNATIVES: EXTERNAL PRESSURES OR INTERNAL COMMITMENTS

In the complacent period prior to Yom Kippur, the deceptive relaxation of external pressures witnessed a distressing increase of internal tensions and troubles: rampant crime rates, quasi-racial frictions between Oriental and Occidental Jews, the poverty gap leading to social unrest, "Black Panthers", and even some intermarriage with Arabs inside Israel, whilst outside Jewish life was plagued by alarming mass-defections, a declining *Aliya*, and anti-Jewish as well as anti-Israel manifestations like the "Jews for Jesus" and the anti-Zionist "New Left" movements—both the first such aberrations ever to be found within the Jewish community. That some of these scourges would automatically disappear in a religious environment scarcely needs labouring. Observant Jews certainly do not consort with missionaries, do not betray their wives and do not engage in drug-traffic or robberies. Bnei Braq, a large and predominantly religious city, has not even a police station!

But more important still are the wider social and national ramifications.

Experience has taught us that there are ultimately only two alternatives for preserving the unity of our people and the Jewish character of the State, enabling it to resist the danger of factional disintegration from within and the currents of assimilation from without: either the hostility of Israel's neighbours compelling us to hold together and remain distinct from them, or our common submission to the Torah, which unifies our people and prevents us from being submerged among the nations. What futility there would be in gaining peace at the cost of losing the Jewish quality of the State and the cohesion of its population, not to mention the resultant rift between Israel and the Diaspora which, once no longer dependent on each other, would be bound to drift apart in the absence of common religious loyalties!

THE COST: TWO MILLION ISRAELIS

We often hear the argument these days, especially in Aliya campaigns, that had Israel now had a population of five million Jews instead of three million, this might have made all the difference to its security, if not also to its economic prosperity. This is obviously true enough. But what is not mentioned, and cannot be over-emphasised, is that Israel *would* today have at least five million Jews if the moral dictates of Jewish law on abortion and birth-control had been observed. And these two million extra Jews who would have been born since the establishment of the State, had one half of these not been smothered in the womb and the other half remained unconceived would all have been native-born Israelis, without any of the problems and costs involved in the transport and absorption of new immigrants totalling at best but a small fraction of that number. Naturally, no one willingly assumes the extra expense and inconvenience of a large family except out of a profoundly religious conscience, as demonstrated by the striking disparity in the birth-rates of strictly observant and other Jews—a factor borne out in this country, too, in the latest report of the statistical unit of the Board of Deputies. Other nations face the problem of population explosion; our problem is population insufficiency!

THE RELIGIOUS MOTIVATION OF ALIYA

Aliya itself, also now more urgent than ever, is likewise affected by religious considerations. It is sad to reflect that during twenty-five years of Jewish independence, Jews driven to Israel by oppression far outnumber those attracted there from the Free World. Most Diaspora Jews living in comfort still look upon the Jewish State—apart from being a source of great pride and self-respect—as a home for the homeless. This finds its echo in the false rendering in an American Conservative *Haggadah* (Prayer Book Press, Hartford, 1959) wherein the words *vehu yolicheinu komemiyut le'arzeinu* ("and may He bring *us* upright into our land") are translated gratuitously as "lead *the homeless of our people* in dignity into our homeland". However small the Aliya rates, immigrants from Western countries came, and will continue to come, disproportionately from groups whose idealism was nurtured by their strong traditional background and education. Again, among immigrants from Arab and Soviet lands, those who remained or became religious eventually presented fewer problems of integration, both because they share a common way of life with their new neighbours and because their religious commitment makes them less liable to social indiscipline and moral fall-out.

The uncertainties created by the Yom Kippur War will greatly accentuate these trends, perhaps even in a shocking new form. Already one hears in Israel of Sabras who are unwilling to expose themselves and their children to the chronic risks of war and insecurity. Unfortunately, some even consider emigration. For them Israel is principally a haven; once they believe its security is in doubt, they will seek the greater safety of foreign lands. No truly religious Jew thinks that way. For him, Israel is primarily the only place where he can live a fully Jewish life. What attracts him there is its holiness even more than its security. The religious commitment will therefore increasingly determine the rate of Aliya from the West, the degree of successful integration from the East, and conversely the rate of emigration from Israel.

THE PURSUIT OF PEACE

To this very limited catalogue of religious principles with a bearing on pressing current issues must be added the overriding quest for peace, the greatest and most oft-repeated Jewish religious yearning of all. As has now been so cruelly demonstrated, even distant borders and military strength do not of themselves secure or guarantee peace. Genuine peace springs not from a balance of power, and certainly not from an imbalance of fear. It slowly grows out of mutual trust, encouraged by each side showing the same understanding of the other's apprehensions and sufferings as it seeks for itself. The traditional Jewish compassion over ancient Egypt's losses in the Red Sea, still marked in our annual Passover observances, well illustrates an approach, the challenge of which hardly lacks contemporary parallels, not least regarding the sensitivity to the plight of Arab refugees, whatever the cause of the problem. Only through an intensely religious conscience can such high moral standards be attained as will eventually reassure our adversaries that they can dwell securely and without fear. Real peace is a state of mind, rather than an expedient accommodation. Little wonder that the Psalmist speaks not of wanting or loving peace, but of "pursuing peace", and that in our synagogue usage, when reciting the prayer for peace at the conclusion of the *Amidah* and *Kaddish*, we draw back three steps before coming forward again.

THE RELIGIOUS COMMUNITY'S SPECIAL TASKS

Whether people do or do not agree with the religious interpretation of our present perlexities, what is clear is that the crisis has fundamental spiritual ramifications far beyond its purely political or military manifestations. It is equally clear that, in guiding the perplexed of our times and insuring that we prevail over our immense difficulties, spiritual leaders and the religious community generally are called upon, as they were throughout our past, to make a decisive contribution towards bringing the ship of our destiny to safer waters. In particular, we are summoned to apply ourselves to three distinct tasks: to provide comfort, hope, confidence and encouragement to those of our people whose faith is tottering in adversity; to explain the meaning of our current tribulations and our response to them in the light of our historical experience and religious insights; and to respond to the intense search for spiritual values evoked by the trauma of the Yom Kippur War by arousing a massive religious re-awakening to restore our people to its timeless purpose and destiny.

In addition, in the Diaspora it is primarily for the religious community and its leaders to stimulate a mass-movement of Aliya, by redirecting Jewish education to this end; by transferring ever more seminars, schools and yeshivot to Israel; by sponsoring projects to encourage all school-leavers to spend at least a year in Israel, with the prospect that out of many thousands going annually, many hundreds will stay; and above all, by cultivating in our youth the faith and idealism which will predispose them to prefer a full Jewish life in Israel, even under conditions of some risk and hardship, to the spiritual hazards of their exilic existence, even in relative prosperity.

VOICE IN THE WILDERNESS

True, many of the cures prescribed by our teachings may be widely unpalatable and even resented. We may be bitterly opposed, if not abused, by those who do not share our commitment and who will not easily submit to an exacting way of life or abandon the little gods and supermen they have fashioned to replace the God of Israel, however disastrous the course they have chosen may be. But, as heirs to the Hebrew Prophets and like them, we must be prepared to expose ourselves to the risk of loneliness, unpopularity and sometimes even derision. They, too, were often ignored and harassed by their contemporaries. Yet their work has remained immortal, and thanks to their reproof and consolation, we are alive whilst others have disappeared. Today, some twenty-five centuries later, our task is, thank God, far easier than theirs. We can build on the foundations of immense good will, on a vast fund of high idealism, self-sacrifice and passionate dedication, as displayed so heroically by the builders and defenders of our Homeland, and by the supporters of Zion's cause throughout the world. The will is there, if only we provide the direction and inspiration for its expression.

STRENGTH AND WEAKNESS OF TORAH COMMUNITY

So far, and especially after the Six-day War, we must admit, we missed the opportunity and defaulted on our obligations. Torn by strife and enmity within our own camp, and usually concerned more with legislation than with persuasion, with questions *created* by our convictions rather than with the broader moral and spiritual problems *solved* by them, we often estranged the masses of our people instead of attracting them to our way of life. Enormously strengthened as the ranks of our Torah scholars and followers became after their near-annihilation in the Holocaust, thanks to the phenomenal growth of our vast network of schools and yeshivot, this powerful element remained inward-looking and prone to a disdain for the world outside their confines, though perhaps understandably so due to their continuing sense of insecurity following their catastrophic losses, by slaughter in Nazi Europe and by assimilation elsewhere. As a result, they were neither able nor willing to engage in any meaningful dialogue with the secularists, and the gap between the two camps has become ever wider through the on-going process of polarisation.

On the other hand, those within the religious community who spurned the path of self-isolation, who remained active and articulate on the national (and communal) scene, suffered the even greater handicap of the institutional-isation and politicisation of religion. In Israel, in particular, the influence of the Torah camp is gravely weakened by the damaging association of religious education and conduct with the party system, itself now widely discredited, and always bound up in political barter, a *quid pro quo*, some call it "horse-trading", compounded by bureaucracy.

RELIGION AND POLITICS

By and large, the secularists resist the extension of religious power and influence not because of any instrinsic objection to traditional Jewish values, the need for which is now widely recognised, but because they are not prepared to raise a potential threat to the voting strength of their parties, or simply because they see in the religious establishment a force which lacks spiritual qualities and non-partisan appeal. Hence I believe that, without separating religion from politics, we are not likely to unite Judaism with the Jewish State, which is imperative for the survival of both.

Mindful of the historic responsibilities devolving on our spiritual leadership at a critical time like this, I have urged the Chief Rabbinate of Israel ever since the Yom Kippur War to convene an informal consultative meeting of leading rabbis to evolve a meaningful response, intellectually as well as in practical terms, to the enormous spiritual challenges now facing us. Such a meeting was eventually held in Jerusalem two weeks ago, with the participation of some twenty principal Rabbis from Israel, Europe, America and S. Africa. From it emerged a common resolve, in great part along the lines of this appraisal, thoroughly to revise our priorities, with a view to promoting the spiritual foundations of Jewish life, the unity of the Jewish people, sober confidence in the future, and the implementation of specific projects to be undertaken by joint action.

TIME FOR NEW PRIORITIES

Of uppermost concern to me were the potentially disastrous effects on Israel's spiritual strength and stability resulting from the absence of any religious teaching or experience for two-thirds of the country's children on the one hand, and the bitterness and divisiveness engendered by the on-going debates on pro- or anti-religious legislation on the other hand. I therefore pleaded with my colleagues to consider a dramatic gesture to replace the present religious policies by a supreme effort to win at least the rising generation for an appreciation of the Jewish commitment, founded on deep faith, intensive learning and devout observance. To this end, I suggested, at any rate during the present emergency, when religious faith and national unity are such indispensable assets to Jewish survival, to press for some regular religious instruction and practice at all schools, and in return to agree to a moratorium on all new legislation of religious significance, such as on conversions, civil marriage, public Sabbath observance or autopsies—all subjects on which fierce divisive controversies continue to rage and which, to my mind, however vital in themselves, are now irrelevant to the overriding need of fortifying our spiritual defences, by raising God-fearing and practising Jews.

I even doubt the wisdom of the "Who is a Jew?" agitation at this time, not because of the foolish argument that Jews outside Israel have no right to meddle in Israeli affairs—for "Who is an Israeli?" is the business of Israelis, whilst "Who is a Jew?" must obviously be of vital concern to every Jew—but simply because I believe this agitation is futile and counter-productive, so long as the majority of Jews do not share our religious convictions. To advance the future prospects of a truly Jewish State, I would rather concentrate all religious efforts on securing the Ministry of Education and forgo all other portfolio claims, than to persist in legislative battles which cannot but further erode Torah influences by hardening anti-religious attitudes, based today primarily on the objection to what is regarded as "religious coercion", now the principal stumbling-block to regaining for our spiritual leadership the confidence of our entire people.

CHANGELESS ESTABLISHMENTS

I place these thoughts before you tonight in the hope that by winning widespread support such a proposal will commend itself to the powers-that-be as a major step towards national reconciliation and religious consolidation in these trying times. For, following my visits to Israel since Yom Kippur, it distresses me to report that the population at large, and particularly the soldiers, thirsting for a spiritual uplift and disillusioned by the policies of the past, seem to be far readier than the leadership at all levels to contemplate radical changes in outlook and conduct. I had the impression that the War had made the least impact on the establishment, whether political, military or even religious. All too often one meets among them the same attitudes and mentality, the same partisanship and quarrels, the same faces and policies as for the past twenty-five years, as if nothing had happened to catapult us into an entirely new era in which yesterday's ideals have become today's snares, and the failings of the past have turned into the challenges of the future.

The master-key to our salvation, then, lies within our grasp. But our campaign for the spiritual regeneration of our people can be successful only if we first put our own house in order, gradually disengage religious activities from political partisanship, and then bring the enlightened insights and moral discipline of our faith to bear on the unprecedented problems which beset us all in common, above all by reclaiming our youth for the priceless heritage which the people and the Land of Israel were chosen to preserve.

TERRITORIAL CONCESSIONS

Omitted so far from my review of the relevance of Judaism to the security and quality of Jewish life is the attitude of Halachah to the ceding of territory now under Israeli control in the quest for peace. The views of rabbis, as of laymen, vary widely on this vexing and fateful question, a subject here left to the end because of its topical importance.

No rabbinical authority disputes that our claim to a Divine mandate (and we have no other which cannot be invalidated) extends over the entire Holy Land within its historic borders and that halachically we have no right to surrender this claim. But what is questionable is whether we must, or indeed may, assert it at the risk of thousands of lives, if not the life of the State itself.

Any religious law is set aside, even fasting on Yom Kippur, if it involves a danger to life. Rabbis, in giving such rulings in respect of individuals, are required to rely on expert medical opinion to determine what constitutes such danger in particular cases. Similarly, it would seem, we are halachically compelled to leave the judgement on what provides the optimum security for Jewish life in Israel to the verdict of military and political experts, not rabbis. Included as a major factor in this difficult judgement must also be the overriding concern to preserve the Jewish character of Israel which may clearly depend on the proportion of Jews within the State. For in the suspension of religious laws for life-saving purposes the threat to Jewish spiritual life and to physical life is considered alike.

Most importantly also to be borne in mind must be some more intangible factors of supreme Jewish religious and moral concern. The present ceding of some territory, if necessary and consistent with security requirements, may conceivably be justified as a ringing act of faith to promote regional, and indeed international, peace and as a goodwill gesture of immense value to establish friendly relations with the neighbouring peoples, ideals of human fellowship to which Judaism is passionately dedicated.

THE UNIQUENESS OF JERUSALEM

In an altogether unique category is Jerusalem. It enjoys a sanctity of its own and is the common possession of all Jews, wherever they may live, the gateway of all their prayers, the symbol of all their hopes, and now happily also the spiritual heart of Jewish learning, circulating inspiration to the most distant parts of our dispersion. To save life, one can amputate a limb or even excise parts of some internal organ. But not the heart!

The Jewish right to Jerusalem should be asserted not only by Israel, but by world Jewry, and especially by the religious community, who have never forgotten, throughout the long and bitter years of exile, the Psalmist's oath to set Jerusalem above their chiefest joy, yearning for its restoration in every prayer, every grace-after-meals, every blessing of joy to bridal pairs and every greeting of comfort to mourners.

We should also expect the Jewish title to Jerusalem—now completely free for the first time to the adherents of all faiths—to be recognised by the community of nations in acknowledgement of the people who originally sanctified it, who have maintained an unbroken association with it for 3,000 years, and who have constituted the majority of its inhabitants for the past 150 years. The recognition of this title will ensure continuing rights of access and freedom of worship for all, as well as the social and economic progress of the Holy City in the best interests of its entire population.

EXODUS FROM EGYPT: THEN AND NOW

Never have our sacred Scriptures been more topical than today. We currently read in our weekly portions-of-the-Law about the Exodus from Egypt three-and-a-half thousand years ago, just as we experience this week the second Exodus of Israel's hosts from Egypt. Like then, the Jewish movement to the Promised Land in our times has been galvanised by the slogan "Let My people go!" This motto has become the leading symbol and the main dynamic of modern Zionism. In pleading for the liberation of our people, for the release of Jewish refugees from the sordid D.P. camps thirty years ago and of our Jewish brethren from Soviet oppression to this day, we have constantly repeated the cry of Moses before Pharaoh.

But here lies the tragic difference between then and now, between success and failure, between truth and falsehood: to protest "Let my people go!" is a grotesque distortion, a base perversion, of the plea by Moses. He never said or meant anything of the kind. What he demanded time and again before Pharaoh was : "Let My people go, *so that they shall serve Me!*" Our liberation, our settlement in the Land sanctified by the consecration of our fathers and the blood of our children, would be meaningless and incapable of fulfilment unless our physical redemption is but the means to the ultimate purpose of "so that they shall serve Me", unless our journey to Zion takes us via Mt. Sinai and its commandments.

May Yom Kippur, the Day of Atonement and its afflictions, bring atonement to our people and reconciliation with our Maker. May He inscribe and seal us, in the words of the Yom Kippur liturgy: "In the book of life, blessing and peace."

ZION—SANCTUARY OR ASYLUM?

By a peculiar quirk of semantics, the English language equates houses of worship with homes for lunatics—sanctuaries with asylums—as places where fugitives from justice can find immunity from the law. The use of the word "sanctuary" as a shelter for criminals goes back to the law of the medieval church which gave criminals protection from arrest in sacred places. This is in complete contrast with Jewish law, which—far from allowing sanctuaries to be used as a refuge for offenders—enjoined "from off My altar shall you take him to die" (Ex. 21:14): criminals shall be removed even from God's altar to be brought to justice. Only idiots were beyond the reach of the law, since they were legally incompetent to stand trial.

To us, then, sanctuaries and asylums are exact opposites—a sanctuary houses the Ark of the Law, whilst an asylum is inaccessible and out of bounds to the law. Yet, in modern usage the terms "sanctuary" and "asylum" converge in Zion as a haven for the homeless, a refuge for refugees, and a home for a people.

In discussing some aspects of Aliyah tonight, I really want to address myself to the question: Which shall it be? Shall Zion be primarily a sanctuary, a place which by its sanctity draws and attracts Jews, or an asylum to which Jews are driven as fugitives from oppression? On the answer to this question, as we shall see, will depend the success of all our Aliyah campaigns and indeed the whole future development and character of the Jewish State.

THE COURSE OF JEWISH HISTORY

Significantly, Jewish history both begins and finds its ultimate fulfilment with Aliyah. The curtain rises on the drama of the Jewish experience when the first Jew was given the first commandment: "Go from your land and from your birthplace, and from the home of your father to the Land which I will show you" (Gen. 12:1), and the curtain will eventually come down with the "ingathering of the exiles", as we read only last Sabbath in the Haphtorah: "And I shall take you from the nations, and I shall gather you from all the lands, and I shall bring you to your land" (Ez 36:24).

Lecture delivered under the auspices of the Aliyah Department of the Jewish Agency at the Royal Institute of International Affairs, London, on 20 May 1974.

In between these starting and concluding points, let us recognise at once, Aliyah has always been a rather halting affair, and only a fraction of our people returned when the opportunity beckoned. Even the most massive original Aliyah of the Exodus was far from embracing all our people. On the verse "And the Children of Israel went up armed (Heb. *vachamushim*) from the Land of Egypt" (Ex. 13:48), our Sages comment *echad mechamishah*, "one out of five", whilst four-fifths of the Jews stayed behind in Egypt. This seems historically borne out of the reference to "Apiru" (Hebrews) in twelfth-century Egyptian papyri.

THE RETURN OF THE FEW

The second great return, from the Babylonian Exile in the sixth century B.C.E., also included only a small part of the exiles. According to the Book of Ezra (2:64), the number of returnees amounted to no more than 42,300, probably bringing the total Jewish population in the Land of Israel at the beginning of the Second Commonwealth to 60,000–70,000, with the majority of Jews remaining outside. The ratio hardly improved by the end of the Second Commonwealth. Before the fall of Jerusalem, the world Jewish population is estimated at 8,000,000 (based on the reported census of Emperor Claudius in 48 C.E. counting 6,944,000 Jews in the Roman Empire, and on other sources). Only about 2,500,000 lived in the Holy Land, whilst Egypt, Syria, Asia Minor and Babylonia each had Jewish communities numbering at least 1,000,000.

After the destruction of the Temple the Land was drained, though never entirely denuded, of Jews. Aliyah was only sporadic, with significant but numerically still quite small movements of resettlement, such as those led by Nachmanides in the thirteenth century and by Karo, Luria and others of the Mystic School in Safed in the sixteenth century when Safed, with 10,000 Jews, had the majority of the Land's Jewish population. Safed, incidentally, remained a major Jewish community until its virtual destruction by earthquake in 1837—a calamity attributed by R. Moses Sopher (the *Chatham Sopher*) to the settlement of its inhabitants there instead of Jerusalem, where they should have moved because of its superior sanctity.

Almost all these successive immigration movements over the centuries were motivated by the ideal of Zion as a sanctuary, by a passionate love of the Land, rather than by flight from persecution or economic deprivation. In fact, quite apart from the arduous hazards of the long journey, these immigrants often faced far greater hardships in the Land than in their countries of origin.

Only since the start of modern Aliyah late in the nineteenth century has the character of immigration begun to change drastically, turning Zion predominantly from a sanctuary attracting Jews in search of holiness into an asylum for Jews seeking freedom and security.

THE RETURN OF THE MANY

Let me here give you, as a background to present Aliyah trends and prospects, a brief statistical analysis of the modern growth of the Yishuv. Modern Aliyah is commonly divided into three main stages. The First Aliyah (1882–1904) provided about 1,000 immigrants a year, rising in the Second Aliyah (1904–1914) to about 3,000 immigrants a year. Altogether during this period, a total of 55,000–70,000 Jews entered the Land, amounting to about 3% of the entire Jewish overseas migration at the time. During the Mandatory Period (1919–1948) the average increased to 16,000 a year, making a total of 485,000 immigrants, representing 30% of the total Jewish migration. Since the establishment of the Jewish State (1948–1970), immigration increased sharply to about 60,000 a year, making a total of 1,360,000 immigrants, by now the great majority of Jewish migrants. But from this figure we must subtract 195,000 who emigrated from Israel during that time.

These migrations resulted in a growing redistribution of the world Jewish population. In 1914 only 0·6% of world Jewry resided in the Land of Israel. By 1948 this had risen to 5·7%, greatly increasing by 1970 to 18%. Now about 20% of the world Jewish population live in Israel—the same proportion of Jews as are traditionally said to have left in the Exodus from Egypt.

More revealing and relevant is the breakdown of Aliyah figures when divided between those fleeing from oppression in Communist and Arab countries and those freely immigrating from the rest of the world. Out of the total of 1,400,000 immigrants from May 1948 to December 1970, about 500,000 came from Eastern Europe (36%), while 708,000 fled from Arab lands in Asia and Africa (50%), representing a total of 86% who came to Israel as a refuge from persecution. Contrast this with the 75,000 who came from Western Europe (5·5%) and 80,000 from America, S. Africa, and Australia (6%). Thus voluntary immigration from the Free World amounted to no more than 11·5% (the rest were unregistered). In other words, only one-eighth of all immigrants were attracted to Israel without any external pressures.

The figures are even more disappointing when related to the percentage of Jews in the various communities who responded to the call of Aliyah. S. Africa leads with 5% of its Jewish community now settled in Israel; closely followed by Latin America with 4·1%. The United Kingdom comes third with 3·4%, while Canada with 1·4% and the United States with 0·6% lag far behind. These figures compare with 60% of all Jews from N. Africa now living in Israel.

When the other day I mentioned these calculations I had made in the presence of the Israeli Ambassador, he pointedly remarked that the figures ought to be pointless: 34% instead of 3·4%—certainly a point which would make them less disappointing!

LINKS WITH THE LAND

Before I turn to some needs and lessons for the future, let me here insert a few remarks on Israel's claim to Jews and every Jew's claim to Israel in Halachic writings. Nachmanides (*Sepher Ha'mitzvot*, additional positive commandments, no. 4), in common with some other early authorities, regards the duty to settle in the Land of Israel as a distinct precept among the Torah's 613 commandments, based on the verse "And you shall take possession of the Land and dwell in it" (Nu. 33:53). He supports this view by relating the following Midrash:

> It once happened that Rabbi Yehuda Ben Betera, Rabbi Mathia Ben Heresh, Rabbi Hanina Ben Achai, Rabbi Joshua and Rabbi Yochanan left for abroad and reached Platum (probably in Italy), and as they remembered the Land of Israel, they raised their eyes and their tears rolled down. They rent their garments and they read the verse "and you shall dwell in your land" and they returned and came back to their place, saying that the duty to reside in the Land of Israel outweighs all other commandments in the Torah (*Sifri*, on Deut. 12:29).

While Maimonides does not consider this duty to be a specific biblical law, he includes in his great code some most detailed regulations on the obligation to live in the Land and the conditions under which one is permitted to leave it (*Mishneh Torah, Hil. Melachim*, 5:9–12):

> It is always forbidden to leave the Land of Israel for abroad, except for the purpose of studying Torah, marrying a woman, or saving oneself from (the pursuit of) non-Jews; but one should return to the Land (as soon as the purpose has been fulfilled). Similarly one may also leave for business. But to dwell outside the Land is forbidden, unless there is a famine to such an extent that a dinnar's worth of wheat rises to the value of two dinnars. . . .
>
> The great among the Sages would kiss the borders of the Land of Israel, kissing its stones and wallowing in its dust, as is written: "For Your servants take pleasure in her stones and love her dust" (Ps. 102:15).
>
> Said the Sages: Whoever dwells in the Land of Israel will have his sins forgiven . . ., and even if he only walked four cubits in it, he will merit a share in the world to come. Likewise, whoever is buried in it will be granted atonement. But being absorbed in life cannot be compared to being received after death. Nevertheless, the great of the Sages would bring their dead there, as you can learn from (the burial of) Jacob and Joseph the righteous.
>
> A person should always dwell in the Land of Israel even in a city where the majority are non-Jews rather than live outside the Land even in a city where the majority are Jews, for whoever leaves the Land is as if he worshipped idols. . . .

In the same spirit, the Mishnah (*Ketubot*, end) rules: "All may be compelled to go up to the Land of Israel, but none may be compelled to leave it." That is, a man may compel his wife and family to join him in taking up residence in the Land, but he cannot force them to accompany him if he leaves the Land.

Just as the Land has a claim on all Jews, so does every Jew have a title to a share in the Land. This is strikingly illustrated in two Rabbinic regulations. On the famous dictum by Samuel, the great Babylonian Sage, "the law of the government is law" (*Nedarim* 28a), i.e. in Jewish Law, the legislation of any civil authority enjoys religious sanction, R. Nissim comments: "This applies only to (laws enacted by) non-Jewish kings, since the land belongs to them, and they can always tell their subjects 'if you will not carry out my commands, I will banish you from the land'. But it does not apply to Jewish rulers, since all Jews are partners in owning the Land of Israel."

Even more remarkable is a special legal enactment made over a thousand years ago and based on every Jew's title to the possession of four cubits in the Land of Israel. According to the Talmud, one can issue to an agent a letter to authorise the collection of funds from a debtor or depositary only if this is accompanied by the transfer of some land to the agent. But few Jews owned land in Middle Ages. Hence, the Geonim enacted that, for this purpose, Jewish businessmen could rely in such authorisations on the claim of each Jew to the ownership of a portion of the Holy Land's soil. This was explained by Hai Gaon: "The Land may have been occupied by gentiles for many generations, but we have an old legal maxim that ownership of land is never lost by illegal seizure, and hence Israel still holds title to the land." This enactment is also mentioned by Maimonides (*Hil. Sheluchim*, 3:7; see S. W. Baron, *A Social and Religious History of the Jews*, vol. v, p. 27f).

ALIYAH PROSPECTS

I made this little digression into the realm of Halacha, since religious attitudes, as we will now see, will have an increasing bearing on future Aliyah prospects. We have found that, since the establishment of the State, the ratio of idealism to persecution as the principal motivation of Aliyah was one to eight. The continued exodus of Soviet Jews, now the main source of Aliyah, is likely to be strictly limited, and the evacuation of Jews from other lands of oppression is virtually complete.

This leaves the Western world as the only unlimited reservoir of human resources to boost Israel's population by Aliyah. Judging by our past performance, it would take another quarter of a century until our total Western immigration reaches barely 300,000. To this disturbing prospect we must add that our own numbers in the Free World are constantly declining, through the erosion of a low birthrate combined with a high intermarriage and assimilation rate. Moreover, since Yom Kippur, the advantage of security, which attracted some settlers from the West, has been neutralised, if not reversed, as already grimly indicated by the widespread talk about emigration from Israel.

In short, unless we succeed in changing the entire image of Israel from being primarily an asylum, a refuge for the homeless and oppressed, into a sanctuary awakening and attracting those who can be infused with intense idealism, the prospects for substantially increasing Israel's population look bleak indeed.

Already Western Aliyah, notably from here and America, consists disproportionately of people whose love of Israel has been nurtured by their religious commitment and traditions, who have had a good Jewish educational background, and who go out, as Abraham did, heeding a Divine call in search of holiness, rather than of security.

I do not feel competent to judge, as some have already ventured to suggest, whether Israel's overall security through greatly increased numbers by large-scale Aliyah may be offset by the Arabs' correspondingly growing fear of Israeli expansionism. A selective qualitative Aliyah to fortify the moral and spiritual fabric of Israel may in the long run hold out no lesser prospects for eventual peace and security than indiscriminate mass-immigration, even if it were available.

But I am qualified to advocate Aliyah, both as a major religious precept and a national ideal, and as an indispensable boost to Israel's morale. Since Yom Kippur, as I have experienced in two visits, nothing so oppresses Israelis as their loneliness and isolation. A single new immigrant freely choosing to share their life and its anxieties and uncertainties gives them more convincing and encouraging evidence of confidence in their future than any financial support.

NEED FOR NEW POLICIES

How, then, can and should we revise our Aliyah policies in the light of our new circumstances to produce the most effective results? Clearly, mere propaganda campaigns are futile. You cannot promote Aliyah through clever advertising as you sell toothpaste or holiday tours. No one will wrench himself from his family and environment to start a new life involving considerable risks and imponderables simply in response to constant coaxing, or even to meet Israel's need for more man-power. This can only be achieved by cultivating an irresistible love of the Land, to the point of preferring a full Jewish life with hardship to a truncated Jewish exilic existence in relative comfort and safety.

To this end, far-reaching adjustments will have to be made in the patterns of Jewish life, both in Israel and the Diaspora.

THE CONTRIBUTION OF ISRAEL

On the Israeli side, Aliyah prospects will increasingly depend on creating maximum attractions for those in search of an intensely Jewish life. For them, even more important than material inducements, such as tax-concessions, will be the spiritual incentives. The others will not come in large numbers anyhow, whatever the inducements.

This all-important argument is distressingly illustrated in a letter just published in the weekly edition of the *Jerusalem Post* (19 March, 1974). While it may well not be typical of everyone's experience, I will read it to you as the expression of a view with a critical bearing on the spiritual ingredients in attitudes to Aliyah:

> As relatively new immigrants from assimilationist U.S.A., we and our children eagerly looked forward to an authentic Jewish holiday programme on Israel Television on Purim night. The Dan Almagor programme obviously tried to oblige us, for its content was a facsimile of a western saloon setting filled with American songs. The programe's ostensible relationship to Purim was the questionable theme of heavy drinking.
>
> My children asked whether we had come to Israel for such "inspiration" and Jewish fulfilment. Is Israeli culture to be only a fourth-rate imitation of American culture, albeit translated into Hebrew? Can't Israel produce a genuine, meaningful modern Jewish culture? If it cannot, why continue the stream of false "Zionist" propaganda, which warns Diaspora Jews of assimilation unless they come to Israel?
>
> Abraham Lincoln's famous statement of failing "to fool all of the people all of the time" is slowly providing us with the reason why American Jews are reluctant to come to Israel.

These sentiments, evidently expressed by recent immigrants who are not necessarily religious, underline my argument that the intense longing for a full Jewish life is a major factor in the motivation of Aliyah. For religious Jews, therefore, the appeal of Aliyah is definitely compromised by serious spiritual deficiencies, such as are manifested in the current conflicts on "Who is a Jew?", public Sabbath observance and autopsies. I have heard of devout Jews, especially the elderly, who hesitate to consider Aliyah out of fear that, should they die in a hospital, they might be subjected to post-mortem operations, since Israel is still about the only civilised country in the world which does not require family consent for such operations in non-coroner cases. Many observant Jews feel their enthusiasm for settlement in Israel dampened by the widespread public desecration of the Sabbath there, or by their anxiety over finding reliably Jewish partners for their children, once immigrants can be officially registered as Jews, even when their conversion cannot be halachically accepted. These arguments may appear somewhat far-fetched and trivial to some, but they are quite real to the very element which is, and will remain, the most likely section within our Western Jewish communities seriously to envisage Aliyah for themselves or at least their children.

Regarding the painful debate on "Who is a Jew?", by the way, it is instructive to remember that our people were faced with a similarly agonising problem on our return from the Babylonian exile when Ezra was compelled to repair by drastic action the damage done by the terrible inroads of intermarriage.

Another important contribution whereby, I believe, Israel might give greater impetus to a mass-Aliyah from the West is to revise the existing absorption policies by giving more encouragement to group settlement. This might well be of particular significance to Anglo-Jewish immigrants, since their somewhat insular and very settled background often makes it more difficult for them than for others to adjust easily to an entirely new environment. Many British Jews might more readily consider Aliyah if they could be assured of resettlement in Israel as a group in an atmosphere in which they could enjoy their familiar and traditional patterns of life, organised around a community centre, a synagogue, a school, a club, etc., which would provide them with their accustomed social and religious services, including the pastoral activities of an Anglo-Jewish minister. It was this method which proved so highly successful in inducing entire Chassidic communities to establish themselves as closely knit groups in Israel, often transferring there hundreds of families at a time.

Altogether, I believe that Israel should abandon the pressure-cooker policies of enforced individual integration. Israel can only be enriched by preserving, at least to some extent, the diversity of aptitudes, customs and special characteristics accumulated by Jews in different parts of the world over the centuries, and it would be an irreplaceable loss to the Jewish people if we allowed these diverse identities to be lost completely in the process of acculturation to a single standard of drab homogeneity.

Indeed, perhaps it would be even wiser to establish Diaspora agencies in Israel to advise on Aliyah policies than simply to maintain Jewish Agency offices in the Diaspora to conduct campaigns.

THE CONTRIBUTION OF THE DIASPORA

In the Diaspora, too, drastic changes and innovations will be required if Aliyah movements are to become a potent force. I believe that really large-scale recruitment can be promoted mainly through two programmes, one long-term and the other short-term, both concentrating on youth.

In the long run, the response to the challenge of Aliyah must lie in the intensification of Jewish education, its Israeli orientation as well as its spiritual appeal. Fluency in Hebrew is only one of the invaluable assets in such a programme, for ignorance of the language can be a considerable impediment to those otherwise interested in Aliyah. In this respect, we have only made a beginning at our Jewish day-schools here. But we are still lagging far behind other communities where Hebrew is already the common language of instruction at most day-schools. Above all, Jewish education must aim at the cultivation of idealism, self-discipline, and Jewish fervour—qualities which will prove of decisive importance in influencing young people to opt for life in Israel. Only the exposure to extra hard work at school will instill a willingness to face hardship for an ideal's sake.

There is also a more immediate prospect which deserves careful consideration and intensive promotion. To most young people, the appetite for settling in the Land comes only from tasting the fascination of its existing life by a prolonged stay there. There should be a drive to enlist all young people for at least one year's experience of living in Israel. Through tireless publicity and well-prepared schemes, it should become the accepted thing in the community for every Jewish boy and girl to devote at least one year, on leaving school and before entering the universities or other occupational training, to study or work in Israel. Out of the thousands who would go, it may be anticipated that 10% to 20% will stay as permanent immigrants. The others will return to enrich the community through their Israeli experience and intensified Jewish knowledge and commitment.

Unlike Israel's youth, our children are not mobilised for three years' army service in the defence of Israel, with all the dangers and sacrifices involved. But at least they ought to accept one year's national service of life in Israel to defend Jewish survival, both in Israel and here.

To boost the Aliyah of Jews living in free and prosperous countries, it will be essential to refurbish the whole image of Israel and to bring about far-reaching changes in the quality of Jewish life, both in Israel and the Diaspora. During the Mandate, the British spoke of Jewish immigration as governed by the country's "economic absorptive capacity", then reckoned as limited to 100,000 Jews. With far greater truth, we can now claim that Aliyah will be governed by the Land's "spiritual absorptive capacity"—its unlimited appeal to those seeking the attractions of a sanctuary which only Israel can offer as a society suffused with Jewish values and immune to the spiritually eroding influences of our exilic existence.

The term *Aliyah* literally means "Ascent". Originally it derived from our ancestors' "going up" from the flat lowlands of Egypt down south to the mountainous terrain of the Promised Land up north. But closely associated with the geographical meaning of this term was always its supreme spiritual significance as an ascent towards the peak of Jewish fulfilment. To scale high peaks requires long and patient training in mountaineering, a skill which cannot be developed without hardihood and constant exercise. If we want to recruit ever more people to rise to the challenge of climbing the very summit of our Jewish aspirations, we must first train them to appreciate the thrills of the adventure and to exercise their spiritual muscles by the continuous experience of intensive Jewish living. Thus will Zion draw her children and protect them in her sanctuary on high.

ZIONISM TODAY: VISION, ILLUSION AND REALITY

To comply with the U.N. resolution proscribing Zionism as "racism", Jews would have to liquidate the State of Israel, itself created by the U.N. Even more significantly, they would have to cripple their religion which has nurtured the yearning for the return to Zion in doctrine, prayer and precept for thousands of years. For Zionism clearly cannot be expunged from Judaism without amputating the heart from the Hebrew Prophets and the Psalms, mutilating the Jewish liturgy and law-codes, and completely truncating the faith which has sustained the Jewish people in its millennial tribulations.

But I suspect Jews will be guided by historical precedent and moral judgement no less than by the instinct of self-preservation in choosing instead to defy this order to liquidate themselves, their State and their faith.

There are ample precedents for Jews braving in utter loneliness the fury of a hostile and brutal world. Jews and Judaism were no less lonesome and hated when they heroically withstood as a tiny island of monotheism the flood of paganism in antiquity, or when they were pitted against the enmity of the Hellenistic and Roman empires, or when they resisted the brutalities of forced conversion by Moslem legions, Christian crusaders and inquisitors, and their assorted modern counterparts.

Through this obstinate defiance of superior numbers and superior might, not only has the Jewish people prevailed over its oppressors, but all mankind has been immeasurably enriched. Had David not challenged Goliath, Jerusalem would never have been sanctified, and it would today be holy neither to Jews nor to Christians and Moslems. Had the small band of Maccabees not preserved Judaism in their grossly unequal battle with Hellenism, Christianity would not have emerged 165 years later nor Islam 600 years after that. Without Jewish perseverance against the most terrifying odds, all humans might still be spiritual cave-dwellers—sans Bible, sans social justice, sans morality, sans everything.

The cost was heavy, sometimes devastating; but the reward was Jewish survival and continuous creativity.

Published in the first issue of L'Eylah (*Winter 5736*), *the magazine of the Anglo-Jewish Ministry issued by the Office of the Chief Rabbi. The article includes extensive extracts from a paper "To be Equal or To be Different" presented by the author to the Seminar on "World Jewry and the State of Israel", convened by President Katzir in the summer of 1975 at his residence in Jerusalem.*

The story is little different today. Nor has the ingratitude of the world changed over the ages. Had Jews, inspired by Zionism, not rehabilitated their ancient homeland, there would have been no massive immigration of "Palestinians" in the present century, and the Arab population would still consist of a few hundred thousand destitute illiterates instead of being socially and culturally the most advanced Arab community today. Indeed, all the newly emerged nations, which mainly promoted the U.N. betrayal, have shamelessly forgotten their debt to Zionism as the forerunner of the national liberation movements to which they owe their own independence, and their debt to Israel as the only developing country to stretch out a hand to many of them with immense aid programmes to which they owe much of their educational, technical, agricultural and military growth.

Altogether the U.N. resolution adds the insult of vilifying Jews and Judaism to the injury of the Jewish people as the principal victim of racism, a term first applied by the Nazis in their diabolical campaign against the Jews, at the cost of six million lives and untold suffering not so long ago. And this defamatory charge against Zionism is now made by the most notorious regimes guilty of blatant racism—oppressing Jews, expelling Asians, discriminating against whites, or simply slaughtering minorities like Biafrans, Kurds or Bengalis in their midst!

For Jews it is gratifying but sad comfort to know that this act of infamy was vigorously opposed by most Western nations. Their rout only highlights the impotence to which the whole Judaeo-Christian civilisation has been reduced in the councils of the world community. Nor is there much comfort in the truism, often asserted by Abba Eban, that if the Arabs were to sponsor a motion that the earth was flat it would be sure to pass with the unfailing support of the Soviet bloc and the Third World.

For the world, the farce of the U.N. may spell its end as an effective instrument to promote peace and human rights. For Jews, it evokes the smell of gas-chambers and the memories of medieval Jew-baiting, even if those who have never experienced pogroms and concentration camps may find it difficult to understand the Jewish "obsession" with security and its antithesis, anti-Semitism.

The double standards applied to Jews and Israel are, alas, all too familiar. One recalls the frequent U.N. condemnations of Israeli strikes against dens of terrorists while ignoring their murderous raids on children, air-passengers and other innocent civilians; or the zealous concern over Israeli building in Jerusalem in stark contrast with the silence over the destruction of all synagogues, the wanton desecration of Jewish cemeteries, and the denial of Jewish access to the holy places (in violation of U.N. resolutions) during the Jordanian occupation of the Holy City; or the call for its internationalisation when Jews held the Old City and the absence of such a call when the Arabs annexed it.

Soon after the Yom Kippur War, I publicly referred to the specious claim, repeated ad nauseam, that territory acquired by war must not be retained, even for self-defence and security: "This claim reeks of particularly odious hypocrisy when it comes from the lips of Arabs whose vast empires across Asia and Africa were all conquered by the sword, or from Russia which still subjugates half of Eastern Europe by annexation or military occupation as a security-belt, or even from France and Britain whose territorial acquisitions by force, some retained to this day, dwarf all conquests made by Jews in 4,000 years of history."

Jews are simply subject to standards not applicable to others. What a hue and cry there would have been if Jews instead of Arabs, by controlling the world's largest oil reserves, had used history's greatest concentration of wealth to plunge the industrial nations into a frightening recession and to threaten the poorer nations with starvation; if Jews had exploited this fortune for political and financial manipulation in a determined bid to impose their will on the rest of the world! The vicious fabrication of the "Protocols of the Elders of Zion" would be child's play against the monstrous reality of such world domination, and no Jew anywhere would be safe. Yet the Arab conspiracy is accepted in docile submission, whilst Jews—the main target of the conspiracy—are once again hounded as outcasts of society in a recrudescence of anti-Semitism on a global scale.

All this (and more) I argue in an effort to refute our detractors and to arouse an indifferent world. The charges against us are so preposterous, and the treatment meted out to us is so patently immoral, that it is relatively easy to present the justice of our cause to non-Jews even if the attempt may make little difference to a world insensitive to the refinements of truth and integrity. Anti-Semitism, moreover, has never been amenable to logic or reason.

But, having gone through the motions of protest and justification, I realise that denunciation and argument are likely to be largely an exercise in futility, as it has proved to be at the U.N. and elsewhere. I also realise that the dynamics of Jewish history are governed more by spiritual forces within the Jewish people than by physical factors inside or outside it.

The more urgent, more difficult, but also more rewarding question therefore is, how do I, as a Jew, react to the new barbarism beclouding the Jewish and the human scene? More specifically, how do I, as a rabbi and an heir to Israel's Prophets, explain and interpret to my own people the renewed loneliness and discrimination to which we are now again exposed, dashing our hopes that the realisation of the Zionist dream would finally release us from our long ordeals of suffering after thousands of years of waiting and praying?

In the search for an answer to these agonising questions I reproduce in the rest of this article the bulk of a contribution I made last summer to a discussion of these issues at a five-day seminar convened by President Katzir in Jerusalem:

My views on the current situation and its travails are founded on my firm commitment to the authentic Jewish teaching that the tortuous course of the Jewish experience, especially as related to the Land of Israel, is determined primarily not by capricious or fortuitous forces beyond our control, but above all by the merit and spiritual fibre of our own people. Our Prophets expressed this in Covenantal terms of the special relationship between Providence and our fortunes or misfortunes, or the doctrine of reward and punishment (invariably applied in the Bible to Jewish existence in the Holy Land).

This is to me the wider significance of the centrality of Israel. This centrality is now increasingly evident not only in Jewish life but also in world affairs and indeed in the consummation of the human purpose. The mere fact that a tiny people restored to a little land, with few natural resources, continues to be close to the very heart of the major political, economic and strategic upheavals besetting the entire world in a universal crisis of unprecedented proportions, affecting the fortunes of super-powers and small nations alike, is itself the surest indication that the timeless drama of God's special relationship with Israel is far from played out. A numerically insignificant people cannot bestride the front pages of the world's newspapers for over a quarter of a century without serving a special purpose in the evolution of man's history.

Morally and existentially, this centrality finds expression in the very "double standards" applied to Jews and Israel by the international community. Instead of simply decrying this abnormal feature in our treatment, we should accept it in part as a tribute by the world to the superior moral standards expected from the Jewish people, and as a Providential reminder that we cannot escape from our historic assignment as moral pioneers and path-finders among the human family in which we are destined to play a unique role to vindicate our equally unique record against all odds as an eternal people.

The all but complete disregard of these considerations, at least as a major factor in appraising the quite extraordinary features of our contemporary condition, is to me as incomprehensible as it is depressing. Since the untimely passing of Yaacov Herzog, I do not know of a single ranking personality in or near the seats of power in Israel or outside who views the convulsive events of our times through specifically Jewish eyes as he did, who interprets current happenings and trends in the light of the forces governing Jewish history and the dynamics of Jewish thought. This deficiency applies not only to secularist leaders who conduct Jewish affairs of state as would statesmen, politicians or diplomats of any other people facing our dilemma. I look vainly even to our religious and rabbinical establishments for an interpretation of our national fortunes and misfortunes which bears the unmistakable hallmark of distinctly Jewish perceptions. Men of piety and learning may have succeeded to the priestly functions of spiritual leadership in biblical times. But the Hebrew Prophets are without heirs today; the whys and wherefores, the questions on how to put the jigsaw pieces of our jumbled world intelligently together, remain unanswered. The perplexed are not guided, at least not by any corporate voice of the Jewish national conscience, and the imperatives of Israel's moral impact on human affairs are altogether ignored in an abrupt disengagement from the Prophetic ideals of Judaism.

The Agranat Commission, assisted by countless pundits, has probed into the causes of the Yom Kippur War set-backs and their traumatic aftermath. But Jewish history does not operate simply in terms of military logistics or political equations. If it did, we would have disappeared long ago. Happily for us, the logistics were illogical, and the equations did not add up. How lamentable, therefore, that there has been no high-level enquiry into some more profound factors responsible for our disastrous reverses, into miscalculations and intelligence errors which transcend the incorrect deployment of troops or electronic gear. What needs to be re-examined in the light of present realities are the premises and visions, the very axioms of faith, on which the Jewish State was built and developed.

The primary motivation of secular Zionism has always been the belief that the restoration of Jewish sovereignty would "solve the Jewish problem" by eliminating the abnormalcy of the Jewish condition. This belief inspired the earliest fore-runners of political Zionism as it galvanised the policies of their successors. Pinsker's *Autoemancipation* was "rooted in the desire to engineer the acceptance of the Jews as equals in the modern world" by removing them "from the situation of abnormality surrounded by hatred to a territory of their own where they would become a normal nation", whilst Herzl in his *Judenstaat* argued that "the Jews could gain acceptance in the world only if they ceased being a national anomaly" (see *Encyclopaedia Judaica*, 16:1043–4). Though later influenced marginally by Ahad Ha-Am's "Cultural Zionism" and pragmatically by Weizmann's "Synthetic Zionism", this remained essentially the Zionist credo to the present day. National equality became the magic formula which would put an end to all the suffering and persecution caused by the "anomaly" of Jewish exilic existence.

Alas, the Yom Kippur War, if not its long antecedents, finally shattered this illusion. Immeasurable as are the Jewish State's achievements for Jews inside and outside Israel—far outweighing the costs exacted—the one thing it could not, and never will, achieve is to turn us into a nation like all other nations, losing our historic identity as a unique people.

The reverse has happened. Far from having "solved the Jewish problem", Israel has highlighted it. Jews are today as different, as "peculiar", and as lonely as they ever were, subjected to the very "double standards" by the international community it was the dream of secular Zionists to eliminate in the process of making us "equals". Indeed, through Israel the "abnormalcy" of the Jewish condition, with all its attendant perils, has now been extended from individual Jews and scattered Jewish communities to the Jewish people as a whole. For on Israel's safety now depends the welfare of Jews everywhere. Only the semantics have changed. Anti-Semitism has become Anti-Zionism, and instead of sporadic pogroms we have periodic wars and the constant threat of terrorist outrages.

The price exacted by this illusion exceeds the failure to "solve the Jewish problem". In pursuing the phantom of equality and the mirage of normalisation, the whole ethos of our national existence was deleteriously affected. Instead of exporting the values peculiar to the Jewish spirit—from humility, integrity, moral excellence and profound faith to the discipline of life trained by the regimen of religious observances—we all too often imported from our exile the base materialism, the social and moral depravities to which we had been exposed.

The drive towards normalisation has perverted many of our national values and aspirations. We take greater pride in what we have in common with others—an army, parliament, universities—than in what distinguishes us, in what sets a religious soldier, or Hebrew law, or the great academies of Jewish learning apart from others. Israeli patriotism is enthusiastically encouraged in sports or beauty contests more than in reducing the crime rate or road accidents in an international competition to assert the dignity and sanctity of life.

Another dimension of the loss incurred by the abandonment of Jewish traditional values directly affects the very security of the State. Take the problem of Arab refugees. Whoever and whatever caused their plight, and even if we could do little or nothing to solve the problem, surely as Jews—faithful to our ethical heritage of special sensitivity to the sufferings of the stranger and the homeless—we should not have left it to gangs of murderous terrorists to draw the world's attention to this stain on humanity. Had we cried out in protest against the intolerable degradation of hundreds of thousands inhumanly condemned to rot in wretched camps for a generation, had we aroused the world's conscience over a tragedy of such magnitude—who knows?—we might have prevented the growth of a monster-organisation which has already destroyed so many innocent lives and which now, with the blessing of the world community, threatens the very existence of Israel more acutely than the Arab armies ever did.

Again, had we not neglected the teachings of Jewish ethics on abortion and birth-control, making the birth-rate among Arabs *inside* Israel more than twice as high as among Jews the Jewish population would now be over five million, including at least two million more Sabras, without any of the colossal costs and problems involved in the transportation and absorption of immigrants amounting to but a fraction of this number.

For those conditioned by decades of secular Zionist teaching and propaganda (including the principal fund-raising campaigns) to limit their vision of Israel's purpose to being merely a haven of Jewish security, the shock-waves likely to be produced by the collapse of this ideology may be devastating. Their first impact is already felt in declining Aliya and increasing Yerida rates, and in the blighting disillusionment which has driven some of our youth, alienated from our traditions long ago, to ask "What are we fighting for?", others to challenge the justice of Israel's cause and yet others to question the purpose of Jewish survival altogether.

Not surprisingly, only the religious element is now immune to this erosion of faith, as it is to the inroads of assimilation on the wider front in the grim battle for survival. Attracted to the Land of Israel by its holiness more than by the security it may offer, and to the Jewish people by the intense love of Judaism rather than by the accident of birth, these skull-capped and decently-clad young men and women now constitute the bulk of Western Aliya. They are the last to swell the emigration or social drop-out rates, and the first in preserving the pristine idealism and pioneering spirit, in war as in peace, which sustained us throughout our martyred history and once enthused the Zionist movement.

The strictly observant are now, of course, also the only segment of our people, inside and outside Israel, to be physically secure against the ravages of shrinking numbers. Enjoying an exceptionally high birth-rate and a virtually non-existent rate of defection by inter-marriage and assimilation, they now effectively increase their proportionate strength compared to other groups by perhaps as much as four or five times the size of the average Jewish growth-rate which for most Jews, in terms of continuity by active identification, is often less than zero. Considering that these "intensive" Jews face scarcely any problems of drop-outs, crime or identity, one may well discern spiritual echos of Darwin's "survival of the fittest".

The lesson seems obvious; yet those in need of it refuse to acknowledge or learn it—at a cost which may soon become catastrophic.

For the problem goes much deeper. The question "Why Jewish survival?" troubles not only some spiritually impoverished Jews; it bedevils the world at large. Why indeed?

History is, and always was, brutal. Nations, like individuals, are born and die. Greater and more powerful peoples than we have disappeared; no one mourns or misses them. Who would grieve if we vanished, especially at a time when millions die from poverty, starvation and violence, in a world overpopulated with problems and undersupplied with compassion? After 4,000 years of existence, already far beyond the lifespan of other nations, we have had a fair run. Even without the Jewish people, science and arts, industry and agriculture, would continue to develop. We are not needed for that.

Jews are today widely regarded as a troublesome nuisance, a principal factor in many of the world's gravest crises and perils; the Middle Eastern powder-keg, the oil boycott, the energy crisis, the threat to detente and trade relations with Russia, not to mention their traditional scapegoat role in times of economic depression. In the public image, we create problems rather than solve them.

What is to justify, then, our claim to national survival, and our demand for the world's support and sympathy, even at the risk of economic collapse and of reaching the brink of nuclear confrontation, as happened in October 1973 and might well happen again? Surely the answer can only lie in making ourselves indispensable in our special role to be "a light unto the nations", as an exceptional people, a model society determined to enrich mankind with incomparable contributions, as we did in the past. Surely our stricken world needs the uplift and inspiration of our unique Jewish heritage no less today than in pagan antiquity when we blazed a lonely trail which was eventually to guide humanity to the uplands of civilisation and moral progress.

If we were the one people on earth—through religious idealism, ethical virtue and moral passion—to have found the formula of how to eradicate crime and licentiousness, how to banish selfishness and social inequality, how to preserve marriages and bridge the generation gap, how to serve others and discipline oneself—in short, how to sanctify life and raise righteousness into a national goal, our image in the world, among Jews and non-Jews alike, would be vastly different and we would not be exercised by the problem of Jewish survival, as the leading item on our national agenda, for the first time in history! It is surely no accident that three entirely novel questions, never previously asked or debated in our long annals, have been raised simultaneously: "Who is a Jew?", "What is Jewish identity?", and "How do we ensure Jewish survival?" The moment we are no longer certain and agreed on who is a Jew and what is a Jew, Jewish survival becomes problematical.

Our fundamental objectives, then, need revision if Jewish survival is not to be both questionable and meaningless. A secular Jewish state, itself a contradiction in terms, simply cannot be viable, Moreover, without reliance on our religious Covenant and Divine promise, we assert neither a legal nor an historical title to the Land for long ruled and occupied by others. It is the future of Judaism, therefore, even more than of the Jewish people who are but its instrument, which is at stake and whose preservation must become the ultimate goal in our present struggle. There can be no Jews without Judaism any more than Judaism without Jews. Without Judaism, Jews not only lose their one common and unifying denominator; they are simply redundant, and today's world cannot afford the heavy price of preserving such a costly antiquity.

The futility of wresting the Jewish experience from its spiritual moorings, now dramatically exposed by the Yom Kippur War, should have been apparent from even the most cursory acquaintance with Jewish history, or indeed from any realistic appraisal of Israel's purpose. Surely our forbears did not endure so much cruel martyrdom "for the sanctification of the Divine Name", nor offer thanks daily to the Almighty that "He has not made us like the nations of the earth nor like all their multitude", in order that in the end we should glory in being a people just like all others, or even boast the finest army in the world! And does it make sense to establish a Jewish State as a bulwark against individual assimilation only to find it turning into a vehicle of national assimilation?

Withal, I gladly acknowledge that there is today much soul-searching and a widespread quest for spiritual values, though evidently more at the grass-roots of popular impatience than at the storm-resistant treetops of national leadership. This search for fresh thinking may indeed be the most hopeful portent to emerge from the agony of the immediate past. But what most are searching for does not exist: a Judaism without religion, a faith without belief, a Torah without Mitzvot. They are chasing shadows, not light; forms rather than substance.

Such are the unfathomable mysteries of Providence and Jewish history that the 1967 and the 1973 wars may yet reverse their hitherto accepted roles in their effect on the consummation of the Jewish purpose. In retrospect, one wonders whether the Six-day War, with all its ecstasy, may not have induced one of the most calamitous recessions of the Jewish spirit in our annals. Political and military attitudes apart, it bred an inflated sense of over-confidence, an immobility of mind, a disdain for the outside world, and an extravagant taste for high living which spilled over into a moral pollution of the national character once distinguished by faith, integrity, selflessness, idealism and frugality. The Yom Kippur War, on the other hand, its heart-break notwithstanding, may well yet release invaluable spiritual energies and in a mighty burst of power redirect our destiny to its historic orbit.

Chapter Two

ANGLO-JEWRY
Tradition in Transition

SPIRITUAL LEADERSHIP—THE HERITAGE OF PRIEST, PROPHET AND KING

 יראתי בפצותי שיח להשחיל,
תבונה חסרתי ואיך אוחיל.

Trembling, I now pour forth speech from my heart,
Wisdom I lack, how shall I start?¹

With these words from our exalted New Year liturgy I inaugurate on this *Rosh Chodesh* Nisan, this "New Year of the Months,"² my new life in the office to which you have called me and the new era to which I am to call you.

No rabbi ever had more reason than I to say with our father Jacob as he returned home after fleeing from his brother's fury "I am too small for all the favours and all the truth which Thou has done to Thy servant"; and I might continue, adapting Jacob's words: כי במקלי עברתי את הירדן הזה "for I once crossed with but a staff the water" of the English Channel, as a refugee fleeing from oppression, ועתה הייתי לשני מחנות "and now I am become two encampments,"³ at home in two continents.

How fervent must be my praise of Him "Who is good and Who does good" to me in thanksgiving for the supreme privilege of serving as Chief Rabbi the very country which once saved and sheltered me; for calling me to preside over the very Beth Din once graced by the inspired but all too brief service of my sainted Father; and for the honour, unique in the history of this office, of installation by the very leader who previously occupied it with such grace and dedication—my revered teacher and mentor, now for the second time inducting me into a Chief Rabbinical office. Only history will record the full measure of his achievement in consolidating the Torah forces at a time of exceptional stress. May he be granted "length of days and years in pleasantness" and in further distinguished service to our faith and people.

I

On this resplendent occasion, usually witnessed but once in a generation,

Address delivered at his Installation as Chief Rabbi of the United Hebrew Congregations of the British Commonwealth of Nations at the St. John's Wood Synagogue, London, on 11 April 1967.

and before this august and uniquely representative assembly—covering the entire spectrum of the community like a colourful rainbow of peace after a storm—permit me to share with you some of the hopes and prayers stirring my heart, as well as a few thoughts agitating my mind on the future of Judaism and British Jewry as we consecrate our partnership.

The first day of Nisan, by an extraordinary coincidence of anniversaries, marks the beginnings of the three classic forms of Jewish leadership: prophecy, priesthood and kingship. On this day, in the first dated event in the history of prophecy, God told Moses and Aaron: "This month shall be unto you the first of months,"[2] proclaiming to the Children of Israel the dawn of freedom when time, the count of months, would belong to them and not to their Egyptian masters as before.[4] On this day, a year later, the Tabernacle was completed[5] and the Jewish priesthood began to function. And on this day, "the New Year of the Kings,"[6] the kings of Israel started to count the years of their reign.

In some respects, the rabbi today is heir to all three roles of leadership. Let me, then, outline my aims and responsibilities in this triple capacity as I see them.

"Who are the kings? These are the rabbis", says the Talmud.[7] Ever since the lapse of temporal sovereignty, Judaism has invested rabbis with certain royal prerogatives in guiding the destinies of our people. They directed its thoughts, inspired its actions, initiated its great historical movements, and gave Jewish life its sense of destiny and moral purpose.

In this capacity, it will be my charge to help in directing the community's internal and external affairs and to suffuse them with religious content.

I will seek to bring the influence of my office to bear on promoting world peace and the moral regeneration of society—our most urgent universal task; on alleviating the religious attrition and communal isolation of our Russian brethren—the most painful Jewish problem of our day; on cementing the bonds of our common heritage between Israel and the Diaspora—our most acute national problem; and on moving with prudence and caution in the uncharted territory of inter-faith understanding and co-operation—the most serious post-War challenge to religious statesmanship. Within our community, I will encourage friendliness in our relations, imagination and originality in our planning, and a constant search for dedicated talent and high idealism in our communal work. I will use every available means of communication with the public in pursuit of my determination always to take the community into my confidence.

In particular, it will be among my major objectives to enhance the status of the Anglo-Jewish ministry. I realise that the intense concentration of rabbinical power and authority in the Chief Rabbinate is bound to stunt the growth of a dynamic ministry. In fashioning my office to meet the needs of our time, I will try to strike a judicious balance between excessive decentralisation, leading to religious chaos, and over-centralisation, stifling ambition and responsibility among ministers, reducing them to mere functionaries. Having myself risen from their ranks and once joined the brain-drain for bigger opportunities abroad, I know their frustrations. I would like our spiritual leaders to assume unquestioned spiritual command in their congregations, and increasingly to participate at the highest level in the direction of the community and its religious policies. Only thus will we attract our finest sons to a rabbinical vocation.

II

Secondly, I am charged to assume some principal functions of the ancient priesthood. Perhaps this gives a little sense to the curious reference to Britain's earlier Chief Rabbis as "High Priests of the Jews". Moses defined the tasks of the priests as: "They shall teach Thy laws unto Jacob, and Thy Torah unto Israel; they shall put incense before Thee, and whole burnt-offerings upon Thine altar."[8] Let me here, then, come to the heart of my responsibilities as teacher and guardian of Jewish law, coupled with the duty to make Judaism sweet as incense and also to exact sacrifices for it.

ותלמוד תורה כנגד כולם. Far above all else will be my obligation to promote the study of the Torah.

I want to assure the inalienable birthright of every Jew to an adequate Jewish education. On this I stake the success of my ministry, for on this will depend Jewish survival. During the post-War period Jewish education has made vast strides in many lands. There are today tens of thousands of Jewish children, even outside Israel, who master Hebrew fluently, to whom immortals like Isaiah and Rashi and Maimonides speak in familiar accents, who have completed several tractates of the Talmud before they leave school, and who freely consult the genius of Judaism for authentic answers to the social, moral and intellectual perplexities of our age. If Jewish education ends, instead of starts in earnest, at Bar Mitzvah age, is it any wonder that the products are juvenile Jews, quite incompetent to assert their faith in an adult world, their love of Judaism too flimsy to resist the temptation of intermarriage and the allurements of pagan philosophies? Just imagine we were to stop our children's natural growth and their secular instruction at thirteen years of age; would they not become physical and intellectual cripples?

Wherein lies the glory of beautiful synagogues if tomorrow they will be empty monuments to our neglect; what is the profit of the finest Kashruth supervision if kosher homes will continue to decline, and of all our Zionist work without committed Jews in the next generation?

In this emergency of appaling defections among our youth, our expenditure in money and energy on Jewish education represents our defence budget in the communal economy, and it must be given the highest priority over every other Jewish effort.

What Judaism is it I will teach and defend? It is the vibrant faith found in synagogues filled every week, and equally evident "when you sit in your home and when you go about" your business, sanctifying life at work and at leisure, as a guide to professional ethics in public and to sexual morality in private.

It is the Judaism which was never in step with the times: which was as much out of date when it preached the brotherhood of man in pagan antiquity as when our martyrs defied the enticing attractions of Hellenistic culture and the savage bigotry of the Middle Ages; the Judaism which will never be in accordance with the times until the times are in accordance with Judaism.

But it is also the Judaism which is ever dynamic and creative, addressing its eternal message to each generation in terms of its needs and accents; the Judaism which produced the Prophets in response to the challenge of immoral paganism; which evolved the Talmud as a reaction to our encounter with Greece and Rome and to our dispersion among the nations; and which created Jewish philosophy to articulate Jewish teachings in an age of scholasticism and theological speculation; the Judaism which will now have to project its teachings in terms of the scientific thinking and intellectual stirrings of our times.

It will be my priestly duty to offer you, as best I can, this Judaism fragrant and refreshing like incense, to make it meaningful and attractive.

But in my priestly charge I must also insist on sacrifices. Do not ask me to make Judaism easier or cheaper, to devaluate its worth to the soft currency of convenience. I can no more offer you a programme without toil and sacrifice than you can offer me a life of ease and leisure. There is no instant Torah, prepared in one or three hours a week of study and practice, no Judaism without tears, just as there is no creation without travail and no triumph without hardship. Remember always, a religion which demands nothing is worth nothing, and a community which sacrifices nothing merits nothing.

Let me here make this quite clear: I am resolved to preserve the Orthodox traditions of my office and the predominantly traditional character of our community. To borrow from the memorable words uttered, in Britain's finest hour, by the man to whom we all owe our lives and our freedom: I have not become Anglo-Jewry's First Minister in order to preside over the liquidation of British Judaism.

I will do my best to serve and unite all sections of the community, but I am not prepared to replace the Torah by an umbrella, either open or closed, as the symbol of my office. In any event, I anticipate fair weather rather than rain or hail, and we should not require any umbrellas.

For, in my priestly capacity I also want to be among the disciples of Aaron in "loving peace and pursuing peace".[9] In my attitude to all my fellow-Jews, I will look to the example of the saintly Rabbi Kook's boundless "love of Israel", and of my revered Father's broad tolerance. In our free society, I cannot ensure that everyone will submit to my decisions, but I can aspire to earn respect for my convictions and for my right to make decisions as my conscience dictates. I cannot bend or compromise Jewish law which is not mine to make or unmake, but I can administer it with compassion and despatch.

To those whose faith in the Divine origin of the whole Torah is weak and who do not accept the discipline of Judaism as entrusted to me, may I say this in all solemnity: Never forget the immense tragedy of our religious differences. Should your and our hearts not bleed with grief when we, your brothers and heirs to a common tradition, cannot worship in your synagogues, cannot eat in your homes, and sometimes cannot even marry your sons and daughters, because laws which we recognise as Divine and sacred have become meaningless to you, because what has united us for thousands of years now enstranges you? I will never cease pleading with you to rediscover the thrills of traditional Jewish living and the awesome magnificence of our faith: The

Divinity of the Torah, the truth of the Prophets, the authority of the Halachah, and the Messianic vision of the future, born of hope and toil. Nor will I ever surrender my firm belief in the promise of our Prophets that eventually the entire House of Israel will be reunited in the service of our Creator.

Meanwhile, it will be my privilege and my duty to do all within my power and authority to close the gaps within our people, and I appeal to all segments of the community for help in this vital effort. To this end I pledge all the skills and resources I command, for God will hold me to account for the failings of any Jew I can influence as well as for my own many shortcomings.

Nevertheless, I recognise dissent as an inescapable fact of Jewish life today. I will seek to befriend those who dissent, and to work with them in Jewish and general causes unaffected by our religious differences. After the devastating losses we have suffered by slaughter, repression and assimilation, every Jew's contribution to the enrichment of Jewish life is now more precious than ever, and I will encourage all British Jews to give of their best to the common good.

III

Finally, I am summoned to provide the vision and inspiration of the prophet, whose mantle, according to the Talmud,[10] was bequeathed to the rabbis from the day the Temple was destroyed. Unlike the priests who expected the people to come to them in the sanctuary, the prophets went out to the people to proclaim their message. I shall likewise seek out my brethren wherever they are. Those who do not visit me in the synagogue I will try to meet in their surroundings, speaking and debating with them wherever they allow me to appear, and writing to vindicate the Torah wherever it is challenged.

As successor to the Prophets, the rabbi today must demonstrate the relevance of Judaism to the contemporary experience. He must also spiritualise the mechanics of Jewish observance, showing the moral grandeur of religious discipline, the stirring uplift of true prayer, and the holiness of lives daily consecrated to God's service.

He must interpret the interplay between faith and reality, between ritual and ethics, between Israel and the nations. He must make manifest the gap between the laws of nature and the moral law, between impersonal science complacently dealing with things as they are and personal religion impatiently dealing with things as they ought to be. He must demand commitment, denounce indifference, and ennoble the aim of life as a quest for living in the image of God instead of the selfish pursuit of happiness and personal success.

Living in the aftermath of the most turbulent age in the annals of man and of Israel, our generation faces a special challenge in matching our gigantic material strides with a commensurate spiritual advance. The past generation experienced unparalleled bloodshed, first in a world war of unprecedented proportions, then in the heinous holocaust which claimed more Jewish lives than all the medieval massacres combined, and finally in the restoration of Jewish rule to Zion. Such an afflicted generation, however heroic, could not evince the capacities, the vision and peace of mind, to concentrate on spiritual endeavours, any more than King David, conqueror of Jerusalem, because he had spilt blood, could build the Temple.[11]

It is our assignment, blessed as we are with peace and prosperity, to complete the rebirth of Israel. As they restored the *soil* of Israel, we must restore the *soul* of Israel.

A generation ago, the Jewish problem was the survival of Jews. Today it is the survival of Judaism. A generation ago, one-third of our people were annihilated. Today, one-quarter of our people is forcibly denied the right to live as Jews, and at least another quarter wilfully abdicates the right to live as Jews, being just as ignorant about Judaism, just as estranged from the synagogue, from Jewish traditions and literature by choice as the Jews of Russia are by compulsion. Even in the most catastrophic periods of the Middle Ages, when the total number of Jews in the world scarcely exceeded one million, and when these were exposed to slaughter, oppression and destitution, no Jew ever worried about Jewish survival as we do now in this age of unequalled freedom, affluence and opportunity. How passionately would our Prophets indict our generation if we now failed to bestir ourselves to rebuilding our destroyed sanctuary, to invest Jewish existence with meaning and to turn the martyrdom of the past into the consecration of the future!

In the broader arena of mankind's tortuous evolution, we have also just passed an age of unrivalled conquest and material advance.

In the process, life has become mechanised, and man the victim of his own inventive genius. Man today lives longer, he has more time through labour-saving gadgets and faster communications, and yet he pants, too short of breath for contemplation and spiritual pursuits, his moral sense blunted by the hunt for pleasure, his vision obscured by the glitter around him, and the temple within him crushed under the weight of his technocracy.

As history's religious pioneers and moral path-finders, we are summoned to reassert our national purpose in ministering to our fellow-men as "a kingdom of priests and a holy people".

If we expect the world to take up our cause when we are in trouble, we must also be prepared to involve ourselves and our teachings in the travails of mankind.

IV

I pray that in the office I now assume I may be granted a humble share in reorienting the aspirations of our people and our fellow-men towards these prophetic goals. I pray especially that Anglo-Jewry may occupy an honoured place within the world Jewish community in the fulfilment of these ideals.

In the past, British Jewry has enjoyed an enviable reputation for stability and service. From these Isles radiated an example of communal solidarity and religious loyalty. From these Isles went forth the great translations of our Jewish classics, casting our sacred Bible, Talmud, Midrash and Zohar into new vessels of understanding from which all may drink. From these Isles came aid and intervention for suffering Jews everywhere. And from these Isles, through their genius and ours, issued the Balfour Declaration fifty years ago—title-deed to Israel's rebirth. As the principal survivor of the

European catastrophe, Anglo-Jewry must now assume an even more eminent position of leadership and responsibility.

In our shrinking and interdependent world, Anglo-Jewry can no more afford to be insular and self-contained than Britain can afford to withdraw from the rest of the world. We must share with, and contribute to, the Jewish experience of other communities. And we must consolidate our part in the upbuilding of the Land of Israel, by encouraging *Aliyah* and by freely aiding the spiritual and material growth of Israel as a land flowing with the milk of Torah and the honey of prosperity.

I pray that I may always be worthy of your support, trust and friendship. I plead with our eminent Dayanim, our learned rabbis and all my distinguished colleagues: Uphold my hands on the right and on the left.[12] Thus will my arms be firm, the one as "a mighty hand" to defend "the Law of Moses and Israel" and the other as "an outstretched arm" to grasp with love those who stray or falter. I call upon our dedicated lay leaders, perhaps with a touch of homiletical licence: תן לי הנפש והרכוש קח לך. You take charge of our administrative wants, supply our material needs, and give me the freedom to devote myself to things of the spirit, as we share in equal parts, like Issachar and Zevulun, the efforts and rewards in building a flourishing Torah society.

I turn with special fondness to our youth, bright hope of our future, whom I am so delighted to see represented here for the first time in such numbers: Make me at home in your midst, stimulate me by your questions, rejoice me by your response, and humble me by your restless search for depth and meaning beneath the shifting sands of passing fads as you prepare yourselves to become tomorrow's guardians of yesterday's heritage.

To all my brothers and sisters in the far-flung dispersion of the Commonwealth I say: Let us seize each other's hands across our distances to form the most wonderful family of communities cheerfully responding to Jewish history's greatest challenge in these exciting times.

Let us so acquit ourselves of our diverse tasks that no Jew will ever spurn his heritage, and that, as promised in the Torah, "all the nations of the earth shall see that the name of the Lord is called upon us".[13]

As for myself, what do I crave in this hour of destiny? Upon King Solomon's accession to his high office, he had a dream in which God said: "Ask what I shall give you." His response is my response: "O grant to Thy humble servant an understanding heart to judge Thy people, to know between right and wrong." [14]

I seek neither power nor authority; for no rabbi today can impose himself upon unwilling people, or enjoy their respect without earning it. Rather do I seek the wisdom to judge and make the right decisions, the inspiration to guide and persuade, the mind to instruct, and the heart to comfort. I crave for the ability to elicit understanding, not submission; to win partners, not subordinates.

We have now reached the end of the beginning. In responding to your call, I am sustained by a vision. In its fulfilment I have abiding faith. And I desire you to come and share with me this vision, as I now impart it to you in the sight of Him Who is the Sovereign of us all:

My vision is "Out of the cruel shall come the sweet."[15]

My vision is that out of the age of monstrous depravity there arises the great vindication of the age-old Jewish faith in the brotherhood of man, now a more universal hope than ever before.

My vision is that out of the religious hatreds of the past, polluted by rivers of Jewish blood, there is born the great confrontation between Judaism and the world, an encounter not of theological parleys, but of the world religions —secure from bigotry within and missionary subversion without—attacking the common enemy of evil and godlessness, and acknowledging their debt to Judaism as the enduring fountainhead of all that has inspired moral progress in the human story.

My vision is that out of the age of soulless materialism and the blasphemy "God's death" there stirs the search for a higher morality transcending reason, a quest for the living God to replace the sham gods made to order by today's pseudotheologians.

My vision is that out of our people's agony there is reborn Zion restored to its glory, radiating the Word of the Lord everywhere, and there prosper Jewish communities living in tranquility and harmony with our fellow-citizens.

My vision is that out of Anglo-Jewry's past tribulations there emerges a happy, forward-looking community, confounding the defeatists and routing the strife-mongers, as a mighty fortress of our spiritual treasures.

And my vision is that out of the clash of opinions, and sparked by the eternal fire of the Torah, there are released the massive energies to raise us to the peak of achievement, towering majestically in a universal panorama of peace and basking in the everleasting sunshine of God's choicest blessings.

May God grant us, in the words of the first and chiefest rabbi consecrating the first sanctuary on this first of Nisan three and a half thousand years ago:

"May the Divine Presence rest upon the labour of our hands."[16]

NOTES

1. First Day *Rosh Hashanah Shacharith* Service.
2. Ex. 12:2.
3. Gen. 32:11.
4. See Sforno, a.1.
5. Ex. 40:17.
6. *Rosh Hashanah*, 1:1.
7. Though usually quoted in this form, the statement reads differently in the Talmud (*Gittin* 62a, based on Prov. 8:15).
8. Deut. 33:10. The first part of this verse begins and ends with the letters making up the name of my Father (יר־אל) and is inscribed on his tombstone.
9. *Avoth*, 1:12.
10. *Baba Bathra* 12a.
11. 2 Chron. 22:8.
12. Ex. 17:12.
13. Deut. 28:10.
14. 1 Kings 3:5, 9.
15. Jud. 14:14.
16. Rashi, Ex. 39:43.

MILESTONES AND MILLSTONES

How goodly are your tents, O Jacob, your habitations, O Israel

A most popular Anglo-Jewish book declares: "After the destruction of Jerusalem in the year 70, when the Central Sanctuary ceased to exist, no irreparable blow was felt by Judaism as a religious system. Its spiritual potentialities, indeed, were strengthened. (For) the Synagogue continued to function regularly."

I open with this quotation not only in order to link the two historic anniversaries we observe within one month: the end of the Temple nineteen centuries ago, and the beginning, a century ago, of our organisation of synagogues built to help replace it. I also use this quotation from the "Jewish Contribution to Civilisation" in reverent tribute to its distinguished author, Dr. Cecil Roth, my own illustrious teacher and friend for many years, whose recent passing has robbed Anglo-Jewry of one of its most prolific immortals.

A FOREST OF CONGREGATIONS

In celebrating, with this festive Centenary Service, the establishment of the United Synagogue, we mark what may well be the most epoch-making single event in the entire history of Anglo-Jewry. From the little acorn planted by Chief Rabbi Nathan Adler in his Sukkah in 1866, and consolidated by the Act of Parliament which received the Royal Assent on this 15th day of Tammuz one hundred years ago, has grown a mighty oak, in fact a whole forest of congregations which, like every new forest, has ensured soil-conservation, has affected the climate of the whole region, and has brought the refreshing fragrance of life and healthy growth to countless people. The United Synagogue has indeed been the principal bulwark to conserve the traditional soil and soul of our community, to influence the religious climate of Anglo-Jewry, and to provide spiritual shelter and nourishment for hundreds of thousands of Jews.

An anniversary is a milestone, a marker between the past and the future, inviting the traveller to look back with gratification on the exertions and

Address delivered at the Centenary Service of the United Synagogue, held at the St. John's Wood Synagogue on 19 July 1970.

achievements behind him, and to look forward to the challenge and adventure of the unfamiliar ground yet to be encountered. Pausing a little in our march through history at this momentous centennial milestone, let us then briefly survey the scene of both the known and the unknown, in retrospect and in prospect.

STABILITY AND MOVEMENT

The late saintly Rabbi Kook, in a comment of poetic beauty, points to the significance of the two parallel terms used for "homes" in our text from yesterday's Sidrah: *ohel*—"tent" describes the impermanence of the human dwelling, ever about to be pitched and dismantled in constant readiness for movement and change; while *mishkan*—"habitation" represents the home at rest between journeys, resisting movement by being built on firm foundations. This contrast, explains Rabbi Kook, symbolises the duality of man: on the one hand, ever striving to reach higher in his quest for perfection, never satisfied or at peace with himself, always restlessly on the move in search of new and nobler achievements; yet, on the other hand, preserving what he has accomplished, standing firm, ready to defy the threat of erosion and collapse, and enjoying peace of mind behind the walls withstanding the storms outside.

There is a similar ambivalence between stability and movement as we review the accomplishments and the prospects, the past triumphs and the future tribulations, of the United Synagogue. In the past, it has certainly proved a *mishkan*, a solid "habitation" of unrivalled strength. From its humble beginnings, it has grown—by increasing its role of participating congregations twenty-fold and thirty times its original membership—into the world's most massive congregational bastion of traditional Judaism. By the latest official count, no less than 90% of all synagogue-affiliated Jews in Britain belong to Orthodox congregations. This ratio is far higher than in any other sizeable community of our dispersion, and the credit is no doubt due chiefly to the United Synagogue and the unmistakably traditional hallmark it has succeeded in imprinting on the pattern of Anglo-Jewish life. Let it be stated quite categorically on this great occasion that no institution can claim a larger credit than the United Synagogue for the number of Jews who identify themselves with our people, for the homes in which the Sabbath and Kashruth are observed, for the children who receive some Jewish education, and for the predominantly Orthodox character which distinguishes our communal life and continues to make the rule of Jewish law supreme in virtually all our national organisations and public functions.

UNIQUE SERVICE TO THE COMMUNITY

Also without rival in Jewish synagogal life anywhere in the world is the variety of institutions and services supported or maintained by the United Synagogue in the public interest. Not content to pioneer a unique concept of communal fellowship by which richer synagogues share their material blessings with poorer congregations, it has selflessly used its vast resources for the community at large, securing for Jews in London and far beyond their Chief Rabbinate, their Beth Din, their largest Jewish education board, an efficient and widespread hospital- and prison-visitation service, a ramified youth and welfare department as well as substantial subventions to numerous causes serving the entire community, ranging from Jews' College and several yeshivot to the distribution of Matzot to the poor. Never in the history of any Jewish community has one synagogue organisation achieved so much for so many.

One of the outstanding features of the United Synagogue is undoubtedly its stability. Any less solid structure could not have withstood those major convulsions which seemed to rock the community over the years. The United Synagogue was no more shaken by the enormous waves of East European immigrants which trebled Anglo-Jewry during the first decades under review and which suddenly transformed the original Anglicised members into a minority than by the theological conflict which threatened to fragment the community during the last decade. On the contrary, it emerged greatly strengthened from both these traumatic experiences. Altogether, no greater tribute could be paid to the vision of its founders than the steadfast passage of the United Synagogue, intact and structurally unchanged, through history's most turbulent century, a century which moved from the hansom cab to the jumbo jet and which witnessed two cataclysmic world wars, the agony of pogroms and the tragedy of the Holocaust, followed by the glory of the rebirth of Jewish statehood, not to mention major revolutions in religion, science, economics, international relations and every other area of human civilisation. The United Synagogue has indeed been Anglo-Jewry's *mishkan* —a "habitation" built on foundations well and truly laid, a "sanctuary" of stability.

GROWING COMMITMENT

If there were gradual changes, particularly in the post-War period, they were all to the good and in the direction of a firmer religious commitment. Gone are the days when nearly half the Constituent synagogues had the mixed boon of mixed choirs, or when the majority of honorary officers refused to practise what they expected their ministers to preach. While saluting the immense services rendered by generations of outstanding leaders guiding the destinies of the United Synagogue with extraordinary dedication, we must confess that nearly a hundred years had to elapse before most of them were Sabbath-observers—an advance which, we hope, will never be reversed again. Today masses of Jewish day-school pupils, numerous Talmud classes, long lines of *lulavim* on Sukkoth and ecstatic rejoicing on Simchat Torah are expansively in evidence in our synagogues, and at many of our congregations there are larger Sabbath attendances, better adult education programmes, more active ladies' guilds, more flourishing youth activities and children's services, more intense Zionist work and altogether greater enthusiasm than ever before. Also, it is often overlooked that out of our synagogues and largely through the endeavours of our Ministers have grown many of our Jewish day-schools. These now cater for some 2,500 children at Cricklewood-

Willesden, Edgware, Golders Green, Hampstead Garden Suburb, Wembley and lately Ilford, as well as of course the Jews' Free School, and to this imposing roll of honour others are soon to be added.

Notable trends towards more genuinely traditional standards are also apparent in the significant evolution of the ministry—itself a professional fraternity peculiar to Anglo-Jewry, cultivated by the United Synagogue and inspired by the more autocratic exercise of the authority vested in my office in earlier times. While thirty years ago only seven out of thirty-eight United Synagogue minister-preachers held a rabbinical diploma—less than one in five, today we have nineteen rabbis among the forty-two spiritual leaders of our congregations—nearly one-half, and by now all our ministerial students at Jews' College aspire to full rabbinical qualifications.

Our various detractors notwithstanding, we can therefore truly exclaim with the Preacher in *Kohelet* as we look back to the past century: "Do not say . . . that the former days were better than these!"

FUTURE CHALLENGES

But as we now turn from the past to the future, even our solid *mishkan*, our sturdy "habitation", is reduced to a modest *ohel*, just a frail "tent" exposed to the fury of the new elements buffeting our age. If we are to survive, we shall need the scout's skill to improvise and to adapt to new conditions; we shall have to learn the art of exploration and the ability to pitch tents and to live in them—tents not only in the sense in which our synagogues will have to become more mobile to keep moving with our Wandering Jews who will not stay put for more than a generation, but tents also as a symbol of mental mobility, of adventure, enterprise and hardihood. If the United Synagogue is to have a second century, the skill to fold up a tent or a synagogue, to demolish old ideas and out-dated methods, will be just as essential as the capacity quickly to put up new synagogues and novel schemes, or to explore fresh, untried paths to success.

A generation after the disaster of the Holocaust and the miracle of Israel's rebirth, the future patterns of Anglo-Jewry are beginning to crystallise. With the phenomenal growth of our day-schools and academies of higher Jewish learning, with the heartening development of a burgeoning Orthodox intelligentsia among students and scientists, and especially with the disproportionately high natural increase and low defection rate among the most committed, as confirmed in recent statistical surveys, no serious observer can any longer doubt that Anglo-Jewry will survive and be regenerated, however appalling our losses may be in the process. But what is open to speculation is the share the United Synagogue will have in this survival if we allow the forces and instruments of regeneration to elude us.

FINANCIAL AND SPIRITUAL SOLVENCY

Let me here utter this warning with every emphasis before this distinguished gathering: If the United Synagogue will ever decline and fall, financial insolvency will not be the cause. We may be certain, as our Sages tell us, "a community never goes materially bankrupt". If we make the priceless values and services we have to offer sufficiently appealing, people will gladly pay for them, just as they generously pay for other causes they really cherish. The United Synagogue will collapse only if we suffer bankruptcy in our religious and human resources, if we cannot generate enough excitement and commitment to fascinate and involve the rising generation as the active members of the future and if we fail to attract our finest sons—and daughters —to breathe fresh air and vitality into the leadership of our religious community. We have nothing to fear except stagnation. The greatest annual event in our United Synagogue calendar, which many consider to be the financial budget night, should be a spiritual budget day, an annual conference to enable ministers and lay leaders to explore in depth ways and means to make our services more meaningful, to intensify Jewish learning among young and old, and to strengthen the fabric and impact of the religious community within Jewry.

STORMS OF CHANGE

This being a Centenary Service, a once-in-100 years occasion, let us boldly confront reality: in this anti-Establishment age, the United Synagogue will be particularly vulnerable to the storms of change. Firstly, more than any other group of congregations, the United Synagogue has relied for its stability on a commodity which is fast disappearing from our new society. Unlike other synagogue groups, whether to the right or to the left of us, which attract their members primarily through some ideological Torah commitment or non-commitment, our synagogues have depended in the main on a sense of reverence for tradition, on filial loyalty, on sons expecting to take the place of their fathers. All this is no more. We no longer have a hereditary nobility in which parents automatically bequeath their titles and their obligations to their children. We have only life peerages, and must now induce our children to earn their own elevation to the House of Israel if we expect them to wear the crown of Torah-living after us.

Secondly, the United Synagogue is founded not only on the stability of tradition, but on a "middle of-road" philosophy. But in this "either-or" age, compromise and half-commitment are no longer the better part of religious virtue, and one recalls the remark of the sainted *Chafetz Chaim*: in the middle of the road only horses walk. We must recognise that we live in an increasingly polarised community, and once again, the United Synagogue will be the principal sufferer from this development. We are caught between two grinding millstones threatening to pulverise us. The upper millstone will squeeze out of our ranks the finest of our synagogue-family, the young religious intellectuals, the idealistic youth who will be drawn to the better day-schools, the yeshivot and girls' seminaries, gravitating from there either to Israel or to congregations more fervent than ours. And the bottom millstone will be littered with the chaff of the indifferent, the drop-outs of our classes and congregations who in their disenchantment with us will sever their last bonds with traditional Judaism. For let us be under no illusion: The United Synagogue as it is today, our organisation, our education, our services, our leadership and our whole philosophy simply does not attract either element; it will reclaim neither the creative grain nor the wind-tossed chaff, and we will be left with the thinning ranks of the old faithfuls who are too stagnant to break with the past or to rally to the future.

Thirdly, at the root of all these perplexities, we face an ominous crisis in leadership, a dearth of competent people to augment and succeed our present spiritual and lay leaders. How are we to meet these gigantic challenges?

NEED FOR GREATER FLEXIBILITY

What is urgently needed in the first place is to loosen the rigidity of our system. Our trouble is that we have today little room for people with fresh ideas, and none for rebels. On the whole, we welcome neither new questions nor new answers, in an age teeming with questions and crying out for answers. Our leadership must be flexible enough to encourage men of high ideals, broad vision and strong will to come forward, by convincing them that they will have a chance to assert their thinking, unconventional as it may be, in the conduct of our affairs. Our congregations, too, will require more autonomy, greater rights to use the fruits of their extra exertions for their own expansion, if we are to provide incentives for local initiative, rewards for harder efforts, and opportunities for more dynamic leaders and members. The prescription for a modern vibrant community is mass participation, some decentralisation and healthy diversity, apart from an imaginative programme of constant improvement and growth.

RECENT ADVANCES

Plans there are aplenty for the revitalisation of the United Synagogue as a forward-looking force of enterprise and relevance. Some have already been implemented lately to achieve significant advances. Thus, the United Synagogue through its Israel Committee has forged new congregational bonds with the Jewish State. It has pioneered the religious response to our student needs by providing most of the means for the first-ever full-time universities chaplaincy at Oxford, to be followed by similar ventures elsewhere. It has just initiated the first regional youth office under a full-time director; and it has recently even assumed, for the first time, a major Mikvah commitment for the increasing number of Jewish families who cherish the sanctifying rule of God's law in the privacy of their intimate lives no less than in the public domain of the synagogue and the school.

UNMET NEEDS

But many other painstakingly prepared plans are still frustratingly blocked in a long pipe-line which needs thorough cleaning. It is time for a real gesture to our younger people by reserving a fixed proportion of all board and committee seats for people under thirty, and possibly by offering people under 25 free membership with full rights, as proposed long ago. It is time to enliven our synagogue services and to secure greater participation in their conduct by our members and even their children, as suggested to our Ministers at various conferences. If we want to have high-calibre spiritual leaders in ten years from now, it is time to offer our present and future Ministers the promise of far more exciting challenges and attractions by radically improving the opportunities for the exercise of leadership and participation in policy-making, for promotion, for specialisation and extra-congregational work, and for earning properly graded and competitive salaries, as urged in the Ministers' Charter submitted for action over six months ago. It is time we put an end to the unedifying spectacle of so many Bar Mitzvah boys receiving high honours from the community one day, only to dishonour it the next day, by insisting on more adequate standards and better Hebrew school attendance records, as already agreed upon by the authorities concerned. And it is also time at last to implement the long completed plans for a communal magazine which will not trivialise, slant or suppress news on progress within the religious community but serve as an honest forum of trustworthy information, creative thought and constructive criticism to cement the bonds of communication with our 40,000 members.

Above all, of course, as I have said so often, the United Synagogue must redirect its thinking and practical planning to the primacy of intensive Jewish education for our children if it is ever to celebrate another great anniversary again. For if we have no children in our tents of learning today, we shall have neither ministers nor worshippers in our sanctuaries of tomorrow.

AT THE CROSSROADS

On this one hundredth birthday, then, we stand not only at a monumental milestone, but also at the crossroads. Let me figuratively describe the choice before us. Whether this Centenary is to be a tragic end or a happy beginning —a *Kaddish* or a *Kiddush*—that is the question. Let me explain:

A couple of months ago I visited the stricken village of Avivim on the Israeli border with Lebanon a few days following the murderous school-bus ambush there. Almost every family had been bereaved, either immediately or less directly, and in one of the most harrowing experiences of my life, I joined the mourners for Minchah and heard an entire congregation saying *Kaddish* for its children. Likewise in Russia today, a whole generation mourns for its children, not for their physical destruction, but for their spiritual desolation enforced by brutal religious repression denying parents the right and opportunity to educate their children as Jews. How awesome, therefore, the question we must answer and which should give us no rest by day and by night: Shall we—Jews in a free society—whose children are not threatened by war or persecution, yet weep over the wholesale defection of our children out of sheer apathy? Shall we, too, become a community saying *Kaddish*'over its children, grieving over our sons and daughters who marry out or opt out because we taught them no better, turning this anniversary into a solemn *Kaddish* over the past?

Or shall this momentous anniversary be a *Kiddush* for the future, a re-dedication to sanctify a new era of Jewish commitment and spiritual re-awakening? Let us shatter the cup of bitterness. We are not mourners over a glorious past that has come to an end. It must not come to an end. Let us rather cheerfully raise the *Kiddush* cup of our salvation to inaugurate future decades of a happy community in which parents and children will— *Yom Tov*-like— sit together and jointly recite the blessing of thanksgiving "for having kept us alive and preserved us, to reach this day".

May it always be said of this great United Synagogue, "How goodly are your tents, O Jacob, your habitations, O Israel," so that we may be worthy to have a share in building the great Temple of peace in Israel, bringing redemption to all mankind.

THE PROVINCIAL CONTRIBUTION TO
ANGLO-JEWRY

Next to the foremost, momentous events governing the course of present-day Jewish life—the Holocaust, the rebirth of the Jewish State, the oppression, re-awakening and exodus of Soviet Jewry and the phenomenal growth of Jewish day-schools and Yeshivot throughout our dispersion—next to these events, I believe the most significant feature of post-war Jewish history is the massive migration of the Jewish people. Ever since the first Jew received the first divine commandment "*lech l'cha*"—"go" and wander from one country to another—we have remained the Wandering Jew to this very day.

Jewish migration across countries and across oceans, from smaller to larger communities within countries, and from urban centres to the suburbs within cities, has radically changed the world distributions of Jews and the patterns of Jewish life. Through these mass migrations the Jewish centre of gravity has shifted numerically as well as spiritually from Europe—which before the war accounted for some 10,000,000 Jews out of the 18,000,000 then living, or for nearly 60% of the whole of world Jewry—to America in numbers and to Israel in orientation. Inside Europe, while countries like Germany and many other previously large centres of Jewish life have but a fraction of their pre-war Jewish population left, France, on the other hand, through immigration from North Africa in the past decade, has doubled the size of its community, having indeed within recent years overtaken Britain which is now only the sixth largest Jewish community in the world—following the United States, Russia, Israel, the Argentine and France in that order.

Considering all the convulsions that have gone on around us, the condition of Anglo-Jewry has remained, in many respects, remarkably steady and stable—sometimes, I think, too static, especially when we reflect that the organisational structure of our community has remained virtually unchanged for over a century. Most of our major institutions and their constitutions— whether the Chief Rabbinate, the Board of Deputies, the United Synagogue of London, or indeed many local congregations—were designed in and for the nineteenth century. They can hardly be expected to meet the dynamic changes and challenges of this twentieth century without some radical adjustments. Among these changes is the continuing flow of our population

---

Address delivered before the Conference of Jewish Representative Councils, held in Hull on 11 March 1973.

from older to newer areas and from smaller to larger communities. Indeed, 75% of British Jewry is now concentrated in this country's five largest cities, and over two-thirds of the total Jewish population of this country now finds itself in London alone. Any communal long-term planning for the future must clearly take these trends into account if we are to preserve and strengthen viable Jewish life wherever it is to be found.

The emergent patterns of our community will pose special problems for the provinces, particularly in view of the growing tendency towards centralisation in our complex society and the resultant gravitation towards London in the direction of Jewish affairs. I thought it appropriate, therefore, on this occasion, to devote my presentation to this assembly of provincial community leaders, to a survey of the relationship between London and the provincial communities, with special reference to the distinct contributions which the Provinces have made, and can continue to make, to enrich the Anglo-Jewish experience, including some proposals on how best to apply whatever resources we command, for the consolidation and revitalisation of Jewish life in the Provinces and through the Provinces, of Anglo-Jewry at large.

Let me begin with just a few historical asides. The Provinces were an important and often, indeed, a major constituent of the Anglo-Jewish settlement since the earliest times, sometimes possibly even holding the majority of Jews to be found in this country. Records of Anglo-Jewish history, both before the expulsion in 1920 and following the resettlement in the middle of the seventeenth century, afford places of honour and considerable importance to cities like Plymouth, York, Lincoln, Norwich, Bristol and Chatham, as well as to London. It is interesting that of the 53 synagogues buildings listed in the last census taken in this country of this nature, which was in 1851, there are only five then listed which are still in use, and of these five only one is in London. The five are Bevis Marks in London, Plymouth, Exeter, Cheltenham and Ramsgate.

Despite their numerical decline, in relation to the capital city, the Provinces have retained many features and qualities superior to their counterparts in London. For instance, the latest report on Anglo-Jewish statistics, just published by Professor Prajs for the Statistical and Demographic Research Unit of the Board of Deputies (and these are always most fascinating documents) gives a striking illustration. In 1970 Britain had 375 synagogues, 199 of them in London. In other words, London, although it has well over two-third or nearly 70% of all Jews in this country, accounts for only 53% of the synagogues to be found in this country. The report estimates that we have 126,000 synagogue seats or, in terms of our total Anglo-Jewish population, one synagogue seat for every three persons. Yet in the Provinces the ratio is nearly twice as many per member as in London, which has only 66 seats per every 100 members, whereas in the provinces you have about double that figure at present available. But, significantly, the proportion varies inside the Provinces; for instance, Manchester, Leeds, Glasgow and Liverpool have an excess of seats over memberships. They have more seats than actual synagogue members. Birmingham has a small deficiency, while Brighton and Southend have deficiencies similar to those in London. Now, of course, partly this is explained by the movement of population from the Provinces towards London and the south-eastern counties which include Brighton and Southend, so that we now find a shortage of seats in the south-east, whereas there is a surplus of them in the communities that are numerically on the decline.

Incidentally, it may be of interest to learn and, I think, of considerable significance that the ratio of the Jewish population to the number of synagogues is about the same today as it was in 1901, over 70 years ago, when 150 synagogues served the 230,000 Jews to be found in this country—which to my mind is a most revealing comment on the Jeremiads of those who defy the Preacher's counsel: "Do not say that the former days were better than these."

Even more remarkable is the disparity in favour of the Provinces in Jewish school enrolments. Among our Jewish primary schools, London accounts for 14·9% of our corresponding Jewish school population, whereas in the Provinces 25·2% of all our Jewish children of primary school age attend Jewish day schools. The contrast is even more striking at the secondary level. In London 9·3% of secondary school pupils attend Jewish secondary schools, as against 10·5% in the Provinces. But these figures have meaning only if it is remembered that all the smaller centres have no possibility of any secondary Jewish schooling, so that in those centres where Jewish secondary schools are to be found, the proportion of Jewish children attending them is far higher than the under 10% to be found in London. In fact, in some provincial communities the figures are many times as high as in London, with well over 50% of all primary school children attending Jewish schools in communities like Sunderland, Liverpool and Manchester, while in Birmingham, Glasgow and Leeds the figures are also in excess of the London percentage. In higher Jewish education the Provinces altogether eclipse London. The great majority of all full-time Yeshiva students in this country study at provincial centres of Jewish learning. That London, therefore, has by no means a monopoly, let alone a prior claim on special communally sponsored facilities, is also demonstrated by the fact that the only full-time university chaplaincies in this country today are to be found in the Provinces—in Glasgow and Manchester—though, of course, half their cost is borne by London.

I mention these figures in order to set the place of the Provinces vis-à-vis London in the proper perspective. I believe it is a fallacy to think that Jewish survival, or even the quality of Jewish life, is dependent on the size of a community. Indeed, there are some indications to the contrary. After all, have we not proclaimed as a people that we have survived and been chosen "*Ki atem ham'at mikol ha'amim*", not because we were a great mass, a great majority, but "because we were the fewest of all peoples". London Jewry today accounts for 3·5% of the population of London. Provincial Jewry accounts for 0·32%, which is less than one-tenth of the density in London. Yet, compare their corresponding and diverse achievements, despite the fact that the number of Jews, in relation to their non-Jewish environment, is so much more diluted throughout the Provinces. Maybe it is just the smallness of numbers which makes Jewish community life more compact and, as a result, more intense, resulting in an increased commitment and in a stronger urge to be creative as well as to enter into community service and into public service. For example, there can be little doubt that the proportion of Jews who have entered into civic and public life, on the one hand, and who have emerged as communal or national Jewish leaders on the other hand, is considerably higher from among our provincial communities than in the case of those produced by the London Jewish community. And where better, and on what more auspicious occasion, than on this, graced as we are by the presence of a Lord Mayor of this fair city, drawn from our own ranks, could I make this specific reference to the fact—I think the undeniable fact—that the Provinces have produced far more Jewish Lord Mayors, Mayors, Aldermen and Councillors, than their corresponding number in London.

The only statistics I have available concerns Jewish Members of Parliament, as I could not find statistics on the civic dignitaries. There are 40 Jewish members of Parliament. Thirty of them represent provincial constituencies. What is even more striking, out of these 40 Jewish M.P.s—and I looked it up in the current *Jewish Year Book* for 1973—eight were born in London, 22 were born in the Provinces, while the remaining 10 do not list their place of origin. Now this, to my mind, is a fantastic tribute to the productivity of the Provinces in relation to London in terms of public service. With London having three times as many Jews, it still produced only 8 Jewish M.P.s compared with 22 who hail from the Provinces!

I have made a similar study in regard to the Anglo-Jewish Ministry, and I found that the majority of British-born Ministers serving the Anglo-Jewish community come from the Provinces. I did this for the first time in 1948, when as the then Minister of the Great Synagogue, Duke's Place, in London, I delivered a lecture on the East End and the Anglo-Jewish community. Of the then 36 Ministers, excluding Chazanim, serving the United Synagogue in its constituent and district synagogues, 15 hailed from the Provinces—that is Ministers serving the United Synagogue *in London*! Fifteen of those 36 came from the Provinces, 11 from abroad and only 10 from London, 7 of them from the East End. Of the Rabbis and Ministers listed in the 1973 *Jewish Year Book*, 25 were born in the Provinces, only 24 in London, and 50 (more than the percentage in 1948) came from abroad—an increase which, as far as I can make out, is largely due to the addition of so many Progressive Ministers who virtually all came from abroad, mostly from Germany. In fact, who does not know of numerous outstanding Ministers and lay-leaders who hailed from tiny little hamlets—from places like Llanelly in Wales? Whole generations of leaders came from very small communities that were dispersed and miles away from the major centres of Jewish life.

Conversely, in many provincial communities, I daresay, our losses by intermarriage and by assimilation are smaller than they are in London. In a smaller, more compact, community it is simply more difficult to get lost as a Jew. You are being traced, somebody knows you and eventually catches up with you.

Hence, we have had a proportionately greater contribution from the Provinces, not only in the supply of leadership and the preservation of Jewish identity. The corporate contribution of provincial communities has also been proportionately larger. I will give you only six items I wanted to list in particular.

There is today from the Provinces a considerably higher rate of Aliyah to Israel than there is from London. Secondly, a greater percentage of members of our community in the provinces are involved in J.P.A. or J.N.F. work than in London. For instance, in Leeds 63% of the community contribute to the J.N.F. which is incomparably higher than the corresponding figure would be in London. Liverpool, is a particularly staunch supporter of all Zionist activity, on a scale far greater and more intense than is to be found in London.

Thirdly, I think of Manchester's pioneering role in the history of British Zionism, and the crucial historic impact which the Manchester School, as we call it today, has made not merely on the fortunes of Anglo-Jewry but on the fortunes of our entire people, through the role it played in the events leading up to the Balfour Declaration and finally to the re-establishment of Jewish statehood in our days. Had we been dependent simply on London and on the leading Jewish institutions, like the Board of Deputies and the United Synagogue as they then were, who knows whether to this day we would have had a Balfour Declaration, or a Jewish State?

Fourthly, I think of the personalities in communal leadership, not just in terms of their geographical origin, but of the quite unique contributions that only they were able to make to the enrichment of Anglo-Jewish leadership. For instance, Professor Brodetsky and Dr. Cohen of Leeds and Birmingham respectively, were the only ones in a whole generation to become the lay-leaders of Anglo-Jewry drawn from the ranks of the intelligentsia, of the academics, on the one hand, and on the other hand from the clergy. We have not produced a single other leader drawn from those two ranks to assume a position of supreme responsibility for the government of our community and its representation before the nation at large.

Think next, fifthly, of the intensity with which in many provincial communities, Soviet–Jewish activities are being conducted, notably through the impact of the local chapters of the "35 Group" of women, as well as other organisations that have made a distinct mark on the life of their communities and indeed of their cities in a manner which we have scarcely succeeded in doing with the same effect in London.

Finally, I may mention as a specific and, I think, quite uniquely valuable contribution of the Provinces, and that is a diversified Jewish press. If it were not for the often very valuable weekly and monthly magazines published in Manchester, Glasgow, Birmingham, Liverpool and elsewhere as part of this diversified press, I believe we would have an entirely different focus, through a purely monolithic monopoly in the Jewish press, on Jewish affairs and particularly on communal affairs than we actually have, thanks to the invaluable contribution made through the diversification of news media which is so vital a feature for the enrichment of Jewish life.

More generally, the Provinces have helped us to preserve certain community traditions which in London have all but died out together. Take, within the religious context, the *Chevra Kadisha* organisations. In London we have forgotten what the *Chevra Kadisha* really means. We have forgotten that we once taught that the highest form of charity, *Chesed shel emmeth*, is the loving-kindness shown to those who can no longer fend for themselves, a service rendered in an honorary capacity and ranking as the highest honour that can be bestowed. This has survived in very large measure in the provincial communities; while in London this noble tradition has become professionalised, resulting in the loss of a dimension of the Jewish soul and spirit which used to enhance the value of human beings and their dignity, even in death—a concept from which we have now, alas, become estranged.

Through the Provinces we also enjoy a much greater diversity of Jewish life which again enriches our communal scene. There are more variations of communal style by virtue of the autonomy, and often independence, of congregations in the Provinces, as distinct from the massive monolith, from the colossus, that governs community affairs in a city like London. Hence, you are much more easily in a position to pioneer new ventures, to go into communal experimentation and innovation. A vast organisation, like the United Synagogue is big, controlled by ancient traditions and administered by a complex machinery; you cannot easily introduce novel ideas, novel concepts, let alone experiments, into communal government and to communal planning or administration. Broken down into manageable proportions, into smaller communities, you can have more of a family spirit uniting a community together than the impersonal relationship that very often characterises the membership in the vast cities, where two people can sit next to each other in *Shool* Shabbat after Shabbat and not even know each other's names!

In the Provinces, as I have said, there are opportunities for exploration, for innovation, for pioneering, that do not exist in the big conglomerations of communities, such as London represents. For instance, I would think that you may much more easily be in a position that we are in London to pioneer efforts to make the Ministry a more rewarding and more exciting vocation than unhappily it is today, with a result that we are going to face a critical problem of recruitment to the Ministry. You can set standards of emoluments and of giving scope to a Minister which it would take us ages in London to reach. For in London, if you make one little change, such as a slight addition to Ministerial salaries, it has to affect many scores of Ministers, and the figures rise to astronomical proportions. Moreover, if London were to modify drastically the rigid system whereby a Minister is a functionary who carries out duties rather than a leader who is expected to make decisions on his own initiative, then of course you affect at once eighty or a hundred Ministers, not all of whom may be in a position to assume these added responsibilities. In an individual congregation you are able to give these greater responsibilities, this wider scope, this greater challenge to men of calibre and thereby attract them.

These facts and assessments should, I hope, convince you that in many respects the provincial Jewish contributions, whether to civic life, to Anglo-Jewish affairs, to our religious traditions, or to Zionism, are—far from being inferior to those of London—in fact, proportionately far greater. They are certainly reflected by the composition and the activities of the only two major communal institutions which link London and the provincial congregations together, one on the lay level—the Board of Deputies of British Jews—itself led by a son of one of our great provincial communities, and the other on the Rabbinic level, the Chief Rabbinate. As for the latter, it may interest you that in 1972 alone, my itinerary included five days in Manchester, three days in Newcastle and Sunderland, two days in Glasgow, two days in Liverpool, and visits to Leeds, Cardiff, Brighton and Bournemouth as well as, among the smaller communities, to Whitley Bay, Reading, Chatham, Cambridge, Epsom and even to Jersey Island. That was just 1972. My office is very deeply involved in the affairs of the Provinces, and I, for one, always find it most exhilarating when I can wrench myself from the pressures of London Jewry and breathe a little of the sunny and refreshing air of our provincial communities with all the problems that beset them.

Now, in the light of the existing assets and the existing deficiencies—especially numerical deficiencies—as I have tried to convey them to you, how can we best husband and exploit our resources? How can we best strengthen the weak and utilise the strength of the strong, by working together for our mutual advantage in a partnership of service, where each gives of his best and contributes something indispensable to our common good? I believe, broadly speaking, the Provinces have proportionately greater resources of manpower and of commitment, while London, absolutely and relatively, has superior financial and organisational assets. Hence we must look to London for bearing a disproportionate financial burden, whilst in return we must look to the Provinces for making a disproportionate contribution to solving some of our manpower problems and especially for making available recruits for training in leadership.

At the same time, any proposals for strengthening Jewish life in the Provinces and enhancing their contribution to Anglo-Jewish vitality in general, must include efforts to consolidate Jewish life in the main centres and to extend a helping hand to the smaller and declining communities. With these objects in view, finally, I would place before you the following suggestions:

(a) A programme of consolidation for the larger centres. For instance, only the other day Newcastle pioneered a novel enterprise in the Provinces by establishing, partly through the help and guidance of the United Synagogue in London, by forming a union, an association of congregations that will now through their united strength rationalise the distribution of their resources and also effect considerable economies. I would think that similar plans should be explored for cities like Manchester, Liverpool, Glasgow, Birmingham and possibly others. What we have, we should consolidate, and we should eliminate losses suffered by undue fragmentation and duplication.

(b) We should introduce systems of regionalisation, wherever feasible. Some time ago we set up a regional "Beth Din of the North" based on Manchester, but embracing Leeds on the one side and Liverpool on the other, acting in co-ordination with one another and taking care of the religious and Rabbinical affairs of the entire area. I would like to see a similar regional Beth Din established for the north-east to comprise the communities of Newcastle, Sunderland and the surrounding communities. We might possibly also consider (at least by way of exploration) the setting up of regional Rabbinates, whereby we would have supreme Rabbinic authorities that can make local decisions and be involved in local affairs on a day-to-day routine basis, without having to rely on advice and guidance from a remote office in London for the solution of local and regional problems.

You have already heard something at this Conference of plans to regionalise

Shechita and Kashrut. I think we may also have to consider the regionalisation of Jewish education—whereby adjoining communities should pool their resources and establish area schools, such as the one now contemplated by possibly merging the Newcastle and Sunderland schools into one viable unit.

(c) The third proposal to which I would like you to give some serious attention is to introduce a system of twinning of large congregations with individually selected small communities whom they would adopt as being their own. We have today a considerable number of very viable large congregational units, both in London and our larger provincial centres, which are well manned with Rabbis, Ministers, teachers, not to mention experienced lay-leaders. Each such major congregation should take it upon itself to find a lost, small, declining community—say within a 50- or 70-mile radius—and say "this little community becomes my adopted child". What should this achieve? For instance, you could think of periodic arrangements to invite children of this small community to become your guests at a major community, invite them for a *Shabbatton*, for a Shabbat-Seminar. Put them up in your homes, let them see vibrant Jewish life in a manner which they cannot otherwise see, having no Minister, no teachers—certainly no qualified and experienced teachers—in their midst. Or you could think of joint youth functions. Send out your youth organisation, your youth club, to your twin community for joint functions. Send out speakers, preachers, teachers, at regular intervals. Let the Minister of the major community once every three months spend, together with his family, a Shabbat in one of the outlying, lost and scattered little communities that face extinction if we do not inject into them from time to time a new booster of Jewish life, by sending them ranking, experienced personalities, who will feel personally responsible for that community and who will be available for counselling, for consultation, for advice on any local problem.

(d) Next, we should organise the better use of the facilities now available in London for the training of personnel and recruits from the Provinces for both the teaching and Ministerial professions, and possibly for Jewish social service in general. We now have two new sixth-form colleges in London, with residential accomodation available. We will supply and find all the financial resources needed. You find the human resources needed. Send us up your best boys and your best girls, who are either taking their O-levels this coming summer, or who are prepared to enter the college proper, and you will have future leaders in your communities and in the community at large. Similarly, we are already engaged in discussions with various provincial communities to extend the scope of our Jewish Educational Development Trust to the Provinces as well. So far, financially at any rate, this has been entirely London-based, but we are negotiating with communities as diverse as Newcastle, Leeds, and Liverpool, with a view to ensuring that we engage in a common effort to expand and intensify Jewish education by joint planning, mutual aid and the judicious deployment of our limited resources.

I hope that this Conference will help to lift the fog that sometimes prevents us from recognising that we are all brothers and sisters in a common enterprise, that we all belong to the same family, that the sunshine of our history has once again risen upon our fortunes and our generation through the restoration of our people to its homeland, through the return of tens of thousands of our brethren in the darkness of Soviet Russia to the bosom of our people, yearning to be reunited not only with the soil but also with the soul of the Jewish people. May we contribute to the fulfilment of the blessing *"ulchol benei Yisrael haya or bemoshvotam"*, that the brightness and the radiance of this sunshine will illumine our lives, that we will recognise one another, serve one another, and try to raise a new generation which indeed will break out from the fetters and the agonies of the past and return to the Land of Promise and to the faith of promise, which is our heritage and which we are here as custodians not merely to preserve but to hand on intact to our children and to those coming after them.

ANGLO-JEWISH MELTING-POT: THE FUSION OF NATIVES AND IMMIGRANTS

This fascinating volume skilfully describes and profusely documents the most formative period in the history of Anglo-Jewry. It provides massive data and perceptive insights no less indispensable for an analytical understanding of today's community than are references to childhood and adolescence experiences for an appreciation of a mature personality.

The 44 years covered in this book witnessed a phenomenal growth, both quantitatively and qualitatively. The mighty waves of immigration, augmented by a fairly high natural increase, more than quadrupled the number of Jews in this country—from about 60,000 in 1870 to a quarter of a million or more at the outbreak of the First World War. An influx swamping the original community on such a scale was bound to leave some indelible marks on the direction and content of Anglo-Jewish life. In fact, this influx was no doubt responsible for the intensity of the religious and Zionist commitment, the diversity, and indeed the sheer survival of the community as we know it today. Without this enormous transfusion of new blood, very few descendants of those resident in this country in 1870 would now maintain their Jewish identity, let alone sustain a vibrant Jewish community.

Nevertheless, what is astounding is the extent to which the principal features of the community and its institutions remained unaffected by the gigantic tide of newcomers. While it led to some marginal proliferation of synagogue organizations—and even these remained very confined in size and influence—the structure of the community withstood, and eventually almost completely absorbed, this tide. The Chief Rabbinate, the United Synagogue, the Board of Deputies, the Board of Guardians and even the chief provincial institutions emerged from this flood virtually unchanged.

This remarkable phenomenon certainly testifies to the stability of Anglo-Jewry, and perhaps also to the oneness of the Jewish people whereby well over 100,000 East European Jews could integrate in a Western community less than half their number without significantly disturbing the patterns of the latter. In the imagery of Pharoah's dream, the lean cows simply consumed the fat ones.

But the phenomenon also demonstrates the essentially conservative

Preface contributed to the new edition (1973) of Lloyd P. Gartner's The Jewish Immigrant in England, 1870–1914, *Simon Publications, London, first published in 1960.*

character of Jewish organisational life, a feature also strikingly borne out in modern Israel where, notwithstanding the quadrupling of the Jewish population by immigration in the past 25 years, such characteristics as the political party system, the organisation of the rabbinate, and the institutionalisation of diverse economic trends have remained substantially unchanged since before the establishment of the Jewish State.

All this is not to say that Anglo-Jewry has not undergone some fundamental changes, in outlook and attitudes, over the decades separating the huge waves of immigration from the present time. In common with Jewish communities all over the world, including Israel, Anglo-Jewry has tended to become far more polarised, increasingly divided as it now is between the spiritual haves and have-nots, breaking up the traditional "middle-of-the-road" centre into those seeking a more intensive commitment and those drifting away from any Jewish anchorage. The preponderant anti-Zionism of the past has given way to an almost unqualified commitment to Israel. The position of the rabbi has certainly changed beyond recognition from that described in this book.

> . . . the status of the London immigrant rabbi was a sorry one. The social and legal conditions of English life inevitably stripped him of most of his traditional functions, such as judicial services and control of marital affairs. He was no longer the central figure of his community. . . . An ultimate indignity required that an immigrant rabbi who entered under the communal canopy surrendered his very title, and in return was designated "the Reverend Mister". Young Rabbi Meir Berlin, remembering the high standing of the East European Rabbi and perhaps also bearing in mind the prestige of his illustrious forebears in his native *yeshiva* town of Volozhin was perhaps too melancholy over the fate of the immigrant rabbis whom he saw in London. These men, he declared, were "robbed . . . both of their rabbinates and their self-respect. It was a great tragedy to see a rabbi in London. Poverty was discernible in his dress and manner."

Today we not only encourage all our own entrants into the ministry to be distinguished by rabbinical titles, but we scan the globe for outstanding rabbis to fill key positions of spiritual leadership in our community.

How incongruous with our attitude nowadays, especially in regard to the emigration of Soviet Jews, is the plea of Chief Rabbi Nathan Marcus Adler in 1888, in a circular letter addressed to his East European colleagues, entreating

> every Rabbi of a community kindly to preach in the Synagogue and house of study, to publicise the evil which is befalling our brethren who have come here, and to warn them not to come to the land of Britain, for such ascent is a descent . . .

—a sentiment then endorsed by other official agencies of the Anglo-Jewish community.

What a contrast, too, between the Jewish day schools described in this volume, designed primarily to Anglicise Jewish immigrant children, and their successors today, meant to Judaise their descendants.

Perhaps what has remained constant over the years is the peculiar tendency of English Jews to denigrate their community and to suffer denigration by others. Ahad HaAm's derisive description of the Anglo-Jewish community as "a cemetery with pretty gravestones" has its indigenous echoes today. Some of the strictures on Anglo-Jewry's cultural, literary and scholarly apathy and stagnation also still remain true.

Yet, out of this alleged graveyard have arisen, like the dry bones in Ezekiel's vision, one of the best organised and most traditional communities in the world, many historic contributions to Zionism and the Jewish State, and lately even in the sphere of religious education, several flourishing seats of intensive Jewish learning. Indeed, Anglo-Jewry is now by far the largest haven of traditional Jewish living and learning in Europe, indicating a reversal of fortunes both sad as a reminder of a past in ruins, and encouraging as a portent of Jewish regeneration.

Chapter Three

WORLD JEWRY

The Quest for Survival and Identity

THE REUNIFICATION OF JERUSALEM AND THE REUNIFICATION OF THE JEWISH PEOPLE

We have come from the four corners of the earth to deliberate together on how best to redirect our enormous resources and energies towards the spiritual regeneration of Jewish life the world over. The key to our tasks ahead is given by Jerusalem, hitherto scarred by the division of barbed wire and now triumphantly reunited by the transformation of its no-man's-land into every-man's-land. That part of the Talmud which is itself named after this city, the Jerusalem Talmud (*Hagigah*, 3:6) comments on the verse: ירושלים הבנויה כעיר שחוברה לה יחדו, "Jerusalem rebuilt, like a city that is joined together": עיר שהיא עושה כל ישראל חברים, "a city which makes all Israel join together as brethren". Through Jerusalem, we are to unite our tribes and sects still divided by barriers through which there is no communication, to become one people of חברים, inspired by a unity of purpose and of brotherhood, transcending our differences of origin and outlook.

May this unique Conference—drawing its strength from all parts of the world and its inspiration from this centre of the earth, the traditional starting-point of creation, the City of Peace and Unity—help to bridge the gulf between Israel and the Diaspora, between Ashkenazim and Sephardim, between religionists and secularists, between synagogues and yeshivoth, and above all between God and His people.

How are we to achieve this rapprochment, to restore the oneness of Israel as we have restored the oneness of Jerusalem? First and foremost, by each side making an effort to understand the other.

Jews in the Diaspora will have to appreciate the radical impact of Israel's rebirth, an impact so far not sufficiently recognised in our religious and educational thinking. It is time that even synagogue services, and not only the Arab states, recognised Israel's existence. Diaspora Jews will also have to accept the fact that Israel's survival will henceforth depend on massive Aliyah even more than on financial support. It is up to our religious leadership and institutions to galvanise the response to the desperate appeal for Aliyah and not to leave this or any other form of Jewish statesmanship only to Zionist organisations and secularist leaders. Only thus can religious Jewry regain its place of pre-eminence in guiding our people's destiny, and incidentally in assuring the growth of the religious component in Israel's population.

Address delivered at the First Conference of Ashkenazi and Sephardi Synagogues, Jerusalem, 9 January 1968.

And Jews in Israel will have to appreciate that their concern for Jewish survival must include a recognition that it is equally endangered by the mass-defections through assimilation and intermarriage in the Diaspora. Any campaigns to ensure Israel's security and prosperity will have to be co-ordinated with equally urgent emergency drives in our own communities to recapture our youth straying from Judaism by the hundreds of thousands. The response to Israel's emergency must be matched in the Diaspora by crash-programmes for better schools, more dynamic congregations and the training of more competent leaders. Both Israel and the Diaspora, now more than ever mutually dependent on one another, will have to learn that we share the same destiny, by worrying together and consulting together to forge a common bond of our joint fortunes and misfortunes.

Ashkenazim and Sephardim should recognise that the geographical accident of our separate wanderings through Europe, whereby incidentally we were named after our people's worst oppressors in modern and medieval times respectively, must not raise barriers of class-distinctions between us, nor hinder our eventual fusion into common communities, now that our physical separation is at an end and we again live together in Israel and in the Diaspora.

The appalling rift between the religious and irreligious elements of our people must be narrowed by calling a halt to the sterile *Kulturkampf* of unreason and mutual denigration in which neither side cares for the other and each glories in the other's disgrace. Instead of denouncing those who are perplexed through ignorance and rebellious through false teachings, we must grieve over their defection, befriend them and open their eyes to the splendours of our spiritual treasures. We must even acknowledge that we are not blameless for the tragedy of their irreligion, for we have failed to communicate our ideals in a language and through leaders they can understand. If Torah leaders do not encourage some of our best *benei Torah* to be trained for leadership, to become rabbis, doctors, lawyers, civil servants or social workers, but leave the strategic positions of government, administration and influence in the hands of the secularists, how can we then complain when the Jewish State, our institutions, our hospitals, and sometimes even our communities are not conducted by the rule of the Torah? We must learn that in this democratic age our convictions can prevail only by persuasion, not by authority or legislation, only by winning the dissidents, not by coercing or ostracising them.

And the anti-traditionalists must learn that the Jewish people divorced from its traditions is a travesty of Jewish history and martyrdom; it is like a tree without roots, or like a building on quicksand, doomed to destruction. They must realise that the days of Orthodox decline have passed. With far more Israeli and foreign students at Israeli yeshivoth than at Israel's secular institutions of higher learning, with virtually all intensive Jewish day-schools throughout the world under Orthodox control, and with a birth-rate among the strictly Orthodox many times as high as among other Jews who vanish because they produce too few and lose too many, combined with the superior tenacity of those steeled by the moral discipline of Jewish life, who can doubt the ultimate triumph of the Torah forces within our people? Our non-religious brothers, to appreciate the Orthodox mentality, must also realise that our religious faith, as the *raison d'être* of our national existence, is no less precious to us than our land or our people. On our beliefs, they must understand therefore, we cannot compromise, nor can we legitimise religious forms alien to historic Judaism without making a mockery of our most sacred convictions.

But on our side, too, we must promote understanding and communication if the awful cleavage between us, sapping the strength of our people through wasteful strife and acrimony, is to be healed. Only if we try just as hard to understand what caused the dissidents to reject our religious heritage as we want them to understand why we cling to it can we begin to communicate creatively and reach out to their hearts. It is our challenge at this Conference to discover how to stimulate such communications within the framework of our synagogues and congregational activities.

This Conference should also call for a closer partnership between synagogues and yeshivoth, the two essential pillars of Jewish life. Today only the most intensive Jewish learning and living can equip our young people to withstand the intellectual challenges and immoral allurements of the modern world—its godless science, it amoral philosophy and its unbridled way of life. Real immunity to these un-Jewish influences only the yeshivoth can provide. But equally, we cannot today maintain the supremacy of the Torah in communal life, nor hold our *Ba'alei Battim* in the Orthodox fold, without flourishing congregations, led by dynamic, highly trained spiritual leaders. While yeshivoth create Jews, as the forum ללמוד וללמד, synagogues preserve them, as the arena לשמור ולעשות, for acting out their learning. Hence, we must now raise the traditional Issachar-Zevulun relationship to an institutional level. Our congregations must accept the obligation to provide communal support for our day-schools and yeshivoth, by taxing our members for essential educational needs as they do for expenditure on synagogues. And in return, yeshivoth must recognise their debt to our congregations, by making available an army of some of their finest *talmidim* for training and service as rabbis, teachers and communal leaders to man our spiritual defences.

And finally, this Conference must help to restore the unity of God, Israel and the Torah—קב"ה וישראל ואורייתא חד הוא. As heirs of our Prophets, we must proclaim to our brothers here and the world over that without a massive religious revival our people cannot prevail. Expanding their religious horizon beyond the restrictions of our Sabbath, Kashruth and marriage laws, we must convince them that some of our most pressing social and national problems cannot be solved except through generating a profoundly religious conscience, for instance, by raising the Jewish birth-rate, or by reducing Israel's phenomenally high abortion rate, which has already smothered more potential Sabra lives since the establishment of the State than the half million Western immigrants now hoped for. Nor can we root out delinquency and other vices without the moral discipline of Torah education and conduct.

No less relevant to sheer physical security is the religious interpretation of contemporary events. Seven months ago we witnessed one of the most dramatic episodes in Jewish history—a threat of utter disaster turned into a victory of truly biblical proportions. For a moment it seemed to all as if "the stars in their courses had fought" our battle. The world was stunned with awe and wonderment. Our enemies were utterly confounded—תפול עליהם, אימתה ופחד while Jews everywhere rose to a pitch of enthusiasm and exhilaration never before experienced. We thought the event would generate a tidal wave of immigration and Jewish unity. We imagined no Arab would ever again dare speak of another round except a round-table conference. And we believed the nations of the world would acknowledge the futility of obstructing the Prophetic fulfilment of Israel's destiny. Today these hopes are all but shattered. Now, only a few months later, the Jewish excitement has faded; our enemies' awe has waned; and the massive wave of world sympathy has been largely dissipated. How did this happen?

I can offer only one explanation. During and immediately after the Six-day War everyone, Jew and non-Jew alike, was convinced that a tremendous miracle had occurred, that Providence Itself had worked on our side. Every Israeli soldier told of some supernatural experience he had personally witnessed, and the Israeli press freely admitted the manifest intervention of the Finger of God and the resultant popular religious stirrings. And then, by a disastrous reversal, all that was changed. References to Providence and miracles were expunged. Israel's press and leading spokesmen, driven by rabid secularism, were at pains to deny that there had been anything miraculous in the victory. In London, for instance, an outstanding general of Israel's heroic army assured a large audience that the victory was due only to Israeli superiority and Arab weakness. Like the first Russian cosmonaut who could not see God in outer space, the brave general had seen no miracles; to which I, speaking on the same platform, could only retort that he had proved the Talmudic maxim (*Niddah* 31a) "one who experiences a miracle does not recognise it".

And once the event was reduced to natural proportions, to the ordinary norms of military and political encounters, both Jewish and the non-Jewish reaction reverted to the normalcy which had obtained before the War. There was little left to get excited about; for the vision of a Providential intervention in Israel's destiny, against which no power on earth could prevail or argue, was exchanged for an ordinary conflict between nations. By denying the religious significance of the Six-day War, the secularists put paid to any hopes that the extraordinary pathos of Jewish ardour and non-Jewish awe could be maintained, just as surely as without "*Al ha-nissim*", Chanukah would have lost its charismatic grip on our people long ago. Once again, then, without a return to our religious values Jewish security cannot be assured, either internally by commitment or externally by our partnership with Providence. It is up to this Conference and its participants never to tire in proclaiming this warning by word and deed.

OUR PEOPLE'S CHALLENGE TO RABBIS

At our rabbinical meetings we usually discuss what we demand of our congregations and our people in general. But, in this lecture, I wish to discuss what the wider public demands of us.

The truth must be admitted: one cannot conceal the painful fact that the rabbinate, whether in Israel or in the Diaspora, finds itself today in a severe crisis. We may as well recognise that during the past few generations the reins of leadership in national matters have passed more and more from our hands into the hands of the secularists and of political leaders. Already for some time there has been a steady decline in the influence of rabbis on the values and lives of that wider Jewish society which hardly cares for the endorsement of Torah opinion or the counsel of its teachers.

Lately, however, an altogether new and fearful phenomenon has arisen. There has come up a new generation of "stubborn and rebellious sons", to whom one can apply the sayings "woe to the generation which judges its judges" and "in the birthpangs of the *Mashiach* impertinence increases". Wide sections of our people no longer look upon us as guarantors for the unity and fellowship of all Israel. Moreover, they do not accept our argument, in the famous phrase of Rabbi Saadya Gaon, that "Israel is not a nation except by virtue of its Torah" and that only through the rule of those faithful to the word of the Lord can the existence and unity of the tribes of Yeshurun in the world be assured; quite the reverse, they now accuse us of fragmenting our people and even of causing hatred among brothers.

We must admit there is a tendency these days towards an ever greater polarisation which constantly widens the gap between the religious and non-religious camps in a frightening manner. While *we* see the principal cause for this in the estrangement of the masses from the traditions and faith of our fathers, the majority do not agree with us. On the contrary, they attribute this abyss, which threatens to tear up our nation into two contending peoples, to what they call our "fanaticism". In particular they ascribe to us plans and schemes to impose the dominance of the rabbinate in all its rigidity on the community against its will by what they term "religious coercion" whereby, according to them, we bring about divisiveness and hatred among brothers.

A slightly abridged translation of a Hebrew lecture delivered to the Conference of European Rabbis in Grindelwald, Switzerland, on 12 December 1972.

We may do well to give serious consideration to these accusations, realising that ultimately the responsibility falls upon us to befriend the estranged and to prevent a final breach within our people.

There is nothing new under the sun, and the experience of the fathers is a lesson to the children. Already at the beginning of the history of our ancestors we find a precedent for our situation—both for the challenge facing us and for the response required of us. I resort to this precedent not as an exercise in homiletics but as a practical teaching in Jewish law and thought. The first incident of hatred among Jewish brothers occurred between Joseph and his brethren. The cause for that hatred did not lie in the dreams which he dreamed about the sheaves on earth and the sun and moon and stars in heaven which bowed down before him. The brothers hated him "for his dreams and *for his words*", that is, because he expressed *in words* and related what he dreamed.

Joseph, we are told, "was 17 years old, being a lad". At this age every young person dreams that he is destined to subdue the world and conquer it. Thus we find today seething rebellion among youth, not because they *dream* about the conquest of society and the social system; they dreamed such dreams in every generation. The present tensions derive from *telling* the dreams. The root of the friction is to be found in the fact that youth nowadays no longer contents itself with silence, keeping its dreams to itself; young people tell their dreams with a loud voice, with commotion and with noisy protests, while in the past they remained quiet. This is precisely what happened to Joseph: only when he told his dreams to his brothers did their hatred of him increase, as they asked with an envy and hostility born out of fear: "Shall you indeed reign over us, or shall you indeed have dominion over us?"

We find ourselves in a similar situation. Masses of our brethren believe that we rabbis entertain dreams of lordship and dominion. They think and suspect this; indeed, they know that we have such dreams since we proclaim our dreams, and out of the question: "will the rabbis indeed reign over us, or will they indeed have dominion over us?", out of this fear they hate us. Nevertheless, just as "a prophet who suppresses his prophecy deserves to die", so are we obliged and commanded to tell our dreams and our visions.

Let us now turn to the solution of our problem. How did Joseph quieten his brothers and turn their hatred into brotherhood and peace without surrendering his rule over them? Joseph pacified his brothers by saying to them: "And now be not grieved, nor angry with yourselves, that you sold me hither; for God did send me before you to preserve life." And he added: "And God sent me before you to give you a remnant in the land, and to save you alive for a great deliverance."

In this assurance we, too, might find a key to opening the bolted door which bars the relations of brotherhood and understanding between us and masses of our brethren. Moreover, perhaps we can see in these verses a kind of summary programme, both positively and negatively, to serve us as a guide in our attitude towards those remote from the paths of truth and righteousness in the light of Torah. If only we could realise the three items Joseph mentioned to his brothers, we would soon subdue our enemies and turn our hands upon our adversaries. Our task is to convince our erring brethren (a) *that God sent us*, that rabbinic authority is based not on popular opinion but on Divine sanction entrusted to rabbis as agents of Providence, "for the judgement is God's", (b) *that we have been sent before them to preserve life*—not to oppress or complicate life, but on the contrary to assure and sustain Jewish life, and (c) *to give them a remnant in the land, and to save a great deliverance*—that only if we fulfil our assignment to draw all the people of Israel to the Torah and Mitzvot is it possible to preserve the security of the nation, both the remnant in the Land and the great remainder in all the places of their habitations.

Permit me to explain the meaning of these words in detail.

From the viewpoint of the wider public, the activities of rabbis and their influence are mainly concentrated on restrictions over the freedom of life. They see in us only a barrier and a brake to the advance of science, technology and social life in general. Almost all the major campaigns and battles which have been joined by the religious forces in recent times were negative or preventive actions, such as to prevent Sabbath desecration or pig-breeding, autopsies or civil marriages. We always appear to work, or protest, *against* something, rather than *for* positive ideals. Even the "Who is a Jew?" affair, which shook the Jewish world everywhere, was basically a negative endeavour to guard the nation against the admixture of some individuals who were not members of our faith according to Jewish law. In the Diaspora, too, most of the arguments between us and the non-Orthodox sprang from our concern not to allow the destroyers to make inroads into the fortifications of our religious observances, by preventing breaches, such as any recognition of the Reformers and their kind, or mixed choirs, or acts of proselytisation and marriage carried out in violation of Jewish law, etc. As a result, our image, in their distorted mirror, reflects the widespread impression of us as power-drunk men who dream by night and scheme by day on how to impose new bans and prohibitions on the community to consolidate our power to reign and hold dominion over them. Out of this a flood of hatred descended into our midst, and we became two camps.

Obviously, I do not dispute the necessity and importance of these struggles. Certainly we are obliged to fight with all our strength against the desecration of Israel's sanctities. However hard the waging of this battle may be, we are not free to desist from it.

Nevertheless, we must consider well the price which we are paying for these campaigns, weighing carefully whether the gain is not set off by the loss. For, what profit is there in our blood—the blood of this battle—when we go down to the pit of the humiliation of the Torah and the decline of our influence, when the circle of law-observers and respecters of rabbis constantly diminishes? And while our intention is to increase the ranks of the most zealous—adding to the lights of the *Menorah* in accordance with the School of Hillel, we lose the lights of Jewish souls which become extinguished one by one—diminishing their number in accordance with the School of Shammai.

In my humble view, there is an escape from this dilemma. The central point is to determine where to put the emphasis in our campaigns so as to regain the confidence of the wider public in our stand as the pilots of the Jewish people's destiny. Today it is readily possible to find common interests which join religious and non-religious Jews together to deal with problems which cry out for spiritual leadership by rabbis as the heirs of the Hebrew Prophets.

Instead of limiting our activities and protests mainly to items regarding which our thoughts are not their thoughts and their ways are not our ways, the demand of the hour calls for concentrating our attention on major problems which are not only as thorns in *our* eyes and as pricks in *our* sides, problems which agitate not only the faithful and which distinguish us from those who err, but rather also with problems which are the cause of anxiety and perplexity to society at large, problems which unite all sections of our people and which cannot be solved except through the teachings and practice of Torah.

How great would be the respect, or at least the recognition, for us if we came to "preserve life" by efforts to enrich and improve the texture of life which has now become empty of all meaning and purpose, the life of masses among Jews, as among the nations, surrendered to the vanities of the world and its amusements, a life without contents and without goals, without the joy of Mitzvot or the satisfaction of work. We may not yet have a generation that thirsts for the word of the Lord, but there are many who genuinely search in the quest to raise the quality of life and the morals of society. It is up to us, if not in common endeavour, at least to relate to them with understanding, to find the formulae for guiding the perplexed of our times.

The emptiness of life leads to lawlessness and depravity. Whoever has eyes in his head will admit that the sanctification of life is a protective fence against the inroads of crime and vice which corrupt and erode the fabric of our society and its security. Why do we not hoist to the mast the fact that in observant Jewish circles there are scarcely any incidents of immoral conduct, violence and drugs among youth? The time has come to raise a world-wide alarm, "warning the great over the small", that is, the leaders of the people concerning the youth, that other than a religious discipline forged in institutions of Torah and in homes illuminated by its light, we have no shield against the peril of certain doom through the rampant lawlessness which has already claimed many thousands of victims to a life of emptiness and mischief. Today even many unsophisticated people recognise that this is a perverse generation. Sons despise fathers, daughters rise against mothers, as confusion stalks the world.

Let me give you a more specific example for the blighting effects resulting from the lack of a religious conscience—and for a vital problem which only we and our teachings can help to ease. We hear complaints about the decline in Aliyah from Western lands, a factor which diminishes the Jewish population in Israel on a frightening scale relative to the increase in the non-Jewish population—so much so that, if present trends remain unchanged, the majority of Israel's citizens in 15 years' time will be non-Jews.

There are only religious answers to this pressing problem: to increase Aliyah, and to reduce the phenomenally high rate of abortions in Israel, estimated at 40,000 annually, as well as the exceedingly low birth-rate generally. We cry out over the desecration of some tens or hundreds of dead bodies, but we pass with silence over the fearful slaughter which, since the establishment of the State of Israel, has already smothered about a million Jewish souls inside their mothers' wombs.

Similarly, as a direct consequence of neglecting Torah ethics, the Jewish birthrate in Israel, and the Diaspora, is now so low that for the first time in Jewish history we have to worry about Jewish survival. Here, too, we have remained almost completely silent and leave it to others to echo the anguished cry of our mother Rachel: "Give me children, or else I am as dead."

Problems such as these cannot be resolved by legislation, or even by appealing to patriotic feelings. No one produces children out of purely demographic motives. These are matters which are surrendered to the heart, regarding which it says "and you shall fear the Lord your God". For without a deep religious conscience no effective means has yet been found to control abortions and birth-prevention. Only through the Torah can we literally "preserve in life a numerous people".

The same applies to Aliyah. As is known, these days most immigrants from Western lands are religiously motivated. The reason is plain. Today the secular idealism of the early pioneers scarcely exists, and the principal motivation for Aliyah, apart from persecution, is the love of the Land generated by religious sentiment. We must drive home the indisputable fact that if we do not succeed in raising in our schools and Yeshivot a new generation faithful to Judaism, the wells of Aliyah will dry up in but a short time, and there will be neither immigrants nor, by the way, contributors to Israel. Indeed altogether there will be no Jews actively identifying with Jewish life.

In the fullest sense of the word, we must prove that we have been sent to save life, to assure "a remnant for a great deliverance!"

Even on broader national issues we should proclaim the teaching of the Torah as the sole means to attain our goals and to fulfil our longing for the nation's security, peace and unity. Surely not only rabbis understand that without a common commitment to the faith which unites us, the bonds between the State and the Diaspora are bound to weaken and finally to snap altogether. The unity of our people depends upon the unity of the Creator, for only if "You are One and Your Name is One" is it possible to declare: "and who is like unto Your people Israel, one nation on earth" (from the Sabbath *Minchah Amidah*).

However, there are matters which are not understood by all and which require interpretation and illumination by spiritual leaders, particularly regarding events which perplex the public and challenge their faith.

Following the terrible tragedy at Munich, for instance, maybe it was incumbent upon the rabbinate of the world to articulate the religious and moral conscience of the Jewish people, at least to the extent of raising the question whether it was altogether right for a Jewish delegation to come to the accursed land from which the voice of the blood of myriads of Jews still cries out to Heaven—especially to Munich, a place destined for punishment, for shame and for betrayal, in order to participate in the very cult of the body and of physical strength against which our Maccabean ancestors fought with such heroism, assuring for the Jewish people an historic victory, whereby the light of Zion prevailed over the torch of alien fire lit on Mount Olympus.

Another subject which calls for wise instruction concerns a matter on which we have lately heard and read much, perhaps too much—the subject of bastardy in Israel. How much ink has been spilled and how many pens broken over this wretched suffering of children for the sins of their parents. No hostile propaganda is required to arouse a feeling of compassion among Torah sages who know well that already in the Midrash the verse from Ecclesiastes "and behold the tears of the oppressed who have no comforter" is interpreted: "These are the *mamzerim*, for what is their sin?" Where will you find a rabbi or a dayan sitting in judgement who has not dealt with such cases and who does not rejoice when he succeeds in liberating any suspect from the fetters of the disqualification to enter into the Congregation of the Lord? In all rabbinical courts throughout the world such problems constantly find attention, and sometimes solutions, without all the bravado that has been heard of late.

Yet, among the thousands of words which have flooded us in commen's on this unsavoury episode, I have not seen a single word which endeavours to interpret the moral foundations of the law of the *mamzer* as a safeguard against immorality and a shield to protect the sanctity of marriage. The law of the Torah in this respect is no different from the law of nature which is also occasionally cruel by exacting punishment from children for the sins of their parents. For example, if a mother negligently allows her baby to fall from her arms, the child may sustain brain damage leading to some permanent injury for the rest of its life. But this being the way of nature, parents feel their responsibility towards their children, knowing the fearful price they would be required to pay for even a moment of negligence; hence, mothers do not drop their babies. In other words, the very cruelty of nature leads to compassion and care in the relations of parents to their children.

So is this matter. So long as every Jew was careful to observe the commandments of the Torah and knew that a child born as a consequence of a surrender to temptation, however fleeting, might carry a terrible punishment for the sin of its parents, by being banned from marriage within the Congregation of Israel, this knowledge served as an absolute deterrent, preventing acts of adultery and sexual irresponsibility. Such abominations were unknown in Israel, there were neither adulterers nor *mamzerim*. Our camp was holy, and no indecent matter was seen in the tents of Jacob. Would that out of this troubled affair, through intelligent enlightenment by spiritual leaders, it may again be said of Jewish homes: "None has beheld iniquity in Jacob, neither has one seen perverseness in Israel; the Lord his God is with him, and the shouting for the King is among them."

More generally, too, it is incumbent upon us to lead our brethren to the conviction that in the end the true security of the nation and its deliverance from terror and all evils threatening us, whether inside the borders of the State or throughout our dispersion, can be achieved in absolute terms only through fulfilling the assurance in Psalms: "If only My people would hearken unto Me, and Israel walk in My ways, I would soon subdue their enemies and turn My hand upon their oppressors." Certainly we require a powerful army and strong defence forces. But through this alone Judah will not yet be saved, nor Israel dwell securely. By this means one might achieve a cease-fire or a truce based on mutual fear. But true peace requires trust springing from mutual respect, from the unwillingness of one people to have designs against another or covet its territory. How much rational meaning and Divine intelligence are manifest in the Scriptural promise: "No man shall covet your land when you go up to appear before the Lord your God three times a year." What a significant statement: every able-bodied man will leave the border fortifications, converging on the capital city in the centre of the land, in order to participate in a supreme religious experience three times a year; yet the State will be secure and the enemy will not even desire to launch war against "the people saved by the Lord". For "by the greatness of His arm, they are still as a stone"; Israel's neighbours, too, will be able to dwell securely, safe in the knowledge that the people faithful to the holiness of worship in Zion as a Kingdom of Priests will not shed innocent blood nor instigate aggressive strife as robbers of lands not its own.

Again, it is our task to prove that our assignment is to "secure life", to contribute to the survival and rebirth of our people, to confound our enemies and to annul the designs of those who hate us, so that even if "some trust in chariots and some in horses", so long as "we will make mention of the Name of the Lord our God", He will save us and answer us on the day we call upon Him.

But, above all, we must adorn ourselves before we adorn others, by keeping in good repair the inside of the royal palace, (and "who are the Kings? they are the rabbis"). The time has come to put an end to the vilifications and anathemas hurled by some rabbis against others. Remembering the verse "if the Children of Israel will not listen unto me, how will Pharaoh listen to me?" we must realise that if religious scholars do not conduct themselves with respect, peace and brotherhood one to another, how can we expect that the plain people will adopt an attitude of reverence and loyalty towards us? Also, the duty devolves upon us to root out the coarse hooliganism, fit for hoodlums of the street, which lately to our pain has erupted from time to time in an ugly manner even in Orthodox circles. "Merit is brought about only through the agency of men of merit." Whoever desires to purify others and to improve them while he himself is soiled in the impurities of hatred and violence, is worse than he "who immerses himself in a ritual bath while holding an unclean reptile in his hand"—for neither he nor his fellow-man will be purified.

Let me conclude by linking the end of my remarks with their beginning. I found a wonderful interpretation on the *Birkat HaMinim* ("the Benediction of the Heretics") by Rabbi Kook of sainted memory in his *Siddur Olat R'iyah*. He quotes the Talmud in *Shabbat* 28b: "Said Rabban Gamliel to the Sages, is there anyone who knows how to compose the Benediction of the Heretics? Thereupon Samuel the Younger arose and composed it." Why did they not arrange this passage like all other benedictions in the *Shmoneh-Esreh*, and were unable to find an author fitted for this assignment until Samuel the Younger arose and composed it? To this Rabbi Kook replies in his inimitable manner: All other blessings in the *Shmoneh-Esreh* are filled with benevolence and love; they seek the grant of bounties from the Almighty, such as forgiveness and healing, the blessing of the land and the rebuilding of Jerusalem, and similar blessings for His people of Israel. But the Benediction of the Heretics is an exception, in that it invokes a curse upon the slanderers and evil-doers. Blessings for good, continues Rabbi Kook in his golden tongue, "can be composed by any Sage worthy of this high station to order fixed prayers for a holy nation, a wise and understanding people. But regarding this benediction, which contains within it words of hatred and imprecation, and man being only human, it is altogether impossible that there should not be found in him some natural hostility towards his enemies and the pursuers of his people; hence, this prayer can be authored only by one who is completely pure and holy unto God, in whose heart there is no disposition towards natural enmity at all, and who entreats the Lord to cast away the wicked only because through their evil and ensnaring work the ultimate destiny cannot be unfolded. But if there remains in the heart the slightest feeling of hatred caused by natural antagonism, even though he was originally moved by the holiest motives, nevertheless there will develop in his heart also a natural enmity beyond the true intention. Therefore Samuel the Younger arose and composed the prayer, since only he was really qualified, as he constantly taught 'When your enemy falls, do not rejoice'. He thus removed from his heart every feeling of hatred even towards his own detractors, and when he was inspired to compose the Benediction of the Heretics, it manifested nothing but the feelings of the purest heart dedicated to the truest common good."

How great and deep are these words, more precious than pearls and fine gold. They precisely delineate the stand we ought to adopt towards our generation and the members of our communities. It is our duty to arrange and formulate the blessings for the peace and success of the House of Israel, whose eyes are fixed upon us and longingly turned towards us, that we teach them what to say and make known to them how to glory, that they neither stumble nor come to grief. But this is the trouble; today the reverse applies. There is no lack of masters of learning and giants of Torah who know how to order a Benediction of Heretics, by invoking words of denunciation, abuse, accusation and blame upon the heads of presumptuous transgressors and even upon sinners who do not know to distinguish between right and wrong like lost children. In their anxiety to safeguard the tittle of the *Yod* in the letter of the law, they disregard the spark of the *Yod* which resides in every Jewish soul, and who knows whether all the words of condemnation and castigation in these Benedictions of Heretics always really spring from a heart pure of every vestige of hatred and free from the slightest natural or political interest. For "the many are not wise" (Job), and not every rabbi is an expert in the composition of Benedictions of Heretics like Samuel the Younger. On the other hand, few are they who have no truck with the curse of heretics, but who compose blessings of love and compassion, to supplicate for mercy on the House of Israel, to teach understanding to those who err, so that the distant will hear and come near to incline with one accord to the service of the Lord.

By all means, let us dream dreams on the elect people bowing down in reverence before its masters and rabbis. But in telling our dreams, let us beware of causing hatred and misunderstanding. In moral reproof, let our words be faithful as the wounds of a friend and not as the arrows of a foe, to draw near with the right hand and to push aside with the left, "and let there be no strife between us, for we are brethren". In order to remove divisiveness and enmity from our midst, we need not remain silent nor withdraw ourselves from judgement or the obligation to reprove, so long as we are mindful of

Rabbi Yehuda's saying in the Midrash: "Great is peace, for even when Jews worship idols and peace prevails between them, it is as if God says He cannot overcome them."

To the extent that we are compelled to go out to battle and to fight for the sanctities of Israel, let our principal objectives concern issues which unite us in a common anxiety to secure the vibrant existence of our people, rather than concentrate on matters which the majority of the public cannot understand or appreciate until we first succeed to draw them close to our Maker and to endear in their hearts the Torah of which it is said: "Its ways are the ways of pleasantness and all its paths are peace."

ORTHODOXY'S STRENGTHS AND WEAKNESSES

The Orthodox community, showing unprecedented strengths and unprecedented weaknesses, may well be the only element to prevail over the ravages of despair, assimilation and shrinking numbers; but it will be the bitter, lonely experience of concentration camp survivors stalking amid the stench of death and desolation, unless we succeed in sharing the shelter of our faith with the rest of our people and in resuming our role as moral pioneers in the world around us.

In the face of our present and future trials, it would become increasingly evident that only the religious community could never be completely broken or demoralised by adversity. Already the strictly observant are the only section of the Jewish people who do not worry about survival or question the Jewish purpose and identity. Their faith is invulnerable, their schools and academies are flourishing, their birth-rate is soaring, their defections are minimal—all because they rigorously uphold their religious convictions.

Yet tragically, Orthodoxy—instead of using its inner strength to unite and uplift our spiritually impoverished brethren—has now all but lost the confidence of our people. Humiliated by unseemly squabbles and often committed to unwise policies lacking insight and foresight, we have so far proved impotent in effecting the national regeneration which is indispensable for our survival and for regaining our people's image as the custodians of man's spiritual strivings.

We have become altogether too inward-looking, with our horizons largely limited within the ghetto-walls we have erected to separate us from the rest of our people and from the human society beyond. We frequently are seen to promote ritual to the exclusion of ethics, partisan interests instead of common ideals, and rights we demand for ourselves more than duties we owe to others.

Following the report of the Agranat Enquiry, the religious community ought to initiate an investigation into the spiritual and moral factors responsible for our predicament in the light of Jewish teachings. We would discover that the dynamics of Jewish history, certainly in the Land of Israel, do not operate simply in terms of military logistics or political equations. Our

---

Address delivered at the Third Conference of Ashkenazi and Sephardi Synagogues, Jerusalem, 12 February, 1975.

tribulations are at least equally attributable to the disengagement of our national ethos from its spiritual purpose and of our religious commitments from Judaism's social and universal concerns.

Among our own people we should therefore concentrate on exposing the now disastrously proven futility of the secularist illusion that the restoration of Jewish sovereignty would of itself "solve the Jewish problem" and make us accepted as equals among the nations. Jewish statehood notwithstanding, we are now as lonely as ever. Only the semantics have changed. Anti-Semitism had become anti-Zionism, and instead of sporadic pogroms we have periodic wars and terrorist outrages. Without our faith, Jewish survival is meaningless as well as questionable. The idols of inflated self-confidence shattered, the majority of our youth, estranged from the solace and idealism of our faith, have little to hold on to in their travail and disillusionment. Orthodoxy should be identified with this lesson rather than with the many petty arguments which fragment us.

Externally, we also have to raise our sights. Preoccupied with the burning problems of our own survival, we have lost sight of our assignment as a light unto the nations. We need this return to our Prophetic ideals not only in order to restore the relevance of the Torah to the perplexities of our times and its spokesmen to their historic role as spiritual guides. At stake are not only the submission of Jews to authentic Judaism or the public stature of rabbis, but the survival of Jews and Judaism alike.

Countless people now associate Jews not with spiritual values or moral advances—with which we had always been identified in the past—but with international tensions and perils, with a threat to the world's energy supplies, to detente between the super-powers, to safety in civil aviation and to freedom from fear of a nuclear confrontation of universal dimensions. If we no longer have a unique and incomparable contribution to make to the enrichment of civilisation, then by what right can we demand the world's support, with all the risks to international peace and prosperity involved, for the sake of preserving a small people which has already outlived the life-span of other nations, especially in these brutal times when millions die of starvation and violence unmourned and unmissed by the world community? Unless Jews are seen to have this moral dimension, this passion for righteousness and social justice which is our heritage, countries now facing enormous economic problems and massive political pressures would wonder whether the sacrifices demanded were worth while to assert Israel's right to exist. Only by giving priceless values to the nations—through creating a model society in Zion which would radiate its message to inspire the world—could we in return exact the price of their support.

Maybe there are some valid reasons why we have neglected these universal aspects of Jewish teachings. Suffering itself excuses us no more than it prevented our Prophets (who also lived in periods of desolation) from encompassing the salvation of the nations in their vision, and their successors throughout the ages from yearning and working for the eventual supremacy of our ethical and spiritual ideals, so that all God's creatures "will become one band to do His will with a perfect heart".

More relevant might be the fact that leadership, particularly religious leadership, is still largely exercised by men whose outlook was conditioned by the cultural isolation of Eastern Europe, or at least by the constriction of perspectives prior to the emergence of the Jewish State which enabled Jewish aspirations to find the broadest corporate expression. This fact, combined with the pressing need to rejuvenate and revitalise the direction of Jewish affairs, renders it all the more urgent to recruit the younger generation for the responsibilities of leadership faster and more effectively than we have done in the past.

The United Synagogue in London recently introduced an imaginative scheme of offering a period of free membership to newly married couples. It is this generation, the most dynamic element we possess, whom we have to attract to the leadership ranks of our people and our communities, if our influence is gradually to transcend the walls of our synagogues and schools, and even of our Land, to restore our image as the trusted guardians of the Jewish destiny within our people and as "a kingdom of priests" ministering to a stricken humanity, thereby vindicating and assuring our survival.

THE ENLARGED EUROPEAN COMMUNITY—
ITS JEWISH SIGNIFICANCE

Nothing could illustrate more dramatically both the dynamics and the pathos of the contemporary condition of Jewry, particularly European Jewry, than the dual welcome it is my privilege to extend this morning.

On the one hand, we are happy to have here delegates from among the scores of communal leaders gathered in London for the Conference of European Communities to deliberate on closer ties between the various components of European Jewry. These leaders represent over one million Jews in countries now drawn together by the epoch-making expansion of the European Economic Community.

On the other hand, we are profoundly honoured to greet Raiza Palatnik, one of the legendary Jewish heroines of our time. She represents in one person some three million Jews in the Soviet Union, virtually all, of course, European Jews, completely cut off from their brethren and sister-communities, incarcerated behind a Curtain of Iron and cruelly subjected to a vicious campaign of spiritual and cultural attrition.

Here, at this service, we see symbolically unfolded before us the entire Jewish drama of our age, with its agony of destruction and suffering, and its ecstasy of reconstruction and rebirth.

Of Europe's total Jewish population in 1939 of nearly ten million, through the murderous ravages of the war period we are now left with only four million. One-quarter of them are represented by numerous delegates from free lands, assembled here to discuss the regeneration and intensification of Jewish life, now showing many signs of vigorous growth and consolidation, with more freedom, more affluence, more Jewish schools, more communal activity and more Zionist commitment than ever before.

The remaining three-quarters of Europe's Jews are enslaved, without a single Jewish school, with no communal organisation and with Zionism branded as an offence against the State. All of these are here represented by the very incarnation of Soviet Jewry's plight and hope—a young lover of Zion, herself just liberated from the ordeal of imprisonment and hunger-strike for Zion's sake, a gallant woman whose age and valour inspired the

---

Upon Britain's formal entry into the European Economic Community at the beginning of 1973, a "European Conference of Jewish Communities" was held in London under the aegis of the World Jewish Congress in January of that year. The following is the special Conference Sermon preached at the Marble Arch Synagogue, London, on 13 January 1973. The service was attended by Raiza Palatnik, whose ordeal in Russia had inspired the formation and the name of the "35-Group" of women working for the release of Soviet Jews.

formation and the very name of the "35 Group" of women who now spearhead the campaign for Russian Jews.

We salute her in our midst, with gratitude for her inspiring example in the past, with fervent blessings for her future, and with profound thanksgiving to God for her deliverance and reunion with her family in Israel.

In now turning to the Conference and its special significance in the light of the historic entrance of Britain and other countries into the Common Market, if I deal with the Jewish ramifications of this event, it is not in the irrelevant sense of the proverbial "Elephant and the Jewish Problem". It is rather on the basis of a homiletical licence, indeed a mandate, provided by today's Torah reading.

Here we find a striking anomaly. The Portions-of-the-Week are usually divided according to subject-matter. But in this case, strangely, the story of the Ten Plagues is broken up into two, with seven plagues in last week's portion and the remaining three in this week's. There may be a logical and profound reason for this unusual division.

The first seven plagues are presented as intended to teach a lesson to Pharaoh and the Egyptians. The purpose is always to demonstrate the might of God "so that you shall know that I am the Lord in the midst of the land", or "so that you shall know that there is none like the Lord our God", or "in order that you shall know that there is none like Me in all the land". But all these attempts to convert Pharaoh and his people to monotheism proved unsuccessful. They remained unrepentant pagans, and after seven attempts, the effort was abandoned as futile.

This week's account of the remaining three plagues opens an altogether new chapter. God's signs and wonders are now addressed to the Jewish people, "so that you shall tell in the ears of your son and your son's son that which I have wrought on the Egyptians and the signs which I have placed among them, and you shall know that I am the Lord". Following the failure to impress the Egyptians, it would suffice if the Jewish people would appreciate the manifestation of God in history for all times. This attempt proved successful, and to this day the Exodus has remained the central feature in the historic consciousness and, indeed, in the religious and ethical legislation of Judaism.

It is our task, then, to discern the significance of world events in the light of Jewish teachings and their impact on the Jewish scene.

As Jews, we have two special and quite unrelated reasons to rejoice over the emergence of the new consortium of nations. When peoples for centuries at war with each other bind their destinies together in a common pursuit of peaceful goals, we are bound to hail the event as a major contribution to the realisation of our Hebrew Prophets' vision. For millennia, we have preached and prayed that the day will come when "nation shall not lift up sword against nation" but live and work together in harmony and fellowship. Even if the present emphasis, regrettably, is still mainly on the material and commercial benefits anticipated by the participants, as expressed in the very names of Common *Market* and European *Economic* Community, we as Jews would betray our historical assignment if we did not stress and promote the spiritual significance of this progress towards the consumation of the ideal of the brotherhood of man.

Secondly, and of equally crucial importance in a Jewish context, the new association of European nations may be expected to contribute significantly to Jewish security in Europe. As a community of nations, it serves as a major safeguard against a repetition of the diabolical events in Nazi Germany, diminishing the possibility of the domination of Europe by a single nation, intent on the destruction of entire peoples and races.

In return, we as Jews might well make a special contribution to European integration and progress. Because of our history and origin, we have long been dedicated to "European thinking". Following the Romans, Normans, Saxons, Danes and others, we were the last Europeans to arrive in Britain, and with the Jewish flair for travel and trade, not to mention our penchant for international conferences, we are in all likelihood proportionately the most frequent visitors to the Continent.

Little wonder, therefore, that we have pioneered efforts at European co-operation long before the European Economic Community became a reality. Even rabbis, so often accused of being behind the times, very successfully established an ongoing and most active Conference of European Rabbis as far back as fifteen years ago on the initiative of my revered predecessor. Only last month seventy European rabbis, together with distinguished delegations from Israel and the United States, met for three days to discuss the intensification and co-ordination of Jewish religious life in Europe.

The new constellation of European nations will, of course, also offer far-reaching opportunities and challenges to Jewish communities. I am thinking not only of much closer co-operation and integration in national Jewish spheres, such as political and financial support for Israel and Soviet Jewry, or concerted action on shechita defence and the distribution of kosher food, or the co-ordination of Jewish educational endeavours, or even some form of partnership among synagogue organisations.

I also have in mind some specific new ventures which are now feasible to meet our common needs. For instance, in view of the acute and growing shortage of trained personnel for community service, especially rabbis, teachers, shochetim, administrators, youth and social workers, we might consider more centralised recruitment drives and training facilities, to replace the current fragmented and often wastefully duplicated efforts. A European clearing-house for the strategic deployment of available personnel on a rationalised basis might be the first step in this direction.

Another suggestion worth exploring might be the launching of what I would call regional aid schemes for Jewishly depressed areas, providing assistance for under-privileged communities, whereby spiritually and materially more prosperous communities would extend a helping hand, through the loan of personnel and even financial support, to smaller and less viable units of Jewish settlement which would otherwise face the threat of decline and extinction.

In all these emerging new patterns, Anglo-Jewry faces a special obligation and opportunity. After all, we are the only major Jewish community in Europe that was left unscathed by Nazi occupation and devastation.

Moreover, although we are no longer the largest Jewry in Western Europe, having been overtaken in recent years by France which has doubled its Jewish population through the mass immigration of North African Jews, Anglo-Jewry still commands the finest communal assets in Europe. We possess the most cohesive communal structure, the most efficient communal organisations, and the best and largest institutions of Jewish learning. With over 16% of all our children attending Jewish day-schools, we no doubt have the highest proportion of young Jews raised with the requisite knowledge and commitment to produce tomorrow's leaders of the community. All these priceless assets are quite apart from the settled traditions and continuous experience accumulated over centuries of Jewish settlement in this country.

Moral considerations, resources and experience alike should therefore challenge Anglo-Jewry to seize the opportunities now open with particular zeal and determination. Shedding our past insularity, we must now rally to the summons of history to assume the responsibilities of leadership in restoring to European Jewry some of the impetus to the enrichment of Jewish life which once emanated so prolifically from this Continent.

Let me conclude with a more general reflection on the spiritual significance of the momentous events shaping contemporary Jewish life. The current Portions-of-the-Law, in relating the quest of our people to be liberated from their Egyptian thraldom, repeat over and over again the famous phrase which has become the most frequently used Jewish slogan of our time: "Let My people go!" This was our constant plea when we sought to rescue our brethren oppressed in Nazi Germany before the War; it was our anguished cry to secure the admission to Palestine of the remnants left over from the Holocaust in the Displaced Persons' camps after the War; and it is now our agonised call for the release of our brethren in the Soviet Union yearning to be allowed to go to Israel.

But "Let My people go!" was only a part of the plea of Moses before Pharaoh, and like all half-truths it is a perversion of the truth.

What Moses said was: "Let My people go *so that they shall serve Me!*" To ask for the deliverance of our people from slavery and their freedom to enter the Promised Land without seeking the encounter with God at Sinai on the way is a travesty of Jewish history. "Let My people go!" is but the means. It would make a mockery of past Jewish martyrdom and our future destiny if this historic cry were mutilated and left incomplete by the omission of its purpose: "so that they shall serve Me!"

Much of our programme under the slogan "Let My people go!" has been fulfilled in the eventful period since the establishment of Israel 25 years ago. Millions of Jews have been let go and now live in the Holy Land as free citizens. Even today, many Jewish endeavours continue to be inspired by the efforts to turn this slogan into an ever greater historic reality. But the second part of the slogan remains to be fulfilled and to engage our primary attention.

May the deliberations of this Conference succeed in now adding this new dimension to the Jewish national striving of our times. May we prosper in making the vision of our Prophets the blue-print for our spiritual rehabilitation as moral pioneers and religious path-finders, helping to guide mankind towards the Prophetic ideals of universal peace and the brotherhood of man under the Fatherhood of God.

THE CRISIS OF SURVIVAL

I did not cross the Atlantic just for this Dinner in order to give you some stirring denunciation of our diabolical enemies and their powerful lackeys, or a ringing affirmation of the justice of our cause. By such an exercise in self-righteousness I would, I presume, be preaching to the converted. Unlike some rabbis, I make no pretentions to competing with politicians or news-commentators in their prognostications, condemnations and warnings. I speak to you simply as a rabbi, addressing myself to, and maybe challenging, those who share with me the burden to provide religious leadership to our stricken people at this momentous time of destiny.

Our Sages always regarded the Holy Land as the centre of the earth. This is true in a geographical sense—as the exact centre of the inhabited part of the globe and as the meeting point of three continents—no less than spiritually. From the Land of Israel once went forth the moral order to civilise man. Now this little land has become the epicentre of a gigantic earthquake. Its shock-waves have convulsed the whole world, changing beyond recognition the entire landscape of Jewish and international affairs. Since that bitter Yom Kippur a year ago, we are beset by a crescendo of crises, which are as awesome as they are unprecedented.

Indeed, history has no parallel for the manner in which the events precipitated by the Yom Kippur War have demonstrated the interdependence of the Jewish and human destinies. They have shown that Israel cannot enjoy security in an insecure world, any more than the nations can have peace without Israel being at peace.

CRESCENDO OF CRISES

There is the world crisis of unparalleled political, economic and moral chaos. It has brought an abrupt end to the affluent society and to the unchallenged hegemony of the industrial nations, in an abject capitulation to medieval serfdoms which still practise slavery and polygamy, threatening the collapse of our civilisation, as frighteningly indicated by the obscene invitation and ovation extended to murderous gangsters by the majority of the world's

Address delivered at the Annual Dinner of the Synagogue Council of America, New York, 20 November 1974.

nations—a staggering betrayal of all human values, perhaps history's most blatant reversal of man's progress, which literally reverts us to the antediluvian state of "and the earth was filled with violence", and which consequently has plunged mankind into a crisis of more universal proportions than any since the days of the Flood.

There is, overshadowing all our thoughts, the crisis of Israel, with potentially greater dangers to the Jewish State and to Jewish life everywhere than any we have experienced during the past 1900 years.

And there is, quite independently, the crisis of Jewish survival, due to an abnormally low Jewish birth-rate and a phenomenally high rate of defections by assimilation and intermarriage. Even in the Middle Ages, when the total number of Jews hardly exceeded 1,000,000, and they suffered continuous persecution, expulsion and massacres, no Jew ever worried about Jewish survival. It was left to our generation, when we count 13,000,000 Jews, most of them living in unprecedented freedom and prosperity, to question and debate Jewish survival for the first time in 4,000 years.

There is the crisis of faith, reflected in the growing gap between Jews and Judaism, and in the terrifying alienation of most Jewish children, in Israel as well as the Diaspora, from any religious knowledge and experience—a spiritual desolation which has already led many of our youth to the brink of despair in Israel's future, or indeed in a Jewish future, and to thoughts about emigration from Israel, and which, again for the first time in our history, now causes some Jews to question the very justice of Israel's cause and the purpose of Jewish self-preservation.

Then there is the crisis of Jewish identity. For 4,000 years this was the one subject on which we had no arguments. Now, we cannot even agree on who is a Jew, let alone what is a Jew, with the result that there are already many thousands who are accepted as Jews by some and regarded as non-Jews by others, in a potentially catastrophic schism splitting our people.

And, perhaps most sinister of all, there is the crisis of Jewish unity. In our extreme peril and anxiety we might have been expected to close ranks and put our differences aside. Instead, we are now more fragmented than ever before, bitterly torn by dissension at every level, within our political, religious, communal and even military establishments, between old and newer immigrants, between Ashkenazim and Sephardim, between traditionalists and Reformers—all in an orgy of divisive strife, ominously reminiscent of "the causeless hatred" which once spelt the doom of the Temple and the Second Jewish Commonwealth.

SPECIAL TASKS OF THE RELIGIOUS COMMUNITY

All these extraordinary travails summon especially the religious community to guide the perplexed of our times and to rebuild the ramparts of our faith—our only ultimate refuge in the future as in the past. As heirs to the Prophets, Sages and traditions of Israel, we are charged, I believe, with four special tasks:

1. To provide comfort, hope, confidence and encouragement to those of our people whose faith is tottering in adversity;

2. To explain the meaning and lessons of our tribulations in the light of our historical experience and religious insights;
3. To restore the unity of our people at a time when disintegration from within may well again prove a greater danger than terror and war from without; and
4. To respond to the intense search for spiritual values evoked by our traumatic experience and to arouse a massive religious reawakening renewing our people's timeless purpose and destiny.

Obviously only a thorough Jewish education can provide a shield against despair, an understanding of the dynamics of Jewish history and continuity, a common loyalty to unite our people and the rediscovery of the ideals which have sustained us in the past. We are, after all, not novices in battling against the most fearful odds, and we have persevered because we are a people steeled by history and forged by religious faith.[1]

THE FALLACY OF "SOLVING THE JEWISH PROBLEM" BY BECOMING LIKE OTHERS

This is not the first time in the modern Jewish experience that the fallacy of seeking security through becoming like others has led to disastrous disillusionment and catastrophe. Let me quote from a remarkable book just published under the title *Concepts of Judaism*, by Yitzchak Breuer, German Orthodoxy's most profound and articulate thinker who died in Jerusalem in 1946. In a chapter on "Judaism and National Home" he compared the early classic Reform movement with secularist Zionism in what may now seem to reveal some truly Prophetic foresight and insight:

> Both Reform and Zionism aspire to a solution of the Jewish problem. Viewed externally, the problem rests on the obvious incongruity between the Jews dispersed among the nations and their non-Jewish environment. The failure of social emancipation, aspired by Reform, led to the attempt at national emancipation, initiated by Zionism. If Reform attempted to normalise the Jewish individual, Zionism proclaimed as its ultimate aim the normalisation of the Jewish community as a whole, i.e. of the Jewish nation. Normalisation means in this context, assimilation. Zionism wished to assimilate the Jewish nation to all other nations. Reform took hold of religion and separated it from the nation.

The parallel, alas, extends further than he could have foreseen. Individual assimilation consisted of turning Judaism into a mere religion like all others, synagogues into churches without crosses, deleting from our prayers references to Zion and the chosenness of Israel, praying in the language others use, eating what they eat, and keeping the Sabbath and Festivals as they observe their holidays.

Significantly, this attempt to gain security and acceptance by making us equals came to grief in Germany, the very country where Reform was born to bring us salvation by blurring the distinction between Israel and the nations, whilst the futility of achieving equality through national assimilation became

---

1. The text here omitted, continued with a summary of the arguments on the futility of solving the Jewish problem by "normalizing the Jewish condition" presented in the address "The Jewish Destiny—the Spiritual Challenge of the Yom Kippur War".

manifest in the Land of Israel, in the very state which was established to end Jewish inequality once and for all, and which has now turned us all into the loneliest people on earth.

Hard as we may have tried, Jonah-like, to flee from our Divine mission, by becoming like all other nations, first through shedding the distinctiveness of the individual Jewish identity, and then through the secularisation of the Jewish national purpose, our recent experiences have shown that if we do not freely accept the uniqueness of Israel, it is Providentially imposed on us against our will. In Israel, the unexpected invariably happens. Some call it surprises, others miracles. I prefer to define it as Special Providence.

JEWISH EDUCATION—THE KEY TO SURVIVAL

This is a time, then, to abandon myths which have been exploded and to embark on a radical reappraisal of our national objectives.

Who, other than the religious community, can chart the new course Jewish thinking and Jewish living will have to take in the light of the grim realities now about us? And what, other than Jewish education, can now give our rising generation the idealism to vindicate our survival, the faith to bear our burdens with fortitude, the joy and pride at being Jewish even in tribulations, the love of our Land even in the absence of security, and the vision of the silver lining of redemption even when the clouds are dark and menacing?

Today, any Jewish child denied an intensive Jewish education is robbed not only of his birth-right, but of the equipment to weather the storms which may threaten his life as a Jew. Such deprivation of religious faith and learning is a sheer invitation to national despair, indeed to suicide. We might well say with the Prophet: טובים היו חללי חרב מחללי רעב—Better, and far fewer, were those slain by the sword, the heroes who fell על קדוש השם, than those slain by hunger, the hundreds of thousands we lose by spiritual starvation על חלול השם, the drop-outs from Judaism who often breed Jewish self-hatred and contribute to our extinction.

In our desperate plight, it is nothing short of criminal treason to raise a generation which is either kept altogether ignorant of our religious heritage and commitment, as are two-thirds of Israel's children and an even greater number in the Diaspora, or stunted in their religious growth at Barmitzvah age to grow up as spiritual cripples with an infantile understanding of Jewish values, unable to stand up to the buffeting of their sophisticated secular education later on in adult life. To reduce this appalling drain in our human resources and spiritual defences now requires the same determination as a military operation to prevent slaughter by war.

JEWISH UNITY

This leads me, finally, to a few remarks on Jewish unity. Mindful of the striking saying in the *Sifri*: "Great is peace, for even though Israel worship idols, so long as there is peace between them, the Satan cannot touch them"— and desperately concerned in the wake of the Yom Kippur War with maintaining the unity of our people and the stability of Israel's government, I pleaded with the religious and rabbinical establishments in Israel a year ago not to break up the Coalition over the "Who is a Jew?" issue. In taking this stand publicly, I was almost alone among the Orthodox rabbis, though many supported me privately. Supremely vital as this issue is, I nevertheless regarded its being raised as a political issue at this grave time as divisive, futile and counter-productive.

"Who is a Jew?" is neither a political nor primarily an Israeli problem. It is a religious issue which affects every Jew. For a genuine conversion turns the convert into a brother of every Jew, just as every Jew becomes his brother in faith. Hence, this is a problem which can only be resolved on a religious level, not by secular legislation or political bargaining.

But while I therefore opposed the official Orthodox stand as unwise, untimely and gravely damaging to Orthodox interests and national unity alike—as, alas, it turned out to be—I believe that the exploitation of this crisis by non-Orthodox groups, in an effort to impose on Israel our religious divisions in the Diaspora, was at least equally divisive and irresponsible, especially when accompanied by threats or hints that support for Israel may otherwise be compromised.

NO JEWISH UNITY WITHOUT THE UNITY OF JUDAISM

Surely, at a time like this, far from accentuating and perpetuating our differences, we ought to make a supreme effort to narrow and eliminate them. If only to find strength and comfort through unity, can we not now draw closer to our common heritage and repair the tragic rifts in our ranks whereby we cannot worship together, we cannot eat in each other's homes, and sometimes not even marry each other's children?

There can be no unity of the Jewish people without the unity of Judaism. Only if אתה אחד ושמך אחד, can we realise ומי כעמך ישראל גוי אחד בארץ that Israel will again be one people, unique on earth.

I know that the barriers between us, built up over the past 150 years, cannot be dismantled overnight. I also appreciate, and constantly proclaim within my own camp, that spiritual objectives nowadays can only be reached by persuasion, not by legislation; by education, not by coercion.

But surely at this critical time we can and must remove at least those divisions which drive a permanent and irreparable wedge between us, cleaving us into two non-identical peoples, unable even to agree on a common definition as to who is a member of our people, and who is eligible for marriage within our fold.

This terrible schism, for long a heartbreak, is now a disaster, eroding the unity of our people, disturbing the internal peace of Israel, sapping our national and communal energies, and breaking up Jewish families and communities everywhere.

After all, even the Reform Movement, which initiated the break with our traditions and thus the disunity bedevilling us today, has already modified many of its radical departures from our historic traditions under the inexorable pressures of recent Jewish history. It has restored references to Zion, encouraged the increased use of Hebrew in prayer and boldly reversed its earlier stand on many traditional observances.

Is it really too much to hope and to demand, for the sake of our very survival, that at least in respect of marriage, divorce and conversion we all accept the unifying discipline of our halachic heritage? For those who have preserved this heritage intact over the ages to this day at the cost of millennial struggle and martyrdom, such an agreement would bring the reward of perseverance and the triumph of tenacity. For the others, it may involve some occasional sacrifice and hardship which hitherto only their more observant brothers cheerfully endured for the sake of handing the torch lit at Sinai safely to the bearers of posterity to illumine the world. For all of us, it would be the great reconciliation between brothers, and thus the reconciliation between us and our Father in Heaven.

You remember the reunion of Joseph with his brethren following their long estrangement. His first dramatic words were: "Is my father still alive?" May we put an end to our estrangement from each other, so that no Jew will be slow to provide a ringing affirmation in response to his brother's question "Is my father still alive"—are the ancestral ideals of our people still vibrant and throbbing with life, ideals preserved by our fathers throughout the ages at the cost of so much blood and tears? Through such reconciliation among ourselves and with our Divine Father, our continued existence will also be reconciled with the world in which we live.

The key clauses of our Covenant with the Guardian of Israel provided: "If you will walk in My statutes and observe My commandments and perform them, then ... I will give peace in the Land ... and the sword shall not pass through your Land." Following the promise of "peace in the Land", why the further assurance that "the sword shall not pass through your Land"? Explain our Commentators: the first blessing refers to internal peace, "that there will be peace among you, and you shall not fight one man against his brother" (Ramban). Only if there is harmony among ourselves, can we look forward to our people being at peace and safe from the threat of war. Through our common loyalty by observing the statutes and commandments assigned to us as our national purpose will we achieve internal unity which in turn will ensure the fulfilment of the Divine promise: "And you will dwell securely in your Land ... and I will rest My Divine Presence in your midst ... and I shall make you walk upright."

VISITING THE SOVIET UNION: TWO ARTICLES

I

The most momentous feature of my visit to Russia may have been, like Columbus's experience in America, the very fact of arrival. But there was scarcely half an hour during the nine-day tour that was not equally full of drama, trauma and excitement.

The picture emerging from wide-ranging travels, meetings and discussions was far more complex than fairly extensive, though fragmentary, information on conditions in the Soviet Union had previously led me to expect. The shadows turned out to be darker, the gleams of light brighter, and the grey areas in between much larger. Some experiences were more heart-rending and others more heart-warming than could have been anticipated. I was impressed by the cordial reception accorded in all quarters, and by the frankness with which I could discuss our concerns everywhere, whether in government ministries or in the homes of "refuseniks".

Of course, many tears were shed. Who could not but weep at Leningrad's mass-graves for 680,000 citizens starved to death in the 900-day German siege, a most awesome sight stretching for the length of a football-field, and now marked by gigantic memorials to remind the world that to a nation which prevailed at the cost of such enormous devastation the word peace assumes an altogether different dimension?

Or at Babi Yar in Kiev on the snow-covered ravines hiding the blood of 100,000 men, women and children (perhaps 200,000—nobody even counted them), the majority Jews, ghoulishly massacred, or burnt or buried alive by the Nazis—a hallowed site where, in Yevtushenko's words: "all screams in silence", and where the imposing monument now being assembled, after 30 years' efforts to suppress the evidence, will omit any Jewish or Hebrew symbol except "a Biblical theme" (based on Michelangelo's *Pieta*) among the

In December 1975 the author paid an official visit to the three principal Jewish communities in the USSR—the first Chief Rabbi from the West to do so. The visit aroused widespread public interest, and feature articles describing the experience and discussing its results were invited by Britain's leading newspapers. The first article, under the heading "Rekindling the Jewish spirit among the agonizing problems of life in the Soviet Union", appeared in The Times *on 6 January 1976; the second was published, in slightly abridged form, in* The Observer *on 18 January 1976 entitled "My journey into Russia—by the Chief Rabbi".*

deeply moving sculptured components depicting terror, grief, heroism and defiance?

And whose throat would not be choked with bitter emotion on visiting a spiritually once flourishing community, still numbering two or three million Jews, but now desolate? In the synagogues, neither children nor their parents are to be found; only a few hundred fast-aging grandparents. No clubs, no organizations, no Jewish literature or culture, not even Jewish social events of any kind. Moscow, with a Jewish population of 400,000—about the size of Anglo-Jewry—has one ailing rabbi. In Leningrad, with more Jews than London, I was shown the grave of their last rabbi, who died three years ago.

The spiritual blight is simply shattering, especially when one recalls that from these lands once came the scholars and writers, the great modern religious, cultural and national movements which nourish Jewish life all over the world to this day.

Or who could remain composed on looking into the despairing eyes of Mrs Mikhail Shtern, whose husband still languishes in prison, a frightful fate shared by a few dozen others despite worldwide protests? Or on meeting leading academics and scientists, stripped of their jobs, and demoralized as outcasts from the scientific fraternity, waiting in seemingly endless suspense, sometimes for five years or more, for exit visas to rejoin members of their families in Israel?

But these harrowing encounters were not without occasional relief, not least by reason of the indications given that much could or might be done to alleviate the situation. Most heartening was the realization that, after more than half a century of spiritual and cultural attrition, some significant expressions of Jewish consciousness had wondrously survived and lately been greatly intensified. This thirst for Jewish identification, for Jewish knowledge and values, sometimes even for a return to our religious traditions, is indescribable. A handshake from a visitor, a word of blessing, a simple Hebrew reader or an elementary textbook on Jewish history, law or literature—these are like precious water on a parched tongue.

One cannot but feel utterly humbled and inspired by the sheer courage with which a growing number of mainly young idealists pursue and spread this reawakening of the Jewish spirit. Nor can one fail to be awed by the living martyrdom of eminent intellectuals who willingly exchange relative prosperity, security and academic recognition for a life of fear, deprivation and "scientific starvation" in their quest to regenerate themselves as Jews. Even the efforts of synagogue leaders, working as they must with the Soviet authorities, to maintain the only semblance of corporate Jewish life which is at present possible, merit understanding.

Some anti-Jewish discrimination undoubtedly exists and apparently increases—in job advancement, admission to universities, social acceptance and virulently in some publications. But I saw no evidence of violent anti-Semitism of the type rampant in the 30s. Nor was this feared by the Jews or officials I met. Most Jews are conscious of the benefits of treatment and opportunity under the present regime compared with the past tyrannies of the Tsars, Hitler and Stalin.

The anti-Jewish campaign is directed against religious and cultural pursuits and all organised Jewish life outside the solitary synagogues, not against Jews whom the authorities would wish to be seen as equals among the amorphous mass of the people, minus the privileges enjoyed by all other nationalities and even the churches.

The stark contrast between hope and despair arises from the ambivalence of the official attitude which leaves the wide grey area between *approved* legality and forbidden illegality largely undefined. It is not illegal to demand exit visas, yet applicants may find themselves intolerably harassed. It is not against the law to receive phone-calls or letters from abroad, but the phones may be disconnected and the mail stopped. It is not unlawful to perform circumcisions or religious marriage ceremonies; to teach Hebrew as a language in schools or provide private religious instruction in homes; or even to publish a religious journal and other literature for those interested. Yet most Jews shrink from any such activities for fear of being branded, with consequences ranging from job dismissal to incarceration.

I visited the headquarters of the Russian Orthodox Church, and its theological seminaries with a total of about 500 students engaged in eight-year courses of intensive studies for the priesthood, in Zagorsk and Leningrad. It publishes and distributes in all its parishes a religious monthly, in both Russian and English editions, and other literary material. If Jews had the freedom, without running personal or communal risks, to enjoy these rights and facilities, it would make a substantial contribution to cementing the cohesion of the widely scattered Jewish community, and to satisfying the craving for spiritual nourishment of those who seek it.

And if the Soviet authorities would recognize, as I repeatedly told them, that the desire to live a fuller Jewish life in Israel, after praying for the return to Zion for 2,000 years, is not a betrayal, detente may eventually include some accommodation with the Jewish people which has shared with the Soviet peoples so much suffering and sacrifice in the struggle against fascism, and which now sees in Soviet policies such a grim threat to its very existence, and to human rights in general.

Was the visit successful? Certainly so, far beyond expectations, in its immediate objectives of effecting a memorable reunion with our long-separated brethren, bringing them a public message of affection and encouragement, opening up invaluable lines of communications and gaining entirely new insights into Soviet Jewry's agonizing problems, as indeed into the condition of Soviet life, culture and attitudes generally. But only time will tell whether some success also attended the wider objectives of exploring and securing ways to remove the grievances which have caused such worldwide concern and agitation, among Jews and non-Jews alike.

II

Soviet Jews are close to the hearts of all Jews throughout the world. We care for them so deeply, not only because they constitute about one-fifth of our people, as the third largest Jewish community in the world, with twice as many Jews as Western Europe. Even more important is the leading role which Jews from those lands have played in recent centuries as the mainstay of Jewish spiritual and cultural life. From here have come our greatest sages, thinkers, writers, artists, historians and world Jewish leaders. Here were generated the principal modern Jewish movements; here flourished the finest academies of Jewish learning; from here came the parents or grandparents of most Jews now living in Britain, America and elsewhere. To this day, our religious and cultural life is inspired by what was created here, and our communites are often still led by rabbis, teachers and communal workers who were born and sometimes even trained here. So we obviously feel a special kinship with Soviet Jews and an exceptional affection for them.

With these words I greeted my hosts on arrival at Moscow airport, to begin my momentous reunion with the Jewish community, separated so long and so painfully from the rest of Jewry.

The nine-day visit materialised after a gestation period of about nine months. It originated with soundings from the Soviet authorities. It was suggested that such a visit might contribute to "a detente with the Jewish people". Following extensive consultations, including all the appropriate official sources, the invitation was accepted in principle, but with certain stipulations.

In September I received a cordial invitation (in Hebrew and Yiddish) from the President and Rabbi of the "Moscow Jewish Community" (i.e. the synagogue and its aged worshippers). I did not accept until two further communications reached me, from Professor Alexander Lerner and Professor Mark Azbel, enthusiastically inviting me to lecture at their homes. There, several dozen scientists and teachers, refused exit visas for Israel and dismissed from their posts, meet regularly for scientific and cultural seminars to overcome the demoralisation of their academic isolation. In some cases they have waited for five years or more and still wait indefinitely.

I eventually sent my formal acceptance; explicitly subject to a programme which would include visits to leading Jewish activists in Moscow, Leningrad and Kiev, as well as meetings with senior Soviet officials in charge of Jewish affairs and with church leaders.

These stipulations were never expressly approved or disapproved, though they were indispensable if I was to attempt to familiarise myself with the widest possible range of Jewish life, explore its amelioration (beyond the exceedingly limited confines of the synagogues) and make contact with non-Jewish agencies affecting it. In the event, my reception everywhere was more than courteous and the entire programme (and much more) was carried out as planned, though not without some ineffectual efforts to curtail the "unofficial" part. There were nagging pressures to do more sight-seeing and pay more theatre visits, and efforts to shunt me off to Leningrad or Kiev for the weekend to prevent me from addressing the 600-strong congregation in Moscow on the Sabbath and the seminars on the following two days. With some persistence, the "unavailable" time, the "unobtainable" train-reservations, or the "lost tickets" to bring me back from Leningrad—turned up. In the end, the official car at my disposal brought me to the very homes of the activists I wished to visit!

I had asked to do all internal travel (some 2,000 miles!) by train so as to get some "feel" of the country and its life. Though this meant spending four of my nine nights on trains (the Moscow–Kiev journey takes 14 hours!), the experience was well worth the extra strain. I picked up an English newscast from Israel (!) on the journey from Kiev whilst fiddling on my transistor, thirsting for the first news in a week, in a language I could understand. On the train to Leningrad, lay a German booklet on the "Jewish autonomous region" in Biro-Bidjan, giving an idyllic account of this "flourishing" outpost in Eastern Siberia—where self-governing Jews by the tens of thousands were intended to rebuild their culture and where now few Jews and even less of their culture are left. But the conversations and encounters en route were even more illuminating.

What did the visit achieve?

The more long-term results, if any, will obviously take weeks or months to discern. If the hopes held out are to be fulfilled, they would be significant and far-reaching, removing or at least modifying many of the sufferings and disabilities presently endured by Soviet Jews. In my long, instructive and constructive discussions at the Department of Cults in Moscow and in Kiev (responsible for all religious affairs in the USSR and the Ukraine respectively) and at the All-Soviet OVIR (in charge of issuing, or refusing, exit visas), we explored in some depth the entire gamut of our anguished concerns, from emigration to harassment, and from the training of religious personnel to the provision of literature in order to halt the all but complete spiritual and cultural starvation which has devasted Soviet Jewry for three generations. A list of specific representations and proposals, I was promised, would be given "serious consideration".

The immediate results were more tangible. By itself invaluable, and exhilarating beyond words, were the opportunities to renew contact with "the Jews of silence" (in Eli Wiesel's eloquent phrase); to be embraced by activists whose names have become legendary and whose courage defies description; to visit their modest homes filled to overflowing and talk (at their request) not about their ordeals but on my specialised subject of Jewish medical ethics (whilst my companion, the Executive Director of my office, discussed their plight and their pioneering activities with numerous individuals, augmented by many discussions in which I later joined); and to witness the miracle of some Jewish reawakening out of the utter desolation to which Jewish life had been reduced through a succession of terror, war and repression.

Some historic experiences alone would have made the visit memorable and rewarding: to boost the morale of many Jews, who have never even seen a rabbi (Leningrad and Kiev have none, whilst Moscow's solitary incumbent is elderly and ailing—yet between the three communities are more than twice Britain's 410,000 Jews!); or to extend a word of hope and comfort to a broken soul like Mrs. Mikhail Shtern, inconsolate at her sick husband's imprisonment for wishing to live as a Jew; or as one of the first foreigners at Babi Yar to shed a few tears on the oceans of blood spilt in the Nazi massacres of 100,000 people (perhaps twice as many; no one knows), mostly Jews.

Hardly less valuable were the opportunities to investigate the Jewish situation against the indispensable background of Soviet life and thought generally and by comparison with the struggle of other religious and national groups to preserve their identity against the atheistic and monolithic pressures of their environment. Desperately searching for relief, and trying to discover how others manage to survive, I spent hours at the Russian Orthodox Church establishments in Zagorsk and Leningrad, and at their seminaries where some 500 theological students receive intensive academic and religious training. There, incidentally, I met the only Israeli citizen I came across in the Soviet Union. Enquiring if they had any English-speaking students, I was introduced to a young man, originally from Greece, who was sent by the Russian Church in Jerusalem to complete his studies in Leningrad before returning permanently to Israel!

It is sadly clear that the Jewish community enjoys even less rights and opportunities than do other nationalities and denominations. There is no authorised expression of Jewish culture, literature or social life of any kind. Nor does the organisational framework exist within which such activities could be sponsored. The synagogues are strictly confined to worship for the fast-disappearing generation which still lives on the Jewish memories of pre-Revolution or pre-War times. Even the small number of children I saw attending church at Zagorsk could not be found in the synagogue; nor could their parents. Hebrew is the one language banished, among the scores of national tongues spoken and taught in the USSR. The Church publishes a very attractive religious monthly for the faithful. Jews produce no magazine whatever, other than the "Sovietish Heimland" appearing in Yiddish (which only some grandparents speak)—a façade of Soviet–Yiddishist culture used to put the stamp of conformity and legality on breaking the last links of Jews with their faith, their heritage, their national homeland and their people.

The great majority of Jews—by now completely ignorant of their traditions, and yet reminded of their Jewish "nationality" in their official documents as well as by widespread discrimination and anti-Semitic propaganda—have given up the active struggle long ago. With memories of even more oppressive tyrannies, they are resigned to integrate into Soviet society at the cost of any meaningful Jewish self-expression. But for the growing number who have rediscovered their Jewish roots, the inability to live as Jews in Russia has increasingly intensified the demand to emigrate. This alternative, too—theoretically open to all seeking reunification with families abroad—is now being denied to anyone except those prepared to face the resultant harassments, which may range from indefinitely waiting without livelihood for an exit visa to arrests, house-searches and imprisonment on the flimsiest charges.

A similar fate awaits the tiny but brave band of activists who, though violating no laws or clearly defined regulations, engage quietly in Hebrew teaching, cultural activities or the distribution of Jewish literary and historical material among small groups seeking such elementary amenities. Jewish activists, it must be emphasised, are not dissidents in the sense that they wish to challenge or change the system. They merely want to assert their legitimate rights as guaranteed by the Soviet constitution and by international agreements to which Russia is a party—whether to study and practise their traditions inside the country, or to rejoin their families elsewhere. Nothing they or their massive supporters abroad demand contravenes Soviet laws.

Why, then, do the authorities presently clamp down so mercilessly on these rights?

The Soviet mentality may be inscrutable to Western minds. Some insights, however vague, can only be gained by seeing the country, its intensely pursued culture and the rigidity of its social fabric. Already one's first superficial impression is significant. Everything is massive—numbers, buildings, crowds, monuments. Against this background, the individual vanishes and individuality becomes deviation.

Without appreciating the inner dynamics of the system, the Western world can recognise neither its peril nor its opportunities for some accommodation. For instance, personal and poignant experiences taught me that one understands far better the Russian mentality and the forming of Soviet attitudes after witnessing the shattering sight of Leningrad's mass-graves for the 680,000 citizens starved to death in the 900-day German blockade. These are now marked by huge monuments immortalising the staggering cost of victory in suffering and devastation. (Similarly one cannot comprehend the Jewish concern with security without visiting the haunting Yad VaShem memorial in Jerusalem immortalising the fearful horrors of the Nazi holocaust.)

Again, only inside the Soviet Union can one begin to sense the quasi-religious fervour, and its distinctly messianic overtones (and therefore its universalist aspirations), with which its brand of socialism is being cultivated. It is sustained by a faith in which the ubiquitous bust of Lenin has replaced the crucifix, and scientists are the new high-priests. Those rejecting the millennium in favour of the decadent West are consequently regarded as guilty of apostasy, if not of "deicide"—echoes of charges all too familiar in Jewish history.

Moreover, the rigidity of the system is such that the most insignificant concessions, especially to minority claims, immediately engender fears of domino reactions with unpredictable consequences to its stability. Where innovations or responses to fresh currents may meet in Britain the resistance of inertia and tradition, they are stultified by the dread of total collapse in Russia. In a society in which back-copies of newspapers are unavailable (except to approved research scholars), contemporary history is meant to be static, and yesterday's ideals and idols must not be seen to differ from today's reality. Messianic fulfilment is incompatible with ongoing human evolution.

On the other hand, the invitation extended to me, and the wide-ranging experiences I had during the visit, seemed to indicate that the Jewish problem does rankle as a major irritant to the Soviet regime—externally as an embarrassing impediment to global strategy on detente, trade, Middle East policies, etc.; and internally as an intractable obstacle in the system's inexorable drive for conformity and facelessness. Evidently still elusive is a formula which, to lessen internal pressures and external agitation, will provide some meaningful relaxations of the present crippling restrictions on the rights of Jews who wish to live or to leave in consonance with the promptings of their Jewish commitment; but a formula which would also not cause damage, real or imagined, to national pride (by appearing to act under duress) or to national stability (by unduly shifting any of the under-pinnings on which the elaborate structure of the society and its faith is erected). The search for such a formula must remain a major feature in the quest for an accommodation.

There are of course subtle changes in Russian attitudes and responses to world opinion. One need only contrast the earlier success in securing the quiet emigration of 120,000 Jews with the failure of the Jackson Amendment to maintain, let alone to increase (as had been agreed with the American Administration before the deal was leaked) the rate of emigration, now reduced to a bare trickle. Notwithstanding detente, the "spirit of Helsinki" and all that, the Russians were prepared to face severe hardships by cancelling massive credit and trade agreements rather than to be seen to surrender to Western pressures in a glare of publicity. Hence my insistent plea on my return from the visit that we constantly reappraise our policies. These certainly require greater flexibility, as well as more sophistication and diversification, if they are to be effective in countering the presently worsening condition of Soviet Jewry.

What, then, are the future prospects of survival for the bulk of Russia's two to three million Jews? Logically none, for it might well be maintained that most Jews have passed the point of no return. But happily Jewish history has never conformed to the laws of logic or nature; otherwise we would have been extinct long ago. Twenty years ago Jewish life in Russia was written off as a dead and beyond resurrection. No one would have believed in the miracle of a reawakening, however limited, which by now has led over one hundred thousand to Zion and caused countless thousands of others to thirst for their Jewish regeneration inside Russia—some through acts of defiant valour which were as unimaginable then as they are now inspiring, evoking the admiration of the world.

By the same inscrutable mystique of Jewish survival, twenty years hence my confidence may be vindicated that Soviet Jews will reclaim their Jewish heritage in ever larger numbers. In the end, they may suffer far fewer losses by defection and assimilation than Jews in the West—if only because the vestiges of anti-Semitism do not allow them to forget that they are Jews, and because even Russia may discover that the Messiah has not yet come, after all.

Chapter Four

RELIGION AND SOCIETY

Beyond our Confines

INTER-FAITH RELATIONS—ADVANCES AND LIMITS

Few of the revolutionary changes which have reshaped the post-War world can be greeted by us with greater satisfaction than the dramatic improvement of interreligious relations generally, and particularly the attitude of Christianity to Judaism. Great faiths, for millennia implacable and often mortal rivals, now reason together. We witness formerly undreamed-of manifestations of tolerance, exemplified here by the Council of Christians and Jews under the patronage of the Queen and the joint presidency of the heads of denominations, and culminating in the Vatican decision to modify age-old teachings offensive to Jews, including the murderous "deicide" charge.

It is no credit to civilisation that these revisions were not effected until well into the twentieth century. Had they come a thousand years earlier, untold millions of human lives might have been saved from degradation and slaughter. Nevertheless, late as they are, these radical developments are obviously welcome.

These new trends challenge as well as relieve the Jewish people. The olive branch of peace and understanding signifies more than an end to the past flood of blood and tears, and the present overtures envisage more than the unilateral rectification of historic wrongs. A new era is being ushered in, with ecumenism as its watchword, aiming at some as yet undefined inter-denominational reconciliation, in which demands will also be made of Judaism. What are these demands, what prompts them, and how far can they be met?

The ecumenical movement, aimed at "Christian Unity", is of course a purely internal affair within Christendom. The forces generating this movement are not born, and cannot be expected to be born, solely out of altruistic motives, any more than the internationalism of the United Nations is sustained without a measure of self-interest by the great powers. With the end of European colonialism diminishing the hopes of converting to Christianity one-third of mankind, and with militant atheism ruling another third, not to mention the rebellion against religion in the remaining Christian world. Christianity is on the defensive for the first time in its history. This momentous turn of the tide is bound to produce pressures for consolidation from within, to compensate for the inroads from outside. Clearly the same

Sermon delivered at the St. John's Wood Synagogue on 12 June 1971. A large extract was published in The Times *two days later.*

pressures also call for some accommodation with Judaism, to strengthen the ramparts of the "Judaeo-Christian patrimony" against the "common foe" of materialism, secularism, atheism and sheer paganism sweeping the world.

From the Jewish point of view, some Jewish and Christian interests converge, while others will always remain irreconcilable. Jews certainly have an interest in Christians being good and faithful Christians, not only because —in the phrase first coined in medieval times—"wie es christelt sich, so juedelt's sich". Judaism obviously cares deeply for the advancement of the moral and religious values promoted by all monotheistic faiths.

There are also many specific areas in which inter-faith co-operation should prove of common interest. Consultations and joint efforts are surely desirable to ensure better religious educational facilities, including aid for denominational schools; to defeat morally unacceptable legislation, from abortion on demand at the start of life to euthanasia at its end; to fight racial or religious discrimination; and generally to cultivate the moral and religious conscience of society.

But traditional Judaism shrinks from inter-denominational activities and debates in areas on which our religious differences impinge. Our aversion to theological dialogues and inter-faith services, for instance, is founded both on practical considerations and on the dictates of Jewish law.

We regard our relationship with God, and the manner in which we define and collectively express it, as being so intimate and personal that we could no more convey it to outsiders than we would share with others our husband-wife relationship. We feel it is improper to expose one's innermost beliefs and mode of worship to the judgement or comparative scrutiny of those who do not share the same religious commitment.

Moreover, any parleys between Judaism and Christianity would be between two essentially unequal partners on several counts, quite apart from the gross disparity in dominance and numbers in Christian lands. Christianity may well have seen a need officially to define its doctrinal attitude towards the faith from which it emerged and eventually broke away. But neither the recognition of this need nor the resultant relationship can be entirely reciprocal. Judaism, antedating Christianity by many centuries, had no occasion or cause to include in its official doctrines any formal views on a faith which sprang up long after these doctrines were formulated in all essentials. It lies in the nature of their history that the New Testament can refer to the Old, whilst the Old cannot refer to the New.

An even more important element of inequality lies in the fundamental divergence of views on evangelism, a subject of special sensitivity to a people already decimated by persecution and assimilation. While Christianity aspires to convert all human beings, uniting them within one universal religion, Judaism has no such aspirations. It is content to remain for all time a minority faith, "the remnant of Israel," restricted to those born into it and the few who may spontaneously seek to embrace it, without any encouragement or inducement. Even if Christians were to foreswear any missionary intent in theological dialogues with Jews, their traditional division into two groups—the one seeking to absorb the other—is historically, if not theologically, so deeply rooted as inevitably to compromise their equality.

Judaism accepts religious diversity and cultural pluralism not just as an inescapable fact of life, or a temporary condition to be tolerated, but as a desirable state to enrich the human experience. Diversity, we believe—in creed, race, nationality, political views and other spheres— is as essential to create the dynamics of human progress as are the distinctions and tensions between male and female or between positive and negative poles, which are required to generate all life and energy. A human race made up of identical beings would be as dull and as uncreative as a symphony played by a single-instrument orchestra.

Judaism teaches that even in Messianic times, when the Kingdom of God will be accepted universally, religious differences will still exist. At "the end of days," in Micah's famous prophecy, "all the peoples will walk each in the name of his God" (4:5). This is the real significance of the verse from Zechariah with which we conclude every Jewish service: "In that day shall the Lord be One and His Name One."

AN INSTRUMENT OF AMITY

In welcoming this uniquely distinguished assembly to this Synagogue hall, may I first of all say how very profoundly we appreciate this gesture to the Jewish community, of holding the Jubilee meeting of this Council on Jewish premises for the first time in the annals of the Council's history. And in particular how deeply I value holding it in the hall of a Synagogue where exactly one month ago today I consecrated myself to my new assignment and where indeed I am now a regular worshipper. In return, as a counter-gesture, I have taken up residence in a district and am worshipping in a synagogue which bears a Christian name!

I am indeed deeply touched by the warmth of the expressions of welcome and good wishes that I received on my election, on my installation and on this historic occasion from the spiritual leaders of this great country who are now my colleagues on the Presidency of this Council. I will endeavour to emulate the example of my predecessors in forging bonds of personal friendship and of interdenominational co-operation built on the bedrock of this Council.

Our generation has borne witness to the most convulsive changes of all times, in every area of human life and knowledge. The emergence of the United Nations, now composed of a growing preponderance of non-Christian nations, has set an altogether new pattern of international relations and shifted the centre of gravity from the Western world which had enjoyed political and cultural hegemony in the evolution of civilisation for nearly two thousand years. The spectacular rise of the Human Rights movement and the liquidation of colonialism have added a new dimension to the quest by nations, races and individuals for freedom and equality. The scientific explosion, whereby we now double, every eight years, the sum total of man's knowledge about the universe in which we live, has radically altered our ways of living and thinking.

No less significant is the advance of the new morality which peremptorily

---

Address given at the "Silver Jubilee" Annual Meeting of the Council of Christians and Jews at the St. John's Wood Synagogue Hall in May 1967. This was the Chief Rabbi's first appearance as a Joint President of the Council, together with the Archbishop of Canterbury, the Cardinal Archbishop of Westminster, the Moderator of the Free Churches and the Moderator of the Church of Scotland, all of whom also attended the meeting.

questions and displaces moral values and traditions that have stood the test of time for millennia. But I believe that, in terms of the long-range impact on the future course of history, by far the most significant revolution has occurred in the sphere of inter-faith relations, whereby the great religions have moved for the first time in history from bitter enmity and rivalry to a friendly understanding and co-operation. I believe that this revolution will leave a more permanent mark on the course of human history than any other revolution that we have witnessed. In this epoch-making development, this Council has played a pioneering role, long before the very word "ecumenism" was known anywhere outside strictly theological circles. To this day the Council, graced as it is by patronage of Her Majesty the Queen, and presided over by the supreme leaders of this country's denominations, represents the highest inter-faith platform to be found anywhere in the world, and no tribute can be adequate to the vision and foresight of our predecessors in evolving this unique instrument of religious amity.

ATTITUDES TO ECUMENISM

For historical reasons evident to anyone familiar with Jewish history, the Jewish response to the more recent overtures of ecumenism and dialogue has been marked by feelings of relief and gratification mixed with some apprehension. It is no secret that there are currently deep divisions among us, between those advocating and those opposing theological dialogues. These divisions are particularly pronounced in the United States. The Jewish hesitation to embrace the ecumenical spirit with unreserved enthusiasm is based in part on our anxious concern, as a small minority, to maintain the distinctiveness of our faith and in part to the deeply ingrained fear of missionary overtones: a fear which cannot be completely eradicated until each religion acknowledges the permanent right to survival and the inviolability of another in its teaching and its practices. I will look to this Council to remove suspicions on both sides on this score.

THEOLOGY AND MORALS

I believe that out of our own Jewish dialogue or dialogues, there is being crystallised an attitude which will distinguish between theological parleying and discussions and common endeavours on social and moral issues confronting all religions. It is to our work together in this latter sphere that I want to give every encouragement and make whatever contribution I can. For instance, there are today under public discussion numerous legislative proposals which impinge upon our religious and moral conscience, and which should see us on common ground in thought and in action. I wonder, for example, whether the renewed debate on divorce might not prompt us to consider abolishing the curious anomaly between marriages and divorces, whereby marriages are being recognised by State authorities even if religiously performed, whilst divorces are surrendered exclusively to the jurisdiction of the State. Perhaps in addition to having civil divorces administered by the Courts, each denomination should be given the right to set up ecclesiastical courts that would likewise enjoy the same rights to dissolve a marriage as they have to solemnise a marriage under State sanction.

REGENERATION OF SOCIETY

Above all, I think we should address ourselves jointly to the evils and immorality rampant in our society. In the Jewish view, all spiritual leaders must assume some degree of personal responsibility for every crime that is committed by people in their care. It is our task to assure the primacy of the moral regeneration of society in the awareness of every citizen.

Some years ago numerous countries banded themselves together in a colossal enterprise known as the Geo-physical Year, lavishing vast resources in brain power and finance on an exciting corporate study of the world's physical features. Perhaps we should propose the proclamation of a Geo-spiritual Year in which nations and governments will co-operate in massive research and moral rehabilitation programmes to devise effective means for the elimination of vice and crime, of marital faithlessness and immorality gnawing at the roots of our common civilisation and our common heritage. May it be granted that we ourselves have a humble share in making a contribution to the dawn of that day when all human beings throughout the world will acknowledge the brotherhood of man.

HUMAN RIGHTS AND HUMAN DUTIES

I must admit that, when just over a year ago I somewhat reluctantly agreed to leave the fleshpots of America for the headaches of the British Chief Rabbinate in response to one of the more unusual bids by Sir Isaac Wolfson, the chairman of the Chief Rabbinate Conference which elected me, I certainly did not realise that the honour of addressing this august Conference of Directors would be part of the bargain.

My presence here at this conference before Britain's captains of industry is not so incongruous as might appear. I am the director of a fairly large and tricky business—the business of selling traditional Judaism to critical and sometimes hesitant buyers in a highly competitive world in which the market is being flooded by many cheaper substitutes which imitate the article I have to offer. And since moreover all the customers I seek—some half a million of them—are Jewish, my powers of salesmanship are severely put to the test.

In America, the title 'chief' conjures up visions of befeathered Red Indians; here, at least in our community, "chief" is associated with bearded rabbis. Otherwise, your organisation might be known as the Institute of Chiefs. Now, I like to be more "rabbi" than "chief". And so, on weekdays I *practise* as "chief" and on Sabbaths and festivals I *preach* as "rabbi".

In this latter capacity, in the course of a sermon during the recent High Holydays, I related the story of three men who, having been doomed by their doctors to die within three months, were asked how they would spend the time left to them. The Scotsman answered that he would cheerfully squander his savings on all the pleasures he had previously denied himself. The Frenchman spoke of the utter abandon with which he would dine and wine to his heart's content. And the Jew simply said, "I would look for another doctor to get a second opinion." I used this story not only to launch my homiletical ship of solemn exhortation with the merry champagne of a little laughter, but also to illustrate the perennial refusal of the Jew to regard anything as final or inevitable. Whenever in our long history others forecast the doom of Jewry, writing off Jewish survival, or talked, in the diabolical language of the Nazis, of "the Final Solution" of the Jewish problem, the Jew—refusing to accept finality—always consulted his faith for a second opinion.

Address delivered at the Institute of Directors Annual Conference at the Royal Albert Hall, London, on 9 November 1976, and subsequently published by the Institute in a special Report of the proceedings.

Herein also lies one of the most characteristic features of Jewish religious belief. Jews still look forward to the coming of the Messiah—finality lies in the future. We refuse to acknowledge any human order as finally settled. How else can one explain the but recent re-emergence of the gallant little State of Israel?

This dissatisfaction with things as they are, constantly challenging the imperfections of the present, fashioned the character of the Jew and his contribution to human progress. Out of this restless defiance of the *status quo* were born the social protest of the Hebrew Prophets in antiquity, the non-conformity of Jewish martyrs in the Middle Ages, and the inventive genius and revolutionary fervour of so many Jews in modern times.

Here I now come to my main theme. Today this restlessness is universal. The oppressive feeling that things are far from what they should be, this critical search for purpose and meaning—all these tides of unsettlement and instability engulf the entire world. This dissatisfaction with the existing order may well be the most characteristic mark of our age. Never before in the history of man have so many people and so many nations wanted so much they do not have. Never before have the discontent with the present and the longing for change been more universal. Gone are the complacent days, which prevailed until the first World War, when people by and large preferred the solid certainty of the *status quo* to the imponderables of change and revolution. The violent winds of change have indeed swept away the old order, but we all realise that these winds of change are likely to persist for quite a while longer until they will have blown themselves out to make way, we hope, for a stable world. Meanwhile, the human society is in a state of unprecedented turbulence, tossed about in the ocean separating hope from reality, and plunging precariously between peace and war, between industrial rest and unrest, between social security and strife, between racial equality and riots, between political universalism and chauvinism, between scientific mastery and human mechanisation, between religious ecumenism and moral impotence.

Somehow all our giant advances in every sphere of human relations and social endeavour have been counter-productive of giant new pressures. In science, the spectacular conquest of nature has left man defenceless against the blighting by-products of automation, against the dreaded invasion of privacy, against the terror of annihilation—to mention but a few of the problems created by science. Our universities, once so called because of the universality of knowledge they taught, are now all too often assembly-lines of specialists who cannot see the wood of culture for the trees of depart-mentalised efficiency.

In religion, the dramatic progress towards inter-faith amity and understanding on the highest level has been offset by the recession of religion at the lower levels, creating a moral vacuum filled by a mini-morality and a hippie-culture which have made the cost of crime and the prevention of crime the nation's biggest industry, have produced millions of human wrecks from rising divorce and illegitimacy rates, and which have turned the pleasure of worship into the worship of pleasure.

The social and human rights movements have gone a long way to securing greater equality in ethnic and industrial relations; yet they have also produced their problems in seriously exacerbating racial and labour tensions in even the most stable democracies.

And, politically, the liquidation of colonialism has brought the boon of independence to scores of new nations together with the bane of continual crisis to both the liberated and the liberators alike. To Britain in particular the renunciation of imperial power has resulted in an agonising search for a new national purpose. Britain has been the traditional tugboat of democracy with an illustrious record of having brought so many national ensigns to safe harbour. But now these are sailing under their own steam, and the tugboat is searching for a new role. Tugboats do not lend themselves for conversion into pleasure-steamers, and to find new outlets for the British genius in towing others across the ocean of history is now the measure or Britain's crisis of purpose.

Much of the current restlessness and discontent irritating human relations in all these areas must no doubt be attributed to the sudden shrinkage of the world. The speed of modern communications may have reduced distances, but it has also widened the gap between the haves and the have-nots. What you do not see or know you do not want. You covet only possessions you see others have. In former days, the poor and the oppressed saw little of how the rich and the free were living. People however deprived, and nations however underdeveloped or exploited, were resigned to their lot because they knew no better. Today, the master-publicists of Madison Avenue and Fleet Street, or the glamour screens of Hollywood, instantly bring the enviable image of carefree affluence into the most impoverished home, thus accentuating the awareness of economic inequality. Vivid pictures and reports of racial demonstrations and riots in any part of the world penetrate without delay into the most sordid ghettoes and into darkest Africa to arouse bitter indignation and violent agitation.

Altogether, the emphasis in our labour-saving, machine-dominated technocracy is on securing fast benefits from reduced efforts, with the result that we all want more for less. It is even being said that some politicians want more power for less criticism, some directors more profits for less competition, and some workers more pay for less hours. There may also be some doctors who want more freedom for abortions for less reasons, and some clergymen more religious observance for less lay interference, while some negroes want more equality for less restraints, and some boys want more girls for less to cover them.

Underlying the malaise of our age, then, is that we want more than we can get, and that today's philosophy of life encourages us to want more than we can get. This gnawing sense of unfulfilment and deprivation frustrates us and bedevils all our human relations, whether personal or collective, whether between individuals or between groups and nations.

What can I, as a spokesman for Judaism, offer as a contribution to mitigating this malaise?

Perhaps the most significant feature of our contemporary social and moral philosophy is that we define our basic human imperatives mainly in terms of rights. We speak and think of human rights, constitutional rights, international rights, political rights, labour rights, student rights, racial rights and what have you. The whole motivation of our social behaviour is galvanised by our clamour for rights which we are pressed to assert as our due. The demand for rights we consider inalienable fuels the machine of our ambitions and kindles the fires of our discontents and frictions.

Now, in Judaism we know of no intrinsic rights. Indeed, there is no word for rights in the very language of the Hebrew Bible and of the classic sources of Jewish law. In the moral vocabulary of the Jewish discipline of life we speak of human duties, not of human rights, of obligations, not of entitlements. The Decalogue is a list of Ten Commandments, not a Bill of Human Rights. In the charity legislation of the Bible, for instance, it is the rich man who is commanded to support the poor, not the poor man who has the right to demand support from the rich. Or, to use its phraseology, it states "Thou shalt surely open thy hand unto thy poor and needy brother". It does not state that the poor man shall open *his* hand to demand his share. Economic and social justice is to be achieved by impressing upon the privileged the duty to give, and not upon the under-privileged the right to demand. Likewise, in labour-relations as in all other laws affecting the social order, the accent is invariably on the debt of him who has, not on the claim of him who has not. Even in Jewish medical ethics, which happens to be my specialised interest, the same principle applies. In Jewish law a doctor is obliged to come to the rescue of his stricken fellow-man and to perform any operation he considers essential for the life of the patient, even if the patient refuses his consent or prefers to die. Once again, the emphasis is on the physician's responsibility to heal, to offer service, more than on the patient's right to be treated.

In a profoundly meaningful passage nearly 2,000 years old, dealing with the sanctity and equality of human life, the Talmud requires witnesses in capital trials to be cautioned with the following argument: "Why was but a single man created as the progenitor of the entire human race? So that no one should say to his fellow: 'My father is greater than your father'." Mark this, it does not say, "So that every man may *claim* 'My father is as great as yours'," but rather that people *shall not* claim "My father is greater than yours." In other words, it is not the one who feels inferior who shall claim equality, but the one who is in a superior position who shall grant equality. We want to teach people to think not in terms of what they may demand from others, but of what they owe to others.

Herein, surely, lies the curse of our age—and its cure. The accent today is on demands, not on obligations. Everyone thinks of what society owes to him, not of what he owes to society. Already our youth are conditioned to ponder on what they can get out of life, and not on what they must put into life. And just as a family in which the relationships between parents and children are predicated on the rights children may demand from their parents rather than on the duties parents owe to their children must flounder, so a society whose catchwords are success instead of service, leisure instead of work, rights instead of duties, must come to grief and disillusionment.

What is needed, then, if we are to reverse the tide of restlessness and frustration is to change radically our focus in human relations. We must expunge the word rights and replace it by duties. If, for instance, management felt that the onus of improving the workers' lot rested more on management granting better conditions than on labour unions demanding them, we would have no strikes, and if the workers sensed the urgency of deliberating on how better to serve the country by increased productivity and a greater pride in work, we would have no economic crisis. If people were trained to regard their obligations to serve others, and not their addiction to personal success and selfishness, as the leitmotif in their preparation of a career, we would not have the growing problems of delinquency and narcotics, not to mention immorality, on our hands, for they all stem from a perverse insistence on rights without duties. If our newspapers and other mass media provided the people with what they need rather than with what they want, public enlightenment and entertainment would encourage service through publicising virtue, and not crime through publicising scandals, vice and agitation. And if the incentives to international trade and agreements were the obligation to help other nations rather than sheer national self-interest, we would have neither war through conflicting interests nor the suppression of war through a balance of terror; we would have peace through the brotherhood of man.

Instead of asserting rights at the expense of others, let us assert duties at our expense. Instead of drifting aimlessly in quest of new purpose and meaning, let our purpose be the service of others and our meaning to secure equality by granting it. In setting our sights on these soaring peaks in the wonderful panorama of human evolution, we may yet confound the prophets of doom who see nothing but strife and disenchantment in store for us. The fatalistic prognosis of so many of our political and social doctors may well be overruled by a superior second opinion, granting a new lease of creative life to ourselves and to all our fellow-men, every one of them a director of our human destiny, created to live in the image of the Divine Director of us all.

MORAL CHALLENGES BEFORE THE MASS MEDIA

The honour done to me in being invited as the Guest of Honour at this year's Annual Luncheon of your Group is greatly appreciated, all the more so since I am, I gather, the first Jewish speaker to be so honoured since Lord Samuel accepted a similar invitation quite a few years ago. Speaking as a purveyor of eternity before those who are professionally purveyors of brevity, I will try my best to strike a reasonable balance between eternity and brevity within the limited time allotted to me, although the temptation is great to exceed these limits on this privileged occasion when I appear before editors who cannot cut or edit my remarks, nor heckle me in the form of rejoinders

My theme is a sensitive subject, challenging to speaker and listeners alike— to the former because some question I will pose may be unanswerable, and to the latter because some answers I will propose may be unpalatable.

FLEET STREET: FLEETING AND PROLIFIC

The moral dilemma of the mass media is dramatised by the inevitable inconsistency between two paradoxical features characterising these media, and particularly the press: their power and their evanescence. The press represents by far the most potent and most prolific literature published today; yet it is the most ephemeral. With a circulation of over 25,000,000 daily newspapers in this country alone, the output of newsprint in one day is probably greater than the combination of all books printed in a week. The average time spent on reading, viewing or listening to news media is far in excess of the time devoted to all other reading matter put together. Nevertheless, this vast literature is dated and obsolete on the day after publication. The Psalmist, if he were living today, might well exclaim: "For a thousand years in Thy sight are but as yesterday's newspaper."

MORAL ASPECTS

The mass media have, of course, enormous moral achievements to their credit. They have made an immense contribution to strengthening the social and moral conscience of mankind. As a direct result of their impact, vast

Address delivered to the Weekly Religious Press Group on 24 January 1969.

strides have been made towards human equality. For the first time in history, they have made people really care for, and become involved in, the sufferings of others thousands of miles away, for example in Vietnam or in Biafra. The President of the Free World's mightiest nation has come to grief through the violent concern with the affairs of a distant country generated by the news media.[1] All over the world, the mass media have helped to break the stranglehold of absolute power derived from class, wealth and privilege.

But these tremendous benefits have been secured at a high, perhaps sometimes even excessive, cost. Much of the restlessness, fear, insecurity and strife afflicting our society must also be attributed to the influence of the mass media.

Let me explain. Lately we have heard a good deal about the "trivialisation of the news". This is, however, a comparatively minor evil. Worse is the distortion of the news inevitably resulting from the accepted rules of journalistic practice.

RULES AND EXCEPTIONS

By way of illustrating what I have in mind, let me relate to you an instructive fable found in Jewish sources, a fable my late sainted father was fond of telling to explain the contrast between the publication of freaks, such as aeroplane accidents, and the silence on normal events, such as safe landings. A lion mother once took her little cub on a walk to teach it a lesson on the facts of leonine life. "We are the kings of the beasts," explained the proud lioness, "we need not be afraid of any other animal. We are even more powerful than human beings whom we can attack without fear." As they walked on, they passed an imposing monument showing Samson tearing up a lion. Exclaimed the frightened lion-cub: "But mother, didn't you just tell me that we had no one to fear and could overpower even man? And look, here is a lion brutally torn to pieces by a human being." "This just proves what I told you," the lioness reassured her child, "if this were a common event, they would not put up any monument to mark it; only because it happened only once, did they immortalise the unusual occurrence in stone!"

Now imagine there would be not just one such monument, but millions of them, to be seen everywhere all the time. Then one might indeed begin to wonder whether the event it commemorated was all that unusual and exceptional.

It lies in the nature of our system of mass communications that, by publicising the freak more than the common, the exceptional becomes the norm. Attention is drawn to that which challenges or breaks the rule rather than to the rule.

ACCENT ON DISSENT

In the often fierce competition for catching the editor's eye, the noisy dissident always has the edge over the quiet upholders of tradition, the criminal over the law-abiding citizen, the disturber of the peace over the pursuer of peace. Those who challenge the established order are bound to be louder and more newsworthy than those who defend it. Consequently, it is the pickets, the strikers, the demonstrators, the rebels—the irritants of society—which are always highlighted, irrespective of their merits or legality. For the excitement of strife and controversy is always more interesting than the tedium of harmony.

The media thus amplify protest and muffle the voice of stability, they advertise vice and crime while reducing the appeal of decency and order.

In this entirely unequal contest between the shrill noise of protest and small still voice of tradition, religious leaders are bound to be among the worst victims, for it is ineluctably their assignment to preserve rather than to change values. The tendency to accentuate dissent has been dramatically demonstrated in the recent ordeal of the Roman Catholic Church. The Anglo-Jewish community, too, is only just beginning to recover from a near-crippling religious crisis fostered by a widely publicised challenge to the beliefs and institutions of the Establishment. In the unavoidable distortions of mass media thirsting for public attention, the devotees of stability and tradition never can stand a fair chance against the advocates of change and rebellion.

THE TRUTH, BUT NOT THE WHOLE TRUTH

The other day I received and read the fascinating Annual Report of the Press Council. It provides a most interesting indication of the variety and complexity of the numerous moral and ethical problems encountered in journalistic practice. But what I want to discuss here is an area of moral challenge not touched upon in the Report. In affirming, or swearing to, the absolute veracity of a statement, three conditions are required: that it be "the truth, the whole truth, and nothing but the truth." Now, professional journalistic ethics, as reflected in the cases before the Press Council concerns itself only or mainly with two of these requirements, namely that anything published be "the truth, and nothing but the truth." However, compelled to excerpt, condense and edit by the limitations of space and time, the news media can never tell "the whole truth". This exigency, however unavoidable, clearly represents a grave compromise with the truth itself. It is aggravated by the kind of "exciting" extracts from "the whole truth" which *will* be chosen for publication!

Think of a photographer or a painter who portrays only a wart or a scar on the face of his subject. The artist certainly reproduces "the truth, and nothing but the truth"; what the portrait shows is the true likeness of the subject. But it does not show "the whole truth." It therefore grossly distorts.

By quoting part of a speech, selected by reason of its newsworthiness rather than by virtue of its instrinsic value or of its characterisation of the whole, journalists may do similar violence to their subject—in this case, the author of the speech. In publishing excerpts at the discretion of the editor or his agents rather than by the free choice of the author, the media deprive authors or speakers of the copyright over their own statements and project a public image of thoughts determined by those who transmit them rather than by the people to whom they are attributed.

One wonders how the Hebrew prophets would have fared if their speeches had been distilled through the editorial filters of the press. Would it be unreasonable to suspect that, instead of the immortal denunciations of injustice and pagan depravity inspiring us with their lofty passion to this day, all that might have been left to posterity would have been lurid descriptions of the very vice and violence, of the lust and lechery they denounced?

SOME PROPOSALS

There are no panaceas I can offer. But I would like to submit one or two broad suggestions for consideration. Some method should be devised to divorce the presentation of news from entertainment. The transmission of science, medicine, law or education is not subject to any popularity contest. Why should just the presentation of the news, perhaps the most crucial factor in shaping attitudes and opinions, be determined by what appeals to the masses? The newsworthiness of stories or statements to be published ought to be gauged by their true value as a contribution to human progress, not by their capacity to attract readers, listeners or viewers. If people want entertainment, let them turn to fiction, to the stage or the screen, not to current news.

I also believe that those whose message and image are projected by the media should be entitled to determine what extracts of their statements are to be published. They should be allowed the right to check the accuracy of any reports on opinions attributed to them. In other words, what an author of speeches or lectures or statements desires to convey to the wider public should be left to the author and not to the sole discretion of editors or reporters whose assessment of what is important or in context may completely distort the intentions of the author.

THE DISINTERESTED USE OF THE PUBLIC INTEREST

Above all, editors should voluntarily invoke "the public interest" not only to justify the publication of questionable material; thus I see the Chairman of the Press Council has acclaimed the "editorial courage" of publishing items even if they are marked "confidential". They should similarly have recourse to "the public interest" to withhold the publication of harmful items, such as anything which advocates or is liable to promote crime, subversion, unrest or indecency.

In assuring the highest moral and ethical standards of the mass media, a special responsibility naturally rests on the religious press. It should play a pioneering role in creating a moral code to guide an industry and a profession which lack such ancient principles as have regulated the practitioners of religion, medicine, law or education for many centuries past.

THE NEWS IN THE PERSPECTIVE OF TIME

Such an effort might well draw its inspiration from the Hebrew prophets, the greatest news-commentators of all times. They contrived to report and interpret contemporary events on a vast canvas stretching over the entire panorama of human history. They saw the shape of the events they witnessed in the perspective of eternity—as an essential link between the past and the future.

It is up to those in whose hands rests the crushing responsibility of establishing the communications between man and man to make manifest the brotherhood of man, and to ensure that we see in our contemporary experience not only a tiny particle of history but an essential bond linking the successes and failures of the past with the hopes and redemption of the future.

NOTE

1. The reference was to President L. B. Johnson.

RELIGION IN PUBLIC LIFE

The proprieties and traditions attaching to my office, as indeed to religious leaders in general, usually impose restraints and restrictions which in part disenfranchise me from the public exercise of free speech—certainly on subjects with political ramifications or overtones.

Pulpits and most other platforms at my disposal simply do not lend themselves to indulgence in controversial opinions and nonconformity. I therefore appreciate all the more this invitation to enjoy the sanctuary of academic freedom within these hallowed precincts of learning, and I hope I will not be charged with ungraciousness or the abuse of hospitality if I exploit this privilege for the expression of some possibly controversial, unconventional or even provocative opinions.

Clearly, I do not subscribe to the rule that clerics should be confined to pulpits, nuptials and burials (much as women were once expected to confine themselve to the kitchen) or that, when outside their normal habitat, and like good children, they should be seen but not heard.

My views, let me state at once, are coloured, perhaps biased, by two quite unrelated factors: my Jewish heritage going back nearly 4,000 years, and my American experience which extended over eight years in New York.

As a Jew, I am an heir to the Prophetic tradition and committed to the Jewish philosophy of life. The Hebrew Prophets were not ecclesiastics. Rather they represented the principal challenge to the political and social establishment of their day. They were the world's most outstanding leaders of the opposition, though they commanded no votes, and were as lonely in their day as they are immortal today. As Buber put it, "The prophet is appointed to oppose the king and, even more, history".

They preached not in temples or synagogues, but in the market place and in royal courts. The Prophets applied their religious insights not to theology or ritual observances but to moral standards in statecraft, international relations and social conduct. Their vision encompassed the entire panorama of history and man's evolution in the consummation of the human destiny towards the perfect world order.

Lecture delivered at the University of Leeds on 15 October 1974. Extensive extracts were published as a feature article in The Times *on 27 January 1975. Also included in this lecture, but omitted here, were some passages on the mass media which are reproduced in the preceding item.*

In contrast to other faiths, Judaism addresses itself primarily to society, not to the individual. Even prayer is complete only if uttered with the congregation in public worship. Again, our classic sources use the term salvation only in a national or universal context, never as a purely personal ideal.

Hence, as I have never tired to remind my own people especially following the trauma of the Yom Kippur War, we look upon the return of Jewish sovereignty to Zion promised by the Prophets primarily as a corporate instrument to promote social justice and the rule of religious faith and moral discipline. Both the means and the end of our national restoration are founded in these ideals. In the immortal words of Isaiah: "Zion will be redeemed through justice and those who return to her through righteousness;" and again as the goal of our redemption: "For out of Zion will go forth the Law and the word of the Lord from Jerusalem."

Now to my American antecedents. I found religion in America, though disestablished and divorced from the State by a rigid "wall of separation", far more potent in its influence on public life than here. It is less discreet and reticent, serving as a major crusading force, perhaps for the very reason that it is not part of the establishment and thus free to challenge it. The Civil Rights movement, the Vietnam protest, and even the moral fervour of the Watergate drama were largely spearheaded by religious leaders. Especially in the mass-media, the voice of religion is prominently vocal, even vociferous, in every public debate—from arguments on divorce or abortion legislation to discussions on strikes or racial integration, often even to the point of intervention in political elections by the endorsement or rejection of candidates from the pulpit; the latter an excessive expression of the extrovert American character which I neither shared while in America nor would advocate for emulation here.

THE COLLAPSE OF CIVILISATIONS

But, quite apart from the impact of my Jewish and American experience, my reading of the contemporary predicament itself indicates the urgent need for the more effective assertion of religious teachings and leadership in the arena of public life.

The world is now faced by an acute crisis of more universal dimensions than any since the Flood. I cannot believe that such a crisis, threatening the very collapse of our civilisation, can occur; I cannot believe that nations can become ungovernable, that technological advances as well as vice and violence have outstripped our capacity to control them; that we witness the end of the era of affluence, and of the hegemony of the industrial nations; I cannot accept that powerful governments must capitulate to the economic and political dictates of a handful of persons ruling over medieval serfdoms which still practise slavery and polygamy; that the majority of the world's nations must agree to confer legitimacy to a murderous organisation dedicated to diabolical terror against innocent air-passengers, sportsmen and school-children—in short, I cannot believe that the civilised world as we knew it is inevitably coming to grief and ruin in a convulsion of unprecedented proportions; simply because some effective political and economic formulae have eluded us and the requisite wisdom has suddenly failed our statesmen and their select teams of skilled advisors and efficient bureaucrats.

The Roman Empire and other past civilisations did not decline and fall simply because some inept heads made the wrong decisions in moments of crisis. Civilisations do not die from headaches, and heads do not usually suffer from fatal pains unless there is something seriously wrong and diseased within the whole organism of the body. One does not have to be a devotee of psychosomatic medicine to realise that the ailments afflicting the body of society today are largely in the intangible domain of the soul and the spirit. Hence the health of our society cannot be regenerated without the kind of moral therapy which religious leaders ought to provide as spiritual healers responsible for diagnosis and treatment alike.

DISTRIBUTION OF THE WORLD'S RELIGIOUS WEALTH

Let me start my listing of a few illustrations with a brief glimpse at the inequitable global distribution of our religious wealth and the resultant tensions. Mankind is now almost equally divided into three camps: the religiously developed, the underdeveloped and the maldeveloped. Perhaps just over a billion people, at least nominally profess one of the three mono-theistic faiths of Judaism, Christianity and Islam. Another billion, spread over vast lands in Asia and Africa, are religious neutrals—uncommitted—neither acknowledging nor rejecting God. And about another billion, alas, are in militant rebellion against God. For the first time in history we have not only individuals but powerful states dedicated—indeed constitutionally committed as a matter of national policy—to the overthrow of all religion and to the eradication of belief in any Deity from the hearts and minds of men.

To my mind, this is fundamentally the crux of the ideological struggle between East and West, even more than differences in social doctrines or economic systems. For, after all, Communism as such teaches a lofty doctrine of human equality and brotherhood; a doctrine not entirely unrelated to our Prophets' passion for social justice. How can we explain, then, that it has nevertheless been perverted into such a mighty instrument of oppression, that it has led to prisons engulfing almost whole continents, to the brutal suppression of freedom of speech and literary creativity, to the degradation of man into a soulless machine?

The answer is quite simple, apparently too obvious to be noticed. There can be no brotherhood of man without the Fatherhood of God. It is only as children of a common God that we humans are brothers. Take away the link, and the chain of human fraternity and understanding disintegrates. Dethrone God, and the dignity of man created in His image is bound to collapse.

That is the ultimate cause of our present-day tribulations.

In staking this claim, I am all too painfully aware of the terrible wars, persecution, intolerance, torture and slaughter so often inflicted in the name of religion—from the medieval Crusades to the intractable agony of Northern Ireland in the present day. But these manifestations of inhumanity are an abuse and perversion of true religion, entitling us to blame and banish religion itself with as much logic as we ought to ban and condemn science because it created an atomic bomb, or to proscribe music and literature because some of history's most evil tyrants resorted to these arts and prostituted them in the pursuit of their fiendish frenzy.

INFLATION OF SELFISHNESS

Let me now turn to the role of religion nearer home, and the vindication of my belief that our contemporary dilemma represents basically a profound moral crisis.

Take our tottering economy as one example. Even worse and more devastating than the inflation of prices and the devaluation of money as a cause for our tribulations is the inflation of selfishness and the devaluation of moral values and ideals.

Our age is conditioned to think only in terms of rights, never of duties and obligations, only of what people can get out of life, not what they must put into it. Contending parties and politicians have only recently told us (in the General Election campaign just held) that we face a crisis which was never so bad—when incidentally they told us not so long ago that we never had it so good. They then proceeded to display an assortment of programmes which would raise Britain out of its economic doldrums, but none dealt with the roots of the crisis which is simply that we do not work hard enough.

We can no longer match the growing demand for rising living standards with the declining will to work, with the waning pride and pleasure in producing the means of personal and national wealth. In today's competitive world, a nation without extraordinary resources cannot prosper on a 30-odd hour working week (interspersed by 2-hourly tea-breaks or afternoons off for golf), periodically disrupted by strikes, and compromised during work by indifference to the job. The real crisis betrays a perverse sense of values, a warped philosophy of life, in which pleasure is the *summum bonum*, in which comfort and the avoidance of work are a greater virtue than diligence, and in which the pursuit of selfish interests is the legitimate road to success and power.

Naturally, an effective challenge to work harder, to place the serving of others above, or at least on a par with, promoting one's own interests, such an unpopular demand can hardly come from those vying for massive votes in popularity contests. Who, if not religious leaders, can advocate the application of the Golden Rule of loving one's neighbour as oneself to the wider sphere of social relations, of caring for the welfare of others as for one's own —now that this may well be a key to economic survival no less than to personal salvation?

INDUSTRIAL RELATIONS: SOCIAL JUSTICE AND STRIKES

Selfishness is also at the root of the increasingly bitter and potentially explosive polarisation of society—or confrontation, in the contemporary parlance. This threatens to lead not merely to economic bankruptcy but to civil strife and political instability of unpredictable consequence.

In this day and age of instant communications, when the wealth and comforts of the rich are constantly portrayed on the screens of the under-privileged and disadvantaged in their very homes, the inequalities between the haves and have-nots, or have-less, are bound to arouse greater envy than ever before and to erupt into desperate, sometimes even violent, action to redress the balance. In the face of these realities, we surely ought not to wait for pickets and demonstrators to denounce and eliminate the social injustices which still maintain an indefensible differential between the wages of some labourers and the incomparably higher earnings of those in management, or entertainment, or other recipients of rewards unrelated to output, training, skill and effort.

The equitable redistribution of wealth should be a powerful moral challenge to unite the nation, not a political slogan to divide it. Its fiercest advocates ought to be the appointed custodians of the nation's moral conscience rather than the partisans of class and party.

At the same time, religious leadership might be expected, by a concerted effort, to help in devising a more civilised and less damaging method for resolving industrial conflicts than by crippling strikes, which cause millions of innocent citizens who are not a party to the dispute—not to mention the national economy—to suffer grievous harm, untold misery and hardship, appalling losses and sometimes even death as a result.

The imposition of such suffering on the whole community for gaining the rights of a section is immoral. A claim of one person or group against another, however justified, never entitles the claimant to hurt or damage a third party. When two individuals have a financial dispute, we do not expect them to resolve it by fighting it out until one has bloodied the other and, for good measure, given a black eye to all bystanders as well. A civilised and morally sensitive society ought not to tolerate using such primitive methods to settle disputes, involving not just thousands of contestants but also millions of by-standers. Religious action might well succeed in finding alternative means to industrial action to secure a morally, socially and economically healthier society. Religious leaders would have to take the lead in both pressing more rigorously for social justice with civic responsibility and helping to find a system of adjudication or mediation which would render arguments between sections of industry amenable to the same orderly and fair process of resolution as we take for granted when individuals have conflicting claims.

THE DEVALUATION OF LIFE

Perhaps an even more disturbing phenomenon calling for the greater involve-ment of religious leaders in public affairs is the problem of the rising tide of violence and its corollary, the cheapening of human life.

Significantly, with the end of the long Vietnam War, and the mercifully short armed conflicts in the Middle East and Cyprus, the world is now without an international war for the first time in decades. But instead of conflicts fought over international frontiers or for military targets, war has now moved into the streets and homes of our cities, into shops and offices, banks and public houses, railway stations on the ground and civilian planes in the skies. Hijacks, kidnaps, car-bombs, letter-bombs, incendiary devices, muggings, vandalism—these words are now among the most common terms in our contemporary vocabulary, bringing the threat of violence in any innocent mailbag to unsuspecting citizens everywhere, and exposing even children as deliberate targets of political blackmail and extortion.

The wave of indiscriminate violence is only one aspect of the current assault on the supreme value of life. There is the threat to life from atomic bomb tests prompted by a false national vanity. There is the ecological peril to our environment which, through our reckless abuse of the bounty of nature in the name of economic progress, threatens to poison our food, pollute our rivers and choke us in the very air we breathe. There is the legalised cheapening of human life; at its inception through wholesale abortions for reasons of personal convenience, at its conclusion through the despatch of the incurably sick and aged urged by the agitators for euthanasia, and—in the period between swaddling clothes and the shroud—through experimentation on humans in the interests of medical science.

If, in an ostensibly civilised society like ours, the absolute sanctity of life can be legally set aside for selfish reasons of national pride, political dogma, material advantage, personal comfort and social convenience, or even for what has been medically justified as "important research procedures", can we be surprised that fanatical or misguided groups or individuals apply the same reasoning, with equal logic, to justify murder and violence for political ends? In a climate of disdain for life, can we wonder there are those who seek political domination or social revolution through terror and anarchy, or engage in extortion by violence to support these or lesser causes?

Worse still, we are now told, often by representatives of the very agencies responsible for the enforcement of law and order, that we will have to learn to live with violence as an accepted fact of modern life.

This is the counsel of despair and the surest prescription for failure. It is like telling a person with a nagging toothache, that he should learn to live with it, instead of repairing to a dentist to have it cured. Or like telling a school committee concerned with the indiscipline of unruly children in a classroom that they must accept the situation, instead of devising ways to improve the training of teachers and children—and perhaps also of parents—in order to eliminate the problem.

The moment society or groups of individuals are prepared to come to terms with injustice, to say "it's too bad; we will have to learn to live with it", then they will indeed have to live—and suffer—with it, for they surrender the will to ameliorate their lot and lose the hope of improving their condition. The great glory of this country in 1940, "its finest hour", was precisely that its people were not prepared to come to terms with evil.

Unless religious teachings help to restore the infinite regard for the sanctity of life, we will face catastrophe; as our cities turn into jungles, and terrorist gangsters, holding up to ransom governments, citizens and including even children, will rule the world at will in an orgy of human self-destruction. I stress religious teachings, for only religion postulates that no life is expendable, that life being infinite in value is indivisible, making one human being worth as much as a million others and conferring on each equally infinite value.

THE PRESENT IN THE PERSPECTIVE OF ETERNITY

I have started with the Prophets and I will conclude with them by reference to the usage of the language in which they spoke and wrote. In classical Hebrew there is strictly no present tense; the verb has only the past and future tenses. The Hebrew genius cannot conceive of the reality of the present except as reflected in the traditions of the past and the destiny of the future. Herein lies the great failing of our society. Living neither on the wisdom of the past nor on the vision of the future, we concern ourselves only with the immediate needs of the present.

Transcending the problems and anxieties of the moment is man's quest for self-preservation and immortality—his contribution to the ultimate realisation of the human destiny.

By consecrating public life no less than individual conduct, religious perceptions and commitments can offer our stricken generation the solace, the strength and the faith to see ourselves horizontally bound together as human brothers in a fellowship of peace and vertically linked with the generations before and after us to consummate our human evolution, from the time we were *created* in the image of our Maker to the time we shall *live* in His image.

LETTER TO THE QUEEN

On 22 April 1975 the Chief Rabbi and his wife were the guests for dinner and an over-night stay at Windsor Castle at the invitation of the Queen. Also present were the Queen Mother, the Duke of Edinburgh and Prince Andrew. The first Chief Rabbi ever to be so honoured, he presented the Queen with a large mounted frame featuring the original Orders of Service issued by his office to mark the Coronations of Herself (1953), her parents King George VI and Queen Elizabeth (1937), her grandparents King George V and Queen Mary (1911), and her great-grandparents King Edward VII and Queen Alexandra (1901) as well as a prayer for her great-great-grandmother Queen Victoria on the occasion of the Indian Mutiny (1858).

April 24, 1975

MADAM,

In searching for adequate words to articulate the feelings of my wife and myself following our exhilarating experience at Windsor Castle, the Psalmist readily comes to my aid: "All glorious is the king's daughter within the palace . . . ; they shall be led with gladness and rejoicing as they enter into the royal palace" (Ps. 45:14, 16).

These verses truly express the sentiments evoked by the unique honour of the invitation, the superb hospitality we enjoyed throughout our stay, including the extraordinary care taken over our religious requirements, the sheer delight of the distinguished company, crowned by the most charming and gracious manner in which Your Majesty and the members of Your Family entertained us and guided us through the splendours of the Castle and its fascinating treasures.

When set against the historical background of our people's millennial tribulations as well as the anxiety and loneliness of so many of our co-religionists today, our visit was for us a particularly moving event. We found in Your noble example of human fellowship the balm of hope and the restoration of faith in the invincible goodness of humanity.

The memento it was our privilege to present to You encapsules our fervent prayer which we constantly recite for You, as we have done for Your Royal Forebears, that the Almighty may bless You, together with Your illustrious Family, "to preserve You in life, guard You and deliver You from all sorrow and trouble"—a prayer now of very deeply personal meaning to my wife and myself, as we will for ever recall and recount our thrilling experience with the most profound gratitude.

With loyal and affectionate respects, I am, Madam,

Most sincerely yours,

(signed)   I. JAKOBOVITS

Her Majesty The Queen
Windsor Castle

Chapter Five

PASSOVER AND NEW YEAR BROADCASTS

PASSOVER AND NEW YEAR BROADCASTS

By a tradition almost as old as religious broadcasting, the BBC has allotted 15 minutes twice a year to successive Chief Rabbis for seasonal talks prior to every Rosh Hashanah and Passover. Lately some of these programmes have been varied to include occasional interviews and discussions on Jewish religious topics.

Passover Broadcast 1967

"Acting Today, Asking Tomorrow"

Just over 30 years ago I experienced a personal Passover. I lived in a country ruled by a tyrant more cruel than any Pharaoh. The "Destroyer" stalked the land and eventually plucked out of life God's first-born by the million—in history's most diabolical slaughter. Providentially, the "Angel of Death" passed over me, allowing me to find refuge in this land of freedom. How great is my joy and pride, therefore, now to return to this land of my salvation, coming here no longer as a refugee but as spiritual head of Britain's historic Jewish community, itself the only major European Jewish community to have been passed over in safety by the fearful holocaust.

Nor can I pass over this first opportunity since taking up my office a few days ago to address myself to a host of fellow-citizens in this gallant country without saluting the courage and compassion of the British people in opening this hospitable island to me and thousands of my co-religionists in Jewry's darkest hour. We shall tell the story of this "Passover" from oppression to freedom to our children and children's children for generations to come, even as we have told our children, at this season, the story of our first Passover in Egypt since times immemorial.

For us it is a religious duty annually to relate the exciting account of that historic episode to our children. We do so at a special service celebrated in our homes known as the "Seder". Let me take you to one of our homes as it will look tomorrow night at the opening of our eight-day Festival. There you will see a festively laid table. Around it are seated all the members of the family, often together with many guests and even strangers. On this occasion we want even the poorest and the loneliest to experience the joys and comforts of a home. In an elaborate ritual, you can watch the entire company re-enacting the actual experiences of our forefathers. We eat the unleavened "Matzah", the bread of affliction, and the "bitter herbs" to dramatise our identification with the past. Into the centre of it all we place our children.

Soon you will hear the youngest child opening the discussion on the Exodus, asking four set questions which begin: *Ma Nishtana Halayla Hazeh Mikol Haleyloth*, "Why is this night different from all other nights?" In the practice of our faith, we want to involve our children, not as onlookers but as participants. We believe that essentially Judaism cannot be taught—it must be caught. We encourage our children to ask questions, for no stimulus to education is more effective than the development of curiosity. Only a questioning, inquisitive mind is drawn to the adventure of study and exploration.

Let me speak to you, then, on the place of questions in religious faith.

The ceremony I have just described, with its emphasis on the children's questions, is based on a biblical verse which reads, literally translated: "And it shall be, when your son asks you tomorrow, saying, what is this? And you shall tell him, with a mighty hand the Lord brought us out from Egypt, the home of slavery." What a strange wording, this, "When your son asks you *tomorrow*." Why doesn't he ask today, now, at the time when he observes all these Passover rites? Why, according to the biblical text, does he wait with his question about the meaning of "all this" ritual until tomorrow? First, it seems to be assumed, the child participates in the paschal celebration; he eats his Matzah, he hears the story, he re-lives the Exodus, and he observes all the religious requirements. And only tomorrow, on the next day, he asks questions and enquires about the why's and wherefore's.

This is exactly how Judaism views the relations between faith and reason, between religious practice and enquiry. We have the same idea in a familiar song sung at the conclusion of every Sabbath and festival service in the synagogue. It starts with the words: "There is no one like our God" and then it continues "Who is like our God?" First the declaration of faith: "There is no one like our God" and only then the questioning of faith: "Who is like our God?" Similarly, when our people three and a half thousand years ago witnessed the revelation of God's law at Mount Sinai, they responded to the Divine summons, in the words of the Bible: *Na'aseh venishma*, "We will do and we will hear". First we shall do, and submit to the law; then we shall hear and understand.

Of course, we want our children to ask questions. Judaism has never shared the view that ignorance is bliss, or that creed and credulity go together. We have always taught that you cannot have religious living without religious thinking. The whole fabric of our religious literature is made up of the warp and woof of questions and answers, of challenge and response, of doubt and resolution. We have never advocated blind faith, shuttered in darkness against the discriminating rays of reason.

But the sequence is crucial. What matters is the "order", the very translation of the Hebrew word "*Seder*". Reason placed before faith blights it. Let me explain: Imagine we were to expect our children to be good and honest only after they understand the reasons why. They would probably become habitual delinquents long before they would recognise the virtues of upright living. You surely know of parents who refuse to give their children proper religious education on the specious grounds that they don't wish to indoctrinate or prejudice them. Let them make up their own minds when they are old enough to make a choice, these parents argue, not realising that their children, brought up without any meaningful religion, never will have a choice. For you cannot choose what you do not know. They would have to be an Abraham or a Moses if they were really expected to discover God and His law on their own.

Within our own community we often hear complaints that the burdens of Judaism are too hard to carry. The observant Jew refrains from working, even from driving or smoking, on the Sabbath, he restricts his food to a special diet, he imposes on his children ten hours or more of religious instruction a week in addition to their secular studies. All this is too irksome, they say. Now, the remarkable thing is that these complaints always come from people who themselves don't observe the law. It is a burden only for those who don't carry it. Jews who practise Judaism don't find these impositions burdensome. On the contrary, they find Jewish living joyful and inspiring, lifting the burdens of life and investing human existence with meaning and cheerfulness.

It all depends, therefore, on what comes first. If critical enquiry precedes religious action, if reason is placed before faith, then the result will be little reason and less faith. Religion from the distance of the outsider looks forbidding and exacting. But if practice comes before questions, the judgement will be quite different, for it is based on experience, not on speculation.

Let me broaden this thought a little, and extend it to the moral discipline of life. We live in a permissive society. Many believe we should leave it to each individual to work out his own salvation without pressures or restraints. They encourage people to question the moral order of the past before accepting it. Little wonder that so many young people, putting reason before practice, never find any reason to practise the moral teachings of the past. Now, isn't it odd that we use this argument only in the spheres of religion and morals? Just think of what our civilisation would look like if we were to use the same reasoning in the realms of science or literature or philosophy; where would we be, if we refused to indoctrinate our children with the accomplishments of earlier generations, saying, let them discover for themselves the laws of nature, or the beauty of poetry, or the rules of logic? Did you ever hear anyone say it is wrong to use modern gadgets unless you discover them for yourself, or to take advantage of the technological marvels of electronics unless you understand their workings? No, we first accept the achievements of the great discoverers, inventors, writers and thinkers of the past, and only then we ask questions on how and why. We know that every person cannot be an Aristotle, or a Shakespeare, or an Einstein, and if we had to discount the heritage of the past and start from scratch in every generation, the human race could never move forward, and we would remain perpetual cave-dwellers and sun-worshippers. Without tradition, without accepting the past before questioning it, there can be no progress, no human civilisation and no moral order. Nor can there be any true and firm religious faith unless we accept and practise it first, and only then search for reasons and meaning.

Let me conclude with a thought which is especially topical this Passover. Usually, the Christian Easter occurs during the week of our Passover, since the dates for both festivals are determined on a similar basis of a complex solar–lunar calculation. But this year is an exception in which Easter and Passover are separated by a month, an exception which last happened in 1959 and will not occur again until 1970. Perhaps this occasional discrepancy is to remind us of what divides us as well as what unites us in our heritage of faith, morals and tradition. However many interests our religions have in common, however close we want to be in promoting inter-faith understanding, the distinctions between us must always remain evident. A world in which all religions lose their distinctiveness would be as dull as one in which all human beings were identical, and as ineffective as a machine in which all parts were equal. It is the very uniqueness of each faith which endows it with an invincible power over man to the point of total commitment in life and martyrdom in death.

That, after all, is what the original Passover was all about: the right of a people to be released from the bondage of uniformity and the freedom to worship God in its own unique manner. Wishing my brethren everywhere a happy and kosher Pesach, I pray that this Passover may strengthen our faith to triumph over all questions and doubts, and that it may proclaim the message of true freedom for all God's children, so that each of us may sing, in the words of the Song of Moses after crossing the Red Sea: "This is my God, and I shall glorify Him; the God of my father, and I shall exalt him."

Passover Broadcast 1968

"Promise and Fulfilment"

The Jewish Passover is probably the oldest continuously observed festival in the world. For well over 3,000 years now we Jews, wherever we lived, have celebrated this festival every year at this season in a more or less identical form, eating the same unleavened bread and bitter herbs, drinking the same four cups of wine, and relating the same story to our children as did our ancestors since time immemorial.

What have we been celebrating for all these many centuries with so much fervour and solemnity, and what are we still celebrating wherever Jewish homes are to be found? Of course, every schoolchild knows—or ought to know—that Passover commemorates the Exodus from Egypt, the deliverance of the Children of Israel from slavery to freedom. Nevertheless, what we recall at this season is not just some outstanding event in our early history. Nor is our Passover merely a kind of Jewish independence festival, marking the anniversary of our people's emergence from the mists of antiquity to appear on the arena where the drama of man is being acted out and in which the Jewish people have been active players ever since.

The real significance of this millennial festival lies far beyond its historical meaning as our national birthday, or even its homage to freedom by recalling our liberation from the bondage to Pharaoh. Above all, Passover celebrates the redemption of a Divine promise. What we stress particularly in our festivities is that the Children of Israel were delivered in response to a pledge God had given to their fathers. The Exodus from Egypt fulfilled God's word to Abraham: "Know for sure that your seed will be a stranger in a land that is not theirs, where they will serve and be afflicted for four hundred years, . . . and afterwards they shall come out." It fulfilled God's word to Jacob two generations later: "Fear not to go down to Egypt; for I will there make of you a great nation. I will go down with you into Egypt and I will also surely bring you up again;" and of the promise to Moses when his people's suffering was at its height: "And I will come down to deliver them out of the hand of the Egyptians, and bring them up out of that land into the land flowing with milk and honey."

There can be few prophecies more extraordinary than these. Here, our people's first ancestor, Abraham, long before his son Isaac was even born, was told that his descendants would endure centuries of oppression and then be liberated. Similar, but perhaps even more striking, is the warning given to the Children of Israel in the wilderness, that if they disobeyed God's law, He would exile them among the nations, followed by the reassurance that God would always remember His covenant with them and eventually restore them to the land of their fathers. There is something almost uncanny in the devastating accuracy with which these forecasts were fulfilled, sometimes thousands of years later.

Just imagine someone were to prophesy and warn the citizens of some modern nation that because of their moral shortcomings they would be utterly defeated by some foreign invaders, deported from their country and scattered all over the world; that even as exiles they would maintain their consciousness as a people belonging together, and then perhaps after a few thousand years return again to their land of origin! That is precisely what the Jewish people were told nearly three and a half thousand years ago, and what incredibly has come to pass.

Passover, then, celebrates primarily the vindication of Divine Providence. We rejoice at this season not just because God redeemed our ancestors but because He redeemed His pledge. Passover protests against the notion that history is just a haphazard string of events. The Festival proclaims that behind the unfolding of the human destiny, that underlying the slow and often tortuous evolution of man's civilisation, lies a master-plan designed by a Creator. History is nothing but the ongoing encounter between God's purpose and man's response, sometimes supporting and sometimes defying this purpose, but always with the eventual triumph of Providence over the worst man can do to impede his progress.

Passover has gripped the hearts of our people to this day more than any other historic celebration for the very reason that it demonstrated the reality of the covenant between God and Israel—or, perhaps more broadly, between Providence and history.

All this may well be a notion rather remote from the ideas and stirrings of our age. Most of our contemporaries believe that history is made by statesmen, not by Divine promises, by popular elections rather than God's election of a people, and by massive protests and demonstrations more than the lonely pleadings of spiritual leaders, however passionate. In our predominantly secularist society there is little room for the hope of human betterment and redemption beyond the yearning for better living standards, for more enjoyment and less work. In the light of the recent bitter debate on coloured immigration in Britain, and of the ghastly racial strife in America during the past week, how many of us on either side of these conflicts have really hoped and prayed in all sincerity for a solution brought about not by a change of laws but by a change of heart, whereby every human being will look upon his fellow, of whatever colour or creed, as a brother whose welfare is as precious to me as my own?

The set-backs to human progress are sometimes so tragic and so staggering that people of faltering faith may be forgiven if they despair altogether of man ever advancing to the goals set for him. The Jewish people certainly, continually exposed to slaughter, hatred and persecution, might have been excused if they had surrendered their confidence in human progress long ago. It is surely not easy to resist the temptation to despair when in a country like Poland, where millions of Jews were done to death only a generation ago in history's worst slaughter, there is now a recrudescence of anti-Semitism against the pitiful remnant of some 20,000 Jews who survived.

And yet, if we had ever given up hope in the ultimate redemption of man we could not have survived. Perhaps I may use a trifling, though topical, analogy to illustrate the point. Think of the tragedy of a farmer who suffered an outbreak of foot-and-mouth disease and the slaughter of his livestock, followed by the re-infection of his newly stocked cattle and their destruction. Could he survive if he were not confident that he would be luckier the third time?

Similarly, human history cannot move forward unless we believe, notwithstanding all our disappointments and set-backs, that in the end the promise of progress and salvation will be fulfilled, that the Divine plan for man's destiny will be realised.

That exactly is what Passover is all about. That is why, to my mind, Jews everywhere were stirred by the outcome of the events in the Holy land of last June to such a peak of solemn exhilaration. For, like Passover, the really stirring significance of the event, at least for religious Jews, lay not in the conquest of territory nor even in the relief of 2½ million Jews from mortal danger, but rather in the vindication of a Divine promise, in the redemption of God's pledge that our people would be restored to Zion and Jerusalem, even if we had to wait, often in martyrdom, for 1,900 long years to witness this fulfilment.

I do not conceal the fact that there are secularists in our midst who failed to appreciate the Providential aspect of this wondrous fulfilment of biblical prophecy and instead saw the whole drama only in political and military terms. Nor can I withhold my pained rebuke of those who are insufficiently touched by the unspeakable misery and indignity of the refugees—whether Arab refugees displaced from their homes in the Holy Land, or deprived Jews in and from Arab lands; at this season need we be reminded of the biblical injunction: "You shall not oppress the stranger, for you were strangers in the land of Egypt"? Nevertheless, I firmly believe that what we witnessed was the unfolding of God's plan as announced through His messengers acknowledged by all monotheistic faiths, and that, however tedious our progress, ultimately Jews and Arabs, unhappily at war for twenty years, will again live creatively together to bring peace and prosperity to the Middle East, just as the prospects of peace have suddenly brought hope to the Far East in a land tortured by war and terror for twenty years.

That, then, is the special challenge of this Passover to Jews and Gentiles alike. History does not make sense unless we believe in some master design assuring its forward thrust to some pre-ordained objective. The miseries of man, the agony of refugees dislodged from their homes, the tribulations of those oppressed because of their faith or colour, the anguish of the poor and the sick—all this would far outweigh and eclipse the benefits of the health, comfort and security enjoyed by some if we did not believe that ultimately out of the travail of human suffering will be born a human order dedicated to freedom and cemented in peace; that in the end every piece in the multi-coloured jigsaw puzzle of our bright and dark experiences will fall into place in accordance with the drawing of its designer. Over three thousand years ago one such piece fell into place; in our own present-day experience others may have been brought into position; and every time any one of us, whether as individuals or as nations, promotes the realisation of God's vision and promise, every time we help to eliminate hatred or crime or oppression and to advance human understanding and unity, we have some share in completing the picture of a human family, created in God's image as we, His children, were meant to be.

With prayers that all men everywhere may soon rejoice in a universal festival of freedom, I greet my Jewish listeners with the blessing for a happy Passover, and the time-honoured wish of the season: "Next Year in Jerusalem Rebuilt!"

"Creation and Judgement"

The message of *Rosh Hashanah*, though thousands of years old, has never been more relevant than in our turbulent age. The Festival combines two distinct aspects: it traditionally marks the anniversary of the creation of the world, as described in the Book of Genesis; and we also observe it as the Day of Judgement before God. On the one hand, it proclaims our *origin* as children of God, and on the other hand, our *destiny* as having to render an account for our actions.

The fact that we are the product not of chance but of choice, that we exist by design and not by accident, renders us liable to judgement. For only that which is deliberately created can be asked why and for what purpose it exists and whether it has fulfilled the intentions of its creator.

Our age is witnessing new creation on a scale more vast and dramatic than ever before. Whether the convulsive events around us represent the death agony of a dying civilisation or the birth pangs of a new era, they certainly indicate the most momentous change from one order to another ever seen in a single generation.

The year we are just concluding in the Jewish calendar has made an especially massive contribution to fanning the storms of change. It was a year in which we heard, as at every birth of new life, much crying; it was an exceptionally noisy year. Throughout the year we heard a cacophany of deafening sounds and shrieks: the murderous bombs and mortar shells exploding in war-torn Vietnam; the rumbling of invading tanks brutally crushing a brave people gasping for freedom; the heart-rending groans of Biafran children starving to death; the shattering explosions of terrorist mines ripping peaceful civilians in Israel, and the nearby cries of despair from Arab refugees drained of all human dignity in the world's worst breeding-grounds of hate; assassins' shots snuffing out the lives of great world leaders; the confused din of wild demonstrations against universities and governments and other assorted symbols of authority or discipline; not to forget the world-wide chorus of fierce press campaigns to drown out the ancient voice of ecclesiastical fiat.

Of course, history never stood still or mute. The world always recreated itself, with change as the only really constant factor in the human experience. But what has changed is the speed of change. Today there are more changes and innovations in a single lifetime than previously in the whole of recorded human history. For instance, it is estimated that we now double the sum total of scientific knowledge every eight years. That means, we gain in eight years as much new knowledge about the universe we live in as was previously accumulated in all the millennia of man's search for knowledge since the dawn of history. In other spheres, too, the acceleration of change is hardly less extreme. Within the last couple of decades we have certainly seen greater changes in some of our religious, moral, social and scientific thinking than had previously occurred in many centuries of slow evolution. Nowadays we all occupy grandstand seats to watch—at closer range than ever before—the birth of a new world, the creation of a new order.

This is where the twin meaning of our New Year comes in. In the Jewish view there can be no creation without judgement. Even God Himself judged what He had created: "And God saw all that He had made, and behold it was very good", as we read at the end of the creation story in Genesis. Hence, the dividing line between the old year and the new one to which it gives birth is the Day of Judgement. How much more so when an entire era expires to pass on the gift of life to a new era.

The knowledge that there must be judgement safeguards the new creation from crippling malformation or premature death. How many fatal blunders, how much misery and failure, could be avoided if only we remembered our liability to ultimate judgement before we act, if only we associated the risk of every creation with the certainty of being judged eventually! Recent events in the world's two mightiest seats of power in the East and in the West provide sad and dramatic evidence. If the Eastern bloc rulers had been aware that they would one day be held to account by their own people for their inhuman betrayal of their Czechoslovak allies just as surely as Stalin was brought to judgement for his crimes and political blunders by his successors, would they not have shrunk back from their cynical abuse of power? And if the Free World's leading ruler had realised in time that the massive judgement before the bar of history would compel him to bow out of his exalted office, might he not have listened to the cooing of the doves at least as sympathetically as to the crying of the hungry hawks?

The same surely applies to all of us, at whatever level of life or society, whether we sit in the cockpit of leadership at the controls in man's flight through history, or we are seated further back as mere passengers, watching the panorama of life fleeting by beneath us. Only by the constant realisation that a judgement awaits us can we ensure that we use our talents and energies to create and not to destroy. Only by remembering always that we are accountable for all our actions, that life is not meant to be just an idle pursuit of carefree relaxation and amusement, can we avoid the irredeemable tragedy of wasted lives, of leaving this world without enriching it, or worse still of impeding man's progress to his destination.

We talked of creation and judgement. Judgement before whom? Who is to judge what to create and what to destroy, what to discard of the old world and what to contrive for the new? Here, too, the symbolism of our New Year is to provide the answer. On this solemn Day of Judgement we shall blow the *Shofar*, the ram's horn, at our Divine services. This ram's horn is to remind us of the ram which once replaced Isaac's sacrifice marking the birth of Judaism, or indeed the genesis of monotheism, the belief in God and the brotherhood of man. Nearly five hundred years later the ram's horn was sounded at Mount Sinai, heralding the proclamation of the Ten Commandments and the revelation of God's law to the Children of Israel, at the birth of the moral order which has governed the progress of human civilisation ever since. This ram's horn is a simple, unsophisticated musical instrument which has not changed over the ages. We use it to usher in every New Year, as a reminder that everything we create and achieve will ultimately be judged by the timeless truths which are as valid today as when they were discovered by Abraham and revealed to Moses.

Lately we hear increasingly about a new voice, called the voice of our conscience, competing with the voice of religion as the judge to determine what is right and what is wrong, to define the difference between good and evil. If you are in any doubt, we are told, on what the moral law requires, for instance, on the complex moral questions involved in heart-transplants or in abortions, or on intimate relationships outside marriage and how many children to have inside it, then just consult your conscience and you will have the answer. The clamour today is to worship not God but our conscience, and when the two conflict, let the conscience prevail.

Judaism, as a reliable guide to human conduct, looks elsewhere; it relies no more on the natural law than on the individual conscience. We believe the rules of the moral law can only be established by God as our Supreme Judge; they are not enshrined in any laws of nature or in the capricious whims of the human conscience. If we are really honest with ourselves, don't we often use our conscience merely as a convenient expedient to justify our self-interest? And do not the judgements of our conscience vary with every age and from one individual to another? How reliable can the conscience be when, as we are told, it now tells many priests and other deeply religious people to reject moral teachings to which only ten years ago their conscience demanded conformity with equal insistence?

Is the conscience not often fickle, swayed by the slightest winds of popular propaganda and personal desire, and easily perverted? In our permissive society the conscience tells thousands of young people that they can shape and twist the moral code to their own specifications, so long as they do it in the name of true love and happiness. Behind the Iron Curtain millions are sincerely convinced by their consciences, after adequate indoctrination, that the freedom of the individual must be sacrificed for the good of the state or the social system, and I have little doubt that many Nazis had genuinely believed they were carrying out the dictates of their conscience when they shoved millions of people into gas chambers to promote their insane doctrines of racial purity.

Of course we cherish the refined conscience as man's noblest possession, so long as it is but the instrument through which the Divine composition of virtue and goodness is being played out. As an inner power stronger than any army or police force, the conscience is meant to keep us away from the brink of evil and temptation and to urge us on to acts of righteousness and moral bravery. It is the very essence of our religious belief that the conscience serves not to *make* moral laws but to *enforce* them. We need our conscience not to tell us what is right but, knowing what is right, to make us act accordingly. This is symbolised by the ancient ram's horn, breaking the sound-barriers of time by transmitting to us the echoes of God's voice rebounding from the mountains of Moriah and Sinai. Truth, virtue, honesty and other moral values, though subject to reinterpretation as circumstances change, would be worthless if they did not speak with the same authentic accents in all ages and to every human society, just as the laws of nature are immutable even if our growing understanding and application of them constantly expand the frontiers of science and technology.

It is this stability in the midst of change, this firm judgement in the adventure of creation, which invests true religion with majesty, guiding like a fixed star in the firmament our storm-tossed ship of life across the ocean of history to its ultimate destination.

According to the Jewish tradition, this same ram's horn will also be sounded to proclaim our eventual redemption, the time when all men will acclaim God as their Judge and their conscience as His law-enforcement agent, when every man will see his own happiness in the happiness of his neighbour, the time when "nation shall not lift up sword against nation, neither shall they learn war any more". May this New Year speed the realisation of this unchanging dream of the ages. May it bring freedom to the oppressed, equality to the deprived, peace to those pursued by war and terror, relief to the sick in body, soul or mind, inspiration to all leaders of men, and the joy of fulfilment to Creator and creatures alike.

New Year Broadcast 1969

"Reaching the Moon; Two Perspectives"

The date for the beginning of our year, just like the beginning of every Hebrew month, is fixed to coincide with the New Moon. On this New Year's eve, we may truly speak of the New Moon in a special sense. For new indeed is the moon bearing the footprints of man on its surface, and equally new are the expanded vistas gained by man's spectacular ascent into the heavens, though different evaluations and appraisals may emerge from this conquest of space.

Some have already hailed the moon adventure as the greatest enterprise in the history of man, easily worth the billions of dollars spent on its accomplishment and eclipsing every previous epoch-making event across the expanse of the centuries. But there are others to whom this colossal enterprise appears to be the most extravagant wastage of human and material resources, an enterprise of which they may say: "Never has so much been contributed by so many for so little." Of course, the many-faceted truth is that there is a measure of validity in both conflicting evaluations. There can be no doubt but that man's successfully reaching for the moon represents both the most glorious tribute of all times to human ingenuity, vision, courage and the quest for knowledge, and, at the same time, possibly the most gigantic monument to vainglorious national ambition, reaching a peak of irrelevance in the context of our earthly problems.

Of infinitely greater significance, however, is a similar divergence of judgement in assessing the present state of our terrestrial world around us from the perspective of the moon.

I well recall a fascinating sermon published nearly a decade ago in the American *Reader's Digest*, giving an imaginary account of what the first man to set foot on the moon would see and experience. The spaceman had landed on the powdery surface of the moon, gazed in wonderment and overpowering solitude at the primeval desolation around him, completed his scientific chores, and then, during a moment of contemplation, heard this message in the silence of his soul:

> "You, Astronaut of Earth, are now standing upon an uncontaminated celestial body. Across these dusty plains and in these towering mountains there is not, and never has been, the slightest stain of sin or evil. No lie has yet been told in this silent world. These rocks are unstained by the blood of war. . . . This is the purity of the universe as it was when it left the mighty hand of God."

> At that moment, continues the author, the astronaut raised his eyes to look upon the most beautiful and amazing sight ever to burst upon the vision of man. Up from the sharp horizon of the moon rose the shining orb of Earth. He stood transfixed. His eye in a single moment swept from the snowcapped arctic to the snowcapped antarctic, with the oceans, the continents and the vast blanket of white glistening clouds in between. . . . From this distance it

looked as pure and beautiful and unstained as the moon upon which he stood.
No sign of sin or greed or selfishness or violence could be seen. . . .

Now, how would a preacher who is inspired by the Jewish ethic—which,
as you know, does not believe in the doctrine of Original Sin—how would
he describe this same experience? I believe he would do it in quite different
terms. He would view the empty wastes of the moon not so much as unstained
by any sin or vice but rather as wastes unsanctified by any virtue or noble
deed. True, no lie has yet been told here; but, more to the point, neither has
any truth ever been told or proclaimed in this lifeless world. Here, in these
barren surroundings, no stone has ever borne witness to a feat of heroism
or to an act of self-sacrifice, no site has been hallowed by prayer or love, and
no grandeur of human creativity testifies to the partnership between God and
His creatures in perfecting the universe He created.

Just as a glass half-filled with water strikes optimists as half-full and
pessimists as half-empty, so do the same phenomena of an as yet incomplete
world strike some for what man has achieved and others for what man has
failed to accomplish. To the Jew, with his perennial optimism which assured
his survival in the face of so much adversity, the brilliant orb of Earth far out
beyond the moon's horizon would have induced a proud feeling of exhilaration, not a morbid mood of depression. He would behold it as the one planet
in the vastness of space around him on which, transcending the strife and
crime and vice plaguing it, countless generations have laboured to build a
highly complex civilisation, with its immortal triumphs of the human spirit,
mind and heart, expressed in religion and literature, in art and science, in
industry and social services.

Of course, he could not fail to see moral decadence abounding in our
modern world. In the spurious name of progress, our permissive society has
reincarnated the spirit of our antediluvian ancestors, with their loose morals,
their caveman-like long hair and scant dresses, and even the wild erotic
contortions of their primitive music.

But beneath these shifting sands of passing fads there is much solid rock
of stability and fertile soil of creativity. The rates of divorce, of crime, of
illegitimacy, of drug addiction may be alarming. Some students may delight
in riots, some workers in reckless strikes, some employers in unethical
exploitation, and some politicians in the abuse of power. But there are still
countless homes which are happy and cheerful. The overwhelming majority
of citizens are decent and law-abiding. Most children are born in wedlock,
most students are responsible and eager to get on with their studies, most
workers and employers are dedicated to their jobs, and—I dare say—most
politicians are honest and concerned to promote the welfare of society.

True, on the world scene today, even if one does not look beyond the
banner headlines of our newspapers, which read almost like a modern
version of the Book of Job, we discover that mankind is tormented by many
festering sores. All the major crisis-spots which afflicted the world a year ago
continue unabated to bedevil human relations. The tragic conflicts in the
Middle East, Vietnam, Biafra, Czechoslovakia and the racial strife in America
have all persisted in wreaking terrible havoc during the past twelve months.
To these travails have now been added the ominous Sino-Russian border

clashes in the Far East and the frightening unrest in Northern Ireland in the Near West, with an assortment of riots and hi-jacks and kidnappings elsewhere thrown in for good measure. Judged by these criteria, the contemporary scene and future prospects on our planet look grim indeed.

And yet, from the distant perspective of a man on the moon, the human situation may appear entirely different. For every country at war or in the grip of terror there are dozens at peace. For every agitator plotting aggression or subversion there are hundreds of ordinary people who want to live in harmony with their neighbours. For every pedlar of hate and mischief there are any number of decent folk who practise justice and kindness, who want to live and let live in security and happiness. Even inside the lands convulsed by strife and terror and oppression there are countless peace-loving citizens who harbour no evil against their neighbours. How many Russians, if they knew the full facts, really desire to see Czech freedom brutally suppressed by military occupation, or their own Jewish fellow-citizens subjected to such heartless discrimination and repression? How many Irishmen want religious bigotry and social inequality driven to the brink of civil war? And how many Arabs among the hundred million ringing Israel really thirst for the annihilation of the Jewish State?

If only we used the tremendous amplifying machinery of our mass communications not to publicise the mischief of the few but rather to broadcast the pursuit of law and order and decency by the many, would not the human condition today look far less bleak and be more reassuring? Would not, as a result, the overwhelming majority of upright and peaceful people manage to contain and prevail over the relatively tiny minority of troublemakers, agitators and war-mongers? How much encouragement and strength would be given to our moral resources if only the press and TV cameras turned their spotlight on those of our youth who heroically resist temptation and defy the pressures of unchaste conformity instead of on those who affront human dignity by their shamelessness or cheap exhibitionism. The best defence against the spread of evil, as of any physical infection, lies in quarantine, in isolating it. Unfortunately, we do the opposite. In the hot competition for public attention in our news media, the advantage is always given to the noisy dissident over the quiet upholder of tradition, to the criminal over the law-abiding citizen, to the disturber of peace over the pursuer of peace, to the lustful beast in man over the disciplined best in man. In a ceaseless hunt for excitement serving to entertain, more befitting to the stage and fiction literature, our mass communications magnify the noise of violence and protest and obscenity, whilst muffling the voice of stability and moral sanity.

A personal experience the other day exemplifies this. Following the recent grievous fire at the Al-Aksa Mosque in Jerusalem, when the world press was full with blazing reports on the hysterical calls for a "holy" war against Israel, I issued a public statement expressing the grief of the Jews in Britain over the damage done to one of Islam's holiest shrines. I appealed to responsible Arabs, and particularly to Muslim religious leaders, not to allow the disaster to be used as an instrument for fanning the flames of war and hatred, hoping that instead they would join us in the search and pursuit of a stable peace to assure the happiness of all peoples and the safety of all holy places in the region we commonly treasured as our national homes and birthplaces. But, alas, although I believe I expressed the yearning of far more people than did those who sought to whip up hatred and violence in the name of religion, the cry for war was more newsworthy and therefore widely publicised, while the plea for peace was all but ignored in the mass media.

Only last week Sir Peter Medawar, in a presidential address before the British Association for the Advancement of Science, justly decried the prophets of gloom who blamed our science and technology for the deterioration of the world. We cannot but endorse his ringing challenge to those who surrendered their faith in human progress, although we may not altogether agree with his assertion that "today we are conscious that human history is only just beginning. Only in the past five hundred years have human beings begun to be, in the biological sense, a success." We believe that the history of human civilisation began when man first resolved to be God-like in making our earth different from the changeless sterility of the moon, and we believe that civilisation will continue to advance so long as there are people yearning and working for a better world in which we rejoice in the happiness of our neighbours as in our own, placing mortal life into the service of immortal creations, knowledge into the service of moral and social advance, and the brotherhood of man into the service of our common Father. May the New Year find us worthy to be His partners in fashioning the world as He intended, a world in which, as our New Year liturgy has it, "The just shall rejoice, the upright shall exult, and the pious shall be jubilant in song, when all wickedness shall be wholly consumed like smoke and the rule of arrogance shall pass away from the earth."

Passover Broadcast 1970

"Racial Equality—What can Jews Contribute?"

"This is the bread of affliction which our fathers ate in the land of Egypt . . ."

With this chant we shall commence our Passover festivities at our Seder tables in Jewish homes all over the world, as we point at the unleavened bread which will be our staple diet for eight days and which symbolises the bondage of our ancestors in Egypt.

In the world of the twentieth century, 3,500 years later, there are many millions in bondage who still eat the bread of affliction and poverty, suffering persecution and discrimination—whether they be coloured immigrants in this country, black people in America and South Africa, or Jews in the Soviet Union who are denied their religious freedom and are severed from the rest of their people. But, alas, the fate of all these is not relieved by redemption nor remembered by any Passover celebrations to make the privileged feel the plight of the underprivileged.

This year the Jewish community in Britain will follow Passover by the observance of a special Sabbath—dedicated to the theme of race relations, and I have asked ministers of synagogues all over the country to devote their sermons that day to this subject.

The two events really belong together, for Passover and race relations are closely connected. The Bible itself relates the experience of the Exodus from Egypt with the humane treatment of the alien and the disenfranchised. "And a stranger you shall not wrong, nor shall you oppress him, for you were strangers in the Land of Egypt." The very Passover laws, as detailed in the Second Book of Moses, stress this cardinal message of the Festival: "One law shall be unto him who is homeborn and unto the stranger that dwells with you."

Racial discrimination is a modern phenomenon. Previously, the oppression of one group by another—which has marred man's history from the beginning —was caused mainly by national, social or religious differences. It was left to our advanced civilisation to add the least consequential and most unreasonable of all human divisions (race or colour) as an excuse for persecution. It is now among the most acute problems confronting us here and elsewhere.

As a people, Jews were the first victims of racial discrimination. Only lately have others adopted terms like "ghetto" or "genocide" from the Jewish experience. Over 3,000 years earlier, Jews were also the first to find and proclaim the antidote to this poison: the doctrine that all men are equal.

In the Hebrew Bible no law occurs more frequently than the consideration due to the non-Israelite; thirty-six times it enjoins us to respect the stranger, to treat him as an equal, and to share one's joy and bounty with him. The Golden Rule of the Law of Moses "Love your neighbour as yourself" is expressly followed by the instruction: "But the stranger that dwells with you shall be unto you as one born amongst you, and you shall love him as yourself." There exists no more ringing and reasoned testimony to the brotherhood and equality of man than the immortal utterances of our Prophets: "Have we not all one Father, has not one God created us?... " and "Are you not as the children of the Ethiopians unto me ... ?" Colour-blindness indeed!

Even religious rights were not to be exclusive. Thus Solomon, in dedicating the Temple, prayed: "Moreover, concerning the stranger that is not of Thy people Israel ... , when he shall come and pray toward this house, hear Thou in heaven ... and do according to all that the stranger calls to Thee for."

The air of racial tolerance breathes through the whole of Jewish law and history. Judaism is in contrast with other faiths which declare theirs to be the sole path to salvation. Spurning missionary designs and regarding devout adherents of any monotheistic faith as "saints of the nations of the world", we even discourage conversions except upon a sincere acceptance of Jewish belief and practice, an absence of ulterior motives, and an awareness of the sacrifices involved in becoming a Jew. But on these conditions admission to Judaism is open to any person without discrimination. Nothing could be more baseless than to brand Judaism as racist; the truth is patently demonstrated by the fact that any person, of whatever race, colour or previous creed, can embrace Judaism.

Consonant with these teachings, the State of Israel today undoubtedly represents the most successful endeavour in the world of the fusion of diverse human elements. Among the Jews there—themselves a conglomeration of many ethnic admixtures, and despite their kaleidoscopic variety of origin and background, covering the entire spectrum from white to dark-skinned, oriental to occidental, and primitive to highly sophisticated people—the process of integration and the elimination of prejudice is already more advanced after two decades than in America and elsewhere after a century of enlightenment. The Arabs, too, enjoy equal rights as citizens, subject only to national security in a land under continuous siege and still facing the threat of terror, invasion and extermination at the terrible cost of so many precious lives on both sides of the tragic conflict.

In this country the Jewish community is also being increasingly involved in the problems of race relations. Many Jewish social workers and philanthropists as well as ministers are rendering valuable services in this field. During the past year the Jewish Board of Deputies set up a special Working Party which has now issued an important Report of findings and recommendations for a campaign to intensify the Jewish involvement, to be launched on the special Sabbath to which I have already referred.

The Jewish attitude, then, in theory and in practice, is unequivocal and uncompromising. Where it may differ from current movements and policies is not on objectives or the urgency to attain them, but on methods and nuances of emphasis. Of course, Judaism is firmly committed to seek racial equality by legislation and education. But it would be an illusion to rely on laws alone as the answer to such a complex human problem. Legislation cannot change hearts. It usually levels down and seldom levels up. Moreover, the cultivation of human relations is an organic process which cannot produce instant fruit.

Equally unrealistic is the sole reliance on protests and demonstrations, particularly when made from a safe distance. Jews played a leading role in sparking and supporting the civil rights movement in America, and they have learnt to their cost how easily such a movement can degenerate into large-scale violence and bitter prejudice in reverse, feeding the very fires of extremism and racial hatred it was meant to extinguish.

But it is on the basic philosophy of human relations that Judaism can and must make its most significant positive contribution. The curse of our age is that it postulates rights rather than duties. People are conditioned to think and clamour of what society owes to them, not of what they owe to society. In the moral vocabulary of Judaism, as indeed in classical Hebrew, there is no word for rights. In the constitution of the Bible there are only obligations, not entitlements. Its Decalogue is a list of Ten Commandments, not a Bill of Human Rights, and its charity legislation obligates the rich to give to the poor, not the poor to demand support from the rich. Why, inquires the Talmud, does mankind derive from a single progenitor, Adam? "So that no man can say 'My father was greater than yours'." The answer is not: "So that every man shall claim 'My father was as great as yours'." Significantly, again, the ideal is not for the "inferior", the underprivileged, to *claim* equality, but for the "superior" to *grant* equality.

The world today is plagued by a restiveness which springs from constant incitement and agitation, focused only on demands. Society will not be healed of this social sickness, nor will it achieve human equality, until we learn to assert duties at our expense before asserting rights at the expense of others.

Jewish history has vindicated this approach. Jews, in the Western world at any rate, have secured their emancipation not by violent activism or noisy protest. They gradually overcame discrimination and prejudice by a passion for education, by fierce patriotism, by ambition to serve society through scientific, commercial and social enterprise, by the extraordinary stability of family life, and by holding the individual responsible for the good name of the community, denouncing any misdeed in public as a "Chilul Ha-Shem", a profanation of the Divine Name.

Judaism clearly insists, then, that we help wipe out the evil of racial discrimination by word and deed—whether by promoting enlightened legislation or by treating our coloured brethren with the same consideration and humanity as we would wish to be accorded to ourselves.

In addition, Jews could and should make three specific contributions:

1. To study and make available the relevant lessons from the Jewish experience in securing civil rights and social integration under conditions similar, though admittedly not altogether analogous, to the colour problem of today.
2. To replace the focus on rights by the emphasis on duties in the moral orientation of our campaigns for social justice. The present imbalance between the demand to take and the willingness to give may well render the price of the resultant strife and bitterness greater than the gain in the struggle for racial equality.

3. To preach and practise the Biblical ideal of the brotherhood of man founded, as it must be, on the Fatherhood of God. Only by strengthening the religious conscience can the heart of man eventually be reformed to accept human equality unreservedly.

Last week's high drama in space stirred the hearts of all men in a curiously contrasting manner. Whilst it sadly proved how much more readily people are excited when things go wrong rather than when they go right, the universal concern and involvement also poignantly illustrated the grandeur of man in making brotherhood a reality.

The festival of Passover provides us not only with the bread of past affliction and ordeal to unite our families and our people. It also looks forward to the ideals of the future when, in the words of the song with which I began, *Leshana Habaa Bnei Chorin*: next year we shall all be free men, redeemed from the scourge of war, hatred and tragedy to enjoy the blessings of peace, liberty and equality.

Passover Broadcast 1971

"The Relevance of Religion"

Passover is our oldest festival. We have celebrated it in essentially the same manner ever since our ancestors were delivered from their Egyptian bondage some 34 centuries ago. The major theme of the festival is freedom: certainly one of the most topical subjects today, when scores of new nations and millions of human beings have tasted liberty for the first time, and when countless other millions still cry out for freedom and equality.

Yet our celebration is really an extraordinary exercise in irrelevance. What can be more irrelevant than to celebrate in 1971 an event which took place about 1,400 years before the Common Era? Year after year, even in the darkest times of persecution and desolation, our people rejoiced at this season in the liberation of our forefathers that occurred in bygone days. They praised God for blessings which were not theirs. Even at this moment, there are numerous Jewish families in Soviet Russia and other lands of oppression who will celebrate Passover in their homes as best they can, hailing the gift of freedom to our ancestors although they themselves groan under its suppression. When they raise their cups of wine in thanksgiving for freedom, could their festivity be more irrelevant to their own experience?

Let me therefore this evening present to you some thoughts on the relevance of religion, for relevance is the big obsession of our times. In art, in literature, in music, in fashions, as in science, economics, politics—it is the contemporary that dominates. Only what is relevant to our present-day experience, to current tastes and needs, really matters. Relevance is also the great gauntlet thrown down in challenge to our religious leadership. People have no use for religion unless it relates to the problems of our daily existence.

Responding to this challenge, spiritual guides of all denominations apply masterly ingenuity to prove the relevance of their faith. This search for relevance is the constant theme of the pulpiteer. For the modern preacher, successful communication is determined, above all, by his skill in relating religious teaching to the contemporary condition of man.

It was not always so. The horizons of past generations were not quite so restricted to the needs and concerns of the moment. Their utopian dreams looked beyond solving the immediate problems besetting their particular age. In their vision of an ideal world they aimed for more than shorter working hours and greater material prosperity—maximum enjoyment with minimum toil. And their religious perspectives, encompassing such distant goals as redemption and the hereafter, could scarcely be further removed from the physical wants of the here-and-now.

This is not to say that in its unworldliness and former unconcern with relevance, religion should not be blamed with major responsibility for tolerating all too long the injustices and social evils rampant throughout the period of religious dominance. But this flashback to the past does contrast all the more strikingly with the present religious obsession with relevance. The desire to be relevant is not only an altogether new phenomenon of very recent times; it has replaced the former stance of irrelevance with a vengeance.

Judaism, it may fairly be claimed, has always striven to strike a balance between these extremes, if not to reconcile them. While completely this-worldly in outlook, its focus is as far removed from the contemporary preoccupation with relevance as it is from Christianity's former irrelevance.

The very range of classical Jewish teachings—from labour legislation to race relations—indicates how immediately and extensively Judaism relates to contemporary issues. The discovery of this relevance is neither contrived to suit the clamour of our times nor prompted by the need to dress up Judaism in a topical garb. Anyone familiar with the Hebrew Bible, the Talmud and all later Rabbinic writings knows that these subjects have always been the principal ingredients of Judaism. No preacher's art is required to reveal the relevance of Jewish law and thought to the most pressing social and moral concerns of our days. Any sourcebook or textbook of Judaism, however dated, will confirm this.

But all this cannot obscure the essentially irrelevant streak in Judaism. It refuses to allow relevance to be used as a yardstick to establish its value, or as a measure to determine what is important and what is worth preserving in our ancestral faith. It emphatically rejects the notion that religion serves primarily as an expedient to solve the problems of our day.

On the contrary. In the past it was the peculiar distinction of the Jew that he saw the purpose of his life not in terms of the contemporary experience in which he suffered or prospered, but in terms of his place in the overall realisation of the Jewish and human destiny. Just as classical Hebrew has no present tense for the verb, speaking of action only as belonging to the past or to the future, so did the Jew eliminate the present as an experience of intrinsic significance. It was regarded as a passing stage between past and future, whereby life assumed meaning only in so far as it perpetuated the traditions of the past and sustained the hope of a perfect future.

Thus, when the medieval Jew yearned and prayed for the return of his people to the Holy Land and the rebuilding of the Temple in Jerusalem, the vision he had in mind had very little relevance to the prospects of a happier and freer life for himself or even his children. He projected his past heritage and future hopes to "the end of Days", however many generations might have to pass before their realisation. He would neither seek nor see any essential relationship between his own fortunes or misfortunes and the ideal society for which his faith induced him to pray and strive. His Judaism was not so utilitarian as to provide promised short-term solutions to problems, however agonising, which bedevilled his generation. Nor did he cherish his religious observances, imposing on himself far-reaching restrictions of diet, work, marriage and other freedoms, by asking himself: "What benefit do I derive from this; how will such a discipline help to make my life easier and happier?" Much as his religion governed his outlook and most of his activi-ties, outside no less than inside the synagogue, the one thing he did not expect from it was relevance in our sense of the word. It was meant simply to add a spiritual and moral dimension to his life. The resultant blessings of personal contentment, of domestic and social stability, of ethnic survival, while often taken for granted, were purely incidental; their attainment was neither demanded nor investigated.

This unconcern with relevance is even more pronounced in the pursuit of Jewish learning. The intensive study of Judaism is to be every Jew's avocation "for its own sake", without regard to professional or other benefits. Moreover, the subject-matter studied is, and always was, irrelevant in the extreme. For many centuries the finest Jewish brains, countless students at the greatest and smallest institutions of learning, devoted their intellectual endeavours to painstaking research into the laws of ritual defilement and the sacrificial Temple cult; they discussed civil and criminal legislation, and regulations on kings and priests long after the destruction of the Jewish State and Temple had deprived these laws of the slightest practical significance, and long before their restoration could realistically be anticipated. The greater part of Maimonides's monumental Code of Jewish Law (the most gigantic enterprise of its kind ever undertaken) deals with subjects which were but of academic interest in his time, and indeed centuries before and after his time. To this day, these subjects form a major part of the intensive Jewish studies pursued by tens of thousands of Jewish children, students and scholars all over the world. History probably knows no parallel to this extraordinary exercise in irrelevance.

It is surely the distinction and the one constant factor of Jewish history that Judaism has never been completely in step with the age. In this sense, the Hebrew Prophets' teachings on social justice were as irrelevant to the concerns of their pagan contemporaries as the Talmud was to the Greek and Roman thinking of the times. Judaism has been just as lonely and at variance with its environment ever since. Indeed, as has been said, "Judaism will never be in accord with the times until the times are in accord with Judaism."

How can an eternal faith, prevailing through numerous layers of diverse civilisations, be anything but irrelevant? Or, indeed, should it be relevant? An analogy may illustrate the point. Imagine a ship far out at sea, unequipped with any mechanical aids to navigation. The skipper relies on the stars to chart his course. One cloudy night he has the bright idea of hoisting a light to the top of the ship's mast to replace the stars obscured from view. Naturally, his guide-light will turn and toss with every movement of the ship. Without readings based on stars fixed and permanent, he will move aimlessly, unable to calculate either his origin or his destination. The function of religion is to help chart the course of history by readings taken from light radiated by fixed teachings. If we are to know whether we move forward or away from our destination, the very value of the light lies in it being unrelated to the fluctuations of our ship as it traverses time.

A religion which is only relevant is worthless; a religion which is totally irrelevant is useless. The difficulty of combining utility with enduring value is inherent in any equation relating time to timelessness. Judaism resolves the difficulty by raising the sights of all ages to goals which are fixed and ultimate. At the same time, it guides each age, in the light of prevalent conditions, to find the way and to remove the obstacles to the attainment of these goals.

Herein lies the message of our Passover festival. We celebrate freedom even if its full achievement may lie in the distant past and the remote future. The festival's fascination is timeless, as revolutionary and as compelling today as it was 3,000 years ago and as it will be to the end of days. It serves not merely as a massive proclamation of justice, but as a forthright rejection of tyranny, slavery and discrimination. In a challenge as stimulating now as it was in the darkest days of our tormented history, it is a resounding declaration of liberty, asserting the human rights of man, the equality of the stranger and the hope of the oppressed.

The thrill of Passover excites the least romantic of minds and has sustained it as one of our most popular festivals. Its ceremony, its warmth, its intensity, its evergreen novelty, provides a spectacle for the eye, food for the mind and refreshment for the soul.

Tomorrow night, as we shall gather round our family table, we shall engage in a dialogue with our children, closing the generation gap and reopening communications with our young critics. Age barriers will be broken down as the young finds himself partnered with the aged in discussing the whys and wherefores of our history and destiny.

Our traditional Passover text read in our homes is designed, above all, to stimulate questions, especially from our children. How meaningful this is for a generation such as ours which, intellectually complacent, has more answers than questions, a generation which, far from being tormented by doubts, is bored by the certainties of its ideologies and has closed its mind behind the barricade of its slogans.

The Passover experience generates an excitement and an affection which harmonises past and future, parents and children, while transcending the individual home to unite all the House of Israel in an identical happening. This is a global demonstration. In countless homes, spread over five continents and 100 countries, over ten million people will simultaneously declare: "Once we were slaves. Now we shall be free." I know of little which can compare in dimension of space and time with a mass rally of this kind.

To my brothers and sisters in this country, and in the distant Commonwealth communities it was recently my privilege to visit; to those in the lands of freedom as well as in the lands to which we address with special anguish the Passover cry "Let my people go so that they shall serve Me"; and to the brave people already returned to the land of our fathers and of so many of our children, I heartily extend the traditional Passover greeting, a happy and uplifting festival, bringing speedy fulfilment to the age-old wish: "Next Year in Jerusalem Rebuilt!"

New Year Broadcast 1971

"The Meaning of Prayer and Confession"

During our forthcoming High Holydays (the New Year and the Day of Atonement) our Divine services in the synagogue will extend to a formidable total of some 25 hours. Even Jews who for the rest of the year are rather remote from religious observances will spend the greater part of this time in the house of prayer.

What do we hope to achieve during these long hours of devotion? Of course, we will pray, reciting many of our standard prayers over and over again; we will listen to numerous biblical passages, ranging from the sacrifice of Isaac to the exciting story of the prophet Jonah. We will be exhorted and uplifted by a number of edifying sermons, on themes and concepts stirring the Jewish conscience at the present time: our yearning for peace in the Holy Land, our anguish over the plight of Soviet Jewry, and our religious and moral responsibilities before God and man. And on the Day of Atonement we shall beat our hearts in contrite remorse, confessing our sins and failings during the past year.

But do we really need 25 hours—the better part of a working week—for these prayers, readings and exhortations? The question is all the more puzzling when we remember that often our synagogue building programme is based on the requirement to contain the vast congregations expected for just these three days in the year.

To begin with, we must understand that the Jewish concept of prayer is quite distinct from the common meaning of the word. In the Jewish view, as the Hebrew term *lehitpalel* clearly implies, prayer is meant to *impress* rather than to *express* ourselves. God does not require to be informed of our wants and needs; He knows them better than we do. No, we pray and pour out our hearts before God for our own sake, to improve and ennoble ourselves by recognising our own impotence and our dependence on our Maker, thus making ourselves worthy of the blessings for which we crave. It may take only minutes to *express* our desires, but it requires hours to change and regenerate ourselves through the *impression* of prayer.

Prayer and all other religious experiences, to be meaningful and effective, require first of all the creation of an atmosphere, a frame of mind, a spiritually responsive mood. Just as a blade of grass, even on the most fertile soil, cannot grow without air, sunshine and rain, so will the soul, or the human conscience, not blossom forth to its full potential unless it first be moved from the polluted environment of everyday existence to an atmosphere warmed by the sunshine of holiness, and refreshed by the rains of faith and rededication, borne on the clouds of inner turbulence and a genuinely distressed spirit.

It takes many hours of hard and sustained effort to produce such a mood. An hour's prayer a few times a year will no more moisten our hearts and cultivate our personality than a passing shower will irrigate a field; it takes days of sustained rain to make the earth yield its fruit.

Moreover, we believe that the necessary mood or environment cannot be created by an individual in isolation. It is a collective experience. It demands of the individual that he merge his identity within that of the community. In the Jewish view it is only as a group, as members of society, that we can effectively approach God and be truly roused by a religious experience. Hence our emphasis on public prayer; in fact, many of our most sacred prayers and readings require the quorum of a congregation and may not be recited in private.

Our sages applied to public worship the biblical proverb: "In the multitude of the people is the glory of the king." The larger the congregation the greater the holiness of God, as it were—or, as we might say, the more can we appreciate His majesty and power, and the greater the resultant religious impact on the worshipper.

Let me develop this a little further and, by reference to a unique feature of Judaism, apply it to our own times. When we confess our sins, we do so neither as individuals nor through any priest or other intermediary. We list a whole catalogue of our failings collectively and directly before God. In our confession, we invariably speak in the plural: "*We* have sinned; *we* have been dishonest; *we* have slandered others; *we* have failed to honour father and mother." Indeed, we mention, and seek forgiveness for, many offences—such as slander or robbery or even incest—which very few in the congregation are likely to have committed. But, if any one of us misconduct himself, we *all* have to plead guilty and seek atonement.

This is based on the cardinal Jewish doctrine that we are all accountable for one another. I am responsible for my neighbours, and they are responsible for me. According to our doctrine of Divine retribution, I will be punished not only for my own wrongs but for the wrongs of the community in which I live, just as the virtues and achievements of any individual bring credit and reward to all. Judaism therefore insists on cultivating not only the individual conscience, but the social conscience, to ensure a deep sense of collective responsibility.

The reason for this doctrine is quite simple. The first recorded question ever asked by man was: "Am I my brother's keeper?" and the answer is: Yes, you certainly are! If anyone in our society defaults in his duties, shirks his obligations, each one of us is held responsible, for we all have a share in his guilt. We should have set a better example, or we should have prevented his misdeed by persuasion and argument, or we should have cared more about community service and the maintenance of law and order, of decency and moral rectitude. In one way or another, by acts of commission or omission, we all aid and abet in any crime, any vice found in our midst, and it is of no avail to plead: "Why should I suffer for the sins of my neighbour?"

Few teachings of our faith have contributed more towards our people's triumph over the vicissitudes of our dispersion. Exiled from one country after another, we frequently had to make a fresh start as new immigrants, ever arriving as aliens on probation. In seeking to make ourselves acceptable and desirable, we were greatly helped by the deeply ingrained feeling of collective responsibility, the awareness that the misconduct of any individual brought the entire community into disrepute. By making every Jew feel that, in committing an offence, he would disgrace not only himself and his family, but his entire people, this sense of collective guilt served as a most powerful deterrent to individual aberrations, amounting in effect to communal sanctions against any delinquents. Any Jew contemplating an illegal or ignoble act knew that he would incur the community's wrath and denunciation for tarnishing the good name of all. Consequently, he would think twice before committing such an act.

By the same token, the corporate social conscience served as an effective incentive to encourage public service and deeds of distinction. The corollary to collective guilt is collective honour, whereby anyone distinguishing himself enables all to share in his glory—an extra inducement to foster acts of outstanding value and service.

This highly developed sense of corporate shame and corporate honour, as a deterrent to vice and an incentive to virtue, clearly proved an important factor in ensuring a notably low rate of crime and fostering a correspondingly high rate of enduring services to humanity, as indicated by the disproportionate number of Jews among Nobel prize winners.

In our shrinking world of instant communication and growing interdependence, the call for collective responsibility is now a major universal challenge. We can no longer isolate the welfare or the ordeals of a country, or of individuals, from the rest of humanity. For the war in far-away Vietnam, or racial discrimination in distant South Africa, or the Arab–Israel conflict, or the trans-Atlantic jitters of the once almighty dollar, bring crisis, turmoil, agitation and insecurity to the whole world. Yet we suffer from such a surfeit of disasters, that we are seldom personally affected by even the most colossal calamities. How many of us really care about the unspeakable horrors suffered in Bengal through the havoc wrought by a frightful civil war compounded by unprecedented floods engulfing millions? Even nearer home, we tend to be hardened to insensitivity by the constant reports on terror in Northern Ireland, stories of violence in our streets, and instances of moral erosion among our youth. When a policeman is gunned down, or when crazy gangs of young people set out on a frenzy of vandalism, or when, less sensationally, countless marriages break up in misery poisoned by the pollution of pornography, or when nearly a million of our fellow-citizens are condemned by unemployment to the misery of want and the indignity of idleness, how many really care?

But in what way can we *all* be held responsible for these evils and how can we prevent them? Let me illustrate the answer by just one or two examples. Just as the flowers of virtue, like the inspiration of prayer, flourish only in a clean atmosphere charged with moral fervour, so do the weeds of evil proliferate in a sick society, muddied by blatant immorality. Violence and agitation breed on publicity and notoriety. We all help in promoting such publicity. If people did not enjoy reading sordid stories of crime, cruelty and the antics of the irresponsibles of society, our newspapers and magazines would not feature them so prominently. They would concentrate on reporting man's successes and not headlining his failures. Similarly, if decent people were outraged with revulsion rather than bored, let alone titillated, by erotic displays and lurid accounts of divorces and adultery, the murky sources of smut and faithlessness would the sooner be cleaned up.

We hear much criticism these days of the silent majority. Although I am not sure that a majority can be anything but relatively silent, nevertheless it should not passively connive at evil by tolerating it or failing to strengthen the defences against it. To preserve law and order is not just the business of policemen; it is the business of every citizen to report crime when he sees it and to extend a helping hand to the victim of violence when he witnesses it. To preach decency and uprightness is not just the business of priests or rabbis; to engage in social welfare is not just the task of social workers, and to instruct our children in morality is not simply the exclusive prerogative of professional teachers; every human owes it to society to reprove others guilty of wrongdoing, to give up some of his time for community service, and to teach his children the difference between right and wrong. If the individual defaults in any of these obligations, he is accountable for the consequences. Even in government and politics, it is ultimately only the concern and the participation of all citizens that can avoid chaos and moral decline. A discriminating electorate ensures discriminating politicians; and a judicious citizenry produces judicious teachers, journalists, scientists, artists and other pace-setters of our community.

I referred earlier to the story of Jonah, our final biblical reading during the solemn Days of Awe ahead of us. Does this story not dramatise our theme on the predicament of the world today and the responsibility of every individual in it? Here we see a prophet of God foiled by disaster in his attempt to flee from his mission and forced to return to his assignment. Here we see the lives of an entire ship's company first threatened and then saved because of the actions of a single individual among them. And here we see a vast city, in which evil was rampant, doomed to destruction and later reprieved. However few the actual criminals, all citizens were held accountable for the city's degeneration, and it was the sincere repentance of the entire population, prodded by the call of just one individual, that finally saved the city.

Today, in our shrunken world, we are all in the same boat; anyone escaping from his mission and shirking his responsibilities endangers us all. Today, moreover, the whole world is one vast Niniveh, corrupted by evil and oppression, and threatened with the doom of chaos, strife and lawlessness.

As we gather in our synagogues to seek the blessings of a New Year on behalf of all our fellow-men, a call goes forth as it did to the inhabitants of Niniveh: Let every man and woman, from the greatest to the smallest, "cry mightily unto God; yea, let them turn every one from his evil way and from the violence that is in their hands. Who knows whether God will not turn and repent, and turn away from his fierce anger, that we perish not?" May we each help to make all worthy of the gifts of life, health and happiness in a year destined, we pray, to bring to the world abundant peace, universal freedom and prosperity for all humans.

Passover Broadcast 1972

"Science—Master or Servant?"

The celebration of Passover is, for us, not merely an occasion for historic recollection. As the Festival of Freedom it sounds an ever-topical note, and it invites us to examine how an ancient festivity speaks to us in contemporary terms.

Indeed, Passover is in a very special category. While *all* our biblical festivals are meant to recall the Exodus from Egypt, Passover does so *par excellence* and, as the first of our festivals, sets the tone to our entire historical, religious and ethical Jewish consciousness. The Exodus from Egypt is the pre-eminent theme not only of the narrative in the Five Books of Moses, but of the legislation contained in them.

Numerous ritual observances as well as ethical laws are motivated by the duty to remember the redemption of our ancestors from Egypt. For instance, when we don the prayer shawl each morning, we do so to recall that "I am the Lord your God who has taken you out from the land of Egypt." When we put on our phylacteries at prayer, we are to be reminded (as the text of the scrolls inside them reads) "For with a mighty hand did the Lord take us out from Egypt." Even in sanctifying the Sabbath, we are told (as the Decalogue in Deuteronomy states) "and you shall remember that you were a slave in the land of Egypt and the Lord your God took you out from there with a mighty hand and an outstretched arm."

In our social relations, too, the experience of our forefathers in Egypt and their redemption are constantly invoked to explain and emphasise such diverse commandments as to champion the rights of the widow and the orphan and the servant, to ensure a livelihood for the poor, not to oppress the stranger, and even not to abhor or hate the Egyptian. In fact, the Pentateuch mentions the Exodus from Egypt in a legal context more than thirty times.

Equally striking and significant is the reference to the Exodus in the first of the Ten Commandments (according to the Jewish listing) proclaiming "I am the Lord your God who brought you out from the land of Egypt, out of the house of bondage." Already some of our classic commentators were intrigued by this definition of God as the Redeemer from oppression rather than as the Creator of heaven and earth. Surely, we might have expected God to reveal Himself above all as Master of the entire universe, rather than as having merely intervened at a certain stage of human history, to liberate a particular people from bondage.

This aspect of Jewish thought and theology was imaginatively expressed nearly two thousand years ago in a remarkable rabbinic homily or Midrash. It relates what may appear at first as a rather fanciful dialogue between God and a letter of the Hebrew alphabet. When, in the biblical account of Genesis, God created the world, starting with the word *Bereshit* (meaning "in the beginning"), the first letter, the *aleph*, or "A", lodged a complaint: "Surely, as the first-born of the letters, this honour should have fallen to me, and not to my junior, the letter *beth*, or 'B'!" Whereupon God comforted the *aleph*: "Be consoled. When the time will come for Me to proclaim the purpose of all creation, the goals and objectives envisaged in My making of heaven and earth; when I will reveal in the Ten Commandments the moral law which is to govern man as the crown of creation, I will start with you, the *aleph*, by opening the Decalogue with the word *Anochi*—'I am the Lord your God'."

What our Sages wished to convey to us, in this poetic imagery peculiar to them, was simply this. The creation of heaven and earth, of all the infinite forces and wondrous mysteries in the universe, manifest only the "B" of God's majesty and power. Greater still than the grandeur of the physical universe, in all its awesome dimensions, is His spiritual creation; the "A" of His supreme majesty lies in the fundamental moral and religious concepts contained in the Ten Commandments, intended to vindicate man's physical existence and to give purpose and meaning to the universe around him.

Consistent with this idea, even our weekly Sabbath is meant to lay less emphasis on God's *creation* of the world, which took six days, than *resting* from His work and stopping His labours on the seventh day; in other words, *controlling* what He had created. Likewise, we humans are summoned to hold dominion over the world, to master and exploit its infinite resources, and to harness its vast powers. But for six days only are we to be masters and creators. On the seventh day, the Sabbath, we are to be creatures, reminded that there is an ultimate Master above us. By liberating the world for one day a week from our domination and releasing nature from its human bondage, we ourselves for once a week become liberated from the slavery to our human creations, from our subjugation to the machines we have constructed, desisting from the generation of light, heat and power or any other creative human labour—the expression of man's domination of nature.

This explains the remarkable contrast between the English term "the Almighty" and the Hebrew equivalent *Shadday*, construed to mean "He who called a halt (*day*) to creation". We see the real might of God not so much in His power to create as in His ability to control what He has created.

Hence, the God we are to worship is not primarily the God who initiated the forces of nature and called all physical matter into existence; He is in the first place the God of history rather than of nature, the God of compassion, who loved freedom so intensely that He intervened in the course of history to deliver His people from oppression and tyranny.

Surely there could be few lessons of greater relevance to the "Weltschmerz" of our times, to the agony of this age, than this repeated emphasis on the primacy of the Exodus in our theological and historical outlook, as highlighted by our forthcoming festival.

We live in a world which worships at the altar of science, consecrating our efforts to material and physical conquests. Our generation is dazzled and dominated by the extraordinary achievements of technology. We often seek to reduce all human problems to the cold calculations of the computer, the soulless impersonal machine. We spend vast resources on research into the physical world and harnessing its boundless energies, on dealing with the material and economic aspects of human relations. But only a tiny fraction of these resources is devoted to metaphysical research, to moral engineering and to spiritual conquests. With all the enormous grants of money and the prolific application of the finest trained brains lavished by governments, universities and other agencies on the material advancement of man and his environment, on the study of nature, the one formula which has still eluded us, the design we have still not discovered, is how to build a human character immune to the scourges of vice, crime, hatred and unbridled passion, how to nurture young people and convince them that they are born not to amuse themselves, but to serve others, not to have a good time, but to make the times good, and how to construct two human homes next to each other in such a way that peace and harmony rule between them, while happiness founded on family stability reigns inside them.

No, the God we worship, if we worship one at all, is still the God of nature, the God who created the physical world, rather than the God of freedom, the Redeemer of the oppressed from bondage. Characteristically, we award Nobel prizes for outstanding discoveries of the human genius mainly in the realm of the material sciences, in physics, chemistry and the tangible aspects of medicine, but not for enduring contributions to the spiritual sciences, in philosophy, ethics or theology. We have no accolade for discoveries which would reduce crime, eliminate the evil of pornography, or prevent the untold misery suffered by countless parents and children through the rampant break-up of marriages on an unprecedented scale. Statesmen, scientists and journalists vie with one another in prophesying the doom of mankind through the pollution of the environment from smoke and the contamination of soil and rivers by noxious products, pleading for the spending of astronomical sums to eliminate these threats to human life. But who really cares with equal passion and resourcefulness about the at least equally destructive effects of moral and spiritual pollution, blighting the growth of healthy, decent and law-abiding citizens, poisoning the relations between nation and nation, race and race, man and man?

In the end, we can be sure, as the story of our own people's extraordinary survival in the face of all odds has shown, that the spiritual stature of man will prevail over his purely mechanical progress in reaching the goals of human evolution. Let me illustrate this by a personal experience of the Exodus of our own times. For some years past, Jews all over the world have drawn the main dynamic of Jewish concern and action from the immortal slogan which sparked the original Exodus from Egypt three-and-a-half thousand years ago, when Moses pleaded to Pharaoh "Let My people go, so that they will serve Me." We have applied this plea to the release of our three million brethren in the Soviet Union from their spiritual bondage. At last, though alas still in the face of great ordeals and frequent set-backs, the cry is beginning to be heard. It was my exhilarating privilege to see this modern Exodus.

What an epic drama unfolded itself before my eyes—perhaps indeed one of the most moving and momentous testimonies of all times to the indomitable triumph of the human spirit and the supreme courage of heroic mould born of hope and faith!

Here I saw Jews who had behind them not 40 years of wandering in a wilderness but over 50 years of religious and cultural repression in a land which sought to stifle their Jewish soul and identity, forbidding them, under pain of imprisonment and often worse, to teach Hebrew or Judaism to their children, to circumcise them, to have any Jewish communal organisations or contacts, let alone to profess any love for the land of their fathers. And yet these Jews, many of them young people, though spiritually tortured and completely cut off from the wellsprings of Jewish life and instruction for over two generations, suddenly now reasserted their Jewish identity with a passionate fervour and often a religious zeal which put me and others in the Free World to shame. I met many Jews who had not seen a rabbi or a Jewish teacher in their lives, had no access to a Jewish book or newspaper; and had yet never desecrated the Sabbath, had meticulously observed the Jewish dietary laws, had tenaciously preserved their religious traditions, and had never lost the hope that they would one day return to Zion and be reunited with their people. Their faith in redemption remained unshaken throughout the long and dark decades of their persecution and tribulations, for they persisted in worshipping the God who liberates the oppressed.

This surely is the universal message of our ancient festival and of the modern miracle of the present-day Exodus. The capacity for spiritual regeneration is infinite and invincible. There resides in every human heart a spark of Godliness which cannot be extinguished, which can at any time burst forth into a mighty flame, defying the tempests of adversity to illumine the path towards mankind's promised land of fulfilment and ennoblement. This capacity of man to rise above the contaminated environment surrounding him, to defy the pressures of conformity and to free himself from the chains of spiritual slavery shackling him, is greater and nobler than his ability to build the tallest skyscraper or to construct the most intricate spaceship.

In wishing all my fellow Jews a *Chag kasher vesameach*, I pray that the message of this festival will strengthen the faith of every human being in the God, to quote our ancient liturgy, "who brought us out from slavery to freedom, from anguish to joy, from sorrow to festivity, and from darkness to great light."

Passover Broadcast 1974

"Constant Exodus"

Only a few weeks ago, Israel's hosts once again went out of Egypt, crossing the same Red Sea and moving into the same wilderness of Sinai as the Children of Israel did 3,400 years ago—a record of history repeating itself, probably unique in the annals of man, a record as singular as Jews being the one people among the nations of the world now living in the same land, professing the same religion and speaking the same language as did their ancestors 3,000 years ago.

In Jewish homes observing Passover this year, therefore, the Exodus from Egypt which the festival celebrates will have an uncannily topical significance.

In my seasonal broadcast talks each year—whether before Passover or the Jewish New Year—I usually try to relate a spiritual message of the festival to contemporary issues within our society generally, and I refer only as an incidental to issues of specific concern to my fellow-Jews. But, this year, I trust I may be excused if I speak firstly to my Jewish friends, and subsequently address myself to the critical problems which we all face and the dangers which threaten our civilisation.

Since the Yom Kippur War nearly six months ago, not only have events affecting the Jewish people been forced on the world's attention, but we have passed through a time of traumatic upheaval. We have experienced intense grief, and have subjected ourselves to profound self-questioning. We have consulted our conscience no less than our history to discern our immediate future and to contemplate our ultimate destiny. In the wake of that cruel 3-week war, with appalling casualties which would in relative terms correspond to the loss of 60,000 soldiers here in this country; in the loneliness of Israel's isolation through the desertion overnight by scores of friendly governments, many former idols have toppled and myths of invincibility and infallibility have been exploded. Less than 30 years after the Nazi Holocaust, which exterminated six million Jews, we were again seized with anxiety for our survival. But in our affliction we were able to turn to all which has sustained us throughout our countless past tribulations for the balm of comfort and the renewal of our faith. We have long historical experience in prevailing over the most daunting odds.

The war which precipitated the renewed disengagement between Egypt's and Israel's forces was hardly less bitter than the experience which preceded the first Exodus. Then it brought an end to centuries of tyranny and slavery which doomed thousands of children to drowning at Pharaoh's behest, and subjected our entire people to misery and desolation. Now it followed an unrelenting sad struggle, fought to regain the Promised Land after centuries of exile, persecution, slaughter and degradation, a struggle which lasted for decades and again claimed thousands of young lives.

Following their deliverance from Egypt, our forebears had a long and arduous path to travel before they eventually secured peace and stability in the land of their destiny. Few will doubt that for our generation too the journey between vision and reality, between hope and fulfilment is still long and the route uncharted.

As we solemnly observe the Passover festival year after year, with its vivid reminders of the tribulations endured by our forefathers, it obviously did not escape our religious thinkers to ask why our national genesis was bound up with so much suffering and hardship. Our Hebrew Prophets, in particular, always concerned to divine the inner meaning of events which outwardly appear senseless and haphazard, directed their inspired mind to the interpretation of seemingly baffling and disconnected experiences in history as essential pieces in a grand master-design for the achievement of ultimate ends which become manifest only in the fulness of time. They compared the birth of a nation to a woman's painful labour in bringing forth a child, and the very encounter with God to the travail of childbirth. In the words of Isaiah, "Is a land born in one day, is a nation brought forth at once?" And again, "Lord, in trouble they sought You, silently they poured out a prayer when Your chastening was upon them. Like as a woman with child, that draws near the time of her delivery, is in pain and cries out in her pangs; so have we been at Your presence, O Lord."

One cannot bring forth new life without pain and the loss of blood, nor refine metal from dross and harden it without the searing heat of fire. Hence the key-role of the Exodus in our historical consciousness to this day. By annually reliving this travail of the Egyptian bondage in our Passover ceremonies and recitations, we are ever reminded of the indispensable conditions of our national birth, our tempering in the crucible of fire which steeled us to undertake our tough assignment as a lonely people destined to endure and serve as a constant spiritual catalyst in a hostile world. The metallurgical simile already occurs in Deuteronomy: "And the Lord has taken you and brought you forth out of the iron furnace, out of Egypt, to be unto Him a people of lasting inheritance, as you are to this day."

It was the immortal grandeur of our Prophets who, unafraid to expose themselves to the unpopularity, contempt and sometimes even persecution of their contemporaries, invariably attributed Israel's troubles and reverses to its own national shortcomings and moral failings, rather than to the might or guile of her enemies. The Prophets had the courage and the vision to say that collective suffering can become the instrument of national regeneration. Shunning the all too human tendency towards self-righteousness, they censured their own people rather than protest against the assaults of Israel's enemies, and did so in impassioned addresses of rebuke and stirring calls for self-improvement. For they were convinced that, in the final analysis, we are collectively all responsible for our own fate. And they were certain, in the perspective of history, that superior spirit and greater fortitude would prove more enduring than superior and greater power.

Prophetical courage and vision are in preciously scant supply today. We prefer to blame our misfortunes on others rather than on ourselves. In political argument, for instance, it is always the other party with whom the fault for domestic failures rests and for ever the other country which causes international tensions.

Following the Yom Kippur War and its grim aftermath, I affirmed both here and in the course of visits to Israel that were our Prophets alive today they would have adopted the same self-critical attitude to explain our reverses that they applied to the cataclysmic happenings of their own times. Refusing to accept the ups-and-downs of history simply as an arbitrary jumble of events without rhyme or reason, the reverses of fortune as a see-saw of fate, or some random twist in the sweepstakes of chance; they would have penetrated beneath the surface of Israel's military and political turmoil to reveal a profound spiritual crisis, a crisis of national identity to determine who the Jew is to be, if his national re-emergence is to restore him to the soul as well as to the soil of his people after 2,000 years of homelessness.

Of course, the Prophets, too, would have recognised and decried the brutal aggression of enemies and the desertion of friends as factors in our predicament. But they would have been far more troubled by deeper questions on the significance of our vicissitudes and they would have probed the very purpose of our existence. They might have asked how we could vindicate our millennial martyrdom and justify our claim to survival after 4,000 years of existence—already far beyond the life-span of so many nations—except by the continued commitment to our special role as "a light unto the nations", striving as a model society to enrich mankind with incomparable spiritual and moral contributions as we did in the past. Now that the whole future of Jewish life and security is again being challenged, and we are once again more as lonely a people as we were when we first emerged as a nation to defy the rest of the world and eventually to inspire it with our teachings, they might have asked what is our *raison d'être* today if not our resolve to cultivate the values and ideals peculiar to the Jewish spirit—humility, family stability, the quest for moral excellence and profound faith as well as the pattern and quiet order of life instilled by the discipline of daily religious observances.

Pointing at the awesome wonders of the latest Jewish Exodus, not only from Egypt but from Russia and indeed from the four corners of the earth fulfilling their vision of the ingathering of the exiles, the Prophets would have interpreted our present travails as an inescapable part in the process of our spiritual rebirth, our moral and religious regeneration, just as they saw in the first Exodus and the tribulations before and after it the pangs out of which were born the spiritual energies which pioneered the concepts of mono-theism, social justice, the brotherhood of man and the moral law in the evolution of man's civilisation. To them, in short, physical survival depended on, and served the purpose of, the fulfilment of Israel's historical destiny. Where this was not accepted freely by choice, Providence imposed the distinction by force.

In our convulsive times, however, the birth-pangs of a new epoch are not confined to any one people. The entire world is in travail, beset by virtually universal crises in national government and family loyalties, in world economics and local industrial relations, in public order and all too often even in personal integrity. In the midst of the daily toll of mounting problems, tragedies and disasters which currently dominate news headlines, all mankind is learning that we evidently cannot magically be transported to the Promised

Land of peace, security and happiness without first experiencing the blows of adversity and physically traversing the wilderness of hardship and deprivation. Yesterday's affluent civilisation is tottering, but it is precisely out of the pressures of today's anguish that we shall generate the energies which can give birth to tomorrow's brave new world.

But will our present ordeals in fact be the *Genesis* of a new age of progress towards the ideals of human fellowship, common prosperity and spiritual greatness? Will the turbulent times through which we are moving prove a worldwide *Exodus* from the oppression, the hatreds and injustices, the crime and violence, the immorality and materialism now threatening human survival, into a *Levitical* epoch in which we will so redistribute mankind's spiritual, intellectual and material wealth that all will share in the bounty of freedom, harmony, education and sufficiency in an unprecedented flowering of the human genius?

In the Hagadah which we recite in our Passover festivities at home, there is a remarkable passage, written many centuries ago, long before there were any ghettos, or pogroms, or concentration camps or gas chambers. The passage reads: "And this is what sustained and strengthened our fathers and us: that not only one man rose against us to destroy us, but that in every generation they sought to destroy us, and the Holy One, blessed be He, saved us from their hands." According to one interpretation, this means that the very attempt to destroy us is paradoxically that which caused us to endure. The sword that was thrust into us was turned into the ploughshare which cultivated our growth and sustained us, transforming the decay of old age into the rejuvenated vitality of flourishing spiritual, literary and intellectual creativeness.

An old Jewish tradition tells us that our ancestors were delivered from ancient Egypt by virtue of their indomitable faith in eventual liberation. A patient's confidence in his recovery is half his cure. Part of our trouble today is that too few people hope, let alone strive, for better times. Redemption comes only to those whose vision extends beyond the wilderness of the present and on to the uplands of fulfilment which remain to be conquered.

May this Passover help to bring us all, in the words of our ancient Seder liturgy, "from oppression to freedom, from sorrow to joy, from mourning to festivity, from darkness to a great light, and from servitude to salvation".

Passover Broadcast 1976

"From the Four Corners"

Within the past four months, in an unusual succession of overseas trips, I have visited the principal Jewish communities of four continents.

These travels began with my momentous experience in Soviet Russia last December as the first Chief Rabbi from the West to visit, by official invitation, our brethren in the USSR—by far the largest Jewish community in Europe, with at least twice as many Jews as in the rest of Europe. A few weeks later I embarked on a pastoral tour of South African Jewry, the leading Jewish community in Africa, and returned via Israel, today the centre of world Jewry. Finally, and quite recently, I spent some days in Canada and in the United States, meeting sections of by far the largest Jewish community ever to be found in a single country at any time in our history. Together these communities account for about 85% of all the 14 million Jews found in the world today.

The contrasts distinguishing these four widely removed concentrations of Jewish life are as striking as the similarities uniting them. There is Israel, reborn out of bitter travail, today as in the past the destination of all our hopes and prayers. Still embattled and subjected to the longest continuous war in modern history, Israel grimly but undaunted faces mounting dangers within and beyond her precarious borders, yet is vibrant and dynamic, galvanising Jewish activity and commitment throughout the world, aglow with the flame of Jewish learning, and calling on Zion's children everywhere, in the Prophet's immortal phrase, "Speedily to make the voice of gladness and rejoicing heard in the streets of Jerusalem and the cities of Judea".

In stark contrast there is Soviet Jewry, about equal in numbers, but prostrate and spiritually desolate, for decades forcibly severed from the rest of our people and involuntarily estranged from our traditions, and yet now showing miraculous signs of reawakening, hungering for Jewish identification and many of them yearning to return to Zion in a bold assertion of the indestructibility of the Jewish spirit which has aroused admiration and support the world over. Indeed, it may be significant that just in Russia, the land officially committed to atheism, a new form of Jewish martyrdom has emerged which has not existed since the Middle Ages when Jews last had the free choice of either purchasing their acceptance as equals through baptism or asserting their Judaism at the cost of brutal persecution. Of course, in more recent times millions were done to death because they were Jews— martyrs who perished in the Nazi concentration camps and gas chambers, and also those who fell in the defence of Israel. But they had no option. Hitler did not give them the alternative of securing survival by renouncing their Judaism, nor would the failure to defend Israel's independence have saved its Jewish citizens from the threat of annihilation. In Russia it is different. There thousands of Jews, many of them of high eminence in the arts and sciences, have willingly sacrificed their livelihood, their reputation and security, exposing themselves to the constant threat of arrest or Siberian exile, simply because they want to live as Jews. This is an entirely new phenomenon, without parallel in modern Jewish history.

In South Africa, again, there is a flourishing community, for long caught on the painful horns of an agonising dilemma. They deeply feel the Jewish moral revulsion against apartheid and yet must strive for toleration within a society based on racial discrimination. Now they are ominously exposed to the storms of change sweeping the Dark Continent and threatening the white enclaves left within it. In some respects, all these three communities (Israel, Soviet Jewry and South African Jewry) now have their very existence imperilled by the spreading power of the mightiest regime of godlessness ever to bestride our world.

Then there is the vast conglomeration of America's six million Jews, a community fragmented but intensely enterprising, culturally stimulating, politically influential, and in some areas religiously resurgent, yet a community deeply troubled by the inroads of apathy and assimilation, by the decline of American morale and power, and by the insidious rise of isolationsim and disengagement from the guardianship of western civilisation and freedom.

All these communities are widely diverse in size and character, in hopes and fears, in their liberties and their disabilities.

Two examples struck me most dramatically as illustrating the glaring contrasts in the conditions of Jewish life. In the United States, and even in South Africa—a community only one-twentieth the size of Soviet Jewry—I met and addressed several thousand children in various Jewish day schools, whilst in Russia I saw only a single Jewish child, and that not in any of the synagogues I visited; there exists, of course, no Jewish school altogether. Again, whilst throughout Jewish communities Hebrew is now widely in use as the ancient and modern language of our people, in Russia it is the one language which is not spoken or taught among the 150 different tongues cultivated among the Soviet peoples.

But these contrasts notwithstanding, the remarkable thing is what unites our communities rather than what divides them. Whether in the Old World or in the New, whether at the centre in Israel or on the periphery of our dispersion, whether spiritually flourishing or languishing, they all share not only a common origin but also common problems, common aspirations and a common destiny. Perhaps the very hostility rampant in so many parts of the world, by unleashing under the guise of anti-Zionism an almost global attack on the very heart of Jewish beliefs and prayers, has drawn Jews more closely together in a community of fate and faith at any time since our dispersion. Never before have Jews everywhere cared so deeply and passionately about other Jews in distant lands, whether in Israel or in Russia. This acute feeling of interdependence, too, is a new phenomenon.

Yet we only have to look at the Passover events we are about to celebrate to discover that the patterns in the contemporary Jewish experience are not so new and unforeseen after all. Passover marks both the beginning and the fulfilment of some of the most extraordinary prophecies of all time. With the Exodus from Egypt *started* one of the most remarkable national histories in the annals of man; and with it also *concluded* one of the most accurate visions of the future ever recorded.

Centuries earlier, Abraham, the father of our people, was told: "You shall know for sure that your descendants shall be strangers in a land that is not theirs; they shall be enslaved and afflicted there for four hundred years, and afterward they shall come out with great substance." I know of no recorded reference to a forecast fulfilled with such precision after the lapse of nearly five centuries—the period which separated Abraham from the Exodus.

But perhaps even more startling are the forecasts by Moses and the Hebrew Prophets on the sequence of fortunes and misfortunes to be experienced by the people of Israel.

At the time of the Exodus, our people was in its infancy. It had just emerged from centuries of foreign bondage and had not yet even reached the national homeland it was promised. And already it was warned by its national leader that, should it fail to live up to its divine vocation as "a kingdom of priests and a holy nation", it would be exiled from its land and be dispersed among the nations. This shattering prophecy was to be realised nearly a thousand years later, with the destruction of the First Temple and the Babylonian Exile, and then again some six hundred years after that, with the destruction of the Second Temple and the fall of Jerusalem under the Romans.

But still more far-sighted, and without parallel in the foretelling of the future, was the assurance given at the same time by Moses, and later by his Prophetic successors, that these long periods of exile and suffering among the nations would not spell the end of the Jews and their peoplehood; they would survive their dispersion and tribulations, and the exiles would eventually be restored to their ancestral homeland from all parts of the earth to regain their national sovereignty. However long it might take, the time would come, in the words of Isaiah, when God "will assemble the dispersed of Israel and gather together the scattered of Judah from the four corners of the earth". Now 2,500 years after Isaiah, we are beginning to witness the realisation, or at least inception, of this forecast.

To appreciate the sheer daring of these prophecies, not to mention the wonder of their fulfilment, just imagine some national leader were to arise today, warning his people that, should they betray the moral order and forsake their national purpose, their country would be invaded by foreign powers and the entire population would be dispersed throughout the world, suffering an indefinite period of terrible persecution, and yet retaining their national and religious identity over centuries or millennia of exile, with the promise to be ultimately restored to their country as an independent nation once again loyal to its original traditions.

Such is the preordained course of Jewish history, initiated with the Passover experience and still being acted out in our own days three and a half thousand years later!

As a people we oscillated between dispersion and ingathering, between being scattered to the four corners of the earth with the explosive force of a shattering catastrophe and then being brought back again with divine compassion to the land of our origin and destiny.

To survive and sustain such convulsive events requires an enormous intake from a source of inexhaustible energy. For us this energy was always provided by the power of our faith. However gloomy the outlook, however hopeless our condition appeared to be, we never surrendered to despair or lost our hope of recovery and redemption. Passover helped us to recharge our batteries of faith and confidence. Brutal and dismal as may have been the world around us, and distant as may have been the prospect of relief, every Jew at his Passover table, recounting the salvation of the past in fulfilment of ancient promises, always exclaimed with unshakable conviction: "Next year we shall be free!"

Today, times are trying and bleak not only for Jews, but for all nations.

In the grim scramble for survival, only the fittest will prevail. The fittest will not necessarily be those with the highest living standards or the best technological equipment. Great, prosperous and advanced civilisations have perished in the past. Our history has taught us that what will in the end determine survival is the tenacity of our faith, the passion of our commitment to universal values like social justice and self-discipline, and the breadth of vision which transcends the ups and downs of momentary successes and reverses to encompass the wider purpose of human existence in ridding the world of vice and violence, of slavery and subjection, in a common fellowship of mutual service, brotherly love and collective ennoblement.

With firm trust in the promise of God and the power of man to re-enact the Passover epic of securing freedom from bondage, I extend my festival greetings to all my brethren in this country and the Commonwealth, indeed to those in the four corners of the earth. Strengthened by our solidarity and inspired by the ageless ideals which have preserved us through the ages, may we be worthy soon to witness the renewed Passover miracle of deliverance, together with all our human brothers, to enjoy the universal blessing of peace and life through righteousness.

Chapter Six

JEWISH EDUCATION AND JEWISH IDENTITY

What Makes and What Is a Jew

A PHOENIX FROM THE ASHES

In some respects Judaism has shared with other faiths the travails and convulsions as well as the renaissance experienced by religion in the postwar era. Common challenges confronting all religious denominations have included the despiritualization of man bred by the cult of science and the mechanization of life, the frivolities of our "pop" culture and the sexual revolution, the disproportionate limelight in our mass media on protest and dissent, the constant incitement to rebellion against authority and all forms of discipline, and maybe even the popular pressures of an egalitarian ecumenism.

There are, of course, also several important features of contemporary society stimulating the growth of religious influence and activity. Thus, religion has no doubt been enriched by the intensified quest for moral guidance to resolve acute new perplexities besetting man, whether on nuclear war, race relations, heart transplants or contraceptive pills. As in Newton's law of motion, to every action there is an equal and opposite reaction: the very rise in the rates of crime, vice, divorce and illegitimacy has helped to encourage the renewed search for religious values in a society irritated by restlessness and insecurity on a scale more universal than ever before.

These degenerative and regenerative forces have affected Judaism and other faiths in more or less similar ways during the past two decades. But these common denominators apart, there are several factors relevant only to Judaism, and I will briefly survey a few of these with particular reference to the Jewish community in this country.

Overshadowing the postwar Jewish experience in every sphere has been the Nazi holocaust which devastated European Jewish life with the slaughter of six million Jews—that is, every third Jew in the world—in Jewish history's worst disaster. The long-term effects of this catastrophe have been numerous and varied. A traumatic cataclysm of such dimensions, aided and abetted as it was by a conspiracy of silence throughout the "civilized" world which is only lately coming to full light, could not but provoke a serious crisis of faith in God and man. From this crisis neither Jews nor Judaism have yet fully recovered to this day. Among the ramifications of the crisis is the Jewish reticence in responding enthusiastically to the overtures to interfaith dialogues

Article published in The Times Educational Supplement, *4 April 1969.*

and in greeting without reservations the historic revisions of the Christian attitude to the Jewish people. These revisions are now of little more than academic interest; had they been made a thousand years earlier they would have saved many millions of lives.

Equally drastic has been the impact of the holocaust in shifting the Jewish centre of gravity from Europe to America and, more recently, to Israel. For centuries right up to the Second World War, Eastern and Central Europe contained the great reservoir of spiritual, religious, cultural and human strength for the Jewish people. From it had sprung all the great creative Jewish movements of modern times—whether Hasidism, Zionism or the various streams of religious and scholarly diversity. From it had poured forth the unceasing flow of reinforcements to replenish, by immigration to America, Britain and other Western communities, the Jewish ranks thinned by assimilation, intermarriage and a low birth-rate. From that reservoir the rest of the Jewish world had drawn most of its sages. In Britain, for instance, until the war virtually all leading rabbis and scholars were born and/or trained in communities destroyed by the Nazis.

With the former spiritual and manpower sources of supply now completely dried up, the surviving Jewish communities have been forced to create and sustain their own resources. Under this pressure of self-preservation, new flourishing Jewish centres of learning have lately sprung up in ever-increasing numbers to replace the outstanding academies martyred during the war. As a result, in countries like the United States, Britain and France—hitherto hardly congenial to this kind of commitment—Jewish studies are today pursued more widely and more intensively than ever before.

While this remarkable rejuvenation of Jewish religious life in the Western world is still, numerically at least, far from balancing or making good the continued drift from Judaism, particularly among the youth, there are certainly incipient signs of a very significant return to traditional loyalties, assuring the survival of many communities that may otherwise have been doomed to extinction by a process of religious and cultural attrition.

The principal factor in the arrest of this process is, of course, the emergence of the Jewish State, an event marking the "equal and opposite reaction" to the holocaust. Israel, though still only the third largest Jewish community (following American and Russian Jewries), is now by far the most dynamic element in Jewish life, both intrinsically and by its impact on Jews and Judaism the world over. Israel's prolific production of scholars, educators and literature—not to mention the massive output of plain Jewish idealists— already represents a well-spring of Jewish vitality on a par with the most vibrant communities found at any time in Jewish history. Moreover, Israel's strivings, her ordeals and her triumphs, are today the most potent force in galvanizing Jewish consciousness and activity wherever Jews live.

What Israel's spectacular military feats accomplished in three wars since 1948 in restoring Jewish self-respect and self-confidence after the shattering humiliation of the holocaust, has been achieved religiously, perhaps even theologically, by the manifestation of a benevolent Providence in literally fulfilling the age-old prophecies and millennial dreams of the Jewish return to the Holy Land, culminating in the reunification of Jerusalem under Jewish sovereignty for the first time in nineteen hundred years. To countless Jews inside and outside Israel this wondrous combination of ancient hope and prayers has vindicated the religious claims of Judaism in a challenge to the secularist philosophy of history scarcely less significant than the opposite effects of the holocaust in rocking the foundations of religious faith a generation earlier.

Out of the combination and interplay of these often conflicting factors, both general and Jewish, have emerged the patterns of Jewish religious life today. They explain, above all, the increasing polarization among Jews everywhere. This process is constantly widening the gap between religious and secularist Jews, as well as between Orthodox and non-orthodox factions. In Britain, for example, what was once a rather homogeneous, middle-of-the-road community of moderate Orthodoxy, with proud insistence on strictly "established" traditions in public and considerable flexibility of observance in private, has become a diversified community in which the religious and communal loyalties of many have appreciably weakened, while among the committed there has been a strong movement towards more exacting standards of Jewish living and learning.

Contemporary Jewish life, then, reflects a peculiar dichotomy. More Jews are being lost as well as reclaimed to Judaism than ever before. The number of children without any Jewish education constantly grows; but so do the enrolment figures in the burgeoning network of intensive Jewish day schools and academies of higher Jewish learning. On the one hand, many Jewish intellectuals now have only the most tenuous ties with Judaism and the Jewish community, turning away disillusioned with the "irrelevance" of Jewish thought to their universe of discourse; and on the other hand, a new synthesis of Jewish and secular values is steadily gaining strength in the remarkable growth of Orthodox student and academic organizations and in the output of sophisticated literature articulating the Jewish approach to current challenges, whether in science or in theology, in social relations or even in politics.

In assessing future prospects, some concrete indications stand out among many intangible factors. What the strict traditionalists currently lack in numbers, popular appeal and trained leadership (since the Jewishly best-educated youth today increasingly shies away from the Rabbinical and even teaching professions) is compensated by their superior dedication and tenacity, by their considerably higher birth rate and by their significantly lower defection rate. Indeed it is this element which at present represents religiously the most creative force in a spiritual and organizational as well as physical sense. Perhaps it is just the challenge of the holocaust on the one hand and of a religiously indifferent world on the other which represents the travail out of which the new vitality is being born, just as all life has its origin in pain and tension, and as all human progress is forged in the crucible of hardship and sacrifice.

JEWISH EDUCATION—IS THE ALARM JUSTIFIED?

This is my God, and I will glorify Him;
My father's God, and I will exalt Him.
Exodus 15:2

Ever since my return to these shores just over two years ago to assume my present high and responsible office, Jewish education has been my major plank. In numerous statements and addresses up and down the country, in virtually all my activities, I have never ceased to emphasise the desperate urgency of revitalising Jewish education in this country. Whether in talks to ordinary members of small congregations or at special sessions before the principal leaders of our community, I have continually raised the alarm, warning Anglo-Jewry that without improving our educational facilities we might face extinction. At the same time, I have initiated a sweeping enquiry into Jewish education, more comprehensive and more painstaking than any similar investigation ever undertaken in the history of our community.

The first Report of some recommendations and findings has just been published. It envisages bold and drastic steps of educational expansion and improvement which will impose upon the community heavy new financial burdens. We are advised that we will require no less than £3,000,000 to be spent over the next five years on our most urgent educational requirements—on more schools, on better instruction, on higher salaries, on teacher-training and on numerous other needs. To raise this kind of money, I will have to expect some members of a congregation such as this to come forward enthusiastically with donations not in the £100 or £1,000 range, but in denominations of £10,000 or more in order to give the proper impetus to the campaign. These are exacting demands, and I will have to justify them if the community is to rally to my support.

I may well be asked, why all this alarm about the present state of Jewish education? Surely, people might say to me, you are not the first Chief Rabbi in our history. Your predecessors, all outstanding leaders of intense dedication, did not belabour the community all the time for their alleged educational failings. They did not refuse—as you do—to consecrate new Synagogue

Sermon delivered at the Marble Arch Synagogue, London, on the Eighth Day of Passover, 10 April 1969.

buildings unless they included special youth or educational facilities; and yet Anglo-Jewry survived. Why should you, then, ignoring the example of those before you, want our community to be any different from what it has always been, and threaten us with dire warnings of disintegration if we did not heed your call?

These are questions and arguments which sound reasonable. Indeed, they constitute an entirely plausible challenge, and I owe the community an explanation to show why I should be different, and why the community will have to be different if it is to survive. Let me, then, this morning make an attempt at meeting this challenge. I will do so by referring first to a famous verse in this morning's superb Haftorah and then to an equally famous extract from yesterday's reading of the Song of Moses.

A few moments ago, we all observed in reverence the sacred *Yizkor*-hour of remembrance for our dearest departed loved ones. I recalled the memory of my revered and sainted father, and in his memory I want to pass on to you an interpretation he was particularly fond of giving this phrase from Isaiah's magnificent vision of the Messianic Age: "For the earth shall be full of the knowledge of the Lord, as the waters cover the sea." Now, what is the meaning of this strange comparison between the universality of the knowledge or the acknowledgement of God in the age of perfection and "the waters covering the sea"? My father explained it this way: If in the end all humans and all peoples alike will recognise the sovereignty of God, if ultimately we will all reach the same destination, then why should some people endure so much suffering and so much hardship for the sake of religion for thousands of years while others will live carefree lives until we reach that common destination? Surely it is inconceivable that those who have made religion their national business, suffering martyrdom and untold agonies to vindicate the belief in God and to promote the rule of religion, should ultimately be no better and no nearer the ideal than those who never cared, who remained pleasure-hunting pagans throughout history, completely indifferent to all religion and interested only in their own fleeting happiness.

Hence, says the Prophet, the knowledge of God in the time to come will be "as the waters cover the sea". These waters have the same level all over the globe only on the surface. Superficially they are all alike. But underneath the surface they vary tremendously in depth. In some parts, the oceans are many miles deep, in others their shallowness can be measured in inches. That is how the understanding of God will be in the Messianic Age. For those who have spent all their energies and lavished their best intellectual resources for thousands of years on studying the law of God, on intensive research into religious thought, on a ceaseless quest for the moral order of self-discipline and ennoblement, for them the acknowledgement of God will be profound like the unfathomable depths of the ocean. But for those who are only newcomers to religion, the knowledge of God will be shallow, just inches deep. Superficially, we will all alike acclaim the sovereignty of God. On the surface, "in that day the Lord will be One and His Name will be One", as His sovereignty will be universally hailed. But underneath the surface there will be enormous differences of depth and shallowness, "as the waters cover the sea".

Similar variations are also to be found in the depths of Jewish scholarship among different Jewish communities the world over. Anglo-Jewry has many outstanding assets and virtues, but profound or popular Jewish scholarship is not one of them. In all the three hundred years of its existence, Anglo-Jewry has produced and trained very few Jewish scholars of international repute. Characteristically, the most outstanding contributions to Jewish literature in this country have been translations, such as the monumental renderings into English of the entire Talmud, Midrash and Zohar. Translations, of course, are essentially the least original works of scholarship; they merely transmit the creative intellectual and literary labours of others. We just cannot compare our indigenous contributions to Jewish scholarship in this country with the highly original output in the creative fields of rabbinics, or theology, or philosophy, or other areas of Jewish thought by the Jewish communities on the European continent before the war, or in Israel and America since the war.

With 95 per cent of all our children receiving no Jewish education at all past the Bar Mitzvah age—and that education consisting often of training for a one-day Synagogue performance which they could just as well obtain from a gramophone record as from a teacher—our standards are bound to be shallow indeed. Anyone who can tolerably conduct a religious service, or recite a passable Haftorah, ranks almost as a *Talmid Chacham*, whilst a person at home in a piece of *Chumash Rashi* is looked upon as a *Gaon*. We have a long way to go, therefore, till we reach some acceptable depths of Jewish scholarship through more intensive Jewish education.

But all this would be of relatively minor significance without my second point. Our text selected from the Song of Moses refers to two kinds of Judaism: there is the faith of *This is my God and I will glorify Him*, in which I uphold Judaism because I have discovered it for myself; and there is the religion of *My father's God and I will exalt Him*, in which I carry out the practices of Judaism and subscribe to its teachings simply out of respect for my father who believed in them. There is a vast difference between the two forms of allegiance. Of "my father's God" it says: "and I will exalt Him"— in Hebrew *va'aromemenhu*, from the root *rom*, meaning "high", "lofty" or "soaring". A God who is not my own but merely "my father's" I worship even if He is "high" above me; a religion confessed simply out of respect for my father, out of filial piety, does not have to make sense to me; even if it is far "above" I will still reverently uphold it. Such a loyalty is generated by a deep sense of tradition, not by the recognition of any intrinsic value in my religious practices.

But if Judaism is to be my own faith and not just my father's, if *This is my God*, then *I will glorify Him*—in Hebrew *ve'anvehu*. According to one Talmudic sage, this word derives from *na'eh* "beautiful". Hence the phrase is interpreted as *hithna'eh lefanav*, "beautify yourself before Him"; perform the *mitzvot* in a beautiful manner, don a beautiful *tallit*, build a beautiful *succah*, take a beautiful *lulav*. In other words, I can only find *my God* and discover Judaism for myself, by seeing in Jewish observances something beautiful, attractive, and meaningful. Another sage interprets the word as "Be like God", explained by Rashi as based on dividing the word *ve'anvehu* into *ani* and *vehu*, meaning "I and He". Only by relating myself to God, by engaging in a dialogue with Him, and by seeing the relevance of the teachings of my faith to the problems and burdens of the society in which I live can God become *my God*. Both interpretations, then, make it clear that Judaism can be truly meaningful to me only if I can discover the *beauty* and the *relevance* of its teachings rather than relying merely on the inertia of preserving my father's observances through a blind attachment to tradition.

This precisely is our present predicament. Anglo-Jewry has always been a community distinguished for its solid devotion to tradition. Until now this strongly conservative trend has served us well and preserved the essentially Orthodox character of our communal patterns and usages. We still have a far higher proportion of kosher homes, and of people affiliated to Orthodox synagogues, than are to be found in almost any other community in the Diaspora. But it was not our own God we worshipped; it was mainly our fathers' God. Children simply carried on the traditions of their parents without asking why. Whether they were Jewishly educated or not, whether they appreciated Jewish values through a profound study of them or not, made little difference to the stablity of their religious loyalties.

All this is now finished, and not likely to return in our lifetime. In our sophisticated and critical world, a Judaism founded on "the God of my father" cannot survive. If, as the many empty seats at today's *Yizkor*-service have so eloquently testified, respect for parents is no longer powerful enough to make children honour them by a single visit to the Synagogue, then how much less can we rely on such respect to make them act as loyal Jews all the year round, outside the Synagogue as well as inside.

We might as well resign ourselves to the grim new fact of Jewish life: either we intelligently teach our youth what Judaism means, or else Anglo-Jewry is going to become one if the lost tribes of Israel. Either we will educate them to proclaim "This is my God", or they will have no God at all.

This is where my challenge differs from that faced by my predecessors. For them better Jewish education was a desirable asset to adorn the community; for me it is an indispensable priority to prevent the decline and fall of Anglo-Jewry. They presided over a stable community in which the traditions of the past were not questioned, in which the authority of the Establishment was not challenged, and in which the religious and communal loyalties of the rising generation were scarcely determined by their understanding of Judaism, whether it was shallow or profound. I have been called upon to take charge of the religious destinies of Anglo-Jewry in vastly different times. On my success in persuading you and other congregations in this country to take Jewish education far more seriously and to adopt imaginative and expensive programmes of educational expansion may depend the survival of Anglo-Jewry.

We should be under no illusion about it; only a thorough and profound understanding of Judaism, of Jewish ethics and philosophy, of Jewish law and theology, of Jewish literature and history, can counter the rebellion, distractions or apathy generated so profusely in the intellectual and social climate of the restless society around us. Without such understanding through education, especially at the post-Bar Mitzvah level, many of our youth will be left defenceless against the allurements of defection and intermarriage; they will opt out of the community. If we are not going to embark immediately on a massive campaign of educational reconstruction, there will be little left to salvage in ten years' time from now. If nothing drastic gets done in the meantime, we shall by then have to close scores of Synagogues for lack of enough regular worshippers to sustain them. Worse still, we shall have no spiritual leaders to guide our congregations. The recruitment situation, already more precarious than is generally realised—with ever more important vacancies we are unable to fill adequately—will be nothing short of disastrous in ten years from now, unless an altogether new attitude to Jewish education and scholarship will again begin to attract some of our most promising young men to dedicate themselves to Rabbinical and teaching careers in the supreme service of our community.

You may now understand why, in contrast to my predecessors, I cannot afford to be patient or reticent in my urgent demands for solving our educational crisis with all the resources at our command. If I fail to arouse you, or if you fail to respond, there may be no further Chief Rabbi after me to have another chance, there may be neither Rabbis nor teachers, neither worshippers nor Zionists, there may be no corporate Jewish life as we have known it until now.

May God grant us the will and inspiration to succeed, so that we may transform the "God of my father" of the past into "This is my God" of the present and the future. We will then have an immortal share in speeding the age when indeed "the earth will be filled of the knowledge of the Lord as the waters cover the sea". That age of universal peace will be characterised, among other blessings, by the reins of leadership passing into the hands of youth, as foretold in the idyllic picture drawn by the Prophet in this Festival's final Biblical message: "And the wolf shall dwell with the lamb, and the leopard shall lie down with the kid; and the calf and the young lion and the fattling together; and a little lad shall lead them." May we do our part in making our little lads, our youth, fit for leading our people and all mankind into an era of peace and happiness for all.

LIFE-LINE TO SURVIVAL

Education lies at the heart of Jewish purpose and without it we perish. Today this is more acutely true than ever before. We have ample experience to prove that no Jewish loyalties can survive in our modern society without a thorough knowledge of Judaism.

When, five years ago, I was called to assume my share of the responsibility for safeguarding the future of British Jewry and its religious traditions, I realised full well that, in the face of the alarming drift threatening the very survival of our community, I would have to concentrate all my resources, above any other commitment, on the development of Jewish education, in quality and quantity.

With tens of thousands of Jewish children receiving no Jewish instruction at all, and 80% of the remainder forsaking their meagre studies at an age when they cannot but remain juvenile Jews for the rest of their lives, it is no wonder that so many of our young people find their Jewishness too crippled and underdeveloped to sustain their loyalty to our faith, to our community, to Israel and indeed to the moral values of society.

The case made within these covers is simple and compelling. The brief historical survey and statistics (the most comprehensive so far assembled) testify to the considerable strides made during the past twenty five years. Out of the near-paralysis of Jewish education in the War years and through the single-minded efforts of a few pioneers, has grown a burgeoning countrywide network of Jewish Day Schools, now embracing one in six of all Jewish children in the primary grades and one in twelve of all Jewish children in the secondary age group.

But this is still far from adequate. Every year our schools are turning away hundreds of applicants, for whom they have no places, simply because the community defaults on its duty to provide full-time Jewish education for all those who seek it. To ensure Anglo-Jewry's continuity and growth, we must double our present capacity in the next ten to fifteen years.

Following several years of intense preparations, the Chief Rabbi launched the "Jewish Educational Development Trust" with the publication of an attractive booklet entitled Let My People Know—Proposals for the Development of Jewish Education *in 1971. The booklet contains a Foreword (reproduced here), a brief history of Anglo-Jewish education, a detailed statistical survey of its growth in the post-War period, and a two-phase programme of expansion and intensification. With the help of the Trust, many of the proposals have since been implemented.*

In Great Britain only in Manchester, Liverpool, Sunderland and Gateshead, and in the London Borough of Hackney, do at least one in three Jewish children attend Jewish Schools. But this is now the rule rather than the exception in most larger European and Commonwealth communities (including Canada, South Africa and Australia). This target is therefore entirely realistic and attainable—all the more when it is remembered that virtually all these overseas communities, unlike our own, maintain their schools entirely out of their own resources, without any State aid.

The target will require not only a colossal new school building programme, but also a corresponding increase in the output of qualified teachers, headmasters and other skilled personnel.

The present proposals outline in some detail the first 5 year phase of the programme, concentrating the building programme mainly on Greater London (where the need—and demand—is greatest, and where two thirds of British Jewry reside), but also featuring national schemes such as teacher training. Phase II of the scheme, spread over the succeeding decade, must be re-evaluated and more precisely formulated as soon as the first projects of the present programme are "off the ground".

On completion of Phase I approximately 13,000 pupils will have places at Jewish Primary and Secondary Schools. Phase II will have to provide at least another 8,000 places. Altogether, we shall have to plan the construction of some twenty new schools throughout Britain.

No attempt is made here to evaluate the contents of Jewish education. But, by including proposals for Teacher Training and for the setting up of Headmasters' and Educational Experts' Conferences, the machinery will be created for promoting greatly improved standards and methods; better co-ordination between the schools; and pooling of resources for text-books, seminars and other common interests. I hope that some of our schools will become Hebrew speaking (and use Ivrit as the exclusive medium of Jewish instruction, from Kindergarten to A-levels) especially when the Israeli part of our teacher training programme gets under way.

Next to Israel, Jewish education must become our principal concern and the top priority in our communal budgeting. Thoroughly modernising our thinking and planning, congregations and individuals will have to accept the new facts of Jewish life already accepted elsewhere—whereby more money is spent on schools than on shools. Shools preserve Jews; schools create them.

JEWISH IDENTITY

1 WHO IS A JEW?

For over 3,000 years, whatever arguments and schisms may have divided some Jews from others, they were agreed on the definition of a Jew. *He was a person born of a Jewish mother or converted to Judaism according to Jewish law.* They asked only *What* is a Jew, and in reply to this question they produced a vast literature setting forth the *Orach Chayim*, the "path of life", on which one must walk to be characterised as a Jew. But they never asked *Who* is a Jew.

It is a curious testimony to the instability of our times that the oldest people on earth, bound by millennial ties of faith, race and history, should now question its own identity. It is even more ironical that this explosive question, which has rocked the Jewish world, should have erupted in, and out of, the State of Israel, established to give the fullest expression to Jewish identity. Can it be that the State intended to exemplify and cement the unity of the Jewish people should now serve to fragment it?

Such fragmentation would, of course, have been inevitable if the extreme secularists in Israel had won the day against the traditionalists over this question, and if the Israeli parliament had not overruled the Supreme Court's decision in favour of conferring Jewish identity on unconverted children born to a non-Jewish mother. There would have been two conflicting definitions of a Jew: one as defined by history and tradition, and the other as contrived by a secular state. Since one group would be unable to recognise the other as Jews, or marry its members, the seeds would be sown for a national disaster on a scale matched only by the division of Solomon's kingdom into Israel and Judah, two distinct and sometimes warring nations, a calamity which eventually led to the loss of ten of the twelve tribes of the Jewish people. Little wonder that the Who is a Jew controversy, touching such a raw nerve of the Jewish conscience, sparked off the gravest internal upheaval in the history of the Jewish State, erupting into several cabinet crises and reverberating bitterly in Jewish communities throughout the world.

Since Israel's establishment, religious Jews have had many, sometimes

---

The following three essays, published by the Jewish Marriage Education Council in 1971, are based on lectures given during the preceding years in London.

vehement clashes with the secularists over the numerous issues that divide them: over military conscription for girls, Sabbath observance, pig-breeding, indiscriminate autopsies and other *causes célèbres*. But these were only skirmishes, relatively speaking. The Who is a Jew controversy is the first serious conflict over what lies at the core of their disagreement—and at the heart of Jewish peoplehood.

It was not only the immediate need to preserve the unity of the Jewish people which raised this controversy to such a pitch of intensity and world-wide agitation. Underlying the conflict was the deeper crisis of Jewish identity which irritated modern Jewish life both *inside and outside Israel*. The incongruity of an essentially secular Jewish state emerging out of, and within, an essentially religious Jewish tradition and history was bound to produce tensions that could not fail to reach some breaking point. Added to these tensions were the secularist pressures on and among Jews in the Diaspora. For many of them, the most meaningful link with the Jewish people had long ceased to be of any religious significance; they identified themselves as Jews only in a purely secularist sense—through social, ethnic, cultural or national bonds.

So long as the forces of assimilation operated only on individual Jews, the crisis could be contained. However great and painful the losses caused by religious defection, they did not affect the corporate continuity of the religious element in Jewish existence. There *was* simply no recognised way to authenticate Jewish identity and to establish personal association with the Jewish people other than the criteria established by the religious community. No Jewish social club, ethnic fraternity, cultural society, or political movement could challenge the exclusive right of religious authorities to determine and confer membership of the Jewish people. Officially, at any rate, Jewish identity remained a religious designation; even individually, while people could opt *out* of the religious community by defining their Jewishness in secular terms, they could not opt *in* to become members of the Jewish people except by entering through the portals of the Jewish religion.

All this changed radically when assimilation to secular patterns found *national* expression in the State of Israel. Here emerged, for the first time in Jewish history, an official agency claiming the power, through its legislature and its judiciary, to enact and interpret laws affecting Jewish status by criteria other than religious allegiance.

Obviously, no one disputes the prerogative of the Jewish State to legislate concerning the national status of its citizens and to determine the conditions for the grant of citizenship. *Who is an Israeli* is the exclusive concern of Israel. But *Who is a Jew* affects the ten million Jews outside Israel no less vitally than the three million inside. Membership of the Jewish people must clearly be the concern of all its members.

So far the immediate crisis has been resolved democratically by the overwhelming majority of Israel's population and parliament favouring the *status quo*, i.e. the traditional definition of the Jew by religious criteria. The religious minority received massive support from the secularist camp not only because Jewish unity was at stake, but also because the overriding anxiety for Israel's military and political security rendered the times unpropitious for a major internal showdown by inviting an open *Kulturkampf*. The pressure exerted by Jewish communities in the Diaspora, too, was bound to weigh heavily on the outcome. But the root-cause of the tensions cannot be eliminated so long as there is the dichotomy of a secular state set in the ethos of a religious tradition and bound to religiously-oriented communities abroad by some common identity. In the long run, the problem is all the more intractable because of the need to include references to Jewishness in Israel's civil legislation, such as in the Law of Return and in the registration of citizens, not to mention the surrender of jurisdiction on personal status to religious courts, themselves subject to the higher jurisdiction of secular courts—a built-in source of friction and contradiction.

The present rather precarious truce based on the *status quo* is not likely to be replaced by an enduring understanding until the very character and composition of the Jewish State undergoes a fundamental change. In the meantime we may be somewhat reassured in the knowledge that this complex issue is but one of the many paradoxes and inconsistencies which have marked the irrational course of Jewish history from the beginning to the present day.

The national ramifications of the controversy, while of primary importance, are obviously not the only ones to be considered. The problem merits equally serious examination from the point of view of the individuals concerned.

In order to discuss the main arguments, let us consider an extreme case. A European Jew married a non-Jewess, and they experienced the horrors of Nazi persecution together. She moreover had a Jewish grandfather and was branded and treated as a Jewess according to the racist Nuremberg laws. They were liberated after the war and settled in Israel. They lived only among Jews and integrated completely into Israel's social life. And their sons served with distinction in the Israeli army. These now declare themselves as Jews, though they refuse to undergo a religious conversion. Why should they be denied Jewish status, and consequently the right to marry Jewish partners?

Let us analyse these claims *seriatim*. By what logic or process shall suffering together with Jews, or even on account of Jews, turn one into a Jew? There were countless Christians, atheists and others in the concentration camps. Shall they all be entitled to be accepted as Jews on request, simply because they shared their ordeal with Jews?

The argument becomes even more unreasoned when used in conjunction with the resort to the Nuremberg laws defining anyone with even a single Jewish grandparent as a Jew. Shall the norms of Jewish law and tradition be revised to comply with the arbitrary whims of a diabolical tyrant? It would surely only add revolting insult to crushing injury to suggest that Hitler replace the Sages of Israel in determining Who is a Jew, and that his racist laws and persecution become a substitute for solemn acts of proselytisation. Such an abject surrender by Judaism to the mad frenzy of its oppressor would forfeit the merit gained from all the martyred generations who defied tyranny and the evil ideologies behind it.

Even subjectively, it is hard to see how joint suffering can ever be a guarantee for a common commitment. People who survived the concentration camps are not likely to be any less diverse in outlook and allegiance than were those who entered them. Judaism may often be conducive to suffering, but suffering of itself can hardly be conducive to Judaism.

Nor can social integration among Jews, on its own, establish Jewish status any more than living among Britons can confer British citizenship. For the sake of mere legality, if nothing else, there must be some manifest act or ceremony to effect such a cardinal change as the transfer from one loyalty (or none) to another. One cannot just lose one's way into Judaism, as it were, dissolving one's identity and imperceptibly merging into another, without some pledge, some formal entry, some acceptance of the rules governing the group to be joined.

Service in the defence of Israel certainly merits the highest recognition and gratitude by Jews everywhere. The award of a prize, a title, the freedom of a city, or even honorary citizenship—by all means. But being a Jew cannot be a kind of a medal, a distinction bestowed for meritorious service. A Jew *honoris causa* is at least as absurd as an honorary rabbi or an honorary physician admitted to practice without any qualifications.

Even less plausible is the suggestion that a person should become Jewish by declaring himself to be so. Would a club or society admit members merely by virtue of a declaration that they regarded themselves as members? It is up to any simple organisation, let alone an historic entity like the Jewish people, to determine its own rules for admission.

Underlying all our objections to these facile arguments is, of course, a much more basic consideration. Any entrance into the fellowship of Jewish peoplehood is a mutual covenant. *A convert joins the Jewish people no less than the Jewish people joins him.* They assume mutual obligations and commitments. Every Jew becomes a brother to him as he becomes a brother to every Jew. Such a covenant can never be unilateral, for it assumes the willingness of all Jews to regard the newcomer as one of them just as much as his agreement to consider himself so. And without a rabbinically sanctioned conversion a large segment of the Jewish people at least, to say nothing of Jewish law, would refuse, and could not be expected, to recognise him as a Jew, so rendering his or anyone else's claim that he is Jewish entirely meaningless.

Finally, turning from Jews by conversion to Jews by birth, we must explain why Jewish status is inherited from the mother and not the father in the event of a mixed marriage. This rule has its origin in a biblical allusion. On entering the land of Canaan, the Jews were warned against marrying with the indigenous population: "And you shall not make marriages with them; your daughter you shall not give unto his son, nor shall you take his daughter unto your son. For he will turn away your son from following Me" (Deut. 7:3–4). "He will turn away your son" evidently refers to a non-Jew, married to a Jewess, seducing their child to idolatry. This child is called "your son", in other words, he is regarded as Jewish though he only has a Jewish mother. But in the reverse case of "his daughter given to your son", it does not state "For she will turn away your son"; hence, the Rabbis deduced that with a non-Jewish mother the child would be longer be "your son" (Rashi).

Several reasons may be given for the rule. A child from a mixed marriage could not legally be a 50% Jew, growing up with a half commitment or a double faith. A choice must be made, and once made, it must be consistently applied in all cases, since no law can be arbitrary or subject to personal variations. Now, in making this choice, the certainty of maternity must be set against the doubt of paternity, however small this doubt may be. In such cases Jewish law invariably invokes the rule "a doubt can never over-rule a certainty".

Even in nature, the mother's bond with her child is, in some respects, firmer than the father's. It was Eve (Hebrew *Chavah*) who was so called "because she was the mother of all living (*chay*)" (Gen. 3:20), whereas Adam was not named "*Chayim*" as "the father of all life". It must also be remembered that Jewish law, unable to sanction or recognise a mixed marriage as religiously valid, technically regards the child as born out of wedlock and therefore legally having a mother only.

In a wider sense, the determination of the child's religious status by the mother may also indicate that she has the superior influence on the child's religious development.

Finally, and equally important, apart from these intrinsic national and personal considerations, the indirect effects of any change in the legislation of Israel on Jewish life the world over must be borne in mind. By giving non-Jews (i.e. particularly the children of mixed marriages with a non-Jewish mother) the right to claim Jewish status without a conversion sanctioned by Jewish religious law, that is, according to the *Halacha*, Israel would deal a devastating blow to efforts to curb the inroads of assimilation and inter-marriage already sorely afflicting Jewish communities in the Diaspora.

At present, the knowledge that such children will not be accepted as Jews—in their home communities or in Israel—without first fulfilling the conditions for conversion is often the only effective deterrent to young Jews contemplating marriage outside their faith. By removing this barrier in Israel, the floodgates still stemming the tide of inter-marriage elsewhere would be breached. Not only would rabbinical authorities in the Diaspora be subjected to intolerable pressures to be "no holier" than Israel in policies on admissions to Judaism, but mixed couples and their children could always assure their recognition as Jews at the cost of a return ticket to Israel where the necessary papers could be legally obtained.

Psychologically, too, any tampering with the traditional and historic definition of Jewish identity in Israel would naturally serve as a disastrous encouragement to inter-marriage. If Israel does not object to such unions and accepts their offspring as Jews, why should Jews elsewhere care or object? In Israel the complete loss of Jewish identity through the secularisation of Jewishness might be partly, and temporarily, checked by the forces of national cohesion and patriotic allegiance; in the Diaspora the consequences of such a break with tradition would inevitably threaten to erode any form of Jewish commitment and identity.

This is recognised even by Israel's principal spokesmen in the secularist camp, as was so eloquently expressed by the Head of Government and the Leader of the Opposition in the memorable Knesset debate which ended in over-ruling the Supreme Court and in reaffirming the traditional definition of

Who is a Jew. This is an extract of the moving speech by the Prime Minister, Mrs. Golda Meir:

> I am not religiously observant, but had it not been for religion, we would have shared the fate of all those peoples who have disappeared. We are fortunate, indeed, that there are still synagogues in Moscow, Odessa and Leningrad serving as the only centre for Jews to come at least on Simchat Torah, as an outlet for their feelings of Jewish identity. I would like to tell you that in 1948 when I attended synagogue on Rosh Hashana and Yom Kippur in Moscow, I did not stir from my place the whole day. I thought to myself that had I stayed longer at my post, I would have gone to synagogue not out of duty, as the representative of the Jewish State, but I, Golda Meir, my place is in the synagogue along with other Jews.
>
> Above all else, in my view and that of the overwhelming majority of the Knesset, the survival of Israel comes first, before the State of Israel, before Zionism. . . . Any price is worth paying for the security of the State of Israel, so long as it is realised that its role is to preserve the Jewish people. Otherwise, it is pointless. The measure may not succeed in reducing the incidence of inter-marriage, but at least it will grant no *Heter* (license) for it.

And this is a part of Mr. Menachem Begin's historic utterance on the same occasion:

> Our people should have by now numbered 200 to 250 million souls. . . . Why have but 13 million survived? There are only two reasons for that—slaughter and assimilation. And who knows if assimilation did not take what slaughter had spared—many millions in each generation. Were it not for the prohibition of inter-marriage, we would have disappeared long ago. . . .
>
> What are your grievances against the Halacha which determines who is a Jew? . . . We interpret the laws of Israel for well over twenty years, in the light of English Common Law. If in the days of Queen Elizabeth I, a British judge passed a sentence, the Israeli judges are still bound by that precedent. . . . What is wrong, what is sinful, with the idea that in the fateful matter, Who is a Jew, we should be bound by the interpretation of the Jewish Common Law—pardon my expression—the Jewish Halacha which is in force thousands of years? What free man can be insulted by that?
>
> I propose the following rule to the entire Knesset without distinction of Party. Here it is: *That Judaism not be forced on any person, and no person be forced on Judaism.* Is this compulsion? . . . Suppose a person does not submit to traditional conversion and is still classified as a Jew; isn't that compulsion? Yes, that would be a compulsion imposed upon the entire Jewish people for generations without end; upon millions no longer alive, upon those who are alive, and upon millions yet unborn.

Since the above was written, more recent developments have prompted me to add the following paragraph.

Persuaded by these arguments, the Knesset conceded the major principle at stake in the Who is a Jew controversy, *viz.* that admissions to Jewish status can be effected by religious conversion only and not by any secular act or agency. But, alas, in revising the law, the Israeli parliament introduced a new element of confusion. The revised law authorises the registration of Jews "by birth or by conversion", without stipulating that such conversion must be "in accordance with the Halacha". Clearly, this omission provides a loophole for the registration as Jews of persons who were not converted according to traditional Jewish law and who could not, therefore, be recognised as Jews by Orthodox Jews the world over. Consequently, officially, there are now persons, however limited in number, whom Israel acknowledges as Jews whilst all traditional Jews would regard them as non-Jews, thus establishing the breach in the definition of Jewish identity it was intended to avert. This breach is both confined and aggravated by the fact that it is of purely civil significance—confined inasmuch as such persons are still subject to Orthodox rabbinic jurisdiction in matters of marriage and divorce in Israeli law, and aggravated, for the very reason that such persons are admitted to Israel as Jews and yet not permitted to marry as Jews there. This inconsistency—not to mention the threat to the unity of the Jewish people resulting from it—remains to be resolved. Meanwhile the debate continues with unabated bitterness.

2 STEMMING INTER-MARRIAGE—WHY AND HOW?

Among Jews there is no word next to *sh'mad* (apostasy) which evokes greater horror than inter-marriage (meaning really extra-marriage or mixed marriage). Even Jews who have reconciled themselves to a *t'rephah* meal or a Sabbath cigar still wince with heartache on learning that their child has decided to marry out. How far can such an attitude be justified, and promoted, in this day and age?

While reliable statistics are difficult to obtain, the estimated rate of inter-marriage—ranging from 15% to 50% or more in different communities—has certainly reached disaster proportions. According to a recent assessment in America, some 70% of all children born of mixed marriages are not raised as Jews altogether. Even of the remaining 30% very few indeed are likely to grow up as committed Jews. Since Jewish boys are about twice as prone to marry out as Jewish girls, two-thirds of the resultant children (since they assume the mother's status) are not even legally Jewish. With the abnormally low Jewish birth-rate already scarcely sufficient to maintain the existing Jewish population, the cumulative effect of inter-marriage among Jews the world over, after one or two generations, is therefore liable to result in losses comparable to the extermination of one-third of our people in the Nazi Holocaust. That is the purely demographic measure of this calamitous problem.

That this process of attrition is infinitely less dramatic than the mass-slaughter of six million Jews only aggravates the situation. When Jews are lost through register-office marriages instead of gas-chambers, no one weeps, protests or demonstrates. There is no enemy to galvanise the defenders into frantic action, and no outburst of anguish to stir the conscience of the survivors. The worst cancer is the painless type; unaware of the danger signals, the patient will not even resort to a doctor for treatment until it is too late. Inter-marriage is such a scourge. It gnaws almost imperceptibly at the vitals of Jewish existence, without raising the alarm to induce our people to seek drastic prophylactic and therapeutic treatment.

The present-day scale of the problem may be unprecedented, but its existence is hardly new. In fact, it has bedevilled the Jewish people at almost all times. It is striking that the Biblical account of Jewish history begins and ends with a protest against inter-marriage. In the very first record of a Jewish marriage, Abraham expresses his anxiety over the problem and charges his trusted servant "not to take for my son a wife of the daughters of the Canaanites in whose midst I live" (Gen. 24:3). History repeats itself in the next generation, when Rebekah tells her husband Isaac: "My life has become repugnant because of the daughters of Heth. If Jacob take a wife, such as these, of the daughters of the land . . . , what is my life worth?" (Gen. 27:46) She sends Jacob away from home, not just to be safe from the murderous fury of his brother, but also from the danger of betraying the ideals which he was born to uphold. Without assuring the continuity of these ideals, life becomes "repugnant" and ceases to have any "worth" for the first Jewish parents.

Again, at the end of the biblical record, Ezra the Scribe confronts the same problem when organising the return of the Babylonian exiles. By now, inter-marriage was widely rampant; as in our own day, it evidently appealed to Jewish men far more than to women, and it penetrated the top echelons of Jewish leadership: "For they have taken of their daughters for themselves and for their sons: so that the holy seed have mingled themselves with the peoples of the lands; yea, the hand of the princes and rulers has been first in this faithlessness" (Ezra 9:2). By Ezra's drastic decree, only those Jews who separated from their non-Jewish partners were permitted to participate in the return to the Land of Israel, and the episode caused great popular grief: "Now while Ezra prayed, and made confession, weeping and casting himself down before the house of God, there was gathered together unto him out of Israel a very great congregation of men and women and children; for the people wept very sore" (Ezra 10:1).

The problem did not abate in post-Biblical times. It is mentioned in the Book of Maccabees at a time when Jewish consciousness was particularly stirred, leading the Maccabean Beth Din to pronounce a special ban on such marriages. This was reinforced by further enactments in the Talmud. Even in the Middle Ages, when mixed marriages encountered Christian as well as Jewish opposition, rabbinic writings frequently reflect the acute concern of communal leaders with this problem.

But these precedents can serve but as cold comfort in an age when the problem has assumed altogether new dimensions. It now not only besets, and often breaks up, Jewish families by the thousands, sometimes even "the best" of them. It not only, as we have seen, makes serious inroads into the prospects of Jewish survival, it also threatens to disrupt many Jewish communities. For all too frequently it is the controversy over accepting inter-married couples and their children that leads to new non-Orthodox congregations being formed, so splintering the established community. Often neither the old nor the new congregation is really viable, and frequently these splits lead to intercommunal strife and bitterness.

In the past three factors, apart from the safeguard of a higher birth-rate which more than compensated for the losses sustained, combined to contain the flood of inter-marriage: an intense love and understanding of Judaism, the deterrent of public disgrace, and a social climate generally unfavourable to mixed marriages. Today, none of these factors operates effectively, and their restoration or replacement merits careful consideration to discover how far they can be applied in the light of the prevailing condition of Jewish life.

When a young man stands on the brink of temptation—drawn there by the attraction of a non-Jewish girl claiming his heart—obviously, the primary and strongest safeguard is a passionate love of Judaism. He can prevail in the ensuing struggle within him only when the love for his faith and people proves the stronger of the two attractions at the critical moment of decision. His Jewish convictions would have to be sound and compelling for him to reject, on purely religious grounds, the partnership with a girl to whom he feels intensely attracted. Nowadays, very few young Jews and Jewesses are equipped to master such a crisis. Because their Jewish education is usually stunted at a juvenile level when they reach the age of thirteen years, it is hardly surprising that some non-Jewish girl encountered by chance on a dance floor or at a coffee bar proves a stronger attraction than the slight bond they have with Judaism.

Classical Hebrew significantly uses the same word *yada* for "to know" and "to love". One can only *love* what one knows, and what is unknown, strange or remote cannot be held dear and cherished. An enduring love for Judaism can only grow out of a thorough knowledge of it, and where this is lacking, the basic insurance against inter-marriage is cancelled. Intensive Jewish education, therefore, is clearly the first necessity for raising a loyal generation of Jews.

Of course, Jewish education covers more than mere abstract learning. It is a life-time process, starting from earliest childhood and including, above all, the constant experience of Jewish living. A cheerful, devout Jewish home, founded on the strict observance of the *Kashrut* laws, is a most potent agent against inter-marriage. By restricting one's eating to homes and establishments serving only *kasher* food, one is likely to avoid the social intimacies that lead to inter-marriage. The splendours of the Jewish Sabbath and the intelligent observance of the laws of Jewish family life all produce the kind of outlook and a commitment that ensures that a young person does not even contemplate finding his life's partner outside the ranks of his faith and people.

The battle against inter-marriage does not begin at the age of sixteen or seventeen, when young people start to "date" seriously. By then the battle is already either won or lost. It begins at least ten years earlier, if not at a still younger age. A little anecdote may illustrate the point:

A young man once stood at a station platform, waiting for a train. "Could you tell me the time, please?" he asked another traveller standing beside him. No answer. He asked again, only to be ignored. Impatient, he rebuked the elderly gentleman: "If you have no watch, you might at least tell me so civilly." The other man replied: "I have a watch, and I could have told you the time. But had I done so, you would have thanked me, and on boarding the train you would have sat down next to me and engaged in conversation with me. Before the journey was over, you would have known where I was living. You would have come to look me up one day, found that I had a very attractive daughter, and eventually proposed to marry her—and I don't want a son-in-law who hasn't even got a watch!''

If one wants to prevent the wrong marriage, one cannot wait until the train has arrived. One must foresee the sequence of events while still waiting for the train—before the journey has begun. According to the Talmud, marriages are determined in Heaven forty days before a child is formed. It is certain that on earth inter-marriages are made or unmade at about that time, determined by the parents' attitude and way of life before the child is born.

The second barrier to inter-marriage, now also widely breached, was the horror it evoked in the Jewish community. The very frequency with which inter-marriages now occur has vitiated this deterrent. Bashfulness and shame —once virtues particularly fostered among Jews as a safeguard against vice— are altogether in short supply in this age of immodesty.

It may be difficult to recreate the communal sense of outrage which often helped to rescue those who might waver, too weak to resist through their own personal resources of will-power and self-discipline. But the onus rests on the community to strive for its own survival and to secure it by any means, short of impinging on the individual's freedom of conscience. However, this freedom does not curtail the community's right, and duty, to insist on reciprocity in its relations with its members. To belong to the community, to enjoy its privileges and honours, is the birthright of every Jew. In turn, he must meet his debt to the community and accept certain responsibilities. On inter-marriage, these responsibilities are renounced, and therefore any claim to communal honours and privileges lapses. By denying these, the community invokes sanctions designed to prevent the breach of faith from being taken for granted, and public honours being given in return for public dishonour and damage.

A community under such stress is also under a special obligation to ensure that societies, clubs and functions organised under its auspices, and supported to serve Jewish interests, will not encourage, or even permit, the kind of mixed membership which, far from stemming the tide of inter-marriage, promotes it.

The obvious dilemma involved in advocating such policies nowadays may be considered in dealing with the third traditional barrier: the non-Jewish objection to inter-marriage which has now also all but disappeared. Not so long ago it was generally accepted that religious groups kept together, and should keep together, without incurring the disapproval of social reformers or popular opinion. Such denominational cohesion was considered to be as natural and proper as the exclusiveness of family bonds—the relationship between husband and wife, or parents and children. Today this restrictiveness is often branded as ghettoism. In our morally permissive and ethnically egalitarian society, it is becoming increasingly difficult to resist the common movement towards blurring all human differences and distinctions.

These present trends pose a double challenge to the Jewish people: how to maintain its identity as a tiny minority swimming against a mighty tide, and how to advocate religious particularism and so risk popular antagonism, if not hostility. Both challenges will demand sacrifice and courage of a high order. They call for a defiance of conformity, and nothing is harder in this age of conformity than to defy it.

The post-Emancipation period has taught us that Jewish survival is no easier, and certainly no more assured, in conditions of freedom than under persecution. Indeed, while the Jewish people have demonstrated the capacity to survive oppression, it has yet to prove that it can survive liberty and equality. What is now needed is nothing short of a new type of martyrdom— a martyrdom not to die for Judaism but, possibly harder still, to live for Judaism at the cost of unpopularity and the risk of rejection. Voluntarily to surrender some of the hard-won boon of social acceptance demands the highest form of idealism. The communal endorsement of policies to counter the ravages of inter-marriage will undoubtedly exact such a price. But it is no higher than the price Jewish communities in the Diaspora will have to pay for their readiness to identify themselves with Israel, even at the risk of incurring the charge of "dual loyalties" and other grave embarrassments.

In the end, however, the choice on whether to marry in or out is a highly personal decision, little influenced by communal policies and attitudes. The real argument to be overcome is: "As long as we are happy together. . . ." It is of little avail to counter such a philosophy of life with statistics. Experience may show, as in fact it does, that the rate of marriage failures and divorces is twice as high in mixed marriages as in endogamous unions. Sociological surveys may also indicate that children brought up in a spiritual no-man's-land are more prone than others to end up in misery and mischief. But no young couple in the flush of love think, or even fear, that theirs will be among the marriages to strike disaster, or that their children will turn out as misfits. Young people no more believe that they will land on the wrong side of the statistics than do inveterate smokers. The rate of casualties may be far higher, but love is an even more irresistible addiction than smoking.

The answer, therefore, will have to be found elsewhere. So long as our sons and daughters are brought up to believe the pernicious doctrine that all that matters in life is to be happy, to have "a good time"—rather than to make the times good—they are bound to grow up as social parasites, doing no good to society or ultimately to themselves. Happiness, like honour, as our Sages said, eludes those who pursue it and pursues those who flee from it. Our children must be taught, if they are to be raised as solid and useful citizens, that we are not born simply in order to amuse ourselves. Life is too precious for that. It is also too sacred to be prostituted by any vice masquerading as a virtue by making the pursuit of happiness into an ideal, thinking that the selfish formula "as long as it makes them happy" can legitimise and whitewash every breach of the moral and social order. Some people are made happy by cheating—betraying their fellow-men's confidence; some by adultery—betraying their marriage; and others by marrying out—betraying their people. Only in a perverse society do the whims of personal happiness determine the norms of right and wrong, and only the most irresponsible parents tell their children to regulate their behaviour by whatever makes them happy.

To Jews this notion is particularly obnoxious. The cult of happiness could have saved the Jewish people two thousand years of agony. Jews could have been as happy as anyone else for the asking. All they had to do to put an end to their suffering and martyrdom was to renounce their religious commitment, to betray their faith. But the thought of purchasing happiness at the cost of their ideals never occurred to them. Jews simply were not brought up to think along those lines. They took it for granted that life served a higher purpose than just to enjoy oneself, and they cheerfully endured hardship and persecution for the sake of values which made life, and even death, worth while.

And because they did not pursue happiness, it pursued them in the end. In all the misery of their circumstances, Jews were probably the happiest people in Western society. Inside their homes they found ample compensation for their suffering outside. Cheered by their Sabbaths and festivals, and rejoicing in the delights of harmonious family bonds, untroubled by any generation gap and but rarely soured by divorce or infidelity, their domestic life and stability became the envy of even their oppressors.

Despite their ordeals, Jews loved life more passionately, they clung to life more tenaciously, and they mourned the dead with greater grief than anyone else. Jewish life, however grim externally, was infinitely precious, beautiful and full of joy. Only when Jewish young people are prepared and conditioned to cherish a similar outlook—placing law above love, and service above selfishness—can they and their people anticipate similar rewards of meaningful living combined with true happiness.

3   TO CONVERT OR NOT TO CONVERT?

No rabbinical act is of more far-reaching consequence than a conversion to Judaism. It crucially determines for all time the convert's personal status, his marital rights and restrictions as well as his religious allegiance, and in the case of a female affecting her offspring for all generations to come. If a pledge of unqualified loyalty to Judaism is subsequently betrayed, the result is disastrous, not least for the rabbi involved, should he have been guilty of an error of judgment in authorising the conversion on insufficient evidence of sincerity. In that event, he is bound to feel some personal responsibility and liability for every violation of Jewish law the convert may commit. For only through his act in conferring Jewish status on the former Gentile do actions like working on the Sabbath or consuming *t'rephah* food become grave breaches of the law. Little wonder that many conscientious rabbis, under the weight of this crushing responsibility, contemplate conversions with extreme, sometimes perhaps excessive, hesitation.

The conditions for admission to Judaism are simple enough in definition. A properly qualified rabbinical court must be satisfied that the candidate is genuinely willing and able to accept the religious discipline of Jewish life without reservation, whereupon the formal act of conversion is carried out by ritual immersion and, in the case of a male, circumcision (which, if previously performed, is religiously validated by drawing a single drop of blood as a "sign of the Covenant"). Conversion under these conditions is open to any person, irrespective of race, colour or previous creed. A person so converted, then has all the rights and obligations vested in any other Jew.

Strictly speaking, the actual conversion from any faith (or none) to Judaism is of course carried out by the proselyte himself. The rabbinic authority, in effect, merely serves to authenticate the change, like a hallmark confirming the genuineness of a precious metal. To effect a total religious commitment which is to endure for a lifetime, and through children beyond, more than a declaration of intent is required. It is brought about by radical changes inside the person's heart determining all his future loyalties, his thinking, feelings and actions, the mould of his very personality, in many respects even more bindingly and incisively than the commitment involved in a bond of marriage or in the adoption of a child. *A conversion, in the Jewish view, is the most delicate heart operation to which a person could ever submit, and the onus rests on the applicant to prove that he is adequately prepared to undergo such an operation.* Some may complete the requisite preparation, in intensive study and environmental experience, in a matter of months; others, lacking in determination or opportunity, may never be ready even after years of fruitless effort. How long this process takes is determined by the candidate, not the rabbi.

The ultimate test is certainly not the applicant's love for a Jewish party he or she seeks to marry. On the contrary, such an ulterior motive will militate against accepting the application. The criterion is the love of *Judaism*, generated by such thorough familiarity and fascination with the Jewish way of life as to render all sacrifices, obstacles and delays worth-while. Only if this love of Judaism, in theory and practice, transcends any other love and loyalty are the conditions for admission truly fulfilled.

But why are these conditions so rigid and demanding? Almost every applicant (and many a Jew) questions their justice with the seemingly plausible argument: why should so much more be expected of a convert than most Jews are prepared to do for their Judaism? Why should converts be more punctilious in their religious observance than are the majority of Jews?

To begin with, we have no special interest in swelling our number by conversions. As a "holy people" charged with onerous tasks of spiritual pioneering, numbers are relatively immaterial to the success of our national mission. True "proselytes of righteousness" are welcome, but converts of questionable loyalty attenuate rather than consolidate our strength. As Jewish history has amply demonstrated, our survival does not depend on numbers, but solely on the intensity of our Jewish commitment!

Moreover, a conversion is a religious naturalisation. Even for a civil naturalisation—though affecting infinitely less significantly the innermost beliefs, the whole personality and the daily routine of life of the applicant—certain rigid requirements are universally accepted. For the grant of citizenship, countries usually require a waiting period of at least two years, fluency in the vernacular, and certainly a ready submission to all the laws of the land. No-one questions these demands. Any alien declaring his readiness to observe all the country's laws *except one* would be refused his naturalisation, and it would not help him to argue that there are many native citizens who also sometimes transgress one regulation or another. In these matters it is all or nothing. Yet when would-be converts are told that it may take two years or more to assimilate the requisite knowledge and atmosphere (which even born

Jews must cultivate through years of Jewish education, plus living in a Jewish environment from birth), that they are expected to have some familiarity with Hebrew, and that they must undertake to observe all the laws of Judaism, they argue, often amid a chorus of popular Jewish applause, why should we have to meet requirements which so many Jews fall short of?

It would be of little avail to an applicant for British citizenship to resort to a similar argument. The incontestable answer would be that anyone born of British parents—whether good, bad or indifferent, whether he knows English and abides by the law or not—is British. Even a criminal's citizenship cannot be disowned. But if a foreigner wants to become British, every effort may and must be made to ensure that he will prove a law-abiding citizen, an asset and not a liability. Likewise parents must accept their natural child, healthy or crippled, upright or delinquent. But in adopting a child, they are free to choose, entitled to take all reasonable precautions to make sure that the child will be a source of pride and joy to them. Surely the arguments in favour of similar safeguards in admitting persons to the Jewish faith and people are no less compelling or convincing.

Within these general principles, there is of course a degree of variation. Since the assessment of a candidate's sincerity and the adequacy of his preparation is subject to a human estimation, there is bound to be a subjective factor in any such judgment. One rabbi may be more credulous, another more suspicious in accepting a declaration of submission to Judaism. Moreover, the law itself is flexible enough to allow for some variety of interpretation, notably on the extent to which unknown mental reservations at the time of the conversion act may be discounted. Diverse local conditions, too, may have an important bearing on the decision to admit proselytes. In Israel, for instance, where all converts will certainly live in a Jewish environment, learn Hebrew, send their children to Jewish schools, and observe the Jewish calendar—at least in great measure—and where there is hardly any opportunity of becoming integrated into non-Jewish society, it is obviously far easier to accept converts (and harder to reject them) than in the Diaspora where these conditions do not obtain. In the light of these variables, the attitude to conversion may differ somewhat even among strictly Orthodox rabbinates. England, for example, has always had a tradition of relative stringency in conversion policies. Already in 1735 an Italian traveller, on visiting London, recorded in his diary:

> I saw during this time two Protestants become Jews and be circumcised, and two ladies likewise embrace the Jewish religion with great devotion. The difficulties that the Jews themselves place in the way of those who wish to become Jews are so great that it would seem impossible that anyone should resolve to take such a step. But when it is resolved, it is not taken for an ulterior motive but because they believe that infallibly they are doing rightly. After all the warnings to proselytes, when nothing remains but the act of circumcision, and the operation is to be performed, they bring out a great knife, like that with which the Jews slaughter cattle, which would put fear in a giant, shining like crystal, then the brave fellows resign themselves to endure the pain in order to embrace the Hebrew religion and to believe in the Hebrew Law as the true Law. (*Remember the Days*, ed. John M. Shaftesley, 1966, p. 104.)

The "great knife" mentioned in this passage was, of course, never used for circumcision, but as a metaphorical knife brandished across the path to conversion, like the "flaming sword" guarding the way to the Garden of Eden, it was no less forbidding in the nineteenth century. A curious but telling piece of evidence comes from a letter dated 1873 by Chief Rabbi Nathan Marcus Adler, advising the Hebrew congregation in Sydney against the formation of a Beth Din, for fear that it would only aggravate the "annoyance and unpleasantness" he already had from the Melbourne Beth Din over the admission of proselytes. He wrote in part:

> I beg to state that my long experience has taught me that in general these mixed marriages, even if the woman becomes a convert, prove unhappy. It is not whether in Cromwell's time a condition had been made that we must admit no proselytes into our faith, but this I must say, that even were such not the case we ought ourselves to act as if it were and do all in our power to prevent them. For this reason we postpone them six months, and afterwards, as you know, we send all these cases if unpreventable to Holland. Under these circumstances I must call your attention that you must not regard having a Beth Din in Sydney a boon but quite the reverse, as it will only induce young men to such marriages having every facility in their way, and you would afterwards reproach yourself having asked for it. (Cited by Moshe Davis, *Beit Yisrael Be-Amerika*, 1970, p. 334.)

To this day the standards set by the London Beth Din are stricter than in many other communities, notably in Israel and also in the United States, where, in the absence of a centralised communal rabbinate, attitudes vary widely from rabbi to rabbi.

Naturally, the circumstances prompting an application will invariably be taken into account. A woman who wants to become Jewish because she has fallen in love with a Jew, seeking to change her religion almost like one changes a passport on being married, will find far less sympathy than parents who wish to convert an adopted non-Jewish child because they could find no Jewish child. Extreme compassion, making the conditions as liberal as the law permits, will also be shown in cases of non-Jewish children from mixed marriages who, through no fault of their own, were brought up to believe that they were Jews, attending synagogue services, going to Jewish schools, etc.

But these are clearly exceptions. As a rule, it will be found that anyone prepared to change his religion neither had a deep religious allegiance before the change nor will have one after the change. Those who can be, and are, admitted to Judaism indeed turn out to be rather exceptional people. They represent a microcosm of the Jewish people itself, the few among the many, individuals endowed with a profoundly religious soul, with the capacity to swim against the stream and to spurn the line of least resistance, and with immense hardihood to sustain a stern discipline of life.

True proselytes live up to the qualifications so consicely expressed by the most famous of them all, when Ruth the Moabite pledged: "Where you go, I will go; and where you lodge for the night, I will lodge"—sharing the misfortunes as well as the fortunes of the Jewish people, the experience of darkness in sympathy with Jews who suffer, no less than the bright joys of their triumphs; "your people will be my people"—identifying with Jewish national aspirations and joining the togetherness of Jews whoever and wherever they are; "and your God will be my God"—serving as a witness to Israel's religious commitment; "where you die, I will die, and there shall I be buried" (Ruth 1:16–17)—defending Jewish beliefs and practices even to the grave.

Anyone prepared to follow Ruth's example of total loyalty will be accepted into the Jewish faith with open arms. But in the absence of such candidates, we should occupy ourselves with the challenge to convert *should-be Jews*, rather than *would-be Jews*, to Judaism.

THE "WHO IS A JEW" CRISIS

Almost since the beginning of the Jewish State the arguments between traditionalists and others on the legal definition of "Who is a Jew?" have erupted periodically into fierce controversies, leading to cabinet crises in Israel and to much bitterness throughout the world. The debate reached its unhappy climax in the wake of the Yom Kippur War, when the National Religious Party (Mizrachi-Hapoel Hamizrachi), in compliance with a ruling requested from Chief Rabbi Goren, left the Government in the midst of the delicate disengagement negotiations and refused to rejoin the Coalition unless the Law of Return would be revised and recognise conversions only if carried out "al pi halacha", i.e. according to Orthodox practice. As a result, Israel was beset by a continuous government crisis for several crucial months until the NRP rescinded its decision without gaining any of the concessions demanded and in defiance of the rabbinical ruling it had sought and obtained. Nearly alone among Orthodox rabbis, the author publicly opposed the NRP stand to forestall a futile confrontation at a time of supreme crisis and to avoid the very humiliation eventually suffered by the NRP, causing incalculable damage to Orthodox interests in Israel and abroad. This Memorandum, circulated in February 1974 with the Newsletter *published by the Office of the Chief Rabbi, sets out the practical considerations which guided his attitude.*

The following elaboration on the "Who is a Jew?" controversy, now vindicated by the National Religious Party's decision to rejoin the Government, is presented in response to several requests for the information of colleagues:

1. By concentrating all public attention on the "Who is a Jew?" issue during the present emergency, our religious leadership lost a unique opportunity for responding to the profound spiritual yearnings evoked by the Yom Kippur War. Instead, this diversion has alienated and embittered large sections of our people at a time when they might have been more receptive to religious influences than ever before. By a concerted effort, unhampered by divisive partisanship, we could well have secured far more important gains, including some religious instruction at all Israeli schools, popular confidence in rabbinic leadership, and an appreciation for Jewish spiritual values. The war revealed a desperate need for religious faith, moral discipline and national solidarity to overcome the despondency, turpitude and fragmentation now rampant in Israeli society.

2. To most Jews the supreme anxiety at this time is Israel's survival and security. By exploiting a fortuitous political bargaining position to extract a religious concession, even at the cost of stalling attempts to form a government, the NRP laid itself open to the charge of neglecting the overriding need for a strong government to safeguard Israel's vital interests in the current crucial peace talks—a charge which might for long haunt religious Jewry in its endeavours to assert the primacy of Torah in Jewish life. It might also further erode the appeal of the religious parties.

3. Sadly, the agitation was doomed to failure. It was hardly realistic to expect the Mapai-dominated government, backed by the secularist majority of Israel's Parliament and population, to capitulate to a demand which, however justified in itself, they were bound to regard as affronting some two-thirds of American Jews by disowning their spiritual leaders. A little foresight would have avoided a futile confrontation, a grave religious set-back and a political humiliation for Orthodox Jewry, not to mention a prolonged internal crisis in Israel.

4. The only real outcome of this unhappy episode has been greatly to strengthen the influence of Reform and Conservative Judaism inside and outside Israel. The dissidents have been given a standing and support they never previously enjoyed in Jewish religious affairs, whilst Orthodox Jewry has been brought into disrepute.

5. This painful debate on the identity of the Jew undoubtedly touches on the very core of the Jewish conscience and the essential unity of the Jewish people. The issue also vitally affects the devastating inroads of intermarriage, by encouraging marriage with non-Jews whose "conversion" cannot be recognised by Jewish Law. The urgency of resolving this problem is not in question. But what is questionable, apart from raising it at this particular time when for years the Mizrachi was content not to precipitate a political crisis over it, is the feasibility, if not the wisdom, of settling the matter through political bargaining or civil legislation in the Knesset, even in normal times, especially in the light of the unsuccessful past efforts to amend the Law of Return. In the final analysis, the religious character of the Jewish State will be determined not by legislation or coercion, but by persuasion, especially by raising the younger generation as God-fearing and practising Jews.

6. The intolerable problem of non-Orthodox "converts", who are regarded as non-Jews by those faithful to Halachic Judaism and as Jews by others, bedevils the Diaspora far more than Israel, where immigrants include but a handful of such "converts" (and where these are in any case subject to Orthodox jurisdiction for marriage purposes), compared with thousands of Reform "converts" in America. Hence, any campaign to eliminate the problem should be conducted outside rather than inside Israel.

7. Even if the amendment *Giyur Ke-halacha* ("conversion according to the Halacha") were passed in the Knesset, it would be fraught with grave dangers to the integrity of Halacha. It would in effect compel Israel's rabbinate to give Orthodox authentication to Reform "conversions", by necessitating a formal "reconversion" which would consist of a *Tevila* without any meaningful *Kabbalat Ol Mitzvot* (strict submission to the laws of Judaism), thus perverting Halacha itself. At present the rabbinate is free not to recognise

non-Orthodox "conversions", but once the State requires *Giyur Ke-halacha*, how can the rabbinate withhold its approval (by an empty ceremonial) from immigrants who will live in Israel and yet refuse to share our religious beliefs and practices? Shall they be compelled to send their children to Arab or Christian missionary schools to avoid being raised as Jews? One would sooner have such "converts" misleadingly entered as Jews on civil identity-cards than be forced to give Orthodox sanction to "conversions" which would make a mockery of Halacha.

8. Moreover, *Giyur Ke-halacha*, even if carried out under Orthodox auspices, provides no absolute guarantee against conversions as worthless as non-Orthodox "conversions". As we know only too well from tragic experiences in this country, "conversions" within a few weeks by "ultra-Orthodox" rabbis in Mea Shearim are available for a financial consideration even to British tourists who afterwards return here with imposing conversion certificates and yet are as remote from *Shemirat Shabbat, Kashrut*, etc., as they were before their trip to Israel.

9. "Who is a Jew?" is a religious matter which concerns all Jews, not a subject for civil legislation by Israelis. The only solution to this long-standing problem is to remove the determination of Jewish status from secular authorities to the jurisdiction of the Israel rabbinate, in so far as immigrants to Israel are concerned. For the rest of the world, and particularly America, renewed efforts should be made (previously initiated by Rabbi J. B. Soloveitchik and now supported by others inside and even outside Orthodox ranks) to devise an agreed formula whereby all matters of personal status will eventually be governed by Halachic norms.

10. In the meantime, during the present emergency, a moratorium on all pro- or anti-religious legislation in Israel should be accepted by all parties to prevent further divisiveness, to promote good will, and above all to concentrate all energies on strengthening the spiritual defences of the Jewish people at this critical time when we determine "Who *will* be a Jew" after us.

Chapter Seven

STUDIES IN JEWISH LAW, THOUGHT AND HISTORY

MARRIAGE AND DIVORCE IN THE SOURCES OF JEWISH LAW

Purpose of marriage

The principal purpose of marriage, as reflected in the provisions of Jewish law, is threefold: (a) to enable man to fulfil the duty of procreation; (b) to prevent lewdness in thought and the suspicion of immoral conduct; and (c) to provide men and women, incomplete and unequal by themselves, with what they mutually require to form harmonious entities in intimate companionship.

Marriage as means to procreation

The law to "be fruitful and multiply"[1] ranks as the first of the Bible's 613 precepts.[2] Karo's great code, in the section dealing with marital matters, opens with the significant words: "Every man is obliged to marry in order to beget children, and whoever refuses to discharge this obligation is as if he shed blood; he diminishes the Divine image and causes the Presence of God to depart from Israel."[3] In Jewish law, therefore, the propagation of the race is a positive and cardinal duty. It is this consideration, above any other, which motivates the objection to birth-prevention or other misuses of man's reproductive faculties.[4]

Technically this obligation is incumbent only upon men,[5] and it is fulfilled with the birth of a son and a daughter.[6] These limitations, though mainly theoretical in themselves, govern many consequential regulations. For instance, only men, but not women, are forbidden to marry partners who cannot have children for reasons of health or age, unless they already have a son and a daughter.[7]

Marriage as check on immorality

The institution of marriage, while primarily designed as a prerequisite means to human reproduction, also serves as the only legitimate expression for the impulses of sexual love. Hence, even when the duty of procreation has been

---

This chapter, here enlarged to include the notes, was originally published in An Introduction to Jewish Law, *ed. Peter Elman, World Jewish Congress, British Section, London, 1958.*

discharged, the obligation to be married devolves upon every man "so that he shall not be tempted to unchaste thoughts", and upon every woman "so that she shall not be suspect".[8]

Marriage as companionship

The great majority of the Jewish marriage regulations are devoted to setting out the mutual rights and duties of married partners to ensure the stablity of their union and the harmonious balance of their joint lives. The law assumes that two incompatible parties cannot be expected "to dwell in a single cage together",[9] and it seeks to eliminate all avoidable causes for disagreement by carefully defining their mutual relations in terms of advice and precept.

Fulfilment of purpose as indispensable condition to durability of marriage

Where these three objectives (procreation, avoidance of sin, and mutual understanding) cannot be achieved, Jewish law would often counsel, and sometimes even enforce, the dissolution of the marriage. Thus divorce is indicated if a union has proved sterile for ten years,[10] if it was illegally contracted[11] or subsequently disturbed by charges of faithlessness,[12] or if the parties could no longer live together in health[13] and happiness.[14]

Choice of partners

Great emphasis is therefore laid on physical as well as cultural compatibility in the selection of marriage partners. A man should see his expected bride beforehand "lest she become repulsive to him" afterwards,[15] and he should reassure himself—by submitting her to a kind of health examination—that she is free from physical defects.[16] There should be no undue discrepancy in the ages of the parties.[17] For eugenic reasons one should not marry into a family disposed to hereditary diseases[18] nor take a partner from a morally blemished family.[19] Above all, one should look for congeniality in religious and intellectual rank. An ignorant person should not marry a girl of priestly stock,[20] nor a pious and learned man be united with a boorish family.[21] The ideal marriage is one of which one may say metaphorically: "Bunches of grapes combined with bunches of grapes, a fine and fitting thing."[22]

Forbidden marriages

Legal impediments to marriage may exist for both moral and purely religious reasons. To the degrees prohibited in the Bible on account of consanguinity or affinity under pain of death,[23] the Talmud added some "secondary" degrees, partly as new prohibitions and partly by extending those mentioned in the Bible in the ascending and descending lines.[24] These degrees are not altogether identical with those prohibited in civil law; for example, Jewish law permits the marriage between an uncle and his niece.[25] Into the same category as incestuous unions belong relations with a married woman, likewise a capital offence.[26] Further prohibitions include marriages with non-

Jews,[27] bastards,[28] certain types of foundlings,[29] and spadones,[30] provided their incapacity is not congenital.[31] A man must not remarry his former wife if, following their divorce, she had been married to another man.[32] No widow or divorced woman may remarry until ninety days after her husband's death or the divorce;[33] if she is pregnant or nursing, twenty-four months should elapse after the child's birth.[34]

Marriages forbidden to priests

Men of priestly descent are required to observe further restrictions.[35] They are debarred from marrying women who are divorced[36] or released from the levirate bond (Halitzah),[37] proselytes,[38] and women born out of any forbidden union or previously a party to such union (with certain exceptions).[39]

Legal consequences

Marriages with non-Jews, and those biblically branded as incest or adultery, are null and void; they require no formal divorce for their dissolution in Jewish law.[40] Other marriages contracted against the law, while valid, must be terminated by divorce.[41] Regarding the status of the offspring born out of forbidden relations, the Jewish laws of illegitimacy are rather at variance from their modern civil equivalents. Illegitimate children (i.e. bastards, or Mamzerim, who may not marry anyone except their like) are only the products of capital acts of incest or adultery.[42] All children of other forbidden unions, including those born out of wedlock, are perfectly legitimate, in the sense that they suffer no marriage restrictions, except their ineligibility for priests, unless either parent was himself or herself a bastard.[43] In the event of unions out of the faith, the religious status of the children—in the absence of a valid marriage between their parents—is determined solely by their mother;[44] there are no "half-Jews" in Jewish law.

Age of marriage

The duty to marry and raise a family devolves upon a man from the age of eighteen years. Marriages at an even earlier age are encouraged, and they should in any case not be delayed until after the twentieth year.[45] Formal marriages contracted by, or on behalf of, boys who have not reached their majority at thirteen years are of doubtful validity[46] and condemned as immoral.[47] A minor girl may be given into marriage by her father,[48] or act on her own if she is no longer under his control and of sufficient understanding,[49] but the rabbis deprecate such marriages and insist that she should rather be married with her free consent after she attains her majority at the age of twelve and a half years.[50]

Marriage procedure

Originally the solemnisation of marriages consisted of two quite distinct acts: the betrothal (Erusin or Kiddushin), establishing the legal bond between the parties, followed—usually a year later during which the bride remained in the home of her father—by the marriage proper (*Nissu'in* or *Huppah*) under the nuptial canopy.[51] Nowadays the two acts are performed in a single ceremony.

Essentials of betrothal act

Biblical Hebrew has no word for "marriage", even as it has none for "religion". The only legal reference in the *Torah* to the act of marrying speaks of a man who "takes" (or "acquires") a wife,[52] and this expression—by analogy with another mention of the same verb in the sense of "purchases"[53]—was taken to define the essential characteristics of the legal bond between husband and wife.[54] In a strictly technical sense, a man "acquires" his bride to be his wife by an act of "purchase". But the contractual basis of this "transaction"[55] is complemented by the idea behind the rabbinic word for marriage: "Sanctification" (*Kiddushin*). While, in the significant phraseology of the *Mishnah*, "the woman is acquired" by her groom,[56] "the man sanctifies" her through the betrothal act.[57] The union between them is thus both legal and spiritual: in order to merge them into a single unit—"one flesh"[58]—the wife becomes a part of her husband, whilst he becomes the subject of her "consecration".

Act of betrothal

This dual aspect is reflected in the two constituents of the betrothal act. First the groom presents his bride an object of value in return for which she is "acquired" by him. This object conventionally takes the form of a plain ring of precious metal.[59] It must be his personal property,[60] and it is placed on the bride's right index finger (with which one would commonly draw or "acquire" things) to indicate that it is given essentially not as an ornament but as "legal tender". He then proceeds to the second part by reciting the marriage formula: "Be thou sanctified unto me with this ring according to the law of Moses and of Israel" (that is, biblical and rabbinic law[61]). After this act the marital bond is absolute and cannot be dissolved except by death or divorce. In both functions (as in the divorce act) the man is the active (giving) partner, and she is the passive (receiving) one, reflecting the relationship between them as ordained by nature. Prior to this act, the betrothal blessing is recited over a cup of wine,[62] and the betrothal is followed by the reading of the *Kethubah*.

"*Kethubah*"

The *Kethubah* is a document, written in rabbinic language, originally instituted to protect the wife against arbitrary divorce at a time when this could be granted by her husband against her will.[63] The document, which is signed by two witnesses on the husband's behalf, provides for the payment to the wife of a certain minimum amount if the bride was a virgin, and otherwise half that amount, in the event of his death or her divorce.[64] In the absence or loss of the *Kethubah* husband and wife must not live together,[65] and a special replacement document (*Kethubah de'irchasa*) must be drawn up on application to the ecclesiastical authorities.[66]

Huppah

The ceremony takes place under a canopy, symbolising the marriage chamber, which is essential to validate the second part of the procedure, the marriage proper (*Nissu'in*).[67] Under it the "Seven Benedictions" are now recited for which the presence of *Minyan* (ten adult Jews) is required.[68] A marriage is a public event, for the family is the basic unit of society. These benedictions, again over a cup of wine from which the bridal pair drink a little, praise God as the Creator of man in His image, of joy and happiness, of groom and bride; and conclude with the prayer that the voice of jubilation may soon be heard "in the cities of Judea and the streets of Jerusalem".[69]

Bridal dress and breaking of glass

Jerusalem and the destruction of the Temple should also be remembered, at this moment of supreme joy, by the sober simplicity of the bridal attire and by the breaking of a glass at the conclusion of the public ceremony,[70] so as to share the feelings of the Psalmist: ". . . if I remember thee not; if I set not Jerusalem above my chiefest joy."[71] The absence of all jewellery or other ornaments is also to indicate the equality between rich and poor under the *Huppah*, where only harmony and sanctity count, not wealth or social standing.[72]

Consummation of marriage

The legal requirements are completed by the couple's retirement, immediately after the ceremony, to a "private meeting" alone and the subsequent consummation of the marriage.[73] Following this, the wife assumes all legal rights as a married (as distinct from merely a betrothed) woman.[74]

Function of rabbis and witnesses

The acts of marriage are not valid unless they are witnessed by two religiously qualified persons,[75] that is, fully observant adult Jews who must not be related to the parties or to each other.[76] Rabbis (or ministers) attend merely as legal experts to ensure that the provisions of Jewish law are correctly carried out. A rabbi does not "marry" a couple any more than a rabbinical court "grants" a divorce: the agent "performing" the act is in both cases the husband.[77]

Consent and proxy

Either the groom or the bride may legally be represented by a proxy at their marriage (as in any legal act), though the law prefers them to carry out the act in person.[78] But the validity of the marriage is in any case contingent upon the free consent of both parties.[79] This condition applies particularly to the woman. *His* agreement to marry given under duress may be valid, but such consent forced upon *her* certainly renders the marriage null and void.[80] The reason for this discrimination in her favour is that in the event of a divorce the woman's consent could be more easily dispensed with than the husband's[81] (see below).

Husband's obligation

Upon marriage, the husband automatically assumes the following basic liabilities towards his wife: He must provide her with maintenance and clothing, and pay the marital dues; these requirements are stipulated in the Bible.[82] Moreover, he becomes liable for the marriage settlement (*Kethubah*), her medical expenses, her ransom from captivity and her burial upon her death. If he dies, his heirs must provide her with food and housing out of his estate until she remarries, maintain her daughters until they are married and give her sons certain preferential rights of inheritance.[83] To these ten liabilities is added his obligation to maintain his children until they come of age, even if they have possessions of their own by inheritance from a maternal relation.[84] If a husband leaves his home for more than three months, his possessions may be sold by the court to provide his wife[85] and minor children[86] with what they need. The minimum amount of the alimony,[87] clothing,[88] domestic[89] and cosmetic articles[90] to which a wife is entitled is fixed by law; but this must be increased to the extent permitted by the husband's resources.[91] In fact, a woman always "rises with her husband but does not descend with him",[92] that is, she shares in the husband's comforts if they exceed her previous means, but she need never claim less than she enjoyed at her father's home.[93]

Wife's obligations

Upon the wife marriage imposes four basic liabilities: She must assign to her husband the income from her work, objects she finds, the profits accruing from her possessions, and any inheritance she leaves on her death.[94] She is also obliged to perform certain domestic duties.[95] In case of poverty the range of such duties is extended and includes the nursing of her children,[96] but she is then entitled to demand special concessions in regard to her food and her work.[97] A wife is not liable for the breakage of domestic vessels.[98]

Mutual rights

The four afore-mentioned rights granted to the husband were rabbinically enacted in exchange for four of the liabilities incurred by him;[99] for instance, his claim to her income in return for his obligation to maintain her. Hence, the wife—but not the husband—may opt to forgo her maintenance and retain her earnings.[100] In respect of the other liabilities either party has the right to stipulate in the marriage contract not to be bound to honour any particular claim, with the exception of the rights to the marital dues, the marriage settlement, and her inheritance, these three rights being absolute.[101] The payment of the nuptial duties—the frequency is determined by law according to the husband's health[102] and occupation[103]—belongs to the inalienable obligations of every marriage, and neither party may renounce or refuse them to the other under normal conditions.[104] A wife may even restrain her husband from business travels, or occupational changes, which would interfere with the regular discharge of this obligation except with her consent.[105] Generally, a husband cannot remove his residence without his wife's approval; if he does, she is not compelled to follow him,[106] except to settle in the Land of Israel,[107] provided there is no danger involved.[108] Either party may object to living in a home among bad neighbours, even if the other is satisfied to stay there.[109] Both may also exclude from their home the other party's relations, but the wife may call her relations if she is ill or in confinement.[110]

Altogether, the law enjoins every husband to honour his wife more than himself, to give her of the best according to his means, and to treat her tenderly and without anger, while she is to comport herself with submissive love and consideration for his moods.[111]

Wife's property

A father is obliged to give his daughter a dowry.[112] This, together with any other personal assets, gifts or inherited possessions she brings into the marriage, remains her inalienable property, though her husband assumes certain powers of trusteeship for the duration of the marriage. The wife's property may consist of three kinds: Firstly, the assets noted in the *Kethubah* as her dowry. While the husband is entitled to the rents, fruits and other profits of this property, he assumes full responsibility for the capital in case of loss or damage and for the return of its entire value to the wife upon the dissolution of the marriage.[113] Neither party can dispose of this property, not even to support the family, save with the consent of the other.[114] The second type consists of possessions which the wife obtained after her betrothal by gift, inheritance or damages for injuries. For the loss or depreciation of these possessions the husband is not liable. But as with the previous type, he is awarded the usufruct of the property[115] in consideration for his liability to ransom his wife from captivity[116] and to enable him to increase the comforts of the home.[117] This property, too, the husband can sell only with his wife's consent,[118] but he may invest it as he pleases to yield more profitable returns.[119] If she sells it, the husband may claim the profits due to him (and possibly even the principal) from the buyer.[120] Their joint sale of the property is, of course, always valid.[121]

Thirdly, there are possessions over which the wife exercises exclusive control. These include her marriage settlement[122] and any gifts she received for her personal use, and she may dispose of them at her absolute discretion.[123] Gifts given to her by her husband, too, belong to her together with their profits, but she must not sell them.[124] The husband must never sell them, even to feed his family, except that such dire necessity does entitle him to dispose of his wife's jewellery, though otherwise not even her festive clothing.[125] Into this category also belongs any property the wife obtained before or during the marriage, if her husband agreed to renounce his rights to it.

She may then sell it or give it away at will, though he is still entitled to the usufruct until its disposal.[126]

Maintaining marriage bond

Jewish law thus provides marital partners with the proper balance between rights and duties, having regard to their differing natural propensities and requirements. The woman seeks from her husband, apart from love, protection and a sense of security. She wants to be sheltered by her mate, become part of him, and yet to make an indispensable, though discreet, contribution to his stature. The law supplies her with these needs, by charging the husband with full responsibility for her and her family's maintenance during and after his life, for the safe and profitable custody of her possessions, and for sharing his property with her. He, in turn, wants trust and personal service from his wife, respect for his management of affairs, and freedom from nagging and irritation. All these requirements are assured to him by the fulfilment of her legal obligations. Jewish law recognises that men and women are not equal by nature or disposition, and that each partner should give what the other needs. It seeks to establish an enduring association between them without doing violence to their characteristic individuality, by requiring them to make joint decisions and giving each the right to object to acts distressing the other. Above all, it insists on regular conjugal relations between them— the most powerful bond guarding the intimacy and stability of their union. All these regulations, however, are flexible enough to allow for adequate adjustments in individual cases, provided they are made by mutual agreement.

Renewing marriage bond

But even the wisest enactments cannot guarantee the permanence of the bond between wedded partners unless their strongest link—their natural attraction to each other—remains constant. The delights of married life can retain their original fascination only if they are not taken for granted, and become neither common nor routine. Marital relations require, therefore, sublimation and regular renewal. To this end, Judaism has enacted a whole corpus of legislation designed to impose a periodic suspension of all physical contacts between the spouses, and to elevate their relations to a spiritual level under religious control. By the strict observance of these laws of "family purity"[127]—the breach of which is branded as a capital offence in the Bible[128] —the wife's personal dignity is respected and the couple's mutual love is constantly regenerated in the cycle of anticipation and fulfilment. In the words of the Talmud: "Why does the *Torah* prescribe a regular period of separation? Because the husband, being accustomed to his wife, may find the relationship repulsive. But the *Torah* decreed that she is forbidden to him for a period so that (every month) she shall become as attractive to him as she was when she entered the marriage canopy".[129]

Breaking marriage bond

Finally, to safeguard the marriage from attack by a third party, Jewish law stipulates the most drastic measures against adultery. It regards any outside intrusion into the sanctity and privacy of a marriage as having caused irreparable damage to it, and it threatens both offending parties with the supreme penalty.[130] To further discourage the temptation of faithlessness, it is forbidden not only to maintain the existing (and broken) marriage but also subsequently to contract a new one between the correspondents.[131] Indeed, a previously married woman must never marry a man who testified to the death of her former husband, or who carried her deed of divorce from him (to prevent collusion);[132] nor may she marry a man who courted her prior to her divorce, or for whose sake her former husband divorced her, so that people should not say "They exchange their wives like presents".[133] Jewish law thus contrasts *toto caelo* with modern civil law which, far from treating adultery as a penal crime, puts a premium on it by requiring it to be proved as a legitimate ground for divorce to pave the way for a marriage between the offenders.

Adultery cannot be committed except by relations between a betrothed or married woman and a man other than her husband.[134] The reason for this is that in biblical law polygamous marriages are tolerated. They were finally banned only by a decree of R. Gershom in the eleventh century.[135]

Right to divorce

The sanctity and stability of marriages can be protected in two ways. Either they are made so attractive and secure that no one would normally wish to avail of any but emergency exits, or all exits are firmly locked, so that, having once entered into the sanctuary of marriage, one can no longer escape, however intolerable the conditions within. Judaism chose the former course. It left the escape routes wide open; yet they were used only in the rarest cases. Jewish law regards marriage as a contract which can be terminated by mutual agreement in the same way as it is established. While the law does everything possible to eliminate causes for friction or disappointment among the parties, it does not seek to foist them on each other once the conditions for a fruitful and happy association—the purpose of every marriage—no longer exist.

Divorce by agreement

Under normal circumstances a divorce can be executed only with the free consent of both the husband and—by a further decree of R. Gershom—the wife.[136] What is, therefore, branded as "collusion" and ruled out as an inadmissible ground for divorce in civil law (until quite recently) is an essential prerequisite in Jewish law. But it is forbidden to enter a marriage with a view to a subsequent divorce.[137] Although no stigma attaches to divorced parties, the dissolution of a marriage is deemed a great tragedy over which even "the altar sheds tears"; it should not be entertained except for very grave reasons, and never merely in order to marry a more attractive partner.[138]

Divorce by compulsion

In certain cases, however, the law exercises compulsion against either party upon the demand of the other, or even against both of them. The ecclesiastical court may then apply pressure on the husband—by ordering him to be socially ostracised, deprived of the rights to communal facilities, burial, trade or any other favours until he agrees to grant the divorce[139]—or on the wife by ignoring the decree against her compulsory divorce.[140]

Forcing both parties to divorce

The law requires the dissolution by divorce of marriages (a) if they were contracted against biblical or rabbinic law[141] (including the union between an adultress and her paramour[142]); (b) if they proved barren for ten years[143] (though this is no longer enforced[144]); (c) if the wife's constant state of "impurity" renders any marital relations impossible;[145] and (d) if the husband suffers from a disease (presumably venereal) which makes conjugal intercourse dangerous.[146] In the last two cases the party whose condition necessitated the divorce must not then remarry until the disability is removed.[147] But there are no restrictions on the remarriage with other partners in the first two cases.[148]

Insanity

Marriages among, or with, insane persons are not valid.[149] A marriage legally contracted cannot be dissolved by the husband whilst he is not fully in control of his faculties,[150] and during his incapacity the court may sequestrate his property to maintain his wife[151] and minor children.[152] The wife, too, should not be divorced whilst she is insane "so that she shall not be treated (callously) as ownerless property" and the husband is obliged to provide her maintenance and medical expenses.[153] But if her incapacity is interminable, he may obtain "the sanction of a hundred rabbis" to release him from the ban of R. Gershom, particularly if he has not yet fulfilled the duty of procreation.[154]

Husband's right to divorce

The husband may, and in some cases should, divorce his wife, even against her will, if she is guilty of licentious conduct;[155] if he has evidence, or she admits, that she misconducted herself with another man;[156] if she refuses him the marital dues for twelve months (and possibly less, unless she pleads some just cause, e.g. his misdemeanour or extravagance);[157] if she became an epileptic (but not for lesser defects);[158] and if she suffers from a protracted illness, though it is then improper to divorce her.[159]

Wife's right to divorce

The wife is entitled to sue for a compulsory divorce from her husband if he is guilty of apostasy or consorts with harlots;[160] if he denies her the marital dues;[161] if she charges him with sterility after ten years' marriage[162] or with impotence, provided she can adduce some evidence;[163] if he refuses to support,[164] house or clothe her;[165] if he contracted epilepsy[166] or some malodorous habit[167] (but not if he sustained a permanent injury[168]); if he engages in certain offensive trades;[169] if he is forced to leave the place of marriage in order to save his life;[170] if he habitually turns her out of his house or beats her;[171] and if he marries her by fraud or deception.[172]

Disposal of property

The divorced parties must not live in each other's immediate vicinity, to prevent any misconduct between them.[173] As a rule, a divorced woman is entitled to the full payment of the marriage settlement as well as to the return of her dowry and property, provided she was the innocent party; otherwise she forfeits her marriage portion, or part of it, and—in cases of grave guilt— even some of her possessions.[174]

Custody of children

While a divorced woman loses her alimony, she is entitled to an allowance for the provision of her children's necessities.[175] She also has the right to their permanent custody; but in the case of sons, the father may stop their allowance after their sixth year unless they return to him, whilst in the case of daughters the court may order their transfer to the father's custody if this is considered to be in their interest.[176]

Annulment of marriage

The annulment of marriage in the usual sense is not known in Jewish law. But it confers on either party the right to stipulate specific conditions at the time of the marriage; their non-fulfilment then renders the marriage invalid.[177] Thus, if the husband discovers certain physical defects in his wife, and he had made it a condition of marriage that she would be free of blemishes, the marriage is null and void.[178] However, the principle of retroactive annulments granted by the court in some specific cases of misdemeanour is recognised in the Talmud. This was done on the premise that "whoever marries, does so with the sanction of the rabbis; hence (if he subsequently abuses their trust by violating their enactments) they reserve the right to cancel his marriage."[179] It is a matter of dispute whether the few such cases specified in the Talmud (which include the forcible betrothal of a woman mentioned earlier) can serve as a precedent for other cases by later enactments.[180]

Separation

There are also no special provisions for the legal separation of married partners. Nevertheless, in a few cases (such as the discovery of physical blemishes) the law, whilst it does not enforce a divorce, grants the parties the right not to live together, for "one does not compel a person to live with another whom he regards as repulsive."[181] On the other hand, a woman who left her husband's home because it was in a disreputable neighbourhood or because he quarrelled with her can claim her full allowance from him, and any debts she incurs for her household must be paid by him, even if she moved to her father's home.[182]

Levirate marriage

Biblical law requires the widow of a man who died without leaving any living issue to be married to his paternal brother (*Yibbum*), "that his name be not blotted out in Israel". If the brother refuses to perform this duty, the widow must not be remarried until he releases her from the levirate bond existing between them by a special ceremony (*Halitzah*).[183] By another decree of R. Gershom, the choice of *Yibbum* is now no longer open to the brother-in-law, and the parties must invariably carry out the *Halitzah*[184] (possibly with certain exceptions[185]). The levir is in duty bound to free the widow for remarriage by this act; if he holds her up to ransom, the promise to pay an agreed sum to him need not afterwards be honoured.[186]

Divorce and "Halitzah" procedures

The divorce and *Halitzah* ceremonies must be carried out in strict accordance with very detailed regulations, based on ancient tradition. They must be performed under the direction of competent rabbinical experts,[187] since the slightest error may render the act invalid, with the gravest consequences to the legitimacy of a subsequent marriage and its issue. The main essentials of a divorce are: The husband, having assured the judges that he wishes to divorce his wife of his own free and unfettered will,[188] commissions a scribe to prepare the divorce document ("*Get*"), which the latter then writes out in exact accord with an ancient formula (the biblical "bill of divorcement"[189]). Finally the document, after its careful examination by the judges and witnesses,[190] is handed over by the husband into the hands of his wife, who raises it, walks away with it, and then surrenders it to the judge for re-examination.[191] Both the husband and the wife, or either of them, may be represented by agents duly appointed by them.

The *Halitzah* ceremony symbolises the formal severance of the bond between the widow and her deceased husband's family and her contempt for him "that doth not build up his brother's house".[192] It is enacted before a rabbinical court of five members,[193] who explain the significance of the act to the parties.[194] The levir is given a special sandal which he puts on his bare right foot.[195] This is then untied and removed by the widow, who casts it aside[196] and expectorates on the floor,[197] exclaiming the biblical *Halitzah* formula followed by the thrice-repeated response of those present.[198] The ceremony is concluded by the judges' prayer: "May it be (God's) will that the daughters of Israel shall be spared the need for either *Halitzah* or *Yibbum*."[199] This act cannot be performed by proxy.[200]

NOTES

This summary of the leading features of the Jewish marital legislation is based mainly on the *Even Ha'Ezer* part of Joseph Karo's final code of Jewish law, the *Shulhan Arukh*, and Moses Isserles's glosses on it. Wherever in these notes figures are given without any source, they refer to chapter and paragraph in the *Even Ha'Ezer*.

1. Gen. 1:28; 9:1, 7.
2. Aaron Halevi, *Hinnukh*, commandment 1.
3. 1:1 Based on *Yevamoth* 63b f.; cf. Rashi, on Gen. 9:7.
4. See I. Jakobovits, "Artificial Insemination, Birth-control and Abortion", in *The Hebrew Medical Journal*, vol. xxvi, part 2 (1953), pp. 174 ff.; *Journal of a Rabbi*, 1967, pp. 213 ff.; and *Jewish Medical Ethics*, 1975, pp. 154 ff.
5. 1:13.
6. 1:5. This is merely the minimum duty; when it is fulfilled, one should still be married and raise further children (1:18).
7. Maimonides, *Hil. Ishuth*, 15:7.
8. 1:8, 13. See Maimonides, *ib.*, 15:16.
9. *Ketuboth* 72a.
10. See note 143.
11. See notes 141 and 142.
12. See notes 131 and 156.
13. See notes 145, 146, 158, 159, 166 and 167.
14. See notes 136, 157, and 171.
15. 35:1.
16. If there are public baths in the bride's place, it is assumed that her groom is aware of any bodily defects she has when he marries her, having been advised of these by his female relations; 117:5, 6.
17. 2:9.
18. 2:7; see I. Jakobovits, "Sterilization and Eugenics in Jewish Law" in *The Jewish Medical Journal*, vol. 27, part 2 (1954) p. 178 ff.; and *Jewish Medical Ethics*, 1975, pp. 153 ff.
19. 2:1–5.
20. 2:8.
21. 2:6.
22. *Pesahim* 49a.
23. Leviticus 18 and 20.
24. 15. See *Jewish Encyclopaedia*, 6:527 f.
25. 2:6.
26. Lev. 20:10.
27. 16:1, 2. Following Deut. 7:3.
28. 4:1. Following Deut. 23:3.
29. 4:30–33.
30. 5:1–9. Following Deut. 23:2.

31. 5:10.
32. 10:1. Following Deut. 24:4.
33. 13:1.
34. 13:11.
35. Following Lev. 21:7.
36. 6:1–5.
37. This is a rabbinical offence; 6:1.
38. 6:8; 7:21.
39. 6:8 ff.
40. 44:6, 8.
41. 154:20; 6:1; 11:8.
42. 4:13 ff.
43. 4:18.
44. 8:4, 5.
45. 1:3. Maimonides (*Hil. Ishuth*, 15:2) puts the commencement age at 17 yrs.
46. 43:1, see *Pithhei Teshuvah*, *a.l.*, 1.
47. 1:3.
48. 37:1. Following Deut. 22:16.
49. 37:2 ff.; Maimonides, *Hil. Ishuth*, 4.7. But such a marriage, being only rabbinically valid, can be dissolved when she comes of age by a mere declaration of refusal to maintain it; 153:1, 3.
50. 37:8; cf. 56:4.
51. See *Jewish Encyclopaedia*, 3:125; cf. 56:1.
52. Deut. 24:1.
53. Gen. 23:13.
54. *Kiddushin* 2a.
55. For a rebuttal of attacks on the "contract" principle of marriage, see L. Loew, "Eherechtliche Studien", in his *Gesammelte Schriften*, 1893, vol. 3, pp. 15 ff.
56. *Kiddushin*, 1:1.
57. *Kiddushin*, 2:1.
58. Gen. 2:24; see Nahmanides, *a.l.*
59. 31:2; 27:1.
60. 28:1 ff.
61. Cf. *Kethuboth*, 7:6. On the history of this formula, see Loew, op. cit., p. 24.
62. 34:1, 2.
63. *Kethuboth* 11a; cf. 66:2. But some hold the institution to be of biblical origin; see Asheri, *Kethuboth*, 1:19.
64. 66:6.
65. 66:1, 3.
66. 66:3. This is a special document,

originally drawn up by R. Gershom;
see *Otzar Yisrael,* 5:305.
67. 61:1.
68. 62:1, 4.
69. See Singer's *Prayer Book,* p. 299.
70. 65:3; *Orah Hayim.* 560:2.
71. Psalms 137:6.
72. Cf. *Ta'anith;* 4:8.
73. 55:1; see also 63:1.
74. 61:1.
75. 62:2–4.
76. 42:5. On the qualifications of wit-
    nesses, see *Hoshen Mishpat,* 33–37.
77. In fact, Israel Lipschuetz (*Tiph'ereth
    Yisrael, Bekhoroth,* 4:6. [1].) suggests
    that such services do not properly
    belong to the functions of a rabbi at
    all, and that he is therefore entitled to
    be paid for them.
78. 35:1; 36:1.
79. 42:1.
80. 1b. see also ANNULMENT below.
81. *Maggid Mishnah, Hil. Ishuth,* 4:1.
82. Exodus 21:10.
83. 69:1, 2: and following chapters.
84. 71:1; 112:1 ff.
85. 70:5–11.
86. 71:2.
87. 70:1–3.
88. 73:1 ff.
89. 73:1.
90. 73:30.
91. 70:3; 73:4.
92. 83:3; following *Kethuboth* 61a.
93. Unless she eats with him; 70:1.
94. 69:3; 80; 84; 85; 90.
95. 80:1–6.
96. 80:6.
97. 80:11, 12.
98. 80:17.
99. Maimonides, *Hil. Ishuth,* 12:4.
100. 69:4.
101. 69:6.
102. 76:3, 11.
103. 76:1, 2.
104. 76:4 ff. For further regulations on
     marital conduct, see *Orah Hayim,* 240.
105. 76:5.
106. 75:1.
107. 75:2, 3, 4.
108. 75:5.
109. 75:2; 74:11, 12.
110. 74:9, 10.
111. Maimonides, *Hil Ishuth,* 15:19, 20.
112. 58: a. fr.
113. 85:2.
114. 90:13, 14; and *Ba'er Hetev, a.l.,* 31.
115. 85:7.
116. 85:1, but see 78:1.

117. *Kethuboth* 69a.
118. Maimonides, *Hil. Mekhirah,* 30:4.
119. 85:13.
120. 90:9; but see also 10, 11.
121. 90:16; see also 10.
122. 105:1.
123. 105:11.
124. 105:7.
125. 90:15.
126. 92:1.
127. For details of these laws, see *Yoreh
     De'ah,* 183–200.
128. Lev. 20:18.
129. *Niddah,* 31b.
130. Lev. 20:10.
131. 11:1; 115:6 ff.
132. 12:1.
133. 142:15; 11:8.
134. Rashi on Exodus 20:13.
135. 1:10.
136. 121.1; 119:5.
137. 2:10; 119:1.
138. 119:3; and *Ba'er Hetev, a.l.,* 3.
139. 154:21.
140. 117:11; see also *Pithhei Teshuvah, a.l.,*
     5.
141. 154:20; 15:1; 6:1.
142. 11:1.
143. 154:10.
144. 1:3.
145. 117:1.
146. 154:1.
147. *Ib.;* and 10:4.
148. 154:16; but see note 39 above.
149. 44:2. Marriages between the deaf and
     dumb are restricted, too; 44:1.
150. 121:1–3.
151. 70:6.
152. 71:3.
153. 70:4; 119:6.
154. On this sanction, see Ezekiel Landau,
     responsa *Noda Biyehudah,* part i,
     Even Ha'Ezer, no. 3.
155. 115:4.
156. 115:6, 7.
157. 77:2, 3.
158. 117:11.
159. 119:3; but see also commentaries, *a.l.*
160. 154:1.
161. 77:1; 154:3.
162. 154:6.
163. 154:7. But the marriage between
     sterile parties is generally valid; 44:4.
164. 70:3; 154:3.
165. 73:5.
166. 154:5.
167. 154:1.
168. 154:4; but see *Pithhei Teshuvah, a.l.,*
     10.

169. 154:1.
170. 154:9.
171. 154:3.
172. 77:3.
173. 119:7.
174. 115–117.
175. 82:6. Nevertheless, the divorced wife herself has a prior claim on her former husband's charity; 119:8.
176. 82:7. The mother can renounce the custody of her children in favour of the father or of the community; 82:8.
177. 38:1.
178. 39:3.
179. *Yevamoth* 90b, 110a; *Kethuboth* 3a; *Gittin* 33a; *Baba Bathra* 48b.
180. See *Talmudic Encyclopedia*, 2:139 ff.
181. 117:11. Cf. note 9 above.
182. 70:12.
183. Deut. 15:5–9; 156–169.

184. 165:1; and *Pithhei Teshuvah, a.l.*, 7. See also *Otzar Yisrael*, 3:318.
185. *Pithhei Teshuvah*, 165:3.
186. 165:1; 169:50.
187. 154, *Seder Haget*, introductory gloss, and 101.
188. *Ib.*, 14.
189. Deut. 24:3.
190. 165, *Seder Haget*, 66.
191. *Ib.*, 85.
192. Deut. 25:9.
193. 169, *Seder Halitzah*, 1, 5.
194. *Ib.*, 29, 30, 47, 50.
195. *Ib.*, 40.
196. *Ib.*, 52.
197. *Ib.*, 53.
198. *Ib.*, 54, 55.
199. *Ib.*, 56.
200. *Ib.*, 12.

THE ASHKENAZI AND SEPHARDI PRONUNCIATION IN PRAYER

Some Historical and Religious Aspects of a Contemporary Argument

I am deeply appreciative of the honour done to me in being invited to open this series of annual Founder's Lectures in memory of the late Rabbi Kopul Rosen who, had he been spared to live, might well occupy my position today, and to whom I am, therefore, particularly proud to be asked to pay this memorial tribute today. Our subject, too, is especially fitting; what could be more appropriate than to discuss the articulation of the Hebrew language in memory of him who may be described as possibly the most articulate exponent of Judaism produced in the midst of our community in recent times?

Moreover, it is apt that this lecture on this particular subject is being given within the precincts of this valuable institution of learning, Carmel College, for a double reason: here was introduced for the first time what I regard as the proper manner of changing over our pronunciation of Hebrew in our prayers following, as was the case, the familiarisation with that accent as part of the programme of Hebrew instruction.

Secondly, by a strange coincidence, Carmel takes its name from the famous promontory overlooking the City of Haifa in the Holy Land, and it so happens that Haifa is mentioned for the very first time in Jewish literature in connection with a question on the pronunciation of Hebrew. As we will see later, it is on the basis of a passage in the Talmud[1] dealing with a difference in the pronunciation of Hebrew between the citizens of Haifa and the rest of Israel at the time that centuries later the halakhic discussions and rulings on the subject of changing the pronunciation evolved.

And, finally, I have chosen this subject for my discourse today also as a tribute to my own revered and sainted father, whose only published Jewish work happens to be a little pamphlet on this very theme printed in Frankfurt in 1936.[2] I, therefore, feel that, in making this choice, I am honouring not only the founder of this College, but at the same time also the founder of my life.

DIVERSE HEBREW ACCENTS IN THE BIBLE AND TALMUD

The history of the differences in the pronunciation of Hebrew goes back to

Founder's Lecture delivered at Carmel College on 29 October 1968

Biblical times. Already in so early a book as the Book of Judges,[3] reference
is made to the people of the Tribe of Ephraim who could not pronounce the
Shin properly and instead said *Sin*, so that the word *Shibolet* was pronounced
by them as *Sibolet*. There was, therefore, already in early biblical times a
distinct group of Jews, one of the tribes of Israel, with a peculiar pronunciation of Hebrew, distinguishing them from the rest of the tribes.

In the Talmud[1] we have the further reference to which I have already
alluded. There it is related that the people of Haifa and of Beth-She'an were
forbidden to ascend the "*Duchan*", if they were of priestly descent, to bestow
the priestly benediction anywhere except in their own localities, because they
confuse the *ayin* with the *alef*. Rashi[4] explains that they were debarred from
publicly reciting the priestly benediction because their prayer would be
defective, being mispronounced, whereas Rabbi Mordecai Jaffe,[5] a much
later authority, said that they would be inadmissible for giving the blessing
because it might disturb the *kavanah*, the devotion of the congregation,
having to listen to a pronunciation with which they were not fully familiar.

EARLY REFORM AGITATION

So far, then, I have given just some references to indicate the antiquity of
the divisions in the pronunciation of Hebrew and the earliest precedents
for the halakhic treatment of our problem. The advocacy of a deliberate
change from one pronunciation to another is, of course, very much more
recent. As Dr. Zimmels, the distinguished Principal of Jews' College, has
pointed out in his masterly work on *Ashkenazim and Sephardim*, where an
entire chapter is devoted to this matter,[6] the first to plead and agitate for
changing the customary Ashkenazi pronunciation into the Sephardi accent
were several Reform leaders in the nineteenth century. He cites in particular
four such advocates, including the famous Rabbi Aaron Choriner, a leading
pioneer of the Reform movement in Hungary, who incidentally also sought
support for the change of accent by referring to the religious services conducted in the Sephardi accent at the home of the Rabbi Nathan Adler.[7]
(This is not the late Chief Rabbi Adler of this country, but a much earlier
Nathan Adler, who lived in Frankfurt in the late eighteenth century and
who was the teacher of R. Moses Schreiber, the *Chatam Sopher*.) Dr. Zimmels
also refers to Rabbi Moses Kunitzer of Budapest who, likewise early in the
nineteenth century, advocated changing over to the Sephardi accent. But
his reasoning was rather more romantic. Since, after all, the Ashkenazim
constituted only a small segment of the Jewish people and since, therefore,
as he had computed it, less than one-eighth of all the Hebrew prayers that
ascended to Heaven were in the Ashkenazi pronunciation, we ought to
surrender that small minority in favour of what he believed to be the uniform
majority.[8]

Already at that time, Orthodox voices were raised against the proposed
change. Thus in 1820 Rabbi Abraham Loewenstamm, Rabbi of Emden in
Germany, contested the advocacy of the Sephardi accent by these Reform
leaders on the basis of numerous counter-arguments. First, he showed that
both the Ashkenazi and Sephardi pronunciations had different advantages

and disadvantages. Moreover, he argued—and this is an argument with a rather modern sound—if we Westerners were to try to adopt the Sephardi pronunciation, the result would probably be a pronunciation which was neither Ashkenazi nor Sephardi but, as some wit had suggested, "Ashkephardi". He also referred to the report on Rabbi Nathan Adler conducting his services at home in the Sephardi pronunciation. Having in fact himself attended some of those services, he could testify that this great sage had actually kept a Palestinian scholar at his home for two or three years for the sole purpose of being taught the Sephardi pronunciation properly. Rabbi Loewenstamm added: "If he, blessed be his memory, in spite of his strong will, phenomenal memory and power of comprehension, had to devote several years to the acquisition of the Sephardi pronunciation, how many years would then be required for us who are not even worthy to be his footstool". For this reason the Chasidim in Eastern Europe, even though they adopted the Sephardi ritual (*Nusach*) in their services, had nevertheless retained the Ashkenazi pronunciation.[9]

ORIGIN OF ASHKENAZI AND SEPHARDI ACCENT

Whether, in fact, the Ashkenazi or the Sephardi pronunciation is the more ancient, or the more correct, way of rendering Hebrew remains to this day the subject of much debate. Let it suffice here to say that so great a scholar in the tradition of the *Juedische Wissenschaft* as Solomon J. Rappaport, one of the founders of the "Science of Judaism", regards the Talmudic discussion on the Haifa accent which I mentioned earlier as proving that, in fact, there existed in those days already a distinction between what we now term the Ashkenazi and the Sephardi pronunciation. Rappaport believes that the Ashkenazi pronunciation of today has its origin in Palestine, whence the Jews eventually moved to the more Northern parts of Europe, while the Sephardi pronunciation, as it is now known, goes back to the usage of the Babylonians, who later emigrated mainly to the Mediterranean countries, where they cultivated the Sephardi pronunciation.[10]

This view is endorsed by Eisenstein, the famous editor of the *Otzar Yisrael* Encyclopedia. He also regards the Ashkenazi as being the closer to the original. Among the reasons he puts forward is that the very words used for the different vowels are based on the Ashkenazi accent. Thus, *qametz*, which means "closed", indicates the *o* sound, while *a* is called *patach*, which literally means "open". These references to the formation of the mouth clearly make sense only if the two vowels are pronounced in the Ashkenazi manner, an indication that at a very early stage the vocalization of Hebrew showed a closer affinity to the Ashkenazi than to the Sephardi pronunciation. Eisenstein adduces some other Talmudic proofs as well for his contention that the Ashkenazi represents the original Palestinian pronunciation of Hebrew.[11]

As against these opinions, Prof. Elbogen, the celebrated authority on the Jewish liturgy, argues that the Sephardi is the more correct and original pronunciation, since it is closer to the pronunciation of Arabic which is, of course, indigenous to the countries of the Orient, as well as to the Greek transliteration of Hebrew in the Septuagint where, for instance, a name like

Abraham appears as *Abraam* and not as *Avrohom*, as it would be in the Ashkenazi pronunciation, which he considers merely as an assimilation to the languages of Eastern Europe.[12] In the *Jewish Encyclopedia*[13] this question is left unresolved and arguments are adduced in favour of both theories. There may, therefore, well be some valid evidence pointing in both and opposite directions.

RELATIVE MERITS OF EACH PRONUNCIATION

It is quite clear that, in some respects at any rate, the Ashkenazi pronunciation is far more articulate than the Sephardi. It makes certain distinctions between different sounds, both vowels and consonants, that do not appear in the Sephardi pronunciation. For instance, the *qametz* must originally have been pronounced differently from the *patach*, as it still is in the Ashkenazi (*o*) but not in the Sephardi (*a*) accent. Otherwise, it would make no sense that a word like *sha'ar* would appear with a double *patach* in the middle of a sentence and with a *qametz-patach* at the end of a sentence, a special pausal form varied for purely euphonic reasons. The different vowel here used was obviously meant to be pronounced differently, corresponding to the Ashkenazi usage.

Similarly, there can be no question that between *tav* and *thav*, between the aspirated and non-aspirated forms of the last letter of the Hebrew alphabet, there must be a distinction of pronunciation, so that the Sephardi way of pronouncing both alike certainly is not as accurate as the distinction made in the Ashkenazi pronunciation.

Moreover, it would be quite wrong to assume that all the Oriental pronunciations of Hebrew necessarily correspond more closely with the Sephardi accent. For instance, the Yemenite pronunciation of Hebrew in many ways comes closer to the Ashkenazi than to the Sephardi. They do make a distinction between *tav* and *thav*. They also pronounce *torah* more like our *tauroh*, or *teirah*, than like the Sephardi *torah*. Linguistic reasons, too, account for this. The *cholem* was doubtless originally a diphthong, a combination of two distinct vowel-sounds. This is indicated in Syriac, where *Joseph* is vocalised *Ya-usef*, corresponding to the Ashkenazi *Yowsef*. Hence the retention of the *vav* (*u*) in Hebrew.

On the other hand, of course, there are likewise advantages in the Sephardi pronunciation, particularly when distinctions such as between *cheth* and *khaf*, or *ayin* and *alef* are made. Unfortunately, by omitting these distinctions many Israelis have adopted the shortcomings of both pronunciations. Nevertheless, to most ears the Sephardi accent sounds more rhythmic, more melodious and certainly more authentically Oriental.

However, it is often forgotten that the differences *within* the Ashkenazi pronunciation are very much greater than the difference between the Ashkenazi and Sephardi accents. For instance, there is clearly a greater dissimilarity between our *borukh* and the East-European *boorikh* than between the Ashkenazi *borukh* and the Sephardi *barukh*.

VARIANT ACCENTS IN ALL LANGUAGES

Obviously such variations are not peculiar to the Hebrew language. They are to be found in every language that has developed over the centuries, especially a language as ancient as Hebrew, which has been spoken or recited over millennia in widely dispersed parts of the world. Much bigger divisions are to be found in the pronunciation of English, say, between a Scotsman or a Welshman and a Londoner, or, for that matter, the American drawl, whether it is from Texas in one form and from New England in another. Climatic, geographic and other conditions are bound to account for variations in the course of time if a common language is eventually spoken over a wide area.

HALAKHIC PRECEDENTS

I will now turn to the Halakhic aspects, that is, to the discussion in our religious literature on the permissibility of changing from one pronunciation to another. The original precedent on which our present-day rulings in this matter are ultimately based is the Talmudic passage[1] already mentioned, according to which priests must not officiate in places where their Hebrew accent is strange or peculiar. But our question today as to whether we should deliberately go out of our way artificially to introduce a new pronunciation for the old traditional one—that, of course, is of fairly recent origin. Let me, then, give you a very brief summary of some of the major sources, drawn principally from my late father's collection of them in the pamphlet[2] to which I have already referred.

To begin with, already the *Shulchan Arukh*[14] extends to any public officiant in the synagogue the prohibition found in the Talmud debarring priests from using a pronunciation not locally customary. In other words, any reader is likewise disqualified from conducting services except in the locally accepted accent or dialect. Nevertheless, some authorities sanction the conduct of services by a reader accustomed to a different pronunciation if no other reader is available,[15] whereas others insist that the reader ought in that case to try to use the local accent.[16]

The first Rabbinic responsum on this subject appears, oddly enough, in answer to the reverse question, i.e. not whether one may change the pronunciation from Ashkenazi to Sephardi, but from Sephardi to Ashkenazi. This is published in a work by R. Samuel Landau, the son of the celebrated *Noda Biyehudah* in a work dated 1827. He was asked by the shrinking Sephardi community in Karlsruhe, a small town in Southern Germany, whether (in view of their declining numbers and the threat that, if they were to maintain their own rite and their own manner of worship, they would eventually die out completely) that small remnant would be allowed to surrender their Sephardi rite and their Sephardi pronunciation and to adopt the forms of the larger Ashkenazi community within which they lived. In his responsum, he permitted this change to take place, since otherwise their synagogue services and the education of their children might not continue altogether.[17]

HEBREW IN THE LAND OF ISRAEL

The current problem was, of course, created by the massive return of our people to the Land of Israel and the adoption there of Hebrew in the Sephardi pronunciation as the vernacular. This led to the question as to whether one might now change one's pronunciation from the traditional Ashkenazi to the Sephardi or Israeli accent.

The first to deal extensively with this matter was the saintly Rabbi Kook, the first Chief Rabbi of the Holy Land, of blessed memory, who devotes a lengthy discussion to this subject. It is found not in his *Responsa* but in his *Letters*. It may be interesting to quote a part of his opinion. He wrote (let me translate it literally): "It is forbidden to change the practice adopted by the earlier generations from one pronunciation to another, since every pronunciation has certain distinct features, both in the stress of the words and in the pronunciation of the letters, which, if someone else were to adopt them, would render his pronunciation defective." He argues that, despite the euphonic advantage of the Sephardi pronunciation, one must not give up the Ashkenazi accent since it is the more articulate pronunciation, distinguishing more clearly between like-sounding vowels and even consonants. Moreover, he was also strongly opposed to the change on the grounds of *al titosh torat immekha*,[18] forbidding any deliberate change in the customary traditions that have come down by way of a long and hallowed heritage. Finally, R. Kook adds that only that which comes about by itself through education is a different matter. Hence if, as a result of raising a new generation of children to whom the Israeli accent will be natural, this will be their pronunciation of prayer, he saw no objection—or at least he left it open whether under such circumstances the change could be affected.[19]

Three years later the problem was again discussed at great length by his colleague, Rabbi Uziel, the Sephardi Chief Rabbi of the Holy Land at the time. He was, of course, somewhat more favourably inclined towards the Sephardi pronunciation and argued that among the immigrants who came into the Land of Israel and were brought up to use the Sephardi pronunciation as their vernacular, there could be no question but that they should change from their customary Ashkenazi to the Sephardi pronunciation in their prayers. In that event, he held, this did not come under the heading of *al titosh torat immekha*, not to change the traditions inherited from earlier generations. It would then be simply the adoption of what had become the customary accent of Hebrew. However, in order to introduce some cohesion and uniformity of pronunciation, R. Uziel urged calling a Rabbinical conference to determine what ought to be the accepted practice for the whole *Yishuv*, for all those newly settled now in the Land of Israel. Needless to say, this conference is still awaiting its realisation.[20]

RECENT RESPONSA

Among the latest Rabbinical opinions on the subject, I will only mention a few of the main responsa. The recently deceased Rabbi Yechiel Weinberg, the former Rector of the *Rabbiner Seminar* in Berlin, included in his three-volume work of Responsa, a ruling permitting a *Bar Mitzvah* boy to use the Sephardi pronunciation in an Ashkenazi Synagogue if he was so trained.[21] Rabbi S. Braun cites several authorities to show that congregants would fulfil their religious obligations of prayer if their services were conducted by someone who, unlike themselves, used the Sephardi pronunciation, so long as this was done only occasionally.[22]

Finally, the opposition to any change in the traditional accent was strongly endorsed by Dayan Weiss of the Manchester Beth Din, probably the greatest living exponent of Halakhah in this country. In a responsum addressed to Chief Rabbi Brodie in the year 1958, he emphatically supports the ruling the Chief Rabbi had given in 1952 in favour of maintaining the Ashkenazi pronunciation. In support of the ruling, Rabbi Weiss refers to the opinion of so early an authority as Rabenu Bachaya[23] as well as of R. Jacob Emden[24] who had a certain preference for the greater articulation of the Ashkenazi pronunciation mentioned before.[25]

Here, then, you have in capsule form some representative Rabbinic opinions and rulings on the matter. It is quite clear that all agree, including such towering sages as Rabbis Kook and Uziel who certainly could not be accused of any anti-Zionist bias, on opposing any artificial change from the Ashkenazi to the Sephardi pronunciation in prayer.

ANGLO-JEWISH PRONOUNCEMENTS

Let us finish this part of our survey by referring to the two Anglo-Jewish pronouncements on the subject. Rabbi Brodie, in 1952, as already mentioned, issued a formal edict, or verdict, in which he said that "for the present the Ashkenazi pronunciation as used in this country hitherto must be retained at all Divine services and throughout the entire service".[26] Ten years later, in a directive issued by the Office of the Chief Rabbi on 12 July 1962, Rabbi Brodie somewhat modified his stand by permitting the Sephardi accent to be adopted at Jewish Day Schools and Hebrew Classes, provided that "the teachers will have had adequate guidance beforehand . . . ," and that the children will also be acquainted with the Ashkenazi pronunciation to enable them to follow the Divine Services in synagogues.

On taking office in succession to Chief Rabbi Brodie nineteen months ago, and being once again exposed to a great deal of agitation and confusion on the subject, I issued not a ruling or an edict, but simply a communication to to my colleagues in the *Newsletter* published for internal circulation by my office. With perhaps some important modifications of the previous ruling, and consonant with the halakhic positions adopted by all the earlier authorities, I set out some guide-lines and explanations for the guidance of my colleagues. I would like to read to you this statement issued just half a year ago, so that you may hear it at first-hand and not through the various garbled versions of it that have been widely publicised. It reads:[27]

1. The Chief Rabbi wishes to bring the attention of colleagues to some guide-lines of policy on the use of the Israeli pronunciation at synagogue services and in religious education.

(a) The question of how to render our prayers at synagogue services is obviously a religious matter. It can be determined only by competent religious authorities in the community; under no circumstances should it be referred to a meeting of the synagogue members for decision by voting.

(b) No general ruling can be laid down for indiscriminate application to the whole community, since there may be some crucial local variations. Consequently, there should be some flexibility within the framework of a general policy. But the Office of the Chief Rabbi should be advised if any change is contemplated in a congregation.

(c) In principle, there should be no change from one customary pronunciation to another unless the majority of regular worshippers are familiar with the new pronunciation to be adopted. It would then be a matter for a Rabbinical decision actually to determine the change-over.

(d) Even where the Ashkenazi pronunciation is currently in use, there is no objection to worshippers normally using the Sephardi or Israeli pronunciation being called up to the Torah, or even reciting the Maftir and Haftarah, if that pronunciation is the more familiar one with them. Under similar circumstances, prayers may also be occasionally conducted in the Sephardi pronunciation. But any regular Reader or *Baal Koreh* should, of course, be fluent in, and publicly use, the pronunciation traditionally accepted by his congregation.

(e) Every encouragement should be given to use the Hebrew language, naturally with the Sephardi pronunciation, as a vehicle of instruction in our day schools and Hebrew classes, wherever possible. But where the hours of instruction are so minimal as to render it impossible to train the children to have any competence whatever in the language, and it is taught solely for synagogue purposes, the Ashkenazi pronunciation should be retained or, at least, should preferably be retained. In any event, a switch-over at the Hebrew classes should never occur unless the teacher is fully at ease in the use of the new pronunciation.

2. The reasoning behind these directives should be presented in terms comprehensible to *Baalei Battim*. Thus, it should be made clear that:

(i) The agitation for the change-over to the Sephardi accent is often noisiest from those who themselves do not render their prayers in either pronunciation, and who moreover very often use this agitation solely for propaganda purposes to denigrate Orthodoxy and its leadership.

(ii) The use of the accent is entirely irrelevant to the commitment to, or identification with, Israel—in the same way as the use of a Scottish or a Cockney accent has nothing whatever to do with a Briton's loyalty to his country.

(iii) Prayer must be rendered in a natural manner. The artificiality of using a pronunciation with which one is not completely at home would destroy its purpose as "a service of the heart".[28]

(iv) What should, above all, be emphasised is the need to understand Hebrew, whatever the accent. Today when the vast majority of our worshippers are no more familiar with Ashkenazi than with Sephardi Hebrew, and indeed know neither any more than they know Latin or Greek, the question of how to pronounce the unknown language is surely a matter of purely academic interest. Hence the stress must be on greatly expanding the facilities among youth and even adults for mastering Hebrew as a language so that the synagogue service will be familiar to them. Once that is achieved, then by all means let the Israeli accent gradually prevail and by sheer common usage become the accepted pronunciation of our public worship as well.

(v) It might also be mentioned that the common preference in favour of the Sephardi pronunciation has no scientific or historical foundation. There is sound scholarly support for the view that the Ashkenazi pronunciation is at least as ancient as the present-day Sephardi accent, as proved, for instance, by the fact that the Yemenite Jews—for thousands of years separated from the rest of our people—pronounce Hebrew in a manner much closer to the Ashkenazi than the Sephardi form. There are also other indications to warrant the opinion that the division between the Ashkenazi and Sephardi pronunciations probably already existed in Talmudic times when the Babylonian Jewry became the origin of the communities that later found their homes in the Mediterranean lands and became the Sephardi segment of our people, whilst the Palestinians populated the more central and northern regions of Europe and became the original forebears of the Ashkenazi communities, each retaining the peculiarities of their pronunciation of Hebrew that they had brought from Babylonia and Palestine respectively during the Talmudic period.

AN EXERCISE IN IRRELEVANCE

Let me now make some concluding remarks on what no doubt is bound to be one of the strangest controversies in the history of Judaism. In these times of challenge to Jewish survival, one might have thought—to be or not to be, that is the question, but others apparently believe—*a* or *o*, that is the question.

In fact, much of this debate goes back to a very odd freak of history. How is it that Israel which was originally settled and developed predominantly by immigrants who came from Ashkenazi-speaking communities—Jews from Eastern and Central Europe—accepted as its official form of Hebrew for daily use the Sephardi in preference to Ashkenazi pronunciation? This came about through a peculiar chain of circumstances. The early Zionist pioneers chose the Sephardi accent because they believed that it was the more "scientific" pronunciation, as it had been adopted at the universities. The textbooks on Hebrew used at the universities were, in fact, using the Sephardi transliteration of Hebrew. That, in turn, is due to the fact that the very first to introduce Hebrew into the universities, the German Renaissance scholar Johann Reuchlin of the fifteenth century, happened to have had a Sephardi teacher, R. Obadiah Sforno of Italy, who used the Sephardi pronunciation because he was an Italian Jew. In other words, it is the sheer accident of a non-Jewish lover of Hebrew, who made Hebrew into a scientifically accepted language by introducing it into the universities, having had a Sephardi instead of an Ashkenazi teacher, that accounts now for the agitation to bring about an artificial change in our mode of prayer.

But it ought to be emphasised that England is about the only country in which this has become a public issue (no doubt due to the partisanship of its monopolistic press). Neither in the vast communities of the United States, Canada and Latin America, nor anywhere else in Europe or in other parts of our dispersion (with the possible exception of South Africa, where very special reasons prevailed, and where the change made in 1948 continues to cause some confusion at synagogue services to this day), does this agitation exist or does the question feature as a public controversy. Nowhere else is even consideration being given to now bringing about this change as a result of the emergence of the State of Israel.

IDEOLOGICAL CONFLICTS BEHIND THE CONTROVERSY

There can be little doubt that the original Zionists who gave the newly settled Land of Israel its characteristic expression and articulation were themselves largely motivated by a spirit of rebellion against the world from which they had escaped, with its ghettos and religious restrictions, a world from which they had run away in an effort to rebuilt Jewish life on secular lines. Therefore, the very choice of the Sephardi pronunciation of Hebrew—though brought about, as I said, by the historical accident of Reuchlin's teacher having been a Sephardi—also betrayed traces of rebellion against an order of life that they wanted to be done with and to be consigned to the limbo of Jewish history.

Of course, several opponents of the change today are no doubt also motivated by some hostility towards political Zionism, as is, for instance, made clear in the Responsum of Dayan Weiss[25] which I cited to you. Nevertheless, I think no honest observer can deny that there are far more agitators in favour of the change exploiting this issue as a stick with which to attack not only a mode of pronouncing Hebrew, but a mentality, a frame of mind, and traditional norms of Judaism in general than there are opponents of the change with ulterior political motives. In this country the controversy has obviously been inflated and constantly raked up for partisan ends. The most vociferous advocates of the change usually pray in neither accent and, even if we brought about change in our synagogues, they would hardly become aware of the difference. Moreover, it is quite clearly a farce to debate in which way we ought to accent a language that is largely unfamiliar to all, just as it is futile to agitate for the abolition of the Second Day of *Yom Tov* before we have secured the observance of the First Day of *Yom Tov*.

REAL AND SPURIOUS BONDS WITH ISRAEL

The ties that unite us with what is quite unquestionably one of the most glorious peaks in the whole panorama of Jewish history will not be strengthened by using an *a* instead if an *o* for a certain vowel in the Hebrew language. They will be strengthened primarily by a deep sense of commitment to the ideals that link us together, to our common acts of worship, of sacrifice, of education, to our common literature, our common history and our common destiny that make us one people and that, whatever diversity there may exist in the manner of pronouncing Hebrew, cannot affect the unity that binds together those who pray in a common language to their common Father.

We might fittingly conclude this survey with a reference to another freak of history relevant to our issue. Many of the very leaders in the movement to revive Hebrew, the exponents of the *Haskalah,* some of the greatest modern Hebrew poets, who have made such an immense contribution towards revitalising our ancient language, themselves wrote their Hebrew poetry on the basis of both the Ashkenazi pronunciation and of the Ashkenazi stress which is usually on the penultimate instead of the last syllable of Hebrew words. Ashkenazi Hebrew is presumed in the poetry of men like Bialik, Tschernichowsky, Schoeneur and Kahan.[29] You could not sing even such a patently Zionist song as the *Hatikvah* itself, except if you adopt the meter that goes with the Ashkenazi pronunciation. Instead of *kol od baleváv penimáh,* as Israeli Hebrew would have it, the words were written to be sung: *Kol owd balévov penímoh,* etc.

If even inspired revivers of our linguistic heritage used their own ancestral pronunciation for the tremendous creations of the Hebrew language in modern times in their poetry, then surely we, in expressing through prayer the link between ourselves and our Creator, need not be deterred by the fact that an accent that has been hallowed by many, many centuries of sacred usage should continue for the time being to predominate at our Divine services.

Having said this, I feel we ought now to redirect the energies wasted in this futile conflict towards securing a return to the familiarity with the Hebrew language whereby our children will gradually become bi-lingual, whereby they will master Hebrew as fluently as they master English and whereby, once Hebrew becomes a second natural language to them, we may also ultimately crown our rededication to the ideals of our own time by joining with our brethren everywhere in the world in using accents which, after all, are meant not to attune God's ear to our prayers, but our ears to. His praise and His teachings.

NOTES

1. *Megillah* 24b.
2. Julius Jakobovits, *Halachisches zur Frage der aschkenasischen oder sephardischen Aussprache,* Frankfurt am Main, 1936 (reprint of two articles in *Israelit*).
3. Judges 12:6.
4. Rashi, *Megillah* 24b.
5. *Levush, Orach Chayyim,* 128:33.
6. H. J. Zimmels, *Ashkenazim and Sephardim,* London, 1958, pp. 308ff.
7. *Kinath Ha-Emeth,* published in *Nogah Hazedek,* Dessau, 1818, pp. 14f., 24; cited by Zimmels, *loc. cit.*
8. *Nogah Hazedek,* p. 27c. The other two Reformers in favour of the change cited by Zimmels (p. 309) are Eliezer Libermann (author of *Or Nogah,* Dessau, 1818) and David Caro (*Berith Emeth*).

9. Abraham ben Aryeh Loeb, *Zeror Ha-Chayyim*, Amsterdam, 1820, pp. 57b ff. For extensive quotations from this polemical work, see Zimmels, *op. cit.*, pp. 309ff., and Jakobovits, *op. cit.*, pp. 7f.
10. S. J. Rappaport, *Igrot Shir*, letter 43/1, pp. 224f., and *Toldot Ha-Kalir*, pp. 208f.
11. J. D. Eisenstein, *Otzar Yisrael*, vol. 6, pp. 89f.
12. I. Elbogen, *Juedisches Lexikon*, vol. 2, pp. 1475f.
13. *Jewish Encyclopedia*, vol. 10, p. 210.
14. *Orach Chayyim*, 53:12.
15. *Pri Chadash, a.l.*; based on Tosaphot, *Baba Metzi'a* 86a.
16. *Birkei Yoseph*, on *Orach Chayyim, loc. cit.*; see also *Mishnah Berurah, a.l.*
17. S. Landau, Responsa *Shivat Zion*, no. 5; cited by Jakobovits, *loc. cit.*
18. Prov. 1:8, as interpreted in the Talmud (*Pesachim* 50b and *Chullin* 93b).
19. A. I. Kook, in *Kol Torah*, Jerusalem, 5693, no. 1-2; also in *Letter* printed in Benzion Uziel, *Mishpetei Uziel*, p. iv; cited by Jakobovits, *op. cit.*, pp. 8ff.; and Zimmels, *op. cit.*, pp. 312f.
20. B. Uziel, *Mishpetei Uziel, Orach Chayyim*, no. 1. See also preceding note.
21. Y. Weinberg, Responsa *Seridei Esh*, vol. 2, *Orach Chayyim*, no. 5.
22. S. Braun, *She'arim Metzuyanim be-Halakhah*, part i, 18:4.
23. Bachaya, on *Vayera* (ed. Chavel, Jerusalem, 1966, vol. 1, pp. 168ff.).
24. Emden, *Siddur Ya'avetz*, Introduction *Sullom Bet El*, no. 1.
25. I. J. Weiss, Responsa *Minchat Yitzchak*, vol. 3, no. 9.
26. See the *Jewish Chronicle*, 8 August 1952, p. 5; cited by Zimmels, *op. cit.*, p. 313.
27. *Newsletter* issued by the Office of the Chief Rabbi, no. 9, Iyyar 5728.
28. "And to serve Him with all your heart" (Deut. 11:13)—"What is called 'service of the heart'? Prayer" (*Ta'anit* 2a).
29. See *Juedisches Lexikon*, vol. 2, p. 1477.

ADDITIONAL BIBLIOGRAPHY

(I am grateful to Miss R. Lehman, Librarian of Jews' College, for her help in compiling this list.)

Cohen, Benno: "Wandlungen der hebraeischen Aussprache" (*Jeschurun*, xi, 1924, pp 457–463). This does not go back to the original division.

Hirschfeld, H.: "The pronunciation of the letter AYN". (*J.Q.R.*, iv, pp. 499–502). 1892.

Idelsohn, A. Z.: "Die gegenwaertige Aussprache des Hebraeischen bei Juden und Samaritanern" (*M.G.W.J.*, lvii, 1913, pp. 527–545 and 697–721).

Plessner, M.: "Neue Arbeiten zur Septuaginta-Forschung" (*M.G.W.J.*, lxx, 1926, pp. 237–250). Deals with transcription and reconstruction.

Speiser, Epharim A.: "Nature of the Hexaplaric material and Origen's manner of transliteration" (*J.Q.R.*, xvi, 1925-6, pp. 350–382). Deals with: errors due to confusion of Greek letters, dittography, haplography, transposition, and other textual changes; also the consonants.

Speiser, Ephraim A.: "The pronunciation of Hebrew based chiefly on the transliterations in the Hexapla" (*J.Q.R.*, xxiii, 1932-33, pp. 233–265). Deals with the laryngals, sibilants, emphatic sounds, semivowels, gemination of consonants.

Speiser, Ephraim A.: "The pronunciation of Hebrew based chiefly on the transliterations in the Hexapla" (*J.Q.R.*, xxiv, 1933-4, pp. 9–46). Deals with the vowels, the main schools of vocalization, the pronunciation of Greek vowels at the time of Origen, the transliteration of full vowels, the a-vowels.

ח. ילון: שבילי מבטאים. (קונטרסים לעניני הלשון העברית, שנה א', שנה ב') ירושלים תשכ"ד

מ. צ. סגל: לתולדות המבטא של הקמץ. (לשוננו א', ע' 9–33) תרפ"ח

ב. קלאר: לתולדות המבטא העברי בימי הביניים. (מחקרים ועיונים, ע' 42–46). תל אביב תשי"ד

ד. רעוול: החלופים בין בני בבל ובין בני ארץ ישראל ומקורות ההלכה של הקראים. (חורב א׳ א׳, ע׳ 20–1) תרצ״ד

ש. מורג: העברית שבפי יהודי תימן. ירושלים תשכ״ג

ש. אסף: בבל וארץ ישראל בתקופת הגאונים. (השלח ל״ד ע׳ 448) תרע״ח

ש. אסף: לצמיחת המרכזים הישראליים בתקופת הגאונים. (השלח ל״ה ע׳ 8, 282, 514) תרע״ח

ש. י. רפאפורט: ערך מלין. ע׳ 227. פראג תרי״ב

אגרת רב שרירא גאון. חיפה תרפ״א

משה בן יצחק: ספר השוהם. ירושלים תש״ו

עמנואל בן יקותיאל: ס׳ לוית חן (פרק שני: בבאור כללי הקמץ). מנטובה שי״ג

יוסף יוזפא האן: ס׳ יוסף אומץ. ס׳ כ׳. פ״פ דמיין תפ״ג

THE RELIGIOUS SIGNIFICANCE OF ISRAEL
INDEPENDENCE DAY

This Foreword, prepared in 1972 for a new edition of the Israel Independence
Day Prayer Book, *was never published. Therein lies its significance, especially
in the light of the subsequent Yom Kippur War and its aftermath. For on its
rejection hangs a tale.*

*The original edition was published by Routledge and Kegan Paul for
Mr. Armin Krausz of Sheffield in 1964 in the hope that it would be accepted
by congregations in the British Commonwealth as the standard text on a
par with the Routledge* Machzor *for Festivals produced in the same format.
To this end Mr. Krausz had prevailed on Chief Rabbi Israel Brodie to confer
upon the new Order of Service his "approval", though not his "authorisation".
But the volume never in fact gained general acceptance except in a few
congregations. Despite repeated requests, the present Chief Rabbi refrained
from issuing a similar endorsement, mainly on the grounds that the proposed
liturgy departed from traditional usage by including parts reserved for Sabbaths
and full Festivals (because worshippers were free from work on those days)
but omitted even on long-established semi- or minor festivals like* Chol
Ha-moed, Chanukah *and* Purim. *However, he agreed to supply a Foreword
for the second edition, provided it could refer to these reservations and to the
various religious views on* Yom Ha'Atzmaut *generally. This Mr. Krausz
refused to accept.*

Even 25 years after the establishment of the State of Israel, there are still
three distinct schools of thought on the religious and eschatalogical significance of this momentous event. These differences are exemplified by corresponding variations of attitude to the celebration of *Yom Ha'Atzmaut*.

Some major Chassidic groups and the greater part of what is now commonly known as the "Yeshiva world", supported by the majority of leading Torah
sages and their followers, do not at all recognise the body politic of the
State as representing a religious phenomenon in fulfilment of our millennial
aspirations. They love and treasure Jewish life in the Holy Land no less
passionately than others. They may even acknowledge the miracle of Israel
as a Providential haven for millions of Jews and as Jewry's principal Torah
centre and therefore encourage settlement of their followers there. But they
cannot see any significance in Prophetic terms of a secular State which they
regard as the very denial of the historical ideals to which our people are

committed. Hence, *Yom Ha'Atzmaut* has not been entered into their religious calendar as a date warranting any religious observance.

By contrast, there are those, notably within the Religious Zionist Movement, who are in no doubt that the restoration of Jewish independence in the Land of Israel marks a most momentous phase in the fulfilment of the promised Return to Zion. They believe that this event must be rated a turning-point of Jewish fortunes of pre-Messianic dimensions. They are certain that the wondrous restoration of Jewish sovereignty to Israel and Jerusalem spells out the design of Providence, as foretold by our Prophets, and as inevitably bound to culminate in the complete realisation of that Prophetic vision. For them, *Yom Ha'Atzmaut* is a major day of celebration in the Jewish calendar to be observed by liturgical usages comparable with other Jewish festivals.

Between these two extremes are numerous rabbis and Jewish communities throughout the world who adopt a somewhat less finalised attitude. While they unreservedly hail the establishment of Israel as an epoch-making event of the most profound religious significance, they reserve judgement on its place in the ultimate Divine scheme of Redemption. Whether the State will prove to be the precursor of the Messianic Age as envisaged by our Prophets is a judgement, they believe, which must be left, in the famous Talmudic phrase, "in suspense until Elijah comes". Hence, they rank *Yom Ha'Atzmaut* as a religiously notable day, worthy of special thanksgiving and festivity, but with reservations which distinguish it from the established cycle of festivals in the Jewish calendar.

The *Independence Day Prayer Book*, devotedly edited by Mr. Armin Krausz, reflects the thinking of the second of these three schools of thought, as endorsed by the present Ashkenazi Chief Rabbi of Israel. The special Order of Service officially adopted in the British Commonwealth by both the Chief Rabbis who have occupied office since the establishment of Israel is substantially similar in form and content, though modified by the omission of such Sabbath and Yom Tov prayers as the additional Psalms and *Nishmat* which are not recited even on other long-established festival days such as *Chol Hamoed*, *Chanukah* and *Purim*.

May the great occasion which has prompted the expression of traditional thanksgiving and praise contained in these pages speedily become an augury of Israel's spiritual fulfilment and complete redemption through the merit of our fathers and through our own worthiness to live in this stirring period of Divine wonders and benevolence.

SAMSON RAPHAEL HIRSCH

A Reappraisal of his Teachings and Influence in the Light of our Times

I

This is not meant to be a biography of Rabbi Samson Raphael Hirsch's towering personality, nor an appraisal of his prolific and epoch-making literary output. The intention is rather to present a critical survey of some of his teachings and achievements, with special reference to their impact on our age.

Hirsch's influence is clearly greater and more widespread today than at the time of his death, over eighty years ago. S. A. Hirsch, a distinguished tutor at Jews' College, wrote of his namesake with remarkable foresight in 1890: "Great as the influence was which he wielded during his life-time, the real fruits of his activity are only just beginning to ripen . . . His works must first become known to a greater circle of readers by translation from the German, partly into Hebrew, and partly into the vernacular tongues of countries outside Germany" (*A Book of Essays*, 1905).

This forecast is now being fulfilled, largely through the immense labours of Hirsch's devotees here, in America and in Israel, especially of Dayan Dr. I. Grunfeld who, by his superb translations and introductions, has done more than anyone else to bring about the renaissance of Hirsch's teachings and writings.

The life of Hirsch is truly one of the great Jewish success stories. Already at the age of 28, he published his historic *Nineteen Letters* which may be regarded as a manifesto outlining his life's programme. As his descendant, Mordechai Breuer, so aptly wrote of the *Nineteen Letters*: "This is the entire Torah of Rabbi Samson Raphael Hirsch, and as for the remainder, go and study." Throughout his long, creative and often turbulent life, Hirsch never veered from the philosophical blueprint set out in his *Nineteen Letters*. In his communal work, he likewise reached his principal goals, establishing the kind of community and the type of school that bore the imprint of his vision at a very young age.

These successes are perhaps all the more impressive against the background of several failures, some of them of quite momentous consequence.

Of particular interest to us was his failure to secure the British Chief

Lecture delivered at Jews' College, London, on 16 June 1971.

Rabbinate for which he had applied together with Rabbi Nathan Marcus Adler and two other candidates. The very first issue of the *Jewish Chronicle* (October 18th, 1844) commented thus on the candidates:

> Far be it from us to underrate either of the four candidates. Pious, good, talented men we have no doubt they are; but eminent they assuredly are not. We hesitate not to affirm that previous to his election as Chief Rabbi of Hanover Dr. Adler was comparatively unknown. . . . Dr. Hirsch was known as the author of controversial pamphlets that evinced more talent than learning, more zeal than charity. . . . We ask are they the most competent that they may be invited to fill the office? And unhesitatingly we answer, assuredly not!

Two rather intriguing asides on Chief Rabbinate elections may here also be mentioned briefly. In 1899 Dr. B. Drachman published a translation of the *Nineteen Letters*—the first rendering into English of any of Hirsch's works. Fourteen years later the same Dr. Drachman competed unsuccessfully against Dr. J. H. Hertz for the position of Chief Rabbi in succession to Dr. Hermann Adler.

And, while Hirsch failed in his bid for the British Chief Rabbinate in 1844, Rabbi Meir Loeb ben Yechiel Michael (the "Malbim") was elected as Chief Rabbi of New York in 1897, though he did not live to assume that office. One wonders how different the history of the English-speaking communities might have been if Hirsch and the "Malbim" would have served as chief rabbis in London and New York respectively!

Also remarkable was the inability of Hirsch to win any leading contemporaries for his cause and to retain the affection of some outstanding personal friends. Two especially fateful examples come to mind. For a time, one of Hirsch's most intimate young friends was Abraham Geiger. They were fellow-students in Bonn and earlier in Heidelberg. Yet Geiger eventually became Hirsch's most bitter opponent, making history as the arch-apostle of extreme Reform Judaism, denouncing the Talmud and ridiculing such fundamentals as the dietary laws and circumcision.

Hirsch became similarly estranged from Heinrich Graetz after an auspicious start in their early relations. Graetz, at the age of 19, was so impressed— one may even say entranced—on reading the *Nineteen Letters*, that he asked to be admitted as a boarder in Hirsch's home in Oldenburg. But in the course of one year's stay with the master, Graetz became increasingly disenchanted. Later, especially on the publication of Graetz's monumental *History of the Jews*, the two engaged in a bitter polemic as their paths diverged and turned in opposite directions.

Altogether, Hirsch was easily given to acrimony and scorn in his voluminous polemics with his opponents. These were not limited to non-Orthodox leaders. A glaring example is the fierce controversy between Hirsch and Rabbi Isaac Dob Bamberger of Wurzburg over the question of the *Ausstritt* (the establishment of separatist Orthodox congregations opting out from the officially recognised Jewish community organisations). The argument persists to the present day, dividing "independent Orthodoxy", represented by "Adass" congregations in many parts of the world, from Orthodox "establishments" existing side by side with these congregations.

II

Even more relevant to an appreciation of Hirsch's place in history and in contemporary thought are certain curious contradictions in his relations with giants of Judaism not of his own time. On the whole, Hirsch rarely mentions or quotes the classic medieval philosophers or exegetes who preceded him, such as Rashi, Ibn Ezra, or Albo. Of those to whom he does relate, taking up a specific position *vis-à-vis* them, there are only three: Maimonides, Nachmanides and Yehuda Halevi. But oddly, Hirsch's attitude to them is in each case the reverse to what we might expect.

Of these three, the most kindred spirit to Hirsch is obviously Maimonides, both as a rationalist and as a philosopher reinterpreting Judaism in terms of his age. After all, the Rambam's *Guide of the Perplexed* was meant to reinforce the Jewish loyalties of his contemporaries in circumstances and in a manner not dissimilar from what Hirsch intended to accomplish in his philosophical writings. The *Mishneh Torah* and the *Horeb* also show significant parallels in the codification of Jewish law. Yet it is Maimonides whom the author of the *Nineteen Letters* attacks with special vehemence:

> He entered into Judaism from without, bringing with him opinions of whose truth he had convinced himself from extraneous sources. He . . . gives expression . . . to opinions concerning the meaning and purpose of the commandments . . . which are utterly untenable. . . . But since the precepts, as practically fulfilled, stand entirely out of connection with these explanations, it was inevitable that their ceremonial fulfilment lost its spiritual basis, and became despised.

Even stranger is Hirsch's preference for Moses Mendelsohn, whom some today regard as the spiritual ancestor of assimilation, if not of Reform Judaism:

> His *Jerusalem* . . . emphasizes, . . . in contra-distinction to the *Moreh*, the practical essence of Judaism, and gives utterances to an opinion concerning the *Eduth*, which, had it been carried out and intellectually comprehended by his successors, might have revolutionised the subsequent period. . . . The science of Judaism was not further developed by him, and his successors, lacking the religious sentiment of the master . . . could do nothing better . . . than to surrender completely to the Maimonidean theories.

On the other hand, Nachmanides and Halevi are Hirsch's heroes, though their thinking is fundamentally opposed to his. Nachmanides was, of course, one of the greatest early Kabbalists, representing a philosophy of Judaism almost entirely alien to Hirsch. Though Hirsch mentions the *Zohar* in some preparatory notes on the *Horeb*, his outlook is a complete negation of the mystical view. He expresses this acidly in his *Nineteen Letters*:

> A perverted intellect comprehended the institutions *which were designed and ordained for the internal and external purification and betterment of man* as mechanical, dynamical, or magical formulas for the upbuilding of higher worlds, and . . . thus the observances meant for the education of the spirit to a nobler life were but too frequently degraded into mere amuletic or talismanic performances.

The contradiction is even more pointed in the case of Halevi, whose

Jewish philosophy is the very antithesis to Hirsch's. For Halevi Israel's choice is the expression of God's love, and enjoys His special spiritual endowment transmitted by heredity. Consistent with this premise, Halevi emphasises over and over again the centrality of the Land of Israel, and regards the commandments not merely as a means to the fulfilment of a mission to the nations, but as the highest stage of the religious experience. Hence he considers the revelational laws superior to the ethical and moral precepts.

Hirsch teaches the opposite. He sees the ultimate Jewish national purpose in the mission to the nations. Hence his affirmation of the *galuth* and his demand for unconditional patriotism in terms we could hardly appreciate today:

> But this outward obedience to the laws must be joined by the inner obedience: . . . to be loyal to the State with heart and mind . . . so that every aim which your country has as its national good shall be achieved and furthered. . . . And this duty is unconditional and not dependent upon whether the State is kindly intentioned towards you or is harsh. Even should they deny your right to be a human being and to develop a lawful human life upon the soil which bore you, you shall not neglect *your* duty . . . which God lays upon you: "Loyalty towards king and country and the promotion of welfare wherever and whenever and however you can."

Again, for Hirsch the hope of the Return to Zion is deferred, to be achieved only by spiritual means:

> Not in order to shine as a nation among nations do we raise our prayers and hopes for a reunion in our land, but in order to find a soil for the better fulfil- ment of our spiritual vocation in that reunion. . . . But this very vocation obliges us until God shall call us back to the Holy Land, to live and to work as patriots wherever He has placed us. . . . But it forbids us to strive for the reunion or the possession of the land by any but spiritual means.

These thoughts outlined in the *Nineteen Letters* are also corroborated in Hirsch's *Pentateuch* commentary on this week's Sidra, where he interprets the halachic concept of the resanctification of the Land culminating in the construction of the Second Temple as merely preparatory to Israel's exile for the fulfilment of its national mission:

> The legal fact, that the effect of "the second conquest" was not ended by the second exile could be ascribed to the fact that, during the whole period of the second Temple, the state was not granted national independence which could be considered to have come to an end by the subsequent exile. The whole of the second Temple appears only to have been a gathering of the people about their Sanctuary of the Torah to equip them in preparation for the centuries of dis- persion that lay before them. Ezra's repossession of the land and sanctifying it as the soil of the Torah was just a taking into possession and sanctification in the exile and for the exile which indeed had not come to a complete end with his return. The catastrophe under Titus was accordingly only a bitter and deeper aggravation of the fate that was still continuing under Ezra . . . (on Nu. 15:18).

Another expression of this argument is the difference in the interpretation of *am segulah* ("peculiar treasure" or "chosen people"). While the Targum, Mechilta, Rashi and Ibn Ezra associate this term with the special quality of

God's love for Israel, Hirsch renders it as "a property exclusively belonging to one owner . . . God has the sole and exclusive claim to Israel's devotions and service."

Equally revealing paradoxes may be found in some other aspects of Hirsch's attitudes and outlook. A few examples may here be given.

Hirsch was the leading fighter against Reform Judaism, providing to this day the most effective rebuttal of its teachings; yet he shares with Reform the central emphasis on the mission to the nations, albeit on very different lines. And, having hoisted to his mast the idea of the mission to the non-Jews, he seems to disdain the mission to the Jews by his whole concept of the *Ausstritt* (separatism). Whatever his intent, the movement he inspired—betraying little evident grief over the progressive drift of Jews outside its congregational orbit—never really supported organised efforts to reclaim them and their institutions for traditional Judaism.

Again, he inveighs furiously against calling Judaism a "religion"; yet he is not disturbed by having his own community known as the "*Religionsgesell-schaft*".

He vigorously denounces those who do not construct Judaism "from within" and who admit foreign influences to its interpretation; yet he is himself the supreme exponent of the synthesis of *Torah im derech eretz*, sublimating the fusion of Judaism with the humanism of his day in his highly original concept of "Mensch-Jissroel". Some scholars have even claimed to detect in Hirsch's writings direct traces of non-Jewish philosophers, notably Hegel, Herder and Fichte—claims which even Dr. Grunfeld refutes only somewhat hesitatingly in his masterly introduction to his translation of the *Horeb*.

But, in a way, the measure of Hirsch's greatness is indicated by the fact that these contradictions met with a response of similar ambivalence and dichotomy in the attitude towards Hirsch by some of his leading contemporaries and successors. We are not speaking now of the lurking admiration for him found here and there among his most severe critics, for instance the Hungarian scholar, Leopold Loew, among many others. We refer rather to the reaction evoked by Hirsch among leading Torah sages in Eastern Europe. On the one hand, there was uninhibited enchantment with his teachings. The enthusiastic acclaim was well epitomized by Rabbi Yitzchak Elchanan Spector of Kovno, in his approbation of the Hebrew rendering of Hirsch's Genesis published in 1908: "Value cannot be set on the many novellae introduced by the Gaon and Sage, great in knowledge as in conveying understanding, lucid and conforming to reason, unifying Torah and tradition . . ."

Alas, the approbation of the Hirschian *system* was meant for German Jews only. Essentially, the Torah scholars and religious leaders of East European Jewry have remained hostile to Hirsch's philosophy. Their schools reject the whole concept of *Torah im derech eretz*, with its affirmation of secular pursuits and the Jewish mission among the nations. All this—as well as the type of schools and congregations Hirsch laboured so hard to build up—was and is utterly alien to those who, from the distance, lavished such high praise on Hirsch and his achievements.

That this attitude still prevails was eloquently demonstrated in a convention address I heard a few years ago before the Union of Orthodox Jewish Congregations of America by its principal spiritual guide and ideologue, Rabbi J. B. Soloveitchik. Attacking the very basis on which Hirsch founded his *Weltanschauung*, he sharply denounced the notion of synthesis and argued that it had always been the destiny of the Jew to scale two separate heights ("*ramatayim*"), to live in two *incompatible* worlds which could never meet or converge. But these severe strictures would not prevent Rabbi Soloveitchik from recognising the genius of Hirsch in freely drawing from his teachings and interpretations.

III

Upon the rich canvas woven together by the diverse strands of Hirsch's personality and teachings, we may now attempt to draw a picture of his role in our world of today. We will find traces of similar contradictions which can only be understood in the light of the antecedents we have discussed.

The overall influence of Hirsch is clearly massive, profound and worldwide. There is probably no single individual who has contributed more to the image and standing of modern Orthodoxy. Hirsch not only forged the principal weapons with which traditional Jews have defended themselves against the onslaught of assimilation and Reform. He contrived to make observant Jews respectable in Western society, and he provided the platform on which they could come to terms with the culture around them.

Moreover, Hirsch dramatically influenced the institutional life of Orthodox Jews in Western lands. He did so not merely by inspiring the creation of all the "*Ausstrittsgemeinden*" now throbbing with vibrant Jewish life in many major communities all over the world—ranging from Israel to Australia. He is equally responsible for their colossal impact on raising the religious standards of established Orthodox communities generally. Our United Synagogue here, and similar Orthodox establishments elsewhere, would not today boast the levels of Jewish learning and observance without the competitive stimulus provided by the superior commitment of congregations made in Hirsch's image. To his influence we may also attribute the foundation of the Agudat Israel organisation which gave political expression to Hirsch's communal ideal of "independent Orthodoxy". Another epoch-making institution which owed its inspiration to Hirsch's vision was the Berlin *Rabbiner-Seminar* whose impact, through its many disciples and kindred institutions, continues to be enormous even now, over thirty years after its destruction by the Nazis.

Hirsch's superb and prolific literary creations represent an immortal contribution enriching our times. Through them countless Jews of our age have discovered treasures of Jewish thought which no other author could present with equal passion, conviction, profundity and magnificence of expression.

Above all, our day schools—by the hundreds now gracing and invigorating Jewish communities the world over—acclaim Hirsch as their progenitor He is really the father of them all. For, to some extent, they are all patterned on the school he established in Frankfurt.

These achievements are tremendous and enduring, still potent in virtually every aspect of Jewish religious life today. But here is the ambivalence in his heritage. As against all this extraordinary growth fertilised and cultivated by Hirsch's genius, we must also recognise the limitations.

His immediate following—those who subscribe fully to the Hirschian *Weltanschauung*—is now strictly contained as a tiny minority, an element no longer dominant or significantly growing in any Jewish community.

This decline is all the more striking, and surprising, when viewed in a comparative light. Present-day Orthodox Jewry may be described as energised by three major forces or movements—all of European origin: the Mussar-Yeshiva movement, represented primarily by the great institutions of Talmudic learning; the Chassidic movements; and *Torah im derech eretz*. Despite the devastating blows they sustained in the Holocaust, the first two have made enormous strides in the post-War world. The strength and influence of the yeshivot and of Chassidism within the total Jewish experience are greater today than ever before. The world of East European Jewry has collapsed, yet the values and movements it created flourish with unprecedented vigour.

The third force, on the other hand, is scarcely a national or communal factor today. Though the product of an environment which is closer to the culture surviving in Western lands, the Hirschian movement has not been able to maintain, let alone to strengthen, its momentum. Even within the scattered German-Jewish "Adass" communities, the rising generation are fast swinging away from the ideological commitment of their parents, attracted as they increasingly are by the stronger magnetism of the yeshivot and even of Chassidism. There now exists not a single institution of higher Jewish learning anywhere in the world with a specifically Hirschian orientation. Even the burgeoning organisations of Orthodox scientists do not really represent intrinsically *Torah im derech eretz* ideals, as did their prototype in pre-War Germany. Their members may combine secular avocations with religious studies, but as a matter of expediency rather than by way of fusion in which each half enriches the other. By and large, Orthodox scientists today, remote from the Hirschian ideal, live indeed in two incompatible worlds, asking few questions and providing few answers on the inner relations and conflicts between their religious and secular commitments.

Why should Hirsch's teachings as embodied in a movement have suffered such an eclipse, notwithstanding the renewed interest aroused in his writings and in many of his concepts? I believe the principal answers are to be found in the two cataclysmic events of recent Jewish history. Firstly, Germany's betrayal of civilisation, culminating in the Holocaust, produced a terrible disillusionment with all Western culture and science. Our generation can no longer accept the inevitability of civilisation's progress and of man's enlightenment, as assumed by Hirsch. Secondly, and equally unforeseen by Hirsch, the rise of Israel as a political reality and the primary focus of Jewish life and thought has not only seriously compromised Hirsch's *Weltanschauung*, with its acclamation of the *galuth*; it has largely removed the dynamic of his concept of Israel's mission to humanity. The emphasis today is on self-preservation and on the reclamation of Jews. All our energies are fully engaged in the mission to Jews, not to mankind. By contrast, the yeshiva and Chassidic movements have gained momentum for the very reason that they are inward-looking, unconcerned with the outside world and the Jewish role in it, even though both these movements, too, still have to come fully to terms with the Jewish State.

In this assessment, no value judgement on Hirsch's ideology is intended. It is meant simply as an attempt to offer some explanation for the baffling phenomenon whereby Hirsch is today left with very few genuine disciples, while the great sages and rebbes of East European origin or outlook now count their followers by the hundreds of thousands in Western countries, including Israel, as a dynamic force of ever increasing potency.

Yet, whatever the reverses suffered by the *Torah im derech eretz* movement, Hirsch is far from being a spent force. In many ways his impact has reached a new peak. Only, his influence no longer lies in providing an ideological banner around which Orthodox Jews and congregations will rally as a movement, any more than the *Guide* of Maimonides provides such guidance today. The value of Hirsch's immortal contributions as a thinker and supreme interpreter is to be found rather in providing unique insights into the Written and Oral Laws and the harmony between them, and as a philosophical pathfinder showing the timeless capacity of Judaism to be topical and applicable in every age and within all cultures, however advanced. His artistry in portraying the incomparable beauty of holiness remains as unsurpassed as his pedagogical skill and his powers of persuasion in teaching the discipline of Judaism to an age distracted by dazzling strides in science and technology, by the agony of the "*Weltschmerz*", and by the allurements of religious nihilism, moral permissiveness and materialistic hedonism. Hirsch may yet prove a mighty factor in the inevitable regeneration of Israel's spiritual glory.[1]

NOTE

1. The bibliography of recent studies on Hirsch and Hirschiana is too extensive to be listed here. A considerable number of valuable contributions can be found in various volumes of the Hebrew periodical *Ha-Ma'yan* (published in Jerusalem since 1953) and *Tradition* (published by the Rabbinical Council of America since 1958). A critical article freely used in the preparation of this lecture is by H. I. Levine, "Enduring and Transitory Elements in the Philosophy of Samson Raphael Hirsch", *Tradition*, vol. 5 (Spring 1963), pp. 278–97. Another, more biographical study of special interest is by Mordecai Breuer, in *Guardians of Our Heritage*, ed. Leo Jung, New York, 1958, pp. 263–99.

CONFORMITY AND DIVERSITY IN THE JEWISH HISTORICAL TRADITION

The association of an academic Chair at this University with my name and my Rabbinical office is more than a personal tribute, an honour I am proud to share with several distinguished Chief Rabbinical colleagues, including my revered predecessor.

There are indeed many significant analogies between rabbinic and academic disciplines and functions. "Doctor" and "rabbi" both literally denote "teacher". Again, the word "chair", in its Greek and Hebrew equivalents of *cathedra* and *kisse*, is applied to the "seat" of authority and jurisdiction occupied by both academics and rabbis, as in a "university chair" and in *kisse ha-Rabbanut*.

The academic-rabbinic parallel is even more striking in the case of chief rabbis. Traditionally, my official Hebrew title is not *rav rashi* but *rav ha-kolel*. Literally, this means the "universal rabbi", or even "the university rabbi", as indicated by the recent usage of the term *kolel* for "an institute for advanced rabbinical learning", and *michlalah* as the modern Hebrew word for "university". *Kolel* and "university" both stand for the "universality" of knowledge. Diversity of studies, covering the "totality" of knowledge and varying in approach and content, was once regarded as the essence of higher learning, both secular and religious.

Unfortunately, present-day *kolelim* and universities have partly surrendered these former characteristics. Through the growing tendency towards specialisation, they teach more and more about less and less, no longer providing a well-balanced comprehension of *kol*, of the "totality" and "universality" of Jewish and human culture and of the inter-play between the various academic disciplines. At the same time, by limiting the diversification of their methods of instruction and their philosophies, or their *darkei ha-limud*—now almost uniformly alike at most universities and *kolelim*—they produce a drab sameness of graduates who neither individually nor collectively represent the "universality" of knowledge as found in past ages.

If the challenge implicit in this critique may be directed generally at all *kolelim* and universities—the former specialising in a severely confined area of talmudic studies, and the latter serving increasingly to mass-produce pro-

Lecture delivered at the Inauguration of the Immanuel Jakobovits Chair in Jewish Law at Bar-Ilan University on 16 April 1974.

fessionals and highly departmentalised research workers—it is of special significance to Bar-Ilan. This University was dedicated at its very foundation to the fusion of the *kolel* and university concepts, to the cross-fertilisation of Jewish and human cultures, exemplified in what Rabbi Samson Raphael Hirsch called *Mensch-Yisroel.*

Of course, the knowledge-explosion of our times has made specialisation inevitable. No single scholar can command the totality of all extant knowledge in Jewish fields, let alone in secular disciplines as well, as Maimonides and other outstanding savants did in former ages. The only substitute is collective universality through diversification, so that at least corporately the entire gamut of the various methods and fields of learning is adequately covered. Such diversity must of necessity also embrace differences of approach and attitude, including the courage to explore new paths of enquiry through originality and innovation.

Significantly, the very first reference to Jewish learning already alludes to the needs for diverse forms of instruction: On the verse "And Jacob was a simple man, sitting in tents" (Gen. 25:27), Rashi, based on a well-known Midrash, explains the plural "tents" as meaning that Jacob studied "in the tent of Shem and the tent of Ever". The source in *Tanchuma Yashan* elaborates: "Jacob would go out from the academy of Shem and enter the academy of Ever". There were two yeshivot for a single student—one a house of learning founded on the ancient traditions of Shem, and another on the newer approach of Ever, four generations later. This remarkable Midrash indicates, then, that learning was regarded as complete and balanced only if it combined various methods or *darkei ha-limud.*

To this theme, I want to address myself: Diversity, or universality, as an essential strain in the human, the Jewish and indeed the Orthodox texture of thought and society. Under this general heading I want to trace aspects of non-conformity, and even dissent, as a constant thread in the fabric of Judaism and of Jewish history, and apply the conclusions to the contemporary scene at three levels, dealing with our external, our inter-Jewish, and our inter-Orthodox relations.

Of all the enduring ideals inspiring Western civilisation, there is only one which is not Jewish in origin or orientation. Monotheism, the brotherhood of man, social justice, neighbourly love, the quest for universal peace and the hope for man's redemption, are all part of our biblical heritage: they reflect cardinal Jewish teachings throughout the ages. The only exception is the ideal of democracy, much as we value it as the best system of government so far devised. This notion of the rule of the people, as determined by the majority, is of Greek origin, as is the term itself. Judaism never vested the exercise of power or the arbitration between right and wrong through legislation in the concensus of superior numbers. On the contrary, in opposition to this view the Book of Job already declared: "The many are not wise" (32:9): Wisdom is not necessarily the prerogative of the majority. The opinion of the majority prevails only among equally qualified experts; for, as the *Sepher Ha-Chinuch* put it, "It would be improper to say that a small group of sages should not outweigh a large group of boors, even if they were as numerous as the participants in the Exodus from Egypt" (*Mitzvah* 78). Otherwise, Judaism always upheld minority rights rather than subjecting all to the absolute will of the majority.

This is how the Jewish people, chosen for its historic assignment of moral leadership "because you were the smallest of all peoples" (Deut. 7:7), became the great non-conformists of history. Conditioned from the start to accept minority status, Jews at all times swam against the stream of conformity and spurned public opinion. The Hebrew Prophets in their days were the loneliest and most unpopular leaders of all times: yet, today they are immortal, and through the impact of their teachings, the mighty flood of paganism which engulfed them has been contained and pushed back. The Maccabees represented a tiny band of idealists pitted against the massive strength of the Greek Empire and its Hellenistic culture. Through their victory and because of their triumph, the great monotheistic faiths survived or came into existence, determining the advance of civilisation and social justice on a global scale ever since. And need we be reminded that, throughout the Middle Ages, right up to our own time, our people defied the blandishments of the dominant faith and the cruel blows of our persecutors, persevering as an insignificant minority, ever ready to pay a fearful price for being out of step from our contemporaries?

The firm commitment of Judaism to non-conformity and diversity also finds striking expression in its attitude to proselytisation. In contrast to the other monotheistic faiths, Judaism never went out of its way to encourage conversions nor did it aspire to become a universal religion. It emphatically rejects the belief that it is, or will ever be, the sole portal to human salvation, holding instead, in the words of the Prophet Micah, "that all the peoples shall walk each one in the name of its god" (4:5). A uniform human society in which all groups and individuals strive to be identical would be as stagnant and unworkable as a machine constructed of equal parts only or as an orchestra in which all instruments are the same. Once the common fundamental imperatives of the moral order are accepted, we do not advocate a merger of man's diverse religions or races or national characteristics and cultures. Any blurring of these distinctions can only have blighting effects on human progress.

The Jewish ideal of gaining human brotherhood and unity through non-conformity and distinctiveness, or blending particularism with universalism, is magnificently expressed in the incomparable *Aleinu*-prayer. Longing for the time "when the world will be perfected under the Kingdom of the Almighty, and when all the children of flesh will call upon Your Name", Jews yet rendered thanks to God that "He has not made us like the nations of other lands, nor placed us like other families of the earth". They rejoiced in being different, unlike any other people among the family of nations, believing that only by being different could they eventually share with all in the blessings of universal peace and understanding under the common Fatherhood of God.

Lately, or at least until Yom Kippur, we were in some danger of losing the distinctiveness of the Jewish national character, of shedding the pride in being different. Altogether, we live in an age of rigid conformity, an age in which nothing is harder than to defy the pressures of uniformity. Through instant global communications, through the all-pervasive indoctrination of the mass media, through the growth of international organisations and combines, national and individual features are being levelled out to produce an amorphous homogeneity of opinions, fashions, tastes, eating-habits, social forms and even moral, or immoral, norms all over the world.

For the Jewish people, for whom the refusal to join the majority is an indispensable condition of national survival and fulfilment, this headlong drive towards nondescript uniformity presents a particularly deadly peril. For some centuries past, in the long struggle for Jewish emancipation, we have fought for the right to be equal. Having gained our emancipation, at any rate in the Western world, we now find it hard to fight for the right to be different, or indeed to assert the wish to be different, with the result that the gravest internal Jewish challenge we now face is the crisis of identity.

Paradoxically, the emergence of the Jewish State, founded as a bulwark against assimilation to fulfil the Jewish national purpose, has aggravated the tendency towards national assimilation through the quest for equality. Notwithstanding its immense contribution to the consolidation of Jewish pride and identification inside and outside the Land, Israel has increased rather than weakened the pressures of conformity. The emphasis in our national Jewish stance is largely on becoming like everyone else. Corporately we take more pride in what we have in common with the nations of the world than in what distinguishes us from them. We boast of a parliamentary system, universities, industrial enterprises, not to mention armed forces, like unto others; but we show less pride in what sets us apart from others, in possessing a religious system, academies of Jewish learning, spiritual values and moral attributes which are uniquely Jewish and unlike any other people's national treasures.

Of course, the problem has its historical as well as contemporary causes. The early secularist pioneers of Zionism were primarily concerned "to solve the Jewish problem", convinced that the Jews could gain acceptance in the world only if they had a state of their own and ceased being a national anomaly, as forcefully argued by Leo Pinsker in his *Auto-Emancipation* in 1882 and in Herzl's *Judenstaat* fifteen years later.

We now know how futile this dream was. Hard as we may have tried, the Jewish State has not "normalised" the Jewish condition; on the contrary, it has highlighted the Jewish problem. Indeed, we have paid a terrible price for the illusion that, flying in the face of the destiny assigned to us by Providence, the termination of Jewish homelessness would eliminate the Jewish predicament. The utter loneliness which we have experienced so dramatically with the desertion of our fair-weather friends since the Yom Kippur War, and the double standards applied to Israel by the international community have demonstrated that if we do not freely accept the uniqueness of Israel, it is Providentially imposed on us against our will. As it is now evident, individually many Jews may opt out, but nationally we cannot escape from our destiny of being "a people that dwells alone".

The question whether to be all alike or different, presses on our internal Jewish relations, too. Two thousand years of exile and scattered dispersion, with some communities almost in complete isolation from the rest of the Jewish people, have produced an endless variety of Jewish types, each with its own brand of customs, traditions, attitudes and ways of life generally. The emergence of Israel obviously calls for, and has already resulted in, a great levelling out of these diverse traits. The restoration of Hebrew as the principal common language of the Jewish people is but one example of Israel's impact as a unifying force both inside and outside the State. In Israel, school attendance and army service are other important instruments of equalisation. Even in the Diaspora, the widespread use of Israeli teachers, the intensity of Zionist fund-raising campaigns and the common affiliation to world Jewish organisations and Israel-orientated political parties, have created a degree of likeness among Jews previously unknown in post-exilic times. Today, you can travel, as I have done in recent years, from London to Brazil, from the Scandinavian countries to the Antipodes, and indeed from New York to Jerusalem, and you will find the basic patterns of Jewish life and activity remarkably similar in content and direction.

But we must now ask ourselves, how far should we encourage this process to go? Do we really want all characteristic differences between one Jew and another, or one community and another, to become crushed by the steam-roller of conformity? For instance, do the interests of Jewish unity really require us to abolish traditional distinctions between Eastern and Western, or Sephardi and Ashkenazi rites of prayer, or do different pronunciations of Hebrew challenge the essential cohesion of the Jewish people any more than Scottish and Cockney accents of English compromise British patriotism and unity?

In strong opposition to this view, Rabbi Abraham Gumbiner, forbidding any change in one's ancestral liturgical usages, cites the interesting statement by Rabbi Isaac Luria: "Everyone must adhere to his own rite, since there are twelve gates in the heavens corresponding to the twelve tribes, each of whom possess his own gate through which his prayer ascends to heaven" (*Magen Avraham, Orach Chayim*, 68; see H. J. Zimmels, *Ashkenazim and Sephardim*, p. 117 f.).

The question goes deeper than this. The ingathering of the exiles has endowed Israeli society with a rich variety of religious, cultural and social patterns. Are we justified, historically and in terms of future interests, in pursuing a policy of *Mizug* or fusion which seeks to homogenise the population until each immigrant community sheds its distinctive features and all components of the population become indistinguishable from each other? I rather doubt both the right and wisdom of such a policy.

After all, throughout biblical times, even the territorial integrity of Israel's tribes was maintained by geographical divisions. Each tribe was expected to contribute its special endowments to the totality of Israel's life. That is why Jacob gave each of his children a different blessing, just as Moses before his death charged each tribe with a distinct assignment. Only through group specialisation in the diverse fields of Jewish endeavour could the spiritual and material prosperity of the nation be promoted.

This encouragement of national diversity was responsible for the extraordinary creativity of the Jewish people ever since. The Palestinians and the Babylonians in Talmudic times, the Jewries of North Africa, Spain, France, Germany, Italy and elsewhere in the Middle Ages, and the divisions between

Ashkenazim and Sephardim, Chassidim and Mithnagdim, the Yeshiva-world and the *Torah-im-Derech-Eretz* society in more modern times—they have all made singular and indispensible contributions to the advancement of Jewish scholarship, law, literature, poetry, philosophy, mysticism and numerous other expressions of the Jewish genius.

Shall this prolific luxuriance of the Jewish spirit now be diminished through the return to Zion? Should we not rather, while enhancing the corporate achievements of the Jewish people through the restoration of sovereignty, also preserve the finest of the varied traditions, aptitudes and specialised experiences accumulated over the centuries by communities now transplanted to the Land of our Fathers? Among numerous immigrants, the new rootlessness has already exacted a heavy toll. Deprived of their ancestral traditions, they lost their communal pride and discipline in the process of their adaptation to the uniform specifications for the *Civis Israelus*. There are surely enduring values of the greatest significance which each immigrant community can bring to bear on the enrichment of Jewish life—whether they be the colourfulness, artistry and simplicity of faith of many Eastern communities, the passion and superb intellectual endowments of Russian Jews, the methodical order and academic flair of German Jews, the penchant for conciliation and organisation among Anglo-Jews, or the enterprising exuberance of American Jews. The preservation of these quasi-ethnic traits—perhaps by giving greater encouragement to group-settlements in Israel, such as the various Chassidic communities have established with considerable success—would also strengthen Israel's bonds with the Diaspora through the retention of common traditions. Moreover, such a policy might well promote Aliyah, particularly from countries where settled conditions of life militate against a prospect of an easy adjustment to the social and cultural milieu prevailing in Israel.

This very occasion furnishes the best example for the enrichment of Jewish life through successful co-existence and the preservation of distinct communal traditions. Since the beginning of the eighteenth century, the offices of the Haham and the Chief Rabbi, working in close association and yet maintaining entirely separate jurisdictions, have been the mainspring of British Jewry's religious and institutional development, and my colleague and I are here to testify both to the harmony of our partnership and to the distinctiveness of the trusts with which we are charged. How gratifying and appropriate also that today's event, apart from demonstrating our personal friendship, marks the opening of a university department for Sephardi Studies, designed to consolidate and increase the rich historic contributions of our Sephardic brethren.

Finally, a few words on inter-Orthodox diversity. Here, too, we seem to suffer today from an unconscionable drive towards conformity. Until the Second World War we had, all within the unimpeachably Orthodox fold, a fairly wide variety of authentic attitudes and philosophies—represented by institutions as diverse as Lithuanian-type Yeshivot, the Berlin *Rabbiner Seminar*, London's Jews' College, and New York's Yeshiva University, and embracing Chassidic Stibles, *Gross-Gemeiden* and *Austritts-Gemeinden* alike. Now we find a growing call for uniformity and a tendency to write off as dissenters or heretics those who do not toe the line drawn by their critics. In the past, every duly qualified rabbi was master in his own house, and his rulings for those under his jurisdiction were unquestioned and unchallengeable. Today, a communal rabbi, however Orthodox, is often subjected to intolerable pressures, or indeed to the denial of his rabbinic competence, if he refuses to conform with the dictates and anathemas of those who regard themselves, and are upheld by their followers, as the sole custodians of Jewish religious authority.

Similar trends now prevail in the educational sphere as well. The raising of disciples individually or in small groups has increasingly given way to the institutionalisation of Jewish learning, frequently in massive, impersonal schools and academies, virtually all pursuing similar programmes and teaching methods. Mass-producing scholars, however erudite, with such unimaginative, dull monotony is bound to stifle originality and innovation— the very seeds out of which the giants of Jewish thought and leadership were bred in the past. *Geonim* and pioneering scholars do not come off assembly-lines; they are custom-made, usually out of recruits fascinated by the exploration of new paths.

Throughout our history the dynamics of Jewish intellectual creativeness were generated out of the tensions of conflict and argument, much as in nature the forces of life and energy derive from the interaction between opposites, whether male and female, or positive and negative charges. The entire edifice of the Talmud and all subsequent Rabbinic literature is founded on debate, on often fierce clashes between opposing schools of thought. Yet, no protagonist of one opinion, however, uncompromising, ever outlawed his opponent as beyond the pale of authentic Judaism, as is so common today. Hillel and Shammai, the Rambam and the Raved, or Hirsch and Bamberger —to mention just three examples, from ancient, medieval and modern times— vehemently as they argued, frequently on fundamentals, never called each other *apikorsim* or cast aspersions on their rival's rabbinic authority. On the contrary, their arguments fertilised the fields of Jewish learning and literature.

More than that, dissent, even when sadly it rejected the Rabbinic tradition, was constructively exploited for the enrichment of Judaism. There never were Jewish sectarians more radically and implacably in conflict with authentic Judaism than the Saducees and later the Karaites. Their heresy, with the bitter schisms they provoked in their time, probably inflicted even deeper and more lasting wounds on the unity of the Jewish people than the defection of today's Reformers. Yet, these sects helped to stimulate some of the most momentous advances of Jewish thought and letters. To the relentless challenge of the Saducees we may well owe much of the vigorous vitality of Judaism embedded in the Talmud. And without the gauntlet thrown down by the Karaites, the Rabbinic tradition might never have cultivated such fields as biblical exegesis, Jewish philosophy and Hebrew grammar, as found in the enduring creations of Saadya Gaon, Ibn Ezra, Kimchi and even Maimonides. Their brilliant literary labours were largely sparked by the need to answer and refute the Karaite charges.

Would that we used the current attacks on our beliefs and practices for a similar intensification of our intellectual labours and literary output. How intensely enriched in depth and scope would traditional Jewish thought be today if we devoted our spititual energies to rebutting the claims and attacks of our latter-day dissenters through superior research and reasoned argument, in fields ranging from Bible-criticism to theology, and from archeology to sociology, rather than lavish our limited resources on futile denunciations and political manoeuverings to defeat the rising tide of heterodoxy.

For the past half-century, the bulk of our people's energies have been devoted to the struggle of securing our national rebirth and our physical survival. We now know that this struggle is far from over; indeed it is likely to be prolonged, if not intensified, in the foreseeable future. Nevertheless, we just cannot afford to suspend our spiritual regeneration indefinitely because all our energies are absorbed by this struggle. The generations before us faced a continuous battle of survival every bit as grim as ours; yet the anxiety for their physical security was never allowed to override the concern for the preservation and enrichment of Judaism. Otherwise, our people would have ceased to exist long ago. For if there is one cardinal lesson to be taught by our history, it is that our physical viability depends on our spiritual strength, rather than the other way round.

With the establishment of the Jewish State we have reached our immediate objective of national rebirth to which our people dedicated its primary attention for several generations past. Our continuing difficulties notwithstanding, we must now strive for another Golden Age of an incomparable spiritual renaissance to give substance and meaning to our national achievement.

A major requisite for such a renaissance is to break the fetters of conformity shackling us. We will have to learn not only to accept diversity as a fact of life but to welcome it as a means to the revitalisation of Jewish life, in accordance with every precedent of Jewish history.

This diversity, to sum up, should creatively manifest itself at three principal levels: the preservation of the Jewish identity and the consummation of the Jewish purpose in man's evolution demand that we restore the Jewish pride in being different and unique. Secondly, the enrichment of the contemporary Jewish experience calls on us to maintain such ancestral group-traditions as will usefully add to the diversification of Jewish life and as are essential to provide immigrant groups with a spiritual, moral and social anchorage. And thirdly, the powerful stimulation of Jewish religious, scholarly and cultural achievement requires the encouragement of diversity in the spirit of *Kin'at sophrim tarbeh Torah*, "Jealousy amongst scholars increases Torah", while even dissent, tragic and divisive as it is, must be made to serve as an incentive to a more searching analysis, a more penetrating appreciation, and a more sophisticated presentation of Jewish values than we currently possess.

The visions inspiring Bar-Ilan and the academic talents at its disposal, justify confidence in its ability to assist in spear-heading this adventure into a new era of creativity expanding the frontiers of dynamic Jewish scholarship, turning it into a truly unique institution cultivating the university and *kolel* concepts in their real meaning of universality and totality. I hope that this ideal will most especially distinguish the Chair in Jewish Law which I am now privileged to see called by my name. May it be said of this Chair:

צדק ומשפט מכון כסאך חסד ואמת יקדמו פניך "Righteousness and justice are the foundations of your chair, love and truth go before You" (Psalm 89:15). May it indeed become a "seat" firmly established, not on one leg but on four, the four diverse and yet complementary ideals of *Chesed Ve-emet*, the combination of spiritual fervour (*chesed*) and scientific fact (*emet*), and of *Zedek Umishpat*, the fusion of the moral (*zedek*) and legal (*mishpat*) constituents of Jewish Law.

THE EVOLUTION OF THE BRITISH RABBINATE SINCE 1845 — ITS PAST IMPACT AND FUTURE CHALLENGES

The centenary of Joseph Herman Hertz's birth, and the publication of this volume to mark the event, may be a fitting occasion to survey the development of the office which he graced with such distinction for nearly a third of a century, and to assess its influence on the British rabbinate and the community in general. As the present incumbent of that office, I am bound to view its history with some subjectivity. But perhaps the resultant imbalance is somewhat redressed by the added perspectives gained through my German origins (covering almost my entire school-life) and my rabbinical experience in Ireland and America (covering three-fifths of my ministerial career). The ensuing pages, therefore, while meant as a personal assessment, seek to present the characteristics of the British rabbinate in a comparative light from the vantage points of communal patterns as they existed to the East and still exist to West of Anglo-Jewry.

I

The story of the British rabbinate is largely the story of the Chief Rabbinate —and the opposition to it. Indeed, in no other country in the world is the overall history of the Jewish community so intimately bound up with the Chief Rabbinate as in Britain. From this office, or in close association with it, or in protest against it, have grown virtually all the major institutions and religious movements in Anglo-Jewry.

Herein, rather than in its form or character, lies the uniqueness of the British Chief Rabbinate. Chief Rabbis today head the Orthodox Establishment in almost every country with organised Jewish life outside America. They are the acknowledged spiritual leaders of Jewish communities as diverse as those in Israel and Ireland, France and Roumania, South Africa and Denmark. Even communities as repressed as Moscow or as small as Luxem-

---

This essay was originally prepared for the planned Dr. Isidor Epstein Memorial Volume. But since this project still awaits realisation after years of fruitless effort, the article (slightly revised) was submitted for publication in the Joseph Herman Hertz Centenary Volume by the Soncino Press.

bourg boast their chief rabbis. They all enjoy powers and representational recognition similar to those vested in the British Chief Rabbinate, but none of them have exercised quite the same all-pervasive influence on the shape and development of their communities.

The reason for this extraordinary influence lies in the restricted status peculiar to the Anglo-Jewish ministry no less than in the positive attributes possessed by the Chief Rabbis of the past. In contrast to the situation in other countries, Britain's Chief Rabbi was never *primus inter pares*. He was neither a chief *minister* nor a *chief* rabbi presiding over colleagues of equal qualifications or rank, however locally limited their jurisdiction. In fact, he was, or sought to be, the only recognised rabbi in his realm, with the Beth Din serving as ecclesiastical "assessors" to "advise" him on matters of Jewish law. He ruled on the pattern of the executive power vested in an American president, while in other countries the function of a chief rabbi in relation to his colleagues might be more analogous to that of a prime minister whose cabinet colleagues would share similar, albeit far more confined, responsibilities.

This disparity was obviously conducive to the disproportionate influence of the British Chief Rabbinate, in the absence of rivals or a diffusion of power. But inevitably there was also an obverse side to this rigid system of centralised control and the suppression of challenges to authority within the Establishment. The system encouraged centrifugal forces of dissent and secession. In Anglo-Jewry the separatist congregations—whether of the Reform and Liberal brand on the left, or the *Austritt* variety on the right—arose primarily as protests *against* the monolithic power structure of the officially "authorised" community. Disaffection was generated by repulsion from the centre rather than by attraction to the extremes; the factors leading to secessions were institutional more than ideological. Elsewhere, notably in Germany and the United States, these movements away from the centre grew out of pressures *for* a commitment to distinct philosophies of Judaism. There (in contrast to conditions in England) these philosophies were represented and nurtured by independent theological seminaries committed to the development of these divergent trends.

The "presidential" power sought and achieved by the Chief Rabbis, especially the Adlers, also lent their office and their conduct of affairs a far more personal imprint than would be found in a less absolutist and more "prime ministerial" system such as prevails in other communities. It is, therefore, germane to this survey to include a few personal features. They reveal some intriguing comparisons and contrasts, indeed several striking paradoxes, which have characterised the century's four previous incumbents and their eras.

Considering the entire period under review, one might discern a cycle no less than an evolution, inasmuch as the present incumbent is probably closest to Chief Rabbi Nathan Marcus Adler in background and outlook, or at least closer to him than to any of his other predecessors. Both assumed office following a serious religious schism in the community leading to the establishment of an independent dissident congregation: the foundation of West London Reform Synagogue in 1841 followed by Adler's appointment in 1845, and the establishment of the New London Synagogue in 1964 followed by the present appointment three years later. Both also share a common land of origin, and both were elected notwithstanding the determined preference of the *Jewish Chronicle* for other candidates.

Each of the intervening three Chief Rabbis featured some remarkable paradox.

Hermann Adler was undoubtedly the most anglicised—one might almost say the most Anglican—of all Chief Rabbis, as expressed in the clerical patterns of his administration, his personal style, garb and even title as the first to assume the dignity of "Very Reverend" (on the suggestion of his friend, the Bishop of Bath and Wells). As patron of the English–Jewish Establishment, he held recently immigrated Jews and their leaders in some disdain, being on record as calling them "uncultivated and uncivilised". Yet he was the only Chief Rabbi ever publicly to turn to a foreign sage for support in an internal communal dispute, when he appealed to the renowned Rabbi Yitzchak Elchanan Spector of Kovno to endorse his ban on the opposition *Shechitah* set up by the newly established Machazikei Hadass in 1891. Even more galling to a man of Adler's authoritarian temperament and monarchic rule, which would not suffer any spiritual leader other than himself to be styled Rabbi, must have been the emergence of so many independent congregational bodies, in opposition to the United Synagogue and the jurisdiction he exercised. Indeed, with the foundation of the Federation of Synagogues in 1887, the Machazike Hadass in 1891, the Adass Yisroel in 1909, and the Liberal Synagogue in 1910, his reign coincided with a greater fragmentation of the London Jewish community than that of any other Chief Rabbi. Again, while Adler opposed Zionism, he witnessed the birth of the Zionist Movement, and on Herzl's death called him "the greatest Jew since Maimonides".

Joseph Herman Hertz, by contrast, though probably the most dynamic of all Chief Rabbis, holding office in the turbulent period covering two world wars and the Holocaust, had the most stable but institutionally least creative tenure. Hertz, the man of action and provocation, who would, as was said, "resort to peaceful methods when all else failed", introduced few major innovations, founded hardly any new organisations, and witnessed, let alone caused, no significant break-away from the congregational empire over which he presided. Even the character of the Anglo-Jewish rabbinate and ministry was left essentially unchanged by his immense influence and petulent energies. Ironically, the most enduring impact of his restless, activist personality was in the still world of letters (bequeathing to English-speaking Jews by far the largest literary heritage left by any Chief Rabbi) and in some historic achievements outside his own community, such as the roles he played in the proclamation of the Balfour Declaration, the "Battle of the Sabbath" against Calendar Reform, and the foundation of the Council of Christians and Jews.

Israel Brodie, too, represented some strange contrasts between his background and temperament and his accomplishments. The only English-born Chief Rabbi, he nevertheless emancipated the Anglo-Jewish rabbinate from its insularity and associated, if not integrated, it with the rest of Europe, through the Conference of European Rabbis, which he founded in 1957 and still leads. Though he never studied at a European-type seminary or reshivah, he did more than anyone else to restore the European pattern of qualified rabbis, rather than "reverends", as spiritual leaders of congregations, particularly through encouraging the reintroduction of the Rabbinical Diploma class at Jews' College. Pacific by nature and mellow by disposition, he yet witnessed and aided a more pronounced swing to the right within the religious community than ever before, and he boldly met the challenge of the most violent religious warfare in Anglo-Jewry's history, without in the process losing a single congregation or minister by secession or defection. Also remarkable is the award of a high royal honour, only several years *after* laying down his office, to the only Chief Rabbi to have rendered notable services to H.M. Forces, long *before* he assumed his supreme office, as chaplain, and later senior chaplain, in two World Wars.

Thus was communal history made by the interplay, not always congruous, between diverse personalities and the equally diverse conditions they encountered.

II

The remainder of the rabbinate may be broadly divided into two quite disparate parts: the "authorised" section, consisting of the "official" Batei Din and communal rabbis operating within the Establishment; and those working independently outside the jurisdiction of the Chief Rabbi.

The former group was the slower to grow into a religious force of any consequence in the evolution of Anglo-Jewry. Functioning at first merely as a minor extension of the Chief Rabbinate, it enjoyed few powers and even less influence in the direction of religious affairs.

Even the London Beth Din (the dominant constituent of the group, and indeed the only one of national significance) rose from very humble beginnings to its more recent eminence only in tedious and often erratic stages. Its Dayanim were originally but private advisers to the Chief Rabbi, maintained at one time out of his private purse. Its stature attained community-wide recognition only with the appointment of a ranking Talmudist like Dayan S. I. Hillman, reaching its peak under the dynamic leadership of Dayan Y. Abramsky's towering personality. His commanding influence extended primarily to improving the standards of Shechitah and Kashrut, (including the ban on the sale of hindquarters), to more severe controls on the admission of proselytes, and generally to moving the Beth Din's previous "middle-of-the road" course strongly and irrevocably to the right. Another great uplift of the Beth Din's standing in the community occurred during the incumbency of Dayan Grunfeld through whose legal training and broad interests the Beth Din became prominently involved in such diverse fields as the rescue of war orphans, divorce legislation, human rights and United Nations activities.

Nevertheless, to this day the Beth Din, now widely acknowledged as one of the world's leading assemblages of rabbinical expertise and Jewish juridical power, is still mainly confined to the administration of religious "ritual", from the supervision of food as it passes from abattoir or factory to the shrinking number of observant consumers, to judgements on marriage, divorce and conversion, with occasional *obiter dicta* on matters relating to the synagogue, the cemetery and, perchance, personal or communal disputes. This venerable institution is still largely outside the classic rabbinic tradition of being involved officially in the wider ramifications of Jewish education, true to the pristine meaning of *rabbi* as teacher. It has not directly sponsored the development of schools or yeshivot (except by sometimes immense *personal* efforts in aid of existing institutions), or the training of ministers and teachers, or the design of religious programmes for youth and students, or even the construction of *mikvaot*.

Outside London regular Batei Din are to be found only in Manchester, Leeds and Glasgow, all looking to the ecclesiastical Establishment in London for their authority—and for relief from the more invidious exercise of rabbinical functions, notably in dealing with applications for conversion. Of all these Batei Din only Manchester has ventured beyond the usual confines, by initiating the provision of a communal Mikva and the establishment of a Kolel for advanced rabbinic studies.

Communal rabbis recognised by the chief Rabbinate have established themselves mostly during the past few decades, in Liverpool, Birmingham and Cardiff, though strangely no such authorities exist in comparable communities like Newcastle, Brighton or Southend which are served by congregational rabbis acting as ministers, rather than by communal rabbis in the accepted sense.

III

Within the official clerical Establishment there remains, of course, the ministry, a class of Jewish spiritual leaders peculiar to Britain and some of its former Dominions. Deprived of rabbinic authority by a dominant Chief Rabbinate, reduced to serve as religious functionaries by sometimes imperious lay readers, discouraged from developing their individuality by the tight and rather uniform congregational system, ministers had but few opportunities to help in shaping the institutional structure of the community or to participate in directing its policies.

Yet they played a predominant role in fashioning the *character* of Anglo-Jewry. From their ranks sprang preachers of outstanding excellence, pastoral workers of supreme competence and, occasionally at least, popular writers commanding considerable skills: men like Simeon Singer, Morris Joseph, A. A. Green and Ephraim Levine. Members of the ministerial fraternity, more than anyone else, were responsible for the Anglo-Jewish predilection for moderation and a "mellow" form of Jewish observance, for the firm commitment to tradition and stability, and for the continued primacy of the synagogue as the expression of Jewish identity among most British Jews. Paradoxically, therefore, it is the least "rabbinical", and certainly the least halachically erudite, segment of the community's spiritual leadership which may well merit the major credit for maintaining the staunchly traditional character of Anglo-Jewry, as exemplified by the most recent estimate that no fewer than 90% of Britain's synagogue-affiliated Jews (themselves accounting for some two-thirds of the Jewish population) belong to Orthodox congregations.

The ministry, too, is thus very largely responsible for preserving the continuity of Anglo-Jewry's institutional structure, itself naturally the product of a strongly traditional disposition among the mass of members. The degree to which the community's major institutions have been perpetuated virtually without change for over a century and often much longer is all the more remarkable in view of the massive waves of immigration which have radically altered the composition of the community since the times when those institutions were founded. Neither the wholesale arrivals from Eastern Europe, which swelled the number of Jews in Britain from around 80,000 to some 140,000 by 1914, nor the huge influx during and after the Nazi era, which increased the total to nearly half a million, have had any significant effect on the constancy of organisations like the Chief Rabbinate, the Board of Deputies, the Board of Shechita and the United Synagogue; even their constitutions have hardly changed over the long years of their existence.

In this respect, once again, Anglo-Jewry is unique. In every other large community the patterns of communal and religious life, whatever they had been among the original settlers, were decisively refashioned by the newer immigrants. This is particularly demonstrated by the diversity and decentralisation of American-Jewish life today. Only among British Jews, though now scarcely any less heterogeneous in origin than American Jewry, has the system of community organisation, devised in a much earlier age of homogeneity, survived and ultimately absorbed the waves of newcomers who outnumbered by many times the indigenous residents.

IV

Almost entirely the outgrowth of the immigrant sector is the "unauthorised" part of the rabbinate, still constituting a rather peripheral element, outside the mainstream of Anglo-Jewish life. In view of the numerical preponderance of immigrants over the descendants of Jews born in this country before 1880, it is striking how confined was the sphere of these rabbis and their congregations. Until the late 1930s their influence in the community at large was quite negligable. Only during, and especially since, the Second World War did they emerge as a potent force, though to this day still marginal to the heartland of religious Jewry and isolated from it by self-imposed barriers of insulation under the slogan of "independence". Within this sector, unlike the rest of the community, it was certainly the individual rabbis who set the imprint of their vision and personality upon the congregations they built up— now among the most vibrant and creative centres of Jewish religious life to be found here. Despite their numerical weakness, their "go-it-alone" independence, and the corresponding denial of "official" recognition to a somewhat "outlandish" element, their impact on the wider religious community is beginning to be considerable and varied.

Already these rabbis and the trends they represent have been a major factor in the increasing polarisation of the community. They have precipitated a syndrome of competitiveness, swinging the committed sharply to the right and hence alienating the less committed, moving them to the maelstrom of apathy, assimilation and intermarriage. These recent developments, now manifest in most Jewish communities the world over and characterised, for instance, by the Beth Din's radical turn to the right since the 1940s, were intensified no doubt by the New Right of "independent Orthodoxy" and the need not to appear less zealous than "they" are. This movement towards more exacting religious standards has carried with it a small, but growing and ever more influential, minority of the Establishment, including some ministers, lay leaders, and especially students and professionals. It has spawned on the Anglo-Jewish scene since the early 1950s such novel groups as Yavneh at the universities and the Association of Orthodox Jewish Scientists. In the 1960s the transfer of lay leadership of bodies like Jews' College and the United Synagogue to mainly Sabbath observers also represents significant straws in the winds of change which began to blow from the distant and still barricaded fastnesses of Gateshead and Stamford Hill.

V

Conversely, however, like Newton's law of physics, this movement has also produced an equal and opposite reaction. The same forces which have attracted a qualitatively significant element towards the right have repelled an element of corresponding quantitative significance from even the modicum of religious loyalties to which they or their parents used to subscribe. There are today countless members within the nominally Orthodox community, especially young people, who (weak as their intellectual commitment to Jewish thought and practice has always been) feel bewildered and estranged by what appears to them as the "rigidity", the "extremism" and the "intolerance" now ever more rampant even inside the official Establishment. Through this reaction tens of thousands of young Jews have been set adrift from their traditional moorings in an unprecedented flight of mass defection. However, it must be recognised that this movement has also been strongly reinforced by general post-War trends entirely beyond the control of forces within the Jewish community.

The process impelled, then, by the "unauthorised" rabbinate and its followers is beginning to dissipate the strength of the powerful moderate centre which characterised Anglo-Jewry in the past. In this respect, the gains and losses caused by these New Right tendencies seem fairly evenly balanced, at least for the moment; the high-calibre minority reclaimed to intensive Jewish living and learning being weighed against the indifferent majority weakening or severing their bonds with the religious community. In the long run, however, the impact of the minority is bound to prevail, not only because of their superior commitment and tenacity, not to mention their far more prolific birth-rate, but simply because they alone will care sufficiently to provide the dynamics, the leadership and direction of Jewish life in the future. The others, whatever their present numerical superiority, will stand aside disinterested or opt out altogether from the organised religious community in their inevitable movement towards self-liquidation. Thus will Jewish life ultimately be regenerated. Like a seed sunk into the ground, the bulk decays and dies, while the tiny seminal kernel strikes root and sprouts forth anew in another generation of flourishing life.

VI

The other momentous contribution of the "independent" rabbinate has been unreservedly beneficial. From it has come the principal thrust in raising the levels of Jewish education in Britain to heights never known before. Sparked by the pioneering efforts of Rabbi Dr. Solomon Schonfeld in building up (on the foundations laid by his father, Rabbi Victor Schonfeld) the Jewish Secondary Schools movement in the 1930s, and strongly reinforced by the self-sacrificing labours of a few enterprising rabbis likewise lacking "official" recognition, this group now boasts a burgeoning network of intensive educational institutions, especially in London, Manchester, Gateshead and Sunderland. Out of their yeshivot, kolelim, seminaries for girls and day schools have already come many thousands of Jews and Jewesses whose standards of Jewish learning and piety often far exceeded those of their own parents.

This colossal achievement is all the greater in that it was accomplished in the face of much hostility, later modified to lukewarm support at best, from the rest of the community. Yet it helped to create a climate of educational concern favourable to the growth of other important ventures during the post-War period, such as the Zionist Day Schools, Carmel College, the North-west London Day School and the revived Jews' Free School—all under Orthodox control in their religious instruction, though varying greatly in intensity of Jewish study and observance.

Nevertheless, many day schools and all yeshivot, however remarkable their progress, continue to operate on the whole, financially and ideologically, outside the mainstream of the "official" community, somewhere on or beyond the perimeter enclosing the wide area governed by the Establishment, at least until very recently. This, too, is a situation prevailing only in Anglo-Jewry. Everywhere else the religious community, and certainly the synagogue leadership, have for long identified themselves with, and usually supported, the day schools, if not also the yeshivot, however "sectarian" the auspices under which they were founded. Consequently, in those communities the great educational enterprises have moved into the centre of Jewish religious concerns, and the budget of schools has now often overtaken the sums expended on synagogues—a far cry from the situation in Britain where Jewish education at all levels still accounts for but a fraction, probably less than 25%, of the total budget for religious services.

This unenviable anomaly requires an explanation. In the first place, it is of course due to the strict division between the "authorised" and the "unauthorised" communities in Anglo-Jewry, with the intensive schools all belonging to the latter. No such rigid line of demarcation exists in other countries, where it is therefore easier for less committed congregations to make common cause with the more committed schools. Here, communal recognition would have required such schools and other academies of learning to be founded or sponsored by the "official" Establishment, and this was not the case for reasons already explored.

But there may also be a deeper cause, rooted in the character of Anglo-Jewry, for this anomaly. The very stability of Anglo-Jewish life and institutions in the past militated against the primacy, or indeed the importance, of Jewish education. The addiction to tradition was so strong and natural that the transmission of religious loyalties from one generation to the next was substantially assured even without anything more appealing than the most perfunctory knowledge of Judaism. Jewish education, beyond some elementary Hebrew class instruction during childhood, was simply irrelevant to the expectation that most children would grow up to marry within the faith, keep kosher homes and carry on as members of their parents' synagogue. The religious traditions of the community faced no serious challenges, and they did not demand intellectual props or justification for survival, as they did elsewhere in the absence of such solid traditions.

VII

Similar reasons may account for the surprisingly limited literary output of the Anglo-Jewish rabbinate, particularly in the field of Halachah. In literature as in business, the demand largely creates the supply, and in a community in which to this day any book of Jewish interest which sells a thousand copies is regarded as a best-seller, the incentive to labour on rabbinic productions is sadly small. British Jewry has never nurtured a regular rabbinical journal for any length of time, apart from some yeshivah publications which may more properly be described as house magazines. While Nathan Marcus Adler's *Nethinah laGer* commentary on the *Torah* and the Hertz *Chumash* have become classics used all over the world in many editions, all Anglo-Jewish responsa works could probably be assembled on a single short shelf. Among them the four-volume *Minchat Yitzchak* by Dayan I. J. Weiss of Manchester today ranks with the best of this genre, and the pamphlets of individual responsa published by members of the London Beth Din as well as Dayan A. L. Grossnass' *Lev Aryeh* are also widely consulted.

The most substantial contributions to Jewish scholarship have, of course, come from the academic staff of Jews' College whose long history covers most of the period here under review. Friedlander, Büchler, Marmorstein, Daiches, Epstein and Zimmels are household names among students of Judaism the world over and will always rank among leading scholars of the last hundred years. But not one of these scholars and authors was born or even mainly educated in Britain, nor has Jews' College on its own produced successors of their academic distinction.

Founded on the initiative of Nathan Marcus Adler and conducted in the Adlerian tradition, Jews' College has been maintained, at least until very recently, primarily as a professional or vocational school for the training of ministers. Not infrequently its alumni continue to serve in careers of great distinction in virtually all countries presently or formerly under the British crown, and lately also in several European and even American communities. Though firmly linked with the Establishment through the *ex officio* services of the Chief Rabbi and the Haham as President and Vice-President respect-ively, its actual contacts with the rabbinate, or even the ministry, have general-ly been tenuous, often limited to one or two ministers serving on the Council, and sometimes also on the academic staff as lecturers, albeit usually in some relatively junior position. But unlike the theological seminaries in America and in pre-War Europe, Jews' College has never played a pivotal role in determining the religious orientations of the community or in sponsoring a rabbinical organisation and its activities, let alone in forging a religious movement in response to contemporary challenges, on the lines on which the Berlin *Rabbiner Seminar* powered the *Torah im derech eretz* movement before the War or New York's Yeshiva University generated "modern Orthodoxy" in America.

VIII

On the whole, the system and institutions of religious leadership have certain-ly served Anglo-Jewry well in the past. The system was peculiar to the com-munity, and well matched to the equally peculiar needs and conditions of the Jews living in Britain during an era of extraordinary stability. What the system lacked in imaginativeness and individual enterprise it made up in endurance and corporate strength. It may have been rigid, autocratic and hide-bound, but it achieved a degree of religious solidity not found in any other community.

Of course, to some extent at least, the structure and features of Anglo-Jewry's religious life reflected the characteristics of the wider environment; they imitated not only some of the patterns of the Anglican establishment but the forms of British society in general. In a country unfamiliar with revolutions and ruled by a system of government that has not changed over centuries, it is not surprising that the Jewish community, too, found little room for rebels and little love for innovation, preferring the tried paths of tradition to the more risky, if more exciting, ways of exploration and origin-ality. The synagogue was as solid as the Rock of Gibraltar, the Chief Rab-binate little less secure than the monarchy, and the kosher diet no more dis-pensable that the Englishman's cup of tea. The intellectual challenges of science, philosophy and modern scholarship troubled the British Jew no more than the Oxford Movement disturbed the sedate peace of the nation of shopkeepers. With the natural defences of Jewish life as wide and as safe as the English Channel, Jewish education could afford to take a back-seat, "reserved for children only" in the arena where the drama of Jewish survival was being played out. Spiritual leaders could afford to specialise in pulpit performances, in marrying and burying people, in visiting their members when they were sick or bereaved and mixing with them when they were well.

But this idyllic state of a community in a haven of tranquillity, securely anchored to the rock-bottom of tradition, has now been swept away in a rising storm of scepticism, dissent and disaffection. This storm has already set tens of thousands of Jewish youngsters adrift and threatens to drown countless others. The new pilots charged to guide the communal ship through the present turbulence will require qualifications and equipment far more sophisticated than in the past.

The spiritual leader of tomorrow will have to exert his influence by persuasion rather than by authority. To exercise such influence he will require status in the community, derived from Jewish and general erudition, combined with a far more potent voice in the counsels of leadership. In an increasingly diverse, better educated and more critical community, the rabbinate will also have to be more diversified through specialisation if it is to meet the ramified intellectual challenges of modern life and to assert its leadership in all areas of communal endeavour. To discover and demonstrate the relevance of Judaism there must be rabbinical experts in theology, philosophy, law, science and other fields of contemporary thought, just as there must be rabbis with special skills in education, youth work, social service and scholarly research, bringing competent Jewish influences to bear on these important aspects of communal activity. The questions posed to rabbis by enlightened laymen will no longer be limited to synagogue ritual, dietary rules or marital status; they will include problems as diverse as race relations and the religious significance of space science, heart transplants and the challenge of humanism, student unrest and the permissive society, commercial ethics and political morality, not to mention the techniques of establishing schools and youth centres, organising adult education, activating identification with Israel, and inspiring numerous other spheres of Jewish concern.

In order to produce a corps of such rabbis, four partners will have to make substantial contributions and adopt a significantly revised orientation: the Chief Rabbinate (including the Beth Din), by encouraging a greater diffusion of authority and an increasing participation by the rabbinate at large in the direction of religious affairs and policies; Jews' College, by providing more intensive and more diversified training; the congregations, by offering more responsibilities, greater incentives and wider scope for leadership; and the rabbis themselves, by utilising these new opportunities with more ambition, imagination and enterprise. The first two of these four have already initiated important moves in this direction, moves which must now be sustained and expanded to achieve the required momentum; the other two have yet to come seriously to grips with the new challenges facing them.

Chapter Eight

HALACHAH IN MODERN TIMES

Applying Timeless Principles to Timely Conditions

HALACHAH IN MODERN JEWISH LIFE

I

Let me first present some prolegomena on the current state of "Halachic Judaism"—itself, I believe, significantly a novel term, unknown and perhaps deliberately avoided until quite recent decades.

It is clearly absurd to argue that strictly traditional Judaism, as presently interpreted, is incompatible with modern conditions of life. Such a claim is patently belied by hundreds of thousands of Jews, especially young people, who live in punctilious accord with all the minutiae of the *Shulchan Aruch*. They include numerous scholars, thinkers and communal leaders, ranking scientists and academicians, successful professionals and business executives. In fact, I daresay that never before in our history have we had so many Jews who combine a thorough rooting in secular science and culture with the strictest adherence to Jewish law and belief as we have today, thanks to our burgeoning intensive Jewish day schools, yeshivot, seminaries and religious universities (almost all sponsored and directed under Orthodox auspices) now counting their aggregate, ever-growing enrolment by many tens of thousands in Israel, America and elsewhere.

If, at the same time, in our increasingly polarised society we also find an alarming and unprecedented rate of defections from traditional Judaism, particularly among our intellectuals, it is not because Halachah is incompatible with modern life, but because it is unknown to them. In Hebrew, the word *yada* means both "to know" and "to love", for the very reason that you cannot love and cherish what you do not know intimately. To expect some rudimentary instruction in infantile Judaism, usually terminated at barmitzvah age, to prevail in adult life against the buffeting of our materialist environment and sophisticated secular education is like expecting an adult to walk normally with one leg fully developed and the other stunted in its growth at the age of thirteen.

The second canard which requires refutation is the generalised allegation that Halachah has ceased to develop since the suspension of the Sanhedrin 2,000 years ago, or since the completion of the *Shulchan Aruch* 400 years ago. The vast output of rabbinical responsa during the post-War period (running into thousands of original verdicts on the most diverse modern questions) bears monumental testimony to the dynamic character of Jewish law and its continued evolution. Only the other day in a lecture I delivered at University College, London, on recent developments in my own specialised field of Jewish medical ethics, I was able to point to significant innovations in Halachic thinking and rulings on such varied subjects as abortion, artificial insemination, euthanasia and heart-transplants, as reflected in rabbinical responsa published in the past fifteen years.

Contribution to a Symposium held at the Conference of the Memorial Foundation of Jewish Culture in Geneva on 10 July 1973.

Nor is Halachah altogether static in other areas, either. Its existing framework is flexible enough to allow for some constant adjustments to meet the exigencies of contemporary life. By tempering the strictest rules of Halachah with the rabbinic elasticity sanctioned by them, neither the army nor other essential public services in Israel had have to suspend vital operations on the Sabbath.

Again, almost all *Agunot* have been freed from the legal chains to their husbands missing without trace after the Holocaust, or through war, or following disasters at sea and in the air. Even with the high rates of adultery and of remarriage without a religious divorce so rampant today, *Mamzerim* (that is, the offspring of all such illicit unions) are so rare that they tend to become a world-wide *cause célèbre* when they do occur. Through rabbinic ingenuity based on the flexibility fo Jewish law, the kind of solution recently found in Israel amid so much bravado and publicity is quietly applied by all *Batei Din* throughout the world year in year out; otherwise we should today have hosts of *Mamzerim* and their descendants debarred from marriage.

It is therefore as spurious to argue that Halachah has remained immovably imprisoned in its ancient or medieval fetters as it is slanderous to suggest that those faithful to its discipline are living vestiges of antiquity or the Middle Ages, unfit or unable to live in modern times.

II

The very word "Halachah" itself connotes both its static and its dynamic qualities. Derived from the root *halach* ("to walk" or "to move") it implies continuous movement and development, as already expressly indicated in the biblical phrase *Im bechukotai telechu*, "if you will *walk* in My statutes".

But, at the same time, all such movement and development must be along the carefully defined path of the law, and any departure from it is branded as a sinful "straying" from the right way.

In other words, Halachah represents a two-dimensional road whose width is confined within immutable limits of legal rules and along the length of which every generation, through the toil of research and original Torah study "*Amal baTorah*", is summoned to move forward towards the ultimate goal of a perfect society under the sovereignty of the Torah. Thus has Halachah proved viable and creative as well as consistently authentic in every age.

Nowadays, it must be conceded, the general attitude of the Halachah's custodians is predominantly ultra-conservative. There is a widespread disinclination to encourage innovation and change. The "status quo" is today's sacred cow in Israel's religio-political set-up no less than in rabbinical orientation. There are several reasons to explain this phenomenon:

First, the effects of the Holocaust. Proportionately, the Torah-community was by far its worst victim. While our people at large lost one-third of its membership, the strictly observant segment suffered the destruction of perhaps 90% of its leaders and followers, its strongholds, its communities and its institutions. This devastating loss resulted in an extreme sense of insecurity among the survivors, bound to breed an uncompromising, hard-line determination to preserve, consolidate and expand the tiny remnants of a world which had collapsed—comparable in religious terms to the Jewish national militancy and intransigence out of which the State of Israel was born following the travail of the War period. Such a siege- or back-to-the-wall mentality operates a defence mechanism and produces an inwardness which is naturally averse to compromise, tolerance or originality; adventures which only those who feel secure and immune to influences of ideological attenuation can afford to countenance.

Secondly, and more generally, spiritual no less than physical forces are governed by Newton's law that every action produces an equal and opposite reaction. The massive drift to the Left, manifested in the rampant growth of secularism, religious indifference, assimilation and inter-marriage, could not but generate an equal and opposite drift to the Right, balancing the extremism of the religiously uncommitted with a corresponding extremism of the committed.

Thirdly, these tendencies towards polarisation so characteristic of our age, combined with the widespread disillusionment with the sham values of our contemporary society and civilisation, especially in the younger generation, have further accentuated the ascendancy of the more rigorous school within the Orthodox leadership and its followers. Both the custodians and the seekers of stable traditional values (conditioned by the grim struggle to maintain their commitments as an embattled minority facing far superior numbers and resources) prefer absolutes to uncertainties, rigidity to moderation, and the security of spiritual insulation to the risks inherent in exploring unknown paths or venturing into alien territory.

This explains the strange phenomenon that, of the principal Orthodox philosophies, the post-War generation has opted for the uncompromising and strongly anti-secular Yeshiva and Chasidic movements of Eastern Europe rather than for S. R. Hirsch's humanistic school of synthesis with Western culture.

This pyschology of self-defence through withdrawal and internal consolidation also explains why the handful of Orthodox rabbis advocating halachic innovations and religious dialogues with the world—Jewish and non-Jewish—around them, find themselves in splendid isolation and incur hostile opposition from the mainstream of rabbinical sages and the great mass of their disciples who are implacably opposed to any such tampering or even arguing with the heritage they have salvaged from the ravages of the Nazi terror in Europe and from the scourge of assimilation in the rest of the world.

However much we may disagree with their attitude, whether on the grounds of conviction or of expediency, we must concede that their policies, pursued with utter single-mindedness and passionate dedication, have proved astoundingly successful, having wrought nothing short of one of the great miracles of our times in completely reversing the pre-War trend of Orthodox decline and disintegration. Up to thirty years ago the Orthodox were the vanishing tribe in the House of Israel, and their future seemed doomed. Today, they are the only tribe among our people which is not vanishing or worried about survival.

Due to a far superior birth-rate and a much lower rate of losses through defection and inter-marriage (both advantages caused by their unquestioning loyalty to the moral and religious dictates of Halachah) and due to their enterprise in promoting a flourishing network of day schools and institutes of advanced Jewish learning, the most strictly observant Jews are now proliferating on a qualitative and quantitative scale which is likely, I am convinced, to make them the dominant element, within one or two generations, in a religiously regenerated, though numerically perhaps reduced, Jewish people of the future—both inside and outside Israel.

Halachic Judaism of the rigid kind, then, will play a decisive role in the revitalisation of Jewish life as well as in the physical preservation of the Jewish people and its traditions.

III

What, now, of the content and direction of Halachah, and the prospects of its response to contemporary challenges and pressures?

I have tried to explain why the administrators of Jewish law, in their overwhelming majority, tend to fight shy of the daring in accommodating Halachah by bold innovations and adjustments sometimes found in former periods of stress and change.[1] With all the continued and gradual evolution to which I have referred, powerful brakes on this process admittedly do leave many modern problems unresolved, notably in the spheres of personal status and of national legislation in an independent Jewish State where Halachah has to bridge the gap of some 1,900 years of national homelessness.

But we must see the resultant problems in their proper perspective, especially in view of their often grossly distorted presentation in the public media and other instruments of public opinion—controlled, as these mostly are, by interests which neither care for nor are familiar with the Halachic system and its philosophy of life.

To begin with we must remember that rabbis, like other legislators, operate the law primarily for those who submit to its jurisdiction. Jews devoutly adhering to Halachah do not complain about its severity; they do not groan under the burden and cost of its impositions. The complaints, and the clamour for relaxations, come mainly from groups and people who do not accept these disciplines in principle, much as the charge that synagogue services are too long is usually made by those who come late or not at all.

So long as the Halachah-abiding community is in a minority, the majority cannot expect to sway the thinking and determine the decisions of those charged by their conscience and their assignment to defend the religious commitment of that minority.

Next, the evolution of Halachah is an organic process which cannot be hastened artificially, or through popular agitation and lobbying. The historical forces governing an eternal faith require maturity and natural development for healthy growth. Four hundred and forty years elapsed between Joshua's entry of the Holy Land and Israel's spiritual fulfilment in the building of Solomon's Temple, while the composition of the Talmud covered a period about twice as long to adjust Jewish law from its Temple-centred form to patterns required by exilic conditions of Jewish life. Perhaps in our impatient age of seeking instant answers to timeless questions, we will just have to learn anew that enduring values and spiritual originality cannot be pressed to meet deadlines, or be poured out like newspapers which are topical today and discarded as obsolete the day after.

If Halachah will have evolved some significant new responses within two or three generations following the restoration of Jewish statehood and the other cataclysmic events of our times, we will have reacted more speedily to the promptings of radically changed conditions than in any previous era.

Equally out of focus is the popular assessment of the credits and debits in the Halachic ledger. Through ignorance or deliberate misrepresentation, people see, or are made to see, the rare exceptions rather than the rule, the few negative instead of the countless positive aspects of Jewish law. For every individual hardship case resulting from the strict application of the Jewish marriage laws, for instance, there are many thousands of Jewish homes ennobled and sanctified by these very laws—homes in which marital unfaithfulness, illegitimacy, drugs, crime and other sordid vices eroding our society are simply unknown. For every problem created by the occasional clash between the Sabbath laws and modern technology, there are thousands of people who, because they conscientously observe these rules, feel once a week liberated from the mechanisation of life, from the enslavement to the machine, the tyranny of the telephone and the television, and from the artificiality of human relations. For them, as they sing with their children around their Friday night tables, and join their congregations at Sabbath services, Halachah bridges the generation gap, unites husbands and wives, and the individual with the society, periodically restores their natural creature function as humans walking on two legs instead of serving as machine extensions propelled on four wheels, and enriches their spirituality by their weekly glimpse of the majestic panorama of values transcending the whims of time and place.

Who can measure the immense contributions to the continuity of Jewish existence of the generations of die-hards who, defying the blandishments, the sneers and smears of their contemporaries in happy submission to their Halachic dictates, fiercely resisted the pressures to give up Hebrew as the language of study and prayer, or to expunge from their prayers the daily pleas for the return to Zion, who were steadfastly determined to remain a nation apart and to live by an exacting moral code?

But alas, most Jews (with one eye blinded by the dazzle of our glittering make-believe world, and the other fixed to a distorting telescope) cannot see the endless wood of Halachic luxuriance for the few trees casting their shadows over its approaches.

IV

However, I cannot absolve our religious leadership from some responsibility for these aberrations.

You recall that earlier on I made a critical reference to the very term "Halachic Judaism". I believe this novel phrase epitomises our failure far more than any alleged slowness in lubricating and reconditioning the machinery of rabbinic legislation and jurisdiction. To talk of "Halachic Judaism" is, to my mind, itself a distortion of Judaism, just as it would be to speak of

"Aggadic Judaism", or "Ritual Judaism", or "Ethical Judaism", or "Philosophical Judaism". Authentic Judaism is, of course, an amalgam of all these. To single out Halachah as comprising our faith violates its integrity in the same manner as to claim that traditional Judaism consists merely of the *Shulchan Aruch* and excludes the *Midrash*, or the *Guide of the Perplexed*, or the *Chovot Halevavot* or the numerous other components of its rich literary mosaic.

It is precisely because of our disproportionate emphasis on the purely Halachic or legal aspect of our heritage, to the virtual exclusion of its moral, philosophical and exegetical teachings, that we have alienated the great mass of our people.

Even within the Halachic context we have engaged, or allowed others to engage us, mainly in controversies that have few, if any, moral or national overtones, thus choosing areas of confrontation furthest removed from the estranged majority. In our encounters with the secularists, we would have elicited far more sympathies and understanding for Halachic principles if, instead of fighting our major battles on public Sabbath observance, on pig-breeding, or on autopsies, we would have concentrated our campaigns on problems they share with us and which cannot be solved without a religious conscience cultivated by Halachic disciplines, such as the evil of pornography, or the scandals of poverty and discrimination between Orientals and Occidentals, or if we had emphasised the value of religious idealism as the principal motivation of Western Aliyah today, not to mention intensive religious education as the sole effective answer to the suicidal secularisation of Jewish life!

How many Jews know, for example, that Halachah embraces some very specific directives on a moral issue like abortion, troubling society everwhere, and that as a direct consequence of defying these rules the Jewish State has lost a million potential Sabras since its establishment, smothered in their mothers' womb at the fearful rate of some 40,000 abortions a year?

Altogether, in a state or in communities where Jews loyal to Halachah constitute the minority, the growth of our influence, I am convinced, depends on persuasion rather than legislation, on education which explains and attracts, more than on coercion which repels. While I firmly uphold the inseparable unity of the *state* and Judaism in Israel—itself one of the most distinguishing features of the Jewish religious conscience and tradition—I wonder whether the time has not come to raise a wall of separation between religion and *politics*,[2] an alliance which no longer makes either politics holy or religion popular, and which, I submit, calls for even more urgent review than Halachic procedures if the rule of Halachah is to prevail eventually.

v

Finally, a few words on the more immediate prospects of applying the Halachic process to current needs.

We have, of course, no hierarchical system whereby religious rulings of universal validity can be laid down by a single authority. Any rabbi's authority extends only over communities or disciples who come under his jurisdiction as their elected or acknowledged spiritual guide. New rulings, interpretations or enactments become more widely accepted only as a consensus of rabbinical opinion emerges, usually out of published responsa on new problems or situations. It is the acceptance of these verdicts by the wider religious community which ultimately invests them with binding authority.

This democratic process of relying on the crystallisation of a majority view among competent rabbinical experts provides the checks and balances to prevent the abuse of power or the absolutist exercise of authority.

Beyond local confines, the submission to a rabbi's judgements will always depend on his personal calibre in scholarship and piety much more than on the office he may hold. Many of our most dominant Halachic guides occupied no formal rabbinical positions at all: men like the *Chofetz Chayim*, the *Chazon Ish*, Rabbi Aaron Kotler of sainted memory, or Rabbi Moshe Feinstein today.

True, historically, we had the Sanhedrin which legislated for the Jewish people at large, though (contrary to popular misconception) its principal function was not to ease but to strengthen the observance of the law. However, its operation required two indispensable conditions, among others: its unquestioned recognition by the majority of our people, and the availability of seventy universally acknowledged sages able and willing to serve on it. Today neither of these conditions can even remotely be fulfilled. In their absence, the premature convocation of a Sanhedrin would only add the insult of mocking a venerated historical institution through popular indifference to the injury of further aggravating the religious strife within the Torah community.

On the other hand, in our shrinking and increasingly interdependent world, religious policies and rabbinic rulings in one community, particularly in Israel, are bound to affect others. To achieve some co-ordination I have urged successive Chief Rabbis of Israel from time to time to convene leading rabbis from major communities throughout the world for informal consultations designed to align their policies and actions, or at least for periodic reviews on the response to problems of common concern.

Thanks to the initiative of my predecessor, a similar purpose had been most effectively served by the Conference of European Rabbis, which has met regularly since 1957. Its influence on the rehabilitation and stabilisation of Jewish religious life in Europe has been very considerable.

But on a global scale (having regard to the present climate of suspicion and radical disagreement on the delicate balance between the static and dynamic elements of Halachah) such consultations could prove constructive rather than divisive only if they were held quite informally and totally removed from the partisanship of publicity, political pressures and institutional interests.

NOTES

1. But the alleged inclination of halachic authorities in former ages to modify the law is often seriously exaggerated in the idyllic reconstruction of a past that never was. Maimonides (the greatest Halachist of all times), for example, did not introduce a single innovation or enactment of Jewish law, as far as I am aware. He simply codified Talmudic and Geonic law as he found it.
2. Including the independence of the rabbinate from the control of government agencies or political parties.

HALACHIC ABSTRACTS

The following items, to the end of this chapter, are extracts from the "Review of Recent Halachic Periodical Literature", a regular department of Tradition *(New York) edited by the author between 1961 and 1967. Compilations of earlier abstracts appear in his* Jewish Law Faces Modern Problems *(New York, 1965) and* Journal of a Rabbi *(New York, 1966; London, 1967, pp. 232 ff.).*

THE SIX-DAY WAR

The cataclysmic events of June 1967 inaugurated a new era for the Jewish people. The high drama of those traumatic days—the like of which can be witnessed only once in two thousand years, or less—released a flood of books and articles, some recounting or analysing the War and its antecedents, others probing into the many new problems created by Israel's deliverance. Into the latter category belongs the fairly sizeable volume of halakhic writings spawned by the War and its aftermath. Halakhic echoes of the June triumph could be found in virtually all Jewish religious, and especially rabbinical journals. It is to these—sometimes noisy, or even discordant—echoes that this survey is devoted.

Most of the numerous responsa on questions resulting from the victory dealt, not unnaturally, with the most significant *religious* aspect of the War: The conquest of Judaism's holiest sites, not only enabling Jews to have access to them for the first time in twenty years, but placing them under Jewish control for the first time in nearly nineteen hundred years. Though only an incidental by-product of what was essentially a struggle against the threat of sheer physical annihilation, the liberation of the Jewish Holy Places—historically comparable to what the Crusades were meant to achieve for Christendom—gave Israel's victory celebrations their peculiarly devout, almost unworldly, character, with the only parades to mark one of history's most spectacular military triumphs being the endless streams of pilgrims wending their way to the Western Wall in reverent exhilaration. But the return of the Holy Places also produced its crop of religious problems—and a few bitter inter-religious controversies.

Among our principal sources are a series of articles by Rabbi Eliezer Yehudah Waldenberg (of the Jerusalem Beth Din) in *Ha-Pardes* (New York, October 1967-February 1968) and by Rabbi Mordecai Hacohen in *Panim-el-Panim* (Jerusalem, July 14th, 1967-November 24th, 1967). The former are responsa setting forth specific rulings, while the latter provide an historical review of the main rabbinic arguments on the subjects treated; but both largely draw on identical sources. Two other valuable responsa, though limited to the first question discussed below, are a contribution by Rabbi

Isaac Jacob Weiss—a leading Halakhist—to the *Siyyum Daf Ha-Yomi Supplement* of the *Jewish Tribune* (London, January 26th, 1968), and an article by Rabbi Kalman Kahane—the foremost rabbinical scholar in the Knesset—published in *Ha-Ma'yan* (Jerusalem, Tamuz 5727) only two weeks after the War.

ENTERING THE FORMER TEMPLE SITE

By far the most immediately acute—and the most acrimoniously debated—religious problem arising from the War concerned the right of Jews to enter the precincts on the Temple Mount now occupied by the Dome of the Rock and Mosque El-Aksa. According to the Mishnah (*Kelim*, 1:8), ascending degress of sanctity attach to various parts of Jerusalem, ranging from the walled part of the city to the site of the Holy of Holies, with correspondingly limited access being permitted by an ascending order of personal purity or holiness. Thus, all persons rendered impure through "unclean" discharges are debarred from the entire Temple Mount area, and those defiled by contact with the dead from the fortification ("*Hel*") within that area, while anyone not properly purified entering the "men's courts" (or "Israelite enclosure") is guilty of a capital offense ("*karet*"). Nowadays all are considered ritually defiled, since the means of purification (e.g. through the ashes of the "red heifer") are no longer available. Hence, it has been the almost undisputed practice of Jews, even in times when access was otherwise possible, never to set foot on the Temple Mount site.

There was, of course, no argument about the right of Israeli soldiers to enter the territory during the battle; in times of conquest, even so grave a ban as the prohibition on eating bacon is suspended for Israel's army (*Hullin* 17a).

But, alone among all leading rabbinical authorities, Rabbi Shlomo Goren, the redoubtable Chief Rabbi of Israel's Defense Forces, sought to extend the sanction, firstly by arguing that the suspension applied to the whole period of conquest and not merely to the actual moment of battle, since the original sanction, too, had extended to "the seven years of conquest" under Joshua (*ib.*). Rabbi Goren further held that the forbidden Temple area was far smaller than the entire Mount site, and that he could establish the lines of demarcation with certainty. Based, moreover, on documentary evidence that Jews did, in fact, visit and worship on that site during the Middle Ages, Rabbi Goren actually led a small army group on a demonstrative pilgrimage there shortly after the War (after they had immersed themselves in a *Mikva* and removed their shoes). He also announced his intention to hold regular religious services close to the Dome of the Rock, a plan foiled only by the mounting rabbinical outcry against it, combined with some more discreet political pressures against thus further inflaming Arab resentment.

The historical evidence cited consists mainly of a report by the 13th century Provencal scholar R. Menachem Meiri affirming "the accepted custom to enter the site, as we have heard" (on *Shavu'ot* 16a) and the following diary entry attributed to Maimonides: "On Tuesday, Cheshvan 4, 4926 (1165) we left Acre for Jerusalem . . . and on Thursday I entered *the great and Holy House* (of worship), vowing that I would mark these days as festivals in prayer and rejoicing." (Introduction to *Commentary* on *Rosh Hashanah*; R. Eleazar Askari, *Sepher Charedim, Mitzvat Ha-Te-shuvah*, 3). According to the researches of several modern historians published in *Zion* (Jerusalem, vols. 2-3, 1928–9), permission was given by the Caliph Omar for the erection of a synagogue which actually stood on that site (originally where the Mosque of El-Aska was later built) for over four hundred years until 1080 (Prof. Ben-Zion Dinur; Prof. Moses Schwarb), which explains why the Western Wall is scarcely mentioned up to that time (Prof. Ezekiel Yehuda). R. Hakohen refers to these claims but is inclined to dismiss them as scientifically unproven, although he does accept as substantiated the statements that Jewish pilgrimages to the Temple site were still held after the Destruction at the time of the Tannaim and Amoraim ("possibly because they then still had ashes of the red heifer for purification") and that Jews in the fourth century, having been permitted by the Byzantine Emperor Julian (361–363) to rebuild the Temple, had actually begun construction on the site when they were interrupted by a "fire from the ground", probably an earthquake (see Dubnow, *History*, vol. 3, pp. 125–6; *Zohar Chadash*, Ruth, 76b).

Nevertheless, rabbinic opinion today is virtually unanimous in seeking to bar Jews from any part of the Temple Mount, as also demanded by the Chief Rabbinate of Israel. The objection is based primarily on the ruling by Maimonides whereby the sanctity of the Temple site, even after its destruction, remains intact for all times (*Hil. Bet Ha-Bechirah*, 6:16). This ruling is contested by his glossator, R. Abraham ibn Daud (*RAVeD, a.l.*), but—according to most commentators—only to dispute capital culpability on entering the site, not the prohibition itself (Kahane, Waldenberg). This conclusion is also indicated by ibn Daud's refusal to qualify the ban on entering the forbidden parts of the Temple Mount even in post-Destruction times, as defined by Maimonides (*ib.*, 7:7).

In any case, the opinion of Maimonides, prohibiting entry under penalty of *karet* for those defiled by contact with the dead, is accepted by virtually all decisors, from the Middle Ages (e.g. *SeMaG, Chinukh, RITVA, Tur, MaHaRIL* and *TaSHBaTZ*) to more recent times (*Magen Avraham* and *Mishnah Berurah*, on *Orach Chayyim*, 561:2). Hence the warning not to trespass "from the gate to the Temple Mount and onwards" was already affirmed by the scholar-traveller Eshtori Haparchi in the 14th century (*Kaftor Va-Ferach*, chpt. 6) as it was in the present century by Rabbi A. I. Kook (*Mishpat Kohen*, no. 96) who also suggested the erection of a large and exquisite synagogue outside the Temple Mount area and close to the Western Wall (*ib.*).

The alleged references to any prayers *on* the Temple Mount by Maimonides and Meiri are therefore rejected as either second-hand ("as we have heard") or applicable only so long as the site's sanctity might have been compromised by non-Jewish occupation (Waldenberg). Moreover, the diary statement ascribed to Maimonides would contradict his own ruling; indeed, a careful reading of it in no way suggests that "the great and Holy House" he visited was on the Temple Mount (Weiss).

While, as we have seen, the strict ban mentioned in the Mishnah covers only a limited area within the Temple Mount confines, its extension to the entire site is necessitated by several considerations. Firstly, even if the limits could be defined with precision, it would be impossible to prevent trespasses in error once any part of the site is legitimately opened to Jewish pilgrims (Waldenberg, Weiss). Secondly, several categories of impure persons (other than those defiled by death) may not set foot within a much wider area, and their requisite purification, though technically possible, would be subject to many detailed ritual requirements not otherwise observed in our time (Weiss).

But above all, it is quite impossible to identify the actual Temple area with any accuracy. According to the Mishnah (*Middot*, 2:1), the walled Temple Mount site measured 500 cubits by 500 cubits, corresponding approximately to 61,256 square meters, whereas, today's site is more than twice that area, with the Eastern and Western walls extending to 480 meters, the Northern to 321 meters and the Southern to 223 meters (Weiss), comprising an area of about 145,564 square meters (Hakohen). Thus the entire area must be out of bounds as being at least possibly the original site, especially since there is some uncertainty even about the identity of the "Rock" under the Dome of Omar with the "Foundation stone" (*Even Shetiyah*), traditionally the place where the Ark in the Holy of Holies was originally found, so that no fixed points from which to measure the distances given are definitely known. The discrepancy in the measurements may also be due to doubts about the length of the "cubit". Already 230 years ago, the Kabbalist R. Emanuel Riki (*Aderet Eliyahu, Kuntres Mei Nidah*, no. 36), after checking the height of ten cubits given in the Talmud for the Eastern Gate against the actual height of the well-preserved gate, concluded that one "holy cubit" (i.e. as used within the Temple precincts) corresponded to 1–2/3 cubits elsewhere. By this reckoning, the 500 × 500 cubit area would, in fact, more or less, encompass the entire Temple Mount site as it is today, and the distance from the Dome of the Rock to the Western Wall would tally with the 111 cubits given in our sources for the distance between the Holy of Holies and the Western extremity of the Temple court-yard. On that basis, the original ban would extend to the whole area, and not only to (a possibly unidentifiable) part of it (Waldenberg).

Rabbinic opinion, then, has come down overwhelmingly and implacably on this side of the wall surrounding the Temple Mount. But the extreme vehemence with which this view has been pressed against the more romantic adventures advocated by Rabbi Goren can, perhaps, only be explained, psychologically at least, as another manifestation of the resistance by Orthodoxy's spiritual leadership to any identification of Zionist achievements, so clearly secularist in their motivation and thrust, with the fulfilment of Messianic hopes. Unfortunately, the impotence of these rabbis in asserting their views is painfully demonstrated by the masses of Jewish visitors and tourists ascending the Temple Mount, undeterred by the warning placards put up by the Chief Rabbinate and the Ministry of Religions forbidding trespass under pain of *karet*.

REBUILDING THE TEMPLE

Access to the site of the Temple is obviously but a precondition to its restoration. That the question whether, with the site now under Jewish control, the Temple could or should be rebuilt has nevertheless aroused far less bitterness is simply due to the fact that no one has seriously advocated such a consummation of the Six-day War. But, at least academically, the question has been widely discussed in the wake of the War, partly stimulated by non-Jewish speculation, and notably again in a comprehensive survey by Rabbi Mordecai Hacohen (*Panim-el-Panim*, October 18th, 1967) and a brief note by Rabbi E. Y. Waldenberg (*Ha-Pardes*, October 1967).

Rabbi Hacohen summarises the seven principal arguments for and against building the Third Temple at the present time:

1. According to some authorities (e.g. *Chinnukh*, no. 95), the precept to build the Temple applies only "at the time when the majority of Jews live upon their land", a condition clearly not yet fulfilled. Against this view, it may be argued that at the time of Ezra the rebuilding of the Temple was undertaken although the number of Jews who returned from the Babylonian exile was far smaller than today, in both absolute and relative terms. Also, the insistence on "the majority of Jews" may have been necessary only so long as the Jewish people were divided into tribes.

2. A more substantial objection is the widely-held belief (Rashi, *Rosh Hashanah* 30a, and *Sukkah* 41a; Meiri, *a.l.*; Tosaphot, *Shavuot* 15b, citing *Tanchuma*) that the Third Temple will be erected in a supernatural way by God Himself. This belief is affirmed in some of our best-known statutory prayers, such as the *Musaph Amidah* for festivals (". . . and in Thy great mercy rebuild *Thou* it . . ."; ". . . rebuild Thine House as at the beginning. . . ."). —This argument (also often used against Zionism in the past—*I.J.*) may be countered by the obvious consideration that prayers for, and trust in, Divine help do not exempt us from making our own efforts towards their fulfilment. (The argument is also refuted by similarly ascribing to God the erection of the First Temple in the *Hagadah*: ". . . and *He* built for us the Temple. . . ."— *I.J.*). Surely the duty to build a Temple, codified as a positive commandment by Maimonides (*Hil. Bet Ha-Bechirah*, 1:1), can no more be meant to rely on prayer and hope only than the realization of the verse "The Lord doth build up Jerusalem; He gathered together the dispersed of Israel" (Ps. 147:2).

3. The building of the Temple requires and presupposes conditions of peace. Hence, this commandment is preceded by the duty to appoint a king and to root out the seed of Amalek (Maimonides, *Hil. Melakhim*, 1:1–2), that is, Israel's enemies. This is implied in the Torah itself (Deut. 12:10–11), and historically borne out by the delay in the construction of the First Temple —though it was a precept incumbent upon Israel immediately on entering the land—until the time of King Solomon 440 years later.—The order given by Maimonides, while representing the ideal, is not necessarily an indispensable condition. There are, in fact, some sources suggesting that the building of the Temple may precede the annihilation of Amalek (*Jer. Ma'aser Sheni*, 5:2; *Yalkut Shimoni*, on Deut. no. 816).

4. The Temple cannot be built except by the word of a true prophet, as expressly taught in a classic commentary on Deut. 12:5 (*Sifri*), and as historically confirmed by the roles of the prophets Nathan and Gad in the building of the First Temple (2 Sam. 24:18–19; cf. Ps. 132:2–5) and of Haggai, Zechariah and Malachi in the Second Temple. The Third Temple, too, as ruled by Maimonides (*Hil. Melakhim*, 11:1), is to be built by "the annointed king" (i.e. the prophetically endorsed Messiah.)—This argument is answered in the very passage of the *Sifri* mentioned above: "You might assume you should wait until a prophet tells you (to build the Temple): therefore it teaches: 'unto His habitation shall ye seek, and thither shalt thou come'— meaning, seek and you shall find, and thereafter let the prophet tell you." In this sense the Sages went so far as to assert: "All the thousands who fell in the days of King David fell only because they failed to demand the (building of the) Temple" (*Midrash Psalms*, 17).

5. The sanctification of the Temple site and premises as such may require the sanction of king, prophet, *Urim ve-Tumim* and Sanhedrin, as suggested by ibn Daud (*Hil. Bet Ha-Bechirah*, 6:14; see also above) and as applicable to the original Sanctuary in the wilderness (*Shavu'ot* 15a; *Jer. Sanhedrin*, 1:3). —This view (in any event based on a minority opinion, as indicated above) seems contradicted by Ezra's sanctification of the Second Temple at a time when the *Urim ve-Tumim* no longer existed. Evidently, then, even those who hold, contrary to the accepted ruling as codified by Maimonides, that the original sanctity of the site has lapsed require for its resanctification the sanction of only one, not all, of the agencies mentioned (*Shavu'ot* 16a).

6. All the measurements of the Temple were revealed to King David in precise detail in a scroll handed to him by Samuel (1 Chron. 28:19) who had himself received this by a tradition going back ultimately to Moses (*Midrash Samuel, a.l.,; Jer. Megillah*, 1:1). These measurements are now unknown or in dispute (cf. above).—Details on the Third Temple are actually given in the Book of Ezekiel, and their study is to serve the very purpose of facilitating the rebuilding of the Temple (Maimonides, Introduction to *Zera'im*). The accessibility of the site should now also render it easier for architects and other experts to resolve whatever doubts and uncertainties formerly existed as best the human mind can. More we need not attempt; for the Torah was not given to superhuman beings.

7. Most decisive may be the final argument: The bulk of our generation is neither ready nor anxious for the restoration of the Temple and its form of worship. Only after Israel's religious reawakening can the Temple fulfill its meaning as the supreme symbol and instrument of God's sovereignty over His people (*Midrash Samuel*, 13; based on Hos. 3:5). Hence the order of our constant prayer: "Have mercy, o Lord our God, over Israel Thy people, Jerusalem Thy holy city . . . and the great and holy House over which Thy name is called."—Yet, even this argument may be falacious. Perhaps just our orphaned and hard-tried generation, which has reached the gateway of redemption after the long ordeal of bitter exile, needs and may expect the spiritual regeneration to inspire, and to be inspired by, the restoration of our national Sanctuary, After all, Herod and his generation were scarcely more deserving, nor were the Babylonian exiles who returned under Ezra, and yet

they rebuilt the Temple—praised in the Talmud as "the most magnificent building ever seen" (*Sukkah* 51b).

Quite different from these neutrally-presented views is R. Waldenberg's fairly comprehensive listing of responsa, all of them opposed to any idea of building the Temple in pre-Messianic times. He also refers to Rabbi Kook who, while he evidently considered in one place the possibility of rebuilding the Temple, though without restoring the sacrificial service (*Mishpat Kohen*, no. 94), elsewhere stressed our inability to identify the proper site (endorsement of R. Obadiah Hadayah's *Yaskil Avdi*, vol. 1, Jerusalem, 1931).

THE WESTERN WALL

The return of the Holy Places also prompted R. Waldenberg (*Ha-Pardes*, October 1967) to mention several rabbinic rulings and customs relating to them. Many authorities doubt whether it is permitted to kiss the stones of the Wall, let alone to place hands or prayer-books upon them, or petition papers between them, since the width of the Wall is invested with the sanctity of the site it encloses (Maimonides, *Hil. Bet Ha-Bechirah*, 6:9). Some, therefore, refrain from touching or even walking close to the Wall. But others of no lesser stature observe none of these restrictions. R. Waldenberg lists a number of responsa discussing these usages in detail.

THE CAVE OR MAHPELAH AND RACHEL'S TOMB

Kohanim should be warned not to enter these burial places and thus defile themselves (*Pe'at Ha-Shulchan*, *Hil. Eretz Yisrael*, 2:18; and others). To prevent such defilement, the marking of Abraham's grave is already mentioned in the Talmud (*Bava Batra* 58a).

In this connection, R. Waldenberg also urges visitors to the Cave not to conduct religious services in what, after all, has been constructed, and is still being used, as a mosque, with displays of Moslem religious inscriptions and emblems, and what must, therefore, be regarded as a non-Jewish house of worship which, strictly speaking, Jews should not even enter (Maimonides, *Mishnah Commentary*, on *Avodah Zarah*, 1:4; *Yoreh De'ah*, 149:1). He considers it certainly wrong to use the same building for Jewish and Moslem prayers, even if the respective services are held there on different days.

There are also objections to using burial places for regular prayers. This question was already raised last century in regard to the prayers recited in Rachel's Tomb (*Minchat Eleazar*, part iii, no. 53), a practice widely accepted among Jerusalem's most pious men, despite the law against reciting prayers within four cubits of a grave (*Yoreh De'ah*, 367:3, 6). But the resting-places of the Patriarchs, and particularly of Rachel who herself prayed for her children from her tomb (Jer. 31:15), may be excluded from this ban (Waldenberg).

JERICHO

R. Waldenberg regards as no longer valid the ban on rebuilding the city of Jericho originally pronounced by Joshua (Josh. 6:17–26) and extended in the Talmud (*Sanhedrin* 113a) to the reconstruction of any city by that name. For, in contrast to a city condemned for idolatry which may never be rebuilt even after its destruction (Deut. 13:17), the ban on Jericho lapsed once a new city had been raised on the ruins of the original site (R. Meir Simchah of Dwinsk, *Meshekh Chokhmah, a.l.*, based on *Sifri, a.l.,*). This may explain why Maimonides makes no reference to the ban.

KERI'AH ON SEEING HOLY SITES

The conquest of large parts of the Holy Land previously inaccessible to Jews, especially the cities of Judaea, the Old City of Jerusalem and the Temple site, naturally again raised the question whether one should tear one's garment on seeing these places. Such a token of mourning is required on seeing these sites "in their destruction" (*Orach Chayyim*, 561:1-2; based on *Moed Katan* 26a), and opinions differ on whether this qualification is to be understood as referring to the continued desolation of these places or to their domination by a non-Jewish power. The latter interpretation is favoured by Karo himself (*Bet Yoseph, a.l.*) as well as by R. Eshtori Ha-Parchi before him (*Kaftor Va-Ferach*, chpt. 6) and several commentators on the *Shulchan Arukh* after him (e.g. *BaCH, Magen Avraham, a.l.*). Accordingly, R. Waldenberg simply rules that the sight of Jerusalem or any other city of Judaea, now that they are under Jewish control, no longer necessitates the tearing or *keri'ah*. But this cannot apply to seeing the Temple site, which is undoubtedly still "in its destruction"; hence, on visiting the Western Wall and/or seeing the Dome built on the Temple site *keri'ah* should certainly be torn (as also stipulated by the wording of *BaCH, loc. cit.* and *Pe'at Ha-Shulchan, Hil. Eretz Yisrael*, 3:1-2). He adds, however, that despite the ruling by Maimonides (*Hil. Ta'a-nit*, 5:16) requiring the tearing of all garments one wears at the time, the prevailing practice is to limit the act to one garment only (following *RAVeD* and Nachmanides).

The question has also been submitted to a more critical analysis in a scholarly article by Rabbi Samuel Weingarten (*Sinai*, Iyar-Tamuz 5727, p. 163). After discussing several complementary passages in the Talmud (esp. also *Berakhot* 58b) and other rabbinic sources, the author concludes that these mourning observances are not related to the degree of sanctity attaching to the various places listed; otherwise they should include any of Israel's walled cities which are also enumerated among the "ten degrees of holiness" (*Kelim*, 1:6). Rather, R. Weingarten suggests (following *RaDBaZ, part* ii, no. 646), the reason for the law is to be found in the anguish experienced on seeing these sacred places in desolation, and the cities of Judaea are specific-ally included because "they were once the principal seat of Israel's royal rule" (*Pe'at Ha-Shulcham, loc. cit.*). With the restoration of Jewish sovereignty over the entire land, anguish on seeing any of these sites should now give way to joy and therefore suspend the *keri'ah* requirement altogether.

In a rejoinder published three months later (*Sinai*, Tishri-Cheshvan 5728, pp. 95 f.), A. Azrieli argued that the Temple site is halakhically and logically in a distinct category, quite different from that of Jerusalem and the Judaean cities—halakhically since having torn *keri'ah* for Jerusalem a separate tear is still required on seeing the Temple site, whilst in reverse on sighting Jerusalem or a Judaean city after making the tear for the Temple site only an extension of the same *keri'ah* is required (Nachmanides and Asheri, on *Moed Katan* 26a), and logically since the return of Jewish rule clearly does not affect the grief over the desolation of the Temple and of the spiritual glory it represents. But both contributors do agree in criticizing the masses of our people, and particularly our religious leaders, for not even yearning for the restoration of the Temple with sufficient earnestness to generate serious study and effort, a failure no doubt springing from the fear of "what will the non-Jews say?"

THE MOUNT OF OLIVES CEMETERY

The saddest feature revealed by the conquests of the Six-day War, next to the complete destruction of all synagogues in the Old City of Jerusalem, was the devastation wrought on the Mount of Olives cemetery where hardly a grave was left unmolested by the Jordanian vandals. To add to the fearful desecration of the oldest Jewish cemetery—which, until twenty years ago, had been in almost continuous use for 2,000 years or more—the Jordanians built a road across it, raised largely of broken tombstones over hundreds of wantonly despoiled graves. May this road be used by vehicles or on foot, and must the graves underneath it be uncovered and restored?

After describing the agony of a visit to the site, where every sod and stone cry out in anguish over the desecration of the human remains they were meant to cover and guard, the author affirms with certainty the obligation to close the road immediately, and thereafter to tear it up, searching carefully for any graves beneath it in order to restore them. This decision is borne out by various older responsa. For instance, Rabbi Jacob Saul Alisher (*Olat Ish, Yoreh De'ah*, no. 9), in reply to an inquiry from Algiers, ruled that any stepping upon graves, let alone the constant use of a thoroughfare upon them, constituted a grave indignity to the dead, however deep the graves were under the surface. The prohibitions here involved were the disgracing of the dead as well as their exploitation. Instructive, too, is the decision of Rabbi David Friedman of Karlin (responsa *Sha'alat David*) requiring the demolition of a house which had been erected on grounds presumed to have had Jewish graves. Among the arguments used was the fact that the burial plots had originally been purchased on behalf of the deceased. This rendered it all the more heinous to rob the dead of the ground belonging to them.

Regarding the respect due to the dead, it makes no difference whether the body is still intact or already in an advanced state of decomposition; man, in whatever condition of physical health or blemish, is created in the Divine image (*Chatam Sopher, Yoreh De'ah*, no. 353). This consideration applies even to single bones.

In conclusion, R. Waldenberg proposed proclaiming a special day of prayer and fasting to seek forgiveness for the revolting offense committed against the dead on the Mount of Olives. Even if those responsible were Israel's oppressors, Jews cannot disclaim all guilt, since "the dead are exhumed (i.e. ravaged) by the sin of the living" (*Yevamot* 63b). (The Israeli authorities have meanwhile closed the road.—*I.J.*)

THE OCCUPIED TERRITORIES

The most far-reaching—to some, perhaps, the most irrelevant—argument generated by the Six-day War concerned the halakhic attitude to any withdrawal from territories occupied during the War. Many leading rabbis, notably Chief Rabbi Nissim and several followers of the Rabbi Kook school of thought, threw the weight of formal religious rulings behind the growing popular campaign against any retreat, whether under pressure of the world powers or as a price for a peace settlement. Others, claiming to blend their patriotism with a measure of realism, felt that such matters of state belonged primarily to political and military experts, not to rabbinical scholars.

The moderates' principal flag-bearer was Rabbi J. B. Soloveitchik. In a widely publicized address for which even the usually unfriendly *Ha-Pardes* (January 1968) gave him effusive editorial praise, he berated the exaggerated importance attached to the Jewish "Holy Places", including the Western Wall, when compared to the deliverance of over two million Jews, and he ridiculed rabbinical interference with what were essentially security problems which could only be determined by Israel's government and army authorities. Any religious precepts not to surrender the Holy Land to non-Jewish control were suspended, as was any other religious law, in the face of any threat to life, in this case possibly the lives of millions (Report in *Amudim*, published by the Kibbutz Ha-Dati, Cheshvan 5728). In a further clarification, he explained that halakhically such political decisions were no different from rulings about fasting on *Yom Kippur* which had to be based on the opinion of medical experts (*Panim-el-Panim*, 13 Kislev, 5728, p. 7).

Leading the more militant camp was Rabbi Zvi Yehudah Kook. In a proclamation under the heading "Ye shall not be afraid" (Deut. 1:17) published by him in the Israeli press, he cited the warning given three hundred years ago that Jewish leaders would be held accountable for the failure to restore God's land to God's people (*Or Ha-Chayyim*, on Lev. 25:25) and argued that the surrender of Israel's territory to others was merely a sign of weak faith, causing Jewish suffering, danger and humiliation. It was the bounden duty of every Jew to prevent any permanent withdrawal from any part of the land historically vouchsafed to Israel, and anything undertaken in contravention of this principle, whether politically motivated or abetted by the hesitations of religious sages, was legally null and void. Rabbi Kook also led a mass demonstration at his Yeshivah "Merkaz Ha-Rav", attended by over a thousand leading citizens, including Israel's President, Chief Rabbi and numerous other dignitaries, culminating in an oath taken by all assembled in the words of "If I forget thee, O Jerusalem. . . ." (Ps. 137:5) and the aged rabbi's cry: "The Torah prohibits the surrender of even a single headbreath of our liberated land. . . . We are not conquering any foreign lands. We are returning to our home, to the inheritance of our fathers. . . ." (*Shanah be-Shanah*, Jerusalem 5728, p. 108f.).

The rabbinical debate was not limited to these rather polarised views. Already two weeks after the War, an Israeli daily published the replies of

Chief Rabbi I. J. Unterman and Rabbi S. Israeli (member of the Chief Rabbinate Council) to questions about the conquered areas (*Hatzofeh*, 15 Sivan, 5727; also reprinted in *Shanah be-Shanah, op. cit.*, pp. 105 ff.). A later symposium on the subject featured the views of several other leading rabbis, including Rabbis Bezalel Zolti (Rabbinical Appeals Court), Shlomo Zevin (Editor, *Talmudic Encyclopedia*) and Abraham Schapiro (Rosh Yeshivah, *Merkaz Harav*), in the same journal (*Hatzofeh*, 5 Cheshvan 5728), while a further opinion was published a little later by Rabbi Nathan Zvi Friedman, another outstanding Halakhist (*Zera'im*, Tevet 5728). Among the unpublished contributions to the controversy is an exchange of letters (circulated by the World Mizrachi Head Office in Jerusalem) between Rabbi Joshua Menachem Aaronberg (Tel Aviv, 14 Cheshvan, 5728) and Mr. S. Z. Shragai (Jerusalem, 18 Cheshvan 5728).

All authorities are agreed that there is a religious ban on the surrender by Jews of any territory within the confines of the Holy Land. This is derived primarily from the precept "thou shalt not favour them" (Deut. 7:2), interpreted in the Talmud (*Avodah Zarah* 20a) and codes (Maim., *Hil. Avodah Zarah*, 10:3–4) as enjoining Jews "not to give them any settlement (rights of possession) in the soil" of the land. While this injunction strictly refers only to the pagan "seven nations" that originally inhabited the Land of Canaan, other relevant Biblical precepts are not so limited. Apposite, for example, is the verse "Every place whereon the sole of your foot shall tread shall be yours. . . ." (Deut. 11:24), which may be considered a law as well as a promise (Israeli). Of greater legal force is the injunction "And ye shall take possession of the land and dwell therein. . . ." (Nu. 33:53), which Nachmanides (*Sefer Ha-Mitzvot*, positive additions, no. 4) counts as a distinct law among the 613 Biblical commandments (Schapiro) and which involves the three obligations (1) to conquer the land, (2) not to surrender its possession to others and (3) not to leave it uninhabited (Friedman).

Some acknowledge, however, that these laws may not be absolute. Already several early authorities (*Kaftor Va-Ferach*, chap, 10; so also *RAVeD*, in *Shitta Mekubetzet*) recognized that "thou shalt not favour them" is inapplicable when it conflicts with Jewish property interests; hence economic factors must also be taken into account (Zolti). This is, in fact, the basis for the sanction (*Avnei Nezer, Yoreh De'ah*) to sell plots in the Holy Land to non-Jews (Schapiro). Dealings in real estate between Jews and non-Jews have always been permitted; nevertheless, national considerations may possibly be altogether different and subject to a separate judgement in the light of the existing circumstances (Unterman).

In any event, the borders within which any of these precepts operate are almost certain to exclude the Sinai peninsula—unless its occupation is essential for Israel's security (Zolti); but there is some doubt whether the Golan heights are within the Biblical territory of the Land of Israel (Schapiro).

Support for the more accommodating attitude is mainly founded on the argument, already mentioned above in the name of Rabbi Soloveitchik, that all religious prohibitions automatically give way in the face of any danger to life, and that the determination of such danger is invariably left to experts, such as doctors in the case of violations of the law for medical reasons. Thus, an absolute refusal to entertain any negotiations on border adjustments, or possibly even on the bulk of the territory occupied in June '67 might well endanger Israel altogether; not to mention the fear that the addition of one million Arabs to Israel's population might in time undermine the character and security of the Jewish State (Zevin). In any case, the whole question is not now acute, since the Arabs adamantly continue to reject any peace talks. Moreover, there were many other religious ideals which could not be realised under present conditions, such as the obligation to rid the Holy Land of any practices or shrines regarded as idolatrous in Jewish law (Zevin). A precedent for the more moderate view may also be found in the armistice negotiations of twenty years ago when no one raised any halakhic objections to the recognition of borders more confined than the limits set for the Land of Israel in the Torah (Unterman).

But others will recognize only a direct threat to Israel's security from one of the principal world powers as a valid indication for any concessions; even such considerations as local security against terrorism or demographic factors would not be sufficient to override the religious ban on any surrender of territory, especially since the political and military experts themselves are by no means unanimous on their assessment of the danger if Israel refused any negotiations for territorial adjustments (Schapiro). It is also argued that the duty not to give up any territory is absolute; after all, the *repeated* miracle of Israel's deliverance from attack by superior military forces may not always be assured, following the pragmatic rule "One must not rely on miracles." It would be indefensible, therefore, to allow the enemy ever again to be close to Israel's life-lines (Friedman).

It may even be questionable whether the suspension rule in the face of danger to life is altogether applicable to the law of waging war for the Jewish occupation of the Holy Land. Otherwise, any danger to life resulting from war or terrorist attacks would justify emigrating from the Land of Israel; nor could one plead for any Aliyah from abroad if such an argument were upheld. Hence, the religious precept to occupy the land, and its obverse not to surrender it, cannot be affected by any risk of life. This point is expressly made in connection with the commandment to wage war, with inevitable losses on both sides, on the original inhabitants of the land (*Minchat Chinnukh*, no. 425). Only if without a partial surrender all would be lost might this consideration be varied (Aaronberg).

The circumstances leading to the Six-day War may also weigh the scales against any concessions. We may today not be under any religious obligation to conquer the land, Yet, once it has been occupied through an action enforced by pure self-defense against the avowed threat of extermination, we have no right to surrender land which was taken from our people 1,900 years ago, and to which we lay historical, moral and religious claims (Israeli).

MITZVAH OBSERVANCE FOR SPACE TRAVELLERS

How are spacemen in orbit to fulfill religious observances which depend on the count of days and nights? This up-to-date—or up-to-the-future—question was discussed at some length and with considerable erudition in a contribution by Rabbi David Shlush in *Torah shebe'al Peh* (Jerusalem 5725), the transactions of the Seventh Congress of the Oral Law published by the Mosad Harav Kook under the editorship of Yitzchak Raphael. Orthodox Jews are not yet among the select ranks of space-travellers, so that the answer here precedes the question. But just as the science-fiction of yesterday has become the science of today, the Halakhah-fiction of today may well turn into the Halakhah of tomorrow.

At the outset the author cites an intriguingly relevant *Midrash* to determine whether the laws of the Torah are altogether applicable outside our planet and its atmosphere, as the Torah—which is "not in heaven"—may be restricted to earth-dwellers. The *Midrash*, on the verse "And he (Moses) was there (on Mt. Sinai) with the Lord forty days and forty nights" (Ex. 34:28), asks "How did Moses know when it was day?" and answers "When he was taught by God the Written Law he knew it was day, and when he was taught the Oral Law he knew it was night" (*Tanchuma, Tissa*, 36). It is not explained, however, why Moses needed to distinguish between day and night.

According to Rabbi J. M. Tucatzinsky (in his book *Ha-Yomam*), Moses needed to know the count of days while on Sinai in order to establish when to observe the Sabbath every seventh day. Hence, he deduces that dwellers at the North Pole, who do not see the sun rise or set for months, should fix their Sabbath following every six periods of twenty-four hours. But a commentator (*Etz Chayyim*, on *Tanchuma, loc. cit.*) understands the Midrash to refer to the recital of the *Shema* in the mornings and evenings.

Rabbi Shlush rejects both explanations, arguing that during his sojourn with God Moses required neither the Sabbath nor the *Shema* to remind him of God's creation and unity. Instead, the Midrash is simply intended to explain the frequent reference to "forty days *and forty nights*," since "forty days" alone would have been sufficient to indicate that Moses did not return from the mountain each night during the forty-day period of his stay with God. Detached from all earthly surroundings and needs (e.g. neither eating nor drinking), Moses recognized the distinction between day and night only by alternating his studies between the Written and the Oral Laws.

While the Midrash, then, may have no direct bearing on the liability to observe *Mitzvot* in outer space, it is evident to the author that the laws of the Torah are incumbent on astronauts since, even in space, they remain bound to the conditions of life on earth, being sustained in their earth-constructed sphere by food and air taken from earth.

To determine the time of the Sabbath, three distinct calculations of days are used according to circumstances:

(1) From sun-down to sun-down. For instance, travellers from East to West count the days by sun-down at the place of arrival, even though a single such day may greatly exceed 24 hours (e.g. for a traveller at the speed of the earth's rotation leaving China at midday on Friday westwards and arriving at the same hour in the Western United States, the Sabbath is not observed until sun-down there, although his Friday will have lasted 37 hours).

(2) According to the place of arrival, without considering either the number of hours or of sun-downs. Thus, if the traveller continued his journey

and reached his starting point in China 24 hours later (i.e. by then midday Sabbath there), he observes the Sabbath only for six hours—from the moment of arrival until sun-down (the local termination of the Sabbath), although his flight made him miss the seventh sun-down that week at the start of the Sabbath.

(3) By 24-hour periods. This applies to dwellers at the Poles who observe no sun-set for six months and who therefore fix their Sabbath following every six 24-hour periods.

After a lengthy discussion of the sources and various opinions on these rulings,[1] the author concludes that astronauts in orbit around the earth should observe the Sabbath between every seventh and eighth sun-down they see during their flight, i.e. for about 90 minutes in every 10½ hours (assuming their orbit is fairly close to earth). He defends this view on the ground that the local determination and the 24-hour period (examples 2 and 3 above) apply only where the Sabbath would otherwise conflict with its local observance (e.g. for the travellers returning to China) or else last for one year in every seven (at the Poles, where sun-down occurs only once a year). In our case, however, the Sabbath is properly determined by the count of sun-downs, however frequently these may be observed while in orbit. For the Torah makes the Sabbath dependent on "your habitations," i.e. local variations, and even the original Sabbath at the time of creation presumably started and ended at different times following the course of sun-set around the world (cf. responsa *RaDBaZ*, no. 76). And since the principal purpose of the Sabbath is to remember God's creation of the world in six days followed by the Sabbath, with each reckoned by "and it was evening and it was morning," the Sabbath "day" should be determined by "day" and "night" as apparent to the satellite "dwellers".

But this consideration does not apply to the festivals which are fixed by the days in the month (see the emphasis in Ex. 12:18 and Lev. 23:32), i.e., by the phases of the moon. Since these phases are the same for men in orbit as for those on earth, the festivals (including *Yom Kippur*) should be observed in space as on earth, starting from the moment the satellite is over a point where the festival begins on the ground and then continuing for 24 hours.

Regarding other observances depending on time, Rabbi Shlush reaches the following conclusions: *Tzitzit*, since one is obligated to wear them only when one can "see them" by natural light, need be worn only during daylight periods in orbit.

Daily prayers, i.e. *Shacharit*, *Minchah* and *Ma'ariv*, should be recited only once every 24 hours, but at times corresponding to morning, afternoon and evening respectively in the orbital day.

Shema, to be read "when thou liest down and when thou risest up", should be recited by astronauts before and after their sleeping periods.

Tephillin should be worn by spacemen while reciting their morning *Shema*, provided this is in their day-time and not their Sabbath or festival.

These rulings may well be subject to further debate before they are applied

---

1. Cf. also "Crossing the International Dateline", in my *Jewish Law Faces Modern Problems*, 1965, p. 25ff.

in practice. Meanwhile it may be good counsel to advise any Jew venturing into outer space to recite *Shema Yisrael* all the time pending his safe return to *terra firma.*

LETTERHEADS

Lately it has become increasingly fashionable, almost as a trademark to authenticate Orthodox authorship, to preface letters, notices, public announcement and any other written or printed texts with the Hebrew letters *B"H* (sometimes even in English characters!) denoting *Barukh Hashem* ("Blessed be the Lord") or *Be'ezrat Hashem* ("With the help of the Lord"). The propriety of this use or abuse of the Divine Name is questioned by Rabbi Meir Blumenfeld in the only contribution of current halakhic interest to the latest issue (Tishri 5726) of *Ha-Darom,* the semi-annual Torah-journal of the Rabbinical Council of America.

The Rogodzover Gaon (Rabbi Joseph Rosin) based his own refusal thus to head even Torah writings on the possibility that the erasure of such letters, even if they constitute only part of the Divine Name, may be an offense against the sanctity of the Name and the prohibition to delete it (citing *Jer. Sotah,* 2 and 3). Hence he warned that one should refrain from writing *B'H* at the head of letters (*Tzophnat Pane'ach,* 196 and 197).

Notwithstanding the illustrious source of this rigid opposition, the custom to introduce letters with *B"H* is, of course, widely observed in the most scholarly circles and must therefore be based on good authority. The source appears to be a passage by R. Moses Isserles at the very opening of the *Orach Chayyim* (1:1, gloss) taken from the *Guide of the Perplexed* by Maimonides (3:52): On the strength of the verse "I have set the Lord always before me" (Ps. 16:8), every action, word and even thought of a person should reflect his awareness of God's presence.

To fulfill this ideal, the Kabbalist R. Isaac Luria suggested that one should draw the image of the Divine Name constantly before one's eyes (*Ba'er Hetev, a.l.,* 3), while others went one step further and wrote the Name on a piece of parchment used as a bookmark in order to be continuously reminded of God and of avoiding idle talk during their studies and prayers (*Sha'arei Teshuvah, a.l.,* 3). But yet others objected to this practice as likely to lead to desecrating the Name and possibly erasing it (*ib.*). In any event, to the extent that the custom of writing *B"H* is founded on these sources, it is designed as a reminder to the writer, not the the recipient of the letter; this could just as well be achieved by facing a piece of paper bearing a reference to God while writing any letters, etc.

Another origin of the custom may be found in Ibn Ezra's commentary on the verse "House of Israel, bless the Lord" (Ps. 135:19): this means that Jews are to use the blessing *Barukh Hashem.*

None of these explanations provides any justification for turning the custom into a fetish, particularly when used as a sanctimonious imprint on such things as newspaper advertisements, bank checks or synagogue placards announcing choral services (though the choir includes Sabbath desecrators!).

Actually, the author believes that the only valid reason for the usage lies in associating *Barukh Hashem* with a date at the head of the letter. This may be based on the verse "Blessed be the Lord, day by day" (Ps. 68:20), interpreted in the Talmud as "Every day give Him the blessing appropriate to the day" (*Berakhot* 40a; see MaHaRSHA, *a.l.*). Even the practice thus to use *B"H* with specific dates cannot be regarded as a *minhag*, let alone a *mitzva*, since there were many outstanding Torah authorities in the past not observing it. Indeed, in purely secular contexts, such a practice may be against the law.

MOURNING LAWS FOR BABIES

A Halakhah-brief by Rabbi N. L. Rabinovitch in the Tishri 5727 issue of *Ha-Darom* concerns the death of a six-week-old child born weak and under-developed (though full-term, according to the mother). The doctors had considered it inviable from birth and had preserved its life in an incubator and by artificial feeding. Must the mourning laws be observed in such a case?

As a general rule, any child that survives thirty days is no longer regarded as a premature or inviable birth (*Yevamot* 80a), and any subsequent death actuates all the laws of mourning, unless it was known to have been born in the eighth month (*Yoreh De'ah*, 374:8). Despite the mother's claim, such knowledge can be established with certainty only if the parents were separated throughout the pregnancy period.

Rabbi Rabinovitch further argues that this child, because of its insufficient development and the doctor's hopelessness, may be considered as *terephah* from birth, and for such the laws of mourning do not apply, on the basis of his interpretation of several rulings by Maimonides (*Hil. Evel*, 1:8; *Hil. Rotze'ach*, 2:8) and other authorities.

STRIKES

The right of workers to strike is once again[1] discussed in a rather brief article contributed by Rabbi Raphael Katzenelenbogen to *Hama'yan* (Jerusalem, Tishri 5725).

Explicit references to strikes are not found in rabbinic writings until quite recent times. The reason for this omission is simple. So long as the social relations of Jews were governed by Jewish law, notably the *Choshen Mishpat*, the occasion to resort to labour strikes did not arise. Any claims or grievances would always be referred to rabbinic judgment or arbitration, and the awards

---

1. See my *Jewish Law Faces Modern Problems*, 1965, p. 96ff.

—reflecting objective norms of justice based on the Torah code—would be binding on both sides. Any party that refused to heed a summons to such a *Din Torah* would be so ostracized from the social and religious life of the community as to compel eventual submission. Only with the secularization of Jewish society, and its conduct even in Israel according to legislations and courts alien to Judaism, has the need for strikes arisen, for the secular law often gives workers no other means to assert their claims effectively.

Since there are, of course, many religious workers in organized labour, the question of the halakhic attitude to strike must be resolved for them. Some argue that strike action can never be condoned by the law of the Torah, as the right of compulsion can only be exercised by a judicial tribunal, including a court of arbitrators accepted by both parties. Others go further, objecting to any association with labor unions that rely on strike laws established by international labor organizations in opposition to Torah and religion. But this extreme opinion requires some clarification and qualification.

True, there is no law granting one party the right to force the other to accept his demands. Hence, any recourse to compulsion without judicial authority violates the law of the Torah.

But in labor disputes the employer may try to hire other workers who will agree to his terms, thus depriving the original workers of their livelihood. The principal question regarding strikes is therefore: May strikers, to safeguard their jobs, prevent another worker from taking their place on terms at variance with their demands?

The answer is based on a responsum by R. Joseph Kolon (MaHaRIK, no. 191) which rules that, while a rabbinical court had no power to exclude a newcomer from a city, the members of such a community could use any means at their disposal, including recourse to the non-Jewish authorities, to keep new settlers from their midst. This ruling, accepted by the *Shulchan Arukh* (*Choshen Mishpat*, 156:7, gloss) and most authorities against some dissenters (see *Pitchei Teshuvah*, *a.l.*, 17), is endorsed by R. Moses Schreiber (*Chatam Sopher, Choshen Mishpat*, no. 44) on the grounds that an economic threat to their livelihood entitles citizens to take such action even if it cannot be sustained by the strict law and its administrators.

Similarly, then, workers cannot be restrained from resorting to strikes if, through their replacement, they would otherwise face the prospect of losing their employment. Obviously, however, they would first be required to submit their claims against their employers to a regular or jointly-appointed court, and only if the employers then refuse to appear before such a court or to abide by its verdict can the workers call a strike and prevent other workers from taking their place. But once the management agrees to adjudication or arbitration, labor is certainly forbidden to take the law into its own hands.

Moreover, in the event of the management's unwillingness to accept arbitration and labor's resultant call of a strike, other workers would definitely be guilty of an offense if they were to displace the strikers under cheaper terms than the latter were prepared to accept. This is borne out by the ruling that "even if a Jew works regularly for a non-Jew, another Jew must not offer his services for less pay, and anyone wishing to do so should be rebuked" (*Choshen Mishpat*, 156:5, gloss), a ruling applying equally to workers with a Jewish employer, as implied in the source for this law (responsa of RaSH-BA, part iii, no. 83).

In a supplementary note, the author adds that there can be no justification in denying wage increases to workers at charitable institutions on the ground that such wages are taken from charity funds. This argument is refuted by the fact that such a right was enjoyed even by those paid out of the funds of the Temple treasury, the most sacred of all funds (citing responsa of MaHa-RSHDaM, *Choshen Mishpat*, no. 372).

CAR FUEL PAYMENT

A rather unusual responsum on a not so unusual question appears among Rabbi N. L. Rabinovitch's Halakhah-briefs in the Tishri 5727 number of *Ha-Darom*. A motorist, with his gas tank empty and the contents of his purse reduced to two dollars, asked at a station for two dollars' worth of gas. However, the station assistant filled up the tank at a cost of six dollars, arguing afterwards that he had misunderstood the motorist. The latter protested that he had only ordered two dollars' worth without mentioning any volume, so that he would either regard the whole tank-full as sold at a cheaper rate or else consider the excess as a gift. But since this was unacceptable to the assistant, the motorist told him: "Then take back the extra gas, and if you cannot remove it from the tank, that is your loss."

Relevant to the claim of the excess as a gift, the author cites the following ruling in the *Shulchan Arukh*: Anything erroneously sold by measure, weight or number must always be returned, for the law of (legitimate and limited) overcharge or undercharge applies only to money (i.e. if the error amounted to less than one-sixth of the value of the purchase) but not to a mistake in the count (*Choshen Mishpat*: 232:1). Now, since gas is obviously sold by the measure, as indicated on the meter, the request for two dollars' worth must be regarded as specifying the volume wanted, so that any excess delivered in error cannot be claimed as a gift by the buyer. Nor can the motorist's argument "Take back your gas, or else suffer the loss" be sustained. For "any person who renders his fellow a service or a favour may claim his due payment and cannot be told 'You rendered it free since I did not order you'" (*Choshen Mishpat*, 264:4, gloss). Also, "if one entered another's field and began planting or building there without permission, and the owner then completed the building or kept the plants indicating that he concurred with what had been done, the intruder has the upper hand [in claiming his due payment]" (*ib.*, 375:3; based on *Bava Metzi'a* 101a). Similarly, in this case, the fact that the motorist subsequently drove his car further and clearly benefited from the extra gas is a clear indication that he was satisfied with what he had received, so that he is obliged to pay for it at the fixed price.

CHILDREN'S SERVICES

A contribution to *Shevilin* (Teveth-Adar 2725) by Rabbi C. P. Tchursch deals with an enquiry from religious school authorities on whether it is proper at services attended only by boys under Bar Mitzvah age to take out, read, be called up to, and recite blessings over, the Torah for educational purposes.

The law clearly states in the Mishnah (*Megillah*, 4:3) and the *Shulchan Arukh* (*Orach Chayyim*, 143:1) that readings from the Torah require a *Minyan*, i.e. ten Jews over thirteen years of age. Consequently, in the absence of a *Minyan*, when the Torah cannot be formally read, it should even be forbidden to move it from the Ark (based on *Gittin* 60a). But once ten adults are present, even minors may be called up to the Torah (*Orach Chayyim*, 282:3, gloss).

However, on further study the author finds that even if the worshippers are all children, they may conduct full services for training purposes. He bases this conclusion on the many similar concessions made in the Talmud and elsewhere on educational grounds. Thus, notwithstanding the general ban on making images of celestial objects or on the practice of sorcery, such activities are permitted if carried out for study purposes (*Rosh Hashanah* 24a; and *Sanhedrin* 68a). Similarly, children may be trained in the use of the *Shofar* even on the Sabbath until they are proficient (*Rosh Hashanah* 33a and b), and the usual ban on writing sections of the Torah by themselves (*Yoreh De'ah*, 283:2) is lifted, at least according to one authority, if this is done for the teaching of children (RIF, on *Gittin* 60a).

For this reason minors may also recite the appropriate Torah blessings in full, just as even women may recite benedictions on the performance of precepts legally not incumbent on them, such as *Lulav* or *Sukkah* (*Tosaphot, Chagigah* 6b). Such blessings by children, once they arise from the obligation to educate them, do not offend against the commandment not to take the name of the Lord in vain (*Tosaphot, Eruvin* 96b).

"The purpose of education is only to accustom the child to make a habit of the proper practice when he grows up" (Rashi, *Chagigah* 6a). It is particularly important nowadays, therefore, when children are exposed to so many irreligious influences, to train them in the practice of Jewish life, so that the habit-forming right conduct may take root in them. Naturally, if a *Minyan* of adults can attend children's services, that is preferable; but if this is not feasible, the children may conduct their own services without restriction. This opinion, states the author, is also endorsed by several leading rabbis.

CHANGING PRAYER RITES

In a brief contribution to the January 1966 issue of *Ha-Maor*, Rabbi Meir Blumenfeld deals with a problem rendered increasingly frequent with the proliferations of small "Shtibl" congregations. At one such new synagogue, where some worshippers were used to the Ashkenazi rite and others to the Sephardi rite, it was decided to do justice to both by having the entire congregation alternate between the two rites every month.

The author rejects this solution as clearly "a practice of ignorant people, erring in the weighing of opinions and opposing all accepted traditions." Any traditional *Minhag* (custom), particularly in liturgical usages, is inviolable and must not be changed. Thus R. Isaac Luria ("Ari") objected to changing any local prayer custom "because there are twelve gates in Heaven parallel to the twelve (Israelite) tribes, and each tribe has its own gate and custom, apart from (the texts) mentioned in the Talmud common to all" (*Magen Avraham, Orach Chayyim*, 68:1; based on *Jer. Eruvin*, 3). This objection applies specifically to any change from the Ashkenazi to the Sephardi rite or *vice versa* (*Peri Megadim*); each group should abide "by its own flag," for "these and those are the words of the living God" (*SHeLAH, Torah shebiktav, Bamidbar*). Hence, the action of the congregants in switching from one rite to another is definitely against the law.

ISRAELI CANTORS

May cantors residing in Israel and hired for a festival season abroad conduct services on the second days of *Yom Tov?* Rabbi Meir Blumenfeld, in a concise responsum featured in the Tishri 5727 issue of *Ha-Darom*, answers this question in the affirmative.

Normally, anyone not obliged to recite a prayer for himself cannot do so for others either. And the whole purpose of the institution of a public reader, who repeats the *Amidah* aloud, is of course to discharge the obligation of prayer on behalf of the congregation, even if the worshippers are themselves able to read the prayers (*Orach Chayyim*, 124:3). The question therefore revolves around the cantor's own obligation to recite the *Yom Tov* prayers while on a visit abroad, especially when he is officially engaged by a congregation to be their reader.

As a rule, travelers from Israel are expected to observe the stringencies both of Israel and of the Diaspora (e.g. wearing *Yom Tov* clothes and yet reciting the weekday *Amidah* and laying *Tephillin* in private), and they should follow the Diaspora rules exclusively only if they intend to remain abroad, or if they travel together with their wives, i.e. "their homes" (see *Magen Avraham, Orach Chayyim*, 496:7; and *Shulchan Arukh Ha-Rav, Orach Chayyim*, 496:8, 10). However, some regard the enactment of the second *Yom Tov* day as applicable to all living in the Diaspora, whether permanently or temporarily (M. Landau, *Peri Ha'aretz*; and *Shulchan Arukh Ha-Rav, Maha-dura Tinyana, ib.*).

Hence, cantors leaving the Holy Land to serve some congregation in the Diaspora for *Yom Tov*, since they know they will thereby be compelled to observe the second day of *Yom Tov*, must be considered as if they had no intention to return, in the same way as one who travels with his wife (and "moves his home") abroad. This would apply in particular to unmarried cantors who thus cannot be considered as "settled" in Israel. Notwithstanding one opinion to the contrary (responsa *Tzophnat pane'ach*, no. 100:4), such visiting cantors would also be free from the duty to wear *Tephillin* on these days, since—like the first *Yom Tov* days—the second days are also a "sign" obviating the need for the "sign" of the *Tephillin*.

THE AGUNAH PROBLEM

By far the most agonizing challenge confronting the rabbinate today is to ameliorate the wretched fate of legal spouses who remain "chained" (*agunot*) to each other and debarred from remarriage, because the spitefulness, avarice, desertion, insanity or unproved death of one partner prevents the release of the other through divorce. These tragic cases, which usually inflict more disabilities on women than on men (since the ban on polygamy and on divorcing a wife against her will is only a rabbinic enactment dating from the 10th century and thus of lesser severity than the corresponding restrictions on women), are becoming increasingly frequent with the widespread recourse to civil divorces and the husband's subsequent failure, refusal or inability to dissolve the religious bond by a religious divorce. The problem has lately been dramatized by the much publicized petitions for relief addressed by various National Councils of Jewish Women to the rabbinates in their respective countries.

The first scholarly response to this challenge has now come from Rabbi Dr. Eliezer Berkovits, of the Jewish Theological College in Chicago, in a book *Tenai b'Nissuin uve-Get* ("Conditional Marriages and Divorces") just published by the Mosad Harav Kook (Jerusalem 5727). We here include some brief references to the contents of this significant work because (1) it was originally written for a halakhic periodical publication in Israel, (2) it deals with a subject of exceptional importance, and (3) it features an introduction of fundamental concern by the late Dr. Yechiel Weinberg.

The gravity, delicacy and complexity of the issues discussed in this 170-page volume render it both impracticable and imprudent to give here even the briefest of abstracts. All that can be attempted is to acquaint the reader with the existence of this book, with the general nature of the far-reaching proposals it tentatively submits to expert consideration by the leading sages of our time, and with the authoritative opinions expressed by so knowledgeable a master as Dr. Weinberg.

After acclaiming the author's extraordinary erudition and industry in composing this profound and unique work, Dr. Weinberg emphasizes the unprecedent pressures of this problem. While the leading scholars of the last generation, which adamantly opposed any legal innovations to meet the situation, merely knew of relatively isolated cases of hardship resulting from the marriage and divorce procedures as currently practised, the problem had been immensely aggravated in recent times, especially with the remarriage of numerous women who had obtained no religious divorce from their first husbands and whose subsequent children were thus branded as *mamzerim* suffering permanent and grave disabilities. This growing evil made it all the more urgent to spare no effort in the search for an acceptable solution.

Moreover, the heated and unanimous rabbinical opposition to a previously suggested innovation (proposed by the French rabbinate about sixty years ago) concerned the automatic annulment of every marriage subsequently dissolved by a civil divorce only; this would have reduced all Jewish marriages into mere "partnership contracts" to be arbitrarily terminated by the courts at the wish of either partner, making the formal "condition" attached to every marriage nothing but a legal evasion to cover up the civil verdict. Dr. Berkovits, on the other hand, limits his proposals for such "conditions" to specific cases without making them dependent on the civil courts.

While Dr. Weinberg felt too ill to determine a definitive affirmative or negative opinion on the book's proposals, he did offer some valuable elucidation of the subject. What prompted the greatest sages of the past generation to reject so uncompromisingly any qualifications or conditions in the marriage contract which might have eased the situation—notwithstanding the more lenient views of such leading authorities as R. Mosheh Isserles, the *Noda Biyehudah* and the *Chatam Sopher*—was the concern not to qualify or undermine the absolute sanctity of the marriage bond and not to encourage any licentiousness among Jews who might claim that the religious marriage was but an empty formality which could be voided by a civil judge. The retroactive annulment of marriages resulting from such prior "conditions", by legally turning all marital relations during the intervening periods into "acts of prostitution", violates the moral conscience of Judaism. Even at the time of the Talmud such enactments were only made in specific cases, and then only to avoid inadvertent encumbrances (*Gittin* 33a).

The fundamental question, therefore, that the book challenges the foremost rabbis of our age to resolve is above all one of principle: Is it more important to maintain the absolute sanctity and permanence of Jewish marriages in the sense of "I will betrothe thee unto me for ever" (Hos. 2:21), so that even in religious circles the purity of marital life should not suffer the slightest impairment, or to consider the widespread evils and hardships today of persons who cannot or will not be given their freedom from their spouses, and who nevertheless often remarry with disastrous consequences in violation of the law? There are weighty arguments for both alternatives, and our leading sages must not withhold their judgment by the most painstaking reexamination of this grave question.

In his exceedingly well-documented dissertation Dr. Berkovits examines with great thoroughness and skill the various legal devices which could be, and have been, considered to alleviate the sad lot of the "chained" spouse. The opinions of numerous early and late authorities—from the Talmud to the present day—are carefully cited, analyzed and weighed in the light of contemporary conditions. On balance they lead the author to the conclusion that, upon further study by the acknowledged rabbinical scholars of our time, several solutions to the problem could be found in accordance with authentic precedents.

The book is divided into four chapters discussing the principal methods under review:

1. *Conditional Marriage*—the proposal to make the validity of marriages contingent, by an express agreement between the parties before their wedding, upon certain conditions, whereby, for example, the marriage would be invalidated if two years following its civil dissolution the husband refused to grant his wife a religious divorce or demanded a ransom for such a divorce. This proposal is based mainly on a ruling by the 15th century R. Israel Bruna, codified in the *Shulchun Arukh* (*Even HaEzer*, 157:4, gloss), permitting a marriage to be made contingent on the wife not being left with an apostate brother-in-law (who could not free her from the levirate bond) upon her husband's death. Many objections have been raised against the principle of conditional marriages, but Dr. Berkovits believes that these could eventually be overcome or outweighed by the specific considerations for the public welfare here involved.

2. *Prospective Divorce*—the proposal to execute or commission a divorce to take effect on the fulfillment of certain conditions after a stipulated time. This method is usually advocated, and has occasionally been applied, in war-time to free the wives of missing soldiers some time after the conclusion of hostilities. The author shows that there may be many legal and moral impediments as well as practical objections to conditional divorces of any kind, whether they are to take effect retroactively from the time of execution of later. The recommended procedure is to commission the requisite officials (scribe, witnesses, etc.) to write and hand over the divorce document on behalf of the husband in the event he does not return after, say, two years following the end of the war. This is based on the Talmud (*Gittin* 76b) and does not involve the attachment of any conditions to the divorce itself.

3. *Annulment.* The Talmud provides for certain cases in which the rabbis could declare a marriage null and void, to prevent fraud and other abuses, on the assumption that "whoever marries does so with the agreement of the rabbis" (*Ketuvot* 3a), i.e. on the implicit understanding that his act accords with the rabbinical enactments; hence the inclusion in the marriage formula of the phrase "according to the law of Moses and Israel" (*Tosaphot*). Opinions among later sages have been widely divided on how far this power can be generally used for the annulment of marriages, especially in cases other than the five specific (and rather technical) instances listed in the Talmud. While several communal enactments exercising this power are known from medieval records (as detailed by A. H. Friedmann, *Seder Kiddushin ve-Nissu'in*, Mosad Harav Kook, Jerusalem, 5705), the *Shulchan Arukh* (*Even Ha-Ezer*, 28:21, gloss) appears to rule out such annulments. One important authority (responsa R. M. Alshaker, No. 48) suggests that such enactments can be made only with the consent of all or most of the communities (and their rabbis) in a country. On this basis, Dr. Berkovits believes, the present facilities in communications and the existence of national communal and rabbinical organizations should render it possible to enact legislation for bringing some relief to today's pressing situation.

The book and its proposals will no doubt meet with much determined opposition, as did similar attempts at modifying legislation in the past, even if the arguments can be halakhically sustained. The evolution of Jewish law is an organic process influenced by numerous social, moral and ideological factors as well as purely legal considerations. It is to be hoped that Dr. Berkovits' painstaking researches will give a powerful impetus to an intensified search for procedures doing justice both to the lofty rules which have "sanctified the people of Israel through *Chuppah* and *Kiddushin*" and to the individuals who occasionally suffer great hardship from the application of these rules.

REFORM MARRIAGES

As a rule, the responsa here reviewed are restricted to those published in current periodical literature. We make an exception on this occasion by including some abstracts from a book of responsa, both as a tribute to one of the most prolific and widely respected Halakhists recently deceased and because of the intrinsic value and topical importance of the subjects discussed. They appear in the third volume of Rabbi Yechiel Weinberg's masterly *Seridei Esh* just published by the Mosad Harav Kook in Jerusalem.

A delicate question lately subjected to much popular and mischievous agitation concerns the religious validity of marriage ceremonies performed by non-Orthodox rabbis, i.e. by officiants who do not themselves subscribe to the unqualified authority of Jewish law. One may wonder, parenthetically, why those who protest their freedom from the restraints of the Halakhah to vindicate their dissent from traditional Judaism are so concerned to have their religious actions sanctioned by those loyal to the traditional "law of Moses and Israel".

Rabbi Weinberg deals with this matter in two responsa (nos. 18 and 19), the first written when he was still Rector of the *Rabbiner Seminar* in Berlin. A man had been married by a Reform rabbi and subsequently wanted a traditional *Ketuvah* issued by an Orthodox rabbi, who enquired whether he could accept the marriage as valid and thus save the only daughter born to the couple from any stigma. In his reply, Rabbi Weinberg refers to a case discussed in the *Chatam Sopher* (no. 100) in which a marriage performed by a rabbi, also serving as a witness together with a *shamash* who was later found disqualified as a relative, was ruled valid in principle, since it could be assumed that other acceptable witnesses were present. On a similar assumption the Reform marriage, too, may strictly be in order. Nevertheless, to avoid all doubts, the responsum in the *Chatam Sopher* urged the private performance of a second ceremony in the presence of two qualified witnesses. Accordingly, Rabbi Weinberg likewise advises his colleague to solemnize the marriage again, explaining, if necessary, that this was required for the writing of the *Ketuvah*, since it was not properly executed at the first marriage. But on no account should the husband be told that the original marriage was invalid, "so as not to arouse any evil talk about the [Reform] rabbi and to prevent the husband and his wife from looking upon themselves as having theretofore lived together illegitimately".

The other responsum, written quite recently, considers as valid, subject to Rabbi Moshe Feinstein's endorsement, marriages performed by a rabbi together with a *shamash* (acting as the second witness) who was later found not to be a Sabbath observer. Rabbi Weinberg bases his ruling on the following considerations:

1. In the *Chatam Sopher* (cited above) it is assumed that even if (disqualified) witnesses had been assigned, the marriage is validated by the presence of other (qualified) witnesses notwithstanding the failure to specify them as such, since the groom and bride obviously want the ceremony to be legal.

2. Generally, witnesses cannot be disqualified except by evidence before a court (see *Choshen Mishpat*, 34:25). This may apply even when a witness is aware of his own disqualification (*Pitchei Teshuvah, a.l.*, 1, citing *Chavat Yair*).

3. According to R. Jacob Ettlinger (*Binyan Zion*, no. 25), Sabbath desecrators nowadays are not automatically disqualified from giving evidence (since their action is no longer an act of defiance or heresy, as it was in former times, when Jews lived almost exclusively in a Sabbath-observing society).

4. The disqualification of non-observant witnesses may extend only to evidence relating to laws they do not observe (R. Aaron Walkin, responsa *Zekan Aharon*, part 1, no. 81, citing *Shiltei Giborim, Sanhedrin*, 3). Violators of the Sabbath, however, may be presumed not to violate marital laws, so that their evidence in matters of marriage should be acceptable.

Hence, Rabbi Weinberg advises against informing couples married under such conditions that their marriages are religiously defective, for this would only lead to a *Chillul ha-Shem* by holding up the solemnization of marriages to scorn and the couples so married to disrepute.

[Neither of these two responsa is, of course, conclusively applicable to marriages performed by Reform rabbis who openly flout some fundamental Jewish marriage laws (e.g., by remarrying parties without a religious divorce) and whose ceremonies are not always witnessed by any religiously qualified witnesses.—I.J.]

REFORM MIXED MARRIAGES

Certainly a most unusual source from which to draw material for this Department is the *Central Conference American Rabbis Journal*. But the item abstracted below is so acutely relevant to contemporary Halakhah and its problems that it merits inclusion here as a matter of great interest to Orthodox readers, too.

In a bold challenge to his Reform colleagues Dr. J. Petuchowski, for long an articulate advocate of some return to halakhic Judaism at the Hebrew Union College in Cincinnati, castigates the Reform Rabbinate for its ambivalent attitude to mixed marriages in a plea which could scarcely be improved upon by any Orthodox writer ("Realism about Mixed Marriages," *CCAR*, *October* 1966, p. 34 ff.). The article is based on a recent survey which revealed that 28% of the Conference members will "officiate" at a "Jewish" marriage with a non-Jewish partner, at least under certain conditions (15% without prior conversion, provided the children will be raised as Jews; 10% without conversion "in certain conditions"; and 3% with no conditions). The ostensible objective of such marriages is "to save the Jewish partner for Judaism," the children for Sunday Schools, and the "rabbi" for "an important pastoral function by calming the conscience of the Jewish partner and [his] parents."

But overlooked in these arguments "is the very nature of *kiddushin*, and the clericalist airs which Reform rabbis are giving themselves by agreeing to 'officiate' at a mixed marriage. When it suits our purpose, we never tire of proclaiming that Judaism is a non-priestly religion. . . . But when it comes to concrete cases, we become more priestly and ecclesiastical than the most rigorous Orthodox fundamentalist" by establishing "the validity" or "Jewishness" of marriages which technically do not need a rabbi at all. The only justification for a rabbi's presence "is his role as representative of the *halakhah* accepted by *kelal yisrael*." Otherwise "he is guilty of *genevat da'at*—unless he specifically states in his wedding address, that the validity of this marriage is recognized only by the state and by some sections of Reform Jewry, though not by Judaism as a whole, and unless he omits the words *kedat mosheh veyisrael* from the *kiddushin* formula." He would have to make it clear "that he is 'officiating' at a 'sacrament' of his own invention, [which] has no connection with what is recognized by the rest of Jewry as a 'Jewish marriage.' "

Dr. Petuchowski adds courageously: "As long as more than one quarter of our members . . . will 'officiate' at mixed marriages, the Orthodox have the better of the argument where, as in England and in Israel, they deny the Jewish validity of Reform marriages. At any rate, they would be justified in instigating rigorous investigations whenever they are confronted by a Reform marriage. After all, as our own statistics indicate, 28 out of every 100 Reform rabbis are willing to 'officiate' at marriages which have no standing whatsoever in Jewish law."

To the question "Why should we be bound by the halakhic understanding of *kiddushin*, [and not have] our own Reform understanding of what a 'Jewish' marriage is?" the writer replies bluntly that such a marriage is, at best, a "Reform Jewish" marriage, "Should we be willing to settle for that, we could save ourselves a great deal of trouble in the State of Israel. Some years ago, Israel's Minister for Religious Affairs assured the Reform Jews that they would obtain complete religious freedom (including the area of marriage and divorce law), if they were to consent to registering as a separate religious denomination. . . . The Reform Jews of Israel rejected the suggestion as preposterous." But judged by the admitted practices of the Reform Rabbinate, and particularly the claim, never officially repudiated, of many younger Reform leaders that "Reform Judaism is a new religion . . . which—more or less by historical accident—shares part of its name with the historical religion of Judaism," the Minister's suggestion "may not have been so preposterous, after all." In fact, Dr. Petuchowski believes that about 25% of the

CCAR members would be ready to assert that Reform Judaism is a new religion in its own right—a percentage liable to increase as time goes on.

The author therefore calls on his colleagues to surrender their present ambivalence and inconsistency in favor of one of two mutually exclusive positions: Either mixed marriages, involving an unconverted non-Jewish partner, are possible in all cases, because the prohibition of them no longer applies in modern times. In that event, we "have radically broken with the law of marriage as understood by historical Judaism; [this] should, logically, make us amenable to the suggestion of Israel's Minister of Religious Affairs that Reform Jewry register as a sect in its own right." Or else, the Conference "will have to take a stand against those of its own members who regard Reform Judaism as a new religion . . . , and it will also have to bear in mind the meaning which the concept of *kiddushin* has for *kelal yisrael*."

We cannot but heartily endorse this bold plea, confident that its conscientious adoption would in one stroke remove a major obstacle to Orthodox-Reform understanding and reduce the awful danger of Jewry being split into two peoples unable to marry within each other—a paramount threat unfortunately altogether overlooked in the author's reasoning to sustain his strictures.

MEDICAL HALACHAH

A comparative study by the present reviewer on the differences and similarities in the medical rulings of Maimonides and R. Joseph Karo is published in the Nisan-Iyar 5726 issue of *Sinai* to mark the four hundredth anniversary of the *Shulchan Arukh*.

In order to evaluate properly the classic codes of Jewish law in relation to their time, it must be remembered that even Karo's definitive work represents essentially a codification of Talmudic law. The examples given in the *Shulchan Arukh*, including most of the terms for diseases, medications and treatments, are usually drawn directly from the Talmud, even when they were no longer known or understood in Karo's time. In only two instances does the *Shulchan Arukh* contradict medical rulings found in the Talmud: it permits the drinking of uncovered liquids despite the prohibition in the Talmud (*Avodah Zarah* 30b), since the danger of poisoning by snakes no longer existed (*Yoreh De'ah*, 116:1), and to dispute the Talmudic assertion (*Niddah* 38b) that a viable child requires a full nine months' term (*Even Ha-Ezer*, 156:4, gloss). In fact, the *Shulchan Arukh*, following R. Amram Gaon and other early authorities, frequently asserts that regarding certain Talmudic tests and operations "we are no longer competent" (e.g. *Orach Chayyim*, 350:5, gloss; *Even Ha-Ezer*, 145:9, gloss; and 172:6, gloss). But in general the codes uncritically embody Talmudic data and illustrations, even when these were completely unknown by the 16th century, including some long-forgotten occult cures.

Despite the common basis, therefore, for the codes of both Maimonides and Karo, they often reveal important differences as well as similarities in medical matters. For instance, by way of adding to Talmudic regulations, they agree, in identical wordings, that no one may whisper an incantation over a scorpion's bite even in the Sabbath "although this is of no avail whatever; but this was permitted to a patient in danger so as not to distract his mind (i.e. as a suggestive remedy)" (*Hil. Avoda Zarah*, 11:11; *Yoreh De'ah*, 179:6). Similarly, Karo (*Even Ha-Ezer*, 5:10) adopts the view of Maimonides (*Hil. Issurei Bi'ah*, 16:9) that included in genital defectives "by the hand of Heaven" who are free to marry are persons whose defect is caused by illness. Both authorities also explain the law on sucking the circumcision wound ("*metzitzah*") as serving "to extract the blood from the [more] remote places, so as to prevent any danger" (*Hil. Milah*, 2:2; *Yoreh De'ah*, 264:3).

The two codes also share certain omissions, such as the lack of any references to the ban on desecrating the dead and on contraception by tampon, notwithstanding their mention in the Talmud (*Chullin* 11b; and *Yevamot* 12b).

On the other hand, there are notable differences, especially in regard to health rules. For example, while the *Shulchan Arukh* completely omits the lists of healthful and harmful items which occupy an entire chapter in Maimonides' code (*Hil. De'ot*, 4), several Talmudic rules enacted to avoid health hazards are mentioned only in the *Shulchan Arukh* and not by Maimonides, such as the law on washing hands between, and not eating together, meat and fish (*Orach Chayyim*, 173:2; *Yoreh De'ah*, 116:3), the practice of burying the placenta (*Orach Chayyim*, 330:7) and the custom to refrain from cupping (or venesection) on certain days (*ib.*, 468:10, gloss). Maimonides, again in contrast to the *Shulchan Arukh*, also omits all references to demons found in the Talmud.

Even more significant is the divergence of the attitude to physicians and the treatment of the sick. While both codes regard the practice of medicine as a religious act, Maimonides bases this ruling on the Biblical injunction to restore one's neighbor's lost property, i.e. including his lost health (*Hil. Nedarim*, 6:8; see *Mishnah Commentary* on *Nedarim* 4:4), whereas Karo uses the Talmudic teaching on "He shall surely cause him to be healed" (Ex. 21:19): "This teaches that permission was given to the physician to heal" (*Yoreh De'ah*, 336:1), though he adds "and this is a religious precept" (*ib.*). But details on professional regulations—the physician's licence, liabilities and fees—appear only in the *Shulchan Arukh* (*ib.*)..

Sometimes the difference between the two codes may be explained by the fact that Maimonides himself was a physician. Thus, the Talmudic law not to visit a patient in the first and the last three hours of the day (*Nedarim* 40a) is codified by Karo with the reason given in the Talmud that the illness in the morning is deceptively mild and in the evening deceptively grave, so that the visitor may either neglect or despair of praying for the patient (*Yoreh De'ah*, 335:4), whereas Maimonides simply explains the same law as intended to avoid disturbing the attendants in looking after the patient's needs during those hours (*Hil. Evel*, 14:5). The laws against male nurses attending women suffering from intestinal complaints (*Yoreh De'ah*, 335:10), and against a physician attending his own wife during her menstrual period (*ib.*, 195:16–17) except in grave circumstances (*ib.*, gloss) are also omitted by Maimonides. Conversely, only Maimonides records the Talmudic ban on settling in a place which has no doctor (*Hil. De'ot*, 4:23; *Hil. Sanhedrin*, 1:10).

On the violation of the Sabbath for patients in danger the *Shulchan Arukh* itself reflects an important difference of opinion. Karo, following Maimonides (*Hil. Shabbat*, 2:3), advises that such services should preferably be rendered by adult and responsible Jews (*Orach Chayyim*, 328:12), while R. Mosheh Isserles prefers asking non-Jews instead unless this would involve any delay (*ib.*, gloss). In this view, the latter is consistent with his general principle that all essential violations of the law in the face of danger to life should always be reduced to a minimum (*Yoreh De'ah*, 155:3, gloss). Maimonides, however, maintains his preference for Jews as demonstrating the sanctity of the Sabbath in other cases.

Of special interest are various rulings in the two codes bearing on the subject of euthanasia. Maimonides, whose code covers the whole gamut of Jewish law, including its criminal legislation, defines murder as embracing even the killing of a patient approaching death; only if the victim had reached that condition by a previous attack "through the hand of man" or had suffered from an incurable affliction is the killer free from capital culpability before a human court, though he is still liable for murder before the Heavenly tribunal (*Hil. Rotze'ach*, 2:7-8). The *Shulchan Arukh*, dealing only with laws applicable after Jewish capital jurisdiction had lapsed, omits all this. But it features another law of some relevance, not mentioned by Maimonides. Based on the *Sepher Chasidim*, it warns against hastening death by any movement of the patient in his final moments, but it does permit the removal of an impediment, such as a hammering noise or salt on the tongue, which does not allow the patient to expire peacefully (*Yoreh De'ah*, 339:1, gloss).

On abortion, Maimonides and Karo rule in identical terms: in cases of a hazard to the mother's life an embryotomy may be performed; but once the child's head has emerged, it may not be destroyed to save the mother "since one does not sacrifice one life to save another" (*Hil. Rotze'ach*, 1:6; *Choshen Mishpat*, 425:2). The latter reasoning agrees with the source of this law in the Mishnah (*Oholot*, 7:6): but regarding the first case both codes base the sanction of embryotomy on the law of the "pursuer" who may be struck down to save his victim, whilst the Mishnah justifies the sanction on the ground that the mother's life has priority over the fetus' life since the child before birth is not yet a "*nephesh*" with the same title to life as the mother (Rashi, *Sanhedrin* 72b).

Finally, to the item on circumcision mentioned above we may add some other elaborations of Talmudic law in the codes. Both Maimonides (*Hil. Milah*, 2:2) and Karo (*Yoreh De'ah*, 264:3) insist that the slitting of the membrane to expose the corona (*peri'ah*) be performed "with the finger-nail". Of special historical interest is the Talmudic law (*Yevamot* 64b) exempting a mother or two sisters who lost two sons through the operation from the duty to have the third son circumcised—evidently by far the first recognition in medical history of haemophilia and its transmission by matriliniar consanguinity. According to Maimonides (*Hil. Milah*, 1:18) and the *Shulchan Arukh* (*Yoreh De'ah*, 263:2), the exemption applies whether the brothers have a common father or not, but Karo (*ib.*) extends it even to brothers who have only a father, not a mother, in common, a view for which there is no Talmudic warrant and which is therefore disputed in principle by Isserles (*ib.*, gloss). Also without Talmudic precedent is the ruling by Maimonides, followed by Karo, that the exemption is only temporary and that such a male should be circumcised "when he has grown up and become strong". Karo, but not Maimonides, codifies the practice (first mentioned in geonic sources) to excise the foreskin of a child that died before its eighth day and to give it a name, "so that it will receive compassion from Heaven and live at the time of the resurrection of the dead" (*ib.*, 5).

ARTIFICIAL INSEMINATION

One of the gravest and most complex moral problems raised by the advance of modern medicine engages Rabbli Y. Weinberg's attention in a responsum (*Seridei Esh*, vol. i. no. 5) distinguished by the conciseness of its presentation and the clarity of its conclusions on a subject beset by numerous highly technical considerations. The author refers only briefly, and from memory, to some of the principal rabbinic writings on this problem, and he urges his questioner to consult these carefully before applying his own ruling in practice.

Although artificial insemination is a fairly recent innovation [the first "test-tube baby" was born only exactly one hundred years ago in the United States], the principles involved were known to, and discussed by, the masters of Jewish law very long ago. In fact, the Talmud—alone in the entire literature of antiquity—anticipated the feasibility of a conception without any physical contact between the parents some seventeen centuries before medical science recognized this. The reference is an affirmative answer given to a question whether a pregnant virgin may be married to a high priest (who is Biblically forbidden to marry any woman other than a virgin), the pregnancy being explained as due to the virgin having bathed in water containing the sperm of a male who had previously used the water (*Chagigah* 15a). A later medieval source, similarly acknowledging the possibility of such an artificial (albeit accidental) insemination, warned women against using the bed-linen of strangers, "lest she be impregnated by absorbing the sperm from another man, as a safeguard against a brother marrying his sister (who, unknown to either, have a common father, viz. the man who may have one child by his wife and another through the accidental impregnation of the woman who used his linen)" (BaCH and TaZ, *Yoreh De'ah*, 195, citing *Hagahot SeMaK*).

In the opinion of most, though not all, authorities these passages clearly indicate that (1) an artificial insemination of a married or closely-related woman does not constitute adultery or incest, (2) consequently a child so conceived is not a *mamzer*, and (3) the donor is the legal father of such a child and may, in fact, have fulfilled the precept of procreation in respect of it. The author adduces several proofs to corroborate the major conclusion (1), among them the explicit statement of Maimonides that the prohibition of incest is limited to sexual contact between the offending parties (*Mishnah Commentary, Sanhedrin,* 7; and *Horiyot,* 2).

In the strictly legal sense, therefore, artificial insemination may not violate any cardinal laws of immorality. Nevertheless, Rabbi Weinberg is implacably opposed to sanctioning the practice, both on moral grounds and for fear of grave abuses, and he condemns it as "an act of hideousness and an abomination" incompatible with the traditional chastity of Jewish womanhood. A child so conceived might unlawfully free its mother, if she were widowed, from the levirate bond on the mistaken assumption that it was fathered by her husband, whereas, in fact he died childless. By the same token, such a child might inherit the putative father and thus deprive his true heirs of their rightful heritage. As a far more serious consequence, the practice might well lead to incestuous marriages and widespread debauchery. Since the operation is always carried out clandestinely and the child born by it fraudulently registered in the name of the mother's husband, its real paternity could never be established and its true blood relatives (by his natural father, i.e., the donor) would be as unknown to the child itself as to anyone else, including the mother and the donor himself. The practice would also provide any adulteress or unwed mother with a convenient alibi, enabling her to claim that her pregnancy resulted from artificial insemination and not from the meretricious relationship of which she was actually guilty.

Certain legal disabilities would also ensue. A woman pregnant by artificial insemination would be debarred from relations with her own husband during the period of the pregnancy and lactation, since she must be regarded as "a woman carrying and nursing a child by another man" thus restricted. The child, again, since its paternity is unknown, would have to be considered a semi-foundling and be subject to the marriage disabilities appertaining to that status.

[With one notable and heatedly debated exception (see R. Mosheh Feinstein, *Igrot Mosheh, Even Ha-Ezer,* no. 10), this unconditional proscription of artifiicial insemination by donor is shared by all leading rabbinical authorities who have dealt with the matter.—I.J.]

However, regarding artificial insemination from the husband (in cases where some physical or pyschological impediment renders a successful impregnation under normal conditions impossible), Rabbi Weinberg inclines to a more lenient ruling, as do most other recent responsa on the subject. Since the semen obtained from the husband to this end directly serves the purpose of procreation, this operation may be permitted with even less qualms than to procure the husband's sample for semen-testing, which has also been sanctioned as serving procreative ends (responsa MaHaRSHaM, part iii, no. 268, and others).

THE BLIND IN JEWISH LAW

An exhaustive article on the place, status and consideration of the blind in the Halakhah appears in the Nisan 5724 number of *Hama'yan*, published by the Isaac Breuer Institute of Poalei Agudat Yisrael. It is a chapter of a larger work by J. Joseph Cohen entitled "The Blind and Blindness in Biblical, Talmudic and Midrashic Literature" prepared by the Rehabilitation Office of the U.S. Department of Health, Education and Welfare—a rather inusual source of Halakhic information.

According to one Talmudic sage, the blind are exempted from all religious precepts, based on an analogy between "commandments and statutes" and "judgments" (Deut. 6:1): just as the blind cannot act as judges, they are free from the observance of laws (*Bava Kamma* 87a). But this is a minority view, later endorsed by only one authority (R. Yerucham ben Meshulam, *Sepher Mesharim, nethiv* 14). The others agree that all religious precepts are incumbent on the blind as on any other Jew (see, e.g., Maimonides, *Hil. Zekhiyah Umatanah*, 5:1; *Choshen Mishpat*, 250:5).

Numerous laws are, however, modified or subject to special interpretation for the blind. Several references to them occur, for instance, in connection with synagogue services. Against the opinion of one dissentient, the general ruling is that even a blind person should recite the blessing to the "Creator of the luminaries" in the daily prayers (*Megillah*, 4:6; *Orach Chayyim*, 69:2; see also 53:14), for, although he cannot himself enjoy the light of the sun, he benefits from it through the ability of others to save him from stumbling (Bartinura, *a.l.*). Blindness is also no impediment to acting as a public reader (*Orach Chayyim*, 53:14). In fact, R. Yair Chaim Bacharach remonstrated with a congregation which once dismissed a blind reader, and he forced them to reinstate him (responsa *Chavat Ya'ir*, no. 176). In Talmudic times those called up to the Torah would each read their own portion; this debarred the blind from an *Aliyah*, since the Torah must not be read by heart. To avoid discriminating between those able and unable to read from the Torah scroll, the entire reading was later assigned to public readers. Yet R. Joseph Karo still excludes blind persons from being called up to the Law (*Orach Chayyim*, 139:3). But his glossator recognizes the change and reverses the ruling: "Nowadays a blind person may be called up, just as we call up ignorant people [who cannot read themselves]" (*ib.*, gloss). Some commentators, however, restrict this concession to blind scholars only (BaCH, *a.l.*). In practice this distinction was rarely observed (see, e.g. R. Mordecai Jaffe, *Levush, a.l.*), against the protests of some rabbis (R. Jacob Emden, *She'ilot Yavetz*, part 1, no. 75).

Blindness poses a different problem in regard to the "raising of hands" (*duchaning*) for the priestly benediction. *Kohanim* with conspicuous physical blemishes, including blindness even in one eye, are disqualified from this rite, not because of any intrinsic deficiency, but so as not to distract the attention of the congregation. Hence, this ban is lifted in respect of any blemished *Kohen*, even if he be completely sightless, whom the worshippers are already accustomed to see, i.e. who has lived among them for at least thirty days (*Orach Chayyim*, 128:30).

According to the Talmud (*Betzah* 25b) and the *Shulchan Arukh* (*Orach Chayyim*, 301:18; 622:1), blind people are not entitled to carry sticks in public domain on the Sabbath or festivals, but some authorities permit this if they would otherwise be completely helpless and unable to move at all (*Ateret Zekeinim, a.l.*, in the name of ROSH and others).

The *shechitah* (ritual slaughter) by a blind person is valid but should be avoided, unless others stand at his side to ensure that all the exacting conditions are fulfilled (*Yoreh De'ah*, 1:9).

In several areas the law makes special concessions to persons stricken with blindness or eye diseases. Thus, certain eye afflictions including any threat to the eye itself, being a vital organ, are among the conditions of potential danger to life warranting the suspension of the Sabbath laws (*Orach Chayyim*, 328:9). [This generalized statement by the author requires some qualification. The automatic suspension of the Sabbath laws is sanctioned only for some particular eye diseases as defined in the Talmud and the codes, and this concession is made not because the eye is a vital organ *per se*, but because the Talmud regards such "defect of the eye-sight as being connected with the heart (or mental faculties)" (*Avodah Zarah* 28b), i.e. as liable to lead to a physical or psychological hazard of life.—I.J.] Even slight eye sickness in an infant requires complete healing before he may be circumcized (*Yoreh De'ah*, 262:2). For psychological reasons, to prevent "distracting her mind," lights may be put on on the Sabbath for a woman in childbirth, even is she is blind (*Orach Chayyim*, 330:1).

The concern for sight in Jewish law is also evidenced by the recent lenient rulings on corneal transplants (R. Meir Steinberg, Responsum on Eye Grafts from the Dead, London, 5717; Rabbi Yechiel Weinberg, *Seridei Esh*, part 2, no. 120), and by Rabbi Moses Feinstein's permissive answer on whether a blind person may take a seeing-eye dog to the synagogue (*Igrot Mosheh, Orach Chayyim*, no. 45).

RABBIS AND DEANS

I

We have previously commented on the present tendency to prefer "pure" Talmudic research to the "applied" pursuit of practical rabbinics, as reflected in current rabbinical journals and in the great preponderance of nonpractising rabbis among the alumni of our Talmudic academies.[1] Some of the ramifications and consequences of this development have now been highlighted in an outspoken article on "The Attitude of Disparagement to

---

1. See *Jewish Law Faces Modern Problems*, 1965, p. 13.

the Rabbinate" contributed by Rabbi Raphael Katzenelenbogen to the Tamuz 5725 issue of *Hama'yan*, published by the Isaac Breuer Institute of Poale Agudat Israel.

The author rightly decries, as a phenomenon as unprecedented in Jewish history as it is damaging to religious interests, the widespread practice to belittle not only individual rabbis as the custodians of Jewish law but the rabbinate itself as an indispensable communal institution. The central spiritual authority in Jewish life has always been the duly appointed local rabbi.[2] In his halakhic judgments he might sometimes defer to the superior scholarship of other sages. Nevertheless, he was invariably acknowledged as the sole and final authority in the religious leadership and jurisdiction of the community and its members. Whatever other scholars he may have consulted in reaching his rabbinic decisions, the "lay" public's contacts were exclusively with the rabbi they had chosen to be their guide and their rabbinical judge. While every *Talmid Chakham* was accorded high respect and honors, it was only to the practising rabbi, holding an official position, that the community—including its *Taldmidei Chakhamim*—looked for the exercise of rabbinic authority and guidance.

Such communal rabbis would often also establish local *Yeshivot* and preside over them. In fact, the deans of all leading *Yeshivot* in the past were the official rabbis of the local communities, such as the MaHaRSHaL (Lublin), P'nei Yehoshua (Cracow), Noda Biyehudah (Prague), R. Akiva Eger (Posen), R. Chaim (Volozin), Chatam Sopher (Pressburg), and more recently the heads of such famous academies as Mir, Slobodka, Telz, Ponewez and Lublin.

Only the Reform movement, in its attempt to wrest authority from the traditional rabbinate, recognised "Jewish scholars" (representing the *Juedische Wissenschaft*) as the interpreters of Judaism and the arbiters of its law. When Prime Minister Ben Gurion sought an "authentic" opinion in the "Who is a Jew?" crisis, he turned to the "scholars of Israel" and obstinately refused to submit this question to practicing rabbis who would be governed by norms of the Halakhah, with but two or three exceptions. This constitutes a deliberate rejection not merely of rabbis but of the rabbinate in principle. Today this hostile attitude is betrayed in circles within the *Yeshivah* "world" itself no less than by indifferent laymen, with at least equally tragic and dangerous results.

Another threat to religious interests ensuing from the denigration of the rabbinate and its usurpation by Torah scholars holding no rabbinical office is to be found in the deviation from traditional halakhic methods and standards. While the classic rabbinical solution to new religious problems always takes into account the rulings and precedents set down in the later commentaries and responsa (*Acharonim*) as well as the codes and early authorities (*Rishonim*), the *Yeshivah* scholars often base their practical decisions on their own interpretation of the original sources, without any reference to the intervening authorities. This process is altogether alien to the historic traditions in determining the Halakhah. It often leads to verdicts quite out of harmony with the consensus established in existing rabbinical writings. The refusal to

---

2. See *ib.*, p. 15f.

consult more recent opinions is also indicative of a self-reliant haughtiness in reaching halakhic decisions, in stark contrast to the caution and humility traditionally exercised by rabbinical masters in rendering such decisions. The *Yeshivah* dean is remote from the community and its problems; he cannot enjoy the intimate, personal contact which a practicing rabbi has with his members and their concerns. In nullifying the rabbinate, therefore, one also eliminates the high regard for the Torah image in the community. Whatever the cause for these unfortunate developments, it is the sacred duty of our spiritual leaders to repair this breach and to restore the historic functions of the rabbinate.

To this bold and critical analysis by Rabbi Katzenelenbogen a few further pertinent considerations may be added by the present writer.

The repudiation of the rabbinate and its gradual displacement by academic Talmudic scholars (now commonly referred to as the *Gedolei Ha-Dor* or "Torah sages") in the supreme leadership of the religious community have shifted the center of gravity in the institutional structure of religious Jewry from *kehillot* (congregations) to *Yeshivot*. The consequences of this shift are now becoming increasingly manifest in a variety of ways.

One result is the attrition of the rabbinate. With its demotion and discreditation at the hands of the *Yeshivah* "world", the scholastic caliber of the men attracted to it has steadily declined to a level of general mediocrity. By now there are very few outstanding halakhic guides left in the active rabbinate. Out of the sparse number of *Yeshivah* alumni who are prepared to take up a rabbinical career, most are ill-equipped for the effective exercise of spiritual leadership under modern conditions. For the *Yeshivot* have adamantly blocked attempts to set up rabbinical seminaries for the training of rabbis in the skills needed to influence and guide the destinies of communities. This attrition explains the unprecedented difficulties lately encountered in filling major rabbinical vacancies in Israel, England and elsewhere. We have simply ceased to produce adequate candidates for these key positions.

In the wake of the decline of the rabbinate has come the decline of religious congregations, notably in Israel where the concept of a *kehillah* as a focal point of religious activity and inspiration has all but disappeared completely. Even in the Diaspora, most traditional congregations, bereft of leaders combining profound learning with professional efficiency, have ceased to provide much more for their members than some liturgical and social facilities. With the great men of Jewish learning now mainly confined to the *Yeshivot*, the communities at large have all but lost their Torah image, formerly represented by the rabbi in their midst.

At the opposite pole on the axis of leadership—among the laiety—a similar loss of Torah influence has resulted from the ascendancy of the *Yeshivah* over the *Kehillah* as the basic unit in the religious structure of Jewish life. Despite the phenomenal increase in the output of learned laymen, thanks to the growth of the *Yeshivah* movement, the Torah element in communal and congregational leadership has, far from increasing commensurately, actually declined. For the *Yeshivot* discourage the pursuit of communal responsibilities no less than the choice of the rabbinate as a career, with the result that the Jewishly best educated laymen gravitate to passivity in little *shtibls* rather than to activity, influence, and leadership in important congregations and in the wider community. Communally speaking, then, most *Yeshivah* products are lost, both as rabbis and as lay leaders.

Finally, all these departures from past traditions have had an impact on the latter day direction of halakhic trends, too. Apart from the variations in the treatment of problems submitted to rabbinic judgment, as detailed by Rabbi Katzenelenbogen, the nature of the problems dealt with has also been affected. Responsa by *Yeshivah* deans or scholars not practising as rabbis are mainly of a personal, and often academic, character. They reflect largely the confined life and concerns of students who, while close to their teachers, are often remote from the perplexities troubling the wider community. This accounts for the relative sparsity of responsa devoted to the great social, moral, intellectual and even political challenges of our cataclysmic times. Active rabbis, exposed to all the pressures and questionings of the society in which they live, are bound to cover a much broader and far more practical range of questions in their responsa. Moreover, judgments rendered in the isolation of *Yeshivot* can afford to be rigid, if not dogmatic, in their reasoning. Rabbis, on the other hand, must endeavor to vindicate their decisions before public opinion. They must also take into account the ramifications and consequences of their rulings on relations and attitudes within the larger community. They must have their feet planted firmly on earth even if their heads reach to heaven in arriving at a verdict on problems posed to them.

The Torah, after all, is "a tree of life". It can grow and flourish only in a vibrant environment which is exposed to the manifold elements and stresses making up the reality of life and its problems. It is time to reinvigorate the rabbinate by inducing the finest *Yeshivah* scholars to train and practice as rabbis, and to charge them with rebuilding congregations as the central axis around which public Jewish life should revolve.

II

Emboldened by the encouraging response from many readers to our earlier observations under this heading, we venture now to expand on this theme and to offer some constructive solutions to the problems posed. The principal criticisms leveled at the existing tendencies in the preceding review may be summarized by the following five points:

1. The denigration and usurpation of the role of practising rabbis by *yeshivah* deans had virtually eliminated the traditional place and functions of the rabbinate in the spiritual government of the religious community, resulting in the disappearance of the public Torah image in the community at large.

2. The transfer of rabbinic jurisdiction from communal rabbis to academic scholars confined to *yeshivot* had severely limited the scope of contemporary Halakhah and caused substantial deviations from the traditional pattern in the methods used to determine Jewish law.

3. These unprecedented developments had led to the displacement by *yeshivot* of *kehillot* as the institutional center of gravity in Jewish religious life.

4. The *yeshivot's* discouragement of rabbinical careers was directly responsible for the spread of mediocrity in the rabbinate and the growing scarcity of candidates for leading rabbinical positions.

5. *Yeshivot*, by tending to stifle rather than to promote a sense of commitment to the wider community, had been equally unsuccessful in raising a community-minded laity, so that public Jewish life became increasingly drained of rabbinical and lay readers alike.

To reverse these baneful trends will require much courage and vision. But the foremost requisite is a willingness by all concerned to engage in a dispassionate debate, to tolerate genuine criticism and dissent, and to sweep away the cobwebs of conformity and stereotyped thinking to make room for honest search and bold correctives. The following observations and suggestions on the above five points are offered in this spirit:

1. The answer to the first challenge is obviously the restoration of rabbinic authority. "Jephtah in his generation is [vested with as much authority] as Samuel in his generation, to teach you that even the most unworthy person, *once he is appointed as a leader over a community*, is like the mightiest of the mighty" (*Rosh Hashanah* 25b). Rabbinical authority, our Sages averred, derives from *communal appointment*, not from mere wisdom or learning. As expressed so forcefully in the incident on fixing the date of *Yom Kippur* (*Rosh Hashanah*, 2:9), a Rabbi Joshua, however superior his scholarship, must submit to the rulings and decrees of a Rabbi Gamaliel as the practicing office-holder. There can be no substitute for, or challenge to, an official and legitimate incumbent of a rabbinical post.

A part of the problem may lie in the current use and abuse of the rabbinical title. *Semikhah* (rabbinical ordination) is traditionally the conferment of power and responsibility to *exercise* rabbinical jurisdiction, as emphasized in its wording *yoreh yoreh*—"he shall surely give rulings". It is the passport to an office, not some honorific title or degree. It is a charge to *practise* rabbinics, a "crown" of sovereignty that confers obligations as well as rights, as the wording of the document implies. It is definitely not just a certificate of academic proficiency. "Any scholar who has attained *hora'ah* (or *semikhah*) and does not exercise it withholds Torah and causes the public to stumble; regarding him it is written: 'A mighty host are all her slain' (Prov. 7:26)" (*Yoreh De'ah*, 242:14), just as a qualified physician who does not practise medicine is deemed guilty of bloodshed (*ib.*, 336:1).

Semikhah ought to be awarded only to candidates for the active rabbinate and not as a kind of higher yeshivah graduation diploma, and the *use* of the rabbinical title should be limited to practising rabbis. It was never meant as an incentive to Talmudical studies. "A man should not say, I will study so that people will call me 'Rabbi' " (*Nedarim* 62a). If any such incentives or rewards are really needed let us reintroduce the time-honoured titles of "*Morenu*" and "*He-chaver*" as a mark of distinction for scholarship and piety. Let outstanding masters be known by the affectionate "*Reb*" or the more eminent "*Hagaon*." Even many Talmudical savants were content to forego any rabbinical appellation, men like Hillel and Shamai, or Abaye, Rava and Samuel, amongst numerous others!

Businessmen, accountants, or insurance agents using the title of rabbi

without exercising it can hardly contribute to the public respect for the rabbinate, especially in our confused society. Historically and halakhically, a
rabbi is an administrator of Jewish law, a spiritual guide and a communal
leader. *Yeshivot*, as the custodians of Torah education, should be the first
to acknowledge the function of rabbis in this capacity, and not merely as
expedient fund-raising agents, if the Torah image and authority are to be
restored in Jewish life.

2. The effectiveness of rabbinical authority today largely depends on
public endorsement. For the first time in our history Judaism must be vindicated in a democratic age. Gone are the days when any *ex cathedra* pro-
nouncement or dogmatic ruling by a rabbi would automatically command
popular respect by virtue of his learning or standing. In the administration
of Jewish law, justice must not only be done, but be manifestly seen to be
done; as far as is possible, the logic of halakhic decisions must be demonstrated before the bar of public opinion to win acceptance. To translate this
essential ideal into practice, three elements are required: (a) relevance, (b)
sweet reasonableness, and (c) a measure of tolerance.

(a) *Halakhah* must be, and appear to be, a guide to human progress, not
a brake on it. All too often rabbinic judgments deal with religious problems
in the light of modern conditions, not with modern problems in the light of
religious conditions. Vast segments of our people are alienated from Torah
life because they believe that *Halakhah* creates problems instead of solving
them. This is bound to result from the emphasis in rabbinic rulings on subjects of little relevance to the average modern Jew rather than on the great
moral, social and intellectual challenges troubling our age. To make Judaism meaningful and true to its primary purpose, halakhic guides must address
themselves increasingly to defining the contribution of Jewish thought and
teachings to such areas of current concern as birth-control, juvenile delinquency, the use of leisure, the economics of automation, Jewish-Christian
relations, and the place of religion in public life. *Halakhah* cannot become a
popular guide to life unless it embraces all life.

(b) In making halakhic decisions, the reasons given are as important as
the conclusions. Even Moses was charged "to trouble himself in making
everyone comprehend the reasons" for his teachings (Rashi, Ex. 21:1), and
the *Shulchan Arukh* forbids rabbis to issue permissive rulings "which astound
the public" because they are unintelligible (*Yoreh De'ah*, 242:10). Today
more than ever before, rabbis must interpret or explain as well as adjudicate
the law if they are to enjoy the fealty of the public. They must serve both as
priests "to teach God's judgments to Jacob and His Torah to Israel" (Deut.
33:10) and as heirs to the Prophets (*B. Batra* 12a) in presenting the moral
and universal aspirations of Jewish existence.

(c) The third requisite, tolerance, is equally indispensable for the restoration of rabbinical authority. Differences of opinion are the dynamics of Jewish
learning and practice. They have always fertilized the very soil of the Torah
"tree of life." The cause of Torah Judaism is hindered rather than helped by
the present tendency towards ever more rigid uniformity, turning stringency
into a fetish and branding all dissent as heresy. The violent agitation against
Rabbi Mosheh Feinstein's ruling on artificial insemination and against the

Manhattan *Eruv*, though both based on unimpeachable authorities, are cases in point drawn from recent experience in New York.

The absence of all these three desiderata is inherent in the exercise of rabbinical jurisdiction by yeshivah deans who are remote from the concerns of contemporary society, shielded from the pressures of public opinion, and conditioned by the unquestioning loyalty of their yeshivah students. Practising rabbis, on the other hand, are necessarily exposed to the broader challenges of real life, required to win consent as well as obedience, and compelled to explore legitimate concessions or to tolerate dissent.

3. Rabbinical offices cannot be filled with incumbents, adequate in quality and in quantity, without training them. A *lamdan* (Talmudical scholar), however learned, is not necessarily a rabbi and may be a far cry from it. To meet the exacting and manifold tasks of rabbinic leadership, especially in our trying times, numerous skills are required in addition to scholarship. The spiritual leadership of a congregation calls for a high degree of proficiency in the presentation of Jewish thought, in the exploitation of public and personal relations for religious ends, in the impressive conduct of religious services and functions, in communal vision and diplomacy, in educational expertise, in some literary finesse, and above all in competently grappling with the intellectual challenges of our age. The exercise of purely rabbinical jurisdiction as a *moreh hora'ah* (an administrator of Halakhah), too, requires far more than mere competence in a few Talmudic tractates and some one hundred chapters of *Yoreh De'ah* dealing with ritual slaughter and *kashrut*, as presently constituting the *semikhah* program. To pass halakhic judgments a rabbi must be at home in all parts of the *Shulchan Arukh*, especially the *Orach Chayyim* and *Even Ha-Ezer*, familiar with the responsa literature and its methods, and proficient in the *shikkul ha-da'at* (weighing of opinions) indispensable for all rabbinic rulings. These skills can be acquired only by years of training and experience (*shimmush*), and through the constant consultation of writings and masters reflecting this experience.

The requirements for rabbinic ordination, therefore, should be amended to include this training, both in theory and in practice. To authorize rabbis to practise rabbinics and to guide congregations by virtue of their Talmudic learning only is as irresponsible as to qualify physicians to treat patients and to administer hospitals merely on the basis of some academic studies in the principles of medical science and without any clinical or hospital experience. *Yeshivot* devoted to theoretical studies in Talmud and parts of *Yoreh De'ah* can no more turn out competent rabbis without the help of rabbinical seminaries than medical schools and textbooks can produce qualified doctors without hospitals.

The rabbinate today demands highly specialized professional skills to be an effective agency of spiritual leadership and halakhic jurisdiction. To ensure an adequate supply of high calibre rabbis professional schools are no less essential than for the training of any other professionals. The *yeshivot* can continue to ignore this need only at the cost of letting countless more spiritual "patients" die for lack of competent healers. The appalling toll of defections from Judaism, of religious casualties, will hardly abate unless rabbinical functions are restored to rabbis equipped to respond to the questions and questionings of our times—men able not only "to learn and to teach" but also "to guard and to act".

4. *Yeshivot* are meant to make Jews, *kehillot* (congregations) to preserve them; the former prepare for Jewish life, the latter act it out. When Moses communicated the main principles of Jewish living to the Children of Israel, he assembled them in "congregations," not in *yeshivot* (Ex. 35:1; Lev. 19:2, and Rashi). For countless centuries congregations led by rabbis have always been the backbone of organized Jewish life. Under their umbrella all other facets of communal activity grew up and operated: education, rabbinical courts (*batei din*), *mikvaot* and welfare services. Today, with the disappearance of *kehillot* as the principal bulwark of Jewish life and their replacement by *yeshivot*, many of these communal amenities are largely either non-existent (such as communal *batei din*), or in unreliable private hands (such as *kashruf* and *shechitah*), or under non-religious control (such as the social services of the federations, etc.), and the religious community is fragmented and impotent in guiding the destinies of our people.

This situation will not be ameliorated until the *yeshivot* orientate their students towards a sense of communal responsibility, as expressed, in the first instance, by active membership in established congregations. So long as our most valuable human resources are absorbed and nullified by communally ineffective *shtibels*, which neither demand nor offer any contribution to the leadership and life of the wider community, the most vital potential for building up the organism of Jewish religious life is frittered away, and the congregations that do exist are religiously emaciated for want of members who are intensely committed and exemplary in their learning and conduct. The allegedly low standards of observance and religious fervor in larger synagogues are no excuse for defying Hillel's maxim, "Do not separate yourself from the congregation" and for surrendering our public institutions to the rule of ignorance and apathy. On the contrary, "where there are no men, you endeavor to be the man!" The decline of our congregations calls for mobilizing the support of our *yeshivot*, not for their withdrawal and indifference. The dearth of Torah-committed members in our major Orthodox synagogues does not excuse the *yeshivot*—it indicts them.

5. The Torah tradition, as "a tree of life to them that strengthen it", has always given equal recognition to the scholar and to the supporter of scholarship, to Issachar and to Zevulun, who shared the rewards and the responsibilities for Jewish learning in identical parts. Hence, it was considered no less important to raise Zevuluns, dedicated to the support of Torah learning and living, than to produce Issachars, devoted to the mastery of Torah studies.

Today this essential balance in Jewish life is being dangerously upset. The *yeshivot*, by their monolithic program aiming at the accomplished *lamdan* as their sole ideal, seek to fulfill one requirement whilst ignoring the other. As the main custodians of public Jewish education, *yeshivot* will have to be more diversified in their curriculum and objectives to meet all our needs. The graduation of a potential Zevulun—a successful and devout businessman or professional—should be as urgent and precious a task as raising a profoundly learned Issachar.

To this end, *yeshivot* (at least the larger ones) should have a dual program of Jewish studies: one, stressing intensive learning designed to train competent scholars, rabbis and teachers, and the other, with an academically more limited scope, aimed at producing dedicated and knowledgeable *ba'alei battim*, distinguished by their piety and public-spiritedness rather than their scholarship. These latter products will eventually swell the ranks of an enlightened and loyal laity from which our lay leaders and Torah supporters are recruited.

Not every *yeshivah* student is fit or willing to be fashioned into a *lamdan*. By focusing the entire educational system on the few who are intellectually and otherwise endowed for Talmudic excellence, the *yeshivot* neglect all others and they are often lost to traditional Judaism later in life. With proper modifications in *yeshivah* policies, aims and methods, this large group could be turned into an element no less vital for the preservation of the Torah community than the most erudite scholars. It is to this group of deeply committed "plebeians," at present completely ignored in the *yeshivah* "world", that we must look for providing our scholars with followers and financial support and for replenishing the thinning ranks of our lay leaders and communal workers. Without Zevuluns, Issachars will eventually disappear, too, and it is up to the institutions of Jewish education to raise the former as well as the latter if creative Jewish living is to be perpetuated, and if the Jewish people is to recover its national purpose as a religious *community*.

Chapter Nine

MEDICAL ETHICS

THE JEWISH CONTRIBUTION TO MEDICAL ETHICS

This is more than an academic exercise in historical research. It is also an attempt to regain for the Jewish people its role and its reputation as moral pioneers and to correct the critical imbalance in the popular image of the Jew. In the eyes of a brutal world we are caricatured today as the people of the sword, not of the book, and of conquest, not of compassion. Embattled Israel's continued exposure to the threat of extinction may demand martial qualities as the price for security. But these sad realities summon our people all the more urgently to cultivate and demonstrate the classic Jewish character of human sensitivity and spiritual nobility, as a people historically committed, above all else, to the advancement of the moral order and the sanctification of life.

In medical ethics converge two of the Jewish people's most notable contributions to the progress of humanity: medicine and ethics. From the beginning, our people have shown a special concern with the healing art. The Bible includes in its religious legislation some revolutionary concepts of preventive medicine and public health. In the Talmud we find, among the numerous medical references almost 2,000 years ago, the earliest mention of such innovations as artificial limbs, some form of artificial insemination, oral contraceptives and Caesarian operations on living mothers. Many authors of the Talmud practised medicine. They were succeeded by what became, in the Middle Ages, the common phenomenon of the rabbi-physician. Indeed, it is estimated that over one-half of the best-known rabbinical scholars and authors in medieval times were physicians by occupation. These historical antecedents no doubt contributed significantly to the extraordinary predilection among Jews in modern times for a medical career. Only an attitude conditioned by centuries of nurture could have produced such a disproportionate preoccupation with medicine as enabled Jews to receive 20% of all Nobel prizes for medicine—a proportion more than 40 times the ratio of Jews in the world! Likewise most leading medical historians were Jews; one recalls names like Neuburger, Castiglioni, Singer and, in Israel, Leibowitz and Muntner.

Paramount throughout this long and highly creative association between

Paper read at the 8th World Congress of the Israel Medical Association in Tel Aviv on 19 May 1970.

Judaism and medicine has been the emphasis on ethics as their common denominator. Building materials for the imposing edifice of Jewish medical ethics came from all strata of our religious literature, while the architects were legal experts who, as we have noted, often combined rabbinical and medical experience. The Bible provided the foundations: the sanctity and dignity of human life, the duty to preserve health, an uncompromising opposition to superstition and irrational cures, including faith-healing, a rigid code of sexual morality, and many basic definitions on moral imperatives in medical practice, including the rights of the dead. By the way, these rights, as defined in Deutoronomy, are specifically conferred on executed criminals, and I need hardly stress how significantly this provision alone contrasts with all the callousness of other legislations, ancient and modern, which treat the bodies of such criminals and of so-called "unclaimed persons" (also specially protected by Jewish law as "*met mitzvah*") as *res nullius* and deny them the claim to dignified burial. The impact of the biblical tradition on the development of medical ethics in Western Society may be understood when it is contrasted with the Code of Hammurabi and other ancient legislations which provided, for instance, for the amputation of a doctor's arm if he proved unsuccessful in an operation on his patient.

On these biblical foundations the Talmud established the legal framework in virtually all fields of medical ethics, setting forth the main principles on such problems as abortion, euthanasia, contraception, sterilisation, malpractice claims, etc. The Talmud, followed by the codes, even enacted certain eugenic laws against marriages suspected to result in physically or morally diseased children. Anyone who has read the famous Oath of Asaph Harofe or the medical writings of other early Jewish notables in the history of medicine will recognise at once how profoundly the spirit of the Bible and the Talmud suffused their ethical outlook. Little wonder that there never existed a Jewish form of the Hippocratic Oath, though there were Christian and Mohammedan as well as pagan versions of it. Jews simply fell back on their own ethical heritage. And it was left to the voluminous rabbinical responsa, issued in increasing profusion over the past 1,000 years, to interpret and apply these principles in the light of contemporary conditions and the advance of medical knowledge and techniques. There are now being published annually, notably in Israel, hundreds of such rabbinical responsa or verdicts—ranging over the entire gamut of ethical problems in medicine, from transplants to artificial insemination, and from experimentation on humans or animals to autopsies. The responsa serve as case-law in the evolution of modern Jewish law. As a consensus of opinion gradually emerges from the many often conflicting judgements given, this is recognised as a valid precedent and embodied in the accepted corpus of rabbinic law.

Let me give you just one example to illustrate this process in rough outline. The Bible does not specifically deal with either criminal or therapeutic abortion. But in legislating on the liability for assaulting a pregnant mother and causing a miscarriage, the text in the Book of Exodus (21:22) indicates that the destruction of an unborn child is not culpable as murder, and that the foetus does not, therefore, enjoy the same absolute title to life as an existing human being. The Talmud takes this an important step further by ruling in favour of an embryotomy where a difficult delivery otherwise threatens the mother's life. In any mortal conflict between mother and child the ruling insists that her life enjoys priority, if necessary at the deliberate expense of the child, provided its head or the greater part of its body had not yet emerged from the birth-canal. Judaism, therefore, in contrast to Catholic teaching, would regard it as a grave offence against the sanctity of life to allow a mother to perish in order to save her unborn child.

This and some other talmudic principles are then used in the numerous rabbinical responsa of the past few centuries, and especially of recent times, to provide judgements in more complicated circumstances, for instance, in cases of rape or incest, or of suspected deformities in the child resulting from the effects of rubella or drugs like thalidomide during early pregnancy. Often differences of opinion still remain unresolved. For example, while Rabbi Waldenberg of the Israel Chief Rabbinate, a specialist on medicine in the Halacha, is inclined to permit the abortion of an embryo in the earliest stage of gestation if the mother contracted German measles, Chief Rabbi Unterman is adamantly opposed to the destruction of any potential human life unless the mother's life is in jeopardy. But virtually all responsa recognise only a strictly medical motivation for abortion, and they would not sanction the termination of a pregnancy unless there is some grave physical, or even psychiatric, hazard to the mother's life, however remote, provided every such capital judgement is most scrupulously considered on the strength of the best available medical evidence and in consultation with competent moral experts.

I chose the example of abortion because it is acutely relevant to Israel today. It is estimated that the number of abortions in Israel may now reach 40,000 a year, a staggering figure confirmed to me by sources within the Israel Medical Association—a figure probably more than half the total number performed under the new permissive laws in Britain with twenty times the population of Israel! This means that since the establishment of the Jewish State the better part of one million potential Sabras may have been smothered in their mothers' wombs, making a mockery of the vast resources, energies and propaganda efforts spent on inducing but a fraction of that number to go on Aliyah from the Western world in response to Israel's grave population needs.

To the catastrophic rate of non-therapeutic abortions—tolerated even in Israel's most reputable hospitals—must be added the disproportionately low Jewish birth rate throughout the world, and especially in Israel where in 1967, according to the latest figures of the Central Bureau of Statistics I have seen, the Jewish rate of 2·5% in the Kibbutzim and only 1·3% in a city like Tel Aviv compares with a non-Jewish birth-rate inside Israel of nearly 5%. Clearly the defiance of Jewish medical ethics, which restricts contraception as well as abortion to sound medical indications may well present a far greater peril to Jewish survival than the threat of aggression from outside or terror from within. It is surely ironic that, while many nations, and indeed humanity at large, are haunted by the terrifying spectre of population explosion, the Jewish people today faces the problems of the "vanishing Jew" because of our refusal to be guided by the ethics of our own faith.

This indictment of the present generation is all the greater when it is remembered that no Jew in the past ever worried about survival. In the Middle Ages the total number of Jews scarcely ever exceeded one million; yet they never doubted that they would survive despite their constant exposure to slaughter, exile and economic oppression, whilst today's 13,000,000 Jews, most of them living in unprecedented freedom and affluence, for the first time in our history call the continuity of Jewish life into question.

In more strictly professional terms Jewish medical ethics is also often at variance from the norms developed in secular law and common practice. To take a classic example, if one sees a two-year-old child drowning in a foot of water, neither a doctor nor any other passer-by is under an obligation to help the child, following the letter of the law. In Jewish law such conduct violates the biblical precept: "You shall not stand upon your neighbour's blood." Hence, the *Shulchan Arukh* rules that to engage in medicine is a *mitzvah*, a religious ideal, and any doctor who refuses to attend to those in need is guilty of bloodshed, just as a qualified rabbi who fails to practise his vocation is held responsible for the spiritual victims slain by his default. Worse still—dare I mention this before this audience?—the *Shulchan Aruch* debars physicians, engaged as they are in the fulfilment of a religious duty, from receiving payment for their skills, just as rabbis were expected to give their religious services free—a practice commonly observed until the rabbinate became professionalised in fairly recent centuries. But you may derive some relief—and profit—from the omission of this rule about physicians in the code of Maimonides who was, of course, himself making a living from medicine because he refused to be paid for his rabbinical work. Physicians and rabbis are also treated alike in respect of the liability for damages caused by negligence or errors of judgement.

In a brief historical survey of such wide-sweeping dimensions in time and subject-matter, I am forced to limit my references to some more modern issues to the barest outline of the principal conclusions. Thus on euthanasia, for instance, any deliberate act to hasten death, whether with or without the patient's consent, is incompatible with the Jewish understanding of the sanctity of life. Judaism regards every human life as being of infinite value. Infinity, by definition, is indivisible, so that any fraction of life, whether ten years or a minute, whether healthy, crippled, or even unconscious, remains equally infinite in value. By attacking the ebbing life of a terminal patient because it is deemed worthless, we would rob all human beings of their absolute claim to life, making it merely relative to their expectancy of life, or their state of health, or their usefulness to society, or to any other arbitrary criterion, and no two human beings would be equal in value. For their worth, being reduced to a finite scale, would depend on any variety of physical or social means tests. Consequently, Jewish law brands direct euthanasia as murder. But under certain carefully defined conditions, it might not require the physician to prolong the agony by artificial or "heroic" methods, permitting him to withdraw such treatment in completely hopeless cases of lingering life. But on the precise verdict in these cases there is still some debate in current rabbinical writings.

And just as infinity cannot be reduced by division, making half a life any less valuable than a full life, so cannot infinity be increased by multi-plication, making a million lives any more precious than one life. We would therefore never be justified in sacrificing or deliberately risking a single life, however many others may thereby be saved, and it is wrong to subject people, even with their informed consent, to possibly hazardous medical experiments, unless the subjects themselves might be helped in a gamble to save their lives in the absence of any tried cures.

Similar considerations apply to the present state of transplant surgery. While Jewish law raises no objection to corneal grafts, with certain safe-guards, nor indeed to any organic transplants in principle, it views with grave concern the indecent haste with which doctors and hospitals have competed in these premature operations at the cost of scores of lives and of the false hopes raised and dashed in thousands of sufferers. Jewish law insists firstly that no vital organ be removed from a donor until death is definitely established by the complete cessation of all spontaneous life functions and not merely by what is termed "clinical death", such as irre-versible brain damage, and secondly that such operations must not be con-tinued unless they have passed the purely experimental stage and offer recipients a reasonably hopeful prognosis.

Let me appropriately end this sketchy encounter with the problems of life and death, ranging from the womb to the tomb, with a few general remarks on the tragic and vexing problem of post-mortems. Tragic, because it has so disastrously bedevilled medico-rabbinical and secular-religious relations, having aroused such passionate bitterness in both camps; and vexing, because there is no easy solution in sight. Having dealt extensively with this issue, particularly while in New York serving as chairman of a joint commission of rabbis and physicians to advise the Jewish hospitals there (which issued the *Jewish Hospital Compendium*—the only Jewish guide of its kind ever published), I know that the situation here is sadly exacer-bated by excessive zeal and recrimination on all sides and by the refusal of either side to appreciate the genuine concerns of the other. There are rabbis who understand as little about the indispensable role of some autopsies in promoting the highest medical standards as there are doctors who do not understand the sincere agony of rabbis in trying to protect the rights of those who can no longer fend for themselves as dictated by their religious convic-tions. The present tensions, suspicions and abuses will not be eliminated until the medical profession renounces the anomaly making Israel, of all places, about the only civilised country in the world not to require family consent, and until the rabbinical authorities redefine halachic rules permitting autopsies in special cases for life-saving needs in accordance with present-day conditions. But above all the situation demands the restoration of con-fidence between rabbis and physicians, so that by joint consultations, built on mutual trust and goodwill, a formula can be devised to ensure health for the living, respect for the dead, and compassionate sympathy for the bereaved.

In our technological age, medicine, like science generally, today threatens to turn *homo sapiens* into *homo mechanicus*, replacing his incomparable nature and dignity with a soulless machine. In our push-button world

scientists, technicians and public-relations experts have usurped philosophers, thinkers and men of the spirit in determining the patterns of human
behaviour and the objectives of man's destiny. In this new dispensation, the
physician, too, is wielding ever greater power. Human life is now at his
bidding. He can generate it out of test-tubes and terminate it out of syringes.
He can regulate the size of families by contraceptive advice and foeticidal
operations, and he can sway emotional responses by drugs and psychiatric
treatment. Together with other scientists he will increasingly control human
life, but who will control the controllers?

"Genetic engineering" may soon surrender the very building blocks of
life itself to the arbitrary whims of technical experts. Only recently Dr.
James Shapiro, a leading researcher at Havard University, said in a widely
publicised statement: "The prospect is that sience will learn how to create
a number of identical human beings exactly as you would breed prize cattle,"
or, I might add, as you manufacture cars on assembly lines. This frightening
statement precisely epitomises the challenge to medical ethics: In our blind
march to mechanical perfection, shall we reduce man to prize cattle, or to
mass-produced machines? New medical skills and insights, such as spare-
part surgery and genetic research, may open up a wonderful chapter in the
history of healing. But without strict moral controls and ethical guide-lines,
it may also herald irretrievable disaster through man's encroachment upon
nature's preserves and the danger of assessing human beings by their value
as tool-parts or sperm-donors or living incubators or guinea pigs when they
are alive, and as medical textbooks or suppliers of "erzatz" organs when
they are dead.

No people and no country should be expected more confidently to meet
this historic challenge than Israel; for none has had a nobler record in moral
engineering and ethical research. I therefore conclude with a plea and a
proposal. Medical schools throughout the world have for long provided
some instruction in medical ethics. I have myself given courses in medical
ethics to medical students at Yale University and lectured at numerous other
medical schools. It is surely anomalous that in Israel, with the broad ethical
overlay to its social and religious structure, no such programme has been
incorporated in its three medical schools. It is time an academic chair in
medical ethics be established, preferably for obvious reasons under the
auspices of a non-university academic body, such as the Israel Academy of
Arts and Sciences or the Scientific Council of the Israel Medical Association.
Until a permanent staff can be engaged, visiting lecturers might be invited to
conduct concise courses for students at each of the three medical schools.
Such lecturers must of course be carefully chosen to combine the necessary
academic qualifications with a definite positive commitment to the values
they seek to impart. The programme should also include original research
on historical and contemporary aspects of medical ethics, as well as the
setting up of inter-disciplinary teams of medical, rabbinical, legal and social
experts to advise on coping with complex problems like transplants, abortion
and autopsies, through both legislation and education.

One thousand nine hundred years ago our people, sustaining blows which
would have proved fatal with any other nation, determined to prove that where

there is life there is hope, preferring to live in abject misery and suffering rather than to chose the euthanasia of a heroic death with glory which they could have had for the asking. Because of that choice, we are here today, 1,900 years later, in Reunited Jerusalem, with our national health restored after 1,900 years of agony. May we now help a stricken humanity likewise to choose a life sustained by the supremacy of the spirit over the body, of ethics over mechanics, so that mankind may be restored to universal health.

I pray that this Congress, inspired by the immense services of Jews and Judaism to medical progress, will help to re-establish the time-hallowed partnership between medicine and Judaism to enable Israel to fulfil its historic mission as a beacon of moral leadership and to enable man to realise his destiny as a unique creation in the image of his Creator.

POPULATION EXPLOSION
The Jewish Attitude to Birth Control

Birth-control certainly ranks among the most controversial and the most explosive subjects dividing human opinion today. It is by far the most delicate, the most far-reaching and the most ramified moral issue now facing mankind. Unlike other widely debated modern problems, such as the morality of heart transplants which, also of a highly complex moral nature, nevertheless affect comparatively but a handful of people, our subject directly and immediately affects virtually every human being on the globe, and it will determine the question of "to be or not to be", in a very literal sense, for countless millions of humans yet unborn.

Some prophets of doom, indeed, believe that man's prolific natural increase is presenting an even more immediate and devastating danger to human survival than the external threat of atomic warfare or the internal menace of crime and violence reducing our cities to ruins.

At the same time, the mass production and the easy availability of contraceptives must drastically change our entire moral behaviour, our morals and consequently the social order as we have known it. The popularity of contraceptives has quite clearly removed the most powerful deterrent to promiscuity. On a universal scale, I would imagine, the human race probably never before faced a moral problem of such magnitude and of such dimensions, both in terms of quantity—of the number of people affected, and in terms of quality—of the degree to which they are affected. It is at once the most intimate and personal of all the moral issues concerning us today, and at the same time of far greater public consequence than any other single problem in our problem-ridden world. The outcome of the present debate, then, will have a crucial bearing not only on the demographic future of the human race, but also on its ideals, its outlook, its mode of life.

BIRTH-CONTROL IN JEWISH LAW

I could describe the halachic attitude to birth-control in relatively very simple terms. By now many hundreds of Rabbinic responsa have been written on the subject. There is scarcely a responsa work published in the last 200

Jewish Marriage Education Council Annual Lecture delivered in London on 28 October 1968.

years or so that does not deal, often at very great length, with the problem of contraception. Virtually all these responsa recognise only the medical motivation as a legitimate ground for the practice of birth-control. In fact, the concensus of Rabbinic opinion permits, or possibly even demands, certain contraceptive precautions if indicated by grave hazards that may otherwise imperil the mother, or even the child that she carries or nurses.[1] Jewish law would never, under any circumstances, advocate or even sanction permanent abstinence within marriage as a solution to the problem of family planning. Under some conditions it would rather counsel divorce than a state in which the marriage cannot be fulfilled—in the sense of the marital dues being duly paid by husband and wife towards each other at regular intervals.

The Rabbinic attitude, then, is clearly far less rigid than the Catholic view as recently reiterated so prominently, a view which will under no circumstances, not even for the most urgent medical considerations, permit any artificial impediment to operate for the prevention of the natural consequences of marital relations. On the other hand, the Jewish attitude is clearly more restrictive than that of most Protestant denominations which leave the matter, as they put it, to be determined by the individual conscience or, if we could express it a little more freely, which abdicate their role as religious guides to morals in this particular issue.

However, their reasoning, whether stringent or lenient, is fundamentally different from the Jewish attitude. Judaism does not recognise the operation, or indeed existence, of any natural law as an arbiter of right and wrong. We do not believe that the determination of moral values is enshrined in any of the laws of nature. In the Jewish view, the only sure guide to the definition of right and wrong in a moral sense is the revealed Law of God. The Jewish attitude to birth-control represents but a ramification of the very first of the 613 commandments in the Torah defining the Jewish way of life—the commandment to "be fruitful and multiply" with which the very emergence of man on the arena of history's record opens. The Jewish rulings on contraception, therefore, derive their form and authority neither from the whims of the human conscience nor from the laws of nature, but simply from the positive Divinely ordained obligation to propagate the race.

ORAL CONTRACEPTIVES IN JEWISH SOURCES

But the severe halachic ban on contraceptives, except for grave medical reasons, extends primarily to mechanical or chemical devices. Oral contraceptives are treated far more permissively in Jewish law. In some very fascinating passages in the Talmud, references to oral contraceptives were being made nearly 2,000 years ago, defining the Jewish attitude at least in principle. The Talmud, by far the first literary work in a legal context to mention an oral contraceptive, refers to a *kos shel ikrin*, commonly translated as a "cup of roots" or a "potion of sterility". Evidently, if taken in certain dosages, this produced immunity to conception both in the male and in the female. The attitude of the Talmud towards the use of this oral contraceptive is exceedingly lenient, and is still ruled to be so in the *Shulchan Arukh* which also refers to this "potion of roots" or "potion of sterility" in a very liberal fashion.[2]

However, I am sure that while this drink was clearly believed to be effective in producing either temporary or even permanent sterility, nevertheless, judging by the context, it was certainly something that was neither mass-produced nor absolutely sure in its efficacy. Therefore, notwithstanding the identification of the modern pill with the talmudic potion, in a technical sense, the social and moral ramifications of the contraceptive pill as used today would of course be vastly different from the *kos shel ikrin* mentioned as a very infrequently used and hardly reliable agent in the Talmudic sources.

In concluding this very cursory survey of the principal rulings of Jewish law, it should be stated that under no circumstances would the Halakhah ever permit the employment of any contraceptive device on the part of the male, nor would it ever tolerate the recourse to contraceptives by unmarried people. Whatever our attitude may be to birth-control within marriage to ensure the regularisation of births, we would never agree to contraceptives of any kind being made available to people outside marriage, for obvious reasons.

As against these stringencies, however, there are certain indications to warrant the view that the notion of the spacing of children, partly even for social or economic reasons, was not entirely foreign in early Rabbinic literature. For instance, there is a source which suggests that the famous ban on polygamous marriages proclaimed by Rabbi Gershom around the year 1000 C.E. was motivated by the desire to reduce the burdens of large families.[3] A later authority makes the interesting suggestion that the biblical insistence on a prolonged period of impurity following childbirth (during which physical intimacies between husband and wife are forbidden), and the subsequent re-imposition of this restriction in the *Shulchan Arukh* according to some opinions,[4] may also have been designed to prevent too close an interval between the birth of one child and that of another; for the ban amounted roughly to a three months' interdiction of any conjugal relationship following each childbirth.[5] Indeed, there was a general reluctance already in the Talmud to encourage any new pregnancy within two years of the preceding birth.[6] All these references may have some considerable bearing on the subject of birth-control in the Halakhah.[7]

CAUSES FOR DECLINE OF JEWISH BIRTH-RATE

In any event, everyone will be ready to concede that the spectacular reduction of the Jewish birth-rate today is not due primarily to medical factors. No one will suggest that health standards have declined so disastrously within the past two or three generations that, while our grandmothers and great-grandmothers managed quite well to survive setting four, five, six or more children into the world, the medical stamina of our mothers has now suddenly become so low that more than two or three births would present a grave health hazard.

If it is not, then, the medical consideration that accounts for our declining birth-rate, what else is it? And here, of course, we come to the core of our subject. The most frequently mentioned motivation in this connection is the fear of a population explosion, a factor very impressively brought home to anyone travelling in parts of the world where widespread starvation demonstrates this all too tragically. So it is the population explosion, then, which not only warrants but demands a reduction in our birth-rate.

It would be idle to deny that the problem of population explosion is a very real and indeed a very explosive problem. One need not be a great statistician to work out almost with mathematical precision the date of Doomsday when there will be standing-room only for our descendants in this world, if—and this is a big if—the present rates of human procreation will be maintained. At the present time the increase in the human population is so tremendous— with the decrease in the mortality rate owing to the advances in medicine not having been matched by a similar decrease in the birth-rate—that it is bound ultimately to trigger the catastrophe dramatised by the very suggestive term "population explosion".

OVER-POPULATION AND UNDER-POPULATION

On the other hand, it would be equally false to ignore the fact that this is a problem which is geographically strictly limited. Looking at the global situation, we must admit that the problem has a long way to go yet before it even begins to become universally acute. Let me here mention only a few facts that ought to be borne in mind to obtain some objective perspective on what has become, largely through very determined propaganda campaigns, a rather distorted picture, with very deep prejudices one way or the other.

I am not a demographer, and I do not propose to weary you with a lot of detailed facts and figures on the growth of food production relative to the growth of the human population. But just a few facts are, I think, pertinent. It is estimated, for instance, that so far only one fourth of the arable world is being cultivated. In other words, with all our modern ingenuity and with all the efforts made to increase the production of food, so far we have managed to exploit only one quarter of the land that is fit for tillage. I need not add that there are still unlimited resources of food and other essentials for human civilisation in the oceans, resources which we have not yet even begun to tap. Maybe this is the significance of the verse which, after commanding us to "be fruitful and multiply", concludes: "and fill the earth *and conquer it*".[8] Only through the conquest of nature, only through mastering the earth and bringing forth its treasures, can we fulfill the first part of the verse, the precept of procreation.

Another aspect, too, deserves some attention if we are to see the problem in a realistic prespective. It is often argued that population pressures are a primary cause for international tensions, leading ultimately to wars. Therefore we should be concerned to reduce these pressures by lowering the birth-rate not only in order to be able to feed all the hungry mouths, but also to prevent the kind of proliferation that so easily escalates into wars. Now this too is, not invariably but largely, a fallacious argument. For all these uneasy post-war years since the conclusion of World War II the world has stood on the brink of an atomic explosion due to tensions, sometimes reaching almost breaking-point, primarily between two countries which both happen to be relatively empty countries. Russia and the United States are seriously underpopulated countries, so much so that, while Europe—not exactly rich with mineral resources—has a population density of about 140 people per square mile, the United States, a country with far richer resources, has much less than half that number per square mile. Take a single State like Wyoming. I have motored through Wyoming and seen the vast tracts of unexploited land. Wyoming is a State twice the size of England and with at least the same natural resources; yet it has a population equal to that of Newcastle-on-Tyne —without even including Gateshead! The population of one medium-sized Provincial city, or of a single London Borough, is there scattered over an area, and a rich area, twice the size of the whole of England! So, if the United States increased its population from the present 200,000,000 to a billion people, one would hardly know the difference. So much about the United States which, after all, is still a populated country. If you consider a country like Canada which is even bigger than the Continental United States, and has more resources, or a whole continent like Australia, both virtually empty lands crying out for immigrants, then you will appreciate how very far we still are from a population explosion on a universal scale.

WHAT MAKES PEOPLE EXPLODE

But my emphasis here is on another aspect. Do you know when the first population explosion occurred in human history? With Cain and Abel. There were only two people in the world, yet the world was not big enough for them. One was constantly stepping on the toes of the other, until eventually the tensions between these two people—who had the whole world to divide between themselves—became so great that one brother struck down the other in cold blood. There is a profoundly meaningful passage in the Talmud in which a husband, seeing his once happy marriage come to grief, said to his estranged wife: "So long as our love was strong, there was room enough for the two of us on the edge of a sword. Now that our love is no longer strong, a bed 60 cubits wide isn't big enough for us!"[9] Whether people explode depends not so much on the amount of territory they have. As everyone knows, one mother can look after ten children, and ten children cannot look after one mother. It depends on how they get on with one another. If there is no harmony among people, then Cain and Abel, two single people in the whole world, over-populate the world and there is bound to be an explosion. And if people do get on with one another, if they behave and live as brothers—saying: come in, I have plenty of room; come and share it with me—then, there is room enough "on the edge of a sword" for the people to find their peace.

Wars are caused, in the main, not by shortage of territory. Wars are caused by people who do not get on with one another, who do not share common ideals and who do not look upon each other as brothers belonging to one family. If mankind were to achieve its ultimate goal in the establishment of the brotherhood of man, if we felt as members of one human family, then we would go to the Chinese or to the Indians, and tell them: "Look, you haven't enough food for your teeming population; we have plenty of open spaces, come and live with us, we will be brothers."

JEWS AND THE POPULATION EXPLOSION

Let us now return to the Jewish context of our subject. For so far the Chinese and the Indians, who certainly face an exceedingly grave population explosion problem, have not yet approached me as a Rabbi and asked me questions on what their moral attitude ought to be. If they did come and challenge me on the Jewish response to their problem, I would find some answers for them. We have a very useful device known as *Pikuach Nefesh*. When human life is at stake, every law has to give way. So, if people are starving and human lives are in jeopardy, we find answers compatible with the overriding claims of life. Moreover, according to most rabbinic authorities, the *mitzvah* of *peru urevu*, the precept of procreation as we define it halachically, is altogether not incumbent on "the Sons of Noah", i.e. on non-Jews.[10] In the remainder of my remarks, therefore, I want to address myself to fellow-Jews, leaving the advice for others until they ask for it. Meanwhile, I will be quite content if Jews follow Jewish moral teachings in this sphere.

Now, any Jew who mentions birth-control and the population explosion in a Jewish context, requires not contraceptive treatment but psychiatric treatment. The problem we are facing today is not that of the "exploding Jew" but of the "vanishing Jew". We are threatened by exactly the reverse of the problem that so many other nations face. In fact, I have no doubt that the gravest threat to Jewish survival today both inside and outside Israel, lies in the alarming decline of Jewish birth-rate. Everywhere in the world, almost without exception, and certainly in all the developed countries, notably including Israel, Jews have a far lower birth-rate than the non-Jews living in the same society. According to recent statistics, censuses and studies conducted in countries as diverse as England, Sweden, Switzerland, Canada and the United States, our rate of natural increase is appreciably lower than that of the non-Jews in whose midst we live.[11] In Israel the situation is even more catastrophic. According to very recent official statistics just published in Israel, the Jewish birth-rate in 1967 varied between 2·5% in the kibbutzim and 1·3% in a city like Tel Aviv. This compares with an average birth-rate for the Arabs living inside Israel of nearly 5%![12] Once again, then, one requires no mathematician or demographer to show that the supreme threat to Jewish survival stems not from any marauding terrorists or any invading armies from outside, but from a simple process of attenuation from within.

Our problem is not only that the practice of birth-control is quite evidently more rampant among Jews than among any other groups of the general population. In addition to producing too few to maintain our numbers, we lose too many out of the few that we do produce—through drift, assimilation and intermarriage. These are the stark realities of our time, showing how real a fear the haunting spectre of the "vanishing Jew" has now become.

SURVIVAL OF THE FITTEST

The only saving grace, if any exists, may lie in the fact that today the only segment of our people virtually unaffected by this catastrophic decline in the birth-rate on the one hand and by the equally catastrophic defection rate on the other hand, is the most staunchly religious element. Only among the strictly Orthodox—whether in Brooklyn, or in Stamford Hill, or in the religious quarters of Israel—is the birth-rate many times as high, often effectively four or five times as high, as that among the remainder of our people. Out of profound religious convictions, these groups spurn the temptations of birth-control and assimilation alike, making them by far the fastest growing sector of our people today. Somehow, it seems, Providence has a way of ensuring the survival of the fittest, at least in a religious sense. Evidently, as throughout our history, something is at work here quite beyond ordinary, natural and rational factors to manipulate our future so as to ensure that religiously the most creative element certainly will not suffer from the scourge and blight of self-obliteration.

I am convinced that eventually the problem of the birth-rate will become so burning an issue of sheer physical survival for the Jewish people, notably inside Israel, that even the most rabid secularists will recognise that one cannot solve this problem except through the cultivation of a religious conscience; for no-one produces children merely for demographic reasons. We may, then, here find one of the key factors in a massive return to fundamental religious values in the maintenance of Jewish life and national existence.

WHY SO FEW JEWS BORN?

From these somewhat negative factors let me now turn to the main positive aspect of our subject. We have found that the decline in the Jewish birth-rate can certainly not be attributed to medical considerations. Equally, we have convined ourselves that the decline is not due to any fears of a population explosion among Jews. These factors do not account for Jews having reduced their birth-rate. What then does account for it? What explains the fact that today most Jewish families have one or two, at the most three children?

Let me try to suggest an answer, first homiletically in the form of a striking Midrash.[13] It tells us that, when Pharoah ordered all Jewish males to be drowned at birth, Amram reasoned it was futile to bring children into such a cruel world; therefore he decided to break up his marriage and to divorce his wife. But Amram's daughter Miriam, who had already been born, started remonstrating with her father, saying: "Father, you are worse than Pharoah; he condemns only the males, you condemn the males and females who will remain unborn. And Pharoah decrees death only in this world, you decree it also in the world-to-come." And, continues the Midrash, Amram was impressed by his daughter's argument, remarried Yochevet his wife—and they produced Moses! In other words, had the argument prevailed which originally caused Amram to divorce his wife, the world would have been deprived of Moses! Moseses are born neither by planning nor by accident. A Moses is born by an act of faith. That is how a Moses is born. And God knows how many Moseses, potential Moseses, were not born into the world because we prevented their birth. and how desperately we could do with a man born as an act of faith to become a leader and comforter of our stricken people today.

Yet this is not really the interpretation of the Midrash with which I am mainly concerned here. I am interested in another aspect of it. Why did Amram divorce his wife? Why did not he simply have recourse to some contraceptive methods? They knew very well what to do, already in the days of Amram. They even knew in the antediluvian days before Noah how to practise birth-control, and to have wives merely for marital enjoyment and not for the fulfilment of their human destiny.[14] So why did Amram not resort to some such preventive precautions and maintain his marriage intact? Evidently this did not occur to Amram. That possibility simply did not dawn on him. If he could not assume the obligations and the hardships, the heartaches and sacrifices of marriage, then he felt that he could not have the enjoyments, the benefits and the pleasures of marriage, either. To have an imbalance whereby one has rights and privileges without corresponding duties and obligations, that was something inconceivable to the parents of Moses.

That is precisely what our age wants. With all the security and all the comforts and all the conveniences that modern life can offer, and can offer in very rich measure compared to the way in which our ancestors had to live, we are unwilling to undertake any corresponding obligations towards future generations. We want the advantages of modern life, but not the responsibilities to pay for them. And that, in a nutshell, is the answer to the problem, even if it may be over-simplified. Perhaps crudely but none the less truthfully expressed, even if it may sound more facetious than it actually is, the alternative open to parents today is to choose between either a larger family or a larger car. For if you spend money on extra children, you have to save it somewhere else. Every child is a bother and a heavy expense. A choice has to be made. Quite clearly, you cannot burn both ends of the candle together. And in this choice, all too frequently the larger car or other luxuries win over the larger family.[15]

DOING WHAT IS "RIGHT IN ONE'S OWN EYES"

Let me now return to my starting-point the role of our conscience in these judgements. This challenge obviously confronts Jewish moral thinking just as much as that of other faiths which believe themselves to be the repository of moral truths. It is argued that decisions on birth-control ought to be left to the discretion of the individual conscience. Recently I have had a more public occasion[16] to enter into some aspects of the Jewish definition of conscience as an arbiter between right and wrong. I pointed out that in the Jewish view, the human conscience—fickle and infinitely diverse as are its judgements —is meant not to make moral laws but to enforce them.

But let me here merely ask: what is really meant by the suggestion to leave such decisions to the individual conscience? How does a person set about using his conscience in this matter? How do you consult the oracle of your conscience to obtain its verdict? What kind of considerations is the conscience to weigh in reaching a reliable conclusion? Every person is bound to be an interested party in the verdict on the size of his family. What criteria other than his self-interest can he use? How can his judgment be objective and morally sound if he is judge and plaintiff at the same time? How, therefore, can the individual conscience, called upon to make capital decisions of this magnitude, avoid the bias of convenience, expediency or other ulterior motives in arriving at the morally right conclusion? I have yet to hear an even remotely reasonable answer to these questions, whereby the individual conscience would turn out to be anything more than a glorified substitute for selfishness.

HOLINESS IN ACTION

According to our Jewish belief, it is especially in this supremely sacred area that the reality of God in our conscience is to be tested. I have entered here into what I may literally call the *Kodshei Kodashim*, the Holy of Holies of Jewish life, the inner sanctum of Jewish existence. Our sages tell us in a remarkable passage that the two *cherubim*, the two figures of gold that were placed into the Holy of Holies of the ancient Temple to guard the Holy Ark, visible only to the High Priest once a year, were formed as male and female in a conjugal embrace.[17] We believe that the highest sanctity in the human experience lies in man and woman becoming literally partners with God in the creation of life itself. Nothing ought to be more directly and immediately governed by God as our guide in life than this very area where the most consequential decisions are being made that any human being can ever be called upon to make, decisions which, as I said, determine whether a human life is to be or not to be.[18]

According to Jewish law, we place a Mezuza on the doors not only of our living-rooms, dining-rooms, kitchens and libraries, but most notably also of our bedrooms. The text inside the Mezuza speaks of love. It commands that, transcending any other love or human emotion, you shall love the Lord your God. It goes on to teach the supreme importance of religious education and its definition, telling us when and where the words of the Torah are to be spoken, heard and acted out. Not primarily in the synagogue, nor mainly while worshipping God in prayers. The purpose of Jewish education is to be fulfilled "when you sit in your home, and when you walk on the way, when you lie down and when you rise up". In public life in the street and in the intimacy of your private life at home, that is where you test the strength and sincerity of your Jewish convictions. Not in the synagogue when others watch us, but when we are all alone, shielded from the prying eyes of strangers and charged with making the most momentous decisions of our lives, that is when we are challenged to prove "whether the Lord is within us or not", whether we really recognise Him as our Master or merely as a rubber stamp to confirm the whims of our conscience.

This recognition will determine our people's spiritual and physical survival alike, ensuring that we will qualitatively "be fruitful" and quantitatively "multiply" to pass on and enrich the heritage of our forbears as a source of blessing to all the families of the earth.

NOTES

1. *Yevamot* 12b. This passage in the Talmud is the first and principal reference to the subject in the sources of Jewish law.
2. *Even Ha'ezer*, 5:12.
3. R. Meir Katzenellenbogen, responsa *MaHaRaM Padua*, no. 16; cited in *Otzar Haposkim, Even Ha'ezer*, vol. i, p. 15 (no. 61).
4. *Yoreh De'ah*, 194:1, gloss, following Lev. 12:2 and 5.
5. R. Jacob Reischer, responsa *Shevut Ya'akov*, part iii, no. 77; cited in *Darkei Teshuvah*, on *Yoreh De'ah, loc. cit.*
6. *Yevamot* 42a, followed by *Even Ha'ezer*, 13:11.
7. For a comparative discussion on the Jewish attitude to contraception, documented by numerous sources, see my *Journal of a Rabbi*, 1967, pp. 146f., 163 and 213–220; and David M. Feldman, *Birth Control in Jewish Law*, 1968. An extensive and up-to-date rabbinic treatise appears in R. Eliezer Waldenberg's responsa *Tzitz Eliezer*, 5727, vol. ix, pp. 208–225.
8. Gen. 1:28.
9. *Sanhedrin* 7a.
10. See *Mishneh Lemelekh*, on Maimonides, *Yad, Hil. Melakhim*, 10:7.
11. See my "The Cost of Jewish Survival", in *Judaism*, vol. xv., no. 4 (Fall 1966), p. 427.
12. *Statistical Abstract of Israel*, published by the Central Bureau of Statistics, Jerusalem, 1968.
13. *Sotah* 12a; see Rashi, on Ex. 2:1. Cf. Rashi, on Gen. 4:24.
14. See *Gen. Rab.*, 23:2 and 4; and Rashi, on Gen. 4:19 and 23; and 38:7.
15. This particular juxtaposition is by no means far-fetched or unrealistic. The *Statistical Abstract* (see note 12 above), after detailing the steep decline of the Jewish birth-rate in Israel, reports: "On the other hand, rising standards of living are reflected in the number of private cars. In 1962, 41 out of a thousand families had a private car, and last year the number was 135 cars per 1,000 families."
16. BBC New Year Broadcast, September 19, 1968; see pp. 157f. above.
17. *Yoma* 54a.
18. A leading American-Jewish sociologist, in a note on how best to guage Jewish religious commitment, writes significantly: "The observance of *mikveh* (periodically forbidding marital relations pending immersion in a ritual bath) . . . is the best single measure for determining who is a committed Orthodox Jew. To the uncommitted, it is inconceivable that so personal a matter should be subject to ritual regulation. To the committed, it is inconceivable that an aspect of life so important as marital relations should not be subject to halakhic regulation" (Charles S. Liebman, "Orthodoxy in American Jewish Life", in *American Jewish Year Book*, vol. lxvi, 1965, reprint, p. 72, note 65).

JEWISH VIEWS ON ABORTION

With the staggering rise in the rate of abortions and with the motives for such operations now including the fear of abnormal births as well as birth control considerations, abortion has become the most widely debated medico-moral subject. What was previously either a therapeutic measure for the safety of the mother or a plainly criminal act is now widely advocated as a means to prevent the birth of possibly defective children, to curb the sordid indignities and hazards imposed on women resorting to clandestine operators, to contain the population explosion, and simply to allow women the right to decide more freely whether or not they will bear children. Under the mounting pressure of these new factors, a crushing responsibility is sought by, and is often conferred upon, medical practitioners. Many of them claim that, within some broad general guidelines, the decisions whether or nor legally to terminate a pregnancy should be left to their judgment.

In the Jewish view, this position cannot be upheld. The judgment that is required here, while it must be based on medical evidence, is clearly of a moral nature. The decision on whether, and under what circumstances, it is right to destroy a germinating human life depends on the assessment and weighing of values, on determining the title to life in any given case. Such value judgments are entirely outside the province of medical science. No amount of training or experience in medicine can help in ascertaining the criteria necessary for reaching such capital verdicts, for making such life-and-death decisions. Such judgments pose essentially a moral, not a medical problem. Hence they call for the judgment of moral, not medical, specialists.

In demanding that they should have the right to determine or adjudicate the laws governing their practice, physicians are making an altogether unprecedented claim, one not advanced by any other profession. Lawyers do not argue that, because law is their specialty, the decision on what is legal should be left to their conscience. And teachers do not claim that, since they are professionals competent in education, the laws governing their work should be administered or defined at their discretion. Such claims are patent-

Chapter contributed to Abortion and the Law, *ed. David T. Smith, Western Reserve University Press, Cleveland, 1967, reprinted (with slight amendments) in* Abortion, Society, and the Law, *ed. David F. Walbert and J. Douglas Butler, Press of Case Western Reserve University, Cleveland, 1973.*

ly absurd, for they would demand jurisdiction on matters completely beyond their professional competence.

There is no more justice or logic in advancing similar claims for the medical profession. A physician, in performing an abortion or any other procedure involving moral considerations, such as artificial insemination or euthanasia, is merely a technical expert: he is no more qualified than any other laymen to pronounce on the rights or legality of such acts, let alone to determine what these rights should be, relying merely on the whims or dictates of his conscience. The decision on whether a human life, once conceived, is to be or not to be, therefore, properly belongs to moral experts, or to legislatures guided by such experts.

I. JEWISH LAW

A. The Claims of Judaism

Every monotheistic religion embodies within its philosophy and legislation a system of ethics—a definition of moral values. None does so with greater precision and comprehensiveness than Judaism. It emphatically insists that the norms of moral conduct can be governed neither by the accepted notions of public opinion nor by the individual conscience. In the Jewish view, the human conscience is meant to enforce laws, not to make them. Right and wrong, good and evil, are absolute values which transcend the capricious variations of time, place, and environment, just as they defy definition by relation to human intuition or expediency. These values, Judaism teaches, derive their validity from the Divine revelation at Mount Sinai, as expounded and developed by sages faithful to, and authorized by, its writ.

B. The Sources of Jewish Law

For a definition of these values one must look to the vast and complex corpus of Jewish law, the authentic expression of all Jewish religious and moral thought. The literary depositories of Jewish law extend over nearly 4,000 years, from the Bible and the Talmud, serving as the immutable basis of the main principles, to the great medieval codes and the voluminous rabbinical *responsa* writings recording practical verdicts founded on these principles, right up to the present day.

These sources, which will be detailed below, specify a very distinct attitude on all aspects of the abortion problem. They clearly indicate that Judaism, while it does not share the rigid stand of the Roman Catholic Church, which unconditionally proscribes any direct destruction of the fetus from the moment of conception, refuses to endorse the far more permissive views of many Protestant denominations. The traditional Jewish position is somewhere between these two extremes, recognizing only a grave hazard to the mother as a legitimate indication for therapeutic abortion.

1. *Abortion in the Bible.* The legislation of the Bible makes only one reference to our subject, and this is by implication:

And if men strive together, and hurt a woman with child, so that her fruit depart, and yet no harm follow, he shall be surely fined, according as the woman's husband shall lay upon him; and he shall pay as the judges determine. But if any harm follow, then shalt thou give life for life. . . .[1]

(a) *The Jewish Interpretation.* This crucial passage, by one of the most curious twists of literary fortunes, marks the parting of the ways between the Jewish and Christian rulings on abortion. According to the Jewish interpretation, if "no harm follow" the "hurt" to the woman resulting in the loss of her fruit refers to the survival of the woman following her miscarriage; in that case there is no capital guilt involved, and the attacker is merely liable to pay compensation for the loss of her fruit. "But if any harm follow," i.e. if the woman is fatally injured, then the man responsible for her death has to "give life for life"; in that event the capital charge of murder exempts him from any monetary liability for the aborted fruit.[2]

This interpretation is also borne out by the rabbinical exegesis of the verse defining the law of murder, "He that smiteth *a man*, so that he dieth, shall surely be put to death . . . ,"[3] which the Rabbis construed to mean "a man, but not a fetus".[4]

These passages clearly indicate that the killing of an unborn child is not considered murder punishable by death in Jewish law.

(b) *The Christian interpretation.* The Christian tradition disputing this view goes back to a mistranslation in the *Septuagint*. There, the Hebrew for "no harm follow" was replaced by the Greek for "[her child be born] imperfectly formed".[5] This interpretation, distinguishing between an unformed and a formed fetus and branding the killing of the latter as murder, was accepted by Tertullian, who was ignorant of Hebrew, and by later church fathers. The distinction was subsequently embodied in canon law as well as in Justinian Law.[6] This position was further reinforced by the belief that the "animation" (entry of the soul) of a fetus occurred on the fortieth or eightieth day after conception for males and females respectively, an idea first expressed by Aristotle,[7] and by the doctrine, firmly enunciated by Saint Augustine and other early Chrsitian authorities, that the unborn child was included among those condemned to eternal perdition if he died unbaptized.[8] Some even regarded the death or murder of an unborn child as a greater calamity than that of a baptized person.[9] Eventually the distinction between animate and inanimate fetuses was lost; and since 1588 the Catholic Church has considered as murder the killing of any human fruit from the moment of conception.[10]

This position is maintained to the present day.[11] It assumes that potential life, even in the earliest stages of gestation, enjoys the same value as any existing adult life. Hence, the Catholic Church never tolerates any direct abortion, even when, by allowing the pregnancy to continue, both mother and child will perish;[12] "better two deaths than one murder."[13]

2. *Abortion in the Talmud.* Jewish law assumes that the full title to life arises only at birth. Accordingly, the Talmud rules:

If a woman is in hard travail [and her life cannot otherwise be saved], one cuts up the child within her womb and extracts it member by member, because her life comes before that of [the child]. But if the greater part [or the head] was delivered, one may not touch it, for one may not set aside one person's life for the sake of another.[14]

This ruling, sanctioning embryotomy to save the mother in her mortal conflict with her unborn child, is also the sole reference to abortion in the principal codes of Jewish law.[15] They add only the further argument that such a child, being in "pursuit" of the mother's life may be destroyed as an "aggressor" following the general principle of self-defense.[16]

This formulation of the attitude toward abortion in the classic sources of Jewish law implies (1) that the only indication considered for abortion is a hazard to the mother's life and (2) that, otherwise, the destruction of an unborn child is a grave offense, although not murder.

3. *Abortion in Rabbinical Writings.* Some of these conclusions, and their ramifications, are more fully discussed in later rabbinical writings, notably the prolific *responsa* literature. Before some of these writings are detailed, it should be pointed out that criminal abortion, as distinct from therapeutic abortion, is scarcely mentioned in Jewish sources at all. This omission seems all the more glaring in view of the extraordinary attention given to the subject in Christian literature and other legislations in ancient, medieval, and modern times. Criminal abortion was, with few exceptions, simply nonexistent in Jewish society. Consequently, the legal and moral problems involved were rarely submitted to rabbinical judgment, and their consideration thus did not enter into the *responsa*, at least not until comparatively recent times.[17]

Elaborating on the law as defined in the Talmud and the codes, the *responsa* add several significant rulings. While very little is written on abortions following rape, several opinions are expressed on the legality of aborting a product of incest or adultery, both capital offenses in Biblical law. One eighteenth-century authority considered the case of an adultress different insofar as her capital guilt would also forfeit the life of the fruit she carried.[18] But others maintained that there could be no distinction between a bastard and a legitimate fetus in this respect, and that any sanction to destroy such a product would open the floodgates to immorality and debauchery.[19] A later *responsum* also prohibited such an operation.[20]

Since the Talmud permits the sacrifice of the child to save the mother only prior to the emergence of its head or the greater part of its body from the birth canal,[21] a widely discussed question concerns the right to dismember the fetus even during the final stage of parturition if it is feared that otherwise both mother and child may die. As the danger to the mother usually is likely to occur before that stage is reached, this is mainly a hypothetical question, but it may be of some practical significance in the case of a breech-birth if the child's head cannot be extracted following the delivery of the rest of the body. Notwithstanding the rule that the child in principle assumes full and equal human rights once the major part is born, and that consequently one may not thereafter save one life (the mother's) at the cost of another (the child's), this particular case may be an exception because (1) the child is liable to die in any event, whether the operation is carried out or not, while the mother can be rescued at the expense of the child and (2) in the Jewish view the viability of a child is not fully established until it has passed the

thirtieth day of its life, so that of the two lives here at stake the one is certain
and established, while the other is still in some doubt. This slight inequality
in value is too insignificant to warrant the deliberate sacrifice of the child
for the sake of the mother if, without such sacrifice, the child would survive;
but it is a sufficient factor to tip the scales in favor of the mother if the alternative is the eventual loss of both lives. Hence, with one exception,[22] rabbinical verdicts are inclined to countenance the intervention, provided the
physician is confident of the success of the operation.[23]

4. *Deformed Children in Rabbinical Writings.* More recently the tragic
problem of abortions indicated by suspected fetal defects has occupied considerable space in rabbinical writings. The recognition of this problem dates
only from 1941, when an Australian medical journal first drew attention to
the incidence of abnormalities resulting from rubella[24] in the mother during
her early pregnancy. Since then, the legal, moral, and religious issues involved
have been widely but still inconclusively debated in medical as well as non-
medical circles. They aroused much public controversy when it was established
that the birth of thousands of deformed babies could be traced to drugs,
notably thalidomide, taken by pregnant mothers and when many such mothers
sought to have their pregnancies terminated for fear they would deliver
malformed children.

Most authorities of Jewish law are agreed that physical or mental abnormalities do not in themselves compromise the title to life, whether before
or after birth. Cripples and idiots, however incapacitated, enjoy the same
human rights (though not necessarily legal competence) as normal persons.[25]
Human life being infinite in value, its sanctity is bound to be entirely unaffected by the absence of any or all mental faculties or by any bodily defects:
any fraction of infinity still remains infinite. (But see the Postscript, below.)

5. *Monster Births in Rabbinical Writings.* The absolute inviolability
of any human being, however deformed, was affirmed in the first *responsum*
on the status of monster births. Early in the nineteenth century, a famous
rabbinical scholar advised a questioner that it was forbidden to destroy a
grotesquely misshapen child; he ruled that to kill, or even starve to death,
any being born of a human mother was unlawful as homicide.[26] Indeed, in a
somewhat less legal context, a twelfth-century moralistic work referred to a
ruling against terminating the life of a child born with teeth and a tail like
an animal, counseling instead the removal of these features.[27]

C. *Arguments against the Destruction of Defectives*

Based on these principles and precedents, the consensus of present-day rabbis
is to condemn abortion, feticide, or infanticide to eliminate a crippled being,
before or after birth, as an unconscionable attack on the sanctity of life.
Further considerations leading to this conclusion include the arguments that,
conversely, the saving of an unborn child's life justifies the violation of the
Sabbath (permitted only when human life is at stake);[28] that such a child is
not in "pursuit" of the mother, thus excluding an important condition for
the right to perform a therapeutic abortion;[29] that the interruption of a pregnancy is not without hazards to the mother, particularly the danger of render-

ing her sterile and the increase in maternal mortality resulting from abortions, as attested by physicians;[30] and that the killing of an embryo, while technically not murder according to a "scriptural decree," nevertheless constitutes "an appurtenance of murder" because "in matters affecting human life we also consider that which is going to be [a human being] without any further action, following the laws of nature."[31]

These considerations would be valid even if it were known for certain that the expected child would be born deformed. The almost invariable doubts about such a contingency only strengthen the objections to abortion in these circumstances, especially in view of the Talmudic maxim that in matters of life and death the usual majority rule does not operate; any chance, however slim, that a life may be saved must always be given the benefit of the doubt.[32]

A similar attitude was adopted in a recent rabbinical article on the celebrated trial in Liege (Belgium) in which a mother and others were acquitted of guilt for the confessed killing of a thalidomide baby.[33] The author denounces abortion for such a purpose as well as the Liege verdict. "The sole legitimate grounds for killing a fetus are the urgent needs of the mother and her healing, whereas in these circumstances the mother's efforts to have the child aborted are based on self-love and plain egotism, wrapped in a cloak of compassion for this unfortunate creature, and this cannot be called a necessity for the mother at all."[34]

D. Psychological Considerations

On the other hand, Jewish law would consider a grave psychological hazard to the mother as no less weighty a reason for an abortion than a physical threat. On these grounds a seventeenth-century *responsum* permitted an abortion in a case where it was feared the mother would otherwise suffer an attack of hysteria imperiling her life.[35] If it is genuinely feared that a continued pregnancy and eventual birth under these conditions might have such debilitating effects on the mother as to present a danger to her own life or the life of another by suicidal or violent tendencies, however remote this danger may be, a therapeutic abortion may be indicated with the same justification as for other medical reasons. But this fear would have to be very real, attested to by the most competent psychiatric opinion, and based on previous experiences of mental imbalance.[36]

II. MORAL AND SOCIAL CONSIDERATIONS

The legalistic structure of these conclusions must be viewed in the context of Judaism's moral philosophy and against the background of contemporary social conditions.

A. The "Cruelty" of the Abortion Laws

It is essential at the outset, in order to arrive at an objective judgment, to disabuse one's mind of the often one-sided, if not grossly partisan, arguments in the popular (and sometimes medical) presentations of the issues involved. A hue and cry is raised about the "cruelty" of restrictive abortion laws. Harrowing scenes are depicted, in the most lurid colors, of girls and married women selling their honor and their fortunes, exposing themselves to mayhem and death at the hands of some greedy and ill-qualified abortionist in a dark, unhygienic back alley. Equally distressing are the accounts and pictures of pitifully deformed children born because our "antiquated" abortion laws did not permit us to forestall their and their parents' misfortune. And then there are, of course, always heart-strings of sympathy to be pulled by the sight of "unwanted" children taxing the patience and resources of parents already "burdened" with too large a brood.

These is, inevitably, some element of cruelty in most laws. To a person who has spent his last cent before the tax bill arrives, the income tax laws are unquestionably "cruel"; and to a man passionately in love with a married woman the adultery laws must appear "barbaric." Even more universally "harsh" are the military draft regulations which expose young men to acute danger and their families to great anguish and hardship.

B. Moral Standards in Society

All these "cruelties" are surely no valid reason for changing those laws. No civilized society could survive without laws which occasionally cause some suffering for individuals. Nor can any public moral standards be maintained without strictly enforced regulations calling for extreme restraints and sacrifices in some cases. If the criterion for the legitimacy of laws were the complete absence of "cruel" effects, we should abolish or drastically liberalize not only our abortion laws, but our statutes on marriage, narcotics, homosexuality, suicide, euthanasia, and numerous other matters, which inevitably result in personal anguish from time to time.

So far the reasoning here, which could be supported by any number of references to Jewish tradition, has merely sought to demolish the "cruelty" factor as an argument valid in itself to judge the justice or injustice of any law. It remains to be demonstrated that the restrictions on abortion are morally sound enough and sufficiently important to the public welfare to outweigh the consequential hardships in individual cases.

C. The Cost in Healthy Lives

What the fuming editorials and harrowing documentaries on the abortion problem do not show are pictures of radiant mothers fondling perfectly healthy children who would never have been alive if their parents had been permitted to resort to abortion in moments of despair. There are no statistics on the contributions to society of outstanding men and women who would never have been born had the abortion laws been more liberal. Nor is it known how many "unwanted" children eventually turn out to be the sunshine of their families.

A Jewish moralistic work of the twelfth century relates the following deeply significant story:

A person constantly said that, having already a son and a daughter, he was anxious lest his wife become pregnant again. For he was not rich and asked how would he find sufficient sustenance. Said a sage to him: "When a child is born, the Holy One, blessed be He, provides the milk beforehand in the mother's breast; therefore, do not worry." But he did not accept the wise man's words, and he continued to fret. Then a son was born to him. After a while, the child became ill, and the father turned to the sage: "Pray for my son that he shall live." Exclaimed the sage: "To you applies the biblical verse: 'Suffer not thy mouth to bring thy flesh into guilt.' "[37]

Some children may be born unwanted, but there are few unwanted children aged five or ten years.

D. Abortion Statistics

Thus there are—even from the purely utilitarian viewpoint of "cruelty" *versus* "happiness" or "usefulness"—two sides to this problem, not just one, as is pretended by those agitating for reform. There are the admittedly tragic cases of maternal indignities and deaths as well as of congenital deformities resulting from restrictive abortion laws. But, on the other hand, there are the countless happy children and useful citizens whose births equally result from these laws. What is the ratio between these two catagories?

If one considers that even with rigid laws there were well over one million abortions performed annually in the United States (most of them by reputable physicians), it stands to reason that the relaxation of these laws will raise the abortion rate by many millions. Even allowing for more widespread recourse to birth control, there can be little doubt that the American abortion rate will soar to at least two or three times its previous level (probably a gross understatement).

Out of the several million pregnancies that will probably be terminated every year, no more than 30,000[38] would have resulted in deformed births; the remaining 99 percent would have been healthy children had their mothers been allowed or forced to carry them to term. One can certainly ask if the extremely limited reduction in the number of malformed children and maternal mortality risks really justify the annual wholesale destruction of several million germinating, healthy lives, most of them potentially happy and useful citizens, especially in a country as underpopulated as America (compared to Europe, for instance, which commands far fewer natural resources.)

E. The Individual's Claim to Life

These numerical facts alone make nonsense of the argument for more and easier abortions. But moral norms cannot be determined by numbers. In the Jewish view, "he who saves one life is as if he saved an entire world";[39] one human life is as precious as a million lives, for each is infinite in value. Hence, even if the ratio were reversed, and there was only a 1 percent chance that the child to be aborted would be normal, the consideration for that one child in favor of life would outweigh any counterindication for the other 99 percent.

But, in truth, such a counterindication, too, is founded on fallacious premises. Assuming one were 100 per cent certain that a child would be born deformed, could this affect its claim to life? Any line to be drawn between normal and abnormal beings determining their right to live would have to be altogether arbitrary. Would a grave defect in one limb or in two limbs, or an anticipated sub-normal intelligence quotient of 75 or 50 make the capital difference between one who is entitled to live and one who is not? And if the absence of two limbs deprives a person of his claim to life, what about one who loses two limbs in an accident? By what moral reasoning can such a defect be a lesser cause for denying the right to live than a similar congenital abnormality? Surely life-and-death verdicts cannot be based on such tenuous distinctions.

F. The Obligations of Society

The birth of a physically or mentally maldeveloped child may be an immense tragedy in a family, just as a crippling accident or a lingering illness striking a family member later in life may be. But one cannot purchase the relief from such misfortunes at the cost of life itself. So long as the sanctity of life is recognized as inviolable, the cure to suffering cannot be abortion before birth, any more than murder (whether in the form of euthanasia or of suicide) after birth. The only legitimate relief in such cases is for society to assume the burdens which the individual family can no longer bear. Since society is the main beneficiary of restrictive public laws on abortion (or homicide), it must in turn also pay the price sometimes exacted by these laws in the isolated cases demanding such a price.

Just as the state holds itself responsible for the support of families bereaved by the death of soldiers fallen in the defense of their country, it ought to provide for incapacitated people born and kept alive in the defense of public moral standards. The community is morally bound to relieve affected families of any financial or emotional stress they cannot reasonably bear, either by accepting the complete care of defective children in public institutions, or by supplying medical and educational subsidies to ensure that such families do not suffer any unfair economic disadvantages from their misfortune.

G. Illegitimate Children

Similar considerations apply to children conceived by rape. The circumstances of such a conception can have little bearing on the child's title to life, and in the absence of any well-grounded challenge to this title there cannot be any moral justification for an abortion. Once again, the burden rests with society to relieve an innocent mother (if she so desires) from the consequences of an unprovoked assault upon her virtue if the assailant cannot be found and forced to discharge this responsibility to his child.

In the case of pregnancies resulting from incestuous, adulterous, or otherwise illegitimate relations (which the mother did not resist), there are additional considerations militating against any sanction of abortion.

Jewish law not only puts an extreme penalty on incest and adultery, but also imposes fearful disabilities on the products of such unions. It brands these relations as capital crimes,[40] and it debars Jewish children born under these conditions from marriage with anyone except their like.[41]

    1. *The Deterrent Effect.* Why exact such a price from innocent children for the sins of their parents? The answer is simple: to serve as a powerful deterrent to such hideous crimes. The would-be partners to any such illicit sexual relations are to be taught that their momentary pleasure would be fraught with the most disastrous consequences for any children they might conceive. Through this knowledge they are to recoil from the very thought of incest or adultery with the same horror as they would from contemplating murder as a means to enjoyment or personal benefit. Murder is comparatively rare in civilized society for the very reason that the dreadful consequences have evoked this horror of the crime in the public conscience. Incest and adultery, in the Jewish view, are no lesser crimes,[42] and they require the same horror as an effective deterrent.

    2. *Parental Responsibility.* Why create this deterrent by visiting the sins of the parents on their innocent children? First, because there is no other way to expose an offense committed in private and usually beyond the chance of detection. But, above all, this responsibility of parents for the fate of their children is an inexorable necessity in the generation of human life; it is dictated by the law of nature no less than by the moral law. If a careless mother drops her baby and thereby causes a permanent brain injury to the child, or if a syphilitic father irresponsibly transmits his disease to his off-spring before birth, or if parents are negligent in the education of their children, all these children will innocently suffer and for the rest of their lives expiate the sins of their parents. This is what must be if parental responsibility is to be taken seriously. The fear that such catastrophic consequences would ensue from a surrender to temptation or from carelessness will help prevent the conception of grossly disadvantaged children or their physical or mental mutilation after birth.

H. *Public Standards versus Individual Aberration*

In line with this reasoning, Jewish law never condones the relaxation of public moral standards for the sake of saving recalcitrant individuals from even mortal offenses. A celebrated Jewish sage and philosopher of the fifteenth century, in connection with a question submitted to his judgment, averred that it was always wrong for a community to acquiesce in the slightest evil, however much it was hoped thereby to prevent far worse excesses by individuals. The problem he faced arose out of a suggestion that brothels for single people be tolerated as long as such publicly controlled institutions would reduce or eliminate the capital crime of marital faithlessness then rampant. His unequivocal answer was: It is surely far better that individuals should commit the worst offenses and expose themselves to the gravest penalties than publicly to promote the slightest compromise with the moral law.[43]

    Strict abortion laws, ruling out the *post facto* "correction" of rash acts, compel people to think twice *before* they recklessly embark on illicit or irresponsible adventures liable to inflict lifelong suffering or infamy on their progeny. To eliminate the scourge of illegitimate children, more self-discipline to prevent their conception is required, not more freedom to destroy them in the womb.

The exercise of man's procreative faculties, making him (in the phrase of the Talmud) "a partner with God in creation," is man's greatest privilege and gravest responsibility. The rights and obligations implicit in the generation of human life must be evenly balanced if man is not to degenerate into an addict of lust and a moral parasite infesting the moral organism of society. Liberal abortion laws will upset that balance by facilitating sexual indulgences without insisting on corresponding responsibilities.

I.   Therapeutic Abortions

This leaves only the concern for the mother's safety as a valid argument in favor of abortions. In the view of Judaism, all human rights, and their priorities, derive solely from their conferment upon man by his Creator. By this criterion, as defined in the Bible, the rights of the mother and her unborn child are distinctly unequal, since the capital guilt of murder takes effect only if the victim was a born and viable person. This recognition does not imply that the destruction of a fetus is not a very grave offense against the sanctity of human life, but only that it is not technically murder. Jewish law makes a similar distinction in regard to the killing of inviable adults. While the killing of a person who already suffered from a fatal injury (from other than natural causes) is not actionable as murder,[44] the killer is morally guilty of a mortal offense.[45]

This inequality, then, is weighty enough only to warrant the sacrifice of the unborn child if the pregnancy otherwise poses a threat to the mother's life. Indeed, the Jewish concern for the mother is so great that a gravid woman sentenced to death[46] must not be subjected to the ordeal of suspense to await the delivery of her child.[47] (Jewish sources brand any delay in the execution, once it is finally decreed, as "the perversion of justice" *par excellence,*[48] since the criminal is sentenced to die, not to suffer.)

Such a threat to the mother need not be either immediate or absolutely certain. Even a remote risk of life invokes all the life-saving concessions of Jewish law,[49] provided the fear of such a risk is genuine and confirmed by the most competent medical opinions. Hence, Jewish law would regard it as an indefensible desecration of human life to allow a mother to perish in order to save her unborn child.

III.   CONCLUSION

This review may be fittingly concluded with a reference to the very first Jewish statement on deliberate abortion. Commenting on the *Septuagint* version of the *Exodus* passage[50] quoted earlier, the Alexandrian-Jewish philosopher Philo, at the beginning of the Current Era, declared that the attacker must die if the fruit he caused to be lost was already "shaped and all the limbs had their proper qualities, for that which answers to this description is a human being . . . like a statue lying in a studio requiring nothing more than to be conveyed outside."[51] The legal conclusion of his statement, reflecting Hellenistic rather than Jewish influence, may vary from the letter of Jewish law; but his reasoning certainly echoes its spirit. The analogy may be more meaningful than Philo could have intended or foreseen. A classic statue by a supreme master is no less priceless for having become defective, even with an arm or a leg missing. The destruction of such a treasure can be warranted only by the superior worth of preserving a living human being.

POSTSCRIPT

Since the composition of this article several years ago, the attitude of Jewish law to abortion has been further discussed in a number of rabbinical *responsa* and other writings—prompted partly, no doubt, by the greatly increased recourse to abortion due to the permissive legislation passed in recent years in America, England, and elsewhere. While the predominant view, as expressed in the latest rabbinical verdicts,[52] reaffirms the Jewish opposition to abortion except in cases involving some grave anticipated hazard to the mother (whether physical or psychological), a few considerably more lenient opinions have also been added. Notable among them are the rulings of the Head of the Jerusalem Rabbinical Court. He is inclined to sanction the operation on a Jewish mother even in the absence of any actual danger to her life, provided there is a serious medical indication for it, as well as in cases of a conception by rape or incest, or of a definite risk that the child may be born physically or mentally handicapped. But such abortions should be carried out preferably within the first forty days of the pregnancy or at least within the first three months.[53] Another recent *responsum* finds no reason to object to the destruction of a hydrocephalic fetus if the mother is unwilling to submit to a caesarian operation for the delivery of the child.[54]

But even these rather isolated opinion do not substantially modify the general Jewish view as given in a public statement issued by the Association of Orthodox Jewish Scientists of America in 1971:

> . . . We appeal to Jewish rabbinic and lay leadership to join us in an educational program, within our Jewish communities, designed to promulgate the Jewish attitudes toward abortion. Jewish law permits abortion only when a potentially lethal deterioration in the mother's health might ensue if pregnancy is allowed to proceed to term. Jewish law prohibits abortion when its sole justification is to prevent the birth of a physically deformed or mentally retarded child. Abortion "on demand" purely for the convenience of the mother or even of society is strictly prohibited and morally repugnant. . . .[55]

NOTES

1. *Exodus* 21:22–23.
2. *Mekhilta* and Rashi. For a translation of these sources, see 3 Lauterbach, Mekhilta 66–67 (1935); Rosenbaum and Silberman, Pentateuch and Rashi's Commentary 112–13 (1930).
3. *Exodus* 21:12. (Emphasis added.)

4. *Mekhilta* and Rashi. For a translation of these sources, see 3 Lauterbach, *supra* note 2, at 32–33; Rosenbaum and Silberman, *supra* note 2, at 110–10a.

5. The mistranslation, also followed in the Samaritan and Karaite versions, is evidently based on reading "zurah" or "surah" (meaning "form") for "ason" (meaning "harm" or "accident"). *See* Kaufmann, Gedenkschrift 186 (1900).

6. *See* Westermarck, Christianity and Morals 243 (1939).

7. Aristotle, De anim. Hist., vii. 3; *see* 1 Catholic Encyclopedia 46–48 (1907).

8. *See* 1 Ploss and Bartels, Woman 483 (1935); 2 Catholic Encyclopedia 266–67 (1907).

9. *See* 2 Lecky, History of European Morals 23–24 (3rd ed. 1891).

10. *See* 1 Ploss and Bartels, *supra* note 8, at 484; Bonnar, The Catholic Doctor 78 (1948).

11. *See*, e.g., Catholic Hospital Association of the United States and Canada, Ethical and Religious Directives for Catholic Hospitals 4 (1949).

12. *See* Bonnar, *supra* note 10, at 84.

13. Tiberghien, *Principles et Conscience Morale*, Cahiers Laennac, Oct. 1946, at 13.

14. Talmud, Tohoroth II *Oholoth* 7:6.

15. Maimonides, Hil. Rotze'ach, 1:9; Shulchan Arukh, *Choshen Mishpat* 425:2.

16. This is based on a discussion of the Mishnah, Talmud, *Sanhedrin* 72b. *See generally* Jakobovits, Jewish Medical Ethics 184–91 (1962).

17. Jakobovits, *supra* note 16, at 181.

18. Emden, responsa She'ilath Ya'avetz, pt. 1, no. 43.

19. Bacharach, responsa Chavath Ya'ir no. 31.

20. Halevi, responsa Lechem Hapanim, Kunteres Acharon, no. 19.

21. *See* text accompanying notes 14–16 *supra*.

22. Sopher, responsa Machaneh Chayim *Choshen Mishpat*, pt. 2, no. 50. Some authorities left the question unresolved; see Eger, Oholoth 7:6; Meir of Eisenstadt, responsa Panim Me'iroth, pt. 2. no. 8.

23. Schick, responsa Maharam Shik, *Yoreh De'ah* no. 155; Hoffmann, responsa Melamed Leho'il, *Yoreh De'ah* no. 69.

24. German measles. *See* Gregg, *Congenital Cataract Following German Measles in Mother*, 3 Transactions of the Ophthalmological Soc'y of Australia 35–46 (1941); *see also* Swan, Tostevin, Mayo and Black, *Congenital Defects in Infants Following Infectious Diseases During Pregnancy*, 2 Medical J. of Australia 201 (1943).

25. *See* Mishnah Berurah, Bi'ur Halakhah, on Orach Chayim 329:4. An idiot can even sue for injuries inflicted on him. Talmud, *Baba Kamma* 8:4. Again, the killing of even a dying person is culpable as murder. Maimonides, Hil. Rotze'ach 2:7.

26. Elezar Fleckeles, responsa Teshuvah Me'ahavah, pt. 1, no. 53. *See* ZIMMELS, Magicians, Theologians and Doctors 72 (1952).

27. Sepher Chasidim no. 186 (Zitomir ed. 1879).

28. Bacharach, *supra* note 19. But there is some rabbinical dispute on this opinion. Jakobovits, *supra* note 16, at 279 n. 38.

29. *See* text accompanying notes 14–16 *supra*.

30. Unterman, 6 No'am (Jerusalem) 1 (1963). Unterman, Chief Rabbi of Israel, refers to medical evidence given him by Professor Asherman, Director of the Maternity Department of the Municipal Hadassah Hospital in Tel Aviv.

31. *Id.*

32. Talmud, Yoma 84; Shulchan Arukh, *Orach Chayim* 329:2.

33. Zweig, 7 No'am (Jerusalem) 36 (1964).

34. *Id.*

35. Mitzrachi, responsa P'ri Ha'aretz, *Yoreh De'ah* no. 21.

36. Unterman, Hatorah Vehamedinah 25, 29 (4th ser. 1952); Friedman, responsa Netzer Mata'ai pt. 1, no. 8; Feinstein, responsa Igroth Mosheh *Orach Chayim* pt. 4, no. 88. These authorities permit the violation of the Sabbath for the sake of psychiatric patients.

37. Sepher Chasidim, *supra* note 27, no. 520.

38. This is the number of defective births resulting from German measles anticipated for 1965 in the United States. To this number may have to be added anticipated abnormalities for other reasons, but from it would have to be subtracted the considerably larger number of cases in which affected mothers would not resort to abortion, either because of their opposition to abortion or because the condition is undetected during pregnancy.

The total of abortions fully justified by actual (not suspected) fetal defects due to factors that could be recognized during pregnancy could thus scarcely exceed thirty thousand.

39. Talmud, *Sanhedrin* 4:5. For this reason, Jewish law forbids the surrender of a single life even if any number of other lives may thereby be saved. Maimonides, Hil. Yesodei Hatorah 5:5.

40. *Leviticus* 20:10–20.

41. *Deuteronomy* 23:3, and Jewish commentaries.

42. Compare the juxtaposition of murder and adultery in the Ten Commandments. *Exodus* 20:13.

43. Arama, Akedath Yitzchak ch. 20, at 41 (b) (ed. Frankfurt a/o 1785).

44. Talmud, *Sanhedrin* 78a.

45. Maimonides acquits such a murderer only before "a human court". Hil. Rotze'ach 2:7–8.

46. In practice Jewish law virtually abolished capital punishment thousands of years ago, as it insisted on numerous conditions whose fulfillment was almost impossible (such as the presence of, and prior warning by, two eye-witnesses).

47. Talmud, *Erakhin* 1:4; Talmud, Tosaphoth, *Erakhin* 7a.

48. Ethics of the Fathers 5:8.

49. Shulchan Arukh, *Orach Chayim* 329:2–4.

50. *See* text accompanying note 1 *supra.*

51. De Spec. legibus 3:108–10, 117–18; De Virtut, 138. But in the latter two passages, Philo himself qualified his statement by calling only a person who killed a child already born "indubitably a murderer".

52. So, e.g., Grossnas, London Beth Din Publications, no. 21, Tishri 5732 (1971); Hubner 28 Hadarom (New York), Tishri 5729 (1968) at 31. For further sources, see 2 Asya (Jerusalem), Shevat 5731 (1971) at 39.

53. Waldenberg, Responsa Tzitz Eliezer, pt. 7, no. 41; and pt. 9, no. 51.

54. Rabinowitch, 28 Hadarom, op. cit. note 52, at 19.

55. 12 Intercom (New York), no. 1 (March 1971), at 4.

MEDICAL EXPERIMENTATION ON HUMANS

Some widespread allegations of unethical practices in medical experimenta-
tions on humans have recently been substantiated and carefully documented
in a report published in the *New England Journal of Medicine*.[1] The article,
which was extensively quoted in the American press, cited twenty-two examples, out of fifty originally submitted, of "unethical or ethically questionable studies" involving hundreds of patients. In the view of the author, "it is
evident that in many of the examples presented, the investigators have
risked the health or the life of their subject". In many cases no "informed
consent" was obtained either at all or under conditions which would render
such consent meaningful. Some of the experiments were performed for
purely academic purposes or "for frivolous ends", occasionally on healthy
subjects or organs "with nothing to gain and all to lose". All the examples
are taken from "leading medical schools, university hospitals, private hospitals, governmental military departments and institutes, Veterans Administration hospitals, and industry". Most people involved in these studies were
"captive groups"—charity ward patients, civil prisoners, mental retardees,
members of the military services, the investigators' own laboratory personnel,
and the like.

Such practices obviously raise grave ethical and moral problems. At
issue here is not only the impropriety of physicians or researchers admini-
stering possibly hazardous treatments without the proper consent of the
subject. Equally questionable is the right of the subject to submit to such
experiments even with his consent. On the other hand, a certain amount of
experimentation is patently indispensable for the advance of medicine and in
the treatment of innumerable patients, How far, and under what circumstances, can such experimentation be ethically justified?

The author, therefore, scarcely comes to grips with the gravamen of the
problem when he suggests that "greater safeguard for the patient than consent
is the presence of an informed, able, conscientious, compassionate, responsible investigator, for it is recognized that patients can, when imperfectly
informed, be induced to agree, unwisely, to many things", or when he recom-
mends "the practice of having at least two physicians (the one caring for the

Article published in the Proceedings of the Associations of Orthodox Jewish Scientists,
New York, vol. i, 1966.

patient and the investigator) involved in experimental situations", or even when he proposes the presentation of difficult ethical problems "to a group of the investigator's peers for discussion and counsel".

These suggestions are valuable as far as they go. They certainly would help to prevent some current abuses, such as the excessive zeal of young ambitious physicians seeking promotion by proving themselves as investigators, or the inordinate rewards, functioning as bribes, held out to participating prisoners, not to mention more common pressures, inducements and misrepresentations which destroy the whole concept of free consent. But these suggestions are inadequate on two major counts. First, they limit the problem to securing the subject's free and informed consent, whereas in fact the subject may have neither the right nor the competence to grant any consent, even if freely given. Second, they assume that the physician or the investigator or their peers can pass such critical ethical judgments, whereas in fact the assessment of ethical and moral values is completely outside the purview of medical science, being properly within the domain of the moral, not medical, expert. No amount of medical erudition or expertise can by itself provide the ethical criteria necessary for verdicts that may involve life-and-death decisions or the sacrifice of one life or limb for the sake of another. Competent medical opinion is essential to supply the factual data on which such decisions are based; but the decisions themselves, since they involve value judgments, require moral specialists or the guidance of independent moral rules. Ability, conscientiousness, compassion and responsibility are no substitute for competent and reliable knowledge of what is right or wrong, ethical or unethical, particularly when human life is at stake—possibly both the life of the subject and the lives that might be saved through the experiment.

At least this certainly is the Jewish view. It emphatically maintains that moral questions of such gravity cannot be resolved simply by reference to the fickle whims of the individual conscience or of public opinion, but only by having recourse to the absolute standards of the moral law which, in the case of Judaism, has its authentic source in the Divine revelation of the Holy Writ and its duly qualified interpretors.

What cannot be stated with the same certainty and precision is the definition of the Jewish attitude to the problem at hand. Since this is a rather new question, there are as yet too few relevant rabbinic rulings published for a firm opinion to be crystalized and authoritatively accepted. All that can here be attempted is to scan the sources of Jewish law for views and judgments bearing on our issue. But is must be stressed that the resultant conclusions are entirely tentative, and any verdict in a practical case would be subject to endorsement or revision by a competent rabbinical authority duly considering all the facts and circumstances involved.

To this writer there appear to be ten baisc Jewish principles affecting the issue and ultimately determining the solution. We will list them *seriatim*, adding to each item the relevant sources and considerations.

1. *Human life is sacrosanct, and of supreme and infinite worth*

Life is of itself the *summum bonum* of human existence. The Divine law was ordained only "that man shall live by it".[2] Hence any precept, whether religious or ethical, is automatically suspended if it conflicts with the interests of human life,[3] the exceptions being only idolatry, murder and immorality (adultery and incest)—the three cardinal crimes against God, one's neighbor and oneself—as expressly stipulated in the Bible itself.[4] The value of human life is infinite and beyond measure, so that any part of life—even if only an hour or a second—is of precisely the same worth as seventy years of it, just as any fraction of infinity, being indivisible, remains infinite. Accordingly, to kill a decrepit patient approaching death constitutes exactly the same crime of murder as to kill a young, healthy person who may still have many decades to live.[5] For the same reason, one life is worth as much as a thousand or a million lives[6]—infinity is not increased by multiplying it. This explains the unconditional Jewish opposition to deliberate euthanasia as well as to the surrender of one hostage in order to save the others if the whole group is otherwise threatened with death.[7]

2. *Any chance to save life, however remote, must be pursued at all costs*

This follows logically from the preceding premises. Laws are in suspense not only when their violation is certain to lead to the preservation of life, but even when such an outcome is beset by any number of doubts and improbabilities.[8] By the same token, in desperate cases even experimental and doubtful treatments or medications should be given, so long as they hold out any prospect of success. (But see also no. 9 below.)

3. *The obligation to save a person from any hazard to his life or health devolves on anyone able to do so*

Every person is duty-bound not only to protect his own life and health,[9] but also those of his neighbor.[10] Anyone refusing to come to the rescue of a person in danger of losing life, limb or property is guilty of transgressing the biblical law "Thou shalt not stand upon the blood of thy neighbor."[11] It is questionable, however, how far one must, or may, risk one's own life or health in an effort to save one's fellow; the duty and possibly the right, to do so may be limited to risking a less likely loss for a more likely gain.[12] In any event, when there is no risk involved, the obligation to save one's neighbor from any danger is unconditional. Hence the refusal of a doctor to extend medical aid when required is deemed tantamount to bloodshed, unless a more competent doctor is readily available.[13]

4. *Every life is equally valuable and inviolable, including that of criminals, prisoners and defectives*

In the title to life and in its value, being infinite, there can be no distinction whatever between one person and another, whether innocent or guilty (except possibly persons under final sentence of death[14]), whether healthy or crippled, demented and terminally afflicted. Thus, even a person's inviolability after death and his rights to dignity are decreed in the Bible specifically in relation to capital criminals, created like everyone else "in the image of God".[15] Insane persons can sue for injuries received, even though they cannot be sued for inflicting them because of their legal incompetence.[16] The saving of physically or mentally defective persons sets aside all laws in the same way as the saving of normal people.[17]

5. *One must not sacrifice one life to save another, or even any number of others*

This follows from the preceding principle (see also no. 1 above). The Talmud deduces the rule that one must not murder to save one's life (except in self-defense) from the "logical argument" of "how do you know that your blood is redder than your neighbor's?", i.e. that your life is worth more than his.[18] This argument is also applied in reverse: "How do you know that his blood is redder than yours?" to explain why one must not surrender one's own life to save someone else's.[19] For reasons given above (no. 1), there also cannot be any difference between saving one or more lives.

6. *No one has the right to volunteer his life*

In Jewish law the right to expose oneself to voluntary martyrdom is strictly limited to cases involving either resistance to the three cardinal crimes (see no. 1 above) or "the sanctification of God's Name", i.e. to die for one's religious faith. To lay down one's life in any but these rigidly defined cases is regarded as a mortal offense,[20] certainly when there are no religious considerations involved.[21] The jurisdiction over life is not man's (except where such a right is expressly conferred by the Creator), and killing oneself by suicide, or allowing oneself to be killed by unauthorized martyrdom, is as much a crime as killing someone else.[22]

7. *No one has the right to injure his own or anyone else's body, except for therapeutic purposes*

Judaism regards the human body as Divine property,[23] surrendered merely to man's custody and protection. It is an offense, therefore, to make any incisions[24] or to inflict any injuries on the body, whether one's own or another person's.[25] One may not as much as strike a person, even with his permission, since the body is not owned by him.[26] Such injuries, including even amputations,[27] can be sanctioned only for the overriding good of the body as a whole, i.e. the superior value of life and health.

8. *No one has the right to refuse medical treatment deemed necessary by competent opinion.*

In view of the ban on the voluntary surrender of life (no. 6 above), the patient's consent is not required in Jewish law for any urgent operation.[28] His lay opinion that the operation is unnecessary, or his declared desire to risk death rather than undergo the operation, can have no bearing on the medical expert's duty to perform the operation if he considers it essential. His obligation to save life and health is ineluctable (see no. 3 above) and is altogether independent from the patient's wishes or opposition. The conscientious physician may even have to expose himself to the risk of malpractice claims against him in the performance of this superior duty.

9.   *Measures involving some immediate risks of life may be taken in attempts to prevent certain death later*

Jewish law specifically permits the administration of doubtful or experimental cures if safer methods are unknown or not available. In fact, the authorities encourage giving a terminal patient a possibly effective drug even at the grave risk of hastening his death should it prove fatal, if the alternative to this risk is the patient's certain death from his affliction later. In that case, the chances of the drug either bringing about his recovery or else accelerating his death need not even be fifty-fifty; any prospect that it may prove helpful is sufficient to warrant its use, provided the majority of the specialists consulted are in favor of its employment.[29] The same considerations would of course apply to doubtful surgical operations in a desperate gamble to save a patient.

10.   *There are no restrictions on animal experiments for medical purposes*

The strict Jewish law against inflicting cruelty on animals[30] is inoperative in respect of anything done to promote human health.[31] This sanction clearly includes essential animal vivisection too,[32] provided always that every care is taken to eliminate any avoidable pain and that such experiments serve practical medical ends, and not purely academic investigations into animal psychology or other purposes without any bearing on human welfare.[33]

From these principles we may now tentatively reach the following conclusions in regard to medical experimentation:

1.   Possibly hazardous experiments may be performed on humans only if they may be potentially helpful to the subject himself, however remote the chances of success are.
2.   It is obligatory to apply to terminal patients even untried or uncertain cures in an attempt to ward off certain death later, if no safe treatment is available.
3.   In all other cases it is as wrong to volunteer for such experiments as it is unethical to submit persons to them, whether with or without their consent, and whether they are normal people, criminals, prisoners, cripples, idiots or patients on their deathbed.
4.   If the experiment involves no hazard to life or health, the obligation to volunteer for it devolves on anyone who may thereby help to promote the health interests of others.
5.   Under such circumstances it may not be unethical to carry out these harmless experiments even without the subjects' consent, provided the anticipated benefit is real and substantial enough to invoke the precept of "Thou shalt not stand upon the blood of thy neighbor."

6. In the treatment of patients generally, whether the cures are tested or only experimental, the opinion of competent medical experts alone counts, not the wishes of the patient; and physicians are ethically required to take whatever therapeutic measures they consider essential for the patient's life and health, irrespective of the chance that they may subsequently be liable to legal claims for unauthorized "assault and battery".
7. Wherever possible, exhaustive tests of new medications or surgical procedures must first be performed on animals. These should, however, be guarded against experiencing any avoidable pain at all times.

NOTES

1. Henry K. Beecher, "Ethics and Clinical Research", in *New England Journal of Medicine*, vol. 274, no. 24 (June 16, 1966), pp. 1354–1360.
2. Lev. 18:5.
3. *Yoma* 85b.
4. *Pesahim* 25a and b; *Yoreh De'ah*, 195:3; 157:1; based on Deut. 6:5 and 22:26.
5. Maimonides, *Hil. Rotzeah*, 2:6.
6. Cf. "Whoever saves a single life is as he saved an entire world" (*Sanhedrin*, 4:5).
7. *Yoreh De'ah*, 157:1, gloss, end. For further details, see my *Jewish Medical Ethics*, 1975, p. 45 ff.
8. *Orah Hayyim*, 329:2–5.
9. *Yoreh De'ah*, 116; *Hoshen Mishpat*, 427:9–10.
10. *Hoshen Mishpat*, 426: 1; 427: 1–10.
11. Lev. 19:16 and Rashi, a.l.
12. *Beth Yoseph*, *Hoshen Mishpat*, 426; for details, see *Jewish Medical Ethics*, p. 96 f.
13. *Yoreh De'ah*, 336:1.
14. See *Orah Hayyim*, *Mishnah Berurah*, *Biur Halakha*, 329:4.
15. Deut. 21:23 and Nahmanides, a.l.; see also *Hulin* 11b.
16. *Baba Kamma* 8:4.
17. See note 14 above.
18. *Yoma* 82b; but see also *Keseph Mishneh*, *Hil. Yesodei ha-Torah*, 5:5.
19. *Hagahoth Maimuni*, *Hil. Yesodei ha-Torah*, 5:7; see *Jewish Medical Ethics*, p. 98.
20. Maimonides, *Hil. Yesodei ha-Torah*, 5:4.
21. See *Jewish Medical Ethics*, p. 53.
22. Based on Gen. 9:5 and commentaries.
23. Maimonides, *Hil. Rotzeah*, 1:4.
24. Lev. 21:5 and commentaries.
25. *Hoshen Mishpat*, 420:1 ff., 31.
26. Tanya, *Shulhan 'Arukh*, *Hoshen Mishpat*, *Hil. Nizkei ha-Guph*, 4.
27. Maimonides, *Hil. Mamrim*, 2:4.
28. Jacob Emden, *Mor u-Ketzi'ah*, on *Orah Hayyim*, 228; see my *Journal of a Rabbi*, 1966, p. 158 f.
29. Jacob Reischer, *Shevuth Ya'akov*, part 3, no. 75; Solomon Eger, *Gilyon MaHaRSHA* on *Yoreh De'ah*, 155:5; see *Jewish Medical Ethics*, p. 263, note 69.
30. *Hoshen Mishpat*, 272:9, based on Ex. 23:5.
31. *Even ha-'Ezer*, 5:14, gloss.
32. *Shevuth Ya'akov*, part 3, no. 71; J. M. Breisch, *Helkath Ya'akov*, nos. 30 and 31. See also *Journal of a Rabbi*, p. 170.
33. See responsa cited in preceding note, and my "The Medical Treatment of Animals in Jewish Law", in *The Journal of Jewish Studies*, London, 1956, vol. v, p. 207 ff.

THE MEDICAL TREATMENT OF ANIMALS
IN JEWISH LAW

This article is limited to a discussion of the conditions under which Jewish law permits the infliction of pain on dumb creatures for medical purposes and, conversely, under which it modifies certain religious precepts in order to prevent or mitigate their suffering. We are not, therefore, here concerned with the general attitude of Judaism to the prevention of cruelty to animals,[1] but a few observations on this subject and some comparative views of Christianity are essential as an introduction to the laws to be dealt with.

Both the Bible and the Talmud emphatically affirm the view that the brute creation, too, is sensitive to physical pain. But this purely physiological recognition assumes its real importance only in conjunction with the far more significant assertion that in the divine order of the cosmos the animal, with its feelings and even its "soul"[2] and its " merit",[3] is an object of compassion and distinct consideration,[4] or—as the Psalmist expresses it—that the salvation of the Lord extends equally to "man and beast"[5] (Ps. xxxvi: 7). In this respect, as Wohlgemuth[6] has shown in the course of his valuable articles on the place of the animal in Jewish thought and law, the outlook of the Hebrew Scriptures, with their many lessons and illustrations drawn from the animal kingdom, is considerably at variance with that of the New Testament in the imagery of which animals, with the exception of the lamb, hardly occur.

This difference of outlook characterises the respective views on the relationship of the animal to the human being as well as to God; it may be epitomised by the contrast between the Lord's argument with Job: "Who provideth for the raven his prey, when his young ones cry unto God, and wander for lack of food?" (Job xxxviii:41) and Paul's reasoning: "Who . . . feedeth a flock, and eateth not of the milk of the flock? . . . For it is written in the law of Moses, Thou shalt not muzzle the mouth of the ox that treadeth out the

Article published in The Journal of Jewish Studies, *London, vol. viii, nos. 3 and 4, 1956.*

For the sake of convenience, references to sources from the Bible and from Joseph Karo's *Shulhan 'Arukh* (the final comprehensive code of Jewish law) are given in the text. For the divisions and commentaries of this code the following abbreviations are used: O.H. (*Orah Hayim*); Y.D. (*Yoreh De'ah*); H.M. (*Hoshen Mishpat*); E.H. (*Even Ha-'Ezer*); M.A. (*Magen Avraham*); TaZ (*Turei Zahav*); and A.H. ('*Arukh Ha-Shulhan*). Encyclopedias are abbreviated as follows: JE (*Jewish Encyclopedia*, New York, 1901-6); OY (*Osar Yisra'el*, Berlin and Vienna, 1924); JL (*Juedisches Lexikon*, Berlin, 1927-30); and ERE (*Encyclopedia of Religion and Ethics*, Edinburgh, 1908-21).

corn. Doth God take care for oxen? Or saith he it altogether for our sakes? For our sakes, no doubt, this is written: that he that plougheth should plough in hope; and that he that thresheth in hope should be partaker of his hope" (1 *Cor*. ix:7, 9–10). Neither of these statements, it is true, may be completely representative of the attitude taken up, respectively, by all Jewish and by all Christian teachers. But the fact remains that the outlook manifested by the question addressed to Job was given concrete expression in a series of Jewish laws designed to guard animals against hunger,[7] overwork,[8] disease and distress, while Paul's questions led Pope Pius IX to object to the formation of an animal protection society because he believed the project to be based on a "theological error".[9]

On the other hand, there can be little doubt as to the definitely subordinate place occupied in Jewish thought by the brute creation in its relation to man. Whether the creation of man to "have dominion over the fish of the sea, and over the fowl of the air, and over every living thing that creepeth upon the earth" (Gen. i: 26 and 28) is to be understood as a divine command or, as Wohlgemuth[10] prefers, as a blessing, Jewish thinkers are agreed in assuming and justifying the subservience of the animal to man.[11] In Talmudic literature, moreover, there is much support for the opinion that the animals were specially created in order to serve man's material,[12] and indeed even moral,[13] needs. Among the purposes thus assigned to animals are, in particular, the medical requirements of man. A midrashic work,[14] probably of the tenth century,[15] expressly declared that "forbidden animals and reptiles were brought into the world only [in order to serve] as medicines for the sons of man upon earth." A similar claim was already made by Philo[16] almost a thousand years earlier. The Talmud, too, appears to subscribe to much the same idea in its statement[17]: "Of all the Holy One, blessed be He, created, there is not one thing for no purpose; He created the snail [as a remedy] for a scab; the fly [in a crushed state to be applied as an ointment] for [the sting of] a hornet; the mosquito [to be similarly applied] for [the bite of] a serpent; the serpent for a sore; and the spider for [the bite of] a scorpion." About a hundred years later, the Church Father St. Jerome[18] likewise maintained that everything was created for the sake of man and that, therefore, "all animals which are not created for food, exist to serve as medicines".

The early Jewish and Christian traditions, then, while they diverged substantially in their evaluation of the animal and of the sympathy due to it, held in common the belief in the utilitarian purpose of the animal creation and especially its uses for medical ends. Consequently, the two religions are in broad agreement on the right of man to exploit the dumb creatures for the promotion of his health. But there is virtually no parallel in Christian teachings for the many religious enactments found in Jewish sources on the claims of animals to kindness and even to the setting aside of various religious laws if these may cause injury or distress to them.

The question of the legality of using living animals for medical purposes arose only in connection with the practice of vivisection. The earliest controversial references to experiments on living beings concern, however, not animals but human objects. In a much discussed passage the first-century writer Celsus[19] accused the Alexandrian physicians Herophilus and

Erasistratos of having practised vivisection on human beings. This charge
was repeated by the Church Fathers Tertullian[20] and Augustine[21] with much
indignation. Some modern medical historians have sustained the charge[22];
other have rebutted it, explaining the accusation as a reflection of the criticism
of dissection in general as practised at Alexandria.[23] In the sixteenth century,
a similar charge was again preferred against the great anatomist Vesalius[24]
who himself complained that "the ecclesiastical caucus would not countenance the vivisection of the brain".[25] Although doctors in the Middle Ages
and after have at least thought of human vivisection,[26] it was left to the Nazis
in the twentieth century actually to practise that abomination on a horrifying
scale.

Vivisection on animals was not employed as an instrument of scientific
enquiry until the dawn of the modern era. Bacon advocated the recourse to
vivisection for medical purposes in terms suggesting that it was not actually
done in his day,[27] but Harvey spoke of it as having contributed to his discovery of the circulation of the blood.[28] As experiments on living animals
became more frequent, the protests of the "anti-vivisectionists" also grew
more vociferous. But the attacks on the practice were generally motivated by
sentimental rather than religious factors. The line usually adopted is well
typified by the fierce onslaught of Johnson: "Among the inferior professors
of medical knowledge", he wrote in 1785,[29] "is a race of wretches, whose
lives are only varied by varieties of cruelty; whose favourite amusement is to
nail dogs to tables and open them alive; to try how long life may be continued
in various degrees of mutilation, or with the excision or laceration of the
vital parts; to examine whether burning irons are felt more acutely by the
bone or tendon; and whether the more lasting agonies are produced by
poison forced into the mouth or injected into the veins. . . . With pretensions
much less reasonable, the anatomical novice tears out the living bowels of an
animal, and styles himself physician, prepares himself by familiar cruelty for
that profession which he is to exercise upon the tender and the helpless . . . by
which he has opportunities to extend his arts of torture, and continue those
experiments upon infancy and age, which he has hitherto tried upon cats and
dogs. What is alleged in defence of these hateful practices everyone knows;
but the truth is, that by knives, fire, and poison, knowledge is not always
sought, and is very seldom attained. . . . I know not, that by living dissections
any discovery has been made by which a single malady is more easily cured.
. . . It is time that universal resentment should arise against these horrid
operations, which tend to harden the heart, extinguish those sensations which
give man confidence in man, and make the physician more dreadful than the
gout or stone." In 1876 the Report on Vivisection by the Royal Society for
the Prevention of Cruelty to Animals also confirmed that the main objections
were not of a religious nature. It was only in that year that statutory restrictions on the practice were introduced in Britain for the first time in the Cruelty
to Animals Act. It limited lawful experiments on living animals to licensees
only, except if invertebrate animals were used. The Act was again found
satisfactory by the Royal Commission on Vivisection which was appointed
in 1906 and which published its reports in 1912.[30]

Only Islam appears to have raised religious objections to vivisection.

According to Meyerhof,[31] the dissection of living animals was forbidden to Arabs, and such experiments were therefore rendered impossible. But in the view of the Church vivisection is permissible if necessary for scientific research.[32] Amplifying the attitude of his Church, a Roman Catholic theologian recently stated that, whilst animals lack reason and personality and cannot therefore be entitled to strict rights,[33] it is unethical to inflict unnecessary pain on them; yet, such action would not involve the violation of any particular virtue (except probably that of temperance) nor constitute a mortal sin or a sin of injustice.[34] This appraisal of the present attitude of Roman Catholicism indicates a slight modification of the views on the rights of animals upheld by Christianity in earlier times. These have been summed up by Henry S. Salt[35] as follows: "There is . . . truth in the statement [by A. Jameson[36]] that 'the primitive Christians, by laying so much stress upon a future life in contradistinction to this life, and placing the lower creatures out of the pale of hope, placed them at the same time out of the pale of sympathy, and thus laid the foundation for their utter disregard of animals in the light of our fellow creatures.' It is certain that during the Middle Ages, when the Roman Catholic Church was dominant, there was, in this respect, little or no progress in humanitarian feeling, the indifference of Roman Catholicism to the claims of animals being broken only by the splendid example of St. Francis of Assisi, whose profound sense of brotherhood with beast and bird is the more remarkable owing to its contrast with the general callousness of his contemporaries.[37] It was this lack of sympathy which, surviving in large measure even to modern times, caused Buddhists to speak of Christendom as 'the hell of animals'."

The main principle governing the attitude to vivisection in Jewish law is already down in the *Shulhan Arukh*. Although it rules that the infliction of pain on animals constitutes a biblical offence[38] (*H.M.*, cclxxii. 9, gloss), yet "anything required for medical or other [useful] purposes" is expressly excluded from the prohibition (*E.H.*, v. 14, gloss). "Hence", adds Isserles, "it is permitted to pluck feathers from living geese[39] without considering [the ban on] causing pain to animals; nevertheless, one refrains [from doing so] as it is [an act of] cruelty" (ib.). Neither Isserles nor the fifteenth century sources[40] on which he based his rulings actually specify any particular medical uses to which living animals can be put. But early in the eighteenth century Jacob Reischer[41] used this ruling to permit a Jewish physician to test the effects of a new drug on an animal (in order to discover whether it might prove injurious or even fatal) before applying it to human beings. It has been argued, however, that Reischer's decision may be limited to the administration of possibly poisonous medicines (because the animal experiences no pain when taking them) without implying a general sanction to perform anatomical experiments on living animals by positive acts of cruelty.[42] Rabbinic opinions expressed during the present century are, on the whole, inclined to permit vivisection for medical research.[43] Wohlgemuth,[44] too, believes that Judaism is bound to justify the vivisection of animals as long as this may be conducive to the saving of human life. But he demands that, in exercising this right, measures be taken to protect the animal from all unnecessary torture and to exclude any operation which has no bearing whatever on the advancement of human health, such as the investigations into animal psychology which seek to resolve the problem of instinct or intelligence through unjustifiable acts of cruelty; for "even science must not emancipate itself from the norms of ethics".

We may now turn to the religious concessions granted in Jewish law for saving animals from pain and distress, and for the preservation of their health. Since the purposeless infliction of physical suffering on animals is, as already stated, regarded as an offence against biblical law (*H.M.*, cclxxii. 9, gloss), any conflict between this law and a rabbinic enactment justifies, in principle, the suspension of the latter.[45] Hence, in the cases to be mentioned here, the laws which may be disregarded out of consideration for the physical well-being of animals are invariably of rabbinic status. There is only one obvious exception: the Mosaic rule "Thou shalt not muzzle the ox when he treadeth out the corn" (Deut. xxv. 4), which covers restraining *any* animal from eating freely whilst engaged in *any* agricultural work (*H.M.*, cccxxxviii. 2), is set aside "if the food on which the animal works is injurious to its bowels, or if it is sick (so that the consumption of food would lead to diarrhoea), because the *Torah* is only concerned with its benefit, whereas it would not benefit [from the application of the usual rule in these circumstances]" (ib.,7).

The examples of laws modified for the sake of animal welfare occur almost exclusively among the Sabbath and festival regulations. As a rule, these concessions are hedged in by limitations similar to those applicable to the treatment of human beings. But in one respect the care for sick animals is even less handicapped by religious considerations than the attention to human ailments. The rabbinical ban on the application of medicines and several other medical cures on the Sabbath[46] is altogether removed for the treatment of animals. Hence, "if [an animal] ate an overdose of horse-beans and feels in pain, one may cause it to run in the yard until it becomes exhausted and [thus] cured" (*O.H.*, cccxxxii. 3), although similar exercises for the relief of man are forbidden on the Sabbath.[47] Again, "if an animal had an attack of congestion,[48] one may place it in water so as to cool it" (*O.H.*, cccxxxii. 4). In both cases the Talmud regards the rabbinical ban as inapplicable because, as Alfasi[49] explains, "a man's excitement over the treatment of his animal is not so great as to lead him to [the offence of] compounding spices [unlawfully on the Sabbath]."

Other relaxations of the Sabbath laws for the sake of sick animals include the permission to capture them[50] (*O.H.*, cccxvi. 2), to anoint their wounds, provided they are fresh and painful[51] (*O.H.*, cccxxxii. 2), and to tell a non-Jew to bleed them if venesection may save their life (ib., 4). Despite the prohibition to inflict a blemish on a first-born clean beast[52] (*Y.D.*, cccxiii. 1), it is lawful to bleed such an animal if it suffers from a "seizure of blood", as long as one does not deliberately aim at causing a permanent mark which would profane the animal and justify its slaughter (ib., 6). On the "intermediate days" of the Passover and Tabernacles festivals any medical treatment of animals, including venesection, is permitted, even if it involves "work" normally forbidden (*O.H.*, dxxxvi. 3). For the prevention of their physical discomfort it is also allowed to cut and adjust the hoofs of horses (ib., 1), although it is the accepted practice not to cut human hand- or foot-nails on these days (*O.H.*, dxxxii. 1, gloss). It is permitteed to remove flies irritating an animal even on the main festival days, notwithstanding the small wound thus caused (*O.H.*, dxxiii. 1).

On the Sabbath one may not deliver the young of cattle (*O.H.*, cccxxxii. 1), because it involves an undue exertion which is incompatible with the Sabbath rest.[53] Such action is also forbidden on festivals; but one may assist by holding the young to prevent it from falling to the ground, by blowing into its nostrils, and by placing the dam's teat into its mouth[54] (*O.H.*, dxxiii. 3). From the discussion in the Talmud[55] on this subject it is not quite clear whether these concessions apply only to festivals or also to the Sabbath.[56] Karo evidently assumes that the permission to render these aids is restricted to festivals, but in the *Turim* code[57] the sanction is expressly extended to the Sabbath as well. The same argument applies to the following regulation: "If an animal rejected its young, it is permitted on festivals to sprinkle the water of its placenta on the latter and to place a handful of salt into its mother's vaginal orifice so that she shall have compassion on it [through being re-minded of her birth-pangs], but it is forbidden to do so with an animal of the unclean species [since this will not help to arouse her pity]"[58] (*O.H.*, dxxiii. 4). To save an animal from suffering pain, it is also permitted to ask a non-Jew to relieve it of milk which may distress it on the Sabbath[59] (*O.H.*, cccv. 20).

The importance of the duty to relieve the sufferings of beasts, even at the cost of violating rabbinic enactments, is illustrated by another significant law. If an animal fell into a canal on the Sabbath, and the water is too deep to enable the animal to be fed on the spot pending its rescue after the termination of the Sabbath, one should bring mattresses or covers and place these under-neath the animal, so that it can raise itself to the surface and escape from its suffering, even though the handling of articles not previously designated for that particular purpose is normally prohibited (*O.H.*, cccv. 19). Yet it is un-lawful actually to lift the animal; one may, however, request a non-Jew to do so.[60] This law, which is of talmudic origin,[61] is of special interest in view of the answer given by Jesus to the question: "Is it lawful to heal on the Sabbath days?" He replied: "What man shall there be among you, that shall have one sheep, and if it fall into a pit on the Sabbath day, will he not lay hold on it, and lift it out?"[62] (Matth. xii. 10–11; cf. Luke xiv. 3 and 5). Although this passage does not accurately reflect the attitude of the talmudic rabbis, it clearly assumes that the healing even of animals on the Sabbath was sanc-tioned by the Pharisees.

The remainder of the Sabbath laws to be considered concern the pro-hibition of the carriage of burdens. Since beasts are expressly included among the beneficiaries of the Sabbath ordinance of rest (Ex. xx. 10; xxiii. 12; and Deut. v. 14), it is obligatory to restrain them from forbidden "work" (*O.H.*, ccxlvi. 3) and, in particular, from carrying any objects on the Sabbath except such as they wear for their protection (*O.H.*, cccv. 1). The codes devote an entire chapter to listing the articles "with which an animal may go out on the Sabbath" (*O.H.*, cccv). This list includes a number of items which, though not belonging to the ordinary outfit of animals, may be carried by them for health reasons or for the prevention of pain. Thus, an animal may go out with a bandage around its wound or a coat of splints to protect a fracture (ib., 11). But it must not wear anything which can easily slip off, such as a sort of shoe to guard its legs against bruises[63] or a bag covering a goat's udder to prevent it from being scratched by thorns (ib.). The same applies to any object not immediately essential for the preservation of its health—for example, the fox tail worn by horses between theirs eyes to ward off the "evil eye" (ib.). Nevertheless, it may be equipped with amulets, provided these are of "proven" efficacy;[64] but an attested human charm is not necessarily efficacious for animals (ib. 17). As a protection against the cold, one may place a cushion on an ass, but not on a horse (since it does not suffer from the cold); it is forbidden, however, to remove the cushion, because the animal experiences no pain if this is not done (ib., 8). Calves and foals, because of their short necks, may suffer physical discomfort if they have to pick up their food from the ground;[65] for their relief it is permitted to suspend a basket with fodder around their neck, though they must not be allowed to walk out of the yard with it (ib., 10).

The strict prohibition of all forms of castration and direct sterilisation is applicable to animals, birds and even fish[66] as well as to humans. In fact, the biblical proscription is originally mentioned only in the context of the exclusion of maimed animals from serving as sacrifices on the altar (Lev. xxii. 24). The Talmud[67] widely extended the scope of this ban to embrace the deliberate sterilisation of all living creatures. Accordingly, it is regarded a biblical offence to impair the reproductive organs of any male animal or bird, though the sterilisation of females creatures is not culpable (*E.H.*, v. 11). The administration of a "sterilising potion" to male animals, too, is forbidden (ib., 12). The prohibition extends also to instructing a non-Jew to carry out the operation on a Jewish-owned beast (ib., 14) and, according to some authorities, even to selling him cattle or fowl when it must be presumed that he will castrate them, unless the operation will not be performed by the buyer himself[68] (ib., gloss). On the other hand, sterility may be brought about by operations not aimed at disabling the reproductive organs directly, such as the removal of a cock's crest (ib., 13, gloss) which was believed to prevent it from mating by depriving it of its pride.[69] Since the castration of animals serves a useful purpose, the question of inflicting pain on them does not arise in this connection. The ban on the practice, as Isserles[70] emphasises, is neither motivated nor supported by this consideration; it involves solely the breach of a distinct biblical law.

It is a moot question whether the biblically valid law against torturing living creatures includes the deliberate inflicting of pain on humans, too.[71] While Azulay[72] can see no reason for discriminating between man and animal in this respect, Ya'ir Bacharach[73] holds the view that "the *Torah* is concerned only about pain caused to brutes, because they lack knowledge and the intelligence to endure suffering, whereas man can choose to ease his mind and to accept with love whatever befalls him."

NOTES

1. On this subject see *JE*, vol. iv, p. 376, s.v. "Cruelty to Animals"; *O Y*, vol. ix, p. 49 ff.; *JL*, vol. v, p. 945, s.v. "Tierschutz"; and especially the articles by J. Wohlgemuth, "Vom Tier und seiner Wertung", in *Jeschurun* (Berlin), vol. xiv (1927), p. 585 ff.; "Das Leid de Tiere", in *Jeschurun*, vol. xv (1928), pp. 245 ff. and 452 ff.; and "Einfuehlung in das Empfindungsleben der Tiere", in *Jeschurun*, vol. xvi (1929), pp. 455 ff. and 535 ff.

2. So, e.g., "The righteous man regardeth the soul of his beast" (Prov. xii. 10); cf. Gen. i. 24. See Wohlgemuth, in *Jeschurun*, vol. xiv, p. 591 ff.

3. Cf. God's "remembrance" of the beasts and cattle in Noah's Ark (Gen. viii. 1) and the significant comments of the *Midrash* on this passage (*Gen. Rabbah*, xxxiii). A similar thought occurs in the divine argument with Jonah on the destruction of Niniveh (Jon. iv. 11) and the aggadic interpretation of it (b*Ta'anith* 16a). With reference to the "merit" of animals, the Talmud states axiomatically: "The Holy One, blessed be He, does not withhold the reward of any creature" (b*Pesahim* 118a); cf. Sa'adyah Gaon, *Emunoth weDe'oth*, iii; and Maimonides, *Guide of the Perplexed*, iii. 18. See also Wohlgemuth, in *Jeschurun*, vol. xvi, p. 460 ff. There is also some support in biblical and talmudic sources for the assumption that animals, too, are held to account and punished for their misdeeds; see Wohlgemuth, in *Jeschurun*, vol. xiv, p. 597 ff. Cf. also Nachmanides, on Gen. ix. 5. Animals were also credited with ethical instincts; for talmudic statements and comparative sources in patristic literature, see Michael Guttmann, in *MGWJ*, vol. lxxviii (1934), p. 180 f. See also Wohlgemuth, op. cit., p. 594 ff.

4. So, e.g., Ps. cxlv. 9, 15, 16; and cxlvii. 9. To illustrate the text: ". . . and His tender mercies are over all His works" (Ps. cxlv. 9), the Talmud relates that R. Judah, the Prince, was smitten with a tooth-ache, because he had rebuked a calf which shielded its head in his lap when taken to the slaughter with the words: "Go, for this reason you have been created!"; he was relieved from his pain only when, on another occasion 13 years later, he asked his mother to spare some young weasels whilst sweeping the house (*Baba Meṣi'a* 85a; cf. *Gen. Rabbah*, xxxiii. 3; and xcvi. 5); ṣee Wohlgemuth, op. cit., p. 606 f.

5. On the significance of this passage, see Wohlgemuth, in *Jeschurun*, vol. xvi, p. 464 ff.

6. Wohlgemuth, in *Jeschurun*, vol. xvi, p. 457 (note). On the attitude to animals of the classic peoples, see W. E. H. Lecky, *History of European Morals*, London, 1911, vol. i, p. 44 ff.

7. A talmudic sage taught that it was forbidden to buy any animal or bird unless one had first assured the necessary supply of its food (j*Ketuboth*, iv. 8). Greater legal force was attached to the teaching derived from the verse: "And I will give grass in thy fields for thy cattle, and thou shalt eat and be satisfied" (Deut. xi. 15): "It is unlawful for man to taste anything until he has provided food for his cattle" (b*Gittin* 62a). Surprisingly, this law is not codified in the *Shulḥan 'Arukh*, although its validity is indirectly assumed (O.Ḥ., clxvii. 6; Gumbiner [M.A., a.l., 18] mentions it expressly). But it is included in several other codes, for example, by Maimonides (*Hil. 'Avadim*, ix. 8) and Abraham Danzig (*Ḥayei Adam*, xlv. 1). On the extension of this law to the feeding of birds, see Azulay, *Birke Yoseph*, O.Ḥ., clvii. 4; and *Sha'are Teshuvah*, O.Ḥ., clxvii. 2.

8. See Ex. xxiii. 5; Deut. xxii. 4; and the talmudic treatment of these laws in b*Baba Meṣi'a* 32a ff. Even the regulation regarding the hired servant: "In the same day shalt thou give him his hire" (Deut. xxiv 15) is homiletically applied to the beast (*Ex. Rabbah*, xxxi. 7).

9. See E. Westermark, *The Origin and Development of the Moral Ideas*, 1906, vol. ii, p. 508.

10. Wohlgemuth, in *Jeschurun*, vol. xiv, p. 601. Cf. also Rashi, a.l.

11. See Wohlgemuth, op. cit., p. 600 ff.

12. This idea often recurs; it is expressed most succinctly in the *Mishnah*: "Were they [i.e. the beasts and birds] not all created in order to serve me?" (m*Qiddushin*, iv. 14). On this assumption the Talmud also explains why man's creation came last and only after that of the lower creatures (see *Tosephta Sanhedrin*, viii. 3)—in terms very similar to

those used by Philo (*De opificio mundi*, §25) and later by several Church writers; see V. Aptowitzer, "Anteilnahme der physischen Welt an den Schicksalen des Menschen," in *MGWJ*, vol. lxv (1921), p. 72 f. The belief that the whole universe was created only for the sake of man was strongly supported by Sa'adyah Gaon (*Emunoth Wede'oth*, iv [begin]; and *Responsa*, ed., Poznanski, no. 11, p. 25) and Abraham ibn Ezra (on Gen. i. 26). Although Maimonides (*Guide to the Perplexed*, iii. 13 and 25; cf. Hans Libeschuetz, "Eine Polemik des Thomas von Aquino gegen Maimonides," in *MGWJ*, vol. lxxx [1936], p. 93 ff.) polemised against this view, it was again affirmed by Isserles (in his philosophic work *Torath Ha'olah*, iii. 22) and Mordecai Jaffe (*Levush*, O.Ḥ., i [begin]) in the sixteenth century. For some further ancient Jewish and comparative sources, see Aptowitzer, op. cit., in *MGWJ*, vol. lxiv (1920), p. 227 f.

13. Thus, the rabbis held that animals, particularly those which "you look upon as super-fluous", were created as agents for the divine punishment of man (*Gen. Rabbah*, x. 5 and 7; cf. also *Sifra, Emor*, ix [end]; b*Ta'anith* 18b; *Semahoth*, viii [end]; and *Midrash Rabbah*, on Eccl. iii. 17); see Aptowitzer, op. cit., p. 309 ff. The idea that man can learn moral lessons from animal behaviour is already expressed in the Bible regarding the exemplary industry of the ant (Prov. vi. 6) and the wisdom of animals generally (Job xxxv. 11). In the Talmud this concept is further elaborated: "If the *Torah* had not been given, we might have learned decency from the cat, [the prohibition of] theft from the ant, [of] incest from the dove, and the proper [marital] conduct from the cock" (b'*Eruvin* 100b).

14. *Tanna d'be Eliyahu Rabbah*, i (end); ed. Friedmann, 1902, p. 6.

15. See *JE*, vol. viii, p. 568; and *JL*, vol. v, p. 864 f.

16. Philo fragment, reproduced by Eusebius, *Praeparatio Evangelica*, viii. 14, 60; see P. Wendland, *Philos Schrift ueber die Vorsehung*, Berlin, 1892, p. 80; cited by S. Krauss, *Talmudische Archaeologie*, 1910, vol. i, p. 711 (note 476).

17. b*Shabbath* 77b. The same statement, with slight variations and attributed to another author, also appears in j*Berakhoth*, ix. 2. Krauss (op. cit., vol. i, p. 257) evidently over-looked these passages when he characterised as genuinely Jewish the assertion by Ben Sirah "God bringeth up medicines from the earth; by them the physician healeth" (Ecclus. xxxviii. 4) in contrast to Philo's belief in the medicinal purpose of the animal creation. Krauss regarded the latter view as "an assumption which had less justification for the Jewish world than for the pagan." Nevertheless, the mainly vegetarian origin of medicinal products was sometimes assumed in classic Jewish sources. Ben Sirah's statement is quoted in *Gen. Rabbah*, x. 6; and a similar assumption appears in the *Targum* on Eccl. ii. 5.

18. Jerome, *Contra Jovinian*, ii. 6; quoted by A. Harnack, *Medizinisches aus der aeltesten Kirchengeschichte*, 1902, p. 22.

19. Celsus, *Proem*.

20. Tertullian, *De anima*, cap. x.

21. Augustine, *De anima et eius origine*, iv. 3 and 6. These passages suggest (probably without justification) that human vivisection was still practised in his day (early fifth century); see L. Thorndike, *A History of Magic and Experimental Science, 1923*, vol. i, p. 147 (note 7).

22. So T. Puschmann, *A History of Medical Education*, 1891, p. 78; and L. Edelstein, "Die Geschichte der Sektion in der Antike", in *Quellen und Studien zur Geschichte der Naturwissenschaften und der Medizin*, 1932, p. 102.

23. See C. Singer, *The Evolution of Anatomy*, 1925, p. 34 f. The justification of the charge is placed in doubt particularly by Galen's silence on it.

24. See J. J. Walsh, *The Popes and Science*, 1912, p. 117.

25. See F. J. Cole, *A History of Comparative Anatomy*, 1944, p. 57.

26. See Edelstein, op. cit., p. 88 (note).

27. See Lecky, op. cit., vol. ii, p. 176 (note).

28. See Lecky, loc. cit., citing Acland's Harveian Oration, 1865, p. 55.

29. Johnson, in *Idler*, no. 17 (August 5, 1758).

30. See *ERE*, vol. xii, p. 626 f.

31. M. Meyerhof, "Science and Medicine", in *Legacy of Islam*, ed., T. W. Arnold and A. Guillaume, 1931, p. 344.

32. See A. Bonnar, *The Catholic Doctor*, 1948, p. 99 (note 2).
33. For the contrast between this and the Jewish view, see note 73 below.
34. See J. McCarthy, in *Irish Ecclesiastical Record*, vol. lxxi (1948), p. 266 ff.
35. Salt, in *ERE*, vol. vi, p. 837.
36. A. Jameson, *Commonplace Book of Thoughts, Memories and Fancies*, London, 1854, p. 209.
37. Cf. Wohlgemuth, in *Jeschurun*, vol. xvi, p. 457.
38. The prohibition is derived from the injunction: "If thou see the ass of him that hateth thee lying under its burden, thou shalt forbear to pass by him; thou shalt surely release it with him" (Ex. xxiii. 5). In the Talmud (b*Baba Meṣi'a* 32a f.) it is a matter of dispute whether this derivation is of biblical or rabbinic status, but our code follows Maimonides (*Hil. Roṣeaḥ*, xiii. 9) in accepting the more stringent view and in considering the infliction of pain on animals as a breach of biblical law (see Karo, *Keseph Mishneh*, a.l.). But for a contrary view, see Joseph Babad, *Minḥath Ḥinnukh*, commandment no. 80.
39. In order to obtain quills for writing purposes. But the consideration of cruelty does not apply if the removal of some feathers from a bird's neck (Y.D., xxiii. 6, gloss) or of some wool from a sheep's neck (Y.D., xxiv. 8, gloss) is essential to prepare the animal for ritual slaughter; see *Be'er Hetev*, Y.D., xxiv. 8; and *Oṣar Ha-Poskim*, E.H., v. 14 (no. 87); vol. i (1947), p. 255. The ritual slaughter of animals, though decreed as a measure to mitigate their pain (Aaron Halevy, *Sepher Ha-Ḥinnukh*, commandment no. 451), may itself be forbidden as an act of cruelty in cases where it does not constitute a religious precept (*Shiṭṭah Mequbbeṣeth*, on *Baba Bathra* 20a).
40. Israel Isserlein, *Responsa*, no. 160; and Jonah Gerondi (?), *Issur weHetter*, no. 59. In more general terms the decision first appeared in *Pisquei Tosaphoth*, *Av. Zarah*, i; based on Tosaphoth, *Av. Zarah* 11a. See Wohlgemuth, in *Jeschurun*, vol. xv, p. 256.
41. Reischer, *Responsa Shevuth Ya'aqov*, part iii, no. 71; see H. J. Zimmels, *Magicians, Theologians and Doctors*, 1952, p. 16.
42. So Jacob Ettlinger, *Responsa Binyan Siyon*, part i, no. 108; quoted in *Oṣar Ha-Poskim*, loc. cit.
43. J. M. Breisch (*Responsa Ḥelqath Ya'aqov*, no. 30), in an elaborate enquiry, came to the conclusion that, while there was no basis in Jewish law for a legal ban on such experiments, they were indefensible for moral reasons. But J. Weinberg, in the same responsa work (no. 31), expressed the view that mere considerations of piety must be waived when the sufferer affected by them will be not oneself but others; moreover, "what right have you to assume that the pain of animals counts more than the pain of sick people who might be helped [by these experiments]?" This view is also shared by J. D. Eisenstein (*OY*, vol. ix, p. 50), albeit with the proviso that "every effort should be made to remove the animal's suffering as far as possible," since "it is known that thousands of persons have already been cured by the discoveries made through anatomical research in this manner." Cf. also Zimmels, op. cit., p. 17.
44. Wohlgemuth, op. cit., p. 248 f.
45. This conclusion is reached in the Talmud (b*Shabbath* 128b) and applied in practice in the codes (see M.A., O.Ḥ., cccv. 11).
46. The ban, which is of mishnaic origin (see m*Shabbath*, xiv. 3, 4; and xxii. 6), is a precautionary measure to guard against the "pounding of spices" on the Sabbath. It prohibits the employment of medicines and various other treatments for people who suffer mere pain (O.Ḥ., cccxxviii. 1 ff.).
47. Such as massages to induce perspiration for relief (ib., 42).
48. J. Preuss (*Biblisch-Talmudische Medizin*, 1911, p. 349) identifies the complaint with plethora.
49. Alfasi, on *Shabbath* 53b. So also TaZ, O.Ḥ., cccv. 2; and M.A., O.Ḥ., ccxxxii. 2.
50. But it is a culpable offence to capture animals on the Sabbath for other purposes including the provision of medicinal preparations (O.Ḥ., cccxvi. 7).
51. The ointment of old (closed) wounds is merely "an enjoyment", not a cure, and therefore forbidden (ib.).
52. See Deut. xv. 19 ff.
53. So Rashi, *Shabbath* 128b.

54. On these aids, see Preuss, op. cit., p. 499; and Krauss, op. cit., vol. ii, p. 114.
55. b*Shabbath* 128b.
56. See A.H., O.Ḥ., cccxxxii. 1 and 2.
57. *Tur*, O.Ḥ., cccxxxii and dxxiii.
58. The explanations added in brackets are based on the source of this law in b*Shabbath* 128b; see Preuss, op. cit., p. 499 f. Krauss (op. cit., vol. ii, pp. 114 and 505 [note 783]) wrongly infers that such "compassion" was shown only *to* clean animals.
59. This is the only law in this category not expressly mentioned in the Talmud. It is first codified by Asheri (*Baba Meṣi'a*, ii. 29).
60. See Maimonides, *Hil. Shabbath*, xxv. 26; and M.A., O.Ḥ., cccv. 11.
61. b*Shabbath* 128b.
62. See Wohlgemuth, in *Jeschurun*, vol. xv, p. 264 (note 1).
63. This appliance was made of metal (b*Shabbath* 59a) and served to shield the animal's feet from stones (so Rashi, a.l.; and on *Shabbath* 53a), or to prevent the animal from slipping (m*Parah*, ii. 3); see Krauss, op. cit., vol. ii, p. 516 (note 907).
64. The Talmud (b*Shabbath* 61a and b) and the codes (O.Ḥ., ccci. 25) set out detailed rules on what constitutes a "tested" amulet which may be worn on the Sabbath for prophylactic or therapeutic reasons. The same "tests" do not of necessity "prove" the efficacy of animal charms because, as the Talmud (b*Shabbath* 53b) explains, man has a guardian angel and thus a chance of recovery from diseases fatal to animals.
65. So Rashi, *Shabbath* 53a. But Krauss (op. cit., vol. ii, p. 126) suggests that without the fodder basket, the old animals would grudge the young ones their food.
66. So Jacob Emden, *Responsa She'ilath Ya'veṣ*, part i, no. 111.
67. b*Shabbath* 110b. See also *Tosephta Makkoth*, v. 6; and *Tosephta Bekhoroth*, iii, 24. Cf. Preuss, op. cit., p. 255 ff.
68. On the operation of these laws in talmudic times, see Krauss, op. cit., vol. ii, p. 115 f.
69. So Rashi, *Shabbath* 110b.
70. Isserles, *Darke Mosheh*, E.H., v.
71. Legally this question arises only when the fulfilment of a religious precept would involve exposure to serious pain or discomfort; for example, if a priest, by leaving his house as soon as a death has occurred in it, must suffer the severe cold outside without adequate protection until the corpse is removed or alternative shelter becomes available. The verdict would then be affected by the status of the offence to inflict pain on human beings; see sources in the following notes.
72. Azulay, *Birke Yoseph*, Y.D., ccclxxii. 2. It has been overlooked that Maimonides (*Hil. Roṣeaḥ*, xiii. 9) evidently also supports this view, since he assumes that legally it is no more lawful to cause pain to another Jew than to an animal; see *Me'irath 'Enayim*, Ḥ.M., cclxxii. 13. For a similar view see also Adreth, *Responsa RaSHBA*, nos. 252 and 257.
73. Bacharach, *Responsa Ḥawath Ya'ir*, no. 191. It is noteworthy that the very argument used by Bacharach (*viz.*, the animal's lack of reason) to *assign* to the animal special rights not enjoyed by man is employed by the Church (see *supra*, note 33) to *deprive* animals of any strict rights. There is also a talmudic parallel to the view that, in some respects, greater legal protection is extended to the animal than to man. The law "Thou shalt not muzzle the ox when he treadeth out the corn" (Deut. xxv. 4) carries the biblical penalty of flagellation only in respect of animals, but not for the imposition of similar restraints on human workers (*Sifri* and Rashi, a.l.; b*Baba Qamma* 88b; and Maimonides, *Hil. Sekhiruth*, xiii. 2), though such action is nevertheless prohibited (Ḥ.M., cccxxxvii. 1; see gloss and commentaries, a.l.; and Elijah Mizrachi, commentary on Rashi, loc. cit.). This discrimination, too, it has been suggested, is due to the fact that "a human worker is different, because he is gifted with intelligence" (A.H., a.l., 2). For a similar reasoning, see also David ibn Zimra, *Responsa RaDBaZ*, part i, no. 728.

TAY-SACHS DISEASE AND THE JEWISH COMMUNITY

Tay-Sachs is a rare congenital infants' disease of the brain and nerve cells, invariably leading to death at between three and four years of age following a long and painful process of degeneration. It occurs only in children whose parents are both latent carriers of it.

Tests in America, Britain and elsewhere have shown that carriers are ten times more common among Ashkenazi Jews than among other Jews or Gentiles—one in thirty Ashkenazi Jews as against one in three-hundred others. When both parents are carriers the risk of their child being afflicted is one in four. That means the chance of a Jewish Ashkenazi Tay-Sachs child being born is one in 3,600 ($30 \times 30 \times 4$); among others it is one in 360,000 ($300 \times 300 \times 4$). In absolute terms, in a recent year out of nine cases in this country three were Jewish, whilst in America (where the proportion of Jews in the population is about four times as high as in Britain) it has been estimated (1971) that 70% of the 52 such patients born annually are Jewish.

In the absence of any known cure, and in view of the Jewish proclivity to the disease, the British Tay-Sachs Foundation proposed in 1972 carrying out a massive screening project among the Jewish community, aimed at examining 10,000 Jews a year (by a blood test) to ascertain whether they are carriers and, if so, to determine by a further (amniotic fluid) test during the fourteenth to sixteenth week of any pregnancy whether it will produce a diseased child, with a view to the termination of such a pregnancy.

A screening operation on such a scale would require the active co-operation of synagogues and other Jewish organisations. To this end, the Foundation turned to the Board of Deputies and to me. Upon consultations with other rabbinical authorities, the Board was advised on 24th August 1972 as follows:

1. According to Jewish law, there is no objection to these tests being carried out within the Jewish community as proposed by the British Tay-Sachs Foundation and to synagogues and other Jewish communal

Article published in L'Eylah (*Summer 1976*), *the magazine of the Anglo-Jewish Ministry issued by the Office of the Chief Rabbi.*

agencies giving whatever assistance they can in the carrying out of this programme.

2. We wonder whether such tests could include single persons, so as to help avoiding the marriage of two carriers of the disease and the resultant chance of children afflicted with the disease being conceived.

3. No general ruling can be given on the termination of pregnancies in cases where the generation of a diseased child is suspected or established. All such cases would have to be submitted to individual rabbinic decisions. But this reservation does not affect the agreement to carry out the programme as proposed.

However, before endorsing and recommending a scheme of such dimensions as requested, I felt that, apart from purely religious and moral considerations, it would be essential to bear in mind some wider communal ramification which required expert medical advice. I therefore wrote in identical terms to Lord Cohen of Birkenhead and Lord Rosenheim as follows:

27th October 1972

The British Tay-Sachs Foundation proposes to undertake a massive "Screening Project" among the Jewish community, having regard to the fact that the disease is disproportionately prevalent among Ashkenazi Jews. In an effort eventually to carry out the requisite blood-tests on some 80,000 Jewish young persons, it is intended to organise this project through the active help of synagogues, Jewish clubs, etc. The Foundation has therefore approached me, as well as the Board of Deputies, to secure the endorsement of the community and the help of Jewish communal agencies through our sanction and encouragement of the proposed enterprise.

From the Jewish religious and moral point of view, I see no reason to withhold my support. The only proviso I have made on religious grounds —and this has been accepted by the Foundation—is that we would much prefer the effort to be concentrated on young people before they marry, so as to discourage marriages between two carriers of the disease, rather than on young married couples, where the tests would be useful as a "preventive" measure to prevent the birth of a Tay-Sachs child only by recourse to abortion.

However, a further factor which should be carefully considered has now been brought to my attention by a medical friend. It might be feared that by subjecting an entire community to these blood-tests, not to mention the attendant publicity which is bound to focus public attention on the Jewish proclivity to the disease, one might induce a communal "neurosis" by creating a state of undue anxiety or notoriety, especially among the less sophisticated members of the community. I understand from the Medical Director of the Foundation that the current annual incidence of the actual disease is estimated at 9 children in the country at large, including 3 Jewish children.

In the light of these considerations, I would deeply appreciate your considered opinion on whether the medical indications to prevent the annual birth of 3 such children outweigh the more intangible social counter-indications to warrant mass-testing of a specific section of the population as proposed. I would not wish to commit myself and the Jewish community to the support of such a massive programme without the endorsement of the community's two most eminent medical personalities. I make this approach to you with the agreement of the Chairman and the Medical Director of the Foundation.

(sgd.) I. Jakobovits

Lord Cohen replied as follows:

1st November 1972

I do *not* consider the proposed screening project should be supported in the form it is presented.

As you write, the current annual incidence of the disease is estimated at 9 in the UK of whom 3 are Jewish; since the duration of life of a child with Tay-Sachs disease is less that 4 years, there can never be more than 12 Jewish cases at any one time. There is no known treatment for the disease so that (unlike phenylketonuria) no benefit to the child follows its detection. Amniocentesis is not unreliable in its results, and the risks of abortion are not negligible.

Even if two heterozygotes marry, the chances of an affected child are only 1 in 4. Thus, the exercise would be, if the requisite blood tests were carried out on 80,000 young persons, of whom of course many might refuse to be tested, a very costly procedure involving a great deal of technical manpower, of which there is a very short supply which could be put to more potentially fruitful projects. I agree with you that the risks of a "communal neurosis" are by no means remote.

May I add one or two further comments:

1. The figures given for gene frequency (by which I think is meant heterozygotes or carriers) appear to me to be taken from New York figures. It would be of interest to know if these are confirmed for the UK. I should think that to test say 1,000 Ashkenazi Jews would be sufficient.
2. Tay-Sachs disease is only one of a group of genetically-determined diseases in which the nerve cells contain abnormal amounts of fatty and other substances which ultimately destroys them.
   A great deal of fundamental research is being carried out on the enzyme deficiencies which are responsible for these conditions. By a curious coincidence, I note in today's *Guardian* a reference to work at Keele University; and the Children's Research Fund, of which I am President, and Chairman of the Council, is supporting similar studies.

I have no objection to your showing this letter to the Chairman of the Foundation, for although the screening project is one which on a cost-benefit basis (apart from the other matter you raise) I could not conscientiously support, I would wholeheartedly urge support for more research into the fundamental mechanisms of this group of genetically-determined metabolic brain disorders.

(sgd.) Cohen of Birkenhead.

From Lord Rosenheim the following two letters were received shortly before his death:

5th November 1972

Thank you for your interesting letter. You ask a series of difficult and penetrating questions.

First of all, I entirely agree with you that if there is a screening method available, this should be offered to young people prior to marriage rather than after.

I have been able to talk about the matter with Professor Harry Harris, who is the Galton Professor of Genetics at University College, London, and Director of the Medical Research Council Unit on Human Biochemical Genetics. He told me that a Tay-Sachs Foundation was already active in the United States, but pointed out that people are more socially and ethnically conscious in the States than they are here. There is certainly a considerable risk of provoking acute anxiety in positive heterozygotes and the possibility of arousing some racial feeling.

On the other hand this condition, in which potential carriers can be detected and in which study of the amniotic fluid early in pregnancy can diagnose an affected infant, is clearly one of the conditions that lends itself best to this form of screening.

As I understood Professor Harris, he calculated that 1 in 3,600 Ashkenazi children might be born with the condition, and I imagine that this is in line with the observed numbers that you wrote to me about. This really raises the question of "Cost-Benefit" with the cost in terms of anxiety rather than hard cash.

(sgd.) Rosenheim

17th November 1972

Further to my letter of November 5th, I have now had a talk with Dr. Philip Evans (the Director of the Foundation) and have also discussed the screening problem with a group of doctors specially interested in screening.

I was impressed by Philip Evans and by the care with which the scheme for screening has been prepared, and I was interested to learn that a pilot trial of the scheme was being started in Wembley.

I am still doubtful about the "cost-benefit" in terms of anxiety and stress, but do appreciate that this is a serious attempt to get rid of a disease that itself causes great distress. I believe that it would be wise to wait for the results of the Wembly trial and would suggest that you should be able to get valuable impressions from the Rabbi and others concerned with encouraging young people to have the test.

I am sorry not to be more helpful. I think that you will note that I am scientifically in favour, but that humanity prompts caution.

(sgd.) Rosenheim

Following these exchanges, a number of pilot schemes were operated at several London synagogues and at Hillel House for students. Despite extensive publicity, including a full-page feature in the *Jewish Chronicle* and letters circulated among 7,000 general practitioners as well as among thousands of synagogue members, the results proved disappointing. Two years' efforts secured only a total of 341 volunteers, of whom 181 were unmarried. Altogether 16 were found to be carriers (1 in 21), and none of the couples tested were at risk.

Further screening projects were abandoned, as the Foundation came to the conclusion that the monitoring of pregnancies in women who already had Tay-Sachs babies was more rewarding. This was done in 20 cases of the infantile type of GM2 gangliosidosis, with 4 positive diagnoses, 4 terminations and 4 diagnoses confirmed. It was found that "at present, in Britain, follow-up of families offers more than mass-screening does". (I am grateful to Dr. Philip Evans, the former Medical Director of the Foundation, for this information.)

*   *   *   *

Since then a great deal of communal screening has been carried out, with varying degrees of success, in several Jewish communities, notably in America, Israel and, for a short time, South Africa. Numerous medical papers have been published on the subject, as have a number of rabbinical responsa and statements. Some of this sizeable literature has quite recently been listed in a comprehensive survey by Dr. Fred Rosner, himself a senior haematologist and currently head of the American Association of Orthodox Jewish Scientists (*Tay-Sachs Disease; To Screen or not to Screen*, in *Tradition*, Spring 1976, pp. 101–112).

On the Jewish religious attitude, Dr. Rosner cited the views of Rabbi Moshe Feinstein (in an unpublished responsum of 1973) and Rabbi J. David Bleich (*Or Ha-Mizrach*, Summer 1973, pp. 216 ff.; and *Tradition*, Winter 1972, pp. 145–148), as well as a statement by the Association of Orthodox Scientists (1973). While they encourage tests before marriage (only Rabbi Bleich prefers childhood or early adolescence; the others by contrast seek to avoid the nervous tension and prolonged anxiety which might result from testing young people not yet contemplating marriage), they all object to amniocentesis and to abortion if the test shows that the foetus is defective.

Dr. Rosner and his Association endorse this prohibition as absolute. But they are evidently unaware of the more permissive verdicts given by other rabbis. Several leading authorities generally sanction the termination of a pregnancy with a high risk of an abnormal birth, e.g. through German measles, provided the abortion is performed within the first forty days, or in special cases even within the first three months (J. Weinberg, *Seridei Esh*, 3:17; S. Israeli, *Amud Hayemini*, 35; E. Waldenberg, *Tzitz Eliezer*, 9:51; see *No'am*, 9:193–213, and 16, *Kunteres Harefu'ah*, 27). Dayan L. Grossnass of the London Beth Din, too, is inclined to permit an abortion if Tay-Sachs is confirmed, since such a child would in any event not be viable (*Lev Aryeh*, 2:205; see also my *Jewish Medical Ethics*, 1975, pp. 262 f. and 274 f.).

EUTHANASIA

On 25 January 1973, a Conference on "Death Control" was held in Westminster Cathedral Hall under the patronage of Cardinal Heenan. In response to an invitation by the Chairman of the Conference for a statement on the Jewish moral code relating to the treatment of the dying, the Chief Rabbi sent the following letter:

"There is little, if anything, in Cardinal Heenan's eloquent statement (as published in the national media) on 'Death Control' which the moral directives of Jewish law would not endorse with equal emphasis and conviction. We, too, would make a fundamental distinction between any deliberate hastening of death, whether with or without the patient's consent, on the one hand, and the withdrawal of *artificial* means to sustain a lingering life in its terminal stages on the other hand, particularly when the recourse to such 'heroic' methods would serve only to prolong the patient's agony. However, the sanction to discontinue treatment would not include the withdrawal of food or other necessities of life.

"By the same token, Jewish law would not object to the use of pain-killing drugs, even when this might involve some risk of life, provided the sole purpose in applying such treatment is to relieve the patient's suffering. His welfare would invariably take precedence over any other consideration, if necessary even including his ability to make his spiritual and temporal preparations for death, so long as the relief from pain and misery is not wittingly purchased at the cost of life itself.

"The basic reasoning behind the firm opposition of Judaism to any form of euthanasia proper is the attribution of *infinite* value to every human life. Since infinity is, by definition, indivisible, it follows that it makes morally no difference whether one shortens life by 70 years or by only a few hours, or whether the victim of murder was young and robust or aged and physically or mentally debilitated".

Chapter Ten

HOMILETICAL MEMORIES OF AMERICA

EXPLORING AMERICA—AND JUDAISM

JUDAISM AND NATURE

Jewish Travels—Past and Present

(Rosh Hashanah—First Day)

Rosh Hashanah marks not only our reunion with God. It is also a reunion among ourselves. Faces we have not seen for months or even a year reappear for these High Holydays. Even for many of our regular worshippers Rosh Hashanah is the day of the great reunion. For, during the summer months we have been dispersed, some resting quietly on beaches or in mountains nearby, and others travelling far and wide to distant parts in the four corners of the world.

This year I, too, was among the travellers, together with my family. Inspired by what we saw and learnt while motoring over 4,000 miles through the spectacular West of this great land, I propose this Rosh Hashanah and Yom Kippur to present to you the message of these Holy Days in the form of a religious travelogue, to give you some thoughts and impressions, some reflections and lessons evoked by five weeks of adventure among some of the grandest works of God and man on earth.

TRAVEL IN JEWISH HISTORY

Jews have always been the most travelled of all peoples. Indeed we are the only nation popularly characterised for its mobility—by being called the "Wandering Jew". Jewish history begins with travel, when God commanded Abraham "Get thee out of thy country, and from thy birthplace, and from thy father's house, unto the land that I will show thee", and it will end with travel, with the "Ingathering of the Exiles", when we are to return to the very land which God once showed as the destination of the first Jew's first journey.

Throughout history we have travelled, sometimes voluntarily and more often driven by force. We have lived not only in mobile homes, but in mobile communities. We have been a people of immigrants and emigrants, of refugees and displaced persons, of pilgrims and travelling merchants and plain tourists,

Five sermons, as "A Religious Travelogue on a Tour of the Western States" by caravan, delivered at the Fifth Avenue Synagogue, New York, on Rosh Hashanah and Yom Kippur 5726 (1965).

not to speak of commuters and *Meshulachim*—travelling collectors and roving participants in international conferences.

Before we reached our own land, we wandered forty years in the wilderness. In the land, we also did not stay put, but travelled three times a year to the Temple in Jerusalem for the three "foot-festivals". Then, when the Temple was destroyed, we journeyed as exiles to the far-flung lands of our dispersion, never remaining for very long before being on the move again, pressed by some new expulsion or oppression.

By the Middle Ages many Jews had developed a *wanderlust* which had important historic consequences. Jews were the great international traders at a time when others never yet ventured out of their countries. Jews became the principal link between East and West, the only bridge between Moslem and Christian culture in medieval Europe, responsible for communicating works of literature, science and medicine from the Orient to the Occident. Many famous Jews enriched literature with celebrated books on their travels; men like Eldad Hadani in the ninth century, who wrote on his adventures in the Far East; or in the twelfth century Benjamin ibn Tudella, famous for the description of his visits to remote Jewish communities, and the renowned sage and poet Abraham ibn Ezra who never stopped travelling and wrote about it in prose and verse. And Jews had a prominent share in the discovery of America by Columbus, providing him with maps, money and some companions for his historic expedition.

JEWISH TRAVELLING TODAY

Even in our more settled modern times, Jews have remained the best customers of travel agencies and transportation companies—on a sufficient scale, even among observant Jews, to compel ships and planes to provide *kosher* meals without extra cost (probably the only places where eating *kosher* costs no more than eating *trepha*).

Yet in all our travels through a land counting six million Jews we found few of them. In the dozens of camping grounds we visited, on mountain trails and desert roads, among the adventurous hikers in the great National Parks and famed scenic attractions, our *yarmulkas* were as unique as the *challas* baked in our trailer.

Through historic circumstances, we have become addicted to the big cities and to crowded resort hotels. Jews are today the most urbanised people on earth, and as a result many of us have become divorced from nature and insensitive to its thrills and quiet inspiration. Most Jews somehow seem to prefer the loud clanging of a dance orchestra to the mystic eloquence of a rushing mountain stream or the sweet, soothing music of a humming-bird. Even when they trot around the world, the exotic stores in teeming cities attract them more than the wonders of God's creation discovered in the captivating loneliness of little-trodden paths.

JEWISH LIFE AND NATURE

There was a time when the Jew lived with nature even in his crowded lacklustre ghetto existence. His whole regimen of life was tied to nature. Wherever he found himself, he first determined the East, like a living compass, to know where to orientate his prayers. In the mornings he would look out for the first signs of the dawning day to fix the earliest time for his *Shacharith* prayers, and in the evenings he would search for a vantage point to view the last rays of the setting sun to establish the latest time for *Minchah*. On Saturday nights he would scan the darkening skies for the first glitter of three stars signalling the termination of the holy Sabbath, and every month he would watch the phases of the moon to bless its renewal in a special prayer while looking at its waxing face. In the autumn, he would remove his residence for a week to a *Sukkah*, peering through its plant-covered roof at the twinkling stars above, and in the spring he would look out for the first trees in bloom to recite the lovely blessing: "Blessed art Thou . . . Who hath not allowed aught to lack in His world, and Who hath created beautiful creatures and beautiful trees to delight with them the sons of man."

Today, with all our freedom, we live artificial, stilted lives, with our horizons narrowed and our vision limited by the very walls our civilisation has erected. We draw the air we breathe from air conditioners, the food we eat from cans and jars, the knowledge we possess from newspapers and magazines, the laughter we enjoy from well-rehearsed professionals, the inspiration of our leisure hours from a pack of cards, and the latest reflections on Judaism from the clichés and trite messages published in *The New York Times*. Our personal prayers are as cold as frozen food, our observances as mechanical and uninspiring as a commuter drive, and our understanding of the breadth and majesty of Judaism as remote as a view of the Hudson River from the choking tunnel underneath it.

EXPLORING JUDAISM

To explore the thrills of Jewish life and thought requires the same spirit of adventure and the same exertions as to explore the wonders of nature. It requires breaking away from crowds and their unthinking, conforming conventions. It requires giving up some comforts and climbing up some rough and steep paths for a while. It requires long journeys, sometimes through parched deserts and sometimes over rugged mountains on lonely trails. It calls for hardihood and a willingness to be different. The search for the infinite vistas of Judaism can no more be successful without hard study and sustained exercise than one can reach the greatest enchantments of nature in armchairs.

Rosh Hashanah, celebrating the creation of nature, invites us to undertake such a tour to explore Judasim. Let us plan and carry out this exciting trip together. We will use our great religious literature as our maps, our beautiful synagogue as our trailer, our Sabbaths and festivals as our camping grounds, our members as our passengers—and leave the driving to me! The trip will involve some hardships, particularly for us as *kosher* travellers, and it will cost some money. But it is better to lose money on an adventure to inspire us for the rest of our lives than on a gambling spree. The money we need will be spent on our trailer—on keeping our synagogue and its activities in perfect running order—and on the exciting enterprise of dedicating our unique resources to the advancement of Judaism in the community at large.

Tomorrow and on Yom Kippur, continuing our travelogue, I will give you a little preview of what we are going to discover on our joint grand tour together—some of the fabulous sights of Jewish vision and inspiration we are going to see.

Meanwhile the ancient *Shofar*, also fashioned by nature without any artificial embellishments, is about to call us all aboard. It calls everyone of us to assemble here at fixed times throughout the year, for services, classes, lectures and other activities—each of them a guided tour to view and learn about some new scene in the vast and magnificent panorama of Judaism. On these tours we shall discover the profound depths of the canyons of Jewish thought, the never-ceasing sparkling fountains of Jewish scholarship, the endless sea of the Talmud, the uplands and lowlands of Jewish history, the broad streams of great Jewish movements, and the fertile fields of Jewish productivity—all in the pure, refreshing air of Jewish ethics and under the infinite skies of our eternal faith.

Let us, then travel together, as Abraham and Isaac once journeyed together to the mountain at the call of God, so that it may be said of us, as it was of them, *vayelkhu sheneihem yachdav*, "and they went together," *belev shaveh*, "with a common heart", father and son, rabbi and congregation, on history's greatest adventure. Then God will assure us, as He assured Abraham after his journey, "Because you have done this thing . . . I will surely bless you, and I will multiply your seed (glittering) as the stars of the heaven and (persevering) as the sand which is upon the sea-shore; and your seed shall possess the gate of his enemies; and in your seed shall all the nations of the earth be blessed" (Gen. 22:16–17).

"HOW GREAT ARE THY WORKS, O LORD"

Grand Canyon, Yellowstone and Redwoods

(Rosh Hashanah—Second Day)

Yesterday the *Shofar* called us to a great adventure: to travel together on an exciting tour to explore the wonders and discover the beauties of Judaism. Today we start.

The first and foremost destination of any trip in search of Jewish beliefs must be God. How does one find God? Where does one discover Him? Through what route can one reach the love and fear of God? Maimonides provides the answer in a striking paragraph of his great law code:

And which is the way to love and fear Him? At the time when a man contemplates His wondrous and great works and creatures, and he sees from them His wisdom which is beyond value and without end, he will immediately love and praise and glorify Him and passionately desire to know the great Lord . . . and when he ponders over these matters, he will immediately be startled and tremble and know that he is but a small creature . . . standing with a puny mind before the perfect Intellect, as David said, "When I see Thy heavens, the work of Thy fingers, what is man that Thou rememberest him?" (Ps. 8:5) (*Hil. Yesodei Hatorah*, 2 : 2).

Let us, then, carefully follow the well-marked roads of this route-map. Maimonides stresses that one discovers God *bema'asav uvru'av hanifla'im hagdolim*, "in the great wonders of creation". Likewise, Jewish law provides a special blessing *oseh ma'aseh bereshith*, praising God, as "the Maker of the creation in the beginning", only at the sight of extraordinary, dramatic natural phenomena. This blessing is to be recited when one sees "mountains or hills which are uncommon, and through which the might of the Creator is manifest", in the words of the *Shulchan Arukh* (*Orach Chayim*, 228:).[1]

We recited this blessing twice on our trip through the West.

GRAND CANYON

First at the Grand Canyon. Here indeed is the most distinct signature of God etched on the surface of our planet, like bold letters of an artist's name emblazoned on a masterpiece he has created.

Here we stood at the rim of a gigantic break in the crust of the earth. an abyss 200 miles long and over one mile deep, flanked by oceans of walls delicately sculptured in the most fantastic rock formations, all draped in a symphony of the most diverse colours, as if illuminated by a million different spotlights—a spectacle changing colour every hour, as the sun's rays penetrate at a different angle into the terraced depths of these bowels of the earth.

There, one mile beneath us, roared the mighty Colorado river, carrying every hour half a million tons of sand and mud, yet looking like a meandering brook amid the massive bluffs engorging it. Were you to place man's tallest edifice, the Empire State Building, at the bottom of the gorge, it would be dwarfed into insignificance in the vastness of the deep.

Here, in the immensity of space, time is at a standstill, as you see laid bare before you in distinct formation geological layers of rocks going back to the infancy of creation, encrusting in its walls the petrified fossils of ocean-life that once covered the region and the footsteps of wild-life long extinct.

Here, in the awesome expanse facing you, all sounds and voices are drowned in an eerie silence resembling the stillness of outer space, and the flimsy movements of humans and birds and clouds seem unreal and lost against the backdrop of this timeless immobility.

Here, indeed, man has relinquished his dominion of the earth, as he stands, puny and overawed, before this wonder, where time and space and power and beauty appear to be infinite.

What human work of art, what masterpiece of music or painting, of architecture or poetry, can arouse you to such ecstasy of awe and ravishment? Who can gaze at this supreme spectacle without exclaiming, in utter humility and reverence, "How great are Thy works, O Lord, how very deep Thy

---

[1] Compare the recognition by our medieval savants that the letters in the Hebrew words *elokim* ("God") and *ha-teva* ("nature") have the same numerical value (86).

thoughts" (Ps. 92:6)? Who can feed his mind and soul with such a surfeit of grandeur, and not sense the irrepressible urge to praise the Maker of it all, *oseh ma'aseh bereshith*?

YELLOWSTONE PARK

We recited this wonderful blessing a second time at Yellowstone, the world's greatest playground of inanimate nature.

Here, the very rocks and sands seem to be quick with life, pregnant with dancing fountains, steaming pools and uproarious cauldrons by the thousands, disgorging their boiling liquids from the womb of the earth in thrilling displays of endless variety and colour, all set in a feast of scenic beauty.

Here, you actually see *oseh ma'aseh bereshith*, the Creator presently at work, as you watch the earth labouring in angry convulsions to give birth to its contours, just as it must have done at the beginning of the universe when, in the opening words of *Genesis*, "the earth was unshaped and void, and darkness was upon the face of the deep, and the spirit of God hovered over the face of the waters".

Here, as you stand in breathtaking wonderment before desolate mounds suddenly spewing out, with almost clockwork regularity, tens of thousands of gallons of scalding water rising high into the sky above, or before bubbling paintpots playing a duet of noise and colour, or before the thundering waterfalls of the Park's rivers tearing gorges of the wildest splendour in their cascading descent to the sea, as you see all this fantastic artistry on the canvas of nature, how can you fail to echo the Psalmist's exclamation "The fool said in his heart: 'There is no God' " (Ps. 14:1); how can you question the reality of the Creator and believe all this pageantry created itself or evolved by chance or accident? An atheist standing against this background looks indeed absurd and incongruously silly, like a retarded child in a maze of computers.

COMMON AND UNCOMMON WONDERS

After one is moved to the adoration of the Creator by such visions of the fabulous and the stupendous, a sober thought begins to puzzle you: Does one really have to travel to the Grand Canyon or to Yellowstone to discover God? Is not the birth of any child as miraculous an event as the eruption of the highest geyser, or the construction of the smallest flower as awesome as the whole Grand Canyon? Is not the flight of a common fly as full of wonder as an eagle soaring in the skies, and a squirrel scurrying across Central Park as marvellous as a bear roaming in Yellowstone? Why did not our Sages ask us to recite the blessing *oseh ma'aseh bereshith* at the sight of the wonders in a blade of grass, or a simple flower, or an ordinary fly?

Obviously because, being common, these experiences have ceased to excite us.

To find God manifest in the spectacular and the extraordinary, in the grandiose and the unusual, rather than in the daily and familiar wonders around us, is surely a human and not a divine limitation.

When we have survived a hazardous operation or recovered from a serious illness, we feel moved to thank God for His favours and recite a special prayer of thanksgiving in the synagogue. But is not the healing of a little cut in a finger just as miraculous, perhaps all the more so because it is common and expected; is this finger's unaided self-repair any less deserving of thankfulness for God's mercies than an uncommon deliverance from acute danger?

And why do we need a spectacular once-a-year religious experience like Rosh Hashanah and Yom Kippur, with its *Shofar* and fasting, to stir us to repentence and spiritual excitement? Is not any common weekday morning or evening service hallowed by prayers as uplifting and inspiring as the lofty liturgy on these days?

The answer is: of course God is as manifest in New York's Central Park as in America's wonderlands; of course a finger repairing an injury by itself is no smaller a miracle or favour than a recovery from major surgery; and of course our prayers every Sabbath and weekday are no less holy than on Rosh Hashanah and Yom Kippur. But familiarity breeds contempt, and what is common we do not appreciate, like a good wife or good health when we enjoy them, or the blessings of peace and freedom when they are abundant.

But these truisms occur to us only *after* we have experienced the unique and the colossal. After a visit to the fabulous West you may recognize the majesty of the Creator nearer home, too. After we recover from a grave illness, we may also appreciate the daily gift of health, and after we have sensed the magic touch of the superb *Aleinu* prayer in the centre of *Musaph* on Rosh Hashanah, we may also become sensitive to its noble spell at the end of every service throughout the year.

Through the experience of the unusual, we learn to value the usual.

NATURE'S AIDS TO UNDERSTANDING THE BIBLE

Living amid the enchanting beauty of nature teaches other religious lessons as well, besides the reality of God's existence. It also promotes the study and perfection of our communication with Him.

Much of the rich imagery of the Bible, the powerful sweep of poetry in the Prophets and Psalms, can only be understood by an intimate familiarity with nature. Take, for instance, Isaiah's phrase *vekhol atzei hasadeh yimcha'u khaf* (35:12), "and all the trees of the field clap their hands", describing the joy with which nature will greet the return of God's people. Who can really visualise the Prophet's ecstatic vision of nature's jubilant response if he has never experienced the solitude of a forest and tuned in his ear to the melodius orchestra of a breeze rustling with a hundred harmonious tunes through the trees clapping their leaves and branches? Who can have a true conception of the invincible yet controlled power blended with infinite grace and rhythmic beauty, depicted by the Psalmist in the verse *mikoloth mayim rabbim adirim mishberei yam adir bamarom haShem*, "above the voices of many waters, the mighty breakers of the sea, the Lord on high is mighty" (93:4), if he has never spent an hour or two in contemplation before the thunderous waves of the ocean smashing their foaming mass against the resisting barriers of rocks and cliffs in a never-ending, deafening contest of power?

And who can fully understand, without a thorough study of bird-life and its mysteries, God's argument with Job on the superiority of Divine Providence over man's intellect, contrasting the hatching habits of the stork and the ostrich:

> *"The wing of the ostrich beateth joyously;*
> *but are her pinions and feathers the kindly stork's?*
> *For she leaveth her eggs on the earth, and warmeth them in the dust,*
> *and forgetteth that the foot may crush them,*
> *or that the wild beast may trample them.*
> *She is hardened against her young one, as if they were not hers;*
> *though her labour be in vain, she is without fear;*
> *because God hath deprived her of wisdom,*
> *neither hath He imparted to her understanding."* (Job 39:13–15)

Or challenging human impotence later in the same chapter:

> *"Doth the hawk soar by thy wisdom,*
> *and stretch her wings toward the south?*
> *Doth the vulture mount up at thy command,*
> *and make her nest on high?*
> *She dwelleth and abideth on the rock, . . .*
> *from thence she spieth out the prey,*
> *her eyes behold it afar off.*
> *Her young ones also suck up blood,*
> *and where the slain are, there is she."* (39:26–29)

NATURE'S AIDS TO PRAYER

If nature, then, teaches us how to understand the word of God and the message of His spokesmen, it also instructs us how to address our words of prayer to Him.

On our tour we found few experiences more exhilarating than to sing our daily prayers surrounded by the charms of God's exquisite nature.

When you stand early in the morning, all alone with your own family, at the rim of the Grand Canyon and exclaim *atta gibbor le'olam haShem*, "Thou art mighty for ever, O Lord", you find it natural to declare with equal conviction the continuation *mechayeh methim atta rav lehoshi'a*, "reviving the dead, Thou art great great in saving".

Or when, high on a cliff overlooking the magnificent Pacific coast on one side and the fertile valleys on the other, and accompanied by the twittering choir of care-free birds breaking the stillness of the morning, you recite the daily Psalm *Hallelu eth haShem min ha'aretz . . .* , "Praise the Lord from the earth, ye sea-monsters and all deeps . . . , mountains and all hills, fruit-trees and all cedars, beasts and all cattle, creeping things and winged fowl" (148:7–10), your words become winged as nature joins you in a panegyric of our common Creator. *Ume'elav yikareh*, the prayers read themselves and well up almost instinctively from the recesses of your heart.

And when you arise before daybreak to await the matchless glory of a sunrise in the desert, standing quite alone among the fragrant shrubs in the vast expanse your eyes behold, and then, as the first glinting rays of the distant fireball illumine your *Tallith* and *Tephillin*, and you think of the nature-

Psalm's description of the sun "as a bridegroom coming out from his chamber, rejoicing as a strong man to run his course" (19:6), you indeed feel elated like an *Unterfuehrer* at a wedding, accompanying the bridal pair of sun and earth in a ceremony of sheer joy and beauty.

When your eyes are raised to scan the towering peaks of a massive mountain range locking heaven and earth together, you can understand why David looked to the mountains to find the assurance of God's strength and providence: *Essa eynay el heharim* . . . , "I lift up mine eyes unto the mountains, from whence shall my help come? My help cometh from the Lord, who made heaven and earth" (Ps. 121:1–2).

And when you travel for long hours through the frightening, parched desert, evidently created to test man's endurance and the power of his faith in God to sustain life out of nothing, you begin to appreciate why the Torah was revealed in a wilderness. There is no place in which you become more conscious of your utter dependence on the Source of all life. Here nothing is alive besides you and God.

THE TESTIMONY OF REDWOODS

From the treeless mountain peaks and the barren, lifeless desert, let me finally take you to a forest of redwoods, the oldest and largest living things on earth.

Among these titans we find ourselves mystically translated into another plane of existence, into a new dimension of time and thinking. Walking in hushed silence on a mattress of needles deposited for over 2,000 years, we have entered into the remnants of a world which is the very antithesis of our rushed age of fast-changing fashion and garish noises, of quick movement and short-lived values.

Here, among these huge, overwhelming ancients, we are in the presence of the last remaining members of a unique race. These very trees you see before you flourished at the time when the Dead Sea scrolls, our oldest existing writings, were written; these trees were grown in the days of Hillel and Shamai, and they were well toward middle age when our Temple was destroyed by the Romans.

These mighty ambassadors of another time have outlasted the rise and fall of empires, and they still stand as strong and majestic today as they did long before anyone except Jews believed in one God. In the presence of these redwoods, even the vainest and most irreverent of men goes under a spell of wonder and respect.

Is this not the image of Judaism, the *etz chayim*, our "tree of life"? Here is a civilisation planted long, long ago, which flourished when Europeans and Americans were still cave-dwellers, which had reached respectable middle age long before any of the other great religions were born, and which today is just as majestic and indestructible, still living—indeed the oldest living faith on earth?

As we traverse the forest of Jewish thoughts and observances, pointing like a sea of redwoods to heaven, should we not be filled with infinite awe and reverence before this unique phenomenon of timelessness?

Of course, just as there are vandals who cut down or mutilate these priceless trees, or who spoil the beauty of the place by thoughtlessly leaving their litter around, so we have heartless Jews with no appreciation for their heritage who cut down Jewish observances or violate them, or who introduce the litter of un-Jewish customs and new-fangled innovations into the sacred territory of our faith.

Rosh Hashanah warns us to preserve our heritage from spoilage and carelessness, so that the generations to come may continue to enjoy the stately beauty, the clean, invigorating air, and the quiet inspiration of the timeless grandeur which the living trees of our faith have provided for the countless generations past, speeding the time when *lo yare'u velo yashchithu bekhol har kodshi* . . ., "they will no longer hurt nor destroy in all My holy mountain, for the earth shall be full of the knowledge of the Lord as the waters cover the sea" (Is. 11:9).

MAN'S CONQUEST OF NATURE

Hoover Dam and Hollywood

(*Yom Kippur—Kol Nidrei*)

> And God said: *"Let us make man in our image, and after our likeness; and let them have dominion over the fish of the sea, and over the fowl of the air, and over the cattle, and over all the earth . . ." (Gen. 1:26).*

In rabbinic literature Yom Kippur is often called *yom hakadosh*, "the holy Day". With this *Kol Nidrei* service we have entered the holiest period in the Jewish calendar. To millions of Jews this service marks the most deeply religiour experience of the year, and to some the only encounter with holiness in the year. Tonight virtually all Jews, whether observant, secular or assimilated, sense the touch of holiness.

You must have been taken aback, therefore, on reading the themes for my sermons this year as a religious travelogue on our tour through America this summer, that I would devote this night to so urbane a subject as the *Ho*over Dam and *Ho*llywood, both of which seem to have little more in common with *ho*liness than the first two letters. Yet what we saw and heard at these two sites may turn out to be highly relevant as a supreme message of this holy hour.

THE JEWISH VIEW OF HOLINESS

Holiness these days is an elusive, vague, almost sanctimonious term. It hardly belongs to the common vocabulary of the twentieth century. Holiness conjures up weird visions of disembodied saints, remote from life; of some ascetic hermits living in the ethereal space of another world. Or else it is associated with the pomp and ceremony of another faith.

In the Jewish view, all this has little to do with holiness. You can live a holy life and yet enjoy all the legitimate pleasures the world has to offer. A Sabbath, when we eat and drink festively, is no less holy than Yom Kippur when we fast and mortify our flesh. Even a weekday can be holy, if we sanctify our home life, our business conduct, and our leisure activities under the law of God.

Kedushah, holiness, means above all to control and sublimate nature, to transcend and ennoble the sensual drives seeking to enslave us, to break the mastery of nature over us, the grip of the brute within us.

Even of God we use the attribute of holiness in this connection: *Mi kamokha . . . ne'edar bakodesh nora thehilloth oseh phele*, "Who is like Thee among the mighty, O Lord, who is like Thee, glorious, in holiness fearful in praises, doing wonders?" (Ex. 15:11). *Ne'edar bakodesh*—His holiness is manifest in *oseh phele*—His ability to perform wonders, to assert His mastery over the laws of nature and to bend them at His bidding.

HOOVER DAM

Applying this to man, we come to Hoover Dam, one of the greatest monuments to man's ingenuity in controlling the blind and often destructive forces of nature. For untold generations the wild and moody waters of the mighty Colorado river went to waste and havoc. People in that region were at the mercy of its capricious whims—in some years suffering from devastating floods, and at other times from equally baneful droughts leading to widespread famine. Nature vanquished man.

Then they built the Hoover Dam, one of the world's most stupendous engineering wonders. And man vanquished nature.

Here, deep in the arid desert, across a precipitous, narrow canyon, they sank more than three million cubic yards of concrete to raise a massive barrier, over 700 feet high, containing a fantastic powerhouse of bustling life and energy, with its thirty miles of subterranean tunnels, its intricate canals and spillways, and its imposing array of giant hydro-electric generators.

Behind the dam, the stored-up water—cleaned of the silt carried in the ravaging river upstream—has formed the largest man-made lake to provide magnificent recreation grounds for three million visitors annually in surroundings of wild beauty, reminiscent of the Gulf of Aqaba at Elat in panorama, colour and climate. And downstream the dam supplies a constant regulated flow of water and power, irrigating without fail over a million acres of rich farmland, reliably meeting the water needs of numerous cities, and feeding millions of homes and factories with electricity.

Thus was a river transformed from a natural menace to thousands through its recurrent floods and droughts into a source of enjoyment and productivity for millions.

HOLINESS AS A MORAL DAM

In moral terms this precisely is the challenge of holiness. Man without barriers and controls is vanquished by nature, subject to its whims and caprice. At times when the surging waters of passion run high, sullied by mud and smut, he cannot contain the flood as it roars on to wreak havoc and devastation in life. And at other times, when the wellsprings of energy and ambition dry up, such a person without a reservoir of moral strength becomes blighted, drained of the will to work and eventually withering in indolence like fields in a drought. Flood and drought—too much unbridled desire and too little urge to work—these are the two major evils responsible for most of the crime, vice, addiction to narcotics and alcohol, broken marriages, dropouts from school, and wasted careers today.

Holiness demands, above all, that we erect a powerful dam within ourselves, that we control our lives by an iron discipline to conquer nature and to master the rampaging torrent of its forces inside us.

Let me give you a few examples of great men who built such dams within themselves:

The Talmud relates the story of some captive women who were accommodated in the loft of the home of a certain great sage, R. Amram. When a shaft of light illumined one of the captives, a particularly attractive girl, this sage, entranced by her exceptional beauty, began to ascend a ladder to reach her. Halfway up, he suddenly cried out: "Help, fire; there is a fire in my home," so as to attract a crowd forcing him to control himself. When his disciples later reproved him, saying "Master, you have shamed us," he replied: "It is better I should disgrace you in this world than that you should be disgraced by me in the next" (*Kiddushin* 81a). This is holiness in action.

Another, more recent example: A famous Chasidic Rebbe lost his father during the festival of Sukkoth. Knowing that *yom tov hi miliz'ok*, the law forbids grieving on *Yom Tov*, he so controlled his emotions that he carried on with the festivities of the holy days as if nothing had happened, even dancing jubilantly on Simchath Torah as in previous years. Then, when the festival terminated, the moment *havdalah* was made, he broke forth in a flood of tears and mourning for the father he had loved and revered so much. This is holiness in action.

Finally, a yet more recent case: The other day a new record of the beautiful Modzitzer Chasidic songs was issued. It included a powerful and moving work called *Ezkerah* from the *Yom Kippur-Ne'ilah* service, composed by Rabbi Israel Taub, the first Modzitzer Rebbe, who has been rated as "the most prolific and original of Chasidic composers." It is said that he began this composition in 1914 in Berlin, where he had come for a leg amputation. Unable to have anesthesia while undergoing the amputation, he drowned his agony by singing the prayer *Ezkerah*—"I will remember Thee, o Lord, and I will tremble." That is the origin of this magnificent composition. This, too, is holiness in action.

Here you have three men who constructed such mighty dams inside them that they could regulate at will the most powerful feelings of passion and grief and pain.

Of course, not every river can have a Hoover Dam, and not every person has the energy to erect a colossus of a barrier such as these three men did. But everyone can and must work at it.

THE DISCIPLINE OF THE MITZVOTH

What are the concrete raw materials with which to construct such a dam?

Our Sages tell us: *lo nitnu hamitzvoth ela letzaref bahen eth habriyoth*, the principal purpose of all the Divine commandments is to refine us (*Gen. Rab.* 44:1), to train us in the art of self-control and discipline.

The *kashruth*-laws, for instance, are a barrier. They allow some foods to pass, and they bar others. The marriage laws are a dam; they regulate relations which are permitted, even with our own wives, and they ban others which we must resist, sometimes even at the cost of life, such as incest and adultery.

These and all other laws accustom the observant Jew to live an even, strictly controlled life, to exercise his power of self-discipline constantly. He holds back his appetite until he has first recited his prayers in the morning and said a blessing over food, and he holds back his sleep until he has read his night prayers. He has a rigid schedule on when to work and when to rest, when to be happy—as on *Yom Tov*—and when to mourn—as on the fast days during the year. He disciplines his life by severe restrictions on the times when he can smoke, on the clothes he wears, the business practices he pursues, the books he reads, and even the shavers he uses.

Such a dam to regulate one's life is a major construction, and it often takes years of hard effort to raise it. But when a man achieves this, what a blessing to himself and to society! Through self-discipline, a barren, empty life is turned into a recreation ground and a source of constructive energy.

How much spiritual air pollution would be cleaned up, how many marriages would be sheer joy, how many homes would be saved from destruction, how many friendships would endure, how much communal activity would be galvanised into action, and how much creative endeavour would be fertilised and sanctified, if people—by constant exercises in self-control—would learn how to keep themselves in check, how to guard their tongue from offensive speech, and how to regulate the flow of life by a code of laws.

HOLLYWOOD

Now let us move on to our next destination in our tour, in our exploration of holiness this night.

If there is any place in the world which may be regarded as the antithesis to holiness it is, one presumes, Hollywood ("would" that it were "holy"); where the stars are not high in heaven, but often low on the murky ground; where the floods of passion and faithlessness and crime are not only left to flow unimpeded but displayed as entertainment for all the world to see. What can this capital of lewdness teach us about the subject of holiness to deserve mention on this holy night?

Well, there were two incidents during our brief visit there which may well provide us with two important moral lessons, one negative and one positive.

We had an introduction to one of the studios to view a film production. On calling to arrange our visit, I was asked if I had any young children with

me, since that particular show included some rather unchaste scenes and
would not be suitable for children. I replied, if it is not fit for children, it
cannot be fit for the parents either.

RELIGION AND MORALITY FOR JUVENILES

Does this not illustrate one of the most curious and perverted notions of
our age? Religion and morality are for juveniles only. Children must be
protected from smutty literature, indecent pictures, immoral thoughts; they
must not drink or gamble. But for grown-ups all this is in order, as if they
were less sensual and more immune to corruption. What sort of a world are
we going to have if goodness and decency were to be the exclusive preserve
of children? What kind of an example are we going to set our children if we
preach virtue for them and practise vice for ourselves?

The same goes for Judaism. Many people seem to think the Torah is a
children's Torah. On Pesach they conduct a *Seder* not for themselves, but
only for the sake of the children. They expect their children to go to Hebrew
classes, but Jewish learning and reading is not for them.

Judaism teaches the reverse. Of course children must be trained in the
virtues of religion and decency and learning to prepare themselves for the
challenges of life ahead. But legally no obligations of any kind are incumbent
on them until they reach *Bar Mitzvah* age—13 years for boys and 12 years
for girls.

Judaism is an adult religion, meant primarily for grown-ups. With Jewish
education often ending instead of beginning in earnest with *Bar Mitzvah* age,
is it any wonder that so many Jews have such a juvenile, primitive notion of
Judaism, that their understanding of Jewish thought—stunted before their
brains matured—is of nursery or elementary school level, and therefore
quite incompetent to cope with the complex intellectual challenges of our
times? With such a childish appreciation of Jewish values, is it surprising
that the flimsiest arguments or distractions encountered on the college
campus are enough to knock down their Jewish loyalties and convictions
like a pack of cards before the slightest breeze?

For holiness, just as for specially "holy" prayers like *Kaddish* and *Kedu-shah*, we require a quorum of adults, not children.

FILMING THE RECORD OF OUR LIVES

Finally, our second experience at Hollywood. Eventually they found a
suitable show for us and our children. We walked through a huge hangar
cluttered up with a maze of wires, switches, lights, cameras and all the para-
phernalia of a make-believe world in which ship cabins never smell the taste
of the sea, in which houses have only two walls, and in which tears come from
artificial eye-drops, not from the heart.

The moment any filming starts, a hushed silence of whisper and tip-toe
walking descends on this beehive of bustling activity. I felt envious, wishing
that worshippers at synagogue services would always observe a similar
decorum.

We watched a one-minute sequence being filmed. It took one full hour to get this little scene right. Six times they had to repeat it before they were satisfied that every detail of movement, speech and lighting was just perfect.

While we observed this painstaking fastidiousness, a saying of our Sages sprang to mind and meaning: "Look at three things, and you will not come into the hands of sin: Know what is above you—a seeing eye, a hearing ear, and all your deeds are written in a book" (*Ethics of the Fathers*, 2:1). We did not have to be told by Shakespeare that

> All the world's a stage,
>
> And all the men and women merely players.

Our Rabbis gave us this analogy as a foolproof formula against sin: Remember that you are actors on the stage of life. Remember that above you is *ayin ro'ah*, a candid, seeing camera, *ozen shoma'ath*, with a sound track, *vekhol ma'asekha basepher nikhtavim*, making a permanent record of every movement you make, every sound you utter and every thought you think. Whether in public or in secret, all our actions are being faithfully filmed and recorded.

One day, when our souls are liberated from the imprisonment and limitations of the body, this film of our life will be played back publicly—for us and all other souls to see.

How great will be our disgrace if that film will show us in scenes shaming us, how will we squirm and blush in humiliation if we and others see ourselves portrayed in unbecoming behaviour; and how immense will be our glory if the film will do us credit and record us acting out our lives in uprightness and decency and virtue!

Should we not, therefore, lavish at least as much care and preparation on how to act every minute of our life, making sure that every action, every word and every thought is just right, as professional actors do for the fleeting moments of a passing show?

This, surely, is the most pressing message of this holy *Kol Nidrei* hour, to guarantee that we can never again fall into the grip of sin: If we constantly remember that whatever we do, or say, or think will once be on display for all to see, then we shall not find it hard to build mighty dams to stop the floods of evil and suffering, and to assure a never-ending flow of the blessings of goodness and health for ourselves and our fellow-men.

MAN'S BEQUEST TO HISTORY

Mesa Verde and an Indian Reservation

(*Yom Kippur—Musaph*)

Remember the days of old; consider the years of every generation (Deut. 32:7).

If to others history is mainly the record of the past, to us Jews it is the guide and inspiration for the future. The greater part of the Hebrew Bible, the blueprint for our lives, is history. From it we draw the mainsprings of Jewish hope and purpose, and by it we measure the success or failure of each generation to fulfil its assigned task and to move us closer to the final goal.

JEWISH AND AMERICAN HISTORY

With the annals of Jewish life extending over nearly 4,000 years and over every civilised land on the globe, our history is timeless and universal, covering an area over which the sun never sets, and a period in which the entries and exits of nations never cease.

By contrast, American history is minute. Indeed, in America everything is vast and of huge dimensions except history. The bounties of nature are immense—the rivers, the mountains, the deserts, the canyons, the trees, the oilfields and other natural resources; and the works of man are colossal—the skyscrapers, the dams, the roads and factories.

Only history is small. If a building stands for fifty years it is old, and if a city was founded a few centuries ago or often less it is historic, a distinction which in the Old World would often require at least a thousand years.

In many parts of this great land history, as we understand it, only began a little over a hundred years ago, when the first white man arrived. What happened, then, before the invasion of the Europeans?

At the time when Columbus landed in America, there were nearly one million Indians here—about as many as there were Jews in the world at that time. Yet compare their respective place in the history of man; compare what the Jews and the Red Indians have bequeathed to America and to human civilisation!

MESA VERDE NATIONAL PARK

During our tour through the West we visited some of the remnants of Indian life, both ancient and modern. The most fantastic of these remains of what was once a flourishing community we saw in the Mesa Verde National Park in the south-west corner of Colorado, where the best preserved cliff-dwellings in America are to be found.

We traversed the high plateau, cut through erosion by deep valleys. For miles not a token of ancient life is to be seen. Then suddenly, signs direct you to narrow paths over the brink of the steep precipice, and you descend precariously on ladders and steps cut into the vertical rock walls to discover one of the weirdest sights your eyes have ever beheld.

There, nestling a thousand feet or more above the valley directly underneath you, in enormous gaping clefts and caves right inside the high and steep cliffs, are whole villages, all over eight hundred years old, with dozens of dwellings two or three storeys high, pit-houses, round towers, ceremonial halls called *kivas*, narrow lanes and plazas. Truly a ghost place if there ever was one. Here, over more ladders and stone steps, you climb into houses, into living-rooms and kitchens and religious assembly halls, abandoned eight centuries ago after teeming with life for a short while.

Modern historians do not know for sure why the Indians built these quaint cliff-dwellings in such inaccessible spots, nor why they left them shortly afterwards; for the Indians left no records.

AN INDIAN RESERVATION

Then, leaving the Park, we travelled through a huge Indian reservation still counting 100,000 residents, most of them illiterates like their ancestors a thousand years earlier, still living in similarly constructed homes and assembling in sand-covered *kivas* for their primitive religious ritual, with its strange beliefs to this day in medicine-men and diseases caused by haunted trees.

Here was a people virtually without history. They, who once ruled this continent unchallenged, have become its prisoners in reservations, like some rare animal species in wild-life reservations or bird sanctuaries. They sold not only Manhattan for $24 but their place in history for some desolate deserts. For countless centuries they had lived here as undisputed masters of America. Yet today we cannot find the slightest trace of their influence in the modern American way of life!

Like their cliff-palaces, they have become a ghost in history, their number reduced to less than half of what it was four hundred years ago, and their share in the evolution of modern culture and civilisation as insignificant as the payment they received for the Island of Manhattan.

How could history be so cruel to a people, and simply by-pass it in the unfolding of its design? The answer is: A people that has no literature, that creates no structures of thought and has no foresight to put the present into the service of the future, such a people is soon reduced to rubble and left to decay in the caves and deserts of history.

At the time when Indian children roamed illiterate in their cliff-dwellings eight hundred years ago, Jewish children exercised their brains in the intricacies of the Talmud. At that time, when the Indians produced hunters and warriors, we produced a Rashi and a Maimonides and countless other giants of the spirit whose works are studied more intensively today than when they were written over eight centuries ago.

As a result, our fortunes were reversed in the course of time: while, when the Indians lived in freedom, we lived in ghetto reservations, now that they live in reservations, we live in freedom in the very land they once dominated.

OUR PLACE IN HISTORY

As we observed, in fascination mixed with pity, the ancient ruins and modern desolation of the Indian people, a frightening thought occurred: how will *we* one day appear in the record of history? How and by what will we be remembered by future generations, and what influence will we, living today, exert on their lives?

Our lovely homes, with all their beautiful furnishings and fittings, will long have decayed, leaving even less behind than the Indians of Mesa Verde. The parties we enjoyed, the cards we played, the gossip we traded will not even survive our own mortal bodies. But do we possess or produce books that will still be read in a hundred years' time? Are we participating in the great creations of the spirit which will outlast us to inspire the future course of Jewish history?

Are we going to leave behind us ghostly cliff-palaces or living institutions? Will our great-grandchildren be Jewish illiterates wasting in a vanishing community, or will they be bearers of a rich Jewish civilisation contributing the experience of 4,000 years of creative history to the advancement of mankind?

Another question should cause us at least equal concern: what will our precious synagogue look like in a hundred years' time? Will its site here just be marked by a plaque outside telling by-passers: "Here stood the Fifth Avenue Synagogue, which provided beautiful services and classes for some two hundred members," or will people a century from now know that we existed because we used our extraordinary resources and prominence to contribute something unique and enduring to Jewish life and thought? Will our existence leave a mark, and not a mere marker, on future Jewish history?

DEAD AND LIVING RECORDS

Historians have two ways of learning about the lives of long-past generations: one way is to dig up or discover ancient homes and implements, some old ruins or broken pottery. That is how we study the history of the Red Indians or the primitive natives of Africa. All we can find about their past are ruins, whether cliff-dwellings or long-hidden sun-temples.

Jewish history is not studied that way. To reconstruct Jewish conditions in by-gone times, you need no spades or ladders. You need a library.

What kind of homes or even synagogues Jews had one or two thousand years ago, what sort of dresses they wore and by what type of work they earned their living, all this does not make the slightest difference to the record of Jewish history. No one can piece together the momentous Jewish contributions to religion and ethics and philosophy and science out of the ruins of of some buildings, however well preserved. No one can reconstruct the story of Jewish heroism and martyrdom out of pieces of pottery or other historic junk.

For the glories and agonies of Jewish life in the past, for an account of the Jewish share in the progress of man, one looks to the Bible, the Talmud and the prolific literature of our people to the present day; one looks to the Jewish ingredients of contemporary civilisation, to the Jewish strands in the fabric of ideas like monotheism, the brotherhood of man, social justice, freedom and human dignity, or to the Jewish participation in the strides of man in philosophy, or science, or medicine, or law, or education.

REMEMBERANCE—BY WHAT?

In this solemn *Yizkor*-hour we plead to God *yizkor*, that "He shall remember" our parents, just as we want one day to be remembered by our children and future generations. But do we want to be remembered as Indians or as Jews?

Shall we bequeath to future historians just some luxurious apartments and beautiful houses of worship, some cliff-dwellings in skyscrapers, some reservations in a spiritual wilderness; or shall we, like the Jews before us, enrich the future by creations which are indestructible and immortal, which can never turn into ruins or rubble?

It is my inescapable charge, as your spiritual guide, to make quite sure that a congregation as distinguished as ours will not one day sink into oblivion, undeserving of an honoured place in history. To this end, we are going to embark on an ambitious adventure to secure for us a leading role in advancing Jewish thought, in making it meaningful and relevant to our perplexed age.

If some are unenthusiastic and prefer us to be cliff-dwellers rather than thought-builders, let them step aside quietly into the limbo of history, and not prevent us from exploiting our unique potential to ensure that history will remember us.

For the day of reckoning will come. Congregations, just as individuals, will be called to account and asked: Have you made of yourself what you could have been? Have you used all your heart, and all your soul, and all your means to serve God and to make others serve God, or did you waste your energies and resorces on hollow enterprises?

May God grant us, collectively and individually, the strength and courage and vision so to live and so to build for the future that *yizkor elokim*, that God and history will remember us, that we shall leave behind not crumbling rubble but monuments of living bridges between the past and the future.

VANISHING JEWS IN AMERICA—AND RUSSIA

Silent and Noisy Reactions

(*Yom Kippur—Ne'ilah*)

We have been on a great trip together. Since Rosh Hashanah we have viewed some of the grandest works of God and man; we have toured some of the finest sights in America and explored some of the noblest vistas of Judaism. As our joint travels on these High Holydays are about to come to an end, we heard, in the final biblical reading of these solemn days, one of the most dramatic travel stories of all times: the story of Jonah's eventful mission to a distant land.

Instead of setting out for Niniveh as commanded by God, Jonah took a boat at Jaffa to go on a Mediterranean cruise where, he thought, he could enjoy some rest from his occupational hazards as a Prophet. At first all went well. The sea was calm and pleasant. Jonah even managed to doze off in a quiet corner below deck. But after a while a savage storm threatened to sink the boat. The passengers became alarmed and pleaded with their gods for deliverance from a cruel death. They awakened Jonah and asked him to what religion he belonged. He answered *ivri anokhi*, "I am a Hebrew."

Strange, isn't it?—so long as things went well and all was quiet on board,

Jonah's Jewish identity was unknown to his pagan fellow-passengers. Presumably he put on his *Tephillin* in the morning and ate his *kosher* sandwiches for lunch in his hidden corner, remote from the rest of the company. He kept his Jewishness to himself. But as soon as the calm was broken and a grave crisis produced pandemonium on board, he publicly proclaimed that he was a Jew.

Something similar, it seems, is happening in our days. American Jewry is currently preoccupied by two major concerns: the fate of Russian Jewry behind the Iron Curtain and the problem of "the vanishing American Jew" here at home. But how differently we react to these two threats!

In Russia three million Jews are subjected to severe religious repression, and we fear for their survival as a vibrant part of our people. The enforced attrition of this vast and once leading Jewish community is admittedly a prospect of catastrophic proportions, particularly after the devastating loss of six million Jews we sustained in the Nazi terror. This threat has aroused the Jewries of the Free World, and although the problem is not of our making and there may be comparatively little we can do about it, we cry out loud. We organise mass demonstrations, we hold protest marches and widely publicised vigils, we lobby governments and churches in a desperate effort to arouse Jewish and world opinion on this calamity, if only on the off-chance that maybe these pressures will prevail upon Russia's rulers to relax their spiritual genocide of our people.

Yet we are little agitated about a threat of exactly the same catastrophic proportions right here at our doorstep in America, where we face the equally devastating loss of three million Jews—only not by force or persecution, but by voluntary desertions, by sheer suicide. In our travels through the West we found a dismal testimony to "the vanishing American Jew". Whole communities are threatened with spiritual extinction. Over the vast area between Denver and the Pacific coast, counting numerous Jewish communities, large and small, there is not a piece of *kosher* meat to be bought and often not a single Sabbath-observer to be found! Jewish learning is as alien to them as, alas, to the Jews of Russia. And here, where the responsibility is ours alone and where we could help if we were aroused, we face this calamity without protest, without demonstrations, without mobilising all our resources to ward off the threatened annihilation of three million Jews as effective bearers of our religious heritage!

Like Jonah, we remain quiet as long as the passage through life is comfortable and unexciting, and we shout and protest our Jewishness only when the going becomes rough and tempestuous.

Whether we can do much to rescue Russian Jewry is at best questionable, for that depends on forces and factors far beyond our immediate control. But certain it is that millions of vanishing American Jews can be saved as surely as Niniveh was saved. What we need are Jonahs who will not run away, but go to the sinking cities all over America to proclaim the word of God. If we but cared for the fate of American Jesw with as much agitation and indignation, with emergency campaigns and the organised arousal of public opinion, as for those beyond our reach, the tide could be turned.

It is tragic enough that three million Jews find themselves cut off from our people behind an Iron Curtain. But at least we have not erected this barrier. But how much more tragic it is to find three million Jews in this land of freedom withering away behind an Iron Curtain we religious Jews have raised around ourselves, isolating us and our influence from the immense wastelands of the American-Jewish dispersion. This is an Iron Curtain which we can and must break down; here are Jews whom we can and must save from being lost to Judaism. All it needs is to put an end to our insular mentality which cares only for our own spiritual welfare and little for what goes on among the rest of the Jews in this great community. Then we shall no longer have to worry about Jews vanishing in America for reasons of sheer indifference on their and on our part alike.

As Yom Kippur—and our tour—now draw to a close, let us pray hard and fervently for the redemption of our brethren in the land of oppression. But let us also be equally sincere in our resolve to liberate our brethren in this free land from their self-imposed alienation to our common heritage. May God grant us a calm and pleasant passage through the year ahead, and may we earnestly acknowledge our Jewish obligations while the sea of life around us is tranquil and not in turmoil, in freedom and not only in the face of oppression. Thus may the time come soon when all the children of our people will be reunited under the banner of our faith, travelling together to reach our ultimate destination: *Leshanah haba'ah biyerushalayim!*

FAREWELL TO AMERICA

THE CHALLENGE TO GO
Rosh Hashanah—First Day

Rosh Hashanah celebrates the creation of man, yet it records the creation of the Jew. Commemorating the beginnings of the universe, it directs our attention to the beginnings of Judaism. In our Torah readings on Rosh Hashanah we hear not the account of Genesis in the beginning but the stories about Abraham, the first Jew; not how the first man came up out of the earth but how the first father went up with his son on a mountain to dedicate him to God.

If the history of humanity is man's quest for meaning and purpose, the evolution of civilisation and the moral order, then true history starts not with Adam but with Abraham. His emergence represented to the record of human progress what Hippocrates meant to medicine, Archimedes to physics, and Einstein to the atomic age.

Just as the history of a synagogue really begins not with the first brick laid at its foundation, but with its consecration and first service, so does the history of man really start, not with the physical foundation of Adam's birth, but with the spiritual consecration of Abraham to the human goals.

That is the meaning of dichotomy between the historical significance of Rosh Hashanah as the anniversary of creation and its Torah readings on the origins of Judaism, between *hayom harath olam*—"this is the day the world was conceived"—and *vatahar Sarah*—"and Sarah conceived" in today's reading.

Equally remarkable is the beginning of Jewish history itself. The drama of the Jew, and the record of Judaism, start with a Divine command to Abraham, a command surprisingly neither religious nor moral, neither ritual nor ethical in character. The very first *mitzvah* which God ever gave to the very first Jew was simply *lech lecha*—"go", move, heed the summons of destiny as it seeks to pluck him out from familiar ground and transplant him to an unknown destination.

Five Sermons delivered at the Fifth Avenue Synagogue, New York, on Rosh Hashanah and Yom Kippur 5727 (1966).

JEWISH RESTLESSNESS

The prominence of *lech lecha* as the introduction to Jewish history, as the gateway through which our people entered on its momentous march through the ages, is surely no accident. *Lech lecha* not merely heads our history, it is its foremost theme. Perhaps even more characteristic of the Jew at all times and in all places than his monotheism or his passion for social justice, is his perennial restlessness, his constant urge for change and movement, his dogged refusal to accept things as they are, to be complacent or resigned.

There is more than mere humour in the story of three men who were doomed by their doctors to die within three months. Asked how they would spend the time left to them, the Scotsman answered that he would squander all his savings on pleasures he previously denied himself, the Frenchman spoke of the utter abandon with which he would dine and wine in lechery, and the Jew simply replied: "I will look for another doctor to get a second opinion."

This Jewish trait of never accepting anything in life as final or inevitable, of always seeking second or third opinions if the first is unacceptable, is responsible for Jewish survival. To others the fate of the Jew may have been settled and doomed. They spoke of "the final solution" to the Jewish problem in very final terms. The Jew knew better, and if he did not know better, he consulted his faith for a second opinion.

Herein, after all, lies the principal difference between Judaism and the dominant faith to which it gave birth. They believe the Messiah has come already, finality lies in the past; we still look forward to his coming, to us finality lies in the future. We refuse to acknowledge any human order as finally settled, any existing state as ultimate and incapable of further movement and improvement.

REVOLUTIONARIES OF MANKIND

But in this trait lies more than the key to Jewish survival. This defiance of convention, this dissatisfaction with the *status quo*, this flight from what others regard as final or inevitable, also fashioned the Jew's moral character and conscience. This trait turned our people into the moral and social revolutionaries of mankind.

Let me read to you a passage from a penetrating analysis of Judaism written recently by a distinguished non-Jewish author:

> The nature polytheisms that surrounded Judaism in ancient times all buttressed the *status quo*. Conditions might not be what the heart would wish, but what impressed the polytheist was that they might be a great deal worse. . . . As a consequence, religion's attention was directed toward keeping things as they were. Egyptian religion, for example, repeatedly contrasted the "passionate man" to the "silent man", exalting the latter because he never disturbs the established order. Small wonder that no nature polytheism has ever produced a major social revolution fired by a high concept of social justice. . . .
>
> In Judaism, by contrast, history is in tension between its divine potentialities

and its present frustrations. There is a profound disharmony between God's will and the existing social order. As a consequence, more than any other religion of the time, Judaism laid the groundwork for social protest. As things are not as they should be, revolution in some form is to be expected. The idea bore fruit. It is in the countries that have been affected by the Jewish perspective on history ... that the most intensive movements for social reform have occurred. The prophets set the pattern. . . . Passionately convinced that things were not as they ought to be, they created in the name of the God for whom they spoke an atmosphere of reform that [quoting Prof. W. F. Albright] "put Hyde Park and the best days of muckraking newspapers to shame." (Huston Smith, *The Religions of Man*, New York, 1958, p. 269.)

The Jews, it has been said, are "the stubborn non-conformists among the nations" (R. T. Herford, *Menorah Journal*, 1919, p. 206). Already the Midrash explained the very name *Hebrew* for Abraham as derived from *Ever*, "the other side": "All the world is on one side, and he is on the other side" (*Gen. R.*, 42:13).

If the Prophets single-handedly denounced, attacked and often modified the iniquities of the existing order in their days, pitting themselves against the might of kings and the opposition to change by their subjects, the people of the Prophets maintained this tradition of dissent and revolution almost to the present time. It is now generally acknowledged by social historians that Jews, ever heeding the call of *lech lecha* for change and movement, played as great and indispensable a role in the rise of capitalism to replace the stagnant feudal system, which had held sway for a thousand years in Western Europe under the influence of the Church opposed to change, as in the emergence of Marxism and Socialism when capitalism was the established order.

This also explains why Jews, constantly in search of new ideas and wider horizons, have played such a disproportionate part in the advances of medicine and science, exemplified by such pioneers as Freud, Ehrlich and Einstein, and lately also in the creative arts.

We began our history with *lech lecha*, with leaving the smug world of our contemporaries, shattering their idols and escaping to find new ideals, and we continued our history with *lech lecha* ever since, constantly challenging the imperfections of the present, dissatisfied with things as they are, and pressing on in quest of new goals for a more perfect society .

HALACHAH AS PROGRESS

Indeed, we have derived the very word for the essence of Judaism from *lech lecha*. *Halachah*, the technical term for Jewish law, comes from *halach*, "to go", "to move". It literally denotes movement, progress, the dynamics of change, as contrasted to the static standstill of the *status quo* advocated by others. Jewish law was conceived as keeping us always on the "move" towards the perfection of man and his society.

He who lives a truly Jewish life disciplined by *halachah*, the legal signposts of the Jewish tradition, is never content with himself or his environment. He never accepts his circumstances as inevitable or beyond improvement. He regards himself as a failure if he is no better this Rosh Hashanah than he was last Rosh Hashanah, and if next year he is not going to live a nobler life than last year. He is always restless, ambitious, critical of the here-and-now and impatient to scale new heights of human idealism, of intellectual prowess and of spiritual fulfillment.

He seeks not merely the Great Society with its victory over poverty, disease and other material wants, but the Good Society with its triumph over evil, crime, faithlessness and godlessness. He wishes not merely a Happy New Year, but *shanah tovah*, "a good New Year". His keyword to the future is not just peace, prosperity and personal happiness, but redemption, for he looks to higher goals than simply security, health, affluence and plenty of leisure for amusement and idleness.

JEWISH COMPLACENCY TODAY

It is perhaps the greatest indictment of contemporary Jewry that the Jew of today has largely lost this trait. For the first time in our history, the Jew—especially the American Jew—feels he has reached his destination. Enjoying unparalleled freedom and affluence, he has nothing more to struggle for. He has ceased to hear history's call of *lech lecha*, the summons for moving on. He likes the *status quo*, he is satisfied—and complacent. His revolutionary fervour is gone, and with it his hopes and yearnings for greater perfection. He is as embarrassed by the call of *lech lecha* to Zion as by the challenge of *lech lecha* to "the land of Moriah", the site of sacrifice and hardship for religious ideals mentioned in the *Akedah*. He wants to stay, not to move.

Two factors are primarily responsible for this sweeping change in the Jewish character: the Emancipation and the fulfilment of the Zionist dream. For two thousand years these were the greatest unmet needs of the Jewish people: the quest for equality; and the quest for the return to Zion. These two ambitions stirred the restlessness of the Jew and galvanised his opposition to the existing order.

But what we forget is that they were merely the means to an end. The Jew did not pray for simple equality as a final goal, nor for the brotherhood of man as an end in itself. He prayed, in the words of our festival liturgy today that "all men shall form one band *to do Thy will with a full heart*". He did not long for his return to the Holy Land by a simple change of address for himself. He yearned, as we repeat daily in our prayers, that "our eyes may behold *Thy return* to Zion in mercy". He saw in the restoration of Jewish sovereignty merely an instrument for the restoration of Divine sovereignty.

Today, having achieved the means of equality and Jewish statehood, we have lost sight of the ends. As a result, we have lost our Messianic drive and hope; or at best we look for the Messiah in the White House or in Wall Street, not in the rule of righteousness or in Zion.

Instead of *ki thetze lamilchamah*, going out into battle wrestling for ideals yet to be realised, we believe *ki thavo el ha'aretz*, that we arrived in the Promised Land already. *Nitzavim*, we stand still, instead of *vayelech*, moving on. Instead of *ha'azinu*, listening to the call of destiny, we think *vezoth haberachah*, that this is the blessing already.

MY CHALLENGE TO GO

By now, my friends, you may have guessed that I have chosen the theme of *lech lecha* to introduce my High Holyday sermons this year, because to me too the call of destiny has come: "Go from your land, your city (the community), and your father's house (the family and friends) to the land which I will show you." I, too, have had to decide whether *ki thetze lamilchamah*, to go out into battle, into the hazards of crisis and heavy burdens and awesome responsibilities, or *ki thavo el ha'aretz*, to prefer the personal happiness, comforts and security of having arrived at my destination; whether *nitzavim*, to remain static and contented with a spiritual standstill, or *vayelech*, to move on to take up new challenges.

To Abraham the call of *lech lecha* was one of the "ten trials" whereby God tested him, and to me this most agonising decision of my life proved no less trying and testing.

Having made the decision and accepted the call of *lech lecha*, I propose to devote my remaining messages on these Days of Remembrance and Judgement to a kind of valediction to the country, community and congregation I will be leaving, God willing, before next Rosh Hashanah comes around.

Meanwhile, I wish to leave with you, as Rosh Hashanah greetings and blessings individually and collectively the benediction Abraham received when he responded to the call of *lech lecha*: "And I will make you into a great people, and I will bless you and increase your name, and you shall be a blessing . . . and in you shall all the families of the earth be blessed."

FAREWELL TO MY COUNTRY

Rosh Hashanah—Second Day

In God's first command to the first Jew opening Jewish history, which we discussed yesterday, the places Abraham was bidden to leave are peculiarly ordered: "Go from your land, from your birthplace, and from your father's house."

Normally we would expect the reverse order. In emigrating to another land, one leaves first one's home, then one's city and only last one's country. Why is the opposite order used in God's message?

Our Jewish commentators gave a significant answer. In a purely local sense, one may indeed depart first from one's home, then one's city, and finally one's country. But subjectively one is severed from one's former environment in the opposite order. The more intimate one's bonds, the longer they last, even after one has left. The ties with your former country go first, your community second, and your family last.

Or, as one commentator (*K'li Yakar*) puts it, God wanted to soften the blow for Abraham. So He told him first to leave his country, which is easiest, next his birthplace, which is harder as it it not so soon forgotten, and finally his home, which is hardest for it is never forgotten.

I feel similarly regarding my call of *lech lecha* to a distant land to which Providence has summoned me.

Subjectively I will leave first the land I have called my own for the past eight years. To go *me'artzecha* and live in another country will be relatively the easiest test. It will be much harder to separate myself *mimoladtecha*, here corresponding to the American-Jewish community with which I have had much closer ties, bonds which will linger on much longer. But hardest of all it will be to depart *mibeth avicha*, from the family of this Congregation within which I found my closest friends and partners, and whose midst I have lived and worked, usually seven days a week, for eight memorable years. To wrench myself from them even physically is the hardest test, for in thought and affection I will never really leave them nor cut my bonds with them.

This synagogue will always be *beth avicha*, my Father's House, the home where I worshipped my Heavenly Father with my brothers and sisters.

Let me, then, in my pre-valedictory messages on these Days of Awe devote myself in the biblical order to these three places I will leave behind, presenting my thoughts on departing *me'artzecha*, on leaving America, on this Rosh Hashanah day—with its more universal overtones as the day of man's creation and judgement, and leaving for Yom Kippur, the day of more specifically Jewish national and individual significance, my thoughts and hopes on taking leave from the American-Jewish community and from my own Congregation.

AMERICA AND JEWISH HISTORY

America has always had an almost uncanny relationship with the history of the Jewish people and the fulfilment of its vision and aspirations.

The very discovery of America in 1492 sets the stage. For in the very year when the largest, most prosperous and most creative Jewish community of the Middle Ages was expelled from Spain to *end* the finest chapter of medieval Jewish history, Columbus discovered the land destined to encompass, nearly five hundred years later, the largest, most prosperous and most creative Jewish community of modern times, thus *opening* the finest chapter of recent Jewish history.

Perhaps America, in sheltering and granting unprecedented freedom and opportunity to history's biggest Jewish community, was only paying its historical debt for the indispensable role Jews had played in the discovery of America, by providing the money, the maps, the nautical instruments and several men for Columbus's expeditions.

Later America became the first and only country in the history of our dispersion which Jews *entered* as equals and without any legal disabilities, for they belonged to a minority like all other immigrants.

Then, just as the worst calamity ever to befall our people claimed 6,000,000 Jewish lives in Europe, America turned out to be the haven of the world's largest community, also numbering nearly 6,000,000 Jews, most of them hailing from the countries devastated by the Holocaust.

A few years later, America again played a crucial and decisive part in Jewish history, when—in a momentous decision by a wise and beneficent President who Providentially happened to occupy the White House at the time—it recognised the new State of Israel on the day of its birth and thus secured its viability.

Equally Providential for Jewish fortunes was the rise of America as the world's mightiest power and the custodian of its freedom just at the time when totalitarianism and oppression threatened to engulf humanity and to imperil the survival of Jews and Judaism everywhere.

RELIGIOUS COMMITMENTS

For me it has been among my most exhilarating experiences to see the workings of this marvellous democracy at close quarters, making the personal acquaintance of numerous public leaders, from the President of this great nation, the Governor of our State and the Mayor of our city down to many judges, law-makers and others involved in the government of the greatest and freest people on earth.

As a Jew, I particularly rejoiced to find in this materialistic age and this pleasure-seeking land innumerable manifestations of our biblical heritage. Beneath the surface worship of material success, money and fun, there is still a deep commitment to the religious and moral values Judaism brought to the world.

A nation which takes its Oath of Allegiance "under God", which imprints "In God we Trust" on its most materialistic symbols of money bills and coins, which exempts from military service those who consecrate their lives to the advancement or study of religion, which makes all religious enterprises tax-exempt, and which even grants clergymen special car licence plates and parking privileges—something unknown in Europe or even in Israel—such a nation can never go religiously or morally bankrupt.

In fact, the two most burning and divisive issues presently besetting the nation—the Vietnam war and the civil rights struggle—are both partly the result of America's almost puritan moral fervour. These two explosive problems are, of course, by themselves entirely dissimilar, especially in so far as they relate to Jews or Jewish convictions.

THE WAR IN VIETNAM

In contrast to most of my American colleagues, I have always maintained that political arguments or comments do not belong to the pulpit. They are much more competently left to the hustings of politicians and the columns of journalists. Vietnam, to my mind, is no exception.

The pulpit should be reserved exclusively for proclaiming the word and law of God, and nobody, not even rabbis, can possibly know God's views on the tragic, costly and perhaps misguided war in Vietnam without being privy to highly classified diplomatic and military information bearing on the security of America and the free world. Whatever opinion individual Jews may legitimately express as citizens in a democracy, I believe it is morally and religiously wrong for rabbis to tell the American government how to conduct its foreign policy.

THE CIVIL RIGHTS STRUGGLE

Civil rights are a different matter. On this the will of God is clear and unequivocal. No civil rights leader could articulate his cause more effectively than the Prophet Amos did when he exclaimed: "Are you not unto Me like the children of the black Ethiopians, O children of Israel, says the Lord" (Amos 9:7), or more rousingly than Malachi's immortal words: "Have we not all one father, did one God not create us, why do we deal treacherously every man against his brother?" (Mal. 2:10).

Of course we are bound to take sides in any contest of human equality. As Jews, we should especially rejoice in this revolution for the dignity of man. After all, our Jewish teachings are being vindicated after thousands of years. Moreover, who knows better than we do the suffering and indignity of those denied their human rights?

What we may question is the wisdom and propriety of the methods used and of the Jewish support for them. If we have a contribution to make as Jews, it should be a Jewish contribution. Indeed, perhaps no one can make a more valuable contribution to this problem than the Jews, for we are the only community who once, before our emancipation in Europe, faced exactly the same problem of exclusion and repression, and we contrived to solve it.

As a matter of fact, it is remarkable that for the first time in our history a term specifically used for Jewish suffering and persecution is now applied to non-Jews. When you now hear of ghettos, you no longer think of Jews confined to a narrow area by walls and chains. This word, still defined as "Jew's quarters" in our dictionaries, now stands for squalid negro quarters.

WHAT JEWS CAN CONTRIBUTE

How did *we* break out of our ghettos and enter the mainstream of society and its privileges? How did *we* secure our emancipation and civil rights? Certainly not by riots and demonstrations, by violence and protest-marches, or by preaching "Jewish power" or even non-violence.

Above all, we worked on ourselves, not on others. We gave a better education to our children than anybody else had. We hallowed our home life. We channelled the ambition of our youngsters to academic excellence, not flashy cars. We rooted out crime and indolence from our midst, by making every Jew feel responsible for the fate of all Jews. We denounced any fellow-Jew besmirching the Jewish name by some misdemeanour as guilty of a *Chillul HaShem*, a desecration of the Divine Name. We did not gatecrash into our Gentile environment; we made ourselves highly acceptable and indispensable to them, by our industrial, intellectual and moral contributions to society.

That is how we gained our freedom and equality, and that benefit of our experience we should impress on our negro fellow-citizens.

Not by "Black Power" but by intellectual and moral power, by educational and cultural progress, will they become accepted and wanted in the rest of society.

YOUTH AND AGE

America's strength and weakness are that it is a young country, a people without deep roots or ancient traditions. This newness has all the advantages and disadvantages of youth; it creates the dynamics of boisterous energy and enterprising enthusiam, but it also makes for superficiality and fickleness.

When I contrast the response in the hundreds of audiences I have addressed all over America with that of European audiences, I find that Americans are far more easily impressed and inspired, they are more open-minded and less settled in their opinions, while their European counterparts, once they have reached adult age, have their minds made up one way or the other, and are therefore much harder to rouse and influence.

It is on the relatively rootless, almost virgin soil of America that our history-tested people and its ancient traditions could make a particularly fruitful contribution, by bringing the old to bear on the new, tried ideals to fill gaping blanks, and seasoned moral experience to supply the guideposts in the current crisis of morality. In no country on earth could we apply our historical know-how in ethics and human relations more constructively than in this New World, still youthfully groping and experimenting in search for the solidity and firm earnestness provided by age.

THE ETERNAL SOUNDS OF THE SHOFAR

What can better symbolise this Jewish contribution to America than the *Shofar* we are about to sound in these modern surroundings of our synagogue?

The *Shofar* is about the oldest musical instrument. Its form has not changed over the millennia, and it will still be the same long after these now modern walls will have been demolished to make room for the newer architecture of the 21st century. Nevertheless, just in this contemporary environment the ancient *Shofar* stirs with the greatest meanings, for it brings to our fickle age the sounds of eternity. Not the most exquisite violin or piano can arouse our hearts as stirringly as the simple, old *Shofar*, for it transplants us into a world that never dies, into a mood that never changes.

In the magnificent contemporary greatness of America, let the Jewish people represent the ancient *Shofar*, rousing like the Prophets of old the moral conscience and religious fervour of the nation by its call to principles which are timeless, to ideals which are immortal, to a brotherhood "under God" Who is eternal, and Who may bless and preserve this land free, brave and glorious.

FAREWELL TO MY COMMUNITY

Yom Kippur—Kol Nidrei

> *By the authority of the Heavenly court*
> *and by the authority of the earthly court,*
> *with the consent of the Almighty*
> *and with the consent of the congregation,*
> *we grant permission to pray with the sinners.*

This strange prayer seems to strike an odd note at the opening of the year's most solemn service. What does this formal sanction for sinners to join us in tonight's holiest exercises mean?

Some may think, quite wrongly, that it refers to this being the only service in the year which everybody attends in time. It would be futile to utter this prayer at the beginning of any other service, for the sinners come late or not at all. The sinners, then, would be the late-comers or absentees on other occasions when, at the beginning of the service, in contrast to tonight, we would only be preaching to the converted.

Actually, the origin of this peculiar text suggests an entirely different meaning. Introduced by Rabbi Meir Rothenburg, the great luminary who lived in thirteenth century Germany, it cannot specifically refer to the Marranos or Spanish crypto-Jews who rejoined their brethren for Yom Kippur, as is commonly believed. For the custom to recite this text before *Kol Nidrei* is much older than the Marranos.

In fact, the formula goes back to a statement already found in the Talmud a thousand years earlier: "Any fast in which the transgressors of Israel do not participate is not a fast; for Scripture included galbanum, although its odour is bad, among the spices of the incense offering" (*Kerithoth* 6b).

This statement itself requires an explanation. Why is a fast without the inclusion of Jewish transgressors no real fast? Why would our Yom Kippur services all over the world not be complete if those who never on other occasions see the inside of a synagogue did not join us tonight?

The answer to this question leads me to my second pre-valedictory theme. Having spoken on Rosh Hashanah of my impending departure *me'artzecha*, my reflections on leaving America, I will muse tonight on my forthcoming farewell *mimoladtecga*, from the American-Jewish community, and deal tomorrow with the hardest parting *mibeth avicha*, from my congregational family.

THE DIVERSITY OF AMERICAN JEWRY

From a religious perspective American Jewry represents the most bewildering diversity of elements ever found in a single community, breaking any number of low and high records. Side by side with large areas more intensely Jewish than the most traditional ghettos of pre-war Europe or the most Chasidic quarters of Jerusalem, you find here vast conglomerations of Jews who cannot distinguish an *aleph* from a *beth*, or Chanukah from Christmas, or an Irish lass from a Jewish girl—Jews whose interest in Jewish matters is aroused more by an anti-Semite like Rockwell than by a Rambam, and who would sooner open their homes to a group of gamblers than to a *meshulach* collecting support for some yeshivah or some poor bride.

American Jewry features at once more intensive Jewish learning *and* more ignorance, more religious gains *and* more religious losses, more contributions to Jewish causes *and* more escapes from communal responsibilities, more sinners *and* more saints, than any other Jewish community.

The only common denominator uniting the two groups—the Jews by commitment and the Jews by default—is that they are mutually indifferent to each other. Neither cares for the other.

That the non-religious Jew does not care for his observant brother is perhaps understandable; after all, to the assimilated Jew the reminder of loyalty to *Kashruth* and Sabbath observance, not to mention the quaint display in public places of yarmulkas, ear-locks and outlandish garbs, is only a source of irritation, embarrassment and provocation. He wants Jews to hide their Jewishness and forget about it.

INDIFFERENCE TO RELIGIOUS DEFECTORS

But quite inexcusable is the complete indifference of religious Jews to the defections of the rest.

A few months ago a Gallup poll published a shocking revelation. Between 73% and 83% of all American Christians of various denominations believe in God "with absolute certainty". Yet only 39% of the Jews interviewed professed a similar belief. What a disaster and what a disgrace! We who discovered God and propagated the belief in Him as our national business, who always glorified the principle of *kiddush ha-Shem*, that our faith is worth more than life itself, we should now be far overtaken by the Gentiles in religious beliefs, with one out of every four or five Christians, but three out of five Jews, doubting the existence of God!

Yet who really cares and weeps with utter shame over this mass-paganism among our people, destined to be "a kingdom of priests"?

Today we have Jewish criminals, Jewish narcotics, Jewish illegitimate children by the thousands, but who is really bothered or disturbed? How many Jews think of themselves as their brothers' keepers, responsible and accountable for one another? Who truly accepts the basic rule *kol yisrael arevim zeh lazeh*, that "all Jews are guarantors for each other"?

That is the significance of the extraordinary way we started our service tonight. "Any fast which does not include the transgressors of Israel is not a proper fast." If we fast here this Yom Kippur and just beat our own hearts in quest for forgiveness, without taking our straying brethren into our hearts, if all we care for is our own salvation and return to God, unconcerned with whether we carry our estranged fellow-Jews with us, then our fasting is no fast before God and Yom Kippur is meaningless.

ORTHODOX ISOLATION

Orthodox Jewry in particular faces a grave responsibility and grave charges of default in this situation. True, we have built up many magnificent synagogues and even more not so magnificent *stibles*, we have erected at enormous cost a flourishing network of day-schools and yeshivoth, we have organised Orthodox scientists among professionals and Orthodox students at the universities. But around us and our institutions we have constructed a "wall of separation" of almost complete indifference to the rest. Many Orthodox leaders have simply written off all others, casting them off from the House of Israel, denouncing and ostracising them, shunning all contact with them, instead of befriending them and bringing them closer to us.

In the past generation the Jewish people have suffered nine million casualties out of a world Jewish population of perhaps eighteen million—six million lost by violent slaughter and another three million lost by spiritual attrition behind the Iron Curtain, not to count the millions more lost in the Free World by assimilation and intermarriage. Today, therefore, every surviving Jew is doubly precious to us, and we cannot afford to count out a single Jew from our people.

Yom Kippur's very first message, then, is to warn us "to pray with the sinners", to acknowledge that the Torah was not given to Orthodox Jews only, that those estranged from our heritage are also our brothers, that we must pray for and with them, and that we are responsible for their return to the fold.

That is Yom Kippur's first message, conveyed at the very moment we began our service tonight.

THE JEWISH MISSION TO THE WORLD

And what is the last biblical message of Yom Kippur to be impressed on us as the fast nears its end tomorrow evening? Our final scriptural reading on these Days of Awe will be the Book of Jonah. It relates a remarkable story. A Jewish Prophet is being sent to a pagan city. There were no Jews living in Niniveh. What does a Hebrew Prophet, a Jewish spiritual leader, have to do in a vast non-Jewish metropolis? Certainly Jonah did not go as a missionary to convert the king and his subjects to Judaism.

No, he merely went as a messenger of God to warn the inhabitants of Niniveh of the doom that would overtake them if they persisted in their godless and immoral ways; he went to stir them to repentance and religious awakening.

At first Jonah was reluctant. Probably he thought that telling the king to order a religious revival would conflict with the doctrine of separation between State and Church. Had he not had second thoughts at the last moment, the great Prophet would have ended his life in the belly of a whale.

Evidently, then, the beginning of Yom Kippur urges us to care for our straying co-religionists, to be concerned "with the sinners", with godless fellow-Jews. And the end of Yom Kippur urges us to care for spiritually corrupt Gentiles, to promote religion among our fellow-men.

It was our national task to be "a kingdom of priests", ministering as God's agents to the peoples of the world. We were charged to spread and strengthen religion and morality, to advance the worship of God in the world.

How do we, American Jews, acquit ourselves of this charge? What contributions do we make to the intensification of the belief in God and of religious worship and practice in the country at large?

JEWS AS PIONEERS OF SECULARISATION IN AMERICA

Ironically, we seem to do the opposite. There is no ethnic or religious community in America today which does more to limit and reduce the sway of religion in this country than the Jews. Jews today spearhead the secularisation of the nation. They have played a major role in the foundation of such areligious movements as Ethical Culture and other substitutes of religion. Jewish agitation and influence and financial backing have taken a leading part in driving God, prayer and the Bible—the greatest Jewish contribution to civilisation—out of the American schools. Jewish leaders and organisations are the most vociferous in objecting to any manifestation of religion in America's public life, and in imprisoning God behind some ghetto "wall of separation" inside the churches and whatever religious homes are still left to withstand the flood of secularisation. Jews even provide the most notorious purveyors of smut and pornography vulgarising the country and demoralising countless citizens.

Of course, all this freedom from religion is being sought in the name of Jewish security and equality. It is argued that the safety of the Jewish-community in American society demands making this "wall of separation" impregnable.

As you know, throughout my eight years here I have taken a strong, consistent and often unpopular stand against this attitude. I am as convinced today as I was eight years ago that this attitude is as un-Jewish as it is un-American, and that far from advancing Jewish security, it threatens to undermine it.

It is un-American because the overwhelming majority of Americans cherish their religious heritage in the nation's public life and schools; 80% of all Americans and almost every governor of our fifty States were opposed to the Supreme Court ruling on prayers in public schools!

It is un-Jewish because to be the apostles of secularism and paganism is the very antithesis to our Prophetic mission in the world. We were chosen to promote the religious conscience of mankind, not to diminish it. We have lived and died, we have suffered persecution, exile and martyrdom so that through our passionate dedication to the supremacy of religion all men would one day acknowledge God and worship Him—kings and rulers as well as subjects and citizens. We were meant to be the pioneers in establishing the brotherhood of man through the Fatherhood of God, realising that without a common Father, there can be no brothers.

Moreover, *"wie es christelt sich, so juedelt's sich"*. The more the non-Jews surrounding us will take their religion seriously, the more intensive will our own religious life be, as proved throughout history of our dispersion. In a general anaemic religious atmosphere, Judaism too becomes anaemic, and prone to all the corrosive influences of assimilation, apathy and inter-marriage. And what is the good of ensuring Jewish security if there will be no committed Jews left to enjoy this security?

THE SECURITY OF JEWS AND JUDAISM

But even the claims of Jewish security are illusory and specious.

If there is any factor discernable today which might one day ignite the fires of anti-Semitism, it is not so much the danger of a Rockwell or of business discrimination as the resentment caused by the already widespread charge that Jews are responsible for depriving Christians of their religion, their prayers and their Bible.

Therefore, if there is anything of significance I want to leave with the great American-Jewish community as my valedictory message, it is this word of caution, this plea not to bury Judaism under a heap of slogans, not to betray Jewish history by promoting a new wave of godlessness, not to sell the innermost soul and highest purpose of our people for a mess of pottage and cliches, and not to arouse the enmity of our neighbours by robbing them of their religious fervour and earnestness.

Let our leaders and all Jews study the Book of Jonah carefully. Perhaps by emulating the Prophet's example of arousing a public religious awakening among the Gentiles, we too might save entire cities from the threat of doom. Otherwise, we may well end up in the belly of a whale of trouble without being spewed out to safety as Jonah was.

American Jewry commands more numbers, more resources, freedom and opportunities than any other Jewish community, past or present. On the whole, these unique assets have been used creatively and creditably in the service of our people. American Jews have built up great institutions of Jewish learning and social service which have enriched not only Jewish life but the canvass of the American experience. We have made immense contributions to Jewish scholarship by an outpouring of books unprecedented in our history. We have helped countless Jews in all parts of the world in distress and persecution. Above all, we have played an indispensable part in the upbuilding of Israel, by financial, moral, political and even religious aid.

Yet withal, we now face a crisis of survival, with "the vanishing American Jew" looming large as a haunting spectre of decline. If we now bring to bear the same energies and sacrifices, the same urgency and idealism, as have made American Jewry great, as have secured Israel's rebirth and growth, and as have helped millions of Jews in need, on making Judaism safe, by crash-programmes of Jewish day school expansion, by Torah corps tours through the length and breadth of the land, by rousing the concern of those who are complacent or resigned, and above all by a personal return to Jewish values, Jewish learning and Jewish living, then this magnificent Jewry will be secure and a source of inspiration to our people everywhere. Then the reassuring words of tomorrow's Haphtorah will be triumphantly fulfilled: "Then shall your light break forth like the dawn, and your healing speedily blossom; your triumph shall go before you, and the Lord's glory shall back you" (Is. 58:8).

FAREWELL TO MY CONGREGATION

Yom Kippur—Musaph

In my Odyssey of *Lech Lecha*—my sermon-theme on these Days of Awe—I have moved *me'artzecha umimoldtecha*, from my country and my community, to reach now the climax of my wrench *mibeth avicha*, from my synagogue-family, from my congregation.

Many of you may remember the most joyful personal occasion I celebrated with you—the Bar Mitzvah of my first-born son. In launching him to independence as a Jew in his own right, I cited the introduction to the blessing our father Jacob gave his children before his departure: "Gather together, and I will tell you what will happen to you in the end of days" (Gen. 49:1), and I gave him Rashi's explanation: "He sought to reveal the end, but the Divine Presence departed from him, and he began talking about other matters."

As a father, I would wish to tell my child what is in store for him, I would want to reveal the future to him. But a veil of secrecy is drawn over my vision, and I must talk about other matters.

Similarly, my congregation, I wished in blessing you on this last Yom Kippur together, I could reveal your future to you. I wished I could tell you what is in store for you; whether the seeds planted here during the past eight years will prosper and bear fruit or not; whether you will meet with success of failure, with joys or sorrows. Alas, I cannot, for Providence hides the future from me as from you, and I must turn to other matters than prognosticating the future.

All I can do in blessing you is, as Jacob and countless Jewish fathers did in blessing their children, to tell you what you *should* be, and what I, as your spiritual leader since your congregational birth, tried to achieve and make of you.

THE THREE FUNCTIONS OF A CONGREGATION

In Hebrew we use three distinct terms for "congregation": *edah* or *adath*, *kahal* or *kehillah*, and *tzibbur*. Each term describes a different aspect of what a Jewish congregation is to stand for, and each is usually linked with a different word for its leader, likewise describing a distinct task facing a congregational leader:

Edah is associated in the Torah with *zaken*, "elder", as in the frequent combination of *ziknei ha-edah*, "the elders of the congregation". *Kahal* is usually connected with *rosh*, "head", when we speak of a *rosh ha-kahal*, "the head of a congregation". And *tzibbur* is used with *shali'ach*, "messenger" or "representative", as in *shali'ach tzibbur*, "the congregation's agent".

Of course, these three terms for leader commonly denote three different persons leading the community. *Zaken*, "elder", stands for *zeh shekanah chochmah*, the scholar, the rabbi, the spiritual leader. *Rosh ha-kahal* is used for the lay leader, the president or *parnas* who secures the material or administrative needs of the congregation. And *shali'ach tzibbur* is the *chazan*, the messenger of the congregation who leads and conveys their prayers as the representative of the worshippers.

However, in a broader sense, all these terms may be applied to the rabbi as defining his functions of spiritual leadership, just as the three terms for congregation describe the three purposes of a community.

THE TESTIMONY OF A CONGREGATION

Edah derives from *ed*, "witness" or *eduth* "testimony." It is also connected with *mo'ed*, "appointed season" or "festival".

The first function of a Jewish congregation is to be a witness, to bear testimony, to the truth of our faith. In Jewish law no *ed echad*, no "single witness", however unimpeachable, can ever be a legal witness at court. In charges against an individual, or in validating legal acts, we must have at least two witnesses, *al pi shnayim edim*. In publicly bearing testimony to God, in *kiddush ha-Shem*—sanctifying His Name, we require more. *Edah* means at least a *minyan*, ten Jews.

No single Jew, however eminent or pious, can ever proclaim the message of Judaism, can ever hallow His Name, as effectively as can any ten Jews worshipping together, however common they are.

Pious, observant Jews have been living in this area as individuals for many years. But the history of Orthodoxy, of bearing witness to the vitality of traditional Judaism in this select district, only began with the foundation of our synagogue.

Our first and foremost task, then, as I saw it, was to be an *edah*, a corporate witness testifying that traditional Judaism is very much alive, and confounding the prophets of doom who forecast long ago that Orthodoxy could not survive in America, certainly not amid the affluence, elegance and modernity of an area as fashionable as ours. I am proud and happy that in this objective we have largely succeeded, in part beyond our wildest dreams. We have demonstrated a *kiddush ha-Shem* in the most public manner for the world to see.

No one, anywhere will ever again be able to say that strict Orthodoxy is incompatible with modern life, that our unadulterated traditions are only for foreigners and old-fashioned people, that you cannot reach the top of the economic ladder and still remain faithful to all our ancient convictions and practices.

We are the *edim*, "witnesses", to prove that it can be done, that Judaism can flourish in Fifth Avenue as in Williamsburg or Jerusalem, in the twentieth century as a hundred or a thousand years ago.

THE RABBI AS TEACHER

It is in association with *edah* that spiritual leaders are called *zekenim*, "elders" or "scholars". My task in helping this congregation to become an *edah* was to present to you, and through you to the community at large, the magnificent vistas of Jewish learning, some insights into Jewish scholarship, to enhance the appreciation for the Jewish faith and observances. I regarded my principal assignment here as being your teacher, so that through knowledge you would be truthful witnesses. For, on what you do not know for sure, you cannot give evidence.

These tasks, yours as an *edah* and mine as a *zaken*, we tried to fulfil together at our *mo'adim*, the "appointed times" when we came together for worship and study, at our services and classes.

Of course, a lot remains to be accomplished. To be an *edah*, a corporate witness to God on earth, every member of the congregation must display an adequate knowledge and observance of Judaism. "For this is your wisdom and your understanding in the eyes of the nations, that when they hear all these laws, they shall say 'What a wise and understanding nation is this great people?' " (Deut. 4:6). A real *adath ha-Shem* brings the *Shechinah* down to earth: *Elokim nitzav ba'adath El*, "God is established in the congregation of the Lord" (Ps. 82:1). Such a congregation makes God manifest among all who enter it, makes them sense the mystic spell of the Divine.

Our success or failure as an *edah*, and mine as its *zaken*, cannot be measured by how many people attended our services or paid us compliments, but ultimately by how many worshippers we inspired to discover God in their souls, faith in their hearts, the thrill of Torah learning in their minds, and the beauty of Mitzvah performance in their deeds. The true test to prove whether we are an *edah* is whether we served as an example to other congregations, whether we have helped to intensify Jewish education, to support charitable causes, to contribute to the well-being and religious vitality of the wider community.

What congregation anywhere has a greater opportunity, more fame and resources to achieve these goals than ours?

A congregation thinking only of itself and its own welfare defaults in its obligations no less than a selfish individual who is unconcerned with the needs of others. To bear testimony, to be a witness, you must convince others, you must carry a jury—or Jewry, in our case—with you. You must serve the public and impersonal cause of justice and truth, of spreading the rule of God and morality.

THE TOGETHERNESS OF A CONGREGATION

Next, a congregation is also called *kahal* or *kehillah*, literally "a gathering" of people. Here the emphasis is on the congregation as an instrument for welding individuals into a community.

The second principal task of a congregation is to give each member a sense of belonging, a loyalty to a larger group, a feeling of togetherness.

THE RABBI AS HEAD

In relation to this function of a congregation, its leader is called *rosh*, "head". Just as the head, with its brain and nerve centre, governs the functions of all organs and limbs, and co-ordinates their movements and activities, so must the rabbi bind the members together to make them feel they belong to one body, he must co-ordinate their thinking and their acting to serve the interest of that body in unison and harmony.

In good measure, we certainly succeeded in creating an intimate fellowship of a closely knit family, but in part the task is far from fulfilled.

The Torah uses the word *kahal* most prominently in the Sidrah bearing the very name *Vayakhel*, when Moses "congregated" the people to announce the Sabbath laws to be observed "in all their habitations" (Ex. 35:1-3). Rashi comments that this occurred "on the morrow of Yom Kippur".

The real test of strength of a congregation as a *kahal* is not on Yom Kippur, when the syngagogue is packed, not on the *mo'adim* at our festive services, but on the following day. The test is determined by how much of Yom Kippur's spirit carries over to the day after, how far our synagogue services on the *mo'adim* influence our home life and hallow our Sabbath observance "in all our habitations". A true congregation does not consist of joint prayers and studies only, but of cementing a partnership, a brotherhood of togetherness, which makes the members remember that they belong to a synagogue even on the day after they attended an inspiring service; which disciplines them to serve God at home or in the office, at work or at leisure, just as devoutly as in the synagogue; and which makes them worry about the congregation's affairs and problems as about their own business.

In serving as your *rosh*, I endeavoured to influence your thoughts and feelings, to direct your movements and to co-ordinate your activities even when you were away from our sanctuary. My greatest joy was when I heard that through my teachings some home had become *kosher;* some people had given up working or riding in the Sabbath; some parents had sent their child to a yeshivah; some boy had taken a worthy Jewish girl to be his wife; or some member had volunteered his services to the congregation.

THE INDIVIDUALS OF A CONGREGATION

Finally, a congregation is a *tzibbur*, from *tzavar*, "to make a heap". This stresses neither the lofty testimony of the *edah* nor the togetherness of the *kahal*; rather it stands for the wants of the individual, the services the congregation renders to each member in his personal needs.

Tzibbur is made up of the initials for *Tzaddikim*, "righteous people", *Beynonim*, "indifferent people", and *Resha'im*, "wicked people". For every community, if you dissect it into its constituent parts, is a heap of saints, sinners and in-betweens.

THE RABBI AS AGENT

Its leader is called *shali'ach*, "messenger" or "representative". For the rabbi must act as the agent of them all, and feel equally close to each of them in their troubles and joys. In this capacity it was my charge to intercede for you when sickness struck, to comfort you in grief, to cheer you in anxiety and to advise you in perplexity, as well as to sanctify your family events, to celebrate your births and Bar Mitzvahs and weddings—to be God's spokesman in your midst and your spokesman before God.

There is little that gave me more gratification than the occasions I had to rejoice with you, or to dry some tear on a care-worn face, or to bring some smile to a patient on the sickbed. In this work there was no difference between sinner and saint or the average in-between. I tried to pray as hard for the daily worshipper as for the person I saw only once a year. All are equally part of the *tzibbur*, and I was responsible equally to be their *shali'ach*.

I was proud to be your *shali'ach* in another sense, too. In all my hundreds of lectures and addresses all over the land, in all my attendances at communal meetings and national conventions, in all my activities on various organisation boards and committees, and in all my writings in books and magazines, I appeared as your representative. I was introduced as your rabbi or greeted as your spiritual leader. The Fifth Avenue Synagogue was the prestigious platform that always travelled with me, even as the White House travels with the President wherever he goes.

I began this series with *lech lecha . . . mibeth avicha*. This phrase "father's house" occurs again two generations after Abraham. On fleeing from his home, Jacob vowed his tribute to God if *veshavti veshalom el beth avi*, "I return in peace to my father's house" (Gen. 28:12). I likewise pray that from time to time I may return to this congregational family of mine and find them *beshalom*, in peace with one another, and in peace with God. May I come to find you, as was said of my namesake Jacob, *vayavo Ya'akov shalem*, "And Jacob came in peace" (Gen. 33:18), literally "in perfection" or "completeness", as explained by Rashi: "Perfect in body, perfect in possessions, and perfect in Torah."

LEAVING IN PEACE

Yom Kippur—Ne'ilah

We have now reached the hour of *Ne'ilah*, "the closing of the gates". With it, our journey, which began on Rosh Hashanah with *Lech lecha* and passed through *artzecha*, *moladtecha* and *beth avichah*, will come to an end.

At this moment of climax and conclusion, of closing and parting, what should our feelings be? Sadness that the great experience we had together is over? Or anxiety lest our spiritual efforts did not succeed? Or fear of what the future may bring to us? No, none of these emotions are in place at this hour.

We read earlier today about the unique Yom Kippur service in the Temple of old, conducted entirely by the High Priest. His was a responsibility and a privilege shared by no other Jew. After an exacting 24-hour long round of ritual functions and vigil, he entered, alone, just this once a year, the Holy of Holies in the Temple, in order there to make atonement "for himself, for his family, and for all the congregation of Israel". On him rested the terrible burden of securing forgiveness for an entire people, of pleading for their welfare, and of guiding their spiritual destiny. This was his moment of truth and supreme challenge, as he stood there, alone with God, on the holiest day of the year, and on the holiest spot on earth, where Abraham was once prepared to sacrifice his "only son Isaac", the spot towards which Jews everywhere and at all times have turned in prayer ever since then.

The burdens of the High Priest were so heavy, and the strains and tensions so great, that people feared for his safety. Since no one else was ever permitted to enter the Holy of Holies, they attached chains to the High Priest before he went in, so that he could be pulled outside if anything happened to him whilst he was inside.

Now, how did he feel when the service was over, when he safely emerged from his spiritual ordeal in the Holy of Holies? Sad that it had come to an end? Or anxious lest he did not succeed? Or fearful of what the future might bring? No, our sources tell us, as we read in our *Machzor* today: "And the High Priest made a *Yom Tov* party for his friends after he had entered in peace (into the Holy of Holies) and came out in peace without incident." He was jubilant, joyfully thanking God for the privilege to lead and represent His people before Him, and for passing through his grave responsibilities in peace and without harm.

I feel likewise at this moment. A rabbi in spiritual charge of a congregation, especially in our turbulent times, carries a crushing burden. His is a high privilege, but also an awesome responsibility. If he can emerge from a term of office serving figuratively in the Holy of Holies, and say "I have entered in peace and I have come out in peace without incident", then he has indeed reason to be jubilant and to celebrate a special *Yom Tov*.

At this hour of *Ne'ilah*, therefore, I joyfully thank God for the honour He bestowed upon me in guiding you, for protecting me from all strife and enmity, for letting me go out in peace as I came in in peace. At this moment I plead for forgiveness for any wrongs I may have done you, and for God's forgiveness and atonement to me, to my family and to all my congregation for the offences we committed against Him and our fellow-men.

The laws of Yom Kippur conclude with the following paragraph: "There is a Midrash stating that on the termination of Yom Kippur a Heavenly voice goes forth and says: 'Go and eat your bread in joy and drink your wine with a happy heart, for God has already accepted your works' (Eccl. 9:7:)" (*Kitzur Shulchan Aruch*, 133:29).

May God's blessings of peace and joy always be with you as a holy congregation ennobling the entire House of Israel.

INDEX

(Major references appear in bold figures.   Names listed here do not include those mentioned only in the Notes and Halachah Abstracts.)

Abortion xii, 120, 127, 140, 316, 332ff., **348ff.**, 379ff.
in Israel 27, 48, 85, 90, 286, 333
Abramsky, Dayan Y. 271
Achad Ha'am 12, 47, 80
Adler, Chief Rabbi Hermann 252, 270
Adler, Chief Rabbi Nathan Marcus 61, 79, 213, 252, 269, 276
Adler, Rabbi Nathan 237f.
Adoption 213
Adultery 92, 222ff., 229, 356f.
Agranat Commission 20, 46, 96
Agunah 282, 308ff.
Aliyah 11ff., 26ff., **34ff.**, 48, 72f., 83, 90, 264, 286
Alkalai, Rabbi Judah 12
America xi, 13, 19, 30, 36, 69, 123, 125, 136, 152, 163, 165, 183f., 190, 194, 205, 213, 217, 269, 342, **387–427**
Anglo-Jewry 18, 36, 40, **53–80**, 101f., 192ff., 264, 268ff.
immigration of 78ff., 190, 194, 273f.
Anti-Semitism ix, 21, 44f., 97, 110, 114, 152
Anti-Zionism 26, 29, 97, 184, 254
Apartheid, *see* Racism
Arabs 3, 5, 18f., 26, 38, 44f., 86, 153, 161, 164, 371
refugees xii, 10, 28, 48, 153, 155
Artificial Insemination 317f., 327
Ashkenazim and Sephardim 26, 83, 84, 104, 238, 264, 307, 379
See also Hebrew, Pronunciation
Australia xi, 36, 198, 213, 342
Autopsies 40, 89f., 200, 335
Azbel, Prof. Mark 112

Babi Yar 109, 113
Bacharach, Rabbi Yair 374
Bachaya 242
Balfour Declaration 5, 13, 58, 73, 270

Bamberger, Rabbi Isaac Dov 252, 265
Baron, Prof. Salo W. 38
Bastards, see *Mamzerim*
Begin, Menachem 204
Ben Gurion, David 12, 321
Beth Din 53, 59, 63, 75, 210ff., 232, 269, **271f.**, 274, 327
Bialik, Chaim Nachman 246
Birnbaum, Nathan 12
Biro-Bidjan 113
Birth-control 48, 221, 315, 333, **338ff.**
Birth-rate 27, 48, 85, 90, 104, 190, 205, 343f.
Blindness 319f.
Board of Deputies 3, 27, 69, 73f., 78, 164, 379f.
Brandeis, Judge Louis 12
Braun, Rabbi S. 242
Breuer, Yitzchak 105
Broadcasts **147–186**
Brodetsky, Prof. Selig 73
Brodie, Chief Rabbi Sir Israel 53, 101, 292ff., 249, 270f., 287
Buber, Martin 135
Buechler, Dr. A. 276

Cantors 307f.
Capital punishment 222f., 358
Chafetz Chaim 65
Charity 128, 305, 424
Chassidism 40, 190, 238, 257, 264, 283, 398
Chief Rabbinate ix, xii, 30, **53ff.**, 63, 69, 74, 78, 125, 242f., **268ff.**
Children 223, 303, 306, 379ff., 399f.
Choriner, Rabbi Aaron 237
Chosen People 105, 254f.
Chovevei Zion 12
Christianity 10, 15, 24, 43, 119ff., 137, 350, 368ff.
Circumcision 111, 210, 212f., 315ff.
Civic service 71f.

Civil Rights 163ff., 414f.
   See also Human Rights
Cohen, Dr. Abraham 73
Cohen, Lord 380f.
Common Market 100
Communism 115, 137, 156, 410
Confession **171ff.**, 180
Conscience 157, 339, 345f., 349, 363
Conversion 5, 107, 164, 200ff., **210ff.**, 215ff., 261, 272
Cosmetics 226
Creation **155ff.**, 175f., 388ff., 408f.
Cruelty
   of laws 92, 353f.
   to animals **368ff.**
   to humans 374

Daiches, Dr. S. 276
Davis, Prof. Moshe 213
Democracy 260, 325
Dissent xi, 57, 114, 131f., 189, **265f.**, 326, 410
Divorce 209, *et passim*
Divorce (laws) 108, 123, **221ff.**, 272, 308ff.
Drachman, Dr. B. 252
Dreyfus Affair 13
Dual loyalties 3, 209

Eban, Abba 44
Education, Jewish ix, 4, 25, 29ff., 41, 55, 62ff., 67f., 104ff., 148, 169, **189–198**, 207, 265, 272, 275f., 306, 400, *et passim*
Eisenstein, J. D. 238
Elbogen, Prof. I. 238
Eliot, George 7
Elizabeth II, H.M. Queen 119, 123, **142ff.**
Emden, Rabbi Jacob 242
Epstein, Dr. I. 276
Ethics 57, 91, *et passim*
Eugenics 222
European Jewry 3, 36, 69, **99ff.**, 189f.
Euthanasia xii, 120, 140, 316, 334, 384
Experimentation
   on humans 140, **362ff.**
   on animals 366, **368ff.**

"Family purity" 228, 340, 347
Feinstein, Rabbi Moshe 287, 312, 318, 320, 325, 383
Friedlander, Dr. M. 276
Fund-raising 4, 13, 47, 73, 101

Geiger, Abraham 252
"Genetic Engineering" 336
Gershom, Rabbenu 229, 232, 340
Goren, Chief Rabbi Shlomo 215, 289ff.
Graetz, Heinrich 252
Green, Rev. A. A. 272
Grunfeld, Dayan I. 251, 255, 271

Grossnass, Dayan A. L. 276, 383
Gumbiner, Rabbi Abraham 263, 307

Hai Gaon 38
Halachah 26, 32, 36ff., 108, 203ff., 215ff., **281–328**, 410f., *et passim*
Halevi, Yehuda 12, 253f.
Halitzah 223, 232
Haskalah 246
Hatikvah 246
Health 221ff., 315, 354f., 393
Hebrew 13, 26, 41, 55, 108, 111, 114, 168, 171, 184, 198, 207, 212, 350, 422
   Pronunciation **236ff.**, 307
Heenan, Cardinal 384
Hertz, Chief Rabbi J. H. 3, 252, 268, 270, 276
Herzl, Theodor 12f., 47, 262, 270
Herzog, Yaacov 46
Hess, Moses 12
Hillman, Dayan S. I. 271
Hirsch, S. A. 251
Hirsch, Rabbi Samson Raphael **251ff.**, 260, 265, 283
Hippocratic Oath 332
Holocaust 3, 8, 13, 29f., 44, 57, 63, 101, 115, 147, 179, 183, 189f., 201, 205, 270, 282f., 413
Holiness **396ff.**, *et passim*
Human Rights 111, 122, **125ff.**, 165, 415

Incest 222f., 318, 356f.
Industrial relations 127f., 138f., 303ff.
Insanity 230, 308, 352, 365
Inter-faith 54, 60, **119ff.**, 126, 150, 189f.
Intermarriage 24, 26, 40, 56, 72, 104, 190, 202f., **205ff.**, 211ff., 222f., 283, 312ff., *et passim*
Islam 15, 24, 43, 137, 161, 294, 370f.
Israel **3–50**, 190f., 227, 282f., *et passim*
   Centrality of 13, 46, 103

Jabotinsky, Vladimir 12
Jaffe, Rabbi Mordecai 237
Jakobovits, Dayan Julius 56, 131, 193, 236ff.
Jericho 294f.
Jerusalem 11ff., **32f.**, 35, 43, 114f., 161, 225, *et passim*
   reunification of 44, **83ff.**, 190, 288ff., 337
Jewish Agency 40
Jews' College 64, 264, 276ff.
Joseph, Rev. Morris 272

Kalischer, Rabbi Zvi Hirsch 12
Karo, Joseph 12, 35, 221, 233, 314ff., 319, 371ff., *et passim*
Kashrut 76, 85, 207, 271, 399, *et passim*
Katzir, President Ephraim 14, 45
Kethubah 224ff.

Kook, Rabbi Abraham Isaac 12, 56, 62, 93, 241f., 290
Kotler, Rabbi Aaron 287
Krausz, Armin 249f.
Kunitzer, Rabbi Moses 237

Landau, Rabbi Samuel 240
Leadership ix, xii, 20ff., 31, **53ff.**, 65, 72, 87ff., 97f., 103ff., 136ff., 167, 196, *et passim*
Lerner, Prof. Alexander 112
Letterheads 302f.
Levine, Rev. Ephraim 272
Lilienblum, Moses Leib 12
Loew, Leopold 255
Loewenstamm, Rabbi Abraham 237f.
Luria, Rabbi Yitzchak 12, 35, 263, 302, 307

Magnes, Judah Leon 12
Maimon, Rabbi Judah Leib 12
Maimonides 19, 37, 167, 253, 290ff., *et passim*
Mamzerim 91f., 223, 282, 357
Marriage **207ff.**, *et passim*
laws 85, 89, 108, **221ff.**, 308ff.
Marmorstein, Prof. A. 276
Medawar, Sir Peter 162
Media 14, 127, 129, **130ff.**, 161f., 189, 252 *see also* Press
Medical Ethics 128, 281, 314ff., **331–384**
Meir, Golda 12, 204
Mendelssohn, Moses 253
Messianism 115f., 121, 126, 193, 250, 291ff., 409, 411
Mikvah 66, 272, 327
Ministry 40, 54f., 72ff., **272ff.**
recruitment 74, 76, 196
Miracles 19, 86, 106, 299
Missionaries 60, 120, 123, 164
Mourning 210, 295, 303
Munich massacre x, **7ff.**, 91

Nachmanides 12, 35f., 108, 253, 296ff.
Nature **378ff.**, *et passim*
Non-Jews 199ff., 222f., 283, 296, 316, 343, 374, *et passim*
see also Intermarriage
Nordau, Max 12

Occupied Territories 32, **297ff.**
Original Sin 160
Orthodoxy 29f., 48, 56, 62, 64, 84, 93, **96ff.**, 107, 191, 195, 205, 215ff., 252ff., 264ff., 268ff., 281ff., 344, 419, 423, *et passim*

Palatnik, Raiza 99
Passover 14, 28, **147ff.**

Peace 27, 91f., 95, 106, 108, 109, *et passim*
Philo 358f., 369
Philosophy 149
Pinsker, Leon 12, 47, 262
Polarisation 65, 87, 138, 191
Prajs, Prof. S. J. 70
Prayer 136, **171ff.**, 236ff., 301, 306f., *et passim*
Press 14, 19, 129, **130ff.**, 155, 173
Jewish 73
Priests 222ff., 237, 294
Pronunciation, *see* Hebrew
Prophets 8ff., 29, 45f., 57, 97, 126, 132f., 135, 141, 169, 180f., 185, 261, 410, *et passim*
Provinces **69ff.**, 198, 272

Rabbis **53ff.**, 72, 79, **87ff.**, 101, 210ff., 225, **268ff.**, 284ff., **320ff.**, 423ff., *et passim*
Rabinovitch, Rabbi N. L. 305
Race relations 152, **163ff.**, 415f.
Racism 43f., 120, 157, 163ff., 173, 184, 201
Rappaport, Solomon J. 238
Reform 56f., 89, 105, 107, 216, 252ff., 269f., 311ff.
Reischer, Rabbi Jacob 371
Religion, in public life **135ff.**, 157, 167ff., 414f.
and politics 30, 215ff., 420f.
Reuchlin, Johann 244f.
Reward and punishment 18, 45, 92, 156f., 172ff., 185, 286
Rosen, Rabbi Kopul 236
Rosenheim, Lord 380f.
Rosner, Dr. Fred 383
Roth, Dr. Cecil 61
Rothenburg, Rabbi Meir 417

Saadya Gaon 87
Sabbath 40, 85, 89, 176, 207, 285, 300f., 312, 372ff., *et passim*
Samuel, Herbert 12
Sanhedrin 287, 293
Schonfeld, Rabbi Solomon 275
Schonfeld, Rabbi Victor 275
Schools 5, 13, 30, 63f., 71, 84, 91, 102, 184, **197ff.**, 242f., 256f., 275, *et passim*
see also Education
Schreiber, Rabbi Moses 35, 304, 321
Science 126, 138, 149, 162, **175ff.**, 189, *et passim*
Secularism xii, 20ff., 47f., 97, 105f., 120, 153, 199ff., 304, 420f.
Septuagint 238, 350, 358
Sforno, Rabbi Obadiah 244
Shaftesley, John M. 212
Shakespeare 401
Shechita 76, 101, 271, 320
Shofar 9, 156, 306, 390, 416

Shtern, Mikhail 110, 113
Silver, Rabbi Abba Hillel 12
Singer, Rev. Simeon 272
Six-Day War ix, x, **3ff.**, 18f., 29, 50, 85f., **288ff.**
Soloveitchik, Rabbi J. B. 217, 256, 297f.
South Africa xi, 30, 36, 163, 173, 183f., 198, 268
Soviet Jewry ix, 5, 9, 13, 38, 54, 67, 73, 76, 79, 101, **109ff.**, 156, 163, 167, 177f., 183ff., 204, 406f.
Soviet Union 18f., 44, 49, 109ff., 156
  visit to x, xi, **109ff.**, 183ff.
Space travel **159ff.**, 299ff.
Spector, Rabbi Yitzchak Elchanan 255, 270
Sterilisation 374
Strikes xii, 129, 138f., 303ff.
Students ix, xi, 66, 160, 169, 191
Synagogues 4, 24, 61ff., 70f., 83, 114, 195f., 198, 204, 275f., 346, *et passim*

Tay-Sachs Disease **379ff.**
Temple, rebuilding of, 292f.
  site of 298ff.
Terrorism xii, 7ff., 44, 97, 139ff., 161, 173f.
Theological dialogues 60, 120, 123, 189, 283
Third World ix
Torah im derech eretz 255ff., 264, 277
Transplants 335
  Eye 320
Truman, President Harry 5, 414

United Nations 5, 43ff., 119, 122, 271

United Synagogue 17, 61ff., 69, 72ff., 78, 98, 256, 270, 273f.
  centenary of x, **61ff.**
Unity 3, 11, 18, 20, 85, 87ff., 104ff., 119, 184, 199ff., 216, 245f., *et passim*
Universities xi, 66, 110, 126, 155, 177, 244, 259ff., 274, 336
Unterman, Chief Rabbi I. J. 298f.
Uziel, Chief Rabbi Ben Zion 241f.

Vivisection 369ff.

Weinberg, Rabbi Yechiel 241, 308f., 311f., 317f., 320
Weiss, Rabbi I. J. 242ff., 276, 289ff.
Weizmann, Chaim 12, 14, 47
Western Wall x, 288ff.
"Who is a Jew" 31, 40, 49, 107, **199ff.**, **215ff.**, 321
Wiesel, Eli 113
Wise, Rabbi Stephen 12
Wohlgemuth, Dr. J. 368ff.
Women 221ff., 308ff., *et passim*

Yeshivot xi, 29, 30, 65, 83ff., 91, 257, 272, 281ff., **320ff.**
Yevtushenko, Y. A. 109
Yom Ha'atzmaut 6, 11ff., 22, **249f.**
Yom Kippur War ix, x, xii, **17ff.**, 44, 103ff., 136, 179ff., 181, 215, 262
Youth 18, 59, 66, 98, 101, 104, 161, 190f., 193ff., 207, 416, *et passim*

Zimmels, H. J. 237, 263, 276
Zionism 11ff., **43ff.**, 73, 80, 105, *et passim*
Zunz, Leopold 7